# Lecture Notes in Computer Science

*Commenced Publication in 1973*
Founding and Former Series Editors:
Gerhard Goos, Juris Hartmanis, and Jan van Lee

Yannis Manolopoulos  Jaroslav Pokorný
Timos Sellis (Eds.)

# Advances in Databases and Information Systems

10th East European Conference, ADBIS 2006
Thessaloniki, Greece, September 3 – 7, 2006
Proceedings

 Springer

Volume Editors

Yannis Manolopoulos
Aristotle University
Department of Informatics
54124 Thessaloniki, Greece
E-mail: manolopo@csd.auth.gr

Jaroslav Pokorný
Charles University
FMP, Department of Software Engineering
Malostranské nám. 25, 118 00 Prague 1, Czech Republic
E-mail: pokorny@ksi.ms.mff.cuni.cz

Timos Sellis
National Technical University of Athens
School of Electrical and Computer Engineering
15773 Zographou, Athens, Greece
E-mail: timos@dblab.ece.ntua.gr

Library of Congress Control Number: 2006931262

CR Subject Classification (1998): H.1, H.2, H.3, H.4, H.5

LNCS Sublibrary: SL 3 – Information Systems and Application, incl. Internet/Web
and HCI

ISSN      0302-9743
ISBN-10   3-540-37899-5 Springer Berlin Heidelberg New York
ISBN-13   978-3-540-37899-0 Springer Berlin Heidelberg New York

Springer is a part of Springer Science+Business Media

springer.com

© Springer-Verlag Berlin Heidelberg 2006
Printed in Germany

Typesetting: Camera-ready by author, data conversion by Scientific Publishing Services, Chennai, India
Printed on acid-free paper      SPIN: 11827252      06/3142      5 4 3 2 1 0

# Preface

The 10th East-European Conference on Advances in Databases and Information Systems was held on September 3-7, 2006, in Thessaloniki, Greece. It was organized by the Aristotle University of Thessaloniki, the University of Macedonia and the Alexander Technological Educational Institute of Thessaloniki.

The main objective of the ADBIS series of conferences is to provide a forum for the dissemination of research accomplishments and to promote interaction and collaboration between the database and information systems research communities from Central and East European countries and the rest of the world. The ADBIS conferences provide an international platform for the presentation of research on database theory, development of advanced DBMS technologies, and their advanced applications.

The conference continued the long tradition of successful ADBIS conferences held in St. Petersburg (1997), Poznan (1998), Maribor (1999), Prague (2000), Vilnius (2001), Bratislava (2002), Dresden (2003), Budapest (2004) and Tallinn (2005). The conference included regular sessions with technical contributions reviewed and selected by an international Program Committee, as well as invited talks presented by leaders in their fields: Serge Abiteboul, Yannis Ioannidis and Pavel Zezula. ADBIS 2006 was also taken as an opportunity to host two other very popular events: the 2nd ADBIS Workshop on Data Mining and Knowledge Discovery (ADMKD) and the 5th Hellenic Data Management Symposium (HDMS).

ADBIS 2006 attracted 126 submissions from 36 countries from all over the world. This volume contains 29 high-quality papers selected during a rigorous reviewing process by an international Program Committee. The papers cover a wide range of topics of database and information systems research, all of them addressing hot research issues. A further 17 papers, which ranked top after the 29 papers presented in this volume, were accepted to be included in a separate volume of research communications published as a local volume of ADBIS 2006 proceedings, and published electronically in the CEUR Workshop Proceedings series at http://ceur-ws.org/.

Many people and organizations contributed to the success of ADBIS 2006. Our thanks go to the authors and invited speakers for their outstanding contribution to the conference and the proceedings. We are very grateful to the Program Committee members for their reviewing and for accepting a heavy workload. Our thanks go also to the additional referees who carefully reviewed the submissions. Without the willingness and enthusiasm of many scientists, who shared their expertise and voluntarily donated their time to thoroughly evaluating the merits of the work submitted, this conference would not have been possible.

We wish to thank all the members of the organizing team, as well as our sponsors, who made the conference possible. Our special thanks go to Apostolos

Papadopoulos and Konstantinos Tarabanis for their general organizational services, Antonis Sidiropoulos and the other members of the Data Eng. Lab of the Aristotle University for maintaining the ADBIS 2006 Web site, and Michalis Vassilakopoulos for the technical preparation of the conference proceedings. We are also grateful to Springer for supporting the publication of the ADBIS 2006 proceedings in their LNCS series. Finally, we would like to express our gratitude to our sponsors: the Ministry of National Education and Religious Affairs, and the IT companies: Altec and G-net.

This volume of proceedings is dedicated with loving memory to Radu Bercary and Alexander Zamulin, members of the ADBIS family, who passed away.

September 2006                                                    Yannis Manolopoulos
                                                                 Jaroslav Pokorný
                                                                 Timos Sellis

# In Memory of Radu Bercaru and Alexandre Zamulin

**Radu Bercaru** was Scientific Director of the National Institute for R&D in Informatics (ICI), Bucharest, Romania, and Secretary of the ICI Scientific Council. He was member of the Program and Steering Committees of the ADBIS conferences. He was author/co-author of more than 40 papers published in national and international journals and proceedings. His areas of expertise were conceptual modelling, development of complex database systems, advanced databases, software engineering, national and international project management and consulting services, and team management in information systems development projects. His international experience consisted in local coordination of EU funded research projects and EU/ PHARE projects. In Romania, he was a member of the Evaluation Board for the Romanian Academy and Ministry of Education and Research Grants, of the Working Groups in charge of the Romanian Information Society Strategy, of the Steering Committee of the Romanian Conferences on Computer Science and Information Technologies, and other committees. He was also Director of the ICI R&D Program "Advanced Technologies and Systems for the Knowledge-Based Information Society". Radu Bercaru died in February 2005.

**Alexandre Zamulin** held several research positions at the Novosibirsk Branch of the Institute of Precise Mechanics and Computing Machines of the Academy of Sciences of the USSR (AS USSR), at the Computing Center of the Siberian Branch of the Academy of Sciences of the USSR (SB AS USSR) and at the Institute of Informatics Systems of the Siberian Branch of the Russian Academy of Sciences (IIS SB RAS). He was also Associate Professor of the Novosibirsk Electrotechnical Institute and Professor of the Novosibirsk State University, where he was head of the System Informatics chair in the Information Technologies Department. Moreover, Alexandre Zamulin was a member of the Inter-Departmental Commission on Databanks of the USSR State Research and Technology Committee, member of the Commission on Databanks of the AS USSR Coordinating Committee on Computing Machines and member of the Scientific Council and the Dissertation Council on physics and mathematics of the IIS SB RAS. Over a long period, he was a co-chair of the International Conference on Perspectives of System Informatics (PSI). For several years, he was a member of the Program Committee of the ADBIS conferences and contributed to ADBIS conferences with a number of articles. In the course of his scientific activities Alexandre Zamulin published over 100 works, including 2 monographs, devoted to the various aspects of constructing information systems, databases, programming languages, and specification languages. In recent years his chief scientific interests were connected with methods of algebraic specification of programming languages and databases. He was also a member of the editorial boards of many international editions. Alexandre Zamulin died in February 2006.

# ADBIS 2006 Conference Organization

## Organizing Institutes

Aristotle University of Thessaloniki
University of Macedonia
Alexander Technological Educational Institute of Thessaloniki

## General Chair

Yannis Manolopoulos, Aristotle University of Thessaloniki

## Program Committee Co-chairs

Jaroslav Pokorný, Charles University of Prague
Timos Sellis, National Technical University of Athens

## Program Committee

Leopoldo Bertossi
Nieves Brisaboa
Albertas Caplinskas
Barbara Catania
Vassilis Christophidis
Alex Delis
Dimitris Dervos
Asuman Dogac
Johann Eder
Georgios Evangelidis
Piero Fraternali
Pedro Furtado
Jarek Gryz
Hele-Mai Haav
Piotr Habela
Mohand-Said Hacid
Theo Haerder
Christian Jensen
Leonid Kalinichenko
Martin Kersten
Mikhail Kogalovsky

Wolfgang Lehner
Peri Loucopoulos
Rainer Manthey
Manuk Manukyan
Esperanza Marcos
Richard McClutchey
Marco Mesiti
Klaus Meyer-Wegener
Tadeusz Morzy
Enrico Nardelli
Pavol Navrat
Nikolay Nikitchenko
Kjetil Norvag
Boris Novikov
Oscar Pastor Lopez
Esther Pacitti
Torben Bach Pedersen
Evi Pitoura
Karel Richta
Tore Risch
Gunter Saake

George Samaras
Heinz Schweppe
Hans-Werner Sehring
Vaclav Snasel
Dan Suciu
Bernhard Thalheim
Yannis Theodoridis
Riccardo Torlone
Can Tuerker
Ozgur Ulusoy
Toni Urpi
Olegas Vasilecas
Michalis Vassilakopoulos
Panos Vassiliadis
Michalis Vazirgiannis
Gottfried Vossen
Robert Wrembel
Marek Wojciechowski
Vladimir Zadorozhny
†Alexander Zamulin

## Organizing Committee Chairs

Apostolos Papadopolos, Aristotle University of Thessaloniki
Konstantinos Tarabanis, University of Macedonia

## Organizing Committee

Yannis Karydis, Aristotle University of Thessaloniki
Dimitrios Katsaros, Aristotle University of Thessaloniki
Maria Kontaki, Aristotle University of Thessaloniki
Alexandros Nanopoulos, Aristotle University of Thessaloniki
Antonis Sidiropoulos, Aristotle University of Thessaloniki
Stavros Stavroulakis, Aristotle University of Thessaloniki

## ADBIS Steering Committee Chair

Leonid Kalinichenko, Russian Academy of Science (Russia)

## ADBIS Steering Committee

Andras Benczur (Hungary)
Albertas Caplinskas (Lithuania)
Johann Eder (Austria)
Janis Eiduks (Latvia)
Hele-Mai Haav (Estonia)
Mirjana Ivanovic (Yugoslavia)
Mikhail Kogalovsky (Russia)
Yannis Manolopoulos (Greece)
Rainer Manthey (Germany)

Tadeusz Morzy (Poland)
Pavol Navrat (Slovakia)
Boris Novikov (Russia)
Jaroslav Pokorný (Czech Republic)
Boris Rachev (Bulgaria)
Anatoly Stogny (Ukraine)
Bernhard Thalheim (Germany)
Tatjana Welzer (Slovenia)
Viacheslav Wolfengagen (Russia)

## Additional Reviewers

Alberto Abelló
César J. Acuña
Ypatios Asmanidis
Qaizar Ali Bamboat
Romas Baronas
Dmitry Buy
José María Cavero
Jordi Conesa
Dolors Costal
Martin Doerr

Philipp Dopichaj
Carles Farré
Elias Frentzos
Anders Friis-Christensen
Ingolf Geist
Gyozo Gidofalvi
Parke Godfrey
Giovanna Guerrini
Stephan Hagemann
Alexander Hampel

Aleks Jakulin
Roland Kaschek
Algirdas Laukaitis
Jens Lechtenboerger
Thomas Leich
Carolin Letz
Sebastian Link
Elena Luciv
Anna Maddalena
Roberto Montagna

Mikolaj Morzy
Lina Nemuraite
Mehmet Olduz
Umut Orhan
Bronius Paradauskas
Paola Podestà
Simonas Saltenis
Eike Schallehn
Klaus-Dieter Schewe

Ingo Schmitt
Anke Schneidewind
Tayfun Sen
Lefteris Sidirourgos
Christian Siefkes
Michal Szychowiak
Ibrahim Tasyurt
Christian Thomsen
Massimo Tisi

Alexei Tretiakov
Belén Vela
Kira Vyatkina
Thomas Weishäupl
Karl Wiggisser
Kevin Xie
Mustafa Yuksel

## Sponsors

Ministry of National Education and Religious Affairs
Altec
G-net

# Table of Contents

## Invited Papers

## XML Databases and Semantic Web

## Materialized Views

# Database Modelling

# Web Information Systems and Middleware

# Query Processing and Indexing

# Data Mining and Clustering

# Modelling and Desing Issues

# Data Ring: Let Us Turn the Net into a Database!

Serge Abiteboul[1] and Neoklis Polyzotis[2]

[1] INRIA-Futurs & LRI-Univ. Paris 11, France
serge.abiteboul@inria.fr
[2] Univ. of California Santa Cruz, USA
alkis@cs.ucsc.edu

**Abstract.** Because of information ubiquity, one observes an important trend towards transferring information management tasks from database systems to networks. We introduce the notion of Data Ring that can be seen as a network version of a database or a content warehouse. A main goal is to achieve better performance for content management without requiring the acquisition of explicit control over information resources. We discuss the main traits of Data Rings and argue that Active XML provides an appropriate basis for such systems.

The collaborating peers that form the Data Ring are autonomous, heterogeneous and their capabilities may greatly vary, e.g., from a sensor to a large database. To support effectively this paradigm of loose integration, the Data Ring enforces a seamless transition between data and metadata and between explicit and intentional data. It does not distinguish between data provided by web pages and data provided by web services, between local (extensional) data and external data obtained via a Web service call. This is achieved using the Active XML technology that is based on exchanging XML documents with embedded service calls both for the logical and physical data model.

Y. Manolopoulos, J. Pokorný, and T. Sellis (Eds.): ADBIS 2006, LNCS 4152, p. 1, 2006.
© Springer-Verlag Berlin Heidelberg 2006

# Future Data Management:
# "It's Nothing Business; It's Just Personal."

Yannis Ioannidis

Department of Informatics & Telecommunications
University of Athens, Athens, Hellas, Greece
yannis@di.uoa.gr

**Abstract.** Conventional data management occurs primarily in central-ized servers or in well-interconnected distributed systems. These are removed from their end users, who interact with the systems mostly through static devices to obtain generic services around main-stream ap-plications: banking, retail, business management, etc. Several recent ad-vances in technologies, however, give rise to a new breed of applications, which change altogether the user experience and sense of data manage-ment. Very soon several such systems will be in our pockets, many more in our homes, the kitchen appliances, our clothes, etc. How would these systems operate? Many system and user aspects must be approached in novel ways, while several new issues come up and need to be addressed for the first time. Highlights include personalization, privacy, informa-tion trading, annotation, new interaction devices and corresponding in-terfaces, visualization, etc. In this talk, we take a close look at and give a very personal guided tour to this emerging world of data management, offering some thoughts on how the new technical challenges might be approached.

Y. Manolopoulos, J. Pokorný, and T. Sellis (Eds.): ADBIS 2006, LNCS 4152, p. 2, 2006.
© Springer-Verlag Berlin Heidelberg 2006

# Scalable Similarity Search
# in Computer Networks

Pavel Zezula

Masaryk University, Brno, Czech Republic
zezula@fi.muni.cz

**Abstract.** Similarity search in metric spaces represents an important paradigm for content-based retrieval of many applications. Existing centralized search structures can speed-up retrieval, but they do not scale up to large volume of data because the response time is linearly increasing with the size of the searched file. Four scalable and distributed similarity search structures will be presented. By exploiting parallelism in a dynamic network of computers, they all achieve practically constant search time for similarity range or nearest neighbor queries in data-sets of arbitrary sizes. Moreover, a small amount of replicated routing information on each server increases logarithmically. At the same time, the potential for interquery parallelism is increasing with the growing data-sets because the relative number of servers utilized by individual queries is decreasing. All these properties are verified by experiments on a prototype system using real-life data-sets. Results are used to establish specific pros and cons of individual approaches in different situations.

Y. Manolopoulos, J. Pokorný, and T. Sellis (Eds.): ADBIS 2006, LNCS 4152, p. 3, 2006.
© Springer-Verlag Berlin Heidelberg 2006

# An XML Algebra for XQuery

Leonid Novak[1,*] and Alexandre Zamulin[2,**]

[1] Institute of System Programming,
Russian Academy of Sciences,
Moscow 109104, Russia
Fax: +7 095 912-15-24
novak@ispras.ru
[2] A.P. Ershov Institute of Informatics Systems
Siberian Branch of Russian Academy of Sciences
Novosibirsk 630090, Russia
Fax: +7 383 3323494
zam@iis.nsk.su

**Abstract.** An XML algebra supporting the XQuery query language is presented. The usage of expression constructing operators instead of high-order operations using functions as parameters has permitted us to remain in the limits of first-order structures whose instance is a many-sorted algebra. The set of operators of the presented algebra substantially differs from the set of operators of relation algebra. It is caused by the complex nature of the XML data model comparing with relational one. Actually, only predicative selection is more or less same in both algebra. Yet, the XML algebra in additttion permits selection by node test. The relational projection operator is replaced by the path expression and navigating functions; the join operator is replaced by unnesting join expressions. In addition, a number of node constructing expressions permitting update of the algebra state are defined.

## 1 Introduction

A formal model of the database state corresponding to the XQuery 1.0 and XPath 2.0 data model [19] and consisting of document trees defined by XML Schema has been presented in [10]. This model regards the database state as a many-sorted algebra composed of the states of individual nodes representing information items of a document. However, no algebra resembling relation algebra for this data model is proposed in [10], and elaboration of such an algebra supporting the XQuery language has been proclaimed as a subject of further research. It should be noted that a number of papers proposing different XML algebras have been published [2,6,5,7,12,15,21].

* The work of this author is supported in part by Russian Foundation for Basic Research under Grant 05-07-90204.
** We are very sad to inform you that Alexandre Zamulin passed away in February 2006, while this article was submitted.

Y. Manolopoulos, J. Pokorný, and T. Sellis (Eds.): ADBIS 2006, LNCS 4152, pp. 4–21, 2006.

Their typical flaws are:

- use of an artificial data model suitable to the authors,
- meaning by algebra something different from what is meant by algebra in mathematics;
- use of functions and predicates as operation arguments, while the algebra is a first-order structure;
- ignoring the fact that the result of a query may belong to an algebra different from the algebra of the query arguments;
- informal description of the algebra ignoring significant details of operations.

One of the aims of this paper is to propose an XML algebra that is free of the above flaws. Another aim is to elaborate such an XML algebra that could support XQuery [17], which is a de-facto standard of an XML query language. Not all features of XQuery are taken into account in the algebra proposed in the paper. We consider that an XQuery interpreter should exist whose task is to interpret an XQuery query in terms of the algebra while performing the work corresponding to the following XQuery features( specification of such an interpreter is not a subject of this paper):

- atomization,
- computation of Effective Boolean Value,
- evaluation of branching (conditional and type switch) expressions,
- evaluation of type-checking expressions (instance of, cast, treat),
- evaluation of content expressions of node constructors.

The remainder of the paper is organized as follows. A brief review of the XML data model presented in [10] is given in Section 2. Basic notions of signatures and expressions are introduced in Section 3. An example database schema used for illustration of XML algebra operations is given in Section 4. Navigating functions used for traversing a document tree are defined in Section 5. Several forms of querying expressions are formally described in Section 6. Different kinds of node constructors changing the database state are defined in Section 7. Related work is reviewed in Section 8, and some conclusions are drawn in Section 9.

## 2 Main Components of the XML Database Model

The data model presented in [10] is described by means of many-sorted algebras [4].

**Definition.** A many-sorted signature $\Sigma$ is a pair $(T, F)$, where $T$ is a set of *sorts* and $F$ a set of *operators* indexed by their *profiles*. An operator is either a symbol or a name, and a profile is either an element of $T$ or $t_1, ..., t_n \to t_{n+1}$, where $t_i$ is an element of $T$.

**Definition.** A many-sorted algebra $A$ of signature $\Sigma = (T, F)$ is constructed by associating

- a set with each element $t \in T$, denoted by $A_t$ in the sequel;
- an element $c^A \in A_t$ with each operator $c$ indexed by the profile $t$;
- a function $f^A : A_{t_1} \times ... \times A_{t_n} \to A_{t_{n+1}}$ with each operator $f$ indexed by the profile $t_1, ..., t_n \to t_{n+1}$.

The family of sets associated with the signature sorts in algebra $A$ is called the *algebra carrier* and denoted by $|A|$. An algebra of signature $\Sigma$ is called a $\Sigma$-algebra.

Since the XML database model presented in [19] intensively uses the notion of *type*, we consider that the set $T$ consists of type names and the set $F$ of operators defined for each type. The function associated with an operator is often called an *operation*. The type system of the model includes a number of atomic types (*xs:Boolean*, *xs:Integer*, etc.), defining atomic values, and the type *xdt:untypedAtomic* denoting atomic data, such as text that has not been assigned a more specific type. It is assumed that each atomic type is equipped with conventional operations. The type system also includes the set type constructor $Set(t)$, the sequence type constructor $Seq(t)$, the union type constructor $Union(t_1, ..., t_n)$, where $t, t_1, ..., t_n$ are types, and the enumeration type constructor $Enumeration(I_1, ..., I_n)$, where $I_1, ..., I_n$ are identifiers.

The following operations are applicable to all sets: "$\cup$" (union), "$\cap$" (intersection), "$\subset$" (inclusion), and "$\in$" (membership) If $s$ is a sequence, then $asSet(s)$ is a set containing the same elements as $s$ without duplicates.

A sequence, like a set, is often defined in this paper by *comprehension*, which generally has the following form: $(f(x_1, ..., x_n) \mid P(x_1, ...., x_n))$, where $x_1, ..., x_n$ are universally quantified variables, $f$ a function name, and $P$ a predicate. Typical sequence type constructors are the empty sequence constructor () and the singleton sequence constructor $(e)$ where $e$ is an atomic value or node. If $s_1$ and $s_2$ are two sequences of the same type, then $s_1 + s_2$ is a *concatenation* of the sequences, such that the first element of $s_2$ follows the last element of $s_1$ (the notation $(v_1, ..., v_n)$ can be considered as a shorthand for $(v_1) + ... + (v_n)$). Also, $s_1 \cup s_2$ is a *union* of the sequences, such that the resulting sequence contains the elements of both sequences (retaining duplicate elements) in an indefinite order. The number of elements of a sequence $s$ is denoted by $|s|$ in this paper. A set can be converted into a sequence by the operation $asSeq$ (the order of the elements is not defined). Several operations are applicable to sets and sequences of numerical values. These are *avg*, *sum*, *max*, and *min*. The operation *count* (number of elements) is applicable to any sequence or set.

The union type constructor plays an important role in the data model since a sequence may consist of items of different types. There are several predefined union types in the data model. The type *xdt:anyAtomicType* is the union of all the atomic types and the type *xdt:untypedAtomic*, and the type *xs:anyType* is the union of all types[1]. The following law exists for "flattening" the union of union types:

$$Union(t_1, ..., t_i, ..., t_n) = Union(t_1, ..., t_{i1}, ..., t_{im}, ..., t_n)$$

---

[1] In fact, the type *xs:anyType* does not include node types in the XQuery data model; it includes them in our data model for generality.

if $t_i = Union(t_{i1}, ..., t_{im})$. The following law permits us to get rid of duplicate component types in a union type:

$$Union(t_1, ..., t_i, ..., t_j, ..., t_n) = Union(t_1, ..., t_i, ..., t_n) \text{ if } t_i = t_j.$$

An XML database schema consists of a number of document definitions. Each individual document consists of *information items* with a definite *document order*. An information item of a document is mapped to a *node* in the database. A node, like an object of an object-oriented database [9], possesses an *identifier* and *state* represented by the values of node *accessors* resembling *observing methods* of an object-oriented database (we mean a node identifier by a node in the sequel). Each node is an instance of type *Node*, which is the union type for the types *Document*, *Element*, *Attribute*, *Text*, *Namespace*, *ProcInstruction*, and *Comment* whose respective instances are document, element, attribute, text, namespace, processing instruction, and comment nodes[2].

Finally, each node and each atomic value are instances of the type *Item*, which is the union of types *xdt:anyAtomicType* and *Node*. Atomic values and nodes are called *items* in the sequel. It is assumed that each data type is equipped with an equality predicate permitting to check for equality two values of the type; the equality of nodes is based on the identity of node identifiers.

All nodes in a database are arranged in linear order in such a way that if a node of one document tree precedes a node of another document tree, then all the nodes of the first tree precede all the nodes of the second tree. The operation $\mathbf{nd_1} << \mathbf{nd_2}$ results in $\mathtt{true}$ if the node $\mathbf{nd_1}$ precedes the node $\mathbf{nd_2}$ (see [1] for an algorithm implementing this operation).

In addition to the types used in [10], we use record (tuple) types in this paper. A record type $\mathtt{rec}\ p_1 : t_1, ..., p_n : t_n\ \mathtt{end}$ is equipped with a record construction operation $rec$ producing a record on the basis of record field values and projecting operations $p_i$ producing field values of a given record. If $p_1, ..., p_n$ are identifiers and $v_1, ..., v_n$ are values of respective types $t_1, ..., t_n$, then $\mathtt{rec}(\mathbf{v_1}, ..., \mathbf{v_n})$ is a record constructing expression of type $\mathtt{rec}\ p_1 : t_1, ..., p_n : t_n\ \mathtt{end}$.

# 3    Signatures and Expressions

A database schema defines a database signature $\Sigma = (T, F)$. $F$ includes, in addition to the operators defined in data types, node accessors defined in [19], all the function names and operators defined in [20], the names of navigating functions defined in this paper and some special constants defined in the sequel. Node accessors used in the paper are *node-kind*, *node-name*, *parent*, *string-value*, *type*, *children*, *attributes*, and *nilled*. Two extra functions with signatures

$$reverse\_order, document\_order : Seq(Node) \rightarrow Seq(Node)$$

are also part of our $F$. The first function orders the argument sequence in document order, and the second one orders it in reverse document order.

---

[2] To save space, we do not consider the last three kinds of nodes in this paper. However, there is no technical problem in taking them into consideration if needed.

Any particular database state is an algebra of this signature as it is explained above. The signature $\Sigma$ (as any other signature) may be *enriched* by new sorts and/or operators. In this case a $\Sigma$-algebra A is extended with new sets and/or functions associated with the new signature components.

Using operators from $F$, we can construct *expressions*. Each expression has a certain type. In a type hierarchy, a subtype expression is also a supertype expression. Given a $\Sigma$-algebra A, an expression can be *interpreted* or *evaluated*, yielding a certain algebra element. However, in contrast to conventional expressions of many-sorted signatures whose interpretation never changes neither the signature nor the algebra, XML expressions may be classified into three groups:

- conventional algebraic expressions written and evaluated in the same signature and algebra;
- expressions written in one signature and interpreted in an algebra of an enriched signature;
- expressions whose interpretation changes the algebra and produces an element of the new algebra.

There is nothing special with respect to the expressions of the first group. The situation with the expressions of the second group is more complex. An example of such an expression in relation algebra is projection of a relation onto a set of attributes or join of two relations. In either case the type of the resulting relation may be different from the relation types defined in the database schema. A query compiler, when parsing such an expression, constructs a new type and enriches the original signature with it. The current algebra is extended by the new type (sort and operations) as well, and the query is interpreted in the new algebra. If a signature $\Sigma$ is enriched to signature $\Sigma'$ and a $\Sigma$-algebra A is extended to $\Sigma'$-algebra A$'$, we use the index A to denote those components of A$'$ that are the same as in A.

An expression of the third group is the most difficult to process because the processing generally produces a side-effect (i.e., the expression, being interpreted in a certain algebra, may change it and produce an element of algebra). An example of this kind of expression is a *node constructing expression* whose interpretation produces a new node in a new algebra. We consider that such an expression is based on a function yielding a pair, an algebra and an algebra element. Note that a node construction expression is an expression and, according to the syntax of XQuery, can be used anywhere an expression is needed. This means that generally the interpretation of any expression may produce a side-effect. To save space, we will indicate this in only in the interpretations of node constructors, the side-effect-producing interpretation of all expressions can be found in [11].

We always write an expression $e$ in italics. Its interpretation in algebra A is written as $\llbracket e \rrbracket^{\text{A}}$. The result of the interpretation is generally written as $\langle \text{A}', \text{e} \rangle$, where A$'$ is a new algebra and e is the evaluation of $e$ in A$'$. However, where there may be no confusion, we write just e for the interpretation of $e$. If $e$ is an expression of type $Seq(t)$, we sometimes write: "$e$ denotes a sequence of items of type $t$". Given a signature $\Sigma$ and a set of variables $X$, we write "$\Sigma$-expression $e$" if $e$

is composed exclusively of operators of $\Sigma$, and we write "$(\Sigma, X)$-expression $e$" if $e$ contains, in addition, variables from $X$. If A is a $\Sigma$-algebra and $\xi : X \rightarrow |A|$ a variable assignment, then the notation $e\xi^A$, or simply $e\xi$, means in the sequel the interpretation of $e$ in algebra A with the variables bound to the indicated algebra elements. The expression syntax is conventional with conventional operator priorities. Generally, an expression is parsed from left to right. The cases where we use special syntax or special parsing order will be mentioned explicitly. The definitions of some functions and expressions use the standard functions defined in [20]. We prefix them by fn.

## 4  Running Example

The examples given in the paper are mainly based on the queries presented in [17] for a database containing documents of the following structure.

```
< bib >...
    < book year = ... >
        < title > ... < /title >
        < author > ... < /author >
        < author > ... < /author > ...
        <publisher>...</publisher>
        < price > ... < /price >
    < /book >. . .
    < proc >
        < title > ... < /title >...
        <editor>...</editor>
        <editor>...</editor> ...
        <article>
            < author > ... < /author >
            < author > ... < /author >...
        </article> . . .
    < /proc > . . .
< /bib >
```

## 5  Navigation Functions

In addition to node accessors, XQuery possesses a number of expressions denoting different parts of a document tree relative to a specified node. For each of these expressions, we define a supporting function producing a node nd of a certain algebra A.

1. *child* : $Node \rightarrow Seq(Node)$ The function yields a sequence containing all children nodes of the argument node if any.
2. *descendant* : $Node \rightarrow Seq(Node)$ The function yields a sequence containing all descendants of a node in the "parent-children" hierarchy if any.
3. *parent* : $Node \rightarrow Seq(Node)$. The function yields a sequence containing the parent of the argument node if any.

4. $attribute : Node \rightarrow Seq(Node)$ The function yields a sequence containing the attribute nodes of the argument element node.

In order to save space we don't give the definintion of other navigating functions: $descendant\_or\_self, ancestor, ancestor\_or\_self, following\_sibling,$ $following, preceding\_sibling, preceding.$ It can be found in [11].

Notation. The call of each of the above functions is written in this paper using the dot notation, i.e., as a call of a method in an object-oriented language; for instance, $nd.child$, $nd.parent$, etc.

## 6   Querying Expressions

In addition to elementary expressions constructed with the use of navigating functions listed above, an XML data model must include facilities for constructing more complex expressions representing data retrieval or update. The set of all possible expressions in an XML data model constitutes an *XML algebra*[3]. Generally, an XQuery query has the following form:

> **for** $\$x_1$ **in** $s_1$, $\$x_2$ **in** $s_2(\$x_1)$, ... , $\$x_m$ **in** $s_m(\$x_1, ..., \$x_{m-1})$
> **let** $\$y_1 := e_1(\$x_1, ..., \$x_m)$, $\$y_2 := e_2(\$x_1, ..., \$x_m, \$y_1)$, ... ,
> $\qquad \$y_n := e_n(\$x_1, ..., \$x_m, \$y_1, ..., \$y_n)$
> **where** $p(\$x_1, ..., \$x_m, \$y_1, ..., \$y_n)$
> **order by** $e(\$x_1, ..., \$x_m, \$y_1, ..., \$y_n)$
> **return** $f(\$x_1, ..., \$x_m, \$y_1, ..., \$y_n)$

where $s_i$ has to be a sequence, and $p$, $e$ and $f$ are expressions involving the variables $\$x_1, ..., \$x_m, \$y_1, ..., \$y_n$. Normally, $s_i$'s are nested sequences. Thus, to represent such a query in XML algebra, we need an expression that evaluates to a sequence of tuples of items belonging to possibly nested sequences (clauses **for** and **let**), an expression that evaluates to a subsequence of a sequence according to selection criteria (clause **where**), ordering expression, and an expression that constructs the resulting sequence (clause **return**). These expressions are defined in the sequel.

### 6.1   Unnesting Join Expression

This expression in fact replaces the *join* operation of the relation algebra because relationships between different sequences of nodes in the XML database are represented by node identifiers rather than by relation keys. First we define three auxiliary expressions serving to support different kinds of FOR and LET clauses. To save space we omit the definition of ordering mode of the resulting sequences of algebra expressions. It can be found in [11].

1. If $y$ is an identifier and $s$ a $\Sigma$-expression of type $Seq(t)$, then $<y : s>$ is an expression of type $t' = Seq(\text{rec } y : t \text{ end})$ of signature $\Sigma'$ obtained by enriching

---

[3] We define special forms of expressions rather than functions to avoid the problem of higher-order functions (a conventional algebra is a first-order structure).

$\Sigma$ by type $t'$. Interpretation. Let $A$ be a $\Sigma$-algebra, $A'$ a $\Sigma'$-algebra extending $A$ by type $A_{t'}$, and $[\![s]\!]^{A'} = s$, then:

$[\![<y : s>]\!]^{A'} = s'$, where $s' = (\text{rec } (v) \mid v \in s)$. This expression supports the FOR clause with a single range variable.

2. If $y$ and $i$ are identifiers and $s$ a $\Sigma$-expression of type $Seq(t)$, then $<y, i : s>$ is an expression of type $t' = Seq(\text{rec } i : integer,\ y : t\ \text{end})$ of signature $\Sigma'$ obtained by enriching $\Sigma$ by the type $t'$. Interpretation. Let $A$ be a $\Sigma$-algebra, $A'$ a $\Sigma'$-algebra extending $A$ by type $A_{t'}$, and $[\![s]\!]^{A'} = s$, then:

$[\![<y, i : s>]\!]^{A'} = (\text{rec } (i, s[i]) \mid i = 1, ..., |s|)$. This expression supports the FOR clause with a range variable and a positional variable.

3. If $y$ is an identifier, and $e$ a $\Sigma$-expression of type $t$, then $<y = e>$ is an expression of type $t' = Seq(\text{rec } y : t\ \text{end})$ of signature $\Sigma'$ obtained by enriching $\Sigma$ by the type $t'$ Interpretation. Let $A$ be a $\Sigma$-algebra, $A'$ a $\Sigma'$-algebra extending $A$ by type $A_{t'}$, and $[\![e]\!]^{A'} = e$, then:

$[\![<y = e>]\!]^{A'} = (\text{rec } (e))$. This expression supports the LET clause with a single variable name.

4. Finally we define an expression supporting any combination of FOR and LET clauses. If $s_1$ is a $\Sigma$-expression of type $Seq(\text{rec } x_{11} : t_{11}, ..., x_{1m} : t_{1m}\ \text{end})\}$ and $s_2$ a $(\Sigma, \{x_{11}, ..., x_{1m}\})$-expression of type $Seq(\text{rec } x_{21} : t_{21}, ..., x_{2n} : t_{2n}\ \text{end})\}$, then $s_1 * s_2$ is an expression of type $t' = Seq(\text{rec } x_{11} : t_{11}, ..., x_{1m} : t_{1m}, x_{21} : t_{21}, ..., x_{2n} : t_{2n}\ \text{end})$ of signature $\Sigma'$ obtained by enriching $\Sigma$ by the type $t'$. Interpretation. Let $A$ be a $\Sigma$-algebra, $A'$ a $\Sigma'$-algebra extending $A$ by type $A_{t'}$, $[\![s_1]\!]^{A'} = s_1$, and $k = |s_1|$. Further, $\forall\ i = 1, ..., k$ let $s_1[i] = \text{rec}(v_{i1}, ..., v_{im})$, $\xi_i = \{x_1 \mapsto v_{i1}, ..., x_m \mapsto v_{im}\}$, $[\![s_2\xi_1]\!]^{A'} = s_{21}$, ... $[\![s_2\xi_k]\!]^{A^{k-1}} = s_{2k}$, $ss_i = (\text{rec } (v_{i1}, ..., v_{im}, w_1, ..., w_n) \mid \text{rec}(w_1, ..., w_n) \in s_{2i})$ then:

$[\![s_1 * s_2]\!]^{A'} = s'$, where $s' = ss_1 \cup ... \cup ss_k$.

**Examples.** If the variable *books* denotes a sequence of book nodes, then

$<x: books> * <y:x.child::element(authors)>$

is an expression evaluating to a sequence of pairs of **book** and **author** nodes so that a book node is paired with its each child author node. The following expression:

$<x: (1,\ 2,\ 3)> * <y: (4,\ 5,\ 6)>$

evaluates in fact to the Cartesian product of the indicated sequences while the expression

$<x: (1,\ 2,\ 3)> * <y = (x+1,\ x+2)>$

evaluates to the following sequence of tuples: $(\langle 1, (2,3)\rangle, \langle 2, (3,4)\rangle, \langle 3, (4,5)\rangle)$. If variable *pets* denotes a sequence ("cat", "dog", "pig", then the expression:

$<t, i:pets>$

evaluates to the following sequence of pairs $(\langle\ 1,\ \text{"cat"}\rangle, \langle\ 2,\ \text{"dog"}\rangle, \langle\ 3,\ \text{"pig"}\rangle)$.

## 6.2   Quantified Expressions

Universal quantification and existential quantification are widely used in XQuery. The corresponding algebra expressions can be defined as follows.

If $t_1, t_2..., t_n$ are types from the signature $\Sigma$, $X = \{x_1, x_2, ...., x_n\}$ a set of variables, $s_1$ a $\Sigma$-expression of type $Seq(t_1)$, $s_2$ a $(\Sigma, \{x_1\})$-expression of type $Seq(t_2)$, ... , $s_n$ a $(\Sigma, \{x_1, ..., x_{n-1}\})$-expression of type $Seq(t_n)$, and $b$ a $(\Sigma, \{x_1, ..., x_n\})$-expression of type $Boolean$ , then

**forall**$(x_1 : s_1, x_2 : s_2, ..., x_n : s_n)!b$ and **exists**$(x_1 : s_1, x_2 : s_2, ..., x_n : s_n)!b$

are expressions of type $Boolean$. Interpretation. The first expression evaluates to **true** if every evaluation of $b$ produces **true**. The second expression evaluates to **true** if at least one evaluation of $b$ produces **true**.

## 6.3   Selection Expressions

A *selection expression* serves for selecting part of a sequence based on a *selection criteria*. In comparison to relational model and object model, the set of selection criteria in XML algebra is much broader and includes node *kind tests* in addition to *predicate tests*. The interpretation of these expressions takes place in an algebra A, and it does not change the algebra.

### 6.3.1 Kind Tests

Let $s$ denote a sequence of nodes. Then:

1) $s :: node()$ denotes the same sequence as s.

2) $s :: element(), s :: attribute(), s :: text()$ denotes a sequence of the nodes of the corresponding type in s.

**Example.** If the variable *books* denotes a sequence of nodes that are descendants of a *bib* node, then *books* $:: text()$ denotes a sequence consisting only of text nodes contained in *books*.

3) $s :: document()$ denotes a singleton sequence containing the document node from s.

4) if $n$ is a QName, then $s :: element(n)$ ($s :: attribute(n)$) denotes the sequence of element (attribute) nodes from s with name $n$.

**Example.** If the variable *book_data* denotes a sequence of nodes that are children of a *book* node, then *book_data* $:: element(author)$ denotes a sequence consisting only of author element nodes of a particular book.

5) if $n$ is a QName and $t$ a type name, then $s :: element(n, t)$ ($s :: attribute(n, t)$) denotes a sequence of element (attribute) nodes from s with name $n$, type $t$, and the value of the node accessor **nilled** equal to **true**.

6) if $t$ is a type name, then $s :: element(*, t)$ ($s :: attribute(*, t)$) denotes a sequence of element (attribute) nodes from s of type $t$.

7) if $n$ is a QName and $t$ a type name, then $s :: element(n, t?)$ denotes a sequence of element nodes from s with name $n$ and type $t$ regardless of the value of the node accessor **nilled**.

8) if $t$ is a type name, then $s :: element(*, t?)$ denotes the sequence of element nodes from s of type $t$.

### 6.3.2 Predicate Tests

Let $t$ be a type the signature $\Sigma$, $s$ a $\Sigma$-expression of type $Seq(t)$, $y$ a variable of type $t$, and $p$ a $(\Sigma, \{y\})$-expression of type $Boolean$, then $\mathbf{select}(y : s) :: p$ is a $(\Sigma)$-expression of type $Seq(t)$. Interpretation. Let A be a $\Sigma$-algebra, $[\![s]\!]^{A} = (v_1, \ldots, v_n)$, i = 1, ..., n, $\xi_i = \{y \mapsto v_i\}$, $[\![p\xi_1]\!]^{A} = p_1$, ..., $[\![p\xi_n]\!]^{A} = p_n$, then
$$[\![\mathbf{select}(y : s) :: p]\!]^{A} = (v_i \mid p_i).$$

**Example.** If the variable *books* denotes a sequence of book nodes, then
  $\mathbf{select}\,(x\colon books) :: typed\text{-}value(x.attribute :: attribute(year)) = 2000$
denotes a sequence of book nodes for the books published in 2000 and
  $\mathbf{select}\,(x\colon books) :: typed\text{-}value(x.child :: element(price)) > 100$
denotes a sequence of book nodes for the books whose price is greater than 100 dollars. The expression can be written in a simpler form if $t$ is a record type[11].

**Example.** If *books* denotes a sequence of book nodes, then
  $\mathbf{select}(<x : books > * < y = x.child :: element(author)>) :: count(y) > 2$
is a selection expression. Note that the local variable $x$ ranges over books, $y$ denotes the authors of a particular book, expression $(<x : books > * < y = x.child :: element(author)>)$ is a sequence of pairs $\langle book, sequence\ of\ authors\rangle$, and the predicate $count(y) > 2$ leaves in the sequence only those pairs where there are more than two authors.

## 6.4   Path Expression

This kind of expression permits one to navigate over a tree by using navigating functions. If $y$ is a variable, $s_1$ a $\Sigma$-expression of type $Seq(Node)$, $t_2$ an atomic/node type, and $s_2$ a $(\Sigma, \{y\})$-expression of type $Seq(t_2)$, then $\mathbf{path}(y : s_1)/s_2$ is a $\Sigma$-expression of type $Seq(t_2)$. The expressions $s_1$ and $s_2$ are called *left step* and *right step*, respectively. Interpretation. Let A be a $\Sigma$-algebra, $[\![s_1]\!]^{A} = (nd_1, \ldots, nd_n)$, i = 1, ...., n, $\xi_i = \{y \mapsto nd_i\}$, $[\![s_2\xi_1]\!]^{A} = v_1$, ... $[\![s_2\xi_n]\!]^{A} = v_n$, then

$$[\![\mathbf{path}(y : s_1)/s_2]\!]^{A} = \begin{cases} \mathtt{f}(\mathtt{asSeq}(\mathtt{asSet}(v_1 \cup \ldots \cup v_n)) & \text{if } t_2 \text{ is a node type} \\ v_1 + \ldots + v_n & \text{if } t_2 \text{ is an atomic type,} \end{cases}$$

where $\mathtt{f}$ is $\mathtt{document\_order}$ if $\mathtt{order\_mode} = \mathtt{ordered}$, and identity function in the opposite case. Note that an ordered set is the result of the interpretation of this expression in the first case and a sequence in the second case.

**Examples:**
  1) The following expression consists of two path subexpressions[4].
  $\mathbf{path}(y : fn : doc(\text{``books.xml''}))/$
      $\mathbf{path}(x : y.child::element(bib))/y.child::element(book);$
The left step is represented in this expression by the function $fn : doc()$, which

---

[4] In this example and henceforth, it is considered that the operator '.' has a higher priority that the operator ':::' which, in its turn, has a higher priority than the operator '/'. There is also no attempt to use any syntactic sugar in expressions.

produces a singleton sequence containing a document node. The right step is represented by another path expression (depending on the variable $y$), which is evaluated for each element of the sequence produced (singleton sequence in this case). In this expression, the left step $y.child :: element(bib)$ gives us an element node at the top of the node hierarchy, which is used by the right step $x.child :: element(book)$ selecting the book elements within the bib elements.

2) If $books$ denotes a sequence of book nodes, then
$$\mathbf{path}(y : \mathbf{select}(x : books) :: typed\text{-}value(x.attribute :: attribute(year)) = 2000)/y.child :: element(title);$$
is an expression evaluating to the titles of the books published in 2000 (note that $x$ ranges over all books and $y$ ranges only over those books that satisfy the selection condition).

3) Let $doc$ denote the following document:
$$< a >\quad < b >< c > 1 < /c >< c > 2 < /c >< /b >$$
$$< b >< c > 3 < /c >< c > 4 < /c >< /b >\quad < /a >,$$
then the expression
$$\mathbf{path}(x : doc.child :: element(a))/$$
$$\mathbf{path}(y : x.child :: element(b))/seq(y.child :: element(c)[2])\text{ evaluates to}$$
$$(< c > 2 < /c >, < c > 4 < /c >)\text{ or }((< c > 4 < /c >, < c > 2 < /c >).$$

### 6.5 Ordering Expressions

In XQuery, the clause **order by** in the FLWOR expression orders a sequence of tuples (records) produced by evaluation of the preceding clauses, based on the values of a number of expressions evaluated for each tuple of the sequence. Therefore, an ordering expression in our algebra serves to order a sequence of tuples (records) based on the values of one or more of *ordering keys*, which are empty or singleton sequences.

Generally, two values of the same ordering key are compared using a predefined operation ">" (greater). However, in case the ordering key has the string type, the name of a specific collation used for ordering may be indicated (as a string value). We will take both options into account.

Let $t$ be a record type $\mathbf{rec}\ x_1 : t_1, ..., x_n : t_n\ \mathbf{end}$, $s$ a sequence of type $Seq(t)$, $e_1, ..., e_l$ be $(\Sigma, \{x_1, ..., x_n\})$-expressions each denoting either an empty or a singleton sequence of type $Seq(t'_k)$ where $t'_k$ is an atomic type, $a_k$ and $b_k$ are one of the symbols '↑' or '↓' ($a$ indicates whether the order is ascending ('↑' or descending ('↓' and $b$ indicates whether the empty sequence has preference ('↑' or not ('↓'), and $c_k$ is a possibly nonempty string if $t'_k$ is the type **string** and the empty string in all other cases, then
$$\mathbf{stable\_order}(e_1[a_1, b_1, c_1], ..., e_l[a_l, b_l, c_l] : s)\text{ and}$$
$$\mathbf{order}(e_1[a_1, b_1, c_1], ..., e_l[a_l, b_l, c_l] : s)\text{ are expressions of type }Seq(t).$$
Interpretation. Let $\mathbf{A}$ be an algebra and $[\![s]\!]^{\mathbf{A}} = \mathbf{s}$. Then
$$[\![\mathbf{stable\_order}(e_1[a_1, b_1, c_1], ..., e_l[a_l, b_l, c_l] : s)]\!]^{\mathbf{A}} = \mathbf{s}'\text{ and}$$
$$[\![\mathbf{order}(e_1[a_1, b_1, c_1], ..., e_l[a_l, b_l, c_l] : s)]\!]^{\mathbf{A}} = \mathbf{s}'.$$
The interpretation of the first expression should produce a sequence $\mathbf{s}'$ containing the same items as $\mathbf{s}$ (i.e., $\mathbf{el} \in \mathbf{s} \iff \mathbf{el} \in \mathbf{s}'$) in the order dictated by $a$, $b$,

and $c$. The second expression differs from the first one in retaining the relative positions of two items having equal values of the ordering key. See the details of interpretation in [11].

**Example.** If *books* denotes a sequence of type $Seq(\text{rec } book : Element, price : Seq(Integer) \text{ end})$, then the following expression indicates ordering the records in the descending order of book prices (records without indicated prices placed last):     **order**$(price[\downarrow, \downarrow, ()] : books)$.

### 6.6 Mapping Expression

This expression denotes the result of a FLWOR query. The constructor of this expression uses a sequence of tuples (records) and an expression and produces a final sequence by evaluating the expression on each tuple of the first sequence. Formally: if $s$ is a $\Sigma$-expression of type $Seq(\text{rec } x_1 : t_1, ..., x_n : t_n \text{ end})$ and $e$ a $(\Sigma, \{x_1, ...., x_n\})$-expression of type $t$, then $s \triangleright e$ is a $\Sigma$-expression of type $Seq(t)$, called a *mapping expression*. Interpretation. Let $[\![s]\!]^A = (\mathbf{r}_1, ..., \mathbf{r}_m)$, $i = 1, ..., m$, $\mathbf{r}_i = \text{rec}(\mathbf{v}_{i1}, ..., \mathbf{v}_{in})$, $\xi_i = \{x_i \mapsto \mathbf{v}_{i1}, ...., x_n \mapsto \mathbf{v}_{in}\}$, $[\![e\xi_i]\!]^A = \mathbf{v}_i$, then
$$[\![s \triangleright e]\!]^A = \mathbf{v}_1 + .... + \mathbf{v}_m.$$

**Example.** Assume the variable *proc* denotes a sequence of proceedings nodes, and we want to pose the following query: *"find the titles of all proceedings whose editors have not have a publication in the proceedings they have edited."*. It can represented by the following expression:
$$\textbf{select}(\lll x : proc \ggg * \lll y : x.child :: element(editor) \ggg *$$
$$\lll z : x.descendant :: element(author)\ggg) :: y \neq z \triangleright x.child :: element(title).$$
The first operator "*" creates a stream of pairs of $(proc, author)$ nodes, the second operator "*" converts it into a stream of triples of $(proc, author, title)$ nodes, the predicate $y \neq z$ selects in the stream those tuples where *editor* and *author* are different nodes, and finally the operator "$\triangleright$" produces the sequence of the titles of the remaining proceedings.

### 6.7 Sequence Expressions

XQuery possesses a number of sequence constructing and manipulating expressions. They are supported in our algebra by several expressions defined as follows.

1. If $e_1, ..., e_n$ are $\Sigma$-expressions of respective types $Seq(t_1), ..., Seq(t_n)$, where $t_i$ is an atomic or node type, then $seq(e_1, ..., e_n)$ is a $\Sigma$-expression of type $Seq(t)$ where $t = Union(t_1, ..., t_n)$. Interpretation. Let $A$ be an algebra, and $[\![e_i]\!]^A = \mathbf{s}_i$, then $[\![seq(e_1, ..., e_n)]\!]^A = \mathbf{s}_1 + ... + \mathbf{s}_n$.

2. If $e_1$ and $e_2$ are $\Sigma$-expressions of type $Integer$, then $range(e_1, e_2)$ is a $\Sigma$-expression of type $Seq(Integer)$. Interpretation. Let $A$ be an algebra and $[\![e_i]\!]^A = \mathbf{s}_i \rangle$, then

　　a) $[\![range(e_1, e_2)]\!]^A = (\mathbf{v}_1, \mathbf{v}_2, ..., \mathbf{v}_n)$,

where $\mathbf{v}_1 = \mathbf{s}_1$, $\mathbf{v}_n = \mathbf{s}_2$, and $\mathbf{v}_{i+1} = \mathbf{v}_i + 1$, for $i = 1, ..., n-1$, if $\mathbf{s}_1 \leq \mathbf{s}_2$;

　　b) $[\![range(e_1, e_2)]\!]^A = ()$, otherwise.

3. If $e_1$ and $e_2$ are expressions of type $Seq(Node)$ then
$$union(e_1, e_2), \ intersect(e_1, e_2), \ and \ except(e_1, e_2)$$

are expressions of type $Seq(Node)$ interpreted as follows. Let $\mathtt{A}$ be an algebra, $[\![e_1]\!]^{\mathtt{A}} = \mathtt{s}_1$, $[\![e_2]\!]^{\mathtt{A}} = \mathtt{s}_2$, then

$[\![union(e_1, e_2)]\!]^{\mathtt{A}} = \mathtt{f}(\mathtt{asSeq}(\mathtt{asSet}(\mathtt{s}_1) \cup \mathtt{asSet}(\mathtt{s}_2)));$
$[\![intersect(e_1, e_2)]\!]^{\mathtt{A}} = \mathtt{f}(\mathtt{asSeq}(\mathtt{asSet}(\mathtt{s}_1) \cap \mathtt{asSet}(\mathtt{s}_2)));$
$[\![except(e_1, e_2)]\!]^{\mathtt{A}} = \mathtt{f}(\mathtt{asSeq}(\mathtt{asSet}(\mathtt{s}_1) \backslash \mathtt{asSet}(\mathtt{s}_2))));$

where $\mathtt{f}$ is $\mathtt{document\_order}$ if $\mathtt{order\_mode} = \mathtt{ordered}$, and identity function in the opposite case.

4. If $s_1$ and $s_2$ are expressions of type $Seq(anyAtomicType)$ and $\odot$ is one of the relation symbols "=", "!=", "<", "<=", ">", or ">=", then $s_1 \odot s_2$ is an expression of type $Boolean$. Interpretation. This expression implements the operation of *general comparison*. See the details of interpretation in [11].

# 7    Node Constructors

This is a set of expressions copying existing nodes or constructing new nodes. The interpretation of these expressions updates the current algebra and produces an element of the new algebra. Therefore, we use a notion of pair $\langle \mathtt{A}, \mathtt{v} \rangle$, where $\mathtt{A}$ is an algebra and $\mathtt{v} \in |\mathtt{A}|$ is an algebra element, as the result of interpretation.

The set of all pairs $\langle \mathtt{A}, \mathtt{v} \rangle$ where $\mathtt{A}$ is a $\Sigma$-algebra and $\mathtt{v}$ a value of type $t$ is denoted by $\mathcal{A}_t(\Sigma)$. The functions $\mathtt{fst}$ and $\mathtt{snd}$ applied to such a pair produce its first and second component, respectively. To save space, we give only informal semantics of the expressions, the formal semantics can be found in [11].

## 7.1    Node Copying

This facility is used in XQuery where parts of existing document trees are used in the construction of new elements or documents. If $nd$ is a $\Sigma$-expression of type $Node$, then $copy\_node(nd)$ is a $\Sigma$-expression of type $Node$, and if $s$ is a $\Sigma$-expression of type $Seq(Node)$, then $copy\_nodes(s)$ is a $\Sigma$-expression of type $Seq(Node)$. In a $\Sigma$-state $\mathtt{A}$ the expressions are respectively interpreted by the functions

$\qquad \mathtt{copy\_node}^{\mathtt{A}} : \mathtt{A}_{\mathtt{Node}} \times \mathtt{A}_{\mathtt{Element}} \to \mathcal{A}_{Node}(\Sigma)$

and

$\qquad \mathtt{copy\_nodes}^{\mathtt{A}} : \mathtt{A}_{\mathtt{Seq(Node)}} \times \mathtt{A}_{\mathtt{Element}} \to \mathcal{A}_{Seq(Node)}(\Sigma)$

as follows[5]: The first function produces a new algebra extending the previous one with a clone of the indicated node, and the second one produces a new algebra extending the previous one with clones of the indicated nodes.

## 7.2    Attribute and Text Node Constructor

These are the node constructing expressions whose interpretation produces a new attribute on the basis of a name and string value supplied in a query or a text node on the basis of a string value.

---

[5] The first argument of both functions is the node/nodes to be copied, and the second argument, if not $\mathtt{NULL}$, is the parent node of each new node.

**Definition.** If $n$ is a $QName$ and $e$ a $String$, then $attribute\_node(n, e)$ is an expression of type $Attribute$.

**Definition.** If $e$ is a $String$, then $text\_node(e)$ is an expression of type $Text$.

## 7.3   Element Node Constructors

There are two forms of element node constructing expressions. The first one constructs an element node with simple content on the base of a string value supplied in a query. **Definition**: If $n$ is a $QName$, $atseq$ an expression of type $Seq(Attribute)^6$, and $e$ an expression of type $Text$ such that $parent(e) = ()$, then $element\_node(n, atseq, e)$ is an expression of type $Element$. By this constructor one can construct a terminal element node.

The second one constructs an element with complex content. **Definition**: If $n$ is a $QName$, $atseq$ an expression of type $Seq(Attribute)^7$, and $elseq$ an expression of type $Seq(Union(Element, Text))$ such that if $type(elseq[i]) = Text$ then $type(elseq[i + 1]) = type(elseq[i-1]) = Element$ (no adjacent text nodes are allowed) and $parent(elseq[i]) = ()$ for any $i = 1, ..., |elseq|$, then $element\_node(n, atseq, elseq)$ is an expression of type $Element$. By this constructor an element node with children is constructed.

**Example.** The following fragment of the XML text:
```
<book> year="2004">
    <title>XQuery: The XML Query Language </title>
    <author>Michael Brundage</author>
    <publisher>Addison-Wesley Professional</publisher>
    <price>34.64</price>
</book>
```
can be represented by the following element constructor:
```
element_node(book, (attribute_node(year, "2004"),
    (element_node(title, (), text_node("XQuery: The XML Query Language")
    element_node(author, (), text_node("Michael Brundage"),
    element_node(publisher, (), text node("Addison-Wesley Professional"),
    element_node(price, (), text_node("34.64")))).
```

A more complex example. The following XQuery query transforms a **bib** document (bound to the variable **$bib**) into a list in which each author's name appears only once, followed by a list of titles of books written by that author. The **fn:distinct-values** function is used to eliminate duplicates (by value) from a list of author nodes. The author list, and the lists of books published by each author, are returned in alphabetic order using the default collation.

---

[6] Constraints: 1) if $n_i = node\text{-}name(atseq[i])$, $n_j = node\text{-}name(atseq[j])$ and $i \neq j$, then $n_i \neq n_j$; 2) $parent(atseq[i]) = ()$. The constrains let one make sure that attributes have different names and none of them is part of an existing tree.

[7] See the above constraint.

```
<authlist>
 { for $a in fn:distinct-values($bib/book/author)
 order by $a return
   <author>
     <name> $a </name>
     <books> { for $b in $bib/book[author = $a]
        order by $b/title return $b/title}
     </books>
   </author>}
</authlist>
```

The query can be represented in the algebra as follows:

element_node(authlist, (), **order**(typed_value(a)[↑,↑,""]:
              <a: fn:distinct-values(**path**(x: bib)/
                    **path**(y: x.child::element(book))/
                      y.child::element(author))>)▷
      element_node(author, (),
        (element_node(name, (), text_node(string_value(a))),
          element_node(books, (), copy_nodes(
            **order**(typed_value(b/title)[↑,↑,""]:
              <b: **path**(x: bib)/
                    **select**(y: x.child::element(book))::
                        a ∈ y.child::element(author) ▷▷
                  b/title))))))

## 7.4   Document Node Constructors

The result of the document node constructor is a new document node whose children are element and/or text nodes.

**Definition:** If *elseq* is an expression of type *Seq(Union(Element, Text))* such that no adjacent text nodes are allowed, then *document_node(elseq)* is an expression of type *Document*.

**Example.** The XQuery query
```
document {
     <author-list>
        fn:doc("bib.xml"/bib/book/author)
     </author-list> }
```
returning an XML document containing a root element named author-list is represented by the following algebra expression:
    document_node((element(author_list, (),
                copy_nodes(fn:doc("bib.xml"/bib/book/author)))))

## 8   Related Work

One of the first works presenting an XML algebra is [5] (an updated version was proposed as a working draft of W3C [16]). The authors show in the paper how nested for-loops can be used to provide restructuring and joining of existing documents and, moreover, how projection can be formally expressed by iteration. There is no algebraic definition of any operation. One can say that just a simple query language is defined that has no relation to XQuery and cannot be used for defining its semantics.

A number of algebras were proposed in the process of design and development of the database system TIMBER [8]. A tree algebra, called TAX, is described in [7]. According to TAX, the database is a collection (set) of ordered labeled trees. For this reason, all operations of this algebra take collections of trees as input and produce a collection of trees as output. The algebra thus uses more complex data structures (trees) compared to our algebra and therefore it is much more heavier. The complexity of the algebra has forced the authors of TAX to design, in addition, a lower-level algebra, called *physical algebra* (reported in [13]), manipulating sequences of trees and serving for implementation of the TAX algebra. However, in the further development of the project the authors practically directly used an updated version of the physical algebra for implementation of a newly designed data structure, Generalized Tree Pattern [3], which represents an XQuery as a pattern consisting of one or more trees. The next step in the project development was the introduction of the notion of a *tree logical class* as a labeled set of tree nodes matching a designated node and development of a new algebra, designed for manipulating tree logical classes [14]. Unfortunately, there is no formal definition of the operations.

An XML algebra for data mining, called XAL, is reported in [22]. An XML document is regarded in XAL as a rooted directed graph with a partial relation on its edges. A XAL operation takes a set of nodes as input and produces a set of nodes as output. The main operations are selection, projection, product, and join. No detailed description of the operations is given.

A logical algebra and a physical algebra reportedly supporting XQuery are presented in [6]. It is claimed that an XQuery query is first translated into the logical algebra and then, after a possible optimization, is evaluated using the physical algebra. Both algebras are described informally. Moreover, since their operations use functions and predicates as operands, they are not algebras in fact.

Another XML algebra, called XAT, is reported in [21]. It is intended to support XQuery like the algebra described in this paper. The XAT data model represents data as hierarchical tables (collections of tuples). The set of XAT operators is divided in three groups: XML operators, SQL operators, and Special operators. All operators as well as translation of the XQuery expressions are described informally, using examples. However, since XAT and XQuery use different data model, the translation is pure syntactical.

Relation-like flat tables are the main data structures used in the Xtasy algebra [15]. Each tuple in a table consists of variable-value pairs also referred to as bindings. The semantics of all the operators are described informally. Only some simple XQuery queries can be represented by the algebra. The tuple-oriented algebra described in [12] resembles the previous one with the exception that the tuple can have a hierarchical structure, i.e., a tuple element can be a set of tuples. The algebra is also informally described.

An XML algebra designed for effective stream processing is briefly described in [2]. The inputs and output of each operator of the algebra are streams represented as tuple sequences. The semantics of the operators are defined by equations using list comprehensions and monoid calculus. Typing details are neglected. Only predicates are used as selection criteria. No navigating function is defined. Differences in paths expressions are not taken into account.

Thus, each algebra is practically capable only syntactically translate some XQuery queries into the algebra. Taking into account that each of them is based on a data model different from XQuery data model, execution of an algebra expression may produce result different from the result produced by direct execution of the corresponding XQuery query.

# 9   Conclusion

We have presented an XML algebra supporting XQuery. The algebra is in fact a number of kinds of expressions (expression constructing operators) algebraically defined. The introduction of kinds of expressions instead of high-order operations using functions as parameters has permitted us to remain in the limits of first-order structures whose instance a many-sorted algebra is.

The set of kinds of expression of the presented algebra substantially differs from the set of operators of relation algebra. The difference is caused by the more complex structure of the XML document compared to the relation. In fact, only selection by predicate test is more or less the same in both algebras. At the same time, the XML algebra in addition permits selection by node test. The projection operator of relation algebra is replaced by the path expression and a number of navigating functions permitting selection of different parts of the document tree. The join operator is replaced by a number of unnesting join expressions permitting creation of a stream of flat tuples on the basis of several possibly nested parts of the document tree.

In addition, we have defined a number of node constructing expressions permitting update of the current algebra by introduction of new nodes and corresponding node accessors. The evaluation of such an expression produces a new algebra as a side effect. Since XQuery allows expressions to be nested with full generality, the evaluation of each expression theoretically may produce a side-effect. For this reason, the semantics of any expression in our approach is a pair, an algebra and a value, which corresponds one-to-one to the semantics of XQuery expressions. Another distinguishing feature of our algebra is that the first operand of many expressions (path, mapping, etc.) provides a context for the evaluation of the second operand, which may help in optimizing query performance. Our algebra does not possess facilities corresponding to the branching and type-checking expressions of XQuery. As we have noted in Introduction, we consider these facilities more appropriate in the XQuery interpreter than in the XML algebra.

# References

1. M. A. Bender,et al. Two simplified algorithms for maintaining order in a list. *Proc. ESA*, 2002, LNCS, vol. 2461, pp. 152-164.
2. S. Bose, et al. A Query Algebra for Fragmented XML Stream Data. *Proc. 9th Intnl. Conference on Databases and Programming Languages*, Germany, September, 2003.
3. Zhimin Chen, et al. From Tree Patterns to Generalized Tree Patterns: On Efficient Evaluation of XQuery. *Proc. VLDB Conf.*, Berlin, Germany, Sep. 2003.
4. H. Ehrig, B. Mahr. *Fundamentals of Algebraic Specifications 1, Equations and Initial Semantics*. EATCS Monographs on Theoretical Computer Science, vol. 6, Springer, Berlin, 1985.
5. M. Fernandez, J. Simeon, and P. Wadler. An Algebra for XML Query. *FST TCS, December 2000*, LNCS, vol. 1974, pp. 11-45.
6. D. Fisher, F. Lam, and R. K. Wong. Algebraic Transformation and Optimization for XQuery. *Advanced Web Technologies and Applications (Proc. 6th Asia-Pacific Web Conference, April 2004)*, LNCS, vol. 3007, pp. 201-210.
7. H. V. Jagadish, et al. Tax: A Tree Algebra for XML. *Proc. Intl. Workshop on Databases and Programming Languages*, Marino, Italy, Sept., 2001, pp. 149-164.
8. H.V.Jagadish, Shurug Al-Khalifa, Adriane Chapman, ea. TIMBER: A Native XML Database. *The VLDB Journal*, Vol. 11 Issue 4 (2002) pp. 274-291
9. K. Lellahi, A.V. Zamulin. An object-oriented database as a dynamic system with implicit state. *Proc ADBIS 2001*, LNCS,vol. 2151, pp. 239-252.
10. L. Novak and A. Zamulin. Algebraic Semantics of XML Schema. *Proc ADBIS 2005*, LNCS, vol. 3631, pp. 209-222.
11. L. Novak and A. Zamulin. An XML algebra for XQuery (preliminary communication). *Preprint No. 117,A.P. Ershov Institute of Informatics Systems* , 2004; http://www.iis.nsk.su/persons/zamulin/preprint_125.ps.
12. Yannis Papakonstantinou, et al. *XML Queries and Algebra in the Enosys Integration Platform*. http://www.it.iitb.ac.in/ prasan/Courses/IT620/MISC/eip.pdf.
13. Stelios Paparizos, et al. *A Physical Algebra for XML*. http://www-personal. umich.edu/ spapariz/publications.html
14. Stelios Paparizos, et al. Tree Logical Classes for Efficient Evaluation of XQuery. *Proc. SIGMOD Conf.*, Jun. 2004, Paris, France.
15. Carlo Sartiani, Antonio Albano. Yet Another Query Algebra For XML Data. *IDEAS 2002*, pp. 106-115.
16. *The XML Query Algebra*, W3C Working Draft, 15 February 2001, http://www.w3.org/TR/2001/WD-query-algebra-20010215.
17. *XQuery 1.0: An XML Query Language*. W3C Candidate Recommendation, 3 November 2005
18. *XQuery 1.0 and XPath 2.0 Formal Semantics*, W3C Candidate Recommendation, 3 November 2005
19. *XQuery 1.0 and XPath 2.0 Data Model*, W3C Candidate Recommendation, 3 November 2005
20. *XQuery 1.0 and XPath 2.0 Functions and Operators*. W3C Candidate Recommendation, 3 November 2005.
21. X. Zhang and E. Rundensteiner. XAT: XML Algebra for Rainbow System. Worcester Polytechnic Institute, Technical Report WPI-CS-TR-02-24, July 2002.
22. M. Zhang, J.T. Yao. XML Algebra for Data Mining. *Proc. of SPIE, Data Mining and Knowledge Discovery: Theory, Tools, and Technology VI*, 12-13 April 2004, Orlando, USA, vol. 5433, pp. 209-217.

# Satisfiability-Test, Rewriting and Refinement of Users' XPath Queries According to XML Schema Definitions

Jinghua Groppe and Sven Groppe

University of Innsbruck, Technikerstrasse 21a, AT-6020 Innsbruck, Austria
{Jinghua.Groppe, Sven.Groppe}@uibk.ac.at

**Abstract.** Writing correct and precise XPath queries needs much effort from users: the user must be familiar with the complex structure of the queried XML documents and has to compose queries, which must be syntactically and semantically correct and precise. Incorrect queries select no data and thus lead to highly inefficient processing of queries. Unprecise queries might select more data than what the user really wants and thus might lead to unnecessarily high processing and transportation costs. Therefore, we propose a schema-based approach to the satisfiability test and to the refinement of users' XPath queries. Our schema-based approach checks whether or not an XPath query conforms to the constraints given in the schema, rewrites and refines the XPath query according to the information of the schema. If an XPath query does not conform to the constraints given in the schema, its results will be every time an empty node set, which is a hint for semantic errors in the XPath query. Our rewriting approach for XPath queries replaces wildcards with specific node tests, replaces recursive axes with non-recursive axes, eliminates reverse axes, and redundant location steps. Thus, our rewriting approach generates a query, which contains more information, and can be more easily refined by the user in comparison to the original query. Our performance analysis shows the optimization potential of avoiding the evaluation of unsatisfiable XPath queries and of processing rewritten and refined XPath queries.

## 1 Introduction

An important issue for query languages is the satisfiability test of a query. The satisfiability test for XPath ([21], [22]) queries can be defined as follows: Given an XPath query Q, the satisfiability test checks, whether or not there exists an XML document D (which conforms to a given schema) so that the evaluation of Q on D returns a non-empty result. Using the satisfiability test can avoid the unnecessary submission and computation of an unsatisfiable XPath query, and thus saves users' cost and evaluation time. As well as for query optimization, the XPath satisfiablity test is also important for consistency problems, e.g. XML access control [5] and type-checking of transformations [15]. Several research efforts focus on the satisfiability test of XPath queries with or without respect to schemas, e.g. [2], [9], [10], [12], [13] and [14].

In the absence of schemas, the satisfiability test can detect errors in an XPath expression, which are inconsistent with the XML data model. For example, the XPath

Y. Manolopoulos, J. Pokorný, and T. Sellis (Eds.): ADBIS 2006, LNCS 4152, pp. 22–38, 2006.
© Springer-Verlag Berlin Heidelberg 2006

query Q1=/parent::a is unsatisfiable, because the root node has no parent node according to the XML data model. The query Q2=//regions/america will be tested as a satisfiable XPath query without respect to a schema. However, according to a given schema, e.g. the schema given in [7], the element regions can have children, which are called namerica and samerica, but cannot have children with name america. Thus, Q2 is unsatisfiable with respect to the given schema. Therefore, we can detect more errors in XPath queries if we consider schema information, which is one of our contributions.

Formulating a query like //a is easy for a user, but the query might often select more data than what the user really wants to achieve. However, writing a query, which exactly specifies the desirable data, might be not trivial for the user as it requires that the user must be familiar with the complex structural constraints imposed by the schema of the input XML document. Thus, there is a need to investigate means to help users to refine their query efficiently. The refinement problem of XPath queries can be stated as follows: Given a satisfiable XPath query Q, we want to find a query R such that for any valid XML document D, the evaluation of R on D returns a subset of the result of applying Q on D, denoted by $R(D) \subseteq Q(D)$, which exactly specifies the data the user wants to achieve. In this paper, we suggest the following refinement approach: Given a query Q, our approach proposes a query Q', which is equivalent to, but which contains more information than Q. For determining Q', we replace wildcards with specific node tests, and replace recursive axes with non-recursive axes. Meanwhile, we eliminate reverse axes, redundant qualifiers and location steps in Q according to the integrity constraints in the schema. This query can be then more easily refined by the user to the query R on the basis of an XPath expression, which is equivalent to, but contains more information than the initial query. Note that in the absence of schemas, the descendant axis can not be replaced with child axes and wildcards cannot be eliminated completely [4].

In comparison to the contributions for the satisfiability test and rewriting of XPath queries with respect to schemas, our approach supports both the satisfiability test and rewriting of XPath expressions, and allows the recursive as well as non-recursive schemas and all XPath axes.

The rest of the paper is organized as follows. Section 2 defines the XML Schema subset and XPath subset supported by our approach. Section 3 develops a data model of XML Schema language for the evaluation of XPath queries on XML Schema definitions. Section 4 presents our approach, including the evaluation of XPath queries on an XML Schema definition, the satisfiability test and rewriting of XPath queries and the complexity analysis of our approach. Section 5 presents the performance analysis based on our prototype. Section 6 describes the related work. This paper ends up with the summary and conclusions in Section 7.

## 2  XPath and XML Schema

XPath queries are used to select a set of nodes in an XML document. In this paper, we consider the basic properties of the XPath language [22][23]. The abstract syntax of the supported XPath subset is defined in EBNF as follows:

Pattern e::= ele | /e | e/e | e[q] | axis::nodetest.
Qualifier q::= e | e=C | e=e | q and q | q or q | not(q) | (q) | true() | false().

axis::=  child | attr | desc | self | following | preceding | parent | ances | DoS | AoS | FS | PS.
nodetest::=  label | ∗ | node() | text().

where label is an element or attribute name and C is a literal, i.e. a string or a number. Furthermore, we write DoS for descendant-or-self, AoS for ancestor-or-self, FS for following-sibling and PS for preceding-sibling. We also use attr as short name for attribute, desc for descendant and ances for ancestor.

The semantics of each pattern is defined in terms of the semantics of its subpatterns. The smallest subpattern is a location step that contains an axis and a node test, with or without qualifiers. An axis identifies a set of nodes, which are related with a given node, called the *context* node. The nodes identified by an axis are filtered by a node-test. A qualifier filters the nodes selected by a pattern.

XML Schema is a language for defining a class of XML documents, called *instance documents* of the schema. We call a schema, which is formulated in the XML Schema language, an *XML Schema definition* (or *XSchema* for short), which is itself an XML document. An XSchema defines the structure of the instance documents, the vocabulary (e.g. the element and attribute names used, and the data types of elements and attributes). In this paper, we support the subset of the XML Schema language, which contains the most important language constructs to express XML Schema definitions, where a given XSchema must conform to the following EBNF rules.

```
XSchema ::= <schema > (elemD|attrGD|groupD|compTD)* </schema>.
elemD ::= <element name='N' occurs? (type='T')?> <complexType (mixed='true')?
             (ref='N')?> complexType? </complexType> (attrR|attrD)* </element>.
groupD ::= <group name='N'> complexType? </group>.
compTD ::= <complexType name='N'> complexType </complexType>.
complexType ::= <all occurs?> complexType?</all> | <sequence occurs?> complexType?
             </sequence> | (elems|groupR)*.
elems ::= (elemD | <element ref='N' occurs? />)*.
groupR ::= <group ref='N'/>.
attrR ::= <attributeGroup ref='N'/>.
attrGD ::= <attributeGroup name='N'> (attrD)* </attributeGroup>.
attrD ::= <attribute name='N' type='T' (use= 'required')?/>
occurs ::= minOccurs=num maxOccurs=(num|'unbounded').
```

**Example 1:** Fig. 1 presents an example of an XML Schema definition web.xsd, which contains the schema information for XML documents describing webpages.

```
(D1) <schema>
(D2)  <group name='pages'>
(D3)   <sequence>
(D4)    <element name='page'
          minOccurs='0' maxOccurs='1'>
(D5)     <complexType>
(D6)      <sequence>
(D7)      <element name='title' minOccurs='0'
          maxOccurs='1' type='string'/>
(D8)      <element name='link'
          minOccurs='0'>
(D9)       <complexType>

(D10)      <group ref='pages' minOccurs='0'
             maxOccurs='unbounded'/>
           </complexType> </element>
          </sequence> </complexType>
         </element> </sequence> </group>

(D11) <element name='web'>
(D12)  <complexType>
(D13)   <group ref='pages'
          minOccurs='0' maxOccurs='unbounded'/>
          </complexType> </element>
          </schema>
```

**Fig. 1.** An XML Schema definition web.xsd

## 3 Data Model for XML Schema

Based-on the data model for the XML language given by [19] and [16], we develop a data model for XML Schema for identifying the navigation paths of XPath queries on an XML Schema definition. The following notations on set and relationships are used to model the XML Schema definition, and are also used to model schema paths (c.f. Section 4). A relationship on types $T_1$, $T_2$, ..., $T_n$, is represented by a function $f$: $T_1 X T_2 ... \rightarrow T_n$. Set(T) indicates the type of a set the elements of which are of type T. We write $\emptyset$ for an empty set, $\in$ for membership and $\cup$ for the union of sets. The transitive closure $f^+$ and reflexive transitive closure $f^*$ of a relationship function $f: T \rightarrow Set(T)$ are defined as follows:

$$f^n(x) = \{ z \mid y \in f^{n-1}(x) \wedge z \in f(y) \}, \text{ where } f^0(x) = \{x\}, f^1(x) = f(x)$$
$$f^+(x) = \cup_{n=1}^{\infty} f^n(x) \text{ and } f^*(x) = \cup_{n=0}^{\infty} f^n(x)$$

An XML Schema definition is a set of nodes of type Node. There are four specific Node types in XML Schema definitions, which are associated with *instance nodes* of the schema: root, iElem, iAttr and iText. Accordingly, we define four functions of Node$\rightarrow$Boolean to test the type of a node: isRoot, isiElem, isiAttr, and isiText, which return true if the type of the given node is a root node, is of type iElem, iAttr or iText respectively, otherwise false.

**Definition 1 (*instance nodes*):** The instance nodes of an XML Schema definition are

- <element name=N> (which is of type iElem),
- <attribute name=N> (which is of type iAttr),
- <complextType mixed='true'> (which is of type iText),
- <element type=T> (which is of type iText), where T is a simpleType.

**Definition 2 (*succeeding nodes*):** A node N2 in an XML Schema definition is a *succeeding node* of a node N1 in the XML Schema definition if

- N2 is a child node of N1, or
- N1=<element type=N> and N2=<complexType name=N> with the same N, or
- N1=<element ref=N> and N2=<element name=N> with the same N, or
- N1=<group ref=N> and N2=<group name=N> with the same N, or
- N1=<attributeGroup ref=N> and N2=<attributeGroup name=N> with the same N.

**Definition 3 (*preceding nodes*):** Node N1 in an XML Schema definition is a *preceding node* of a node N2 in the XML Schema definition if N2 is a *succeeding node* of N1.

Fig. 2 defines the relation functions of Node$\rightarrow$Set(Node), which relate a schema node to other schema nodes. For instances, root(x) returns the root node of the document in which x occurs; iChild relates a node to its instance child nodes. For computing iChild(x), an auxiliary function S(x) is defined, which relates the node x to the self node and all the descendant nodes of x, which occur before the instance child nodes of x in the document order. iDesc relates a node to all its instance descendant nodes and is defined to be the transitive closure iChild$^+$. The relation function iSibling(x) relates the node x to its instance sibling nodes. iBranch(x) relates node x to all the instance element nodes excluding any ancestors and descendants of the node x. iPS(x) relates the node x to its instance sibling nodes that occur before node x in the document order, and iPreceding(x) relates node x to its instance branch nodes that occur before node x in the document order. We write y<<x to indicate that the node y occurs before the node x in the

document order of an instance document. The document order of an instance document is computed from an XML Schema definition in the following way: if a set of elements is declared as sequence with the attribute maxOccurs set to 1, the document order of elements is the order in which they are defined; if it is declared as all or as sequence with the attribute maxOccurs set to be greater than 1, any element of this set of elements can occur before any other elements of this element set in an instance document.

$root(x) = \{ y \mid isRoot(y)\}$

$succe(x) = \{ y \mid y \text{ is a } succeeding \text{ node of } x \}$

$prece(x) = \{ y \mid y \text{ is } preceding \text{ node of } x \}$

$S(x) = \cup_{i=0}^{\infty} S_i$, where $S_0 = \{x\}$, $S_i = \{ z \mid y \in S_{i-1} \wedge z \in succe(y) \wedge \neg isiElem(z) \wedge \neg isiAttr(z) \}$

$P(x) = \cup_{i=0}^{\infty} P_i$, where $P_0 = \{x\}$, $P_i = \{ z \mid y \in P_{i-1} \wedge z \in prece(y) \wedge \neg isiElem(z) \wedge \neg isiAttr(z) \}$

$iChild(x) = \{ z \mid y \in S(x) \wedge z \in succe(y) \wedge ( isiElem(z) \vee isiText(z) ) \}$

$iAttribute(x) = \{ z \mid y \in S(x) \wedge z \in succe(y) \wedge isiAttr(z) \}$

$iParent(x) = \{ z \mid y \in P(x) \wedge z \in prece(y) \wedge isiElem(z) \}$

$iSibling(x) = \{y \mid z \in iParent(x) \wedge y \in iChild(z)\}$

$iBranch(x) = \{y \mid y \in iChild^+(root(x)) \wedge y \notin iParent^+(x) \wedge y \notin iChild^+(x) \wedge \neg isiAttr(y)\}$

$iDesc(x) = \{z \mid z \in iChild^+(x)\}$

$iAnces(x) = \{z \mid z \in iParent^+(x)\}$

$iDoS(x) = \{z \mid z \in iChild^*(x)\}$

$iAoS(x) = \{z \mid z \in iParent^*(x)\}$

$iPS(x) = \{y \mid y \in iSibling(x) \wedge y << x\}$

$iFS(x) = \{y \mid y \in iSibling(x) \wedge x << y\}$

$iPreceding(x) = \{y \mid y \in iBranch(x) \wedge y << x \}$

$iFollowing(x) = \{y \mid y \in iBranch(x) \wedge x << y\}$

**Fig. 2.** Used relation functions

Let NodeTest be the type of the node-test of XPath. An auxiliary function $attr(x, name)$ retrieves the value of the attribute name of the node x. The function NT: Node × Node-Test→Boolean, which tests a schema node against a node test of XPath, is defined as:

- $NT(x, *) = isiElem(x) \vee isiAttr(x)$
- $NT(x, \textbf{Node}()) = true$
- $NT(x, \textbf{text}()) = isiText(x)$

- $NT(x, \textbf{label}) = (isiElem(x) \wedge (attr(x, name)=label))$
  $\vee (isiAttr(x) \wedge (attr(x, name)=label))$

# 4   Schema Paths, Satisfiability Test and Rewriting

In this section, we first present our *XSchema-XPath* evaluator, which evaluates an XPath query on an XML Schema definition and returns a set of schema paths. We then describe the satisfiablity test and the rewriting mechanisms based on the determined schema paths of the XPath query.

## 4.1   Evaluation of XPath Queries on an XML Schema Definition

A common XPath evaluator is typically constructed to evaluate XPath queries on XML documents. Our approach modifies the common XPath evaluator in order to evaluate XPath queries on XML schema definitions rather than the instance documents of the schema. Instead of computing the node set of XML documents specified by an XPath query, our XSchema-XPath evaluator computes a set of schema paths to the possible resultant nodes, when the XPath query is evaluated by a common XPath evaluator on XML instance documents. If an XPath query cannot be evaluated completely, the schema paths for the XPath query are computed to an empty set of schema paths.

### 4.1.1 Schema Paths

**Definition 4 (*Schema paths*):** A schema path is a sequence of pointers to either the schema path records <XP', N$^a$, z, lp, f> or the schema path records <o, {f, ..., f}>, where

- XP' is an XPath expression,
- N is a node in an XML Schema definition,
- a is a label,
- z is a set of pointers to schema path records,
- lp is a set of schema paths,
- f is a schema path list, or a qualifier expression q', and q' ∈ {true(), false(), self::node()=C}, where C is a literal, i.e. a number or a string, and
- o is a keyword.

XP' is the part of a given XPath expression, which has been evaluated; N is a resultant node of a schema whenever XP' is evaluated by our XSchema-XPath evaluator on the schema definition; a is a label associated with the schema node N, indicating an XPath axis, i.e. child, parent, FS, PS or self, from which the node N is generated, or indicating the text node-test text() of XPath. a is needed for rewriting. z is a set of pointers to the schema path records in which the schema node is the parent of the schema node of the current record. Note whenever a record is the first record of a loop, the record has more than one possible parent record. lp represents loop schema paths; f represents either a schema path list computed from a qualifier q that tests the node N, or the qualifier q itself that does not contain location steps like true() or false(), but also including self::node()=C. o represents operators like or, and and not.

**Example 2:** Our XSchema-XPath evaluator evaluates the XPath query Q=//page[title or author]/parent::link on the XML Schema definition in Fig. 1 and computes a set of schema paths from Q (cf. Fig. 3). Fig. 4 is the graphical representation of Fig. 3, in which we only present the schema node item of the schema path records. An empty set of schema paths is computed from another query Q2=//link/title[AoS::page], since the element title is not a child of the element link.

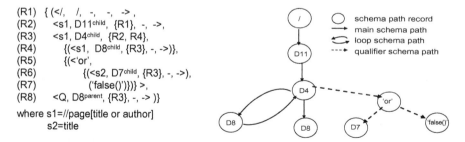

```
(R1)  { (</,  /,  -,  -,  -> ,
(R2)    <s1, D11child, {R1}, -, ->,
(R3)    <s1, D4child, {R2, R4},
(R4)      {(<s1, D8child, {R3}, -, ->)},
(R5)      {(<'or',
(R6)          {(<s2, D7child, {R3}, -, ->),
(R7)          ('false()')})} >,
(R8)    <Q, D8parent, {R3}, -, -> )}

where s1=//page[title or author]
      s2=title
```

**Fig. 3.** Schema paths of the query Q

**Fig. 4.** Graphical representation of schema paths of Fig. 4

### 4.1.2 Computation of Schema Paths

We use the technique of the denotational semantics [18] to describe our XSchema-XPath evaluator, and define the following notations. Let $z$ be a pointer in a schema path and $d$ is a field of a schema path record, we write $z.d$ to refer to the field $d$ of the record to which the pointer $z$ points. We use the letter $S$ to represent the size of a schema path $p$, thus $p(S)$ to represent the last pointer, $p(S\text{-}1)$ to represent the pre-last pointer and so on.

The denotational semantics of the XSchema-XPath evaluator is specified by a function $L$, which is defined in Fig. 5. The function $L$ takes an XPath expression and a schema path as the arguments and yields a set of new schema paths, and is defined recursively on the structure of XPath expressions. For evaluating each location step of an XPath expression, our XSchema-XPath evaluator first computes the axis and the node-test of the location step by iteratively taking the schema node $p(S).N$ from each schema path $p$ in the path set as the context node. The path set is computed from the part $xp''$ of the XPath query, which has been evaluated by the XSchema-XPath evaluator. For each resultant node $r$ selected by the current location step $xp_l$, a new schema path is generated based on the old path $p$. The auxiliary function $\vartheta(r, g)$ generates a new schema path record $e=\langle xp', r, g, \text{-}, \text{->}$ (where $xp'=xp''/xp_l$ and $g$ is a set of pointers to schema path records), adds a pointer to $e$ at the end of the given schema path $p$ and returns a new schema path.

In the case of recursive schemas, a loop is identified whenever the XSchema-XPath evaluator revisits a node $N$ of the XML Schema definition without any progress in the processing of the query. In order to avoid an infinite search, we do not continue the search after the node $N$, once a loop has been detected. We detect loops in the following way: Let $r$ be a visited schema node when evaluating the part $xp'$ of an XPath expression. If there exists a record $p(i)$ in $p$, such that $p(i).N=r$, and $p(i).XP'=xp'$, a loop is detected and the loop path segment is $lp = (p(i), ...,p(S))$. $lp$ will be attached to the schema node $p(i).N$ where the loop occurs. A loop might occur when an XPath query contains the axis desc, ances, preceding or following, which are boiled down to the recursive evaluation of the axis child or parent respectively. For computing $L\lceil desc::n\rfloor(p)$, we first compute $p_i | p_i \in L\lceil child::*\rfloor(p_{i-1})$ where $p_1=L\lceil child::*\rfloor(p)$. If no loop is detected in the path $p_i$, i.e. $\forall k \in \{1, ..., S\text{-}1\}$: $p_i(k).N \neq p_i(S).N \vee p_i(k).XP' \neq p_i(S).XP'$, $L\lceil self::n\rfloor(p_i)$ is then computed in order to construct a possible new path from $p_i$. If a loop is detected in the path $p_i$, i.e. $\exists k \in \{1,.., S\text{-}1\}$: $p_i(k).N=p_i(S).N \wedge p_i(k).XP'=p_i(S).XP'$, a loop path segment, i.e. $\{p_i(k), ..., p_i(S\text{-}1)\}$ is identified. The function $X$ modifies the record, which is the head of the loop, by adding the loop path into the record, i.e. $X(p_i(k), (p_i(k),...,p(S\text{-}1)))$, and returns true. Furthermore, although the schema nodes in two records are the same, i.e. $p_i(k).N=p_i(S).N$, these two nodes have different parents, i.e, $p_i(k).z \neq p_i(S).z$. Therefore, the new parent $p_i(S).z$ has to be recorded and this is done by the function $Z$, which adds a parent pointer into the record $p_i(k)$, i.e. $Z(p_i(k), p_i(S).z)$, and returns true.

The schema paths of a qualifier are attached to the context node of the qualifier. When computing the schema paths of a qualifier, the XSchema-XPath evaluator initializes a schema path variable $f$ with null, which is logically concatenated with the main path $p$, denoted by $p+f$, for the need of both finding the context node of the qualifier and finding the nodes specified by reverse axes in the qualifier, which occur before the context node of the qualifier in the document order. Let $F = \{f_1,..,f_k\}$ be computed from a set of qualifier expressions $q_1..q_k$, where $f_i$ is either a schema path list computed from a qualifier expression $q_i$, or is the qualifier expression $q_i$ itself when $q_i$ does not contain location steps. Let i be an integer indicating the position of a pointer in a schema path p. The function $A(F, i, p)$ writes F into the field $p(i).f$ and returns the modified schema path p. The node $p(i).N$ is the context node of these qualifiers. $q_i$ is evaluated to false if $q_i$ is computed to an empty set of schema paths with the exception of $not(q_i)$, which is computed to true in this case. When the qualifier is evaluated to false, the main schema path is computed to an empty set of schema paths. For the qualifier [q1 and q2], we first generate a schema path with only one record, i.e. f=(<'and', ->), then we compute two sets of the schema paths from q1 and q2, i.e. $L(q_1)(p'+f_1)$ and $L(q_2)(p'+f_2)$, and attach two sets of schema paths to 'and', i.e. f=(<'and', { $L(q_1)(p'+f_1)$, $L(q_2)(p'+f_2)$}>). Finally, the path f is attached to the node in the main path, which is the context node of the qualifier. $L\lceil e[q_1$ and $q_2]\rceil(p)$ is computed to an empty set of schema paths if $q_1$ or $q_2$ is evaluated to false.

L: XPath expression × schema path → set(schema path)

- $L\lceil e_1|e_2\rceil(p) = L\lceil e_1\rceil(p) \cup L\lceil e_2\rceil(p)$
- $L\lceil /e\rceil(p) = L\lceil e\rceil(p_1) \wedge p_1=(</,/,-,-,->)$
- $L\lceil e_1/e_2\rceil(p) = \{ p_2 \mid p_2 \in L\lceil e_2\rceil(p_1) \wedge p_1 \in L\lceil e_1\rceil(p)\}$
- $L\lceil self::n\rceil(p) = \{ \vartheta(p(S).N, p(S).z) \mid NT(p(S).N, n)\}$
- $L\lceil child::n\rceil(p) = \{\vartheta(r, p(S)) \mid r \in iChild(p(S).N) \wedge NT(r,n)\}$
- $L\lceil^* self::n\rceil(p) = \{ p \mid NT(p(S).N, n)\}$
- $L\lceil desc::n\rceil(p) = \{ p' \mid p' \in \cup_{i=1}^{\infty} L\lceil^* self::n\rceil(p_i) \wedge$
  $\forall k \in \{1, ..., S-1\}: p_i(k).N \neq p_i(S).N \vee p_i(k).XP' \neq p_i(S).XP'$
  where $p_i \in L\lceil child::*\rceil(p_{i-1}) \wedge p_i \in L\lceil child::*\rceil(p)$, or
  $p' \in \cup_{i=1}^{\infty} L\lceil^* self::n\rceil(p_{i-1}) \wedge X(p_i(k), (p_i(k),...,p_i(S-1))) \wedge$
  $Z(p_i(k), p_i(S).z)) \wedge \exists k \in \{1,.., S-1\}: p_i(k).N=p_i(S).N \wedge$
  $p_i(k).XP'=p_i(S).XP'$, where $p_i \in L\lceil child::*\rceil(p_{i-1}) \wedge$
  $p_{i-1} \in L\lceil child::*\rceil(p_{i-2}) \wedge p_i \in L\lceil child::*\rceil(p)$.
- $L\lceil parent::n\rceil(p) = \{ \vartheta(r, x) \mid r=Z1.N \wedge Z1 \in p(S).z \wedge$
  $x=Z1.z \wedge NT(r,n)\}$
- $L\lceil ances::n\rceil(p) = \{ p' \mid p' \in \cup_{i=1}^{\infty} L\lceil^* self::n\rceil(p_i) \wedge$
  $\forall k \in \{1,.., S-1\}: p_i(k).N \neq p_i(S).N \vee p_i(k).XP' \neq p_i(S).XP'$,
  where $p_i \in L\lceil parent::*\rceil(p_{i-1}) \wedge p_i \in L\lceil parent::*\rceil(p)$, or
  $p' \in \cup_{i=1}^{\infty} L\lceil^* self::n\rceil(p_{i-1}) \wedge X(p_i(k), (p_i(k),...,p_i(S-1))) \wedge$
  $Z(p_i(k), p_i(S).z)) \wedge \exists k \in \{1,.., S-1\}: p_i(k).N=p_i(S).N \wedge$
  $p_i(k).XP'=p_i(S).XP'$, where $p_i \in L\lceil parent::*\rceil(p_{i-1}) \wedge$
  $p_{i-1} \in L\lceil parent::*\rceil(p_{i-2}) \wedge p_i \in L\lceil parent::*\rceil(p)$.

- $L\lceil DoS::n\rceil(p) = L\lceil self::n\rceil(p) \cup L\lceil desc::n\rceil(p)$
- $L\lceil AoS::n\rceil(p) = L\lceil self::n\rceil(p) \cup L\lceil ances::n\rceil(p)$
- $L\lceil FS::n\rceil(p) = \{ \vartheta(r, p(S).z) \mid r \in iFS(p(S).N) \wedge NT(r,n)\}$
- $L\lceil following::n\rceil(p) = L\lceil AoS:: */FS :: */DoS::n\rceil(p)$
- $L\lceil PS::n\rceil(p) = \{ \vartheta(r, p(S).z) \mid r \in iPS(p(S).N) \wedge NT(r,n)\}$
- $L\lceil preceding::n\rceil(p) = L\lceil AoS:: */PS :: */DoS ::n\rceil(p)$
- $L\lceil attr::n\rceil(p) = \{ \vartheta(r, p(S)) \mid r \in iAttr(p(S).N) \wedge NT(r,n)\}$
- $L\lceil e[q]\rceil(p) = A(\{L\lceil q\rceil(p'+f)\}, S, p')$, where $f=\varnothing \wedge p' \in L\lceil e\rceil(p)$
- $L\lceil e[q_1[q_2]]\rceil(p) = A(\{L\lceil q_1[q_2]\rceil(p'+f)\}, S, p')$,
  where $f=\varnothing \wedge p' \in L\lceil e\rceil(p)$
- $L\lceil e[self::node()=C]\rceil(p) = A(\{ 'self::node()=C'\}, S, p')$,
  where $p' \in L\lceil e\rceil(p)$
- $L\lceil e[e_1 = C]\rceil(p) = L\lceil e[e_1[self::node()=C]]\rceil(p)$
- $L\lceil e[q_1][q_2]\rceil(p) = A(\{A(\{L\lceil q_2\rceil(p'+f_2), L\lceil q_1\rceil(p'+f_1)\}, S, f)\}$,
  $S, p')$, where $p' \in L\lceil e\rceil(p) \wedge f=(<'and', ->) \wedge f_1=\varnothing \wedge f_2=\varnothing$.
- $L\lceil e[q_1$ and $q_2]\rceil(p) = L\lceil e[q_1][q_2]\rceil(p)$
- $L\lceil e[q_1$ or $q_2]\rceil(p) = A(\{A(\{L\lceil q_2\rceil(p'+f_2), L\lceil q_1\rceil(p'+f_1)\}, S, f)\}$,
  $S, p')$, where $p' \in L\lceil e\rceil(p) \wedge f=(<'or', ->) \wedge f_1=\varnothing \wedge f_2=\varnothing$.
- $L\lceil e[q_1 = q_2]\rceil(p) = A(\{A(\{L\lceil q_2\rceil(p'+f_2), L\lceil q_1\rceil(p'+f_1)\}, S, f)\}$,
  $S, p')$, where $p' \in L\lceil e\rceil(p) \wedge f=(<'=', ->) \wedge f_1=\varnothing \wedge f_2=\varnothing$.
- $L\lceil e[not(q)]\rceil(p) = A(\{A(\{L\lceil q\rceil(p'+f_1)\}, S, f)\}, S, p')$,
  where $f=(<'not', ->) \wedge p' \in L\lceil e\rceil(p) \wedge f_1=\varnothing$.

**Fig. 5.** Formulas for constructing schema paths

### 4.2 Testing the Satisfiability of XPath Queries

Since the satisfiability test of XPath queries in the presence of schemas is undecidable for the XPath subset supported by our approach [2], we present a fast, but incomplete satisfiability tester, i.e. for the satisfiability test of XPath queries, our satisfiability tester computes to one of the following results: {*unsatisfiable, maybe satisfiable*}. Whereas we are sure that the XPath query is unsatisfiable, whenever our satisfiability tester returns *unsatisfiable*, we cannot be sure that the XPath query is satisfiable if our satisfiability tester returns *maybe satisfiable*.

**Definition 5** (*satisfiability of XPath queries*): A given XPath query Q is satisfiable according to a given XML Schema definition XSD, if there exists an XML document D, which is valid according to XSD, and the evaluation of Q on D returns an non-empty result. Otherwise Q is unsatisfiable according to XSD.

**Proposition 1** (*Unsatisfiable XPath queries*): If the evaluation of an XPath query Q on a given XML Schema definition XSD by the XSchema-XPath evaluator generates an empty set of schema paths, then Q is unsatisfiable according to XSD.

**Proof.** The XSchema-XPath evaluator is constructed in such a way that the XSchema-XPath evaluator returns an empty set of schema paths, if the constraints given in Q and the constraints given in XSD exclude the constraints of the other. Thus, there does not exist a valid XML document according to XSD, where the application of Q returns a non-empty result.

If the XSchema-XPath evaluator computes a non-empty set of schema paths for an XPath query, the XPath query is only *maybe* satisfiable, since the satisfiability test of XPath expressions formulated in the supported subset of XPath is undecidable [2]. Furthermore, we do not consider the conflict of the constraints from the XPath expression itself, e.g. //a[@b=1][@b=5]. This kind of constraints can be checked by a rule-based approach for testing the satisfiability without schema information like proposed in [10]. The next generation of satisfiability tester may combine satisfiability tester using schema information (as described in this paper) and rule-based approaches (as proposed in [10]) to benefit from the advantages of both approaches,

### 4.3   Rewriting and Refinement of XPath Expressions

After the computation of the schema paths of an XPath query, we can construct an XPath query, which is equivalent to the original one, but in which redundant location steps are eliminated, wildcards are replaced with specific node-tests, and reverse axes and recursive axes are eliminated wherever possible. The rewriting approach of XPath queries includes mapping a set of schema paths to a (regular) XPath expression, and optimizing the mapped XPath expression by a set of equivalence rules.

#### 4.3.1   Mapping Schema Paths to (Regular) XPath Expressions
The mapping function M[L] maps a set of schema paths L={$p_1$,...,$p_m$} into an XPath query Q'. The mapping function M[p] maps a schema path p = ($r_1$,...,$r_n$) (where p∈L) into a sub-expression e of the query Q'. The mapping function M[r] maps a schema path record r (where r∈p) into a pattern of the sub-expression e. The patterns are concatenated in the correct order with '/' to form the sub-expression e=M[p]=M[$r_1$]+'/'+ ...+'/'+M[$r_n$], where we use '+' to denote concatenation of strings. Disjunctions of the sub-expressions form the mapped query Q'=M[L]=M[$p_1$]+'|'+ ...+'|'+M[$p_n$]. In order to compute a pattern from a schema path record <XP', $N^a$, z, lp, f> or <o, {f,...,f}>, we need the following functions. The function S(N, a) computes the axis and the node-test of a pattern; function R(f) computes a qualifier; and the function D(lp) computes the union of loop patterns. Let us assume that B is a pattern, then we define $B^*$ as a loop pattern, in which the Kleene star denotes an arbitrary repetition of the pattern B. As an example, if B = a, then $B^* = (a^0$ | a | a/a | a/a/a |...), where $a^0$ is the empty expression ⊥. The auxiliary function attr(N, 'name')

retrieves the value of attribute 'name' of the node N, which is the name of an element or attribute appearing in an instance document.

Let L be a schema path list, p be a schema path and r be a schema path record, $L=\{p_1,...,p_m\}$ and $p=(r_1, ..., r_n)$, where $p \in L$. The semantics of the mapping function M, which maps a list of schema paths into a (regular) XPath expression, is defined in Fig 6. Note that in the mapping functions of Fig. 6, the two fields XP' and z in a schema path record r are left out since they do not contribute to the computation of the mapping.

If we use the function $M^r[<N^a, lp, ->]$, we get a regular XPath expression with loop patterns using the Kleene star *, which is not a standard XPath operator, and if we use the function $M[<N^a, lp, ->]$, we get a standard XPath expression, which conforms to the XPath specification ([21], [22]), without loop patterns. Since loop patterns are not supported by the XPath language, instead of computing loop patterns, $M[<N^a, lp, ->]$ computes a desc or ances axis from a path record containing loop schema paths.

$$M[L] = M[p_1]+'|'+ ...+'|'+M[p_m]$$
$$M[p] = M[r_1]+M[r_2]+'/'+...+'/'+M[r_n], \text{ if } r_1.N='/'$$
$$M[p] = M[r_1]+'/'+... +'/'+M[r_n], \text{ if } r_1.N\neq'/'$$
$$M[<N^a, -, ->] = S(N, a)$$
$$M[<N^a, -, f>] = S(N, a)+'['+R(f)+']'$$
$$M[<N^a, lp, ->]$$
$$= \text{'desc::'}+attr(N, \text{'name'}), \text{ if } a = \text{'child', or}$$
$$= \text{'ances::'}+attr(N, \text{'name'}), \text{ if } a = \text{'parent'}$$
$$M^r[<N^a, lp, ->] = D(lp)+'/'+S(N,a)$$
$$M[<N^a, lp, f>] = M[<N^a, lp, ->]+'['+R(f)+']'$$
$$M[<\text{'not'}, \{f\}>] = \text{'not'}+R(f)$$

$$M[<\text{'and'}, \{f1, f2\}>] = R(f1)+\text{'and'}+R(f2)$$
$$M[<\text{'or'}, \{f1, f2\}>] = R(f1)+\text{'or'}+R(f2)$$
$$M[<\text{'='}, \{f1, f2\}>] = R(f1)+\text{'='}+R(f2)$$
$$S (/, a) = \text{'/'}$$
$$S(N, a) = a+\text{'::'}+attr(N, \text{'name'}), \text{ where}$$
$$a \in \{\text{'child', 'parent', 'FS', 'PS', 'self', 'attr'}\}$$
$$S(N, \text{'text'}) = \text{'child::text()'}$$
$$R(f) = M(f), \text{ if } f \text{ is a schema path list}$$
$$R(f) = f, \text{ if } f \text{ is a qualifier expression}$$
$$D(lp) = D(\{lp_1,...,lp_k\}) =$$
$$\text{'('+('+M[lp_1]+')*'+'|'...'|'+('+M[lp_k]+')*'+')'}$$

**Fig. 6.** Mapping functions that map a set of schema paths to a (regular) XPath expression. Note that in these mapping functions, the two fields XP' and z in a schema path record r are left out since they do not contribute to the computation of the mapping.

**Proposition 2:** Let S be a set of schema paths, let XP$^r$ be the regular XPath expression mapped from S (where a schema path record with loop schema paths is mapped using the function $M^r[<N^a, lp, ->]$) , and let XP be the standard XPath expression mapped from S (where a schema path record with loop schema paths is mapped using the function $M[<N^a, lp, ->]$). The evaluation of XP returns the same node set as XP$^r$ for all possible XML documents.

**Proof.** As mentioned earlier, a loop occurs only when our XSchema-XPath evaluator processes the location steps, which contains the axis descendant or ancestor to which all recursive axes like following and preceding are boiled down to. All the descendant nodes (or ancestor nodes respectively) of the context node of the location step will be visited. The descendant (or ancestor respectively) nodes are logged into the corresponding schema path records whenever these nodes fulfil the constraints of the current location step and the following locations steps. The function $M[<N^a, lp, ->]$ retrieves the nodes P, which we divide into three different types of nodes: the first type of nodes fulfils the constraints of the current and following location steps and the constraints of the loop patterns, i.e. the nodes retrieved by the $M^r[<N^a, lp, ->]$ pattern; the second type of nodes fulfils the constraints of the current and following location steps, but does not fulfil the constraints of the loop patterns, i.e. these nodes contained in the result of the mapped subqueries of some of the other successfully detected schema paths of Q; the third type of nodes fulfils the constraints of the current location step, but does not fulfil the constraints of following location steps, i.e. these nodes are not logged into any schema path and will be filtered when XP is evaluated. Acording to the XPath language, the result of an XPath query does not contain any duplicates. Therefore, the total mapped XPath expressions using either M or $M^r$ return the same node set for all possible XML documents.

### 4.3.2 Optimizing Mapped (Regular) XPath Expressions

The mapped XPath query can be furthered optimized by eliminating redundant location steps, which are mainly the location steps containing the reverse axis parent. For this optimization, we develop a set of rewriting rules. Different from the rewriting rules presented in [16], which eliminates reverse axes based-on the symmetry of the XPath axes, we eliminate reverse axes mainly based-on the symmetry of the schema paths. For example, [16], which offers a rule-based approach to eliminate reverse axis without considering schema information, eliminates the parent axis by generating a self axis. In comparison, our rules eliminate the parent axis without generating expressions containing the self axis, as we have already considered the schema information when generating the schema paths. The reverse axes, which are remaining after the elimination of redundant location steps, can be eliminated using the rule-set in [16].

Let a be an axis, n be a node-test, e be a pattern and q be a qualifier. The rewriting rules, which eliminate redundant location steps in the XPath expressions mapped from a set of schema paths, are defined in Fig. 7.

$e/attr::n_1/parent::n_2 \equiv e[attr::n_1]$

$e/child::n_1/parent::n_2 \equiv e[child::n_1]$

$e_1/child::n_1/e_2/parent::n_3 \equiv e_1[child::n_1/e_2]$,
   where $e_2$ contains only the axes FS and PS

$e_1/attr::n_1[parent::n_2/e_2] \equiv e_1[e_2]/attr::n_1$

$e_1/child::n_1[parent::n_2/e_2] \equiv e_1[e_2]/child::n_1$

$e_1/child::n_1/e_2/[parent::n_2/e_3] \equiv e_1[e_3]/child::n_1/e_2$,
   where $e_2$ contains only the axes FS and PS

$e_1[child::n_1/parent::n_2/e_2] \equiv e_1[child::n_1][e_2]$

$e_1[attr:n_1/parent::n_2/e_2] \equiv e_1[attr::n_1][e_2]$

$e_1/(e_2/child ::n_1)*/child ::n_2/parent ::n_3 \equiv$
   $e_1/(e_2/child::n_1)*[child::n_2]$

$e/self::n \equiv e$

$e[a::n][a::n] \equiv e[a::n]$

$e[a::n]/a::n \equiv e/a::n$

$e[true()] \equiv e$

$e[q \text{ and } true()] \equiv e[q]$

$e[q \text{ or } true()] \equiv e$

$e[q \text{ or } false()] \equiv e[q]$

$e*/child::n \subseteq desc::n$

$e*/parent::n \subseteq ances::n$

**Fig. 7.** Rewriting rules, which optimizes the XPath queries mapped from schema paths

Note that in Fig. 7, e*/child::n is the pattern, which is mapped by $M^r[<N^a, lp, ->]$ when a = 'child', and desc::n is the pattern, which is mapped by $M[<N^a, lp, ->]$ when a = 'child'. As shown in Proposition 2, although desc::n retrieves a superset of the node set retrieved by e*/child::n, the entire XPath query, which is rewritten from the mapped XPath query, returns the same node set for all possible XML documents when using either desc::n or e*/child::n.

**Example 3:** The schema paths in Fig. 3 is mapped to the regular XPath expression $Q^r$=/web/(page/link)*/page[title or false()]/parent::link and the standard XPath expression

Q'=/web/desc::page[title or false()]/parent::link, and further pruned as Q$^r$=/web/(page/link)* [page[title]] and Q''=/web/DoS::link[page[title]].

**Example 4:** Assume that a user wants to refine a query C = //page[not(parent::web)]/*. Our XSchema-XPath evaluator evaluates the query C on the schema definition web.xsd of Fig. 1 and generates the following XPath query C$^r$ = e$^r$/title | e$^r$/link, where e$^r$= /web/(page/link)*/page[not(parent::web)]. Based on this XPath expression, the user might refine the query as C'= /web/page/link/page/title.

### 4.4 Complexity Analysis

Let $a$ be the number of location steps in query Q and let N be the number of *instance nodes* in an XML Schema definition. Each schema path contains at most $a*N$ nodes, each of which can be the start node of at most $O(\Sigma_{i=1}^{N-1}(N!/(N-i)!))$ different schema paths of length 1 to N in the worst case of a preceding or a following axis until we recognize a loop. Thus, for each schema path of the result of the previous location step, we can detect at most $O(a*N*\Sigma_{i=1}^{N-1}(N!/(N-i)!))=O(a*N*N!)$ different schema paths as the result of the current location step. For all locations steps, we can detect at most $O((a*N*N!)^a)$ different schema paths, each of which contains at most $O(a*N)$ schema nodes, for Q. Therefore, the worst case complexity of both, the runtime and the space, is $O(a*N*(a*N*N!)^a)$.

We assume that the typical case is characterized as follows: Each instance schema node in an XML Schema definition has only a small number of successor nodes. Furthermore, we assume that the query Q specifies a small node set so that we only detect a small number, which is less than $k$, of schema paths. Therefore, the complexity of both runtime and space is $O(k*a*N)$ for the typical case.

The complexity for the construction of the rewritten query is the same in the worst case, i.e. $O(a*N*(a*N*N!)^a)$, and in the typical case, i.e. $O(k*a*N)$, as the construction of the rewritten query is linear to the number of stored nodes in the set of schema paths.

## 5  Performance Analysis

We have implemented a prototype of our approach, including the XSchema-XPath evaluator, satisfiability test and rewriting of XPath queries, in order to verify the correctness and effectiveness of our approach. The test system for all experiments is an Intel Pentium 4 processor 2.4 Gigahertz with 512 Megabytes RAM, Windows XP as operating system and Java VM build version 1.4.2. We use the XQuery evaluators Saxon version 8.0 (//saxon.sourceforge.net) and Qizx version 0.4pl (//www.xfra.net/quizxopen) in order to evaluate the XPath queries.

We have used the XPathMark benchmark [7] as the source of our experimental data. We have transfomed the benchmark DTD benchmark.dtd into the XML Schema definition benchmark.xsd by using the tool Syntext Dtd2xs-2.0 (//freshmeat.net/projects/ syntext_dtd2xs/). We have generated data from 0.116 Megabytes to 11.597 Megabytes by using the data generator of the XPathMark benchmark.

The performance analysis, which deals with the detection of unsatisfiable XPath queries by our XSchema-XPath evaluator and the evaluation of these unsatisfiable queries by common XPath evaluators, has been presented in [9], which shows the optimization potential of avoiding the evaluation of unsatisfiable queries, and a speed-up factor up to several magnitudes is possible. Therefore, in this paper, our performance study focuses on the rewriting overhead and refinement potential. Given an XPath query Q, our approach rewrites Q into a set of more specific (regular) XPath expressions, from which we generate a refined query R. We then use common XPath evaluators to evaluate the queries Q and R on the XML documents with different sizes. We compare the number NQ of the nodes selected by the original query Q and the number NR of the nodes selected by the refined query R, i.e. NR/NQ. We also test the rewriting time of the original queries and the evaluation time of the refined queries.

Fig. 8 presents the original queries Q and their according refined queries R used in our experiment. Fig. 9 presents the result of NR/NQ. Fig. 10 and Fig. 11 present the rewriting time of the original query Q5 by our XSchema-XPath evaluator on the XML Schema definition benchmark.xsd, and the evaluation time of the according refined query R5 on different documents when using the Qizx evaluator and when using the Saxon evaluator respectively. Note that other refined queries have comparable results. The results show that the refined query selects a smaller set of nodes in most cases so that we can save processing and transportation costs. Although the time of rewriting is more than the time of query processing, when the size of the queried data is small, the absolute overhead of the rewriting approach is quite low, less than 1 second in all considered cases.

Q1: //item $\Rightarrow$ R1: /site/regions/africa/item
Q2: //education $\Rightarrow$ R2: /site/people/person/profile/education
Q3: //edge[attribute::*] $\Rightarrow$ R3: /site/catgraph/edge[attribute::from = "J" or attribute::from = "S"]
Q4: //person[child::*] $\Rightarrow$ R4: /site/people/person[homepage]
Q5: //open_auction/child::*/child::* $\Rightarrow$ R5: /site/open_auctions/open_auction/bidder/date

**Fig. 8.** The original queries Q and their according refined queries R

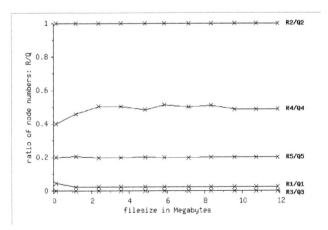

**Fig. 9.** Ratio of the node numbers selected by the refined query and by the original query

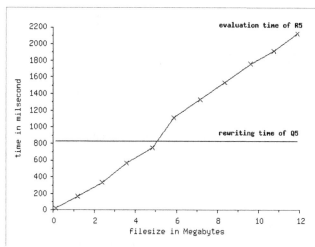

**Fig. 10.** The evaluation time of R5 by Qizx evaluator on different sizes of data and the rewriting time of Q5 by our XSchema-XPath evaluator on the XML Schema definition benchmard.xsd

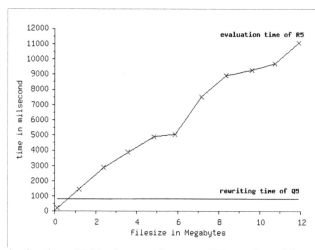

**Fig. 11.** The evaluation time of R5 by Saxon evaluator on different sizes of data and the rewriting time of Q5 by our XSchema-XPath evaluator on the XML Schema definition benchmard.xsd

## 6 Related Work

Several contributions focus on the satisifability problem of XPath queries. [2] theoretically studies the complexity problem of XPath satisfiability in the presence of DTDs, and shows that the complexity of XPath satisfiability depends on the considered subsets of XPath expressions and DTDs. We present a practical algorithm for testing the satisfiability of XPath queries. [12] investigates the satisfiability problem of XPath expressions in the absence of schemas, whereas we present an approach based on schema information. [14] examines the satisfiability test of tree pattern queries (i.e. reverse axes are not considered) with respect to a non-recursive schema. We support all XPath axes and recursive schemas. Furthermore, the approaches presented in [2], [12] and [14] cannot rewrite XPath expressions. In contrast, our approach can rewrite an XPath expression as well as test the satisfiability of XPath expressions. [11] filters the unsatisfiable XPah queries by a set of simplification rules while we use the constraints given by an XML Schema definition to check the satisfiability of XPath expressions.

[13] suggests an algorithm for rewriting and satisfiability test of XPath expressions in the presence of DTDs. Different from [13], which enumerates all possible paths from a DTD, we directly generate the paths for a given XPath query by evaluating the XPath query on the XML Schema definition. Furthermore, we support recursive schemas that are not considered by [13]. We consider all XPath axes, but the axes that depend on document order are not supported by [13].

A number of research efforts are dedicated on rewriting of Path expressions. [4] suggests an approach to minimize wildcards in the absence of schemas. In comparison to [4], we support to eliminate wildcards completely in XPath queries. [16] eliminates reverse axes in XPath expressions according to the axis symmetry of XPath, while we eliminate reverse axes based on the symmetry of schema paths as well as of XPath axes. Thus, we can eliminate reverse axes without adding additional location steps. [6] develops an algorithm to rewrite XPath queries to regular XPath queries on recursive DTDs, but only forward axes are considered and the reverse axes and the axes depending on the document order are not allowed. Our approach can rewrite an XPath query to regular and standard XPath queries in the case of recursive schemas, and supports all XPath axes. Furthermore, similar to [13], [6] enumerates all the paths from a DTD regardless of input queries, but we construct only the paths from an XML Schema definition for a given XPath query. [1], [17] and [20] reduce redundant location steps of tree pattern queries relying on the equivalence and containment analysis of two sub-patterns. [8] reformulates XPath expressions according to XSLT stylesheets in order to reduce the amount of data transmitted and transformed.

[3] models XML Schema with the goal to give a formal description of XML Schema language, whereas our XML Schema model is used to identify the navigation paths of XPath queries on an XML Schema definition.

We extend our contributions in [9] and [10] by rewriting, refinement as well as satisfiability-test of users' XPath queries and a performance analysis, which shows the optimization potential of using our approach in query optimization.

# 7 Summary and Conclusions

We propose a schema-based approach to the satsifiability test, rewriting and refinement of XPath queries. For this purpose, we develop an XML Schema data model to identify the navigation paths of XPath queries on an XML Schema definition so that we can support all XPath axes. Our approach evaluates XPath queries on (recursive) XML Schema definitions rather than the instance XML documents and generates a set of schema paths. If the set of schema paths is computed to an empty set, the XPath query is unsatisfiable, otherwise it is *maybe* satisfiable. Based-on the schema paths, our approach rewrites a given XPath query to a more specific (regular) XPath query by eliminating wildcards, recursive axes, and reverse axes wherever possible. Thus, users can easily refine their query based on the rewritten query of the original query.

We present the experimental results of our prototype, which shows the optimization potential of the satisfiability test and refinement. Our approach can remarkably decrease the processing time of queries by filtering unsatisfiable XPath queries, and a speed-up factor up to several magnitudes is possible. Our approach can significantly reduce the number of nodes selected by refining the original queries and thus the users can save processing and transportation costs.

We are of the opinion that our presented approach can be used to optimize XQuery expressions and XSLT stylesheets, which embed the XPath language.

# References

1. S. Amer-Uahis, S. Cho, L.K.S. Laksmanan, D. Srivastava: Minimization of tree pattern queries. In SIGMOD 2001.
2. M. Benedikt, W. Fan, F. Geerts: XPath Satisfiability in the presence of DTDs. In PODS 2005.
3. A. Brown, M. Fuchs, J. Robie, P. Wadler: MSL: A model for W3C XML Schema. In Proceedings International WWW Conference, Hong-Kong, 2001.
4. C.Y. Chan, W. Fan, Y. Zeng: Taming XPath Queries by Minimizing Wildcard Steps. In VLDB 2004.
5. W. Fan, C. Chan, M. Garofalakis: Secure XML querying with security views. In SIGMOD 2004.
6. W. Fan, J.X. Yu, H. Lu, J. Lu, Y. Zeng: Query Translation from XPath to SQL in the Presence of Recursive DTDs. In VLDB 2005.
7. M. Franceschet: XPathMark – An XPath benchmark for XMark. Research report PP-2005-04, University of Amsterdam, the Netherlands. 2005.
8. S. Groppe: XML Query Reformulation for XPath, XSLT and XQuery. Sierke-Verlag, Göttingen, Germany, 2005. ISBN 3-933893-24-0.
9. J. Groppe, S. Groppe: A Prototype of a Schema-based XPath Satisfiability Tester. In DEXA 2006.
10. J. Groppe, S. Groppe: Filtering Unsatisfiabile XPath Queries. In ICEIS 2006.
11. S. Groppe, S. Böttcher and J. Groppe: XPath Query Simplification with regard to the Elimination of Intersect and Except Operators. In XSDM'06.
12. J. Hidders: Satisfiability of XPath Expressions. DBPL 2003. LNCS 2921, pp. 21–36.
13. A. Kwong, M. Gertz: Schema-based optimization of XPath expressions. Techn. Report University of California, 2002.
14. L. Lakshmanan, G. Ramesh, H. Wang, Z. Zhao: On Testing Satisfiability of Tree Pattern Queries. In VLDB 2004.
15. W. Martens, F. Neven: Fronties of tractability for typechecking simple XML transformations. In VLDB 2004.
16. D. Olteanu, H. Meuss, T. Furche, F. Bry : XPath: Looking Forward. XML-Based Data Management (XMLDM), EDBT Workshops. 2002.
17. P. Ramanan: Efficient algorithms for minimizing tree pattern queries. In SIGMOD 2002.
18. D.A. Schmidt: The structure of Typed programming languages. MIT Press, Cambridge, MA, USA. 1994.
19. P. Wadler: Two semantics for XPath. Tech. Report. 2000.

20. P.T. Wood: Minimising Simple XPath Expressions. In WebDB 2001.
21. W3C: XML Schema Part 1: Structures Second Edition. W3C Recommendation, www.w3.org/TR/xmlschema-1, 2004.
22. W3C: XPath Version 1.0, W3C Recommendation, www.w3.org/TR/xpath/, 1999.
23. W3C: XPath Version 2.0, W3C Working Draft, www.w3.org/TR/xpath20/, 2003.

# X-Warehousing: An XML-Based Approach for Warehousing Complex Data

Omar Boussaid, Riadh Ben Messaoud, Rémy Choquet, and Stéphane Anthoard

Laboratory ERIC - University of Lyon 2
5 avenue Pierre Mendès-France
69676, Bron Cedex – France
omar.boussaid@univ-lyon2.fr, rbenmessaoud@eric.univ-lyon2.fr,
{remy.choquet, stephanea}@gmail.com
http://eric.univ-lyon2.fr

**Abstract.** XML is suitable for structuring complex data coming from different sources and supported by heterogeneous formats. It allows a flexible formalism capable to represent and store different types of data. Therefore, the importance of integrating XML documents in data warehouses is becoming increasingly high. In this paper, we propose an XML-based methodology, named X-Warehousing, which designs warehouses at a logical level, and populates them with XML documents at a physical level. Our approach is mainly oriented to users analysis objectives expressed according to an *XML Schema* and merged with XML data sources. The resulted XML Schema represents the logical model of a data warehouse. Whereas, XML documents validated against the analysis objectives populate the physical model of the data warehouse, called the *XML cube*.

## 1 Introduction

With the recent popularity of Internet and new ways of communication, enterprises are collecting huge amount of heterogeneous data. These data are quite complex since they concern different types of information, coming from different sources, and presented on different supports. For instance, in medical sector, a case study of a patient may contain general information about the patient (age, sexe, etc.) as well as scanned images, recorded interviews and expert's annotations. Since enterprises aim at integrating these data in their Decision Support Systems (DSS), some efforts are needed to structure them and to make them homogeneous as well as possible. The XML (eXtensible Markup Language) formalism has emerged as a dominant W3C[1] standard in describing and exchanging data among heterogeneous data sources in a semi-structured way. Its self-describing hierarchical structure enables a manipulative power to accommodate complex, disconnected, and heterogeneous data. Further, XML documents may be validated against an XML Schema. It allows to describe the structure

---

[1] http://www.w3.org

Y. Manolopoulos, J. Pokorný, and T. Sellis (Eds.): ADBIS 2006, LNCS 4152, pp. 39–54, 2006.
© Springer-Verlag Berlin Heidelberg 2006

of a document and to constraint its contents. Nowadays, in most organizations, XML documents are becoming a usual way to represent and to store data. Therefore, new efforts are needed to integrate XML in classical business applications. Populating data warehouses with XML documents is also becoming a challenging issue since multidimensional data organization [1] is quite different from semi-structured data organization. The difficulty consists in carrying out a multidimensional design within a semi-structured formalism like XML.

In this paper, we propose an XML based approach, named X-Warehousing, to warehouse complex data. We include a methodology that enables the use of XML as a logical modelling formalism of data warehouses. This methodology starts from analysis objectives defined by users according to a multidimensional conceptual model (MCM). We use MCM in order to easily represent multidimensional structures of a data warehouse through what users can express future analysis objectives at a conceptual level. The data warehouse is then modelled at a logical level with an XML Schema, which defines a *reference data cube model*. Our approach also allows to populate the designed data warehouse with XML documents that reflect the latter analysis needs over complex data. In fact, the reference data cube model is matched with complex data presented under XML documents. Note that, we focus on analysis needs rather than data sources themselves. In order to match the reference model with XML documents, they are both presented by XML Schemas. Then, we transform them into *attribute trees* [2] to make them comparable. Therefore, these attribute trees will be merged according to a fusion function by *pruning* and *grafting* [3]. Finally, our approach outputs XML documents valid as well as possible against the reference cube model. Each output XML document respects the user constraints required on its data content and represents a real OLAP (On-Line Analytical Processing) fact. The whole set of the warehoused documents corresponds to the physical model of the data warehouse named *XML Cube*.

The rest of the paper is organized as follows. We address a survey of related work in Section 2. In Section 3, an overview and the context of our approach are given. Section 4 provides a necessary formal background for our X-Warehousing proposal. Section 5 details the methodology of building *XML Cubes* from initial XML sources. We present, in Section 6, a *Java* application we implemented. A case study on a real complex data is illustrated in Section 7. Finally, we conclude and propose future work in Section 8.

## 2   Related Work

Some proposals regarded multidimensional modelling by using XML as a base language for describing data warehouses. Krill [4] affirms that vendors such as *Microsoft*, *IBM*, and *Oracle* will largely employ XML in their database systems for interoperability between data warehouses and tool repositories. Nevertheless, we distinguish two separate approaches in this field.

The first approach focuses on physical storage of XML documents in data warehouses systems. XML populates warehouses since it is considered an efficient technology to support data within well suited structures for interoperability and information exchange. Baril and Bellahsène introduced the *View Model* [5], which is a method capable of querying XML databases. A data model is defined for each view to organize semi-structured data. An XML warehouse, named *DAWAX* (*DAta WArehouse for XML*), based on the *View Model* was also proposed. In [6], Hümmer *et al.* proposed an approach, named *XCube*, to model classical data cubes with XML. *XCube* consists of three kinds of XML Schemas: (1) *XCubeSchema* to hold the multidimensional schema; (2) *XCubeDimension* to describe hierarchical structure of involved dimensions; and (3) *XCubeFact* to describe facts. Nevertheless, this approach focuses on the exchange and the transportation of classical data cubes over networks rather than multidimensional modeling with XML.

The second approach aims at using XML to design data warehouses according to classical multidimensional models such as *star schemes* and *snow flake schemes*. *XML-star schema* [7] uses *Document Type Definitions* (DTDs) to explicit dimension hierarchies. A dimension is modelled as a sequence of DTDs that are logically associated similarly as the referential integrity does in relational databases. Golfarelli *et al.* introduced a *Dimensional Fact Model* [8] represented via *Attribute Trees* [2]. They also use XML Schemas to express multidimensional models by including relationships with *sub-elements*. Nevertheless, Trujillo *et al.* think that this approach focuses on the presentation of the *multidimensional XML* rather than on the presentation of the structure of the MCM itself [9]. They claim that an *Object Oriented* (OO) standard model is rather needed to cope all multidimensional modeling proprieties at both structural and dynamic levels. Trujillo *et al.* provide a DTD model from which valid XML documents are generated to represent multidimensional models at a conceptual level. Nassis *et al.* propose a similar approach where OO is used to develop a conceptual model for *XML Document Warehouses* (XDW) [10]. An XML repository, called *xFACT*, is built by integrating OO concepts with XML Schemas. Nassis *et al.* also define *Virtual dimensions* by using XML and UML package diagrams in order to help the construction of hierarchical *conceptual views*.

The X-Warehousing process is entirely based on XML: it designs warehouses with XML Schemas at a logical level, and then populates them with valid XML documents at a physical level. Further, since it uses XML, our approach can also be considered a real solution for warehousing heterogenous and complex data in order to prepare them for future OLAP analysis.

## 3   Overview and Context of Our Approach

Since we need to prepare XML documents to future OLAP analysis, storing them in a data repository is not a sufficient solution. We rather need to express through these documents a more interesting abstraction level completely oriented to analysis objectives. X-Warehousing builds a collection of homogeneous XML documents. Each document corresponds to an OLAP fact where the XML formalism structures data according to a multidimensional model. In order to do so, we propose to match and validate XML documents against a MCM (*star* or *snow flake* schema) modelled via a reference XML Schema.

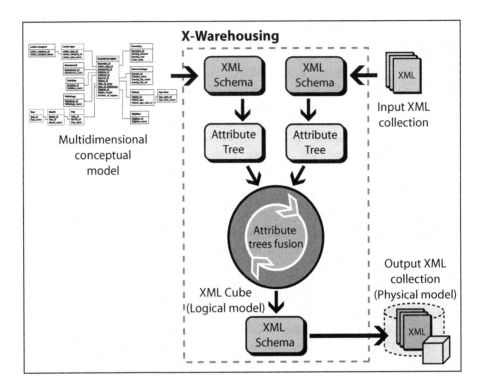

**Fig. 1.** Overview of the X-Warehousing approach

As presented in Figure 1, the **X-Warehousing** approach accepts a reference MCM and XML documents in input. In fact, through the reference MCM a user may design a data warehouse by defining facts, dimensions, and hierarchies. This MCM reflects analysis objectives needed by the user. This model is then transformed to a logical model via an XML Schema (XSD file). Once the reference model is defined, we can submit XML documents to populate the designed warehouse. XML Schemas are initially extracted from input XML documents. We transform the XML Schemas of reference model and XML documents into attribute trees [2] in order to make them comparable. In fact, two attribute trees can easily be merged together through fusion based on *pruning* and *grafting* functions [3]. At this stage, two cases are possible: (1) if an input document contains a minimum information required in the reference MCM, the document is accepted and merged with the MCM. An instance of the XML documents is created according to the resulted XML Schema and validated. This new XML Schema represents the logical model of the final *XML Cube*; (2) otherwise, if a submitted document does not contain enough information to represent an OLAP fact according to the reference MCM, the document will be rejected and no output is provided. The goal of this condition is to obtain an homogeneous collection of data with minimum information capable to populate the final *XML Cube*.

The interest of our approach is quite important since organizations are treating domains of complex applications. In these applications, a special consideration is given to the integration of heterogenous and complex information in DSS. For example, in *breast cancer researches*, experts require efficient representations of mammographic exams. Note that information about a mammogram come from different sources like texts, experts annotations, and radio scanners. We think that structuring such a set of heterogenous data within XML format is an interesting solution for warehousing them. Nevertheless, this solution is not sufficient for driving future analysis. It is necessary to structure these data in XML format with respect to a multidimensional reference model of a data warehouse. Output XML documents of the X-Warehousing process represent the physical model of the data warehouse. Each output document corresponds to a multidimensional structured information of an OLAP fact.

In the following, we base our study on a running example about the *breast cancer* domain. A collection of input XML documents describing suspicious regions of cancer tumors is already created from the *Digital Database for Screening Mammography*[2] [11].

## 4   Formal Background

In this section, we provide a formalization for our X-Warehousing approach. We recall conceptual aspects of typical data warehouse models, i.e., *star schema* and *snow flake schema*. Then, we propose a logical model of data warehouses extracted from the conceptual model, and represented by both XML Schemas and attribute trees [3].

### 4.1   Conceptual Warehouse Models

In general, the conceptual model of a data warehouse is a description of dimension and fact tables. *Star schema* and *snow flake schema* are two main variants of this approach. From a relational point of view, a *star schema* consists in one fact table surrounded by independent dimension tables, i.e., there is no particular relations between dimension tables.

**Definition 1.** *(Star schema)*
*Let $\mathcal{D} = \{D_s, 1 \leq s \leq r\}$ be a set of r independent dimension tables. Each table $D_s$ has $D_s.PK$ as a primary key. $F$ is a fact table with d multi-part keys. A "star schema" is defined by the couple $(F, \mathcal{D})$ which satisfies the following conditions :*

- *$\forall t \in \{1, \ldots, d\}$, it exists exactly one $s \in \{1, \ldots, r\}$ such as $F.K_t = D_s.PK$;*
- *$\forall s \in \{1, \ldots, r\}$, it exists one or many $t \in \{1, \ldots, d\}$ such as $F.K_t = D_s.PK$.*

According to the previous definition, each multi-part key from a fact table is linked to exactly one dimension table. Whereas, a dimension can be linked to one or many multi-part keys in the fact table. This situation can be encountered in many real world modeling problems. For instance, a *Sale* fact can be characterized by an *Origin Country* and a *Destination Country*.

---

[2] http://marathon.csee.usf.edu/Mammography/Database.html

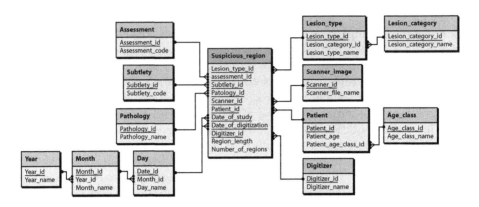

**Fig. 2.** Conceptual model of the *Suspicious Region* data cube

In OLAP analysis, we usually need more than a single granularity level of information in one dimension. For example, to learn about the detailed *Origin* of a *Product*, a multidimensional data model is supposed to cope information as well about the *State* of the *Product* as its *Country*, its *District*, and its *Office*. In order to do so, a dimension may be expressed through a multi-level hierarchy. From a conceptual point of view, a hierarchy with $l$ levels is generally represented by a set of $l$ tables $D_1, \ldots, D_t, \ldots, D_l$, where $\forall t \in \{2, \ldots, l\}$ the primary key $D_t.PK$ of $D_t$ is an attribute (foreign key) in $D_{t-1}$. In other terms, tables of a hierarchy are linked by a semantic inclusion: $D_1 \subset \cdots \subset D_{t-1} \subset D_t \subset \cdots \subset D_l$. For example, one tuple from table *Office* is semantically included to another tuple from table *District*. In the same way, a *District* is semantically included to a *Country*, and so on. We assume that the primary key of a hierarchy corresponds to the the primary key of its first table $D_1$, which represents the finest granularity level of the dimension.

**Definition 2.** *(Snow flake schema)*
*Let $\mathcal{H} = \{H_s, 1 \leq s \leq r\}$ be a set of $r$ independent hierarchies. Each hierarchy $H_s$ has $H_s.PK$ as a primary key. $F$ is a fact table with $d$ multi-part keys. A "snow flake schema" is defined by the couple $(F, \mathcal{H})$ which satisfies the following conditions:*

- $\forall t \in \{1, \ldots, d\}$, *it exists exactly one* $s \in \{1, \ldots, r\}$ *such as* $F.K_t = H_s.PK$;
- $\forall s \in \{1, \ldots, r\}$, *it exists one or many* $t \in \{1, \ldots, d\}$ *such as* $F.K_t = H_s.PK$.

A *snow flake schema* is quite similar to a *star schema*. It consists in one fact table surrounded by a set of dimensions, where each dimension is represented by a hierarchy instead of a single table. For example, the MCM of Figure 2 displays a data cube of *suspicious regions* (tumors detected on mammographic screens) organized according to a *snow flake schema*. The conceptual representation of data warehouses is a way through what users can easily define future analysis objectives. We emphasize that the relational formalism as used here aims at representing both multidimensional data structure and analysis objectives.

## 4.2   Modelling a Warehouse with XML

An XML document consists in nested element structures, starting with a root element. Each element can contain sub-elements and attributes. Both elements and attributes are allowed to have values. Attributes are included, with their respective values, within the element's opening declaration (tag). Between an opening and a closing tag of an element, any number of sub-elements can be present. According to these properties, we propose to represent the above conceptual models (*star schema* and *snow flake schema*) of XML warehouses. More precisely, we use XML Schemas to define the structure of a data warehouse.

To formalize a *star schema* of an XML warehouse, we define the concept of an *XML star schema* as follows:

**Definition 3.** *(XML star schema)*
*Let $(F, \mathcal{D})$ be a star schema, where $F$ is a fact table having $m$ measure attributes $\{F.M_q, 1 \leq q \leq m\}$ and $\mathcal{D} = \{D_s, 1 \leq s \leq r\}$ is a set of $r$ independent dimension tables where each $D_s$ contains a set of $n_s$ attributes $\{D_s.A_i, 1 \leq i \leq n_s\}$. The "XML star schema" of $(F, \mathcal{D})$ is an XML Schema where:*

- *$F$ defines the XML root element in the XML Schema;*
- *$\forall q \in \{1, \ldots, m\}$, $F.M_q$ defines an XML attribute included in the the XML root element;*
- *$\forall s \in \{1, \ldots, r\}$, $D_s$ defines as many XML sub-elements of the XML root element as times it is linked to the fact table $F$;*
- *$\forall s \in \{1, \ldots, r\}$ and $\forall i \in \{1, \ldots, n_s\}$, $D_s.A_i$ defines an XML attribute included in the XML element $D_s$.*

Since the XML formalism allows to embed multi-level sub-elements in one XML tag, we use this property to represent XML hierarchies of dimensions. Let $H = \{D_1, \ldots, D_t, \ldots, D_l\}$ be a dimension hierarchy. We can represent this hierarchy by writing $D_1$ as an XML element and $\forall t \in \{2, \ldots, l\}$, $D_t$ is writing as an XML sub-elements of the XML element $D_{t-1}$. The attributes of each tables $D_t$ are defined as XML attributes included in the XML element $D_t$. Therefore, we can also define the notion of *XML snow flake schema*, which is the XML equivalent of a conceptual *snow flake schema*:

**Definition 4.** *(XML snow flake schema)*
*Let $(F, \mathcal{H})$ be a star schema, where $F$ is a fact table having $m$ measure attributes $\{F.M_q, 1 \leq q \leq m\}$ and $\mathcal{H} = \{H_s, 1 \leq s \leq r\}$ is a set of $r$ independent hierarchies. The "XML snow flake schema" of $(F, \mathcal{H})$ is an XML Schema where:*

- *$F$ defines the XML root element in the XML Schema;*
- *$\forall q \in \{1, \ldots, m\}$, $F.M_q$ defines an XML attribute included in the the XML root element;*
- *$\forall s \in \{1, \ldots, r\}$, $H_s$ defines as many XML dimension hierarchies as times it is linked to the fact table $F$, like sub-elements of the XML root element.*

Based on XML formalism properties, XML Schemas enable to write a logical model of a data warehouse from its conceptual model. Our approach does not only use the XML formalism to design data warehouses (or data cubes), but also populates them with data. We use XML documents to support information relative to the designed facts. As an XML document supports values of elements and attributes, we assume that it contains information about a single OLAP fact. We say that an XML document supports an *XML fact* when it is valid against an *XML star schema* or an *XML snow flake schema* representing a logical model of a warehouse. For instance, Figure 3 shows an example of an *XML fact* associated to the conceptual model of the "Suspicious Region" data cube presented in Figure 2. Note that at a physical level, the *XML Cube*, introduced in Section 3, corresponds to a set of *XML facts*.

```xml
<?xml version="1.0" encoding="UTF-8" ?>
<Suspicious_region Region_length="287" Number_of_regions="6">
        <Patient Patient_age="60" >
                <Age_class Age_class_name="Between 60 and 69 years old" />
        </Patient>
        <Lesion_type Lesion_type_name="calcification type round_and_regular distribution n/a">
                <Lesion_category Lesion_category_name="calcification type round_and_regular" />
        </Lesion_type>
        <Assessment Assessment_code="2" />
        <Subtlety Subtlety_code="4" />
        <Pathology Pathology_name="benign_without_callback" />
        <Date_of_study Date="1998-06-04">
                <Day Day_name="June 4, 1998">
                        <Month Month_name="June, 1998">
                                <Year Year_name="1998" />
                        </Month>
                </Day>
        </Date_of_study>
        <Date_of_digitization Date="1998-07-20">
                <Day Day_name="July 20, 1998">
                        <Month Month_name="July, 1998">
                                <Year Year_name="1998" />
                        </Month>
                </Day>
        </Date_of_digitization>
        <Digitizer Digitizer_name="lumisys laser" />
        <Scanner_image Scanner_file_name="B_3162_1.RIGHT_CC.LJPEG" />
</Suspicious_region>
```

**Fig. 3.** An example of an *XML fact*

### 4.3  Attribute Trees

The concept of attribute trees was first introduced by Golfarelli *et al.*. An attribute tree is a directed, acyclic and weakly connected graph that represents a warehouse schema. In [3], Golfarelli and Rizzi have proposed a general framework for data warehouses design, where a warehouse may be represented by an attribute tree on which it is possible to apply algorithms in order to transform it. For more details about attribute trees, we refer lectures to [2].

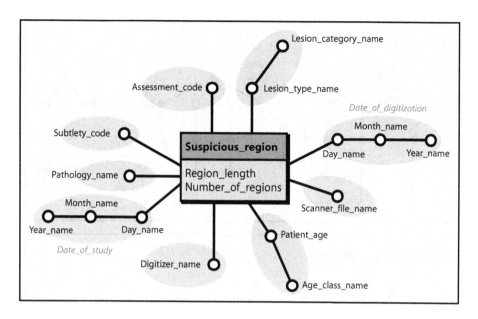

**Fig. 4.** Attribute tree associated to the *Suspicious Region* data cube

In order to handel data warehouses and to be able to transform their schemas, we also represent their logical model via attribute trees. For example, Figure 4 shows the attribute tree associated to the multidimensional model of the "Suspicious Region" data cube presented in Figure 2.

## 5   Building XML Cubes

Recall that our approach starts from a reference MCM corresponding to user's analysis objectives. The reference MCM will be matched with complex data presented in XML documents. In order to make them comparable, both MCM and XML documents are transformed into attribute trees. As explained in Subsection 5.1, the comparison of attribute trees is realized by fusion operations according to *pruning*, and *grafting* functions [3]. Nevertheless, an XML document which does not contains sufficient information according to defined analysis objectives is naturally rejected from the final warehouse. Thus, we introduce in Subsection 5.2 the concept of *Minimal XML document content*.

### 5.1   Fusion of Attribute Trees

The *pruning* and the *grafting* functions provide from two input attribute trees a merged one which contains the maximum of common attributes with respect to their relative relationships.

The fusion by *pruning* is carried out by dropping any uncommon subtree starting from the root vertex. Dropped attributes are not included in the merged

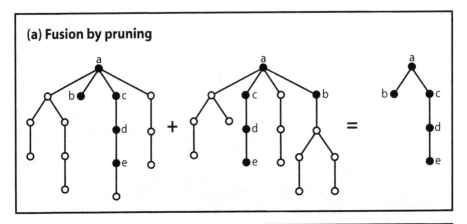

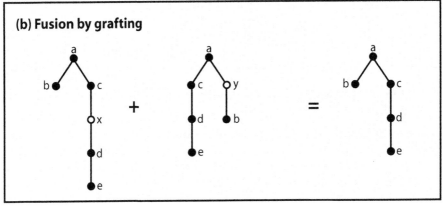

**Fig. 5.** Examples of fusion of two attribute trees by (a) *pruning* and by (b) *grafting*

tree. For example, in Figure 5(a), only common vertexes (black circles) in the two input trees are kept in the resulting tree. All other uncommon vertexes (white circles) are therefore dropped with their subtrees.

The fusion by *grafting* is used when common subtrees do not have a same structure of relationships in two input trees. In this case we need to pick up common attributes by preserving their general relationships. When an uncommon vertex is dropped, the grafting function checks wether its descendants contain common vertex or not. The common descendants are therefore preserved in the merged tree. For example, in Figure 5(b), uncommon vertexes x and y are dropped, but since their respective descendants (d, e and b) are common, they are kept in the merged tree.

## 5.2   Minimal XML Document Content

In some cases, when an input XML document does not contain enough information required by the analysis objectives, the fusion provides a poor output

XML document, which represents an OLAP fact with missing data. It is naturally useless to populate the warehouse with such a document. In order to check wether an input XML document contains enough information to populate the warehouse or not, we introduce the *Minimal XML document content*. The *minimal XML document content* is an information threshold entirely defined by users when submitting the MCM to express analysis objectives. At this stage, a user can declare for each measure, dimension, and dimension hierarchy wether it is mandatory or optional according to his analysis objectives needed in the final *XML Cube*. The *minimal XML document content* corresponds to the attribute tree associated to mandatory elements declared by the user when submitting the data cube model.

Recall that our approach aims at building a data cube with XML sources that allows future OLAP analysis. It is naturally not possible to decide with an automatic process which element in a future analysis context may be optional or not. It is entirely up to the user to define the *minimal XML document content*. Nevertheless, by default, we suppose that all measures and dimensions attributes of a submitted data cube model are mandatory in the final *XML Cube*. We also suppose that not all measures can be optional elements in the data cube. Indeed, in an analysis context, OLAP facts without a measure could not be exploited by OLAP operators such as aggregation. So, users are not allowed to set all the measures to optional elements. At least one measure in the submitted data cube model must be mandatory.

At the fusion step, the attribute tree of an input XML document is checked. If it contains all mandatory elements required by the user, it will be merged with the attribute tree of the data cube model. Else, it will be rejected, the fusion process will be canceled, and therefore no output document will be created.

# 6    Implementation

The core programm of the X-Warehousing application is developed with *Java* and runs on all Java-enabled platforms (Figure 6(b)). The application contains two main modules: the *Model Loader Module* and the *Model Merger Module*.

## 6.1    Model Loader Module

A reference data cube model can be submitted by a manual input or by loading an XSD file associated to a MCM. In the case of a manual submission, the loader module transforms the data cube model into an XML Schema and then into an attribute tree. The attribute tree is saved into an XSD file, which will be displayed within a hierarchical tree (Figure 6(b)) via a *JTree Object*. If a user loads an XSD file, an algorithm parses it and populates an internal attribute tree object structure. We consider each XSD file as a *JDOM* document type. Then, we use the *JDOM API* to scan the document and build attribute trees. On the other hand, the *Model Loader Module* loads input XML documents containing data and their underlying structure. It also extracts the XSD file and the attribute tree corresponding to an input XML document.

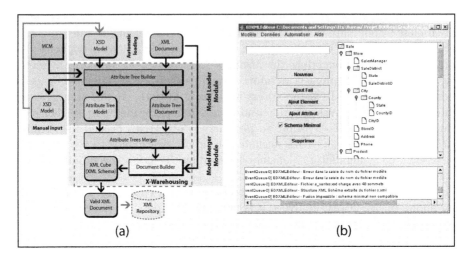

**Fig. 6.** (a) Architecture (b) Interface of the X-Warehousing application

## 6.2 Model Merger Module

Once a data cube reference model and input XML documents are loaded, the *Model Merger Module* can run according to an *automatic* or a *manual* mode. The two modes use the same core algorithms. Nevertheless, the automatic mode picks up XML documents from a specified directory, validates them against the reference model and saves them in an XML repository automatically within a looping mode. The *Model Merger Module* works with the help of fusion functions presented in Section 5. Figure 7 shows function MergeTree which merges two attribute trees. This function goes through each branch of the tree, reads the tree of the data cube model and the tree of an input XML document and populates a new XML document with the resulted model structure. When a vertex from the reference tree does not match with the document tree, MergeTree sets the arc value to zero. Then, it re-writes the tree with only non-null arcs.

```
Function MergeTree(tree1,tree2)
    tree3=DuplicateTree(tree1)
    While Not(end(nodeList(tree3)))
        vertex1=GetVertex(tree3)
        While Not(end(nodeList(tree2)))
            vertex2=GetVertex(tree2)
            If vertex2=vertex1 Then vertex1.arc = 0
        End While
    End While
    Tree3=WriteTree(tree3)
End Function
```

**Fig. 7.** The function MergeTree

## 7    Case Study

We run our X-Warehousing approach on a real world application domain. We consider the *screening mammography* data cube, presented in Figure 2, a reference MCM. We use a collection of 4 686 XML documents as input data to be warehoused [3]. All these documents have the same structure and are valid against the same XML Schema. Therefore they have the same attribute tree. Figure 8 shows the attribute tree associated to these input XML documents. Once the reference MCM and the input XML documents are submitted, our application achieves the fusion of *attribute trees* displayed in Figures 8 and 4. The result of this step closely depends on the *minimal XML document content* defined at the submission of the reference MCM.

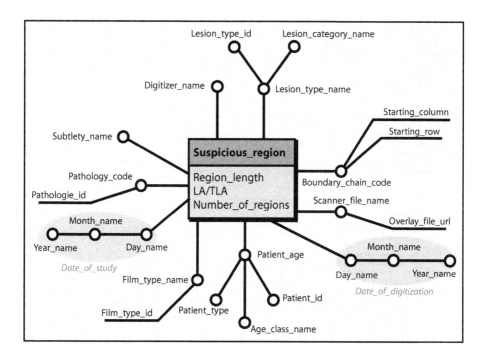

**Fig. 8.** Attribute tree of input XML documents

For example, let set to mandatory all the dimensions and all the measures of the reference model. In this case, all the input XML documents will be rejected and no output will be obtained. In fact, note that the *Assessment_code* attribute is absent in the attribute tree of input XML documents. Therefore, as this attribute is mandatory in the reference model, the *Attribute Tree Merger* will reject each XML document that does not include it.

---

[3] The collection of XML documents is available at: http://eric.univ-lyon2.fr/ ~rbenmessaoud/?page=donnees&section=3

```
<?xml version="1.0" encoding="UTF-8" ?>
<xs:schema xmlns="http://www.w3schools.com" >

  <xs:element name="Suspicious_region" >
    <xs:complexType>
      <xs:sequence>
        <xs:element name="Patient" type="Patient_Type" />
        <xs:element name="Lesion_Type" type="Lesion_Type_Type" />
        <xs:element name="Subtlety" type="Subtlety_Type" />
        <xs:element name="Pathology" type="Pathology_Type" />
        <xs:element name="Date_of_study" type="Date_Type" />
        <xs:element name="Date_of_digitization" type="Date_Type" />
        <xs:element name="Digitizer" type="Digitizer_Type" />
        <xs:element name="Scanner_image" type="Scanner_Type" />
      </xs:sequence>
      <xs:attribute name="Region_length" type="xs:integer" />
      <xs:attribute name="Number_of_regions" type="xs:integer" />
    </xs:complexType>
  </xs:element>

  <xs:complexType name="Patient_Type" >
    <xs:sequence>
      <xs:element name="Age_class" >
        <xs:complexType>
          <xs:attribute name="Age_class_name" type="xs:string"/>
        </xs:complexType>
      </xs:element>
    </xs:sequence>
    <xs:attribute name="Patient_age" type="xs:integer"/>
  </xs:complexType>

  <xs:complexType name="Lesion_Type_Type" >
    <xs:sequence>
      <xs:element name="Lesion_category" >
        <xs:complexType>
          <xs:attribute name="Lesion_category_name" type="xs:string"/>
        </xs:complexType>
      </xs:element>
    </xs:sequence>
    <xs:attribute name="Lesion_type_name" type="xs:string"/>
  </xs:complexType>

  <xs:complexType name="Subtlety_Type" >
    <xs:attribute name="Subtlety_code" type="xs:integer"/>
  </xs:complexType>

  <xs:complexType name="Pathology_Type" >
    <xs:attribute name="Pathology_name" type="xs:string"/>
  </xs:complexType>

  <xs:complexType name="Date_Type" >
    <xs:sequence>
      <xs:element name="Day" >
        <xs:complexType>
          <xs:sequence>
            <xs:element name="Month" >
              <xs:complexType>
                <xs:sequence>
                  <xs:element name="Year" >
                    <xs:complexType>
                      <xs:attribute name="Year_name" type="xs:integer"/>
                    </xs:complexType>
                  </xs:element>
                </xs:sequence>
                <xs:attribute name="Month_name" type="xs:string"/>
              </xs:complexType>
            </xs:element>
          </xs:sequence>
          <xs:attribute name="Day_name" type="xs:string"/>
        </xs:complexType>
      </xs:element>
    </xs:sequence>
    <xs:attribute name="Date" type="xs:date"/>
  </xs:complexType>

  <xs:complexType name="Scanner_Type" >
    <xs:attribute name="Scanner_file_name" type="xs:string"/>
  </xs:complexType>

</xs:schema>
```

**Fig. 9.** Logical model of the *Suspicious Region XML Cube*

Suppose now that we define a more flexible *minimal XML document content* by setting *Assessment* dimension to optional. In this case, the lack of the *Assessment_code* attribute in input XML document would not prevent the fusion step of attribute trees. Therefore, the *Model Merger Module* provides a logical model of an *XML Cube* represented by the XML Schema of Figure 9. Further, for each input document, an *XML fact* (XML document) is generated.

Note that, in this case study, as all the input XML documents have the same structure, all the generated *XML facts* are valid against the same *XML Cube* of Figure 9. Note also that uncommon attributes in attribute trees of Figures 8 and 4 are pruned by the *Attribute Trees Merger* component of our application. For instance, the attributes *Lesion_type_id*, *Boundary_chain_code*, and *Patient_id* are dropped, and therefore do not exist in the *XML Cube*.

Finally, through this case study, we show the capability of our approach to use XML both to design and to store complex data according to a multidimensional structure that reflects analysis objectives required by users. XML can therefore be considered as a logical and physical description platform for future analysis tasks on complex data.

## 8   Conclusion and Future Work

In this paper, we proposed a methodology entirely based on the XML formalism to warehouse complex data. Our **X-Warehousing** approach does not simply populate a repository with XML documents, but also expresses an interesting abstraction level by preparing XML documents to future analysis. In fact, it consists in validating documents against an XML Schema which designs a data warehouse. We defined a general formalization for modelling *star* and *snow flake schemas* within XML. We also use the concept of attribute trees [2] in order to help the creation and the warehousing of homogeneous XML documents by merging initial XML sources with a reference multidimensional model. Constraints on the created XML documents can be required and expressed by users. To validate our **X-Warehousing** approach, we implemented a Java application which loads in input a reference multidimensional model and XML documents. It provides a logical and a physical model of an *XML cube* composed of homogeneous XML documents where each document corresponds to an OLAP fact which respects data required constraints. A case study on *breast cancer* domain is provided to show the interest of employing our approach in a real world field for designing and warehousing complex data by using XML.

For future work, a lot of issues need to be addressed. The first is devoted to a performance study of OLAP queries in order to achieve analysis on XML documents as provided in the *XML Cube*. The second issue deals with experimental tests on the reliability of the developed application. This includes studies on complexity and processing time of loading input XML documents, building attribute trees, fusion of attribute trees, and creation of output XML documents. Third, some optimization are also needed on the *Model Loader Module* architecture. For instance, when we submit a collection of XML documents having the same structure, the application does not need to generate an XML Schema and an attribute tree for each input document. Finally, we plan to study the problem of updating the *XML Cube* when the reference MCM is modified in order to attend new analysis objectives.

# References

1. Kimball, R.: The Data Warehouse Toolkit. John Wiley & Sons (1996)
2. Golfarelli, M., Maio, D., Rizzi, S.: Conceptual Design of Data Warehouses from E/R Schema. In: Proceedings of the $31^{st}$ Annual Hawaii International Conference on System Sciences (HICSS 1998), Washington, DC, USA, IEEE Computer Society (1998) 334–343
3. Golfarelli, M., Rizzi, S.: Designing the Data Warehouse: Key Steps and Crucial Issues. Journal of Computer Science and Information Management **2**(3) (1999) 88–100
4. Krill, P.: XML Builds Momentun as Repository Standard. InfoWorld **20**(25) (1998) 6
5. Baril, X., Bellahsène, Z.: Designing and Managing an XML Warehouse. In: XML Data Management: Native XML and XML-Enabled Database Systems. First edn. Addison Wesley Professional (2003) 455–474
6. Hümmer, W., Bauer, A., Harde, G.: XCube: XML for Data Warehouses. In: Proceedings of the $6^{th}$ ACM International Workshop on Data Warehousing and OLAP (DOLAP 2003), New Orleans, Louisiana, USA, ACM Press (2003) 33–40
7. Pokorný, J.: Modelling Stars Using XML. In: Proceedings of the $4^{th}$ ACM International Workshop on Data Warehousing and OLAP (DOLAP 2001), Atlanta, Georgia, USA, ACM Press (2001) 24–31
8. Golfarelli, M., Rizzi, S., Vrdoljak, B.: Data Warehouse Design from XML Sources. In: Proceedings of the $4^{th}$ ACM International Workshop on Data Warehousing and OLAP (DOLAP 2001), Atlanta, Georgia, USA, ACM Press (2001) 40–47
9. Trujillo, J., Lujàn-Mora, S., Song, I.: Applying UML and XML for Designing and Interchanging Information for Data Warehouses and OLAP Applications. Journal of Database Management **15**(1) (2004) 41–72
10. Nassis, V., Rajugan, R., Dillon, T.S., Rahayu, J.W.: Conceptual Design of XML Document Warehouses. In: Proceedings of the $6^{th}$ International Conference Data Warehousing and Knowledge Discovery (DaWaK 2004), Zaragoza, Spain, Springer (2004) 1–14
11. Heath, M., Bowyer, K., Kopans, D., Moore, R., Jr, P.K.: The Digital Database for Screening Mammography. In: Proceedings of the $5^{th}$ International Workshop on Digital Mammography, Toronto, Canada, Medical Physics Publishing (Madison, WI) (2000)

# SDQNET: Semantic Distributed Querying in Loosely Coupled Data Sources

Eirini Spyropoulou and Theodore Dalamagas

School of Electr. and Comp. Engineering
National Techn. University of Athens,
Athens, GR 15773
{ispirop, dalamag}@dblab.ece.ntua.gr

**Abstract.** Web communities involve networks of loosely coupled data sources. Members in those communities should be able to pose queries and gather results from all data sources in the network, where available. At the same time, data sources should have limited restrictions on how to organize their data. If a global schema is not available for such a network, query processing is strongly based on the existence of (hard to maintain) mapping rules between pairs of data sources. If a global schema is available, local schemas of data sources have to follow strict modelling restrictions posed by that schema.

In this paper, we suggest an architecture to provide better support for distributed data management in loosely coupled data sources. In our approach, data sources can maintain diverse schemas. No explicit mapping rules between data sources are needed to facilitate query processing. Data sources can join and leave the network any time, at no cost for the community. We demonstrate our approach, describing SDQNET, a prototype platform to support semantic query processing in loosely coupled data sources.

## 1 Introduction

Web communities, e.g. concerning e-science, e-learning, art and culture, are popular means of exchanging data and queries for collaborative work. Such communities are based on a network of loosely coupled data sources characterized by heterogeneity and autonomy. A community member in any data source should be able to pose queries and gather results from all the other data sources in the network, where available. At the same time, data sources should have limited restrictions on how to organize their data. Also, a data source should be able to leave/join the network at any time, with no additional global maintenance cost for the community.

Traditional information integration architectures, like virtual databases [9] and mediators [10], provide an arrangement of heterogeneous data sources with a global aspect of the underlying information, independent of its schema and location. However, both architectures are not directly applicable to communities of loosely coupled databases. This is due to their requirement for the existence

Y. Manolopoulos, J. Pokorný, and T. Sellis (Eds.): ADBIS 2006, LNCS 4152, pp. 55–70, 2006.

of a global mediated schema and mappings between that schema and the (local) schemas of the data sources. A global schema must be prepared carefully and globally, and is usually hard to maintain. Data sources are not autonomous enough to significantly change their schemas. The ad-hoc extensibility of data sources is missing. Thus, even for small-scale loosely coupled data sources, data and query exchanging is difficult to achieve.

Peer-to-peer data management systems (PDMSs) [2] provide an information integration framework closely related to that of loosely coupled databases. PDMSs support decentralized sharing and management of data using data sources that have client and server functionality at the same time. A PDMS consists of a set of data sources. Each one maintains a local schema. Queries are initiated by a data source and propagated to other ones for evaluation.

In case a global schema is available in a PDMS, local schemas are usually views of that global schema. In this case, query routing, i.e. finding which sources are able to answer a query, can be supported by schema indexes built for the local schemas of all sources, like in [1]. Those sources will receive and then process the query. While the existence of a global schema makes query routing and processing easier, it does not provide the necessary flexibility needed to support loosely coupled database communities. The reason is that data sources have to follow strict modelling restrictions imposed by the unique global schema.

In case a global schema is not available, each source maintains a list of neighbouring source. Mapping rules should be provided between a source and its neighbours. Queries initiated by a source are sent to its neighbouring sources. Each one of those sources sends the query to its neighbours, and so on. The mapping rules are used to reformulate the query to match the local schema of each source reached. However, such rules are difficult to maintain. For example, every time that a new source joins the system, new mapping rules should be created and several current mapping rules should be changed manually.

**Our Approach.** In this paper we suggest an architecture to provide better support for distributed data management in loosely coupled data sources. The suggested architecture gives the necessary flexibility to employ diverse schema descriptions in data sources, without the need to maintain mapping rules between data sources.

We demonstrate our approach describing SDQNET, a prototype platform to support semantic query processing in loosely coupled data sources. In SDQNET, schema information is organized in three levels: *local schemas, community schemas* and *global schema*. Local schemas (level 1) are the schemas of data sources. Community schemas (level 2) are RDFS schemas available in the community, relevant to a specific domain. They are used to wrap the local schemas of the data sources that want to join the community. The reason for picking-up RDFS is that it can capture easily schema descriptions that range from simple tagged data to relational descriptions and even to complex class/subclass hierarchies. Finally, community schemas are parts of a global RDFS schema (level 3). However, as it will be shown in the next sections, we note that the task of joining a community is based on exploiting the community schemas available and not the global schema. The global schema just ensures that community schemas are consistent to each other. This gives better flexibility to support loosely coupled database communities and enables query transformation.

To join a community, a data source should agree to exploit schema information from a variety of community schemas and not from only one global schema. Specifically, it should determine an RDFS schema $R$ to wrap its local schema. The $R$ (a) can be part of any available community schema, or (b) can be constructed by applying *schema operators* on the available community schemas. Those schema operators can produce integrated RDFS schemas based on union, intersection and difference semantics.

Once a data source determines an RDFS schema $R$, it wraps its local schema to $R$. Wrapping is performed by mapping its local schema primitives to $R$'s primitives (e.g. relational tables to classes, and attributes to properties), and converting local data to RDF resources (e.g. tuples to RDF resources).

Any data source that has joined a community in SDQNET can initiate queries using the RDFS schema which wraps its local schema for that specific community. Queries are initiated and propagated to other data sources in the network to gather results. Query processing does not require the existence of mapping rules between pairs of data sources.

**Contribution.** The main contribution of this work is an architecture for distributed data management in loosely coupled data sources. The suggested architecture provides the necessary flexibility to support loosely coupled database communities, and it lies between the following two extremes: (a) 'having a global schema for easy query processing, at the expense of the flexibility needed for defining local schemas in nodes' and (b) 'do not have a global schema to give the needed flexibility for defining local schemas in nodes, at the expense of maintaining mapping rules'. Specifically:

- We provide a flexible wrapping mechanism, based on RDFS schemas, for data sources that employ diverse local schema information.
- We exploit schema operators for such wrapping. The operators are applied on RDF schema graphs available for the community, and produce new, integrated ones. Such integration is based on set-like semantics and gives an intuitive way in wrapping data sources.
- We design a query processing technique that does not require the existence of mapping rules during the propagation of the query in the data sources. Under this technique, we are also able to retrieve answers, even in the case a query does not exactly match the schema of a local data source.
- We present SDQNET, a platform that integrates the above ideas to support semantic query processing in loosely coupled data sources.

**Related Work.** The Piazza system [2] supports decentralized data management in a network of loosely coupled bases. Each node in Piazza can maintain a local schema without any restriction. Query processing is based on reformulating the initial query using mapping rules. In the Edutella [3] system, nodes can either agree to use the same schema or use different schemas. The Edutella Mapping

Service is responsible to handle the mappings between different schemas and use them in order to translate queries from one schema to the other.

However, as we point out in the previous paragraphs, mapping rules are difficult to maintain. When for example a new node joins the network, new mapping rules should be created and several current mapping rules should be changed. Similar problems appear in case a node leaves the network.

The SQPeer system [1] uses the Semantic Overlay Networks (SONs) technology, according to which peers sharing the same schema information about a community domain are clustered together to the same SON. The active schema of the peer is a subset (view) of a unique global SON schema for which all classes and properties are populated in the peer base. The SQPeer system identifies peers that can answer a query by maintaining indexes on schema information in peers. Thus, query processing is not based on query reformulation.

In our approach, data sources do not have to follow strict modelling restrictions imposed by the unique global schema. This is due to the existence of community schemas, and the set of schema operators available which provide the necessary flexibility considering schema selection for the wrapping tasks.

## 2   Application Scenario

In this section we present an application scenario that exploits SDQNET to set up a community network. Based on the scenario, we identify the key features of SDQNET and its functionality to support distributed data management in loosely coupled data sources.

Consider a web community for exchanging information about movies. This community involves a set of data sources and a set of *community RDFS schemas* shown in Figure 1. The oval labelled nodes represent classes. The rectangular labelled nodes denote literals, like string, integer, etc. The plain labelled edges with the solid arrow represent properties. The other arrowed edges define an $isA$ hierarchy (class/subclass) of classes.

To join a community, a new data source should determine, with the help of SDQNET, a schema in order to wrap its local data. In our example, we consider three new data sources. We assume that all data sources maintain relational schemas. Suppose that community schema $S_3$, shown in Figure 1, fits perfectly the wrapping needs of the first data source $DS_1$. Thus, $DS_1$ selects $S_3$ to wrap its local data.

Suppose now that $S_2$ fits the wrapping needs of the second data source $DS_2$, but it also contains schema information not needed in $DS_2$. For example, $DS_2$ does not want provide information about action and science fiction movies. So, $DS_2$ considers only a part of schema $S_2$, presented as schema $S_4$ in Figure 2.

Finally, assume that both $S_1$ and $S_3$ contain schema information needed by the third data source $DS_3$. For example, $DS_3$ provides information not only about actors, but also about producer of movies. Source $DS_3$ decides to merge $S_1$ and $S_3$ to get the appropriate RDFS schema to wrap its data. The merged schema $S_5$ is shown in Figure 2. Summarizing, $DS_1$ maintains schema $S_3$ to wrap its local data, $DS_2$ maintains $S_4$ and $DS_3$ maintains $S_5$.

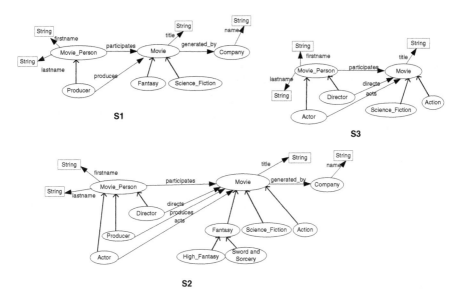

**Fig. 1.** Community RDFS Schemas

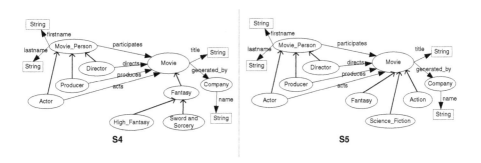

**Fig. 2.** RDFS schemas that wrap data sources

Source $DS_2$ initiates a query to find director names for "High Fantasy" movies generated by "JAK Productions". This query reaches both $DS_1$ and $DS_3$. However, $DS_1$ cannot reply to the answer since it does not contain the class `Company`. Similarly, at first glance, $DS_3$ can not reply to the answer. However, knowing from the community schemas that "High Fantasy" is a subclass of "Fantasy", we can still get answers, though more general. In fact, the SDQNET gives the option for the user to select whether to get such general answers or not.

Based on the functionality described in the application scenario of this section, we next address the following issues:

1. How a new data source joins the community?
2. How a data source wraps its local schema to community schemas?
3. How a data source initiates a query and how the query is processed?

## 3   Joining the Community

When a data source joins a community network, it determines an RDFS schema $R$ to wrap its local schema. To assist the creation of $R$, SDQNET provides a set of *community schemas*. Community schemas are RDFS schemas relevant to the domain addressed in the involved community network, and are used to create $R$. Specifically, $R$ is created by integrating community schemas under union, intersection and difference semantics. Community schemas are RDF schemas which are *subsets* (discussed later) of a given RDF schema, called *global RDF schema* which ensures that community schemas are consistent to each other.

The construction of $R$ is based on the usage of *schema operators* suggested in [6] to support manipulation of RDF schemas as full-fledged objects. The operators are applied on RDF schema graphs and produce new, integrated RDF schema graphs. The key feature is that such integration is based on set-like semantics. We exploit three binary operators (union, intersection, difference) that can be applied on RDF schema graphs as a whole, and produce new ones. We also exploit a unary operator that can be applied on one RDF schema graph and return a part (subset) of it. In the following subsections, we discuss background issues concerning those schema operators originally presented in [6].

### 3.1   Modelling Issues

RDF schemas provide a type system for RDF. The primitives of RDF schemas are classes and properties. Classes describe general concepts and entities. Properties describe the characteristics of classes. They also represent the relationships that exist between classes. Classes and properties are primitives similar to those of the type system of object-oriented programming languages. The difference is that properties in RDF schemas are considered as first-class citizens and are defined independently from classes. Formally, an RDF schema is defined in [6] as follows:

**Definition 1.** *An RDF schema (RDFS) is a 5-tuple $(C, L, P, SC, SP)$ representing a graph, where:*

1. $C$ *is a set of labelled nodes. Each node in $C$ represents an RDF class.*
2. $L$ *is a set of nodes labelled with data types defined in XML schema [7], e.g. integer, string etc. Each node in $L$ represents a literal.*
3. $P$ *is a set of directed labelled edges $(c_1, c_2, p)$ from node $c_1$ to node $c_2$ with label $p$, where $c_1 \in C$ and $c_2 \in C \cup L$. Each edge in $P$ represents an RDF property $p$ with domain $c_1$ and range $c_2$.*
4. $SC$ *is a set of directed edges $(c_1, c_2)$ from node $c_1$ to node $c_2$, where $c_1, c_2 \in C$. Each edge in $SC$ represents an isA relationship between classes $c_1$ and $c_2$ (i.e. $c_1$ is a subclass of $c_2$).*
5. $SP$ *is a set of directed edges $((c_1, c_2, p_1), (c_3, c_4, p_2))$ from edge $(c_1, c_2, p_1)$ to edge $(c_3, c_4, p_2)$, where $(c_1, c_2, p_1), (c_3, c_4, p_2) \in P$. Each edge in $SP$ represents an isA relationship between property $(c_1, c_2, p_1)$ and property $(c_3, c_4, p_2)$ (i.e. that is $(c_1, c_2, p_1)$ is a subproperty of $(c_3, c_4, p_2)$).*

Let $\preceq_C$ be a relation on $C$: $c_1 \preceq_C c_2$ holds if $c_1$ is a subclass of $c_2$. With $\preceq_C^+$ we denote the transitive closure of $\preceq_C$. We consider $c_1$ to be an *ancestor* of $c_2$ (or $c_2$ to be a *descendant* of $c_1$) if $c_2 \preceq_C^+ c_1$. Similarly, let $\preceq_P$ be a relation on $P$: $(c_1, c_2, p_1) \preceq_P (c_3, c_4, p_2)$ holds if $(c_1, c_2, p_1)$ is a subproperty of $(c_3, c_4, p_2)$. With $\preceq_P^+$ we denote the transitive closure of $\preceq_P$. We consider $(c_1, c_2, p_1)$ to be an *ancestor* of $(c_3, c_4, p_2)$ (or $(c_3, c_4, p_2)$ to be a *descendant* of $(c_1, c_2, p_1)$) if $(c_3, c_4, p_2) \preceq_P^+ (c_1, c_2, p_1)$.

We next present the concept of the *subset* relation for RDF schemas introduced in [6]. Intuitively, an RDF schema $R_1$ is a subset of an RDF schema $R_2$ when $R_1$ contains some of the elements (i.e. classes, properties, etc.) of $R_2$, and it does not violate the *isA* hierarchy of classes and properties maintained in $R_2$.

**Definition 2.** *Let $R_i = (C_i, L_i, P_i, SC_i, SP_i)$ and $R_j = (C_j, L_j, P_j, SC_j, SP_j)$ be two RDF schemas. $R_i$ is a subset of $R_j$, denoted by $R_i \subseteq R_j$, if:*

1. *$C_i \subseteq C_j$.*
2. *$L_i \subseteq L_j$.*
3. *for each edge $(c_1, c_2, p_1) \in P_i$ there is an edge $(c_3, c_4, p_2) \in P_j$ with $(c_1 \equiv c_3$ or $c_1 \preceq_{C_j}^+ c_3)$ and $(c_2 \equiv c_4$ or $c_2 \preceq_{C_j}^+ c_4)$ and $p_1 = p_2$.*
4. *for each pair of nodes $c_1, c_2 \in C_i$,*
   *if $c_1 \preceq_{C_i} c_2$ then $c_1 \preceq_{C_j}^+ c_2$ and*
   *if $c_1 \preceq_{C_j}^+ c_2$ then $c_1 \preceq_{C_i}^+ c_2$.*
5. *for each pair of edges $(c_1, c_2, p_1), (c_3, c_4, p_2) \in P_i$,*
   *if $(c_1, c_2, p_1) \preceq_{P_i}^+ (c_3, c_4, p_2)$ then $(c_1, c_2, p_1) \preceq_{P_j}^+ (c_3, c_4, p_2)$ and*
   *if $(c_1, c_2, p_1) \preceq_{P_j}^+ (c_3, c_4, p_2)$ then $(c_1, c_2, p_1) \preceq_{P_i}^+ (c_3, c_4, p_2)$.*

Figure 3 shows the RDF schema $R_1$ which is a subset of $R$, since it satisfies all conditions of the definition. For example, having $C_1 = \{A, B, C, E, G\}$ and $C = \{A, B, C, D, E, F, G\}$, $C_1 \subseteq C$. Also, for each pair of nodes in $C_1$ the fourth condition of the above definition holds (e.g. $A \preceq_{C_1} E$ and $A \preceq_C^+ E$ hold, and $A \preceq_C^+ E$ and $A \preceq_{C_1}^+ E$ hold as well for nodes $A, E$ in $C_1$).

Finally, we give some definitions which are useful to the discussion that will follow [6]. All subsequent definitions refer to an RDF schema $R = (C, L, P, SC, SP)$.

**Definition 3.** *The* extended domain *of a property $(c, s, p) \in P$, denoted by $\mathcal{D}^+((c, s, p))$, is the set of classes $\{c, c_1, \ldots c_n\}$, where $\{c_1, \ldots c_n\}$ are all descendants of $c$.*

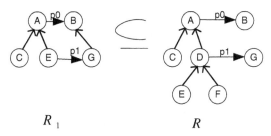

**Fig. 3.** An example of RDF schema subsets

Using the *extended domain* of a property we refer to all classes which can be applied to a property as a set. Similarly, we define the *extended range* of a property to refer to all the classes from which a property can take values as a set.

**Definition 4.** *The* extended range *of a property* $(e, c, p) \in P$, *denoted by* $\mathcal{R}^+((e, c, p))$, *is the set of classes* $\{c, c_1, \ldots c_n\}$, *where* $\{c_1, \ldots c_n\}$ *are all descendants of* $c$.

In SDQNET, community schemas are RDF schemas which are subsets of a given RDF schema, called *global RDF schema*. The global schema just ensures that community schemas are consistent to each other.

**Definition 5.** *Let* $\mathcal{S} = \{R_1, R_2, \ldots R_n\}$ *be a set of RDF schemas. A* global RDF schema *for S is an RDF schema R such that* $R_i \subseteq R, 1 \le i \le n$.

### 3.2  Schema Operators

The operators available to construct the RDFS schema $R$ for a data source to join a community network are summarized as follows (a detailed description of the operators is presented in [6]):

1. **Projection.** Given a set of RDF classes, the projection extracts the part of an RDF schema that involves those classes. Consider the RDF schema R in Figure 4. Projecting R with $C_s = \{C, D, G, F\}$ results in an RDF schema which includes classes $A$, $B$, $C$, $D$, $G$, $F$ and the involved properties $(A, B, p_1)$ and $(D, B, p_2)$.
2. **Union.** The union operator merges two RDF schemas $R_1$ and $R_2$. Union can be implemented as a projection on a class set built from the (set) union of class sets of $R_1$ and $R_2$. An example of the union operator is shown in Figure 5.
3. **Intersection.** The intersection operator results in an RDF schema that contains common elements from both schemas. Intersection can be implemented as a projection on a class set built from the (set) intersection of class sets of $R_1$ and $R_2$.
4. **Difference.** The difference operator results in an RDF schema that contains elements of one schema that are not present in the other. Difference can be implemented as a projection on a class set built from the (set) difference of class sets of $R_1$ and $R_2$.

Users in a data source can create an RDFS schema to wrap its local data, and join the community network, using schema creator wizards provided by SDQNET. Thus, the task of joining a community is based on exploiting the community schemas available and not the global schema. The global schema just ensures that community schemas are consistent to each other. This gives better flexibility to support loosely coupled database communities.

When a data source joins the network, it establishes a neighbouring relationship with some data sources (randomly). Such a relationship will be exploited during the query processing phase. (see Section 5).

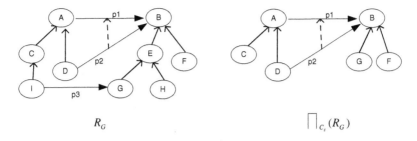

$$R_G \qquad\qquad \sqcap_{C_s}(R_G)$$

**Fig. 4.** Projecting $R_G$ with $C_s = \{C, D, G, F\}$

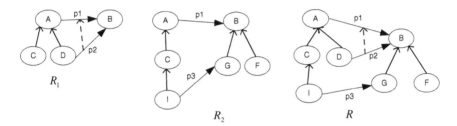

$$R_1 \qquad\qquad R_2 \qquad\qquad R$$

**Fig. 5.** An example of union operation: $R = R_1 \cup R_2$

## 4   Wrapping Local Schemas

Next we describe how a data source wraps it local schema to the RDF schema $R$ constructed by the data source as shown in the previous section. In SDQNET, we assume that all data sources employ relational schemas. However, our prototype can be easily extended to handle data sources with schema descriptions that range from simple tagged data to complex class/subclass hierarchies.

The SDQNET performs wrapping based on a mapping between relational model primitives and RDFS model primitives. Users can define such a mapping using wrapper wizards provided by SDQNET. The process includes two steps:

1. First, user defines an SQL view on the relational data available in her data source. Such a view actually determines which data will be offered to the network by the specific data source.
2. Then, the user maps the attributes of the view created in the previous step to certain class properties of the RDFS schema $R$ used by the data source. Those properties have literals as range. Figure 6 shows the wizard provided by SDQNET to define mappings between an SQL view and $R$ on a data source.

Formally, a mapping between an SQL view and an RDFS schema $R$ is defined as follows:

**Definition 6.** *Let $V(a_1, a_2, \ldots, a_n)$ be an SQL view for a data source, and $P = \{(c_1, l_1, p_1), (c_2, l_2, p_2), \ldots, (c_k, l_k, p_k)\}$ a set of properties of an RDFS schema*

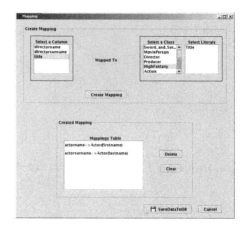

**Fig. 6.** An example of a mapping between an SQL view and $R$ in a data source

$(C, L, P, SC, SP)$, where $c_1, c_2, \ldots, c_k \in C$ and $l_1, l_2, \ldots, l_k \in L$. A mapping $\mathcal{M} :$ $\mathcal{V} \to \mathcal{P}$ is a set of correspondences of the form $a \sim p$, where $a \in \{a_1, a_2, \ldots, a_n\}$ and $p \in \{p_1, p_2, \ldots, p_k\}$.

For example, in Figure 6, the mapping between the SQL view and the RDFS schema is $\{(actorname \sim firstname), (actorsurname \sim lastname)\}$.

After a mapping is established between the SQL view and the RDFS schema $R$ of the data source, data included in that view are converted to RDF resources. Specifically, all tuples in the view are transformed to RDF resources.

### 4.1   SQL View-to-RDF Conversion

The SQL view-to-RDF conversion is based on the mapping between the SQL view and the RDFS schema. The result of the conversion is an XML encoded RDF file $F$ [8] which wraps the data of the SQL view. More specifically, we use (a) the RDFS schema of the data source to define the structure of $F$, and (b) the mapping to fill the values of the RDF class properties that appear in $F$ with the values from the corresponding SQL view attributes. Next we present the conversion algorithm in detail.

**Algorithm**
Consider:
$R = (C, L, P, SC, SP)$: RDFS schema to wrap local schema,
$V(a_1, a_2, \ldots, a_n)$: SQL view,
$P' = \{(c_1, l_1, p_1), (c_2, l_2, p_2), \ldots, (c_k, l_k, p_k)\}$
where $C' = \{c_1, \ldots, c_k\} \subseteq C$ and $L' = \{l_1, \ldots, l_k\} \subseteq L$,
$\mathcal{M} =$ the set of mappings $a \sim p$,
$ClassesToWrite$: it keeps the start tags for RDFS classes to be written (vector, initially empty)
$WrittenClasses$: it keeps the end tags for RDFS classes to be written (vector, initially empty)

*ClosedClasses*: it keeps the end tags for RDFS classes already been written (set, initially empty)

*ClosedProperties*: it keeps the end tags for RDFS properties already been written (set, initially empty)

```
1  for every tuple of V
2    for every class c_i ∈ C'
3      put c_i in ClassesToWrite
4      while ClassesToWrite is not empty
5        if the RDF/XML file is empty
6          write the class c_i start tag
7        else
8          find the property p ∈ P such that (d, c_i, p), where d ∈ C'
9          write the start tag of the property p
10         write the start tag of the class c_i
11       end if
12       for every p_i ∈ P'' ⊆ P', P'' = {c_i, l_1, p_1), (c_i, l_2, p_2), …, (c_i, l_k, p_k)}
13         find a such that a ~ p_i and its value from V
14         write at the RDF/XML file p_i and the value of a
15       end for
16       put c_i in WrittenClasses
17       remove c_i from ClassesToWrite
18       for every p_i such that (c_i, r, p_i), r ∈ C'
19         put r at the beginning of the ClassesToWrite
20       if there isn't any p_i such that (c_i, r, p_i), r ∈ C'
21         for every wc_i in WrittenClasses, beginning with the last one
22           for every p_i such that (wc_i, r, p_i), r ∈ C'
23             if r ∈ ClosedClasses
24               write the property end tag
25               put p in ClosedProperties
26             end if
27           end for
28           if there is no p_i such that (c_i, r, p_i), r ∈ C' and p_i ∉ ClosedProperties
29             write the end tag of the class wc_i
30             put wc_i in ClosedClasses
31           end if
32         end for
33       end if
34     end while
35   end for
36 end for
```

For example, consider that a user of the data source $DS_1$ (see Section 2) wants to wrap its local data using $S_3$ (see Figure 1). First, the user defines the SQL view shown in Table 1. Then, she defines the mapping: $Name \sim firstname$, $Surname \sim lastname$, $Movie \sim title$ ($firstname$, $lastname$ and $title$ are properties whose domain are classes $Actor$, $Actor$ and $ScienceFiction$ respectively). The resulting RDF file in XML encoding follows:

```
<sref:Actor rdf:about="#Item0">
   <sref:firstname>Jodie</sref:firstname>
   <sref:lastname>Foster</sref:lastname>
   <sref:acts>
     <sref:ScienceFiction rdf:about="#Item1">
       <sref:title>Contact</sref:title>
     </sref:ScienceFiction>
   </sref:acts>
   ...
</sref:Actor>
```

**Table 1.** SQL View

| Name | Surname | MovieTitle |
|------|---------|------------|
| Jodie | Foster | Contact |
| ... | ... | ... |

We first write the start tag of the class *Actor* (lines 5,6). Then, we write the properties of *Actor* which have literals as range and their values according to the mapping (lines 12-14). The class *ScienceFiction* is the only class contained in the *ClassesToWrite* vector (lines 18,19). So, this is the next class we consider. This class belongs to the range of *acts* property. So, we first write the start tag of *acts* and then the start tag of *ScienceFiction* (lines 8-10). Next, we write the properties of *ScienceFiction* which have literals as range. Since *ScienceFiction* has not any properties which have a class as range, we start closing the tags at the reverse order we opened them (lines 20-32).

In SDQNET, we maintain RDF resources and RDFS schemas for data sources using the ICS-FORTH RDFSuite[1].

## 5   Querying

A query is initiated by a data source and propagated to its neighbours in the community network for evaluation. The neighbours propagate the query to their own neighbours and so on. We next describe how queries are formulated and processed.

The queries are initiated in a data source using the SDQNET query wizard. Figure 7 illustrates an example of a query that searches for movie titles as well as for the names of their directors.

**Definition 7.** *Let an RDF schema $R = (C, L, P, SC, SP)$. A query $Q$ on $R$ is formed as $\{\{c_1(P_1), p_1, c_2(P_2), p_2, \ldots, p_{n-1}, c_n(P_n)\}, \mathcal{C}\}$ where:*

1. *$c_i \in C$ and $p_i \in P$ $(1 \leq i \leq n)$,*
2. *$p_k$ is the domain of $c_k$ and has $c_{k+1}$ as range $(1 \leq k \leq n-1)$,*
3. *$P_i$ is a list of properties $\in P$ that have $c_i$ as domain and literals as range $(1 \leq i \leq n)$,*

---

[1] http://www.ics.forth.gr/isl/RDF/index.html

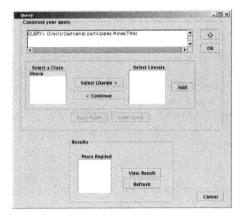

**Fig. 7.** A query example in SDQNET

4. $C$ *is set of conditions of the form* $c.p\{=,>,<,<>\}constant$, *where* $p$ *is a property that has* $c \in C$ *as domain and a literal as range.*

Note that $\{c_1(P_1), p_1, c_2(P_2), p_2, \ldots, p_{n-1}, c_n(P_n)\}$ (from now on: query schema) is actually an RDFS schema, and, in particular, it is a subgraph of $R$.

A query $q$ matches an RDFS schema $R$ if the RDFS graph that corresponds to $\{\{c_1(P_1), p_1, c_2(P_2), p_2, \ldots, p_{n-1}, c_n(P_n)\}$ (i.e., query schema) is subset of $R$ (see Definition 2). In this case we say that $q$ is satisfiable.

If the query is satisfiable on the RDFS schema $R$ that wraps a data source $DS$, then it is evaluated on $DS$. Query evaluation is done using RQL [4], a query language for RDF bases. If the query is not satisfiable then SDQNET applies a query transformation algorithm exploiting semantic information. We next describe the algorithm.

**Query transformation algorithm**
Consider:
The data source RDFS schema $R = \{DC, DL, DP, DS, PS\}$
The query schema $QS = \{QC, QL, QP, \emptyset, \emptyset\}$
The global RDFS schema $GS = \{GC, GL, GP, SC, SP\}$
$\mathcal{R}^+$: The extended range of a property

1 if $c_1 \notin DC$
2    find the nearest superclass $sc$ of $c_1$ with $c_1 \preceq^+_{GC} sc$
    such that $sc \in GC$ and $sc \in DC$
3    if $sc$ exists and $LP' \subseteq LP$ with $LP = \{lp \in LP | (sc, l, lp)$ and $l \in DL\}$
    and $LP' = \{lp' \in LP' | (c_1, l', lp')$ and $l' \in QL\}$
4      substitute $c_1$ with $sc$ in the query schema
5    end if
6    if $p_1 \notin DP$
7     find the property $sp$ with $(sc, c, sp)$, $c \in GC$ and $sp \in GP$
    such that $sp \in (p_1 \cup P' : \forall p' \in P', p_1 \preceq^+_{GP} p')$

8      if $sp$ exists then substitute $p_1$ in the query schema with $sp$
9    end if
10 end if
11 for every $c_i \in QC$ and every $p_i \in QP$, $i \geq 2$ do
12    if $c_i \notin DC$
13        find the nearest superclass $r$ of $c_i$ with $c_i \preceq^+_{GC} r$
          such that $r \in \mathcal{R}^+$ of $p_{i-1}$ and $r \in DC$
14        if $r$ exists and $LP' \subseteq LP$ with $LP = \{lp \in LP|(r,l,lp)$ and $l \in DL\}$
          and $LP' = \{lp' \in LP'|(c_i,l',lp')$ and $l' \in QL\}$
15            substitute $c_i$ with $r$
16        end if
17        if $p_1 \notin DP$
18            find the property $sp$ with $(c_i,c,sp)$, $c \in GC$ and $sp \in GP$
              such that $sp \in (p_i \cup P' : \forall p' \in P', p_i \preceq^+_{GP} p')$
19            if $sp$ exists then substitute $p_i$ in query schema with $sp$
20        end if
21    end if
22 end for

For example, consider the data source $DS_1$ of the application scenario in Section 2, and the query $q$:

*Director(firstname,lastname).directs.High_Fantasy.generated_by.Company(name),*
*Company.name="JAK Productions".*

$DS_1$ maintains schema $S_3$ to wrap its local data (see Figure 1). The query is not satisfiable in $DS_1$ because the query schema $(QS)$ is not subset of $S_3$. Also, $q$ cannot be transformed because there isn't any superclass of *Company* (line 13).

Moreover, the query $q$ is not satisfiable in $DS_3$ because the query schema $(QS)$ is not subset of $S_5$ ($DS_3$ maintains schema $S_5$ to wrap its local data - see Figure 2). According to the transformation algorithm *Director* $\in DC = \{Actor, Producer, Director, MoviePerson, Fantasy, Science\_Fiction, Action, Movie, Company\}$ (line 1) so we next consider *High_Fantasy* class (line 11). *High_Fantasy* $\notin DC$ (line 12). We now search for the nearest superclass of *High_Fantasy* that belongs to the $\mathcal{R}^+$ of *directs* (line 13). The class *Fantasy* satisfies these criteria. In addition, class *High_Fantasy* in $QS$ does not have any properties with literals as range, so $LP' \subseteq LP = \{title\}$ (line 14). Thus, class *Fantasy* is substituted by class *High_Fantasy* in $q$ (line 15). The property *generated_by* exists in $DP = \{participates, directs, produces, acts, generated\_by\}$ (line 17). We now consider class *Company*. *Company* $\in DC$ (line 12), so the algorithm terminates and no other substitution is performed. The reformulated query is therefore:

*Director(firstname,lastname).directs.Fantasy.generated_by.Company(name),*
*Company.name="JAK Productions".*

This new query is satisfiable in $DS_3$, since the new query schema is subset of $S_5$.

# 6   Conclusion

We presented an architecture for distributed data management in community networks of loosely coupled data sources. The suggested architecture is flexible enough for such kind of networks, since it lies between the following two extremes: (a) 'having a global schema for easy query processing, at the expense of the flexibility needed for defining local schemas in nodes' and (b) 'do not have a global schema to give the needed flexibility for defining local schemas in nodes, at the expense of maintaining mapping rules'. No explicit mapping rules between data sources are needed to facilitate query processing. Data sources can join and leave the network any time, at no cost for the community.

Our ideas are being implemented in SDQNET, a platform that supports semantic query processing in loosely coupled data sources. We exploit schema operators applied on RDF schema graphs available for the community. The new, integrated schemas produced are used to wrap data sources. We described a wrapping mechanism based on RDFS schemas for data sources that employ diverse local schema information. We presented a query processing technique that does not require the existence of mapping rules during the propagation of the query in the data sources. Under this technique, we are also able to retrieve answers, even in the case a query does not exactly match the schema of a local data source.

For further work, we plan to extend our wrapping engine to support data sources that maintain different types organization (e.g., DTDs, flat files, etc). Also, we are working on exploiting SDQNET to set up a real community network to provide art information involving various diverse data sources.

# References

1. Giorgos Kokkinidis and Vassilis Christophides.   *Semantic Query Routing and Processing in P2P Database Systems: The ICS-FORTH SQPeer Middleware* . In *Proc. of the P2P DB'04 International Workshop, Heraklion, Greece*, 2004.
2. Alon Y. Halevy, Zachary G. Ives, Peter Mork and Igor Tatarinov.   *Piazza: Data Management Infrastructure for Semantic Web Applications*. In *Proc. of the WWW'03 International Conference, Budapest, Hungary*, 2003.
3. Wolfgang Nejdl, Boris Wolf, Changtao Qu, Stefan Decker, Michael Sintek, Ambjorn Naeve, Mikael Nilsson, Matthias Palmer and Tore Risch.   *EDUTELLA: a P2P Networking Infrastructure based on RDF* . In *Proc. of the WWW'02 International Conference, Honolulu, Hawaii, USA*, 2002.
4. Gregory Karvounarakis, Sofia Alexaki, Vassilis Christophides, Dimitris Plexousakis and Michel Scholl. *RQL: A Declarative Query Language for RDF*. In *Proc. of the WWW'02 International Conference, Honolulu, Hawaii, USA*, 2002.
5. Sofia Alexaki, Vassilis Cristophides, Gregory Karvounarakis, Dimitris Plexousakis and Karsten Tolle. *The ICS-FORTH RDFSuite: Managing Voluminous RDF Description Bases*. In *Proc. of the SemWeb'01 International Workshop, Hong-Kong*, 2001.
6. Zoi Kaoudi, Theodore Dalamagas and Timos Sellis. *RDFSculpt: Managing RDF Schemas under Set-like Semantics*. In *Proc. of the ESWC'05 International Conference, Heraklion, Greece*, 2005.

7. W3C Recommendation. XML Schema Part 2: Datatypes Second Edition, 2004. http://www.w3.org/TR/xmlschema-2/.
8. W3C Recommendation. RDF Primer, 2004. http://www.w3.org/TR/rdf-primer/.
9. Amihai Motro. *Superviews: Virtual Integration of Multiple Databases.* In *IEEE Transactions on Software Engineering, 13(7)*, 1987.
10. Hector Garcia-Molina, Yannis Papakonstantinou, Dallan Quass, Anand Rajaraman, Yehoshua Sagiv, Jeffrey Ullman, Vasilis Vassalos and Jennifer Widom. *The TSIMMIS approach to mediation: Data models and Languages.* In *Journal of Intelligent Information Systems*, 1997.

# Multi-source Materialized Views Maintenance: Multi-level Views*

Josep Silva, Jorge Belenguer, and Matilde Celma

Computer Science Department
Technical University of Valencia
Camino de Vera s/n
E-46021 Valencia – Spain
{jsilva, jorbefa, mcelma}@dsic.upv.es

**Abstract.** In many information systems, the databases that make up the system are distributed in different modules or branch offices according to the requirements of the business enterprise. In these systems, it is often necessary to combine the information of all the organization's databases in order to perform analysis and make decisions about the global operation. This is the case of Data Warehouse Systems. From a conceptual point of view, a Data Warehouse can be considered as a set of materialized views which are defined in terms of the tables stored in one or more databases. These materialized views store historical data that must be maintained in either real time or periodically by means of batch processes. During the maintenance process the systems must perform selections, projections, joins, etc. that can affect several databases. This is a complex problem since making a join among several tables requires (at least temporarily) having the information from these tables in the same place. This requires the Data Warehouse to store auxiliary materialized views that in many cases contain duplicated information. In this article, we study this problem, and we propose a method that minimizes the duplicated information in the auxiliary materialized views and also reduces the response time of the system.

**Keywords:** Data Warehousing, materialized views, multi-source views, view fragmentation, multi-level views.

## 1 Introduction

The use of Data Warehouse systems is becoming one of the critical factors that determine the success of many companies and organizations. The information gathered in the Warehouse can be used to make decisions about the processes of the organization, and should therefore be consistent. The information should also be as up-to-date as possible. Having the information of the operational systems up-to-date makes the results of the queries carried out on the Warehouse Database to be closer to the reality of the organization.

---

* This work has been partially supported by the EU (FEDER) and the Spanish MEC under grant TIN2005-09207-C03-02, by the ICT for EU-India Cross-Cultural Dissemination Project ALA/95/23/2003/077-054, and by UPV under grant TAMAT.

Y. Manolopoulos, J. Pokorný, and T. Sellis (Eds.): ADBIS 2006, LNCS 4152, pp. 71–80, 2006.

Many previous approaches [3, 6, 7, 8, 12, 13, 14, 15] consider that the information of a Data Warehouse System consists of a set of materialized views that store information from one or more databases that the organization uses in its operational systems. The process of loading this information is usually done using daily batch processes at night in order to avoid the slowdown of the operation systems. However, in some cases, the organization needs to compare the historical information in the Warehouse with the most recent information available in the operational system and therefore the Warehouse must be maintained in real time.

Maintenance of materialized views in general, and of Data Warehouses in particular, is a very relevant problem that has been studied in many works. For instance, [14, 15] deal with the problem of updating materialized views in real time, and [5, 7, 12] outline the general maintenance problem of materialized views. Unfortunately, none of these works have studied the case in which each independent view has been defined over multiple sources of data. In this case, the problem is more complex since each single materialized view can involve several operational databases. In [13] we proposed a qualitative solution to the problem; however the solution left the quantification of the different cases for future study. In this article we propose a quantitative approach to the problem and we analyze the most efficient solution for each case.

The article is organized as follows: In section 2, the statement of the problem is presented along with the current state of the art. In section 3, the different parameters for quantifying the problem are studied. Also, different ways of measuring the time and the space required in the maintenance of the materialized views are analyzed. In section 4, the different cases are analyzed and the most efficient solution for each one is presented. Section 5 concludes.

## 2   State of the Art

The updating of materialized views in real time is usually performed by first establishing a communication channel between the Warehouse and the underlying operational systems. This is done so that every time a modification takes place in the tables of the operational systems, these systems inform the Warehouse of the changes by sending the updates that are necessary to maintain the consistency of the materialized views.

When a view is defined on tables from databases of different operational systems, neither the Warehouse nor any of the operational systems can make a join among the tables to solve the view. This is because all the necessary information must be (at least temporarily) in the same location. At first glance, this may appear to be a problem of small granularity; however, this is not always the case. Many times business enterprises have branch offices located in different parts of the world that share the same Data Warehouse. In this context, the volume of data needed for maintaining the views might contain millions of tuples.

The solutions that have been proposed [7, 9, 12] and used to solve the problem of the multi-source views are based on the duplication of information [5, 6]; the definition of maintenance transactions [10]; or the redefinition of the original views, in an attempt to avoid (if it is possible) the joining of tables from different databases [2]; or establishing a hierarchy of auxiliary multi-level views [13].

As it was stated in [13], in many cases the most appropriate solution consists of extending the materialized views definition with a hierarchy of views whose top level are the original views. Although this proposal solves the problem, it has only been defined at a qualitative level, and has left the quantification for future work. An outline is presented in Figure 1, where the solution to this problem is presented.

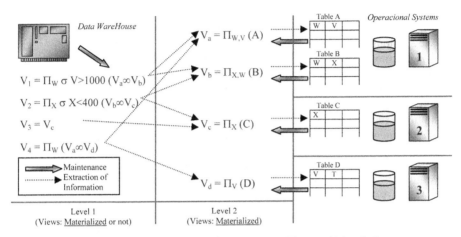

**Fig. 1.** Data warehouse maintenance using auxiliary multi-level views

Figure 1 shows three operational systems with tables (A, B, C, D) and a Data Warehouse with four materialized views ($V_1$, $V_2$, $V_3$, $V_4$) defined as follows:

> $V_1 = \Pi_W \, \sigma \, V>1000 \, (A \infty B)$

> $V_2 = \Pi_X \, \sigma \, X<400 \, (B \infty C)$

> $V_3 = \Pi_X \, (C)$

> $V_4 = \Pi_W \, \sigma \, (A \infty D)$

Views $V_2$ and $V_4$ introduce a problem because they include joins on tables from different databases that are in different locations. To solve this problem, we have defined four new views ($V_a$, $V_b$, $V_c$, $V_d$) to extract the necessary information from tables A, B, C and D. The original views have been redefined from these new views (see definition in Figure 1) in such a way that none of the views include joins on tables from different databases. So the maintenance of the original views is now possible because they are defined over local views (single source); and also the maintenance of auxiliary views is possible because they are defined over a single (remote) source. This maintenance could be achieved by using the ECA (Eager Compensating Algorithm) [15].

This leads to the question of how many level 2 views should be defined for each table of the operational systems in order to duplicate and maintain the smallest quantity of information possible, and at the same time minimize the response time of the system. This question does not have an easy answer, since the answer not only depends on the definition of the views, but on other parameters such as the transmission speed and the volume of data stored in the table. The main goal of this work is to find the answer to this question based on the study of all the possible cases where this problem occurs.

## 3   Problem Statements: Study of Influential Parameters

If we analyze the outline of views in Figure 1, it seems quite clear that there should be at least one view for each database in the operational systems. In the simplest case, this view belongs to the last level in the view hierarchy, and it contains information from one or more tables of this database. It is also clear that it is not always possible to represent all the necessary information from one database in a single view. In general, by defining a subview for each table included in the views of the first level, we have all the necessary information for maintenance. Each subview stores the minimum necessary information of each table, and by joining them, all the Data Warehouse views can be computed. Sometimes it is more appropriate to define more than one view for each table in order to avoid storing and maintaining unnecessary information. As an example, consider Table A in Figure 2, and views $V_1$, $V_2$, $V_4$ and $V_5$. Views $V_1$ and $V_2$ maintain the same information than $V_4$ and $V_5$. Nevertheless, while $V_1$ and $V_2$ maintain redundant information ($\Pi_Q \, \sigma C(A)$), $V_4$ and $V_5$ do not.

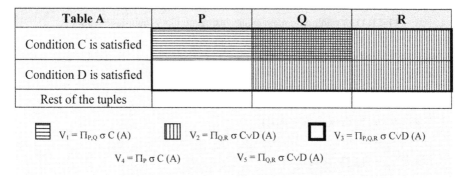

Fig. 2. Removing spare data using several views

A table can be represented as a space of two dimensions where dimension Y represents the tuples of the table and dimension X represents the fields of this table. Each view defined in this table represents a subspace that includes both the fields in its projection and the tuples defined in its selection. In this sense, two different subspaces defined by two different views can be grouped in a single new view. However, information that does not belong to any of them could be included in this new view.

Figure 2 shows two opposed problems that can appear during maintenance. When using a single view $V_3$, unnecessary information can be stored (spare information).

When using views $V_1$ and $V_2$ the same information is stored twice (redundant information).

Data Warehouse designers must determine the number of views for each database and each table of the operational systems. This decision is crucial to ensure that the volume of data stored in the auxiliary materialized views and the maintenance time of the Data Warehouse are minimized. To address this problem, we study quantitatively all the different cases that a designer can find. For this purpose, the designer should take into account the following variables:

**Table 1.** Metrics and variables

| Name | Description |
|------|-------------|
| M | Number of sent messages. |
| C | Global temporal maintenance cost (taking into account input-output operations, bits transference, etc.). |
| Card V | Cardinality of view V. |
| Grad V | Number of attributes (fields) in view V. |
| $M_T$ | Number of updates (insertions, modifications, deletions) on table T. |
| $m_T$ | Percentage of $M_T$ which corresponds with modifications on table T. |
| $\rho$ | Number of updates (on average) that are relevant for several views. |
| k | Average of the maintenance cost (messages + index maintenance + etc) of an operation. |
| s | Number of updates before the view is recomputed. |

In [15], the authors propose to compute the number of messages between the operational systems and the Data Warehouse as a metric of the maintenance cost of a materialized view. This metric corresponds with $M$ in Table 1. For its computation, they propose the following formula whose performance evaluation can be found in annex D in [15]:

(1)
$$M = \left\lceil \frac{M_T}{s} \right\rceil \times 2$$

In this metric, $M_T$ represents the total number of updates in the source; and for every $s$ updates, the operational system sends (and receives) one message to the Data Warehouse. Then, assuming that the message is sent after each update ($s=1$), two messages are generated by each update in the source.

It is clear that measuring the maintenance cost by only considering the amount of sent messages can be too rough. For this reason, we propose a different metric that takes into account other factors such as the view size, the probability that the modifications in the sources will affect the materialized views, etc. The formula that defines this metric is:

$$(2) \quad C = M_T \cdot \frac{Card(V_1) \cdot Grad(V_1) + ... + Card(V_n) \cdot Grad(V_n)}{Card(T) \cdot Grad(T)} \cdot k + \rho \cdot k$$

where $T$ is the table in the operational system on which the views $V_1...V_n$ are defined. The meaning of the rest of variables is explained in Table 1.

This metric takes into account the spare information as well as the redundant information. In the case that the intersection of two or more views is not the empty set, that is, there is redundant information, this redundancy is taken into account in the cost since it is computed several times in different pairs $Card(V_i) \cdot Grad(V_i)$. The spare information is computed in the corresponding pair in the same way. Hence, the component $(Card(V_1) \cdot Grad(V_1) + ... + Card(V_1) \cdot Grad(V_1)) / Card(V_T) \cdot Grad(V_T)$ represents the probability that an arbitrary update in $T$ could affect one of the views.

The redundant maintenance is computed with the second expression of the formula; $\rho \cdot k$ represents the cost associated to all the operations caused by the change of a tuple from one view to another during maintenance. It is of special importance to realize that, in the case of disjoint views, this change of view cannot be caused by an *insert* or *delete* operation, but rather can only be caused by a *modify* operation. Therefore, when views do not have redundant tuples we use the parameter $\rho_m$ which only refers to modifications. Assuming that every field in the views has the same probability to be modified, $\rho_m$ can be computed by the formula:

$$(3) \qquad\qquad \rho_m = \sum_{i=1}^{n} N'_{Vi}$$

where $N'_{Vi}$ is the number of modifications that affect the view $i$.

Parameter $\rho$ represents the number of times that one update on a materialized view produces another update on any other view. In order to validate the correctness of Formula (3), for simplicity, we can assume that every field in table $T$ has the same probability to be updated by one of the $M_T$ updates (in practice, we use a statistical distribution or a weight). Then, the probability that the view $V_i$ was affected by an update is:

$$(4) \qquad\qquad P_{Vi} = \frac{Card(V_i) \cdot Grad(V_i)}{Card(T) \cdot Grad(T)}$$

The probability that the update affects to the set of views $V_1...V_n$ is given by:

$$(5) \qquad\qquad P_{V1.Vn} = \frac{Card(\bigcup_n^{i=1} V_i) \cdot Grad(\bigcup_n^{i=1} V_i)}{Card(T) \cdot Grad(T)}$$

Using (4), the number of updates which affect the view $V_i$ is:

$$(6) \qquad\qquad N_{Vi} = M_T \cdot P_{Vi} = M_T \cdot \frac{Card(V_i) \cdot Grad(V_i)}{Card(T) \cdot Grad(T)}$$

The number of modifications which affect the view $V_i$ is the number of modifications over the tuples of $V_i$ plus the number of modifications over tuples not belonging to $V_i$ which after the modification belong to $V_i$. Formally,

(7)
$$N'_{Vi} = (N_{Vi} \cdot m_T) + (M_T \cdot m_T \cdot (1 - P_{Vi}) \cdot P_{Vi})$$

The generalization of (7) is:

(8)
$$\rho_m = \sum_{i=1}^{n} N'_{Vi}$$

## 4 Case-Based Reasoning

There is not only one solution to the problem described in the previous section. The solutions depend on different factors that are related to the definition of the views (for example the number of fields and tuples of a table used in several views); and they also depend on architectural factors such as the average speed of the information transmission, the average number of transmissions which are necessary to perform maintenance, the volume of information to maintain, etc. In this section, we study all the possible combinations that can take place in the definition of diverse views on a table. For each case we analyze which solution is the most appropriate according to the mentioned parameters.

| Conditions | | | Field W | Field X | Field Y | Field Z |
|---|---|---|---|---|---|---|
| Condition A | Condition C | Condition F | | | | |
| | Condition D | Condition E | | | | |
| Condition B | Condition F | Condition D | | | | |
| | Condition E | | | | | |

**Fig. 3.** Table T with 4 fields and 6 conditions defined over the tuples space

Figure 3 shows a hypothetical table T with 4 fields (W, X, Y, Z) and 6 conditions dividing the tuples space in 4 disjoint sets. Two views defined over this table necessarily hold in one of the following cases:

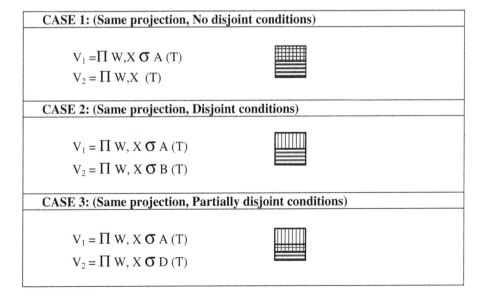

**CASE 1: (Same projection, No disjoint conditions)**

$V_1 = \Pi\ W,X\ \sigma\ A\ (T)$
$V_2 = \Pi\ W,X\ (T)$

**CASE 2: (Same projection, Disjoint conditions)**

$V_1 = \Pi\ W,\ X\ \sigma\ A\ (T)$
$V_2 = \Pi\ W,\ X\ \sigma\ B\ (T)$

**CASE 3: (Same projection, Partially disjoint conditions)**

$V_1 = \Pi\ W,\ X\ \sigma\ A\ (T)$
$V_2 = \Pi\ W,\ X\ \sigma\ D\ (T)$

**CASE 4: (Distinct projection, No disjoint conditions)**

$V_1 = \Pi\ W, X\ \sigma\ B\ (T)$

$V_2 = \Pi\ Y, Z\ \sigma\ F \wedge D\ (T)$

**CASE 5: (Distinct projection, Disjoint conditions)**

$V1 = \Pi\ W, X\ \sigma\ E\ (T)$

$V2 = \Pi\ Y, Z\ \sigma\ C\ (T)$

**CASE 6: (Distinct projection, Partially disjoint conditions)**

$V1 = \Pi\ W, X\ \sigma\ E\ (T)$

$V2 = \Pi\ Y, Z\ \sigma\ B\ (T)$

**CASE 7: (Partially disjoint projections, Same conditions)**

$V1 = \Pi\ W, X\ \sigma\ B\ (T)$

$V2 = \Pi\ X, Y\ \sigma\ B\ (T)$

**CASE 8: (Partially disjoint projections, Disjoint conditions)**

$V1 = \Pi\ W, X\ \sigma\ F\ (T)$

$V2 = \Pi\ X, Y\ \sigma\ E\ (T)$

**CASE 9: (Partially disjoint projections, Partially disjoint conditions)**

$V1 = \Pi\ W, X, Y\ \sigma\ F\ (T)$

$V2 = \Pi\ X, Y, Z\ \sigma\ B\ (T)$

For each case, we have computed the cost taking into account all the possibilities (using different number of views). The whole analysis can be found in a publicly available technical report in http://www.dsic.upv.es/~jsilva/research.htm#techs.

From this analysis, we conclude that in cases 1, 2, 3 and 7 the best solution is to consider one single view. In cases 4, 5, 6 and 8 the best solution depends on the parameter $\rho$ and on the cardinality of the views:

o   If $\rho > M_T$ (*Card $V_3$ · Grad $V_3$ – (Card $V_1$ · Grad $V_1$ + Card $V_2$ · Grad $V_2$) ) / Card T · Grad T*)
then the cost of using one view is smaller than the cost of using two views.

o  If $\rho = M_T (Card\ V_3 \cdot Grad\ V_3 - (Card\ V_1 \cdot Grad\ V_1 + Card\ V_2 \cdot Grad\ V_2)\ )\ /\ Card\ T \cdot Grad\ T)$ then the cost of using one view or two views is the same. In this case only one view is used.

o  If $\rho < M_T (Card\ V_3 \cdot Grad\ V_3 - (Card\ V_1 \cdot Grad\ V_1 + Card\ V_2 \cdot Grad\ V_2)\ )\ /\ Card\ T \cdot Grad\ T)$ then the cost of using two views is smaller than the cost of using one view.

Here, $V_3$ represents a view which contains all the information (and maybe more) stored by $V_1$ and $V_2$.

Case number 9 is more complex since it needs 3 views for maintaining all the information without redundancy. The computation of the cost for this case is shown in a technical report accessible at http://www.dsic.upv.es/~jsilva/research.htm#techs.

# 5  Conclusions

There are many works [3, 5, 6, 8, 10, 14, 15] which deal with the use of materialized views in Data Warehouse systems or with the problem of maintenance of these materialized views. However, surprisingly, not much effort [7, 9, 12] has been spent to address the problem of multi-source materialized views. This is an important problem since, for example, it is not possible —or it is really very expensive due to the necessity of duplicate the tables— to maintain in real-time a view that joins tables from different sources. In [13], we proposed to extend the original views with a set of intermediate views that extract information from just one determined source. But in that work we did not consider how to find out which is the optimal configuration of views taking into account the maintenance costs.

In this paper we have carried out this study analyzing each possible case from the point of view of required space and time consumed for maintenance. To achieve this goal, ECA (Eager Compensating Algorithm) could be used in order to maintain the auxiliary single-source (top level) views.

# Bibliography

1. Ashish N., Knoblock C.A., Shahabi C: *"Selectively materializing data in mediators by analyzing user queries"*. In Proceedings of the 4th IFCIS International Conference on Cooperative Information Systems (CoopIS), Edinburgh, Scotland, September 1999.

2. Colby L.S., Griffin T.G., Libkin L., Mumick I.S., Trickey H.: *"Algorithms for Deferred View Maintenance"*. In Proceedings of the SIGMOD: pp. 469-479, June 1996.

3. Ding L., Zhang X., Rundensteiner E.A.: *"Enhancing Existing Incremental View Maintenance Algorithms Using the Multi-Relation Encapsulation Wrapper"*. Technical Report WPI-CS-TR-99-23: pp. 9-11, Worcester Polytechnic Institute, Dept. of Computer Science, August 1999.

4. Gupta H.: *"Selection of Views to Materialize in a Data Warehouse"*. In Proceedings of the International Conference on Database Theory (ICDT 1997): 98-112, Delphi, Greece; January 1997.

5. Gupta A., Mumick I.S.: *"Maintenance of Materialized Views: Problems, Techniques, and Applications"*. In the IEEE Data Engineering Bulletin Vol. 18 N[er]. 2, June 1995.

6. Kuchenhoff V.: *"On the efficient computation of the difference between consecutive database states"*. In Proceedings of the 2nd International Conference on Deductive and Object-Oriented Databases (DOOD), December 1991.
7. Moro G., Sartorio C.: *"Incremental Maintenance of Multi-Source Views"*. In Proceedings of the 12th Australasian of Electrical and Electronics Engineers (ADC 2001), 2001.
8. Quass D., Gupta A., Mumick I.S., Widom J.: *"Making Views Self-Maintainable for Data Warehousing"*. In Proceedings of the Conference on Parallel and Distributed Information Systems (PDIS '96), 1996.
9. Samtani S., Mohania M., Kumar V., Kambayashi Y.: *"Recent Advances and Research Problems in Data Warehousing"*. ER Workshops, 1998.
10. Stanoi I.R., Agrawal D., El Abbadi A.: *"Modeling and Maintaining Multi-View Data Warehouses"*. In Proceedings of the 18th International Conference on Conceptual Modelling (ER '99), November 1999.
11. Valluri S.R., Vadapalli S., Karlapalem K.: *"View Relevance Driven Selection of Materialized Views in Data Warehousing Environment"*. In Proceedings of the 13th Australasian Database Conference (ADC 2002), Melbourne, Australia 2002.
12. Widom J.: *"Research Problems in Data Warehousing"*. Computer Science Department, Stanford University. In Proceedings of the 4th International Conference on Information and Knowledge Management (CIKM); November 1995.
13. Silva J., Belenguer J., Celma M.: *"Materialización de Vistas Multi-Origen: Vistas Multinivel"*. In Proceedings of the 7th Jornadas de Ingeniería del Software y Bases de Datos (JISBD'02), El Escorial, Madrid, Spain; 2002.
14. Zhuge Y., Garcia-Molina H., Wiener J.L.: *"The Strobe Algorithms for Multi-Source Warehouse Consistency"*. In Proceedings of the 4th International Conferences on Parallel and Distributed Information Systems (PDIS'96), Miami Beach, Florida, USA; 1996.
15. Zhuge Y., Garcia-Molina H., Hammer J., Widom J.: *"View Maintenance in a Warehousing Environment"*. CSD - Stanford University; SIGMOD Conference 1995: pp. 316-327; 1995.

# Clustering-Based Materialized View Selection in Data Warehouses

Kamel Aouiche, Pierre-Emmanuel Jouve, and Jérôme Darmont

ERIC Laboratory – University of Lyon 2
5, av. Pierre Mendès-France
F-69676 BRON Cedex – France
{kaouiche, pjouve, jdarmont}@eric.univ-lyon2.fr

**Abstract.** Materialized view selection is a non-trivial task. Hence, its complexity must be reduced. A judicious choice of views must be cost-driven and influenced by the workload experienced by the system. In this paper, we propose a framework for materialized view selection that exploits a data mining technique (clustering), in order to determine clusters of similar queries. We also propose a view merging algorithm that builds a set of candidate views, as well as a greedy process for selecting a set of views to materialize. This selection is based on cost models that evaluate the cost of accessing data using views and the cost of storing these views. To validate our strategy, we executed a workload of decision-support queries on a test data warehouse, with and without using our strategy. Our experimental results demonstrate its efficiency, even when storage space is limited.

## 1 Introduction

Among the techniques adopted in relational implementations of data warehouses to improve query performance, view materialization and indexing are presumably the most effective ones [15]. Materialized views are physical structures that improve data access time by precomputing intermediary results. Then, user queries can be efficiently processed by using data stored within views and do not need to access the original data. Nevertheless, the use of materialized views requires additional storage space and entails maintenance overhead when refreshing the data warehouse.

One of the most important issues in data warehouse physical design is to select an appropriate set of materialized views, called a configuration of views, which minimizes total query response time and the cost of maintaining the selected views, given a limited storage space. To achieve this goal, views that are closely related to the workload queries must be materialized.

The view selection problem has received significant attention in the literature. Researches about it differ in several points: (1) the way of determining candidate views; (2) the frameworks used to capture relationships between candidate views; (3) the use of mathematical cost models *vs.* calls to the query optimizer; (4) view

Y. Manolopoulos, J. Pokorný, and T. Sellis (Eds.): ADBIS 2006, LNCS 4152, pp. 81–95, 2006.

selection in the relational or multidimensional context; (5) multiple or simple query optimization; and (6) theoretical or technical solutions.

The classical papers in materialized view selection introduce a lattice framework that models and captures dependency (ancestor or descendent) among aggregate views in a multidimensional context [2,10,13,21]. This lattice is greedily browsed with the help of cost models to select the best views to materialize. This problem has been firstly addressed in one data cube and then extended to multiple cubes [16]. Another theoretical framework called the AND-OR view graph may also be used to capture the relationships between views [8,5,9,14,22]. The majority of these solutions are theoretical and are not truly scalable. In opposition to these studies, we exploit a query clustering involving similarity and dissimilarity measures defined on the workload queries, in order to capture the relationships existing between the candidate views derived from this workload. This approach is scalable thanks to the low complexity of our clustering (log linear regarding the number of queries and linear regarding the number of attributes).

A wavelet framework for adaptively representing multidimensional data cubes has also been proposed [18]. This method decomposes data cubes into an indexed hierarchy of wavelet view elements that correspond to partial and residual aggregations of data cubes. An algorithm greedily selects a non-expensive set of wavelet view elements that minimizes the average processing cost of the queries defined on the data cubes. In the same spirit, Kotidis et al. proposed the Dwarf structure, which compresses data cubes [17]. Dwarf identifies prefix and suffix redundancies within cube cells and factors them out by coalescing their storage. Suppressing redundancy improves the maintenance and interrogation costs of data cubes. These approaches are very interesting, but they are mainly focused on computing efficient data cubes by changing their physical design. In opposition, we aim at optimizing performance in relational warehouses without modifying their design.

Other approaches detect common sub-expressions within workload queries in the relational context [3,6,15,19]. The problem of view selection consists in finding common subexpressions corresponding to intermediary results that are suitable to materialize. However, browsing is very costly and these methods are not truly scalable with respect to the number of queries.

Finally, the most recent approaches are workload-driven. They syntactically analyze the workload to enumerate relevant candidate views [1]. By calling the query optimizer, they greedily build a configuration of the most pertinent views. A workload is indeed a good starting point to predict future queries because these queries are probably within or syntactically close to a previous query workload. In addition, extracting candidate views from the workload ensures that future materialized views will probably be used when processing queries.

Our approach is also workload-driven. Its originality lies in exploiting knowledge about how views can be used to resolve a set of queries to cluster these queries together. For this purpose, we define the notion of query similarity and dissimilarity in order to capture closely related queries. These queries are grouped in the same cluster and are used to build a set of candidate views. Furthermore, these candidate views are merged to resolve multiple queries. This merging process can be seen as iteratively building a lattice of views. The merging process time can be expensive when the number of candidate views is high. However, we apply merging over candidate views present in each cluster instead of the whole set of candidate views as in [1]. This reduces the complexity of the merging process, since the number of candidate views per cluster is significantly lower.

The remainder of this paper is organized as follows. We first present in Section 2 our materialized view selection strategy. Then, we show in Section 3 how we build a candidate view configuration through our merging process. Next, we detail in Section 4 the cost models used for building the final configuration of views to materialize. To validate our approach, we also present some experiments in Section 7. We finally conclude and provide research perspectives in Section 8.

# 2   Strategy for Materialized View Selection

The architecture of our materialized view selection strategy is depicted in Figure 1. We assume that we have a workload composed of representative queries for which we want to select a configuration of materialized views in order to reduce their execution time. The first step is to build, from the workload, a context for clustering. This context is modelled as a matrix having as many lines as the extracted queries and as many columns as the extracted attributes from the whole set of queries. We define similarity and dissimilarity measures that help clustering together relatively similar queries. We apply a merging process on each query cluster to build a configuration of candidate views. Then, the final view configuration is created with a greedy algorithm. This step exploits cost models that evaluate the cost of accessing data using views and the cost of their storage.

## 2.1   Query Workload Analysis

The workloads we consider are sets of GPSJ (Generalized Projection-Selection-Join) queries. A GPSJ query $q$ is composed of joins, selection predicates and aggregations. As such, it may be expressed in relational algebra over a star schema as follows: $q = \pi_{G,M}\sigma_S(F \bowtie D_1 \bowtie D_2 \bowtie \ldots \bowtie D_d)$, where $S$ is a conjunction of simple range predicates on dimension table attributes, $G$ is a set of attributes from dimension tables $D_i$ (grouping set), and $M$ is a set of aggregated measures each defined by applying aggregation operator to a measure in fact table $F$. For example, query $q_1$ in Figure 2 may be expressed as follows: $q_1 = \pi_{sales.time\_id,sum(quantity\_sold)}\sigma_{fiscal\_day=2}(sales \bowtie times)$.

The first step consists in extracting from the workload the attributes that are representative of each query. We mean by representative attributes those that are present in **Where** (join and selection predicate attributes) and **Group by** clauses. We also save for each query their aggregation operators and joined tables. A query $q_i$ is then seen as a line in a matrix composed of cells that

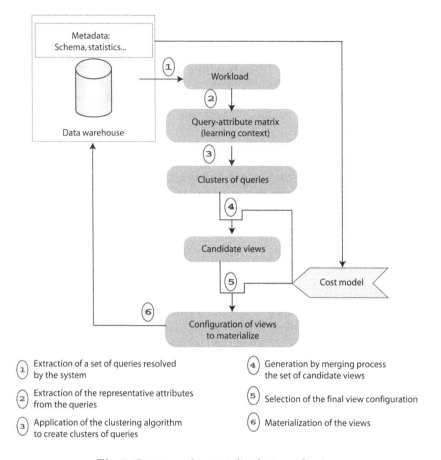

**Fig. 1.** Strategy of materialized view selection

correspond to the representative attributes. The general term $q_{ij}$ of this matrix is set to 1 if the extracted attribute is present in the query and to 0 otherwise. This matrix represents our clustering context. Moreover, we store in an appendix matrix the existing associations between the join attributes and queries, in the same manner. We illustrate this step by an example: from the workload shown in Figure 2, we build the clustering context depicted in Figure 3.

## 2.2   Building the Candidate View Set

In practice, it is hard to search all the views that are syntactically relevant (candidate views) from the workload queries, because the search space is very large [1]. To reduce the size of this space, we propose to cluster the queries. Indeed, we group in a same cluster all the queries that are closely similar. Closely similar queries are queries having a close binary representation in the query-attribute matrix. Two closely similar queries can be resolved by using only one

$(q_1)$ **select** sales.time_id, sum(quantity_sold) **from** sales, times
   **where** sales.time_id = times.time_id **and** times.fiscal_day = 2
   **group by** sales.time_id;
$(q_2)$ **select** sales.prod_id, sum(amount_sold) **from** sales, products, promotions
   **where** sales.prod_id = products.prod_id **and** sales.promo_id = promotions.promo_id **and**
   promotions.promo_category = 'newspaper'
   **group by** sales.prod_id;
$(q_3)$ **select** sales.cust_id, sum(amount_sold) **from** sales, customers, products, times
   **where** sales.cust_id = customers.cust_id **and** sales.prod_id = products.prod_id **and**
   sales.time_id = times.time_id **and** times.fiscal_day = 3 **and** customers.cust_marital_status
   ='single' **and** products.prod_category ='Women'
   **group by** sales.cust_id;
...

**Fig. 2.** Example of workload

|       | $a_1$ | $a_2$ | $a_3$ | $a_4$ | $a_5$ | $a_6$ | $a_7$ | $a_8$ | $a_9$ | $a_{10}$ | $a_{11}$ | $a_{12}$ |
|-------|---|---|---|---|---|---|---|---|---|---|---|---|
| $q_1$ | 1 | 1 | 1 | 0 | 0 | 0 | 0 | 0 | 0 | 0 | 0 | 0 |
| $q_2$ | 0 | 0 | 0 | 1 | 0 | 1 | 1 | 1 | 1 | 0 | 0 | 0 |
| $q_3$ | 0 | 0 | 0 | 1 | 0 | 1 | 1 | 1 | 1 | 1 | 1 | 1 |
| .. |   |   |   |   |   |   |   |   |   |   |   |   |
| .. |   |   |   |   |   |   |   |   |   |   |   |   |

$a_1$ times.time_id  $a_2$ times.fiscal_day
$a_3$ sales.time_id  $a_4$ products.prod_id
$a_5$ products.prod_category  $a_6$ sales.promo_id
$a_7$ promotions.promo_id  $a_8$ sales.prod_id
$a_9$ promotions.promo_category  $a_{10}$ sales.cust_id
$a_{11}$ customers.cust_marital_status  $a_{12}$ customers.cust_id

**Fig. 3.** Example of clustering context

materialized view. Used within a clustering process, the similarity and dissimilarity measures defined in the next section ensures that queries within the same cluster strongly relate to each other whereas queries from different clusters are significantly distant to each other.

**Similarity Measure.** Let $QA$ be a query-attribute matrix that has a set of queries $Q = \{q_i, i = 1..n\}$ as rows and a set of attributes $A = \{a_j, j = 1..p\}$ as columns. The value $q_{ij}$ is equal to 1 if attribute $a_j$ is extracted from query $q_i$. Otherwise, $q_{ij}$ is equal to 0. We describe query $q_i$ by a vector of $p$ values $q_i = [q_{i1}, ..., q_{ip}]$. These $p$ values describe respectively the presence ($q_{ij} = 1$) or absence ($q_{ij} = 0$) of attribute $a_j$. This description model helps comparing two queries. Then, for example, we can consider queries $q_1$ and $q_2$ as closely similar if vectors $[q_{11}, ..., q_{1p}]$ and $[q_{21}, ..., q_{2p}]$ have the majority of their cells equal. This introduces the notion similarity and dissimilarity between queries.

**Similarity and Dissimilarity Between Queries.** We define the notion of similarity and dissimilarity between queries by two functions $\delta_{sim_j}(q_k, q_l)$ and $\delta_{dissim_j}(q_k, q_l)$ that measure the similarity between two queries $q_k$ and $q_l$ with respect to attribute $a_j$.

$$\delta_{sim_j}(q_k, q_l) = \begin{cases} 1 \text{ if } q_{kj} = q_{lj} = 1 \\ 0 \text{ otherwise} \end{cases}$$

This first function defines the notion of similarity between $q_k$ and $q_l$ following attribute $a_j$: two queries $q_k$ and $q_l$ are considered similar regarding attribute $a_j$ if and only if $q_{kj} = q_{lj} = 1$, i.e., attribute $a_j$ is extracted from both queries.

$$\delta_{dissim_j}(q_k, q_l) = \begin{cases} 0 \text{ if } q_{kj} = q_{lj} \\ 1 \text{ if } q_{kj} \neq q_{lj} \end{cases}$$

This second function defines the notion of dissimilarity between queries $q_k$ and $q_l$ according to attribute $a_j$: two queries $q_k$ and $q_l$ are considered dissimilar according to attribute $a_j$ if only and if $q_{kj} \neq q_{lj}$, i.e., if one and only one of the queries does not contain $a_j$. Note that there is not a complete symmetry between the notion of similarity and dissimilarity: non similar queries according to an attribute are not necessarily dissimilar according to this attribute. For example, let $q_1$ and $q_2$ be queries such that $q_{1j} = 0$ and $q_{2j} = 0$, respectively. Then we have $\delta_{sim_j}(q_1, q_2) = 0$ ($q_1$ and $q_2$ are not considered similar) and $\delta_{dissim_j}(q_1, q_2) = 0$ ($q_1$ and $q_2$ are not considered dissimilar). This absence of full symmetry underlines the fact that the absence of the same attribute in two queries does not give an element of similarity or dissimilarity between these queries.

These measures can be extended to an attribute set $A = \{a_1, \ldots, a_p\}$ such that we get the degree of global similarity and dissimilarity between two queries: $sim(q_k, q_l) = \sum_{j=1}^{p} \delta_{sim_j}(q_k, q_l)$ and $dissim(q_k, q_l) = \sum_{j=1}^{p} \delta_{dissim_j}(q_k, q_l)$, where $0 \leq sim(q_k, q_l) \leq p$ and $0 \leq dissim(q_k, q_l) \leq p$. Hence, the closer $sim(q_a, q_b)$ (resp. $dissim(q_a, q_b)$) is to $p$ the more $q_a$ and $q_b$ can be considered globally similar (resp. dissimilar).

**Similarity and Dissimilarity Between Query Sets.** As we do for two queries, we introduce two functions that take into account the degree of similarity and dissimilarity between two query sets. A set of queries (subset of $Q$) is denoted $C_a$. In order to translate the level of similarity (resp. dissimilarity) between query sets, we use function $Sim(C_a, C_b)$ (resp. $Dissim(C_i, C_j)$) that determines the number of similarities (resp. dissimilarities) between two different sets of queries $C_a$ and $C_b$ ($C_a \neq C_b$):

$$Sim(C_a, C_b) = \sum_{q_k \in C_a, q_l \in C_b} sim(q_k, q_l)$$

$$Dissim(C_a, C_b) = \sum_{q_k \in C_a, q_l \in C_b} dissim(q_k, q_l)$$

where $0 \leq Sim(C_a, C_b) \leq card(C_a) \times card(C_b) \times p$ and $0 \leq Dissim(C_a, C_b) \leq card(C_a) \times card(C_b) \times p$. Hence, the closer $Sim(C_a, C_b)$ (resp. $Dissim(C_a, C_b)$) is to $card(C_a) \times card(C_b) \times p$ the more $C_a$ and $C_b$ can be considered similar (resp. dissimilar).

**Similarity and Dissimilarity Within a Query Set.** The notion of similarity (resp. dissimilarity) within a query set corresponds to the number of similarities (resp. dissimilarities) between queries of a same set $C_a$. It consists of an extension of the similarity and dissimilarity functions defined between query sets: $Sim(C_a) = \sum_{q_k \in C_a, q_l \in C_a, k<l} sim(q_k, q_l)$ and $Dissim(C_a) = \sum_{q_k \in C_a, q_l \in C_a, k<l} dissim(q_k, q_l)$, where $0 \leq Sim(C_a) \leq \frac{card(C_a) \times (card(C_a)-1) \times p}{2}$ and $0 \leq Dissim(C_a) \leq \frac{card(C_a) \times (card(C_a)-1) \times p}{2}$. Hence, the close $Sim(C_a)$ (resp.

$Dissim(C_a))$ is to $\frac{card(C_a) \times (card(C_a)-1) \times p}{2}$ the more $C_a$ contains queries that are globally similar (resp. dissimilar).

**Query Clustering.** Clustering involves the determination of groups of objects (here: queries) that reveal the the internal structure of data. These groups must be such as they are composed of objects with high similarity and objects from different clusters present a high dissimilarity.

Let us consider clustering $P_h$ of a query set, a quality measure of this clustering can be built as follows:

$$Q(P_h) = \sum_{\substack{a=1..z, \\ b=1..z, a < b}} Sim(C_a, C_b) + \sum_{a=1}^{z} Dissim(C_a)$$

$$0 \leq Q(P_h) \leq \sum_{i=1..z, j=1..z, i<j} card(C_i) \times card(C_j) \times p + \sum_{i=1}^{z} \frac{card(C_i) \times (card(C_i)-1) \times p}{2}$$

This measure permits to capture the natural aspect of a clustering. Hence, $Q(P_h)$ measures simultaneously similarities between queries within the same cluster and dissimilarities between queries within different clusters. Thus, $Q(P_h)$ evaluates simultaneously the homogeneity of clusters as well as the heterogeneity between clusters. Therefore, the clustering presenting a high intra-cluster homogeneity and a high inter-cluster disparity has a weak value of $Q(P_h)$ and thereby appears as the most natural.

Jouve and Nicoloyannis proposed such a solution in the Kerouac clustering algorithm and its associated clustering quality measure [11]. We have chosen this algorithm because it has several interesting properties: (1) its computational complexity is relatively low (log linear regarding the number of queries and linear regarding the number of attributes) ; (2) it can deal with a high number of objects (queries) ; (3) it can deal with distributed data [12].

## 3   View Merging Process

If we materialize all the different views derived from the query clusters obtained in the previous step, we can obtain a high number of materialized views, especially if the number of queries within the workload is high. A view configuration obtained this way would not be very relevant if the storage space allotted by the data warehouse administrator was limited. Instead of materializing each view, it is better to only materialize views that can be used to resolve multiple queries. To solve this problem, we must enumerate the space of views that can be merged, determine how to guide the merging process, and finally build the set of merged views. View merging is relevant if the queries are strongly similar. As we cluster together closely similar queries, it is logical to apply the merging process on the set of queries present in each cluster. This significantly reduces the number of possible combinations when merging views. We detail in the following sections how we merge two views and then generalize this process to many views.

**Merging of View Couples.** The merging of two views must ensure these conditions: (1) all queries resolved by each view must also be resolved by the merged view, and (2) the cost of using the couple of views must not be significatively greater than the cost obtained when using the merged view. Let $v_1$ and $v_2$ be a couple of views of the same cluster and $s_{11}, \ldots, s_{1m}$ the selection predicates that are in $v_1$ and not in $v_2$. In a dual way, let $s_{21}, \ldots, s_{2n}$ be the selection conditions present in $v_2$ and not in $v_1$. Merged view $v_{12}$ is obtained by applying Algorithm 1.

---

**Algorithm 1** $Merge\_View\_Pair(v_1, v_2)$

1: put $v_1$ and $v_2$ aggregation operations in $v_{12}$ operation aggregations
2: put the union of projection and group by attributes $v_1$ and $v_2$ in projection and group by clause of $v_{12}$
3: put all attributes $s_{11}, \ldots, s_{1m}$ and $s_{21}, \ldots, s_{2n}$ in the group by clause of $v_{12}$
4: put the selection predicates shared between $v_1$ and $v_2$ in the selection predicate clause of $v_{12}$

**Algorithm 2** $Mergin\_View\_Generation$

1: $M = V_1$
2: **for** $(k = 2; V_{k-1} \neq \emptyset; k++)$ **do**
3:     $C_k = \texttt{View\_Gen}(V_{k-1})$
4:     $M \leftarrow M \cup C_k$
5:     **for all** (view $v \in M$) **do**
6:         Remove the parents of $v$ from $M$
7:     **end for**
8: **end for**
9: **return** $M$

---

The merging of two views $v_1$ and $v_2$ is effective if $cost(v_{12}) \geq ((cost(v_1) + cost(v_2)) * x)$. Cost computation is detailed in Section 4. The value of $x$ is fixed empirically by the administrator. If it is small (resp. high), we privilege (resp. disadvantage) view merging.

**Property 1.** *The view obtained by merging views $v_1$ and $v_2$ is the smallest view that resolves the query resolved by both $v_1$ and $v_2$.*

*Proof.* To show that the view obtained by merging views $v_1$ and $v_2$ is the smallest view, we have to show that there is no view $v_{12}'$ such as the data within $v_{12}'$ are also included within $v_{12}$. We denote respectively views $v_1$, $v_2$ and $v_{12}$ $\pi_{G_1, M_1} \sigma_{S_1}(F \bowtie \ldots)$, $\pi_{G_2, M_2} \sigma_{S_2}(F \bowtie \ldots)$ and $\pi_{G_{12}, M_{12}} \sigma_{S_{12}}(F \bowtie \ldots)$, respectively, where:
- $G_1$, $G_2$ are respectively the attribute set of the group by clause of views $v_1$ and $v_2$;
- $S_1$, $S_2$ are respectively the attribute set of the selection predicates of $v_1$ and $v_2$;
- $G_{12} = G_1 \cup G_2 \cup (S_1 \cup S_2 - S_1 \cap S_2)$ is the attribute set of the group by clause of merged view $v_{12}$;
- $S_{12} = S_1 \cap S_2$ is the set of attribute selection predicates within merged view $v_{12}$.

Note that sets $G_{12}$ and $S_{12}$ are obtained by applying lines 1 and 2 of Algorithm 1. Let us now assume that the data in view $v_{12}'$, denoted $\pi_{G_{12}', M_{12}'} \sigma_{S_{12}'}(F \bowtie \ldots)$ are all in $v_{12}$. This means that both of the following conditions hold: (1) $G_{12} \subset G_{12}'$, (2) $S_{12} \supset S_{12}'$.

From the first condition, there is at least one attribute $x$ such that $x \in G_{12}'$ and $x \notin G_{12}$. As we have $x \notin G_{12}$, then $x \notin G_1$, $x \notin G_2$ and $x \notin S_1 \cup (S_2 - S_1 \cap S_2)$ because $G_{12} = G_1 \cup G_2 \cup (S_1 \cup S_2 - S_1 \cap S_2)$. As $x \notin G_1$ and $x \notin G_2$, then $x$ is not in any clause of $v_2$. This means that $x \notin G_{12}'$, which contradicts condition $x \in G_{12}'$.

From the second condition, there is at least one attribute $y$ such that $y \in S_{12}$ and $y \notin S_{12}'$. As we have $y \in S_{12}$, then $y \in S_1$ and $y \in S_2$ because $S_{12} = S_1 \cup S_2$. As $y \in S_1$ and $y \in S_2$, then $y$ must be in all the predicates of the views obtained by merging $v_1$ and $v_2$. This means that $y \in S_{12}'$, which contradicts condition $y \notin S_{12}'$.

**Merged View Generation Algorithm.** The algorithm of view generation by merging is similar to algorithms searching for frequent itemsets. A frequent itemset lattice looks like a lattice of views within a given cluster. The lattice nodes represent the space of views obtained by merging.

**Algorithm 3** *Function  View_Gen($V_{k-1}$)*
1: $C_k = \emptyset$
2: **for all** (view $v \in V_{k-1}$) **do**
3:   **for all** (view $u \in V_{k-1}$) **do**
4:     **if** $(v[1] = u[1] \wedge \ldots \wedge v[k-2] = u[k-2] \wedge v[k-1] < u[k-1])$ **then**
5:       $c =$ Merge_View_Pair $(v,u)$
6:       **if** $(cost(c) \geq ((cost(v)+cost(u))*x))$ **then**
7:         $C_k = C_k \cup \{c\}$
8:       **end if**
9:     **end if**
10:   **end for**
11: **end for**
12: **return** $C_k$

**Algorithm 4**
*View_Configuration_Construction*
1: $S \leftarrow \emptyset$
2: **repeat**
3:   $v_{max} \leftarrow \emptyset$
4:   $F_{max} \leftarrow 0$
5:   **for all** $v_j \in V - S$ **do**
6:     **if** $F_{/S}(v_j) > F_{max}$ **then**
7:       $F_{max} \leftarrow F_{/S}(v_j)$
8:       $v_{max} \leftarrow v_j$
9:     **end if**
10:   **end for**
11:   **if** $F_{/S}(v_{max}) > 0$ **then**
12:     $S \leftarrow S \cup \{v_{max}\}$
13:   **end if**
14: **until** $(F_{/S}(v_{max}) \leq 0$ or $V - S = \emptyset)$

The algorithm of view generation by merging (Algorithm 3) uses an iterative approach by level to generate a new view. It explores the view lattice in breadth first. The input of the algorithm is $V_1$, a set of candidate views extracted from a given cluster. This algorithm outputs a set of candidate views obtained by merging. In the $k^{th}$ iteration, view set $V_{k-1}$ obtained by merging the $k - 1^{th}$ level's views from the lattice (computed in the last step) is used to generate the set $C_k$ of $k$-candidate views. This set is added to set $M$ (line 4). The parents of each view obtained by merging are then removed from set $M$ (lines 5 to 7).

The function for view generation by merging View_Gen($V_{k-1}$), called on line 3, takes as argument $V_{k-1}$ and returns $C_k$. Two views $v$ and $u$ within $V_{k-1}$ form a $k$-view $c$ if and only if they have $(k - 2)$ views in common. This is expressed using a lexicographic order in the condition of line 3. We denote by $v[1] \ldots v[k - 2]v[k-1]$ the merged views in the $k^{th}$ iteration that are used to derive $v$. Function Merge_View_Pair($v,u$) (Algorithm 1) called on line 5 of View_Gen generates a new view $c$. The condition of line 6 ensures, after generating a $k$-view from two $k - 1$-views, that the candidate view does not have a cost greater than the cost of its parents.

## 4   Cost Models

The number of candidate views is generally as high as the input workload is large. Thus, it is not feasible to materialize all the proposed views because of storage space constraints. To circumvent these limitations, we use cost models allowing to conserve only the most pertinent views. In most data warehouse cost models [7], the cost of a query $q$ is assumed to be proportional to the number of tuples in the view on which $q$ is executed. In the following section, we detail the cost model that estimates the size of a given view.

Let $ms(F)$ be the maximum size of fact table $F$, $|F|$ be the number of tuples in $F$, $D_i\_ID$ be a primary key of dimension $D_i$, $|D_i\_ID|$ be the cardinality of the attribute(s) that form the primary key, and $N$ be the number of dimension tables. Then, $ms(F) = \prod_{i=1}^{N} |D_i\_ID|$.

Let $ms(V)$ be the maximum size of a given view $v$ that has attributes $a_1, a_2, \ldots, a_k$ in its group by clause, where $k$ is the number of attributes in $v$ and $|a_i|$ is the cardinality of attribute $a_i$. Then, $ms(v) = \prod_{i=1}^{k} |a_i|$.

Golfarelli *et al.* [7] proposed to estimate the number of tuples in a given view $v$ by using Yao's formula [23] as follows:

$|v| = ms(v) \times \left[ 1 - \prod_{i=1}^{|F|} \frac{ms(F) \times d - i + 1}{ms(F) - i + 1} \right]$, where $d = 1 - \frac{1}{ms(v)}$. If $\frac{ms(F)}{ms(v)}$ is sufficiently large, then Cardenas' formula [4] approximation gives:

$|v| = ms(v) \times \left( 1 - \left( 1 - \frac{1}{ms(v)} \right)^{|F|} \right)$, where $d = 1 - \frac{1}{ms(v)}$.

Cardenas' and Yao's formulaes are based on the assumption that data is uniformly distributed. Any skew in the data tends to reduce the number of tuples in the aggregate view. Hence, the uniform assumption tends to overestimate the size of the views and give a crude estimation. However, they have the advantage to be simple to implement and fast to compute. In addition, because of the modularity of our approach, it is easy to replace the cost model module by another more accurate one.

From the number of tuples in $v$, we estimate its size, in bytes, as follows: $size(v) = |v| \times \sum_{i=1}^{c} size(c_i)$, where $size(c_i)$ denotes the size, in bytes, of column $c_i$ of $v$, and $c$ is the number of columns in $v$.

## 5   Objective Functions

In this section, we describe three objective functions to evaluate the variation of query execution cost, in number of tuples to read, induced by adding a new view. The query execution cost is assimilated to the number of tuples in the fact table when no view is used or to the number of tuples in view(s) otherwise. The workload execution cost is obtained by adding all execution costs for each query within this workload.

The first objective function advantages the views providing more profit while executing queries, the second one advantages the views providing more benefit and occupying the smallest storage space, and the third one combines the first two in order to select at first all the views providing more profit and then keep only those occupying the smallest storage space when this resource becomes critical. The first function is useful when storage space is not limited, the second one is useful when storage space is small and the third one is interesting when storage space is larger.

### 5.1   Profit Objective Function

Let $V = \{v_1, ..., v_m\}$ be a candidate view set, $Q = \{q_1, ..., q_n\}$ a query set (a workload) and $S$ a final view set to build. The profit objective function, noted $P$, is defined as follows:
$P_{/S}(v_j) = \left( C_{/S}(Q) - C_{/S \cup \{v_j\}}(Q) - \beta \, C_{maintenance}(\{v_j\}) \right)$, where $v_j \notin S$.

- $C_{/S}(Q)$ denotes the query execution cost when all views in $S$ are used. If this set is empty, $C_{/\emptyset}(Q) = |Q| \times |F|$ because all the queries are resolved by accessing fact table $|F|$. When a view $v_j$ is added to $S$, $C_{/S \cup \{v_j\}}(Q) = \sum_{k=0}^{|Q|} C(q_k, \{v_j\})$ denotes the query execution cost for the views that are in $S \cup \{v_j\}$. If query $q_k$ exploits $v_j$, the cost $C(q_k, \{v_j\})$ is then equal to $C_{v_j}$ (number of tuples in $v_j$). Otherwise, $C(q_k, \{v_j\})$ is equal to the minimum value between $|F|$ and values of $C(q_k, \{v\})$ (executing cost of $q_k$ exploiting $v \in S$ with $v \neq v_j$).

- Coefficient $\beta = |Q|\, p(v_j)$ estimates the number of updates for view $v_j$. The update probability $p(v_j)$ is equal to $\frac{1}{number\ of\ views} \frac{\%update}{\%query}$, where $\frac{\%update}{\%query}$ represents the proportion of updating $vs.$ querying the data warehouse.
- $C_{maintenance}(\{v_j\})$ represents the maintenance cost for view $v_j$.

### 5.2   Profit/Space Ratio Objective Function

If view selection is achieved under a space constraint, the profit/space objective function $R_{/S}(v_j) = \frac{P_{/S}(v_j)}{size(v_j)}$ is used. This function computes the profit provided by $v_j$ in regard to the storage space $size(v_j)$ that it occupies.

### 5.3   Hybrid Objective Function

The constraint on the storage space may be relaxed if this space is relatively large. The hybrid objective function $H$ does not penalize space–"greedy" views if the ratio $\frac{remaining\_space}{storage\_space}$ is lower or equal than a given threshold $\alpha$ ($0 < \alpha \leq 1$), where $remaining\_space$ and $storage\_space$ are respectively the remaining space after adding $v_j$ and the allotted space needed for storing all the views. This function is computed by combining the two functions $P$ and $R$ as follows:

$$H_{/S}(v_j) = \begin{cases} P_{/S}(v_j) \text{ if } \frac{remaining\_space}{storage\_space} > \alpha, \\ R_{/S}(v_j) \text{ otherwise.} \end{cases}$$

## 6   View Selection Algorithm

The view selection algorithm (Algorithm 4) is based on a greedy search within the candidate view set $V$. Objective function $F$ must be one of the functions $P$ or $R$ described previously. If $R$ is used, we add to the algorithm's input the space storage $M$ allotted for views.

In the first algorithm iteration, the values of the objective function are computed for each view within $V$. The view $v_{max}$ that maximizes $F$, if it exists ($F_{/S}(v_{max}) > 0$), is then added to $S$. If $R$ is used, the whole space storage $M$ is decreased by the amount of space occupied by $v_{max}$.

The function values of $F$ are then recomputed for each remaining view in $V - S$ since they depend on the selected views present in $S$. This helps taking into account the interactions that probably exist between the views.

We repeat these iterations until there is no improvement ($F_{/S}(v) \leq 0$) or until all views have been selected ($V - S = \emptyset$). If function $R$ is used, the algorithm also stops when storage space is full.

## 7   Experiments

In order to validate our approach for materialized view selection, we have run tests on a 1 GB data warehouse implemented within Oracle 9*i*, on a Pentium 2.4 GHz PC with a 512 MB main memory and a 120 GB IDE disk. This data warehouse is composed of the fact table `Sales` and five dimensions `Customers`, `Products`, `Times`, `Promotions` and `Channels`. We executed on our data warehouse a workload composed of sixty-one decision-support queries involving aggregation operations and several joins between the fact table and dimension tables. Due to space constraints, the data warehouse schema and the detail of each workload query are available at `http://eric.univ-lyon2.fr/~kaouiche/adbis.pdf`. Our experiments are based on an ad-hoc benchmark because, as far as we know, there is no standard benchmark for data warehouses. TPC-R [20] has no multidimensional schema and does not qualify, for instance.

We first applied our selection strategy with the profit function. This function gives us the maximal number of materialized views (twelve views) because it does not specify any storage space constraint. This point gives us the upper boundary of the storage space occupation. Then, we applied the profit/space ratio and hybrid functions under a storage space constraint. We have measured query execution time with respect to the percentage of storage space allotted for materialized views. This percentage is computed from the upper boundary computed when applying the profit function. This helps varying storage space within a wider interval.

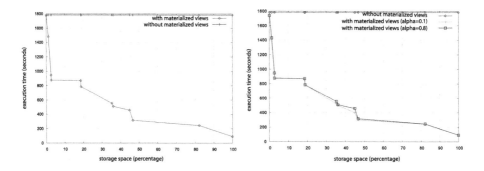

**Fig. 4.** Profit/space ratio function          **Fig. 5.** Hybrid function

**Ratio Profit/Space Function Experiment.** We plotted in Figure 4 the variation of workload execution time with respect to the storage space allotted for materialized views. This figure shows that the selected views improve query execution time. Moreover, execution time decreases when storage space occupation increases. This is predictable because we create more materialized views when storage space is large and thereby better improve execution time. We also observe that the maximal gain is equal to 94.86%. It is reached for a space occupation of 100% (no constraint on storage space). This case is also reached when using the profit function, because it corresponds to the upper boundary.

**Hybrid Function Experiment.** We repeated the previous experiment with the hybrid objective function. We varied the value of parameter $\alpha$ between 0.1 and 1 by 0.1 steps. The obtained results with $\alpha \in [0.1, 0.7]$ and $\alpha \in [0.8, 1]$ are respectively equal to those obtained with $\alpha = 0.1$ and $\alpha = 0.8$. Thus, we plotted in Figure 5 only the results obtained with $\alpha = 0.1$ and $\alpha = 0.7$. This figure shows that for percentage values of space storage under 18.6%, the hybrid function with $\alpha = 0.1$ and $\alpha = 0.8$ behaves as the ratio function. When the storage space becomes critical, the hybrid function behaves as the ratio profit/space function. On the other hand, for the percentage values of storage space greater than 18.6%, the results obtained with $\alpha = 0.8$ are slightly better than those obtained with $\alpha = 0.1$. This is explained by the fact that for the high values of $\alpha$, the hybrid function chooses the views providing the most profit and thereby improving the best the execution time. The maximal gain in execution time observed for the values 0.1 and 0.8 of $\alpha$ is equal to 96%.

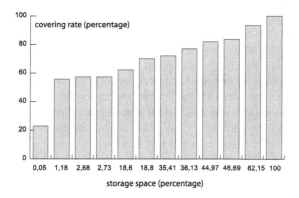

**Fig. 6.** Query covering rate by the selected materialized views

**Selected View Pertinence Experiment.** In order to show if our strategy provides pertinent views for a given workload, we measured the covering rate of the workload query results by the selected views. We mean by covering rate the ratio between the number of queries resolved from the materialized views and the total number of queries within the workload. Thus, the highest the rate value, the most pertinent the selected views. In this experiment, the percentage of storage space is also computed from the upper boundary. We plotted in Figure 6 the covering rate according to storage space occupation. This figure shows that the covering rate increases with storage space. When storage space gets larger, we materialize more views and thereby we recover more query results from these views. When materializing all the views (100% storage space occupation), all the data corresponding to query results are recovered from the materialized views. This shows that, without storage space constraint, the selected views are pertinent. For example, for 0.05% storage space occupation, 22.95% of the query results are recovered from the selected views. This shows that, even for a limited storage space, our strategy helps building views that cover a maximum number of queries. This experiment shows that materialized view selection based on workload syntactical analysis is efficient to guarantee the exploitation of the selected views by the workload queries.

# 8   Conclusion

In this paper, we presented an automatic strategy for materialized view selection in data warehouses. This strategy exploits the results of clustering applied on a given workload to build a set of syntactically relevant candidate views. Our experimental results show that our strategy guarantees a substantial gain in performance. It also shows that the idea of using data mining techniques for data warehouse auto-administration is a promising approach.

This work opens several future research axes. First, we are still currently experimenting in order to better evaluate system overhead in terms of materialized view building and maintenance. The maintenance cost is currently derived from the query frequencies (Section 4). We are envisaging a more accurate cost model to estimate update costs. We also plan to compare our approach to other materialized view selection methods. Furthermore, it could be interesting to design methods that select both indexes and materialized views, since these data structures are often used together. More precisely, we are currently developing methods to efficiently share the available storage space between indexes and views. Finally, our strategy is applied on a workload that is extracted from the system during a given period of time. We are thus performing static optimization. It would be interesting to make our strategy dynamic and incremental, as proposed in [13]. Studies dealing with dynamic or incremental clustering may be exploited. Entropy-based session detection could also be beneficial to determine the best moment to run view reselection.

# References

1. S. Agrawal, S. Chaudhuri, and V. Narasayya. Automated selection of materialized views and indexes in SQL databases. In *26th International Conference on Very Large Data Bases (VLDB 2000), Cairo, Egypt*, pages 496–505, 2000.
2. E. Baralis, S. Paraboschi, and E. Teniente. Materialized views selection in a multi-dimensional database. In *23rd International Conference on Very Large Data Bases (VLDB 1997), Athens, Greece*, pages 156–165, 1997.
3. X. Baril and Z. Bellahsene. Selection of materialized views: a cost-based approach. In *15th International Conference (CAiSE 2003), Klagenfurt, Austria*, pages 665–680, 2003.
4. A. F. Cardenas. Analysis and performance of inverted data base structures. *Communication in ACM*, 18(5):253–263, 1975.
5. G. K. Y. Chan, Q. Li, and L. Feng. Design and selection of materialized views in a data warehousing environment: a case study. In *2nd ACM international workshop on Data warehousing and OLAP (DOLAP 1999), Kansas City, USA*, pages 42–47, 1999.

6. J. Goldstein and P. Larson. Optimizing queries using materialized views: a practical, scalable solution. In *ACM SIGMOD international conference on Management of data (SIGMOD 2001), Santa Barbara, USA*, pages 331–342, 2001.
7. M. Golfarelli and S. Rizzi. A methodological framework for data warehouse design. In *1st ACM international workshop on Data warehousing and OLAP (DOLAP 1998), New York, USA*, pages 3–9, 1998.
8. H. Gupta. Selection of views to materialize in a data warehouse. In *6th International Conference on Database Theory (ICDT 1997), Delphi, Greece*, pages 98–112, 1997.
9. H. Gupta and I. S. Mumick. Selection of views to materialize in a data warehouse. *IEEE Transactions on Knowledge and Data Engineering*, 17(1):24–43, 2005.
10. V. Harinarayan, A. Rajaraman, and J. D. Ullman. Implementing data cubes efficiently. In *ACM SIGMOD International Conference on Management of data (SIGMOD 1996), Montreal, Canada*, pages 205–216, 1996.
11. P. Jouve and N. Nicoloyannis. KEROUAC: an algorithm for clustering categorical data sets with practical advantages. In *International Workshop on Data Mining for Actionable Knowledge (DMAK'2003, in conjunction with PAKDD03)*, 2003.
12. P. Jouve and N. Nicoloyannis. A new method for combining partitions, applications for distributed clustering. In *International Workshop on Paralell and Distributed Machine Learning and Data Mining (ECML/PKDD03)*, pages 35–46, 2003.
13. Y. Kotidis and N. Roussopoulos. DynaMat: A dynamic view management system for data warehouses. In *ACM SIGMOD International Conference on Management of Data, (SIGMOD 1999), Philadelphia, USA*, pages 371–382, 1999.
14. T. P. Nadeau and T. J. Teorey. Achieving scalability in OLAP materialized view selection. In *5th ACM International Workshop on Data Warehousing and OLAP (DOLAP 2002), McLean, USA*.
15. S. Rizzi and E. Saltarelli. View materialization vs. indexing: Balancing space constraints in data warehouse design. In *15th International Conference (CAiSE 2003), Klagenfurt, Austria*, pages 502–519, 2003.
16. A. Shukla, P. Deshpande, and J. F. Naughton. Materialized view selection for multi-cube data models. In *7th International Conference on Extending DataBase Technology (EDBT 2000), Konstanz, Germany*, pages 269–284, 2000.
17. Y. Sismanis, A. Deligiannakis, N. Roussopoulos, and Y. Kotidis. Dwarf: shrinking the petacube. In *ACM SIGMOD International Conference on Management of Data (SIGMOD 2002), Madison, USA*, pages 464–475, 2002.
18. J. R. Smith, C.-S. Li, and A. Jhingran. A wavelet framework for adapting data cube views for OLAP. *IEEE Transactions on Knowledge and Data Engineering*, 16(5):552–565, 2004.
19. D. Theodoratos and W. Xu. Constructing search spaces for materialized view selection. In *7th ACM international workshop on Data warehousing and OLAP (DOLAP 2004), Washington, USA*.
20. Transaction Processing Council. *TPC Benchmark R Standard Specification*, 1999.
21. H. Uchiyama, K. Runapongsa, and T. J. Teorey. A progressive view materialization algorithm. In *2nd ACM International Workshop on Data warehousing and OLAP (DOLAP 1999), Kansas City, USA*, pages 36–41, 1999.
22. S. R. Valluri, S. Vadapalli, and K. Karlapalem. View relevance driven materialized view selection in data warehousing environment. In *30th Australasian conference on Database technologies, Melbourne, Australia*, pages 187–196, 2002.
23. S. B. Yao. Approximating block accesses in database organizations. *Communication in ACM*, 20(4):260–261, 1977.

# Non-blocking Materialized View Creation and Transformation of Schemas

Jørgen Løland and Svein-Olaf Hvasshovd

Dept. of Computer Science, NTNU, Trondheim, Norway
{jorgen.loland, svein-olaf.hvasshovd}@idi.ntnu.no

**Abstract.** In existing systems, user transactions get blocked during materialized view creation and non-trivial database schema transformations. Blocking user transactions is not an option in systems with high availability requirements. A non-blocking method to perform such tasks is therefore needed.

In this paper, we present a method for non-blocking creation of derived tables, suitable for highly available databases. These derived tables can be used to create materialized views and to transform the database schema. Modified versions of well-known crash recovery techniques are used, thus making the method easy to integrate into existing DBMSs. Because the involved tables are not locked, the derived table creation may run as a low priority background process. As a result, the process has little impact on concurrent user transactions.

## 1 Introduction

As applications change over time, the database schema is required to change as well. In a study of seven applications, Marche [19] reports of significant changes to relational database schemas over time. Six of the studied schemas had more than 50% of their attributes changed. The evolution of the schemas continued after the development period had ended. A similar study of a health management system [26] came to the same conclusion. Two ways to let a database evolve is to add materialized views and to transform the database schema.

*Materialized views* (MVs) may be added to a database to speed up processing of frequently used queries. During the last couple of decades, many authors have suggested methods to maintain consistency between MVs and the base tables they collect data from. The goal of their research (e.g. [1,3,9,25]) has mainly been to interfere as little as possible with other transactions using the system. The community has not shown the same interest in the initial creation of MVs, however. Thus, in today's systems, the MVs are created by read and insert operations that effectively block concurrent transactions from updating the involved tables.

A *database schema transformation* changes the table structure of a database. An example is to merge records from two tables into one, thus resulting in a table containing a full outer join of the original records. In current DBMSs, non-trivial schema transformations are executed by an *insert into select* statement. The effect of this is the same as MV creation: read and insert operations block other transactions from updating the source tables.

Y. Manolopoulos, J. Pokorný, and T. Sellis (Eds.): ADBIS 2006, LNCS 4152, pp. 96–107, 2006.

The blocking MV creation and schema transformation methods described may take minutes or more for tables with large amounts of data. Databases with high availability requirements should not be unavailable for long periods of time. Such databases, often found in e.g. the telecom and process regulation industries, would clearly benefit from mechanisms to perform these tasks without blocking. Although databases used in e.g. webshops, airline reservation systems and banking may be less critical, downtime should always be avoided to maintain good customer relations.

Both MV creation and schema transformations can be performed by materializing a derived table (DT). In this paper, we present non-blocking methods to materialize DTs using six relational operators. These are vertical merge (full outer join) and split, horizontal merge (union) and split, difference and intersection. The two first methods are enhancements of algorithms previously published by the authors [18], the remaining four are new.

The DT materialization method presented is based on log redo. This means that log records from the source tables are redone to the DTs in a similar way as normal crash recovery, but with redo rules adapted to each DT operation. We assume that the DBMS produces redo log records, and that undo operations produce Compensating Log Records (CLR) [4] as described for the ARIES method [21]. With CLR, all operations (including undo), are found in the same sequential log and with all the information necessary to apply the operations to the DTs. Furthermore, it is assumed that Log Sequence Numbers (LSNs) are used as state identifiers, and that the LSNs are associated with records in the database [10]. LSNs are commonly used in commercial systems, e.g. in SQL Server 2005 [20].

The paper is organized as follows: Section 2 describes other methods and research areas related to non-blocking DT creation. An overview of the framework and details for how to apply it to the six relational operators are presented in Sections 3 and 4, respectively. Finally, in Section 5, we conclude and suggest further work.

## 2   Related Work

Non-blocking creation of derived tables that involve any of the six operators has to the authors' knowledge only been researched in a schema transformation setting. Ronström [24] presents a non-blocking schema transformation method that uses both a reorganizer and triggers within user transactions. The method is able to perform vertical and horizontal merge and split, but methods for difference and intersection are not presented. Sagas [5] are used to organize the transformations. The reorganizer is used to scan the old tables, while triggers make sure that updates to the old tables are executed immediately to the transformed table. When the scan is complete, the old and transformed tables are consistent due to the triggered updates.

No implementation or test results have been published on Ronströms method, but triggers are used in a similar way to keep immediate MVs up to date. The extra workload incurred by using triggers to update MVs is significant, and other update methods are therefore preferred whenever possible (see e.g. [3,15]).

Fuzzy copy is a technique to make copies of a table without blocking update operations [2,11]. A *begin-fuzzy mark* is first written to the log. The records in the source table are then read without setting locks, resulting in a *fuzzy copy* where some of the

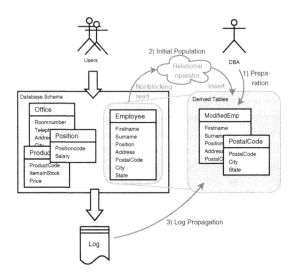

**Fig. 1.** The first three steps of derived table materialization

updates that were made during the scan may not be reflected. The log is then redone to the copy in a similar way as in ARIES [21] to make it up to date. LSNs on records ensure that the log propagation is idempotent. When all log records have been redone to the copy in ascending order, it is in the same state as the source table. An *end-fuzzy mark* is then written to the log, and the copy process is complete. The method requires CLRs to be used for undo processing.

Materialized views store the result of a query. They are used to speed up query processing and must therefore be consistent with the source tables. To the authors' knowledge, no method for non-blocking MV creation has been published. At first glance, maintenance of MVs has much in common with the non-blocking DT materialization method presented in this paper. However, all MV maintenance methods require the MVs to be consistent with a previous state of the source tables [1,3,6,7,8,9,15,22,25,28]. Thus, since a fuzzy copy is not consistent with the source table, the MV update methods are not applicable.

Existing database systems, including IBM DB2 v8.2 [13,14], Microsoft SQL Server 2005 [20], MySQL 5.1 [27] and Oracle 10$g$ [17], offer some simple schema transformation functionality. These include removal of and adding one or more attributes to a table, renaming attributes and the like. Complex tranformations like the ones presented in this paper are not supported.

## 3   General Framework

The goal of the DT materialization framework is to provide a way to create a derived table without blocking other transactions. At the same time, the efficiency of concurrent transactions should be degraded as little as possible. After materialization, the DTs can be used as MVs or to transform the schema. Using relational operators enables us to make use of existing, optimized code (like join algorithms) for parts of the process.

All DT materialization methods presented have four steps. As illustrated in Figure 1, the first three steps are to create the new tables, populate them with fuzzy copies of the source tables and then use modified recovery techniques to make the derived tables up to date with the source tables. The fourth step, *synchronization*, ensures that the DT has the same state as the source tables, thus making the DT ready for its intended use. The four steps are explained in general below.

### 3.1    Preparation Step

Before materialization starts, the derived tables must be added to the database. The tables must as a minimum include an LSN for all contributing source records and the attributes used to identify them in the log. In this paper, we use a Record ID (RID) as identifying attribute, but any unique identifier will work. Record IDs are commonly used internally by commercial DBMSs, e.g IBM DB2 UDB v8.2 [12]. Depending on the operator, other attributes like join attributes in the case of vertical merge, may also be required. If any of the required attributes are not wanted in the DT, they must be removed *after* the materialization has completed.

Constraints, both new and from the source tables, may be added to the new tables. This should, however, be done with great care since constraint violations may force the DT materialization to abort. Any indices that are needed on the new tables should also be created at this point. In particular, since RIDs from the source tables are used to identify which records a logged operation should be applied to in the DTs, all six operators should have indices on source RID to speed up log propagation. Indices created during this step will be up to date when the materialization is complete.

Some of the relational operators require information that is not stored in the DTs. In these cases, an additional table may be required during the DT materialization process. This is commented on when needed.

### 3.2    Initial Population Step

The newly created DTs have to be populated with records from the source tables. This is done by a modified fuzzy copy technique, so the first step of populating DTs is to write a *fuzzy mark* in the log. This log record must include the transaction identifiers of all transactions that are currently active on the source tables, i.e. a subset of the active transaction table. The source tables are then read fuzzily, returning an inconsistent result since locks are ignored [11]. Once the source tables have been read, the relational operator is applied and the result, called the *initial image*, are inserted into the DTs.

### 3.3    Log Propagation

Log propagation is the process of redoing operations originally executed on source table records to records in the DTs. All these operations are reflected in the log, and are applied sequentially. By redoing the logged operations, the DTs will eventually have records with the same state as the source table records.

Log propagation starts when the initial images have been inserted into the DTs. Another fuzzy mark is first written to the log. This log record marks the end of the current log propagation cycle and the beginning of the next one. Log records of operations that may not be reflected in the DTs are then inspected and applied if necessary. In the first iteration, the oldest log record that may contain such an operation is the oldest log record of any transaction that was active when the first fuzzy mark was written. Later log propagation iterations only have to read the log after the previous fuzzy mark.

When the log propagator reads a new log record, affected records in the DTs are identified and changed if the LSN indicate an older state than the log record represents. The effects of the propagation depend on the operator being used and are therefore described individually in Section 4.

If a schema transformation is the goal of the DT materialization, locks are maintained on records in the DTs during the entire log propagation process. By doing this, the locks are in place when the next step, synchronization, is started. Since locks are only needed when user transactions access both source and derived tables at the same time, they are ignored for now.

The synchronization step should not be started if a significant portion of the log remains to be propagated because it involves latching the source tables. Each log propagation iteration therefore ends with an analysis of the remaining work. Based on the analysis, either another log propagation iteration or the synchronization step is started. The analysis could be based on, e.g. the time used to complete the current iteration, a count of the remaining log records to be propagated, or an estimated remaining propagation time.

The log propagator will never finish executing if more log records are produced than the propagator can process in the same time interval. If this is the case, the DT materialization should either be aborted or get a higher priority.

## 3.4  Synchronization

When synchronization is initiated, the state of the DTs should be very close to the state of the source tables. This is because the source tables have to be latched during one final log propagation iteration that makes the DTs consistent with the source tables.

We suggest three ways to synchronize the DTs to the source tables and thereby complete the DT materialization process. These are called blocking commit, non-blocking abort and non-blocking commit synchronization.

*Blocking commit* synchronization blocks all new transactions that try to access any of the source tables involved. Transactions that already have locks on the source tables are then allowed to complete before a final log propagation iteration is performed, making the DTs consistent with the sources. Depending on the purpose of the DT creation, either the source tables or the DTs are now available for transactions.

*The non-blocking abort* strategy latches the source tables for the duration of one final log propagation. Latching these tables effectively pauses ongoing transactions that work on them, but the pause should be very brief (less than 1 ms in the prototype implementation [18]). Once the log propagation is complete, the DTs are in the same state as the source tables.

If the newly created DTs are to be used as materialized views, the preferred MV update strategy (e.g. [3,9]) is used from this point. If the DTs are materialized to perform a schema transformation, the locks that have been maintained on the DTs since the first fuzzy log mark are made active. Records that are locked in the source tables are now also locked in the DTs. Note that locks forwarded from source tables conflict with locks

**Table 1.** Summary of information needed to make the transformations self-maintainable

| Operator | Additional Information Needed |
|---|---|
| Vertical Merge | Attribute: LSN and RID of $S_l$ and $S_r$ records |
| Vertical Split | Attribute: Counter |
| Horizontal Merge (dup. rem.) | Table: LSN and RID of duplicates |
| Horizontal Merge (dup. incl.) | |
| Horizontal Split | Table:Records not matching select criterion |
| Difference | Table: LSN of records in $T_{int}$ and $T_{comp}$ |
| Intersection | Table: LSN of records in $T_{diff}$ and $T_{comp}$ |

set directly on a DT but not with each other [18]. Once the DT locks have been activated, transactions are allowed to access the unlocked parts of the DTs whereas transactions that operate on the source tables are forced to abort. Source table locks held in the DTs are released as soon as the propagator has processed the abort log record of the lock owner transaction.

*Non-blocking commit* synchronization works much like the previous strategy in that latches are placed on the source tables during one final log propagation. In contrast to the previous strategy, however, transactions on the source tables are allowed to continue processing once the tables have been synchronized. If used for MV creation, there is no reason not to choose this strategy. For schema transformations, however, this strategy enables transactions on the source tables to aquire new locks. These locks must be set on all involved records in the DTs as well as in the source tables, resulting in overhead and more locking conflicts. The non-blocking abort strategy may therefore be a better choice, especially in transformations where one DT record is composed of multiple source records, like join.

# 4 Descriptions for Derived Table Materialization Operators

The following sections describe how to materialize DTs by using standard relational operators. These are vertical merge (full outer join) and split, horizontal merge (union) and split, difference and intersection.

The methods differ in whether the DTs contain all necessary information to identify transformed records and their state or not. The information that is not found in the DTs is summarized in Table 1. By adding this information, the log propagator is able to correctly update the DTs without accessing the source tables. This is known as the self-maintainability property [23], and renders the methods useful also in distributed database systems.

## 4.1 Vertical Merge (Full Outer Join)

Vertical merge transforms two source tables, $S_l$ (left source) and $S_r$ (right source), into one derived table $T$ by applying the full outer join operator. An example merge of "Employee" ($S_l$) and "PostalCode" ($S_r$) is shown in Figure 2. For readability it is assumed that the join attribute of table $S_r$ (attribute $PCode$ in Figure 2) is unique, i.e.

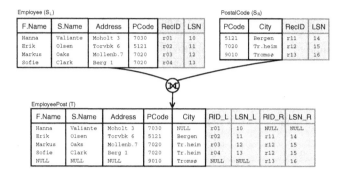

**Fig. 2.** Example of vertical merge DT creation. Grey attributes are used internally by the DT materialization process, and are not visible to other transactions. The reverse operation is an example of vertical split DT creation. The grey attributes are incorrect in a split context.

there is a one-to-many relation between the source tables. A merge of many-to-many relations is possible with minor changes to the described method.

The Derived Table, $T$, must as a minimum include the record IDs and LSNs from both source tables. In Figure 2, these are denoted RID- and LSN- left and right. The join attributes must also be included. With this information, DT materialization satisfies the self-maintainability requirement.

In addition to the indices on source record IDs (see Section 3.1), an index should be added to the join attributes of $T$. These indices provide fast lookup on $T$−records that are affected by any logged operation.

After creating the table, the full outer join operator is applied to the fuzzy read source tables, and the result is inserted into $T$. Special $S_l-$ and $S_r-$ NULL records, denoted $s_l^{null}$ and $s_r^{null}$, are joined with records that otherwise would not have a join match, as illustrated in Figure 2.

Once the initial image is inserted, the log propagator is started. The propagator ignores insert log records if the record already exists in $T$. Otherwise, if a join match is found, the record is joined with it and inserted. In the case that there are no join matches, the record is joined with a NULL record.

If a record joined with a NULL record in $T$ is deleted, the whole record is simply removed. If it is joined with another record, that record must be joined with a NULL record if it is not represented in at least one more record in $T$.

Update log records that do not change the join attributes are propagated straightforward by updating attribute values of all duplicates of the record in $T$, provided that the log has a higher LSN. If the join attributes are changed, however, the update is treated as a delete followed by an insert.

Synchronization is performed as described in Section 3.4. After this, a simple transformation can be used to remove attributes like the additional LSNs that are no longer in use. As mentioned in Section 2, simple transformations like attribute removal exist in commercial systems.

An alternative approach for vertical merge transformation has previously been presented by the authors [18]. The alternative approach did not include the extra LSN and source record ID attributes, thus requiring slightly less storage space. In contrast to the method presented here, however, it was not able to handle delta updates [16] (e.g. "increment").

## 4.2 Vertical Split

Vertical split is the reverse of the full outer join method described in the previous section. The method transforms one source table $S$ into two new tables $T_l$ (left result) and $T_r$ (right result), each containing a subset of the source table attributes. An example vertical split operation is that of splitting EmployeePost in Figure 2 into Employee and PostalCode. Note, however, that the grey attribute values are incorrect in a vertical split context.

In most cases, the source table $S$ contains multiple records with equal $T_r$−parts, e.g. multiple people with the same postal code. These records should be represented by only one record in $T_r$. Furthermore, a record in $T_r$ should only be deleted if there are no more records in $S$ with that $T_r$−part. To be able to decide if this is the case, a *counter*, similar to that of Gupta et al. [8], is associated with each $T_r$−record. When a $T_r$− record is first inserted, it has a counter of 1. After that, the counter is increased every time an equal record is inserted, and decreased every time one is deleted. If the counter of a record reaches zero, the record is removed from $T_r$.

The DTs are created during the preparation step, and must include the record IDs and LSNs from the source tables. The initial population and synchronization steps work as described in Section 3, but log propagation must be described in more detail.

When insert operations are encountered in the log, $T_l$ is checked to see if the record exists there. If so, the logged operation is already reflected in both DTs. Otherwise, a record is inserted into $T_l$ and $T_r$. If an equal $T_r$−record existed, its counter is increased. The LSN is then set to the highest value of the logged operation and the existing record.

Delete and update operations are ignored if the record does not exist in $T_l$, or if the LSN of that record is higher than that of the log. Otherwise, in the case of delete, the $T_l$−record is deleted, and the counter of the matching $T_r$−record is decreased. The LSN of the $T_r$−record is changed if the log record has a higher LSN value. If the counter reaches zero, the $T_r$−record is removed as well. In the case of update, the $T_l$−record is simply updated. If the key attribute of $T_r$ is not updated, updating the $T_r$−record is straightforward as well. If the key attribute is updated, however, the update is treated as a deletion of the old $T_r$−record followed by an insertion of the updated one.

Whether or not two $T_r$−records are equal has so far not been discussed. If the split is performed with the notion that "equal" means that all attribute values are the same, the algorithm described above is sufficient. There are, however, cases where equal primary keys would be a better criterion to determine equality. The described split of EmployeePost into Employee and Postal Code is a good example since for most applications, postal code should be unique. Thus, a problem arises if multiple $S$−records that contribute to the same $T_r$−record are not consistent. To continue the example, if a record with postal code 7020 existed that had a different city than "Tr.heim", e.g. "London", there would be an inconsistency. A solution to this problem has been presented by the authors [18]. The method uses primary key as equalness criterion, and flags records that may be inconsistent. Flagged records are checked regularly, and are unflagged if all contributing source records are consistent. Since source table records have to be read,

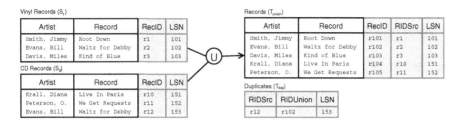

**Fig. 3.** Union Derived Table with Duplicate Removal. Grey attributes are used internally by the DT materialization process, and are not visible to other transactions.

the method is not self-maintainable. The solution forces the DBA to manually update inconsistent records since the DBMS has no notion of which attribute values are correct.

### 4.3   Horizontal Merge (Union)

Horizontal merge adds records from two source tables $S_1$ and $S_2$ into $T_{union}$. If duplicate records are included in $T_{union}$, the method is straightforward. All source records are represented unmodified in $T_{union}$, and the source RIDs and LSNs therefore identify the records and record states in $T_{union}$. Thus, the log propagation rules are applied like normal crash recovery.

Union transformation with duplicate removal is more complex. Duplicate records from the source tables are represented by only one record in $T_{union}$, and logged operations may merge new duplicates and split former duplicates into multiple records. The main problem is that the DT alone does not have LSNs and RIDs of duplicate records. Figure 3 illustrates a horizontal merge with a duplicate pair with RID $r2$ and $r12$. RecID denotes the record ID in the DT, and RIDSrc denotes the ID the record has in the source table. The Figure also shows a table "duplicates" ($T_{dup}$) used to store information on duplicate records. The necessary information is the record ID from the source table and from $T_{union}$, in addition to the LSN. With this information, the log propagator can determine if a logged operation on a duplicate record is already reflected, thus making log propagation possible. In addition to the index on source RID in $T_{union}$, indices should be added to both source and union RID in $T_{dup}$.

Logged insert operations insert a record into either $T_{union}$ or $T_{dup}$, depending on the existence of a duplicate record. If, however, the same source record ID already exists in either $T_{union}$ or $T_{dup}$, the log record is ignored.

Delete operations remove a record from $T_{dup}$ or from $T_{union}$. If the record is deleted from $T_{union}$ and one or more duplicates of the record exists, one of the duplicates must be moved from $T_{dup}$ to $T_{union}$. This can be done by deleting the record from $T_{dup}$ and then update the LSN and source record ID attributes of the record in $T_{union}$ to that of the deleted duplicate.

Update operations may create or remove duplicates: if a record with duplicates is updated, the operation is applied as a delete followed by an insert. If a new duplicate is formed as a result of the update, the method works like described for insert of duplicates. Otherwise, when neither the old or updated record images have duplicates, the update is applied straightforward.

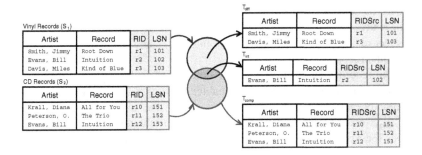

**Fig. 4.** Difference and intersection transformation. Grey attributes are used internally by the DT materialization process, and are not visible to other transactions.

### 4.4 Horizontal Split

Horizontal split is the reverse of union. The transformation takes records from one source table, $S$, and distributes them into two or more tables $T_{1..n}$ by using a selection criterion. Example criterions include that of splitting an employee-table into "New York employee" and "Paris employee" based on location, or into "high salary employee" and "low salary employee" based on a condition like "salary > \$40.000". The selection criterion may result in non-disjunct sets, and may even not include all records from the source table.

All derived tables must include the source RIDs and LSNs from $S$. A temporary table equal to the DTs is used to store records that do not fit any of the select criterions, if any. As an example, consider the employee table that was split into New York and Paris offices. An employee in London would not match any of these. If the log describes an update reflecting that the employee has moved to the Paris office, however, the log propagator will need the pre-update state of the record before inserting it into the correct table to be self-maintainable. The temporary table is removed once the synchronization step has completed.

With source RIDs and LSNs included in the DTs, log propagation for horizontal split is similar to normal crash recovery. The only difference is that the DTs the log records is applied to has to be identified first. For insert operations, the attribute values used in the selection criterions are included in the log record. Thus, the DTs to insert into are found in the log record directly. For update and delete operations, a search is necessery to identify all involved records. The reason for this is that the log records of these operations do not include the value of the selection attributes. Delete operations and update operations that do not change select criterion attributes are applied straight-forward when first found. If the attribute(s) used in the select criterion are updated, however, the record may have to be deleted and inserted into other DTs.

### 4.5 Difference and Intersection

Difference and intersection are so closely related that the same method is applied to materialize both DTs. Figure 4 shows the involved tables: $S_1$ is compared to $S_2$, and difference and intersection sets are inserted into $T_{diff}$ and $T_{int}$, respectively. In addition, the records from $S_2$ are stored into $T_{comp}$.

The derived tables must store the source record IDs (RIDSrc in Figure 4), and LSNs. When the source tables have been fuzzily read, records from $S_2$ are inserted into $T_{comp}$, whereas records from $S_1$ are inserted either into $T_{diff}$ or $T_{int}$, depending on the existence of equal records in $T_{comp}$.

Since the records stored in the DTs are unmodified and contain both source RIDs and LSNs, log propagation is self-maintainable: Insert of $S_1$−records are ignored if the record already exists in either $T_{diff}$ or $T_{int}$. Otherwise, an equal record is searched for in $T_{comp}$ to determine which of the two tables it should be inserted into. Delete operations for $T_1$ removes the record from whichever table it resides in. Updates may require a record to be moved between $T_{diff}$ and $T_{int}$.

The deletion of a record from $S_2$ is propagated as a delete from $T_{comp}$, and may require a record in $T_{int}$ to move to $T_{diff}$. The opposite may be the result of an insert into $S_2$. Finally, update operations affecting a record in $T_{comp}$ may require records to be moved between $T_{diff}$ and $T_{int}$.

## 5    Conclusion and Further Work

A method to perform non-blocking derived table materialization for six common relational operators has been developed for relational databases. Once created, these derived tables can be used as materialized views or for non-trivial schema transformations. In contrast to the method described in this paper, current commercial DBMSs block the involved tables during these task which may take minutes or more when large source tables are involved. Two of the operators are enhancements of methods previously suggested by the authors [18] while the remaining four are new. In contrast to the previously published methods, the enhanced methods can handle delta updates.

The method has been shown to incur little response time and throughput interference to normal transactions executing concurrently with the vertical merge and split methods previously published [18]. All described operators will be tested with the same prototype to verify these results. Since all operators use the same technique, however, the results are expected to be very similar in all cases.

## References

1. J. A. Blakeley, P.-A. Larson, and F. W. Tompa. Efficiently updating materialized views. In *Proceedings of the 1986 ACM SIGMOD Conference on Management of Data*, pages 61–71, 1986.
2. S. E. Bratsberg, S.-O. Hvasshovd, and Ø. Torbjørnsen. Parallel solutions in ClustRa. *IEEE Data Eng. Bull.*, 20(2):13–20, 1997.
3. L. S. Colby, T. Griffin, L. Libkin, I. S. Mumick, and H. Trickey. Algorithms for deferred view maintenance. In *Proceedings of the 1996 ACM SIGMOD International Conference on Management of Data*, pages 469–480. ACM Press, 1996.
4. R. A. Crus. Data Recovery in IBM Database 2. *IBM Systems Journal*, 23(2):178, 1984.
5. H. Garcia-Molina and K. Salem. Sagas. In *Proceedings of the 1987 ACM SIGMOD International Conference on Management of Data*, pages 249–259. ACM Press, 1987.
6. T. Griffin and B. Kumar. Algebraic change propagation for semijoin and outerjoin queries. *ACM SIGMOD Record*, 27(3):22–27, 1998.

7. A. Gupta, D. Katiyar, and I. S. Mumick. Counting solutions to the view maintenance problem. In *Workshop on Deductive Databases, JICSLP*, pages 185–194, 1992.
8. A. Gupta, I. S. Mumick, and V. S. Subrahmanian. Maintaining views incrementally. In *Proceedings of the 1993 ACM SIGMOD international conference on Management of data*, pages 157–166. ACM Press, 1993.
9. H. Gupta and I. S. Mumick. Incremental maintenance of aggregate and outerjoin expressions. *Information Systems*, In Press, 2005.
10. S.-O. Hvasshovd. *Recovery in Parallel Database Systems*. Verlag Vieweg, 2nd edition, 1999.
11. S.-O. Hvasshovd, T. Sæter, Ø. Torbjørnsen, P. Moe, and O. Risnes. A continuously available and highly scalable transaction server: Design experience from the HypRa project. In *Proceedings of the 4th International Workshop on High Performance Transaction Systems*, 1991.
12. IBM. *IBM DB2 Universal Database Glossary, Version 8.2*. IBM.
13. IBM. *IBM DB2 Universal Database Administration Guide: Implementation, version 8.2*. IBM.
14. IBM. *IBM DB2 Universal Database SQL Reference, Volume 2*. IBM, 8 edition.
15. A. Kawaguchi, D. F. Lieuwen, I. S. Mumick, D. Quass, and K. A. Ross. Concurrency control theory for deferred materialized views. In *Database Theory - ICDT '97, Proc of the 6th International Conference*, volume 1186 of *Lecture Notes in Computer Science*, pages 306–320. Springer, 1997.
16. H. F. Korth. Locking primitives in a database system. *Journal of the ACM*, 30(1):55–79, 1983.
17. D. Lorentz and J. Gregoire. *Oracle Database SQL Reference 10g Release 1 (10.1)*. 2003.
18. J. Løland and S.-O. Hvasshovd. Online, non-blocking relational schema changes. In *Advances in Database Technology – EDBT 2006*, volume 3896 of *Lecture Notes in Computer Science*, pages 405–422. Springer, 2006.
19. S. Marche. Measuring the stability of data. *European Journal of Information Systems*, 2(1):37–47, 1993.
20. Microsoft Corporation. Microsoft sql server 2005 books online, http://www.microsoft.com/technet/prodtechnol/sql/2005/downloads/books.mspx (december 6, 2005).
21. C. Mohan, D. Haderle, B. Lindsay, H. Pirahesh, and P. Schwarz. Aries: a transaction recovery method supporting fine- granularity locking and partial rollbacks using write-ahead logging. *ACM Transactions on Database Systems*, 17(1):94–162, 1992.
22. X. Qian and G. Wiederhold. Incremental recomputation of active relational expressions. *Knowledge and Data Engineering*, 3(3):337–341, 1991.
23. D. Quass, A. Gupta, I. S. Mumick, and J. Widom. Making views self-maintainable for data warehousing. In *Proceedings of the Fourth International Conference on Parallel and Distributed Information Systems, 1996, USA*, pages 158–169. IEEE Computer Society, 1996.
24. M. Ronström. On-line schema update for a telecom database. In *Proc. of the 16th International Conference on Data Engineering*, pages 329–338. IEEE Computer Society, 2000.
25. O. Shmueli and A. Itai. Maintenance of views. In *Proceedings of the 1984 ACM SIGMOD International Conference on Management of Data*, pages 240–255. ACM Press, 1984.
26. D. Sjøberg. Quantifying schema evolution. *Information and Software Technology*, 35(1):35–44, 1993.
27. M. Widenius and D. Axmark. *MySQL 5.1 Reference Manual*. 2006.
28. Y. Zhuge, H. Garcia-Molina, J. Hammer, and J. Widom. View maintenance in a warehousing environment. In *Proceedings of the 1995 ACM SIGMOD international conference on Management of data*, pages 316–327. ACM Press, 1995.

# Relationship Design Using Spreadsheet Reasoning for Sets of Functional Dependencies[*]

János Demetrovics[1], András Molnár[2], and Bernhard Thalheim[3]

[1] MTA SZTAKI, Computer and Automation Institute
of the Hungarian Academy of Sciences
Kende u. 13-17, H-1111 Budapest, Hungary
demetrovics@sztaki.hu
[2] Department of Information Systems, Faculty of Informatics,
Eötvös Loránd University Budapest
Pázmány Péter stny. 1/C, H-1117 Budapest, Hungary
modras@elte.hu
[3] Computer Science and Applied Mathematics Institute, University Kiel,
Olshausenstrasse 40, 24098 Kiel, Germany
thalheim@is.informatik.uni-kiel.de

**Abstract.** Entity-Relationship and other common database modeling tools have restricted capabilities for designing a relationship of higher arity. Although a complete and unambiguous specification can be achieved by traditional functional dependencies for relational schemata, use of the traditional formal notation in practice is rare. We propose an alternative way: designing or surveying the properties of a non-binary relationship among object classes or attributes is considered by spreadsheet reasoning methods for functional dependencies. Another representation by the semilattice of closed attribute sets can also be used in parallel due to convenient conversion facilities.

## 1 Preliminaries

### 1.1 Introduction

The Entity-Relationship (ER) model (eg. [12,13,11,21]) is the most widely used graphical tool for database schema design. The design procedure is based on identification of entity classes and relationships among them. Relationships are usually binary, ie. they connect two entity classes, but higher arities (eg. ternary, quaternary) are allowed and should be used whenever convenient. The model allows specification of cardinalities of entities participating in relationships.

During database design we observe a separation of complexity. The arity of entity types (number of attributes) is often higher than the arity of relationship

---

[*] This work was supported by the Hungarian National Office for Research and Technology under grant RET14/2005 and the German Academic Exchange Service (DAAD) research scholarship A/05/10580 in cooperation with the MÖB (Hungarian Scholarship Committee).

Y. Manolopoulos, J. Pokorný, and T. Sellis (Eds.): ADBIS 2006, LNCS 4152, pp. 108–123, 2006.

types (number of component types of the relationship type and the number of attributes of the relationship type). This separation of type complexity may lead to two different design principles: requirement of full knowledge of all functional dependencies that are valid for a relationship type and tolerance of incomplete knowledge of functional dependencies of entity types. Since relationship types are usually of small arity we need tools which allow to develop the complete set of functional dependencies[1] and allow to detect when we gained the complete knowledge.

ER and other common modeling tools have restricted capabilities for designing a relationship of higher arity. Therefore, binarization is often performed even if higher arity relationships would provide a more suitable model. In fact, the complexity of such relationships can be high and different types of ternary, quaternary relationships are not characterized (as opposed to binary cases) [9]. The complete and unambigous specification can be achieved by recalling database constraints, and relationship construction can be achieved through relation schema design. To achieve this, the database developer must master semantics acquisition, while nowadays, dependency theory at schema design is usually applied only to determine keys and decompose schemata into normal forms (eg. [5,6,4,7]). At the same time, a simple and powerful decomposition theory that might be applied to relationship types and will lead to simpler and better to survey schemata is not yet known. This theory can be developed if we have a facility for reasoning on the entire set of functional dependencies of a relationship type.

We focus on relationships that can be described by sets of functional dependencies. The notion of these dependencies was introduced in [3] for the relational database model [14], mainly to provide a way for specification of the properties of valid, acceptable instances of a relational schema. Classical database design is based on a step-wise extension of the constraint set and on a consideration of constraint sets through generation by tools. The theory developed in [7] provides a tool to decompose relationship types within the notions of the extended ER model [21]. In this case a relationship type may be decomposed by pivoting.

The traditional formal notation considers dependencies one-by-one including trivial and redundant ones. The implication is not effective enough in most cases. There is usually a strong inter-dependence among constraints. All these lead to an inconvenience in using the formalism with the traditional axiomatization. Therefore, simple and sophisticated means of representation and reasoning for constraint sets are needed. [18] proposed an approach for graphical representation of sets of functional dependencies for small relation schemata that supports reasoning. Based on similar theoretical considerations, we give in this paper another means of representation, the spreadsheet representation that might be more convenient for some designers, especially for designing relationships with arity higher than three. More details on both representations can be found in

---

[1] During constraint acquisition it is also important to collect those dependencies which are known to be invalid in general. They can be represented by *negated (or excluded) functional dependencies* [21].

[17]. We present the spreadsheet representation parallel with the semilattice approach of closed attribute sets discussed in [16]. They are likely to complement (compensate) each other because the more dependencies we have in the spreadsheet, the less edges we have in the semilattice graph.

The proposal of spreadsheet representation of constraint sets provides a possible solution of the problem of defining a pragmatical approach that allows simple representation of and reasoning on database constraints. It is crucial since typical algorithms such as normalization algorithms can only generate a correct result if specification is complete. Therefore, the database design process may only be complete of all integrity constraints if one specifies the missing constraints that cannot be derived by those that have already been specified.

## 1.2  On the Complexity of Relationship Types

For the binary case, three different basic relationship types exist (without considering optionality and exact cardinalities): one-to-one, one-to-many, many-to-many. If we fix the role of the two components, the many-to-one version must be included additionally. These relationship types can be described by sets of functional dependencies, treating components as attributes of a relational schema. With the generalization of this concept to higher arities, the different possible types of relationships correspond to the different closed sets of functional dependencies.

Denote by $\mathcal{SD}_n$ the set of closed sets of functional dependencies for a relation schema with $n$ attributes (with constant attributes disallowed). This corresponds to the different relationship types for components with fixed role (asymmetric types counted more that once). Furthermore, let $\tau$ the equivalence relation on these sets classifying them into different types or cases (for two equivalent sets there exists a permutation of attributes transforming one set to another). The number of different classes $(\mathcal{SD}_n/\tau)$ exactly correspond to the number of relationship types if the attributes do not have a fixed role (an asymmetric relationship type is counted only once). If we allow attributes to be stated as constants (which is, however not likely in schema design), it yields a larger set that is exactly the set of Moore families [19] for $n$, denoted by $\mathcal{SD}_n^0$ and its equivalence classes $\mathcal{SD}_n^0/\tau$. For each $n \in \mathbb{N}^+$, $\left|\mathcal{SD}_{n+1}^0/\tau\right| = \left|\mathcal{SD}_{n+1}/\tau\right| + \left|\mathcal{SD}_n^0/\tau\right|$ easily follows, as well as $\left|\mathcal{SD}_n^0\right| = \sum_{i=0}^{n}\binom{n}{i}\left|\mathcal{SD}_i\right|$ where $\left|\mathcal{SD}_0\right| = 1$.

With these notations, Table 1 shows the number of different cases for known arities and demonstrates the combinatorial of the search space. The first five rows were computed by a PROLOG program [18,17] and the third column was also obtained by [20]. The number of Moore families for six elements was presented in [19] and the first column can be calculated from that by the summarization formula above. The number of different equivalence classes for the sixth row is still unknown.

Although the number of different relationship types for $n$ attributes is still unsolved[2], it can be seen from the table that the complexity is already high for

---

[2] Estimations exist, see [8,16].

**Table 1.** Number of closed sets of functional dependencies for $n$ attributes

| $n$ | $|\mathcal{SD}_n|$ | $|\mathcal{SD}_n/\tau|$ | $|\mathcal{SD}_n^0|$ | $|\mathcal{SD}_n^0/\tau|$ |
|---|---|---|---|---|
| 1 | 1 | 1 | 2 | 2 |
| 2 | 4 | 3 | 7 | 5 |
| 3 | 45 | 14 | 61 | 19 |
| 4 | 2 271 | 165 | 2 480 | 184 |
| 5 | 1 373 701 | 14 480 | 1 385 552 | 14 664 |
| 6 | 75 965 474 236 | ? | 75 973 751 474 | ? |

small arities. Therefore, suitable tools are sought for a complete specification of a relationship with functional dependencies.

### 1.3   Motivating Example

Figure 1 shows an ER model of a university lecture proposal as a relationship with arity seven. To give a complete specification for the structure of this relationship in terms of functional constraints directly seems to be hard. For a better design, one may seek decomposition possibilities (separation of aspects). A possible solution is presented on Figure 2. [3] In this case we have still the question of describing the type, ie. the inner structure of the relationships. It is simple for the two binaries, 'Side condition' and 'History of proposal', they are many-to-many and many-to-one, respectively, but we need to determine the type of the ternary relationships 'Lecture proposed' and 'Course proposed' by choosing one of the 45 possibilities for each (see Table 1). One may also have relationships in the decomposed schema with higher arities that need complete type specification.

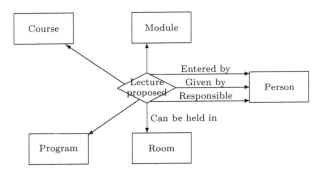

**Fig. 1.** ER schema for a university lecture proposal as a single relationship

Let us consider the specification of one of the ternary relationship types in the decomposed schema as a running example.

---

[3] HERM model, see [21].

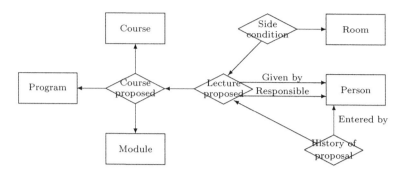

**Fig. 2.** Decomposed extended ER schema of lecture proposal by pivoting

**Example 1.** *'Course proposed': Assume a course determines its module, moreover, there can only be one course proposed for a module and program. It is formalized as two functional dependencies {Course → Module, Program Module → Course}. The complete specification can be reached by a constraint acquisition process.*

## 2  Classical, Lean and Graphical Reasoning

### 2.1  Traditional Logical Approach

We adopt the traditional notation for functional dependencies (eg. [3,16,1,21]) with the correspondence that a relationship type can be interpreted as a relation schema and its component types as attributes. Besides functional dependencies (FDs), we use *excluded functional constraints* (also called *negated functional dependencies*) as well: eg. $X \nrightarrow Y$ states that the functional dependency $X \longrightarrow Y$ is not valid.[4]

Traditional axiomatization of functional dependencies is the following, Armstrong implication system. It can be extended for negated dependencies by five more rules [21].

Axiom

$$XY \to Y$$

Rules

$$(1) \quad \frac{X \longrightarrow Y}{XVW \longrightarrow YV} \qquad\qquad (2) \quad \frac{X \longrightarrow Y, \ Y \longrightarrow Z}{X \longrightarrow Z}$$

However, this traditional formalism has inherent redundancy that might be confusing if one tries to find the derived dependencies of an initial set.

---

[4] Negated functional dependencies are considered with *weak semantics*, ie. a negated dependency may be valid in a particular instance but invalidity is taken as the normal situation for instances of the schema.

**Example 2.** *Recall Example 1. The functional dependency Course Program →
Module easily follows by rule (1). However, at this point only trivial (and
pseudo-trivial)*[5] *dependencies can be derived as a next step and it is not easy
to see whether further nontrivial dependencies can be derived. If one adds
Course Module → Program as an extra initial dependency for the sake of example, this situation remains unchanged. However, in the latter case Course →
Program is a nontrivial consequence that can only be reached via derivation of
a (pseudo-) trivial dependency, eg. by first deriving Course → Course Module
by (1) and then using the transitive rule (2).*

In the above example the question is still open: Is there any other nontrivial dependencies that can be derived? The only way to answer that with the
above axiomatization seems to be first to derive all trivial and redundant dependencies like *Course → Course, Course → Course Program, Course →
Module Program*, etc. and see what may follow further by the rules. It becomes
more complicated when we add the rules for negated functional constraints [21].

One may use the closure algorithm [1] instead, which is effective but does not
provide a representation and reasoning system for the whole set of dependencies.
Moreover it can not deal with negated dependencies which is necessary to collect
the possible remaining dependencies which should be checked against the real
world to achieve a complete specification of the relationship type.

## 2.2   A Simplified Logical Approach

For a more suitable logical framework, we propose a simplification, bearing in
mind that the aim is to consider sets of dependencies and not dependencies one-
by-one. The redundancy and unnecessary complexity of the above formalism lies
in the following aspects: First, all the symbols occuring in the rules denote attribute sets and not single attributes. Moreover, these sets may not be disjoint.
This raises the number of the possible instantiations of the rules. Second, dependencies with more than one attribute on their right-hand sides are inherently
redundant since they can directly be decomposed to *singletons*, ie. which have
only one attribute on their right-hand side.[6] (Pseudo-)Trivial dependencies do
not hold extra information either.

**Functional Constraints, Excluded Functional Constraints and their
Dimension.** To give a proper formal basis for our spreadsheet representation,
we simplify the above formalism and deal with nontrivial singleton functional

---

[5] A trivial constraint has a subset of its left side as its right side. A pseudo-trivial
  constraint has at least one attribute that appears on its both sides. Since we focus
  on sets of constraints, we treat pseudo-trivial dependencies as trivials for the sake
  of simplicity.

[6] A non-singleton functional dependency can be decomposed into singletons. A non-
  singleton negated dependency, however, represents a disjunction. We do not consider
  such dependencies since their relevance is usually not high and by using our simplified implication system they are not needed as intermediate results either (during
  derivation of singleton constraints).

constraints (both functional dependencies and their negated versions) only, without loosing relevant expressive power of functional constraints.

In most of the cases, we focus on *closed* sets of functional dependencies. A finite (singleton, nontrivial) constraint set $\mathcal{F}$ is closed iff $\mathcal{F}^+ = \mathcal{F}$ where $\mathcal{F}^+$ is the *singleton, nontrivial closure* of $\mathcal{F}$, i.e. contains all implied singleton, nontrivial constraints.

*Dimension of a constraint* is simply the size of its left-hand side, i.e. the number of attributes on its left-hand side. Dimension allows a natural grouping of possible singleton, nontrivial functional constraints over an attribute set.

For a single attribute $A$, given a set of functional dependencies $\mathcal{F} \subset \mathbb{D}_c^+$, the *dimension of $A$* is denoted by $[A]_{\mathcal{F}}$ (or just simply $[A]$) and defined as $[A]_{\mathcal{F}} \stackrel{\text{def}}{=} \min_{X \to A \in \mathcal{F}^+} |X|$. This definition is extended with $[A]_{\mathcal{F}} \stackrel{\text{def}}{=} \infty$ for the case when no $X \to A$ exists in $\mathcal{F}^+$. The dimensions of attributes can be used to classify the sets of functional dependencies.

**The ST and PQRST Implication Systems and the Order of Rule Application.** We base our spreadsheet reasoning on the following sound and complete axiomatization of nontrivial and singleton constraints [18,17].

In the following rules, $Y$ denotes a set of attributes (allowed to be empty) and $A, B, C$ are different attributes not occurring in $Y$.

$$(S) \quad \frac{Y \to B}{YC \to B} \qquad\qquad (T) \quad \frac{Y \to A, YA \to B}{Y \to B} \qquad\qquad (P) \quad \frac{YC \nrightarrow B}{Y \nrightarrow B}$$

$$(Q) \quad \frac{Y \to A, Y \nrightarrow B}{YA \nrightarrow B} \qquad (R) \quad \frac{YA \to B, Y \nrightarrow B}{Y \nrightarrow A} \qquad (\square) \quad \neg(Y \to B, Y \nrightarrow B)$$

- The *ST implication system* for positive constraints contains rules (S) and (T) and no axioms,
- The *PQRST implication system* for both negative and positive constraints has all the presented rules and the symbolic axiom ($\square$), which is used for indicating contradiction.

The implication systems introduced above have the advantage of the existence of a specific order of rules which provides a complete algorithmic method for getting all the implied functional constraints starting with an initial set[17]. The order for positive dependencies is first to use (S) only as many times as possible and then use (T) as many times as possible. We may call it *ST method*. It can be fine-tuned by taking dimensions into account: start with lower-dimensional instantiations of rule (S) and move towards higher dimensions. When applying rule (T) the opposite should be done: start with the highest-dimensional cases possible and end with the lowest-dimensional. The method is extended for excluded functional constraints by applying (R) until no changes occur, then (P) and (Q) in an arbitrary order until no changes occur. This is called *STRPQ method*.

### 2.3   Triangular Graphical Representation and Reasoning

[18] proposed a graphical representation for sets of (nontrivial, singleton) functional constraints for small number of attributes, which has a similar theoretical background. Functional dependencies and excluded functional constraints are represented as filled circles at the nodes of geometrical figures (circles and crossed circles, resp). Rules of the PQRST system can be graphically interpreted and implied constraints are denoted by empty circles. Although it can be generalized to higher number of attributes, the representation is best for ternary cases. In such a case, the diagram consists of a triangle and three separate edges. Triangular nodes represent FD's that have two attributes on their left sides. One-to-one constraints correspond to nodes of separate edges. For instance, Figure 3 shows the case of Example 1 on the left: the initial functional dependencies {$Course \rightarrow Module$, $Program\,Module \rightarrow Course$} as filled circles and the implied functional dependency $Course\,Program \rightarrow Module$ as an empty circle. The right side is an extension by the negated dependency $Program \nrightarrow Module$ and its implication $Program \nrightarrow Course$ (by (R)). For higher number of attributes higher dimensional representations exist (eg. tetrahedral for 4 attributes) that may be transformed into two dimensions (eg. quadratic for 4 attributes). Some designers may find the spreadsheet notation we present in this paper more convenient (especially for more than 3 attibutes) but both can be used in parallel.

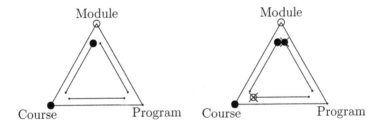

**Fig. 3.** Examples of the triangular representation

## 3   Spreadsheet Representation and Reasoning

### 3.1   The Spreadsheet Notation of Sets of Functional Dependencies

A set of functional dependencies over a specific set of attributes can be represented as a row of a table where columns correspond to the possible functional dependencies and a digit 1 or 0 in a column indicates the presence or absence of the corresponding dependency in the set. This representation is a brief but still convenient way to present a larger amount of sets and can also be used for reasoning on a particular set of constraints.

Dependencies are grouped according to their dimensions. Since our main focus is on schema design, we ignore cases with zero-dimensional constraints (specifying constant attributes), so the possible dimension values for $n$ attributes are

$\{1, 2, \ldots, n-1\}$. The number of possible (singleton, nontrivial) dependencies with dimension $d$ is $\binom{n}{d}(n-d)$. Therefore, the number of columns of the spreadsheet for $n$-ary cases is $\sum_{d=1}^{n-1}\binom{n}{d}(n-d)$. It equals 2 for 2 attributes, 9 for 3 attributes, 28 for 4 attributes and 75 for 5 attributes.

**Sets of Functional Dependencies for Small Relation Schemata.** The number of different types of ternary relationships is 14 (see Table 1). Table 2 shows the spreadsheet representation of the sets with their generating systems and attribute dimensions indicated. The two dimension groups of dependencies are separated by triple lines.

The possible 165 quaternary cases are presented in [17].

**Table 2.** The sets of functional dependencies for the ternary case, grouped by dimensions of attributes

| Case # | BC→A | AC→B | AB→C | B→A | A→B | C→A | A→C | C→B | B→C | Generating system of functional dependencies | Dimension of attributes [A] | [B] | [C] |
|---|---|---|---|---|---|---|---|---|---|---|---|---|---|
| #0 | 0 | 0 | 0 | 0 | 0 | 0 | 0 | 0 | 0 | $\emptyset$ | ∞ | ∞ | ∞ |
| #1 | 1 | 0 | 0 | 1 | 0 | 0 | 0 | 0 | 0 | $\{B \to A\}$ | 1 | ∞ | ∞ |
| #2 | 1 | 0 | 0 | 1 | 0 | 1 | 0 | 0 | 0 | $\{B \to A, C \to A\}$ | 1 | ∞ | ∞ |
| #3 | 1 | 1 | 0 | 0 | 0 | 1 | 0 | 1 | 0 | $\{C \to B, C \to A\}$ | 1 | 1 | ∞ |
| #4 | 1 | 1 | 0 | 1 | 0 | 1 | 0 | 1 | 0 | $\{C \to B, B \to A\}$ | 1 | 1 | ∞ |
| #5 | 1 | 1 | 0 | 1 | 1 | 0 | 0 | 0 | 0 | $\{A \to B, B \to A\}$ | 1 | 1 | ∞ |
| #6 | 1 | 1 | 0 | 1 | 1 | 1 | 0 | 1 | 0 | $\{C \to B, A \to B, B \to A\}$ | 1 | 1 | ∞ |
| #7 | 1 | 1 | 1 | 1 | 1 | 0 | 1 | 0 | 1 | $\{A \to C, A \to B, B \to A\}$ | 1 | 1 | 1 |
| #8 | 1 | 1 | 1 | 1 | 1 | 1 | 1 | 1 | 1 | $\{A \to B, B \to C, C \to A\}$ | 1 | 1 | 1 |
| #9 | 1 | 1 | 1 | 0 | 0 | 1 | 0 | 1 | 0 | $\{AB \to C, C \to B, C \to A\}$ | 1 | 1 | 2 |
| #10 | 1 | 1 | 0 | 1 | 0 | 0 | 0 | 0 | 0 | $\{AC \to B, B \to A\}$ | 1 | 2 | ∞ |
| #11 | 1 | 0 | 0 | 0 | 0 | 0 | 0 | 0 | 0 | $\{BC \to A\}$ | 2 | ∞ | ∞ |
| #12 | 1 | 1 | 0 | 0 | 0 | 0 | 0 | 0 | 0 | $\{BC \to A, AC \to B\}$ | 2 | 2 | ∞ |
| #13 | 1 | 1 | 1 | 0 | 0 | 0 | 0 | 0 | 0 | $\{BC \to A, AC \to B, AB \to C\}$ | 2 | 2 | 2 |

## 3.2   Extension to Spreadsheet Reasoning

Consider the spreadsheet representation for three attributes. Generalization of the following issues for higher number of attributes is straightforward.

To use the spreadsheet for reasoning, we extend the notation as follows. Let 1 and 0 indicate the functional dependencies and excluded functional constraints of the initial set, respectively. We put a '.' to each of the columns corresponding the constraints whose state is not known. As we get an implied positive constraint (functional dependency) during the deduction process, we replace the corresponding '.' with $\vdash 1$ if the state of the implied constraint was previously unknown. Similarly, an implied negated constraint is indicated by $\vdash 0$.

**Table 3.** Example of the spreadsheet derivation of functional constraints: Rules of the PQRST implication system in the spreadsheet form

| BC→A | AC→B | AB→C | B→A | A→B | C→A | A→C | C→B | B→C | Implication impact of detected functional constraints |
|---|---|---|---|---|---|---|---|---|---|
| . | ⊢ 1 | . | . | 1 | . | . | . | . | (S) $A \to B \vdash AC \to B$ |
| . | . | 1 | . | 1 | . | ⊢ 1 | . | . | (T) $AB \to C,\ A \to B \vdash A \to C$ |
| . | 0 | . | . | ⊢ 0 | . | . | ⊢ 0 | . | (P) $AC \not\to B \vdash A \not\to B,\ C \not\to B$ |
| . | . | ⊢ 0 | . | 1 | . | 0 | . | . | (Q) $A \to B,\ A \not\to C \vdash AB \not\to C$ |
| . | . | 1 | . | ⊢ 0 | . | 0 | . | . | (R) $AB \to C,\ A \not\to C \vdash A \not\to B$ |

Table 3 shows how rules of the PQRST implication system can be represented in the spreadsheet form for the ternary case. For cases with more attributes $C$ has to be syntactically replaced in the rules with each possible attribute set. The STRPQ algorithm presented above provides a possible way for derivation of the full knowledge a partial set holds. Other implication systems can also be used but *PQRST* has the advantage that the rules are simple to instantiate in terms of the spreadsheet representation. A rule application corresponds to the choice of one or two columns (depending on the rule) with proper content (0 or 1, depending on the rule) and writing the result in one target column (implied 0 or 1). Dimensionality ensures that the involved columns for a rule instantiation are not far away from each other, even for higher arities: we must consider two neighboring dimension groups only.

The spreadsheet can be used for deriving contradictions as well. Contradictions occur whenever new constraints are introduced and the implication system allows to derive the opposite. We may indicate the contradiction by the symbol ↯. The first case on Table 4 is due to the rule system in the extended Armstrong axiomatization (reversed transitivity). The second one is obvious due to rule (Q) of the PQRST system.

**Table 4.** Deriving contradiction by spreadsheet reasoning

| BC→A | AC→B | AB→C | B→A | A→B | C→A | A→C | C→B | B→C | Implication impact of detected functional constraints |
|---|---|---|---|---|---|---|---|---|---|
| . | . | . | . | 1 | . | 0 | . | ⊢ 0 ↯1 | $\{A \to B, A \not\to C\}\ ↯\ \{B \to C\}$ |
| . | . | ⊢ 0 ↯1 | . | 1 | . | 0 | . | . | $\{A \to B, A \not\to C\}\ ↯\ \{AB \to C\}$ |

## 3.3 Managing Sets of Functional Dependencies

**Inserting a Functional Constraint into a Closed Set.** We can now derive from a set of given constraints all constraints that are implied and that are contradicted. We, thus, obtain a number of constraints whose validity is still open. Using the approach of [2] we can generate sample data and provide them to the designer with the question whether these data support a certain functional dependency or not. At this point, a new constraint is inserted and only the new implications needed to be generated in the spreadsheet, involving a contradiction check. This way sets of functional dependencies can be definitively developed.

The following recursive algorithm adds a (positive) functional dependency to a closed set:[7]

$Add(\mathcal{F}, A_1 A_2 \ldots A_k \to B)$ :
   if $A_1 \ldots A_k \nrightarrow B$ then $\lightning$, stop
   else if $A_1 \ldots A_k \to B$ then return
   else declare $A_1 \ldots A_k \to B$ as implied and
   1. (S): $\forall C : Add(\mathcal{F}, A_1 \ldots A_k C \to B)$
   2. (T): $\forall C :$ if $A_1 \ldots A_k B \to C$ then $Add(\mathcal{F}, A_1 \ldots A_k \to C)$
   3. (T support): $\forall i :$ if $A_1 \ldots A_{i-1} A_{i+1} \ldots A_k \to A_i$ then
      $Add(\mathcal{F}, A_1 \ldots A_{i-1} A_{i+1} A_k \to B)$
   4. (R support): $\forall i :$ if $A_1 \ldots A_{i-1} A_{i+1} \ldots A_k \nrightarrow B$ then
      $Add(\mathcal{F}, A_1 \ldots A_{i-1} A_{i+1} A_k \nrightarrow A_i)$
   5. (Q support): $\forall C :$ if $A_1 \ldots A_k \nrightarrow C$ then
      $Add(\mathcal{F}, A_1 \ldots A_k B \nrightarrow C)$
   end if
end.

To insert a negated constraint, the algorithm looks like this:

$Add(\mathcal{F}, A_1 A_2 \ldots A_k \nrightarrow B)$ :
   if $A_1 \ldots A_k \to B$ then $\lightning$, stop
   else if $A_1 \ldots A_k \nrightarrow B$ then return
   else declare $A_1 \ldots A_k \nrightarrow B$ as implied and
   1. (R): $\forall C :$ if $A_1 \ldots A_k C \to B$ then $Add(\mathcal{F}, A_1 \ldots A_k \nrightarrow C)$
   2. (Q): $\forall C :$ if $A_1 \ldots A_k \to C$ then $Add(\mathcal{F}, A_1 \ldots A_k C \nrightarrow B)$
   3. (P): $\forall i : Add(\mathcal{F}, A_1 \ldots A_{i-1} A_{i+1} A_k \nrightarrow B)$
   end if
end.

The algorithms work by searching all possible consequences and support cases of each constraint recursively based on the implication system PQRST. Their efficiency is proportional to the number of newly implied constraints multiplied by the number of attributes of the schema. It is due to the simplicity of the rules: the number of possible instantiations given one of their prerequisite constraints (i.e. when $Y$ and $B$ fixed) is bounded by the number of attributes – one free parameter remains which is an attribute (eg. $C$ for rule (S) and $A$ for rule (T)). This is not true for the Armstrong implication system. Since there are constant number of rule application types after adding a single constraint (5 for a positive and 3 for a negative constraint), complexity of the whole recursive algorithm is bounded by a constant (five or three) times the number of attributes multiplied by the total number of added constraints.

---

[7] Universe of quantification $\forall C$ contains all the attributes except $A_1 \ldots A_k$ and $B$. Universe of quantification $\forall i$ is $[1 \ldots k]$. Quantifications can be implemented by *for* loops.

**Deleting a Constraint.** Could be performed by a same type of recursion. However, an implied constraint cannot be removed so the first step is to check whether it is implied by other constraints. This should be done for all implications as well. Since mutual implications may exist, deletion can only be carried over by a two-phase method: first flag all the implied constraints in the spreadsheet that can be derived using the one to be deleted and then check which of them can be derived using other, remaining constraints. This may cause some flags to be removed (some constraints not to be deleted). After this procedure is completed, flagged constraints can be removed from the constraint set and the set remains closed.

### 3.4   An Example

**Example 3.** *Recall our running example (Example 1) and from now on, let us abbreviate the components of the relationship with their initials: C for Course, P for Program and M for Module. Table 5 shows the steps of constraint acquisition process with spreadsheet reasoning. The first two steps were depicted on Fig. 3 as well.*

**Table 5.** Constraint acquisition with spreadsheet reasoning

| Step # | CP → M | MP → C | MC → P | C → M | M → C | P → M | M → P | P → C | C → P | Implication impact of detected functional constraints |
|---|---|---|---|---|---|---|---|---|---|---|
| #1 | ⊢1 | 1 | . | 1 | . | . | . | . | . | (S)  $C \to M \vdash CP \to M$ |
| #2 | ⊢1 | 1 | . | 1 | . | 0 | . | ⊢0 | . | (R)  $P \nrightarrow M,\ CP \to M \vdash P \nrightarrow C$ |
| #3 | ⊢1 | 1 | ⊢0 | 1 | . | 0 | ⊢0 | ⊢0 | 0 | (Q,P) $C \nrightarrow P, C \to M \vdash MC \nrightarrow P \vdash M \nrightarrow P$ |
| #4 | ⊢1 | 1 | ⊢0 | 1 | 0 | 0 | ⊢0 | ⊢0 | 0 | no new implication and no ↯ |

*The initial assumption is the same as in Example 1, ie. $MP \to C$, $C \to M$. From this initial set, $CP \to M$ follows by rule (S) as shown in the first line of Table 5. As a second step, $P \nrightarrow M$ is inserted and the recursive implication process yields the only implication $P \nrightarrow C$. In the third step, the possible dependency $C \to P$ is chosen from the still unknown columns and declared as invalid. Rule (Q) is applicable and we get $MC \nrightarrow P$. It immediately implies $M \nrightarrow P$ by (P) and no other new implications exist. As the fourth step the last missing constraint is declared as negated too, and its possible implications are checked whether they contradict some of the constraints already specified. There is no contradiction in this case.*

## 4   Spreadsheet Reasoning and the Semilattice of Closed Attribute Sets

We know from [16] that the set of closed attribute sets wrt a set of functional dependencies is closed under intersection so they form an intersection-semilattice (meet-semilattce, SL). This can be reversed: each set of attribute sets containing the full set (of all the attributes of the schema) that is closed under intersection forms an SL and there exists a set of functional dependencies whose closed attribute sets are exactly the items of the SL. This way we get an alternative representation of functional dependency sets and so, of relationship types.

The semilattice can be represented by a graph [15,10]: labelled nodes correspond to closed attribute sets and the (nontransitive instances of) set containment are represented by edges. Since the attributes are 'inherited' along the edges, it is enough to indicate the new attributes at each node only. For the sake of clarity, we indicate all the attributes but put the inherited ones in brackets. Figure 4 shows the semilattice graph corresponding to Example 1 and 3. [8]

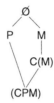

**Fig. 4.** Semilattice graph of closed attribute sets for Example 1,2,3 and 4

The semilattice graph corresponds to a different point of view than the spreadsheet: the more positive dependencies we have, the less vertices the graph has. This is of course not a strict proposition since we may have redundant dependencies. However, adding a nonredundant dependency always destroys at least one closed set, ie. removes one or more nodes from the graph. The semilattice graph notation becomes simple in some cases while considering the set of functional dependencies is complicated in the spreadsheet. In other cases the situation is reversed. Therefore, by designing or surveying a relation schema, both representations may be used in parallel, focusing on the one more convenient.

### 4.1   Conversion Between Representations

**Obtaining the Closed Attribute Sets from a Closed Set of Functional Dependencies.** Whether or not a specific attribute set is closed can be seen from the spreadsheet representation of a closed constraint set in the dimension group corresponding to the size of the attribute set. To construct the semilattice graph of all the closed sets needs systematically collecting the closed sets. It is performed on the basis of the following rules:

1. The set of all attributes is always closed.
2. If a set $X$ is closed and no dependency $Y \rightarrow A$ holds where $Y \subset X$ and $A \in X \setminus Y$ then $Y$ is closed.
3. If two sets $X$ and $Y$ are closed then $X \cap Y$ is closed.

---

[8] If some dependencies remain unknown then a semilattice graph can still be constructed but some closed attribute sets will be (and must be marked as) uncertain.

We start with the full set with size $n$ (first rule). Then look at each attribute sets with size $n-1$ whether the dependency holds whose left-hand side is that set (simply displayed as the highest dimension group in the spreadsheet). If the dependency does not hold, the set is added to the closed attribute sets (second rule). Then we add the intersections of the obtained sets as closed sets (third rule). This process is repeated with the possible sets in decreasing order by their sizes. The third rule ensures once a closed set is found, determining whether a subset of it is closed needs only to check existence of dependencies completely inside (and not pointing outside) of the set. The whole process can be done also by hand for small relation schemata using the spreadsheet representation.

**Transforming the Semilattice Graph into a Closed Set of Functional Constraints.** Given the semilattice of the closed attribute sets, negated functional constraints can be obtained: if a set $X$ is closed, then $X \nrightarrow A$ holds for each $A \notin X$. These are declared as initial constraints in the dimension group of the spreadsheet corresponding to the size of $X$. All other negated constraints can be derived afterwards by the negated reduction rule (P). All the remaining nodes correspond to positive functional dependencies.

**Example 4.** *Consider the graph on Figure 4. We construct line 4 of Table 5 (implication signs may differ). $MC$ is closed, therefore a 0 must be entered into the column of $MC \rightarrow P$. It implies $M \nrightarrow P$ and $C \nrightarrow P$ by (P). The closedness of $M$ means $M \nrightarrow C$ must be declared additionally and due to the closedness of $P$ $P \nrightarrow M$ and $P \nrightarrow C$ must be declared. Finally, all the remaining columns must be filled with 1's.*

# 5   Conclusion, Future Work and Open Problems

We have proposed a spreadsheet representation for reasoning on sets of functional constraints (functional dependencies and excluded functional constraints) as well as conversion algorithms between this type of representation and the semilattice of closed attribute sets that can be used as a support for spreadsheet reasoning. The main focus is on considering sets of constraints as a whole instead of constraints one-by-one as in the traditional notation. Inherent redundancy of the traditional syntax is eliminated by not considering trivial and nonsingleton dependencies. A simple and powerful implication system PQRST convenient for the spreadsheet representation is taken as a basis for reasoning. There exists a specific order of rule application to derive all implied dependencies and we have also given a recursive method for inserting a dependency into a closed set whose efficiency reflects the simplicity of the rules.

Implementation of the discussed methods can give a software tool support for designing relationships by sets of functional constraints. Future work may include the construction of a spreadsheet method for other types of constraints like multivalued or inclusion dependencies.

The different possible sets are generated for up to 5 attributes [17]. We know the number of possible sets for 6 fixed attributes from [19]. However, it is still open for six attributes how many different types of relationships are possible (the number of cases up to permutation of attributes). No exact numbers for more than 6 attributes are known, according to our knowledge. However, a deeper analysis of the known cases (ternary, quaternary, quinary) is also promising in order to have more sophisticated reasoning facilities on types of relationships.

# References

1. S. Abiteboul, R. Hull, and V. Vianu. *Foundations of databases*. Addison-Wesley, Reading, MA, 1995.
2. M. Albrecht, E. Buchholz, A. Düsterhöft, and B. Thalheim. An informal and efficient approach for obtaining semantic constraints using sample data and natural language processing. In *Proc. Semantics in Databases, LNCS 1358*, pages 1–28. Springer, Berlin, 1998.
3. W. W. Armstrong. Dependency structures of data base relationships. In J. L. Rosenfeld, editor, *Information Processing 74, Proceedings of IFIP Congress 74*, pages 580–583, Stockholm, Aug. 5-10,1974, 1974. North-Holland, Amsterdam.
4. J. Biskup. Boyce-codd normal forma and object normal forms. *Information Processing Letters*, 32(1):29–33, 1989.
5. J. Biskup. *Foundations of information systems*. Vieweg, Wiesbaden, 1995. In German.
6. J. Biskup, J. Demetrovics, L. O. Libkin, and M. Muchnik. On relational database schemes having a unique minimal key. *J. of Information Processing*, 27:217–225, 1991.
7. J. Biskup and T. Polle. Decomposition of database classes under path functional dependencies and onto contraints. In *Proc. FoIKS'2000*, LNCS 1762, pages 31–49. Springer, 2000, 2000.
8. G. Burosch, J. Demetrovics, G. O. H. Katona, D. J. Kleitman, and A. A. Sapozhenko. On the number of databases and closure operations. *TCS*, 78(2):377–381, 1991.
9. R. Camps. From ternary relationship to relational tables: A case against common beliefs. *ACM SIGMOD Record, 31(2)*, pages 46–49, 2002.
10. N. Caspard and B. Monjardet. The lattices of closure systems, closure operators, and implicational systems on a finite set: a survey. *Discrete Applied Mathematics*, 127:241–269, 2003.
11. Chen & Associates, Baton Rouge, LA. *ER-designer reference manual*, 1986–1989.
12. P. P. Chen. The entity-relationship model: Toward a unified view of data. *ACM TODS*, 1(1):9–36, 1976.
13. P. P. Chen, editor. *Proc. 1st Int. ER Conf., ER'79: Entity-Relationship Approach to Systems Analysis and Design*, Los Angeles, USA, 1979, 1980. North-Holland, Amsterdam.
14. E. F. Codd. A relational model for large shared data banks. *CACM*, 13(6):197–204, 1970.
15. J. Demetrovics and N. X. Huy. Translations of relation schemes and representations of closed sets. *PU.M.A.Ser. A*, 1(3-4):299–315, 1990.
16. J. Demetrovics, L. O. Libkin, and I. B. Muchnik. Functional dependencies and the semilattice of closed classes. In *Proc. MFDBS'89, LNCS 364*, pages 136–147, 1989.

17. J. Demetrovics, A. Molnar, and B. Thalheim. Graphical and spreadsheet reasoning for sets of functional dependencies. Technical Report 0404, Kiel University, Computer Science Institute, http://www.informatik.uni-kiel.de/reports/2004/0404.html, 2004.
18. J. Demetrovics, A. Molnar, and B. Thalheim. Graphical reasoning for sets of functional dependencies. In *Proceedings of ER 2004, Lecture Notes in Computer Science 3288*, pages 166–179. Springer Verlag, 2004.
19. N. Habib and L. Nourine. The number of moore families on n=6. *Discrete Mathematics*, 294(3):291–296, 2005.
20. A. Higuchi. Note: Lattices of closure operators. *Discrete Mathematics*, 179:267–272, 1998.
21. B. Thalheim. *Entity-relationship modeling – Foundations of database technology.* Springer, Berlin, 2000. See also http://www.informatik.tu-cottbus.de/~thalheim/HERM.htm.

# Modeling and Storing Context-Aware Preferences

Kostas Stefanidis, Evaggelia Pitoura, and Panos Vassiliadis

Department of Computer Science, University of Ioannina, Greece
{kstef, pitoura, pvassil}@cs.uoi.gr

**Abstract.** Today, the overwhelming volume of information that is available to an increasingly wider spectrum of users creates the need for personalization. In this paper, we consider a database system that supports context-aware preference queries, that is, preference queries whose result depends on the context at the time of their submission. We use data cubes to store the associations between context-dependent preferences and database relations and OLAP techniques for processing context-aware queries, thus allowing the manipulation of the captured context data at different levels of abstractions. To improve query performance, we use an auxiliary data structure, called context tree, which indexes the results of previously computed preference-aware queries based on their associated context. We show how these cached results can be used to process both exact and approximate context-aware preference queries.

## 1 Introduction

The increased amount of available information creates the need for personalized information processing [1]. Instead of overwhelming the user with all available data, a personalized query returns only the relevant to the user information. In general, to achieve personalization, users express their preferences on specific pieces of data either explicitly or implicitly. The result of their queries are then ranked based on these preferences. However, most often users may have different preferences under different circumstances. For instance, a user visiting Athens may prefer to visit *Acropolis* in a nice sunny summer day and the *archaeological museum* in a cold and rainy winter afternoon. In other words, the results of a preference query may depend on context.

*Context* is a general term used to capture any information that can be used to characterize the situation of an entity [2]. Common types of context include the *computing context* (e.g., network connectivity, nearby resources), the *user context* (e.g., profile, location), the *physical context* (e.g., noise levels, temperature), and *time* [3]. A *context-aware* system is a system that uses context to provide relevant information and/or services to its users. In this paper, we consider a *context-aware* preference database system that supports preference queries whose results depend on context. In particular, users express their preferences on specific attributes of a relation. Such preferences depend on context, that is, they may have different values depending on context.

Y. Manolopoulos, J. Pokorný, and T. Sellis (Eds.): ADBIS 2006, LNCS 4152, pp. 124–140, 2006.

We model context as a finite set of special-purpose attributes, called *context parameters*. Users express their preferences on specific database instances based on a single context parameter. Such *basic preferences*, i.e., preferences associating database relations with a single context parameter, are combined to compute *aggregate preferences* that include more than one context parameter. Context parameters may take values for hierarchical domains, thus different levels of abstraction for the captured context data are introduced. For instance, this allows us to represent preference along the location context parameter at different levels of detail, for example, by grouping together preferences for all cities of a specific country. Basic preferences are stored in data cubes, following the OLAP paradigm.

Although, aggregate preferences are not explicitly stored, we cache the results of previously computed preference queries using a data structure called *context tree*. The context tree indexes the results of queries based on their associated context. The cached results are re-used to speed up the processing of queries that refer to the exact context of a previously computed query as well as of queries whose context is similar enough to those of some previously computed ones. We provide initial experimental results that characterize the quality of the approximation attained by using preferences computed at similar context states.

In summary, in this paper, we make the following contributions:

- We provide a logical model for context-aware preferences that is based on a multidimensional model of context.
- We propose storing the results of previously computed preference queries using a data structure, the *context tree*, that indexes these results based on the values of the context parameters.
- We show how cached results can be used to compute both exact and approximate context-aware preference queries.

## 2   A Logical Model for Context and Preferences

### 2.1   Reference Example

Consider a database schema with information about *points_of_interest* and *users* (Fig. 1). The *points_of_interest* may for example be museums, monuments, archaeological places, zoos. We consider three context parameters as relevant to this application: *location*, *temperature* and *accompanying_people*. Users have preferences about *points_of_interest* that they express by providing a numeric score between 0 and 1. The degree of interest that a user expresses for a *point_of_interest* depends on the values of the context parameters. For example, a user may visit different places depending on the current temperature, for instance, user *Mary* may give *Acropolis* that is an open-air place, a lower score when the weather is *cold* than when the weather is *warm*. We consider temperature to take one of the following values: *freezing, cold, mild, warm,* and *hot*. Furthermore, the location of users may also affect their preferences, for example, a user may prefer to visit places that are nearby her current location.

Similarly, the result of a query depends on the *accompanying_people* that might be *friends*, *family*, and *none*. For example, a *zoo* may be a better place to visit than a *brewery* in the context of *family*.

*Points_of_Interest(<u>pid</u>, name, type, location, open-air, hours_of_operation, admission_cost)*
*User(<u>uid</u>, name, phone, address, e-mail)*

**Fig. 1.** The database schema of our reference example

## 2.2  Modeling Context

Context is modeled through a finite set of special-purpose attributes, called *context parameters* $(C_i)$. For a given application $X$, we define its context environment $CE_X$ as a set of $n$ context parameters $\{C_1, C_2, \ldots, C_n\}$. For instance, the context environment of our example is {*location, temperature, accompanying_people*}. As usual, a *domain* is an infinitely countable set of values. A *context state* corresponds to assigning to each context parameter a value from its domain. For instance, a context state may be: $CS(current) = \{Plaka, warm, friends\}$. The result of a context-aware preference query depends on the context state of its execution. It is possible for some context parameters to participate in an associated *hierarchy of levels* of aggregated data, i.e., they can be viewed from different levels of detail. Formally, an *attribute hierarchy* is a lattice of attributes – called *levels* for the purpose of the hierarchy – $L = (L_1, \ldots, L_n, ALL)$. We require that the upper bound of the lattice is always the level $ALL$, so that we can group all values into the single value '*all*'. The lower bound of the lattice is called the detailed level of the parameter. In our running example, we consider *location* to be such an attribute as shown in Fig. 2 (left). Levels of *location* are *Region, City, Country*, and *ALL*. *Region* is the most detailed level, while level *ALL* is the most coarse level.

## 2.3  Contextual Preferences

In this section, we define how context affects the results of a query. Each user expresses her preference for an item in a specific context by providing a numeric score between 0 and 1. This score expresses a degree of interest: value 1 indicates extreme interest, while value 0 indicates no interest. We distinguish preferences into basic (involving a single context parameter) and aggregate ones (involving a combination of context parameters).

**Basic Preferences.** Each basic preference is described by (a) a value of a context parameter $c_i \in dom(C_i)$, $1 \le i \le n$, (b) a set of values of non-context parameters $a_i \in dom(A_i)$, and (c) a degree of interest, i.e., a real number between 0 and 1. So, for a context parameter $c_i$, we have:

$$preference_{basic_i}(c_i, a_{k+1}, \ldots, a_m) = interest\_score_i.$$

In our reference example, besides the three context parameters (i.e, *location*, *temperature* and *accompanying_people*), the set of non-context parameters are attributes about *points_of_interest* and *users* that are stored in the database. For example, assume user *Mary* and the point-of-interest *Acropolis*. When *Mary* is in the *Plaka* area, she likes to visit *Acropolis* and gives it score 0.8. Similarly, she prefers to visit *Acropolis* when the weather is *warm* and gives *Acropolis* score 0.9. Finally, if she is with *friends*, *Mary* gives *Acropolis* score 0.6. So, the basic preferences for *Acropolis* and *Mary* are:

$$preference_{basic_1}(Plaka, Acropolis, Mary) = 0.8,$$
$$preference_{basic_2}(warm, Acropolis, Mary) = 0.9,$$
$$preference_{basic_3}(friends, Acropolis, Mary) = 0.6.$$

For context values not appearing explicitly in a basic preference, we consider a default interest score of 0.5.

**Aggregate Preferences.** Each aggregate preference is derived from a combination of basic ones. An aggregate preference involves (a) a set of of $n$ values $x_i$, one for each context parameter $C_i$, where either $x_i = c_i$ for some value $c_i \in dom(C_i)$ or $x_i = *$, which means that the value of the context parameter $C_i$ is irrelevant, i.e., the corresponding context parameter should not affect the aggregate preference, and (b) a set of values of non-context parameters $a_i \in dom(A_i)$, and has a degree of interest:

$$preference(x_1, \ldots x_n, a_{k+1}, \ldots, a_m) = interest\_score.$$

The interest score of the aggregate preference is a *value function* of the individuals scores of the basic preferences. This value function prescribes how to combine basic preferences to produce an aggregate score. In general, this may be any computable function specified by the user. In this paper, we assume that the interest score of an aggregate preference is simply a weighted sum of the corresponding basic preferences. Users just specify a weight $w_i$ for each context parameter $C_i$, such that, $\sum_{i=1}^{n} w_i = 1$. For instance, in the previous example, if the weight of *location* is 0.6, the weight of *temperature* is 0.3 and the weight of *accompanying_people* is 0.1, *preference(Plaka, warm, friends, Acropolis, Mary)* gets score 0.81.

We describe next two approaches for computing the aggregate scores when the value for some parameters in the preference is '*'. The first one assumes a score of 0.5 for those context parameters whose values in the preference is '*'. Then, the *interest_score* for the preference $preference(x_1, \ldots x_n, a_{k+1}, \ldots, a_m)$ is computed as:

$$interest\_score = \sum_{i=1}^{n} w_i \times y_i$$

where $y_i = preference_{basic_i}(x_i, a_{k+1}, \ldots, a_m)$, if $x_i = c_i$ and $y_i = 0.5$, if $x_i = *$.

The other approach includes in the computation only the interest scores of those context parameters whose values are specified in the preference and ignores those specified as irrelevant. In this case, the *interest_score* for the preference $preference(x_1, \ldots x_n, a_{k+1}, \ldots, a_m)$ is computed as follows. Assume without loss of generality, that for the first $k$ parameters $x_i$, $1 \leq i \leq k$, it holds $x_i = c_i$, for $c_i \in dom(C_i)$ and for the remaining $n - k$ parameters, $x_i$, $k < i \leq n$, it holds $x_i = *$. Then,

$$interest\_score = \sum_{i=1}^{k} w'_i \times y_i$$

where $w'_i = \frac{w_i}{\sum_{j=1}^{k} w_j}$, $y_i = preference_{basic_i}(x_i, a_{k+1}, \ldots, a_m)$, if $x_i = c_i$ and $y_i$ = 0.5, if $x_i = *$.

For instance, $preference(Plaka, *, friends, Acropolis, Mary)$ has score 0.69 when using the first approach and score 0.77, when using the second one.

It is easy to see that the orderings produced by each approach are consistent with each other [4]. That is, both approaches order the tuples (e.g., the *points_of_interest* in our example) the same way, since in both cases their aggregate score depends on the values of the context parameters that are specified, i.e., are not irrelevant. In the following, we assume that the second approach is used.

To facilitate the procedure of expressing interests, the system may provide sets of pre-specified profiles with specific context-dependent preference values for the non-context parameters as well as default weights for computing the aggregate scores. In this case, instead of explicitly specifying basic and aggregate preferences for the non-context parameters, users may just select the profile that best matches their interests from the set of the available ones. By doing so, the user adopts the preferences specified by the selected profile.

### 2.4   Preferences for Hierarchical Context Parameters

When the context parameter of a basic preference participates in different levels of a hierarchy, users may express their preference in any level, as well in more than one level. For example, *Mary* can denote that the monument of *Acropolis* has interest score 0.8 when she is at *Plaka* and 0.6 when she is in *Athens*.

For a parameter $L$, let $L_1, L_2, \ldots, L_n, ALL$ be the different levels of the hierarchy. There is a hierarchy tree, for each combination of non-context parameters. In our reference example, there is a hierarchy tree for each user profile and for a specific *point_of_interest* that represents the interest scores of the user for the *points_of_interest*, according to the location parameter hierarchy. In Fig. 2 (right), the root of the tree corresponds to level $ALL$ with the single value *all*. The values of a certain dimension level $L$ are found in the same level of the tree. Each node is characterized by a score for the preference concerning the combination of the non-context attributes with the context value of the node.

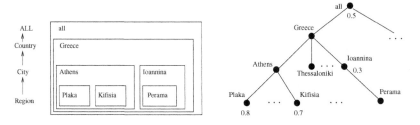

**Fig. 2.** Hierarchies on *location* (left) and the hierarchy tree of *location* (right)

If the context in a query refers to a level of the tree in which there is no explicit score given by the user, there are three ways to compute the appropriate score for a preference. In the first approach, we traverse the tree upwards until we find the first predecessor for which a score is specified. In this case, we assume that a user that defines a score for a specific level, implicitly defines the same score for all the levels below. In the second approach, we compute the average score of all the successors of the immediately following level, if such scores are available, else we follow the first approach. Finally, we can combine both approaches by computing a weighted average score of the scores from both the predecessor and the successors. In any case, we assume a default score of 0.5 at level *all*, if no score is given.

## 3  Storing Basic Preferences

We store basic user preferences in *hypercubes*, or simply *cubes*. The number of data cubes is equal to the number of context parameters, i.e., we have one cube for each context parameter. Formally, a *cube schema* is defined as a finite set of attributes $Cube = (C_i, A_1, \ldots, A_n, M)$, where $C_i$ is a context parameter, $A_1, \ldots, A_n$ are non-context attributes and $M$ is the interest score. The cubes for our running example are depicted in Fig. 3. In each cube, there is one dimension for the *points_of_interest*, one dimension for the users and one dimension for the context parameter. In each cell of the cube, we store the degree of interest for a specific preference.

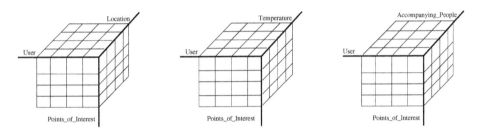

**Fig. 3.** Data cubes for each context parameter

A relational table implements such a cube in a straightforward fashion. The primary key of the table is $C_i, A_1, \ldots, A_n$. If dimension tables representing hierarchies exist (see next), we employ foreign keys for the attributes corresponding to these dimensions. The schema for our running example which is based on the classical *star schema* is depicted in Fig. 4. There are three fact tables, *Temperature*, *Location* and *Accompanying_People*. The dimension tables are: *Users* and *Points_of_Interest*. These are dimension tables for both fact tables.

Regarding hierarchical context attributes, the typical way to store them is shown in Fig. 5 (left). In this modeling, we assign an attribute for each level in the hierarchy. We also assign an artificial key to efficiently implement references to the dimension table. The denormalized tables of this kind suffer from

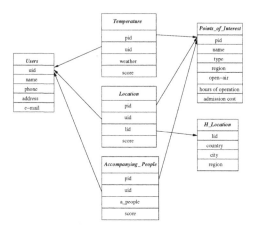

**Fig. 4.** The fact and dimension tables of our schema

the fact that there exists exactly one row for each value of the lowest level of the hierarchy, but no rows explicitly representing values of higher levels of the hierarchy. Therefore, if we want to express preferences at a higher level of the hierarchy, we need to extend this modeling (assume for example that we wish to express the preferences of $Mary$ when she is in the city of $Thessaloniki$, independently of the specific region of $Thessaloniki$ she is found at). To this end, we use an extension of this approach, as shown in the right of Fig. 5. In this kind of dimension tables, we introduce a dedicated tuple for each value at any level of the hierarchy. We populate attributes of lower levels with $NULLs$. To explain the particular level that a value participates at, we also introduce a level indicator attribute. Dimension levels are assigned attribute numbers through a topological sort of the lattice.

To compute aggregate preferences from simple ones we need also to store the weights used in this computation. Weights are stored in a special purpose table $AggScores(w_{C1}, \ldots, w_{Ck}, A_{k+1})$. The value for each context parameter $w_{Ci}$ is the weight for the respective interest score and the value $A_{k+1}$ specifies the user who gives these weights. For instance, in our running example, the table $AggScores$ has the attributes $Location\_weight$, $Temperature\_weight$, $Accompanying\_People\_weight$, and $User$. A record in this table can be ($0.6$, $0.3$, $0.1$, $Mary$).

Aggregate preferences are not explicitly stored. The main reason is space and time efficiency, since this would require maintaining a context cube for each context state and for each combination of non-context attributes. Assume that the context environment $CE_X$ has $n$ context parameters $\{C_1, C_2, \ldots, C_n\}$ and that the cardinality of the domain $dom(C_i)$ of each parameter $C_i$ is (for simplicity) $m$. This means that there are $m^n$ potential context states, leading to a very large number of context cubes and prohibitively high costs for their maintenance. Instead, we store only previously computed aggregate scores, using an auxiliary data structure (described in Section 4).

| G_ID | Region | City | Country |
|------|--------|------|---------|
| 1 | Plaka | Athens | Greece |
| 2 | Kefalari | Athens | Greece |
| 3 | Perama | Ioannina | Greece |
| ... | | | |

| G_ID | Region | City | Country | Level |
|------|--------|------|---------|-------|
| 1 | Acropolis | Athens | Greece | 1 |
| 2 | Kefalari | Athens | Greece | 1 |
| 3 | Polichni | Thessaloniki | Greece | 1 |
| ... | | | | |
| 101 | NULL | Athens | Greece | 2 |
| 102 | NULL | Salonica | Greece | 2 |
| ... | | | | |
| 120 | NULL | NULL | Greece | 3 |
| 121 | NULL | NULL | Cyprus | 3 |
| ... | | | | |

**Fig. 5.** A typical (left) and an extended dimension table (right)

An advantage of using cubes to store user preferences is that they provide the capability of using *hierarchies* to introduce different levels of abstractions of the captured context data through the *drill-down* and *roll-up* operators [5]. The *roll-up* operation provides an aggregation on one dimension. Assume, for example, that the user has executed a query about Mary's most preferable point-of-interests in *Plaka*. However, this query has returned an unsatisfactory small number of answers. Then, Mary may decide that is worth broadening the scope of the search and investigate the broader *Athens* area for interesting places to visit. In this case, a *roll-up* operation on *location* can generate a cube that uses *cities* instead of *regions*. Similarly, *drill-down* is the reverse of roll-up and allows the de-aggregation of information moving from higher to lower levels of granularity.

## 4   Caching Context-Aware Queries

In this section, we present a scheme for storing results of previous queries executed at a specific context, so that these results can be re-used by subsequent queries.

### 4.1   The Context Tree

Assume that the context environment $CE_X$ has $n$ context parameters $\{C_1, C_2, \ldots, C_n\}$. A way to store aggregate preferences uses the *context tree*, as shown in Fig. 6. There is one context tree per user. The maximum height of the context tree is equal to the number of context parameters plus one. Each context parameter is mapped to one of the levels of the tree and there is one additional level for the leaves. For simplicity, assume that context parameter $C_i$ is mapped to level $i$. A path in the context tree denotes a *context state*, i.e., an assignment of values to context parameters. At the leaf nodes, we store a list of ids, e.g., *points_of_interest* ids, along with their aggregate scores for the associated context state, that is, for the path from the root leading to them. Instead of storing aggregate score values for all the ids, to be storage-efficient, we just store the $top - k$ ids (keys), that is the ids of the items having the $k$-highest aggregate scores for the path leading to them. The motivation is that this allows us to provide users with a fast answer with the data items that best match their query. Only if more than $k$-results are needed, additional computation will be initiated. The list of ids is sorted in decreasing order according to their scores.

The context tree is used to store aggregate preferences that were computed as results of previous queries, so that these results can be re-used by subsequent queries. Thus, it is constructed incrementally each time a context-aware query is computed. Each non-leaf node at level $k$ contains cells of the form $[key, pointer]$, where $key$ is equal to $c_{kj} \in dom(C_k)$ for a value of the context parameter $C_k$ that appeared in some previously computed context query. The pointer of each cell points to the node at the next lower level (level $k + 1$) containing all the distinct values of the next context parameter (parameter $C_{k+1}$) that appeared in the same context query with $c_{kj}$. In addition, $key$ may take the special value $any$, which corresponds to the lack of the specification of the associated context parameter in the query (i.e., to the use of the special symbol '*').

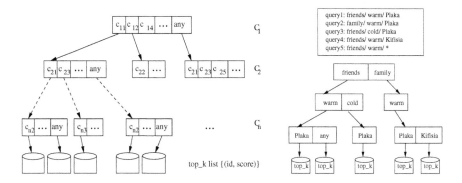

**Fig. 6.** A context tree (left) and a set of aggregate preferences and the corresponding context tree (right)

In summary, a context tree for $n$ context parameters satisfies the following properties:

- It is a directed acyclic graph with a single root node.
- There are at most $n+1$ levels, each one of the first $n$ of them corresponding to a context parameter and the last one to the level of the leaf nodes.
- Each non-leaf node at level $k$ maintains cells of the form $[key, pointer]$ where $key \in dom(C_k)$ for some value of $c_k$ that appeared in a query or $key = any$. No two cells within the same node contain the same key value. The pointer points to a node at level $k + 1$ having cells with key values which appeared in the same query with the key.
- Each leaf node stores a set of pointers to data sorted by their score.

For example, Fig. 6 (right) shows a set of context states expressed in five previously submitted queries and the corresponding context tree. Assume that the three context parameters are assigned to levels as follows: *accompanying_people* is assigned to the first level, *temperature* to the second and *location* to the third one. Leaf nodes store the ids of the $top - k$ *points_of_interest*, that is the places with the $top - k$ highest aggregate scores.

The context tree provides an efficient way to retrieve the *top-k* results that are relevant to a preference query. When a query is posed, we first check if there exists a context state that matches it in the context tree. If so, we retrieve the *top-k* results from the associated leaf node. Otherwise, we compute the answer and insert the new context state, i.e., the new path and the associated *top-k* results, in the tree. Thus a query is a simple traversal on the context tree from the root to a leaf. At level $i$, we search a node for a cell having as key value the $i^{th}$ value of the query and descend to the next level following the appropriate pointer. For a context tree with $n$ context parameters $(C_1, C_2, \ldots, C_n)$, if each parameter has $|dom(C_i)|$ values in its domain, the maximum number of cells that are required to be visited for a query is $|dom(C_1)| + |dom(C_2)| + \ldots + |dom(C_n)|$, while the number of nodes is equal to the height of the tree.

The way that the context parameters are assigned to the levels of the context tree affects its size. Let $m_i$, $1 \leq i \leq n$, be the cardinality of the domain, then the maximum number of cells is $m_1 * (1 + m_2 * (1 + \ldots (1 + m_n)))$. The above number is as small as possible, when $m_0 \leq m_1 \leq \ldots \leq m_k$, thus, it is better to place context parameters with domains with higher cardinalities lower in the context tree.

Finally, there are two additional issues related to managing the context tree: replacement and update. To bound the space occupied by the tree, standard cache replacement policies, such as LRU or LFU, may be employed to replace the entry, that is the path, in the tree that is the least frequently or the least recently used one. Regarding cache updates, stored results may become obsolete, either because there is an update in the contextual preferences or because entries (points-of-interests, in our running example) are deleted, inserted or updated. In the case of a change in the contextual preferences, we update the context tree by deleting the entries that are associated with paths, that is context states, that are involved in the update. In the case of updates in the database instance, we do not update the context tree, since this would induce high maintenance costs. Consequently, some of the scores of the entries cached in the tree may be invalid. Again, standard techniques, such periodic cache refreshment or associating a time-out with each cache entry, may be used to control the deviation between the cached and the actual scores.

## 4.2  Querying with Approximate Results

We consider ways of extending the use of the context tree to not only providing answers in the case of queries in exactly the same context state, but also providing approximate answers to queries whose context state is "similar" to a stored one. One such case involves the '*' operator. If the value of some context parameter is "any" (i.e., '*'), we check whether results for enough values of this parameter are already stored in the tree. In particular, if the number of the existing values of this parameter in the same node of the context tree is larger than a threshold value, we do not compute the query from scratch, but instead, merge the stored results for the existing values of the parameter. We call this threshold, *coverage approximation threshold* (*ct*). Its value may be either system defined or given as input by the user.

Another case in which we can avoid recomputing the results of a query is when the values of its context parameters are "similar" with those of some stored context state. For example, if one considers the near-by locations *Thisio* and *Plaka* as similar, then the query *friends/warm/Thisio* can use the results associated with the stored query *friends/warm/Plaka* (Fig. 6 (right)).

To express when two values of a context parameter are similar, we introduce a *neighborhood approximation threshold* ($nt$). In particular, two values $c_i$ and $c'_i$ of a context parameter $C_i$ are consider similar up to $nt_i$, if and only if for any tuple $t$ with score $d_i$ for $C_i = c_1$ and $d'_i$ for $C_i = c'_i$, it holds:

$$|d_i - d'_i| \leq nt_i \tag{1}$$

for a small constant $nt$, $0 \leq nt \leq 1$.

The threshold $nt_i$ may take different values for each context parameter $C_i$ depending for instance, on the type of its domain. As before, the threshold may be either determined by the user or the system. To estimate the quality of an approximation, we are interested in how much the results for two queries in two similar context states differ, that is how much different is the rating of the results in the two states, thus leading to a different set of *top-k* answers. We have proved [4] the following intuitive property that states that for any two tuples, the difference between their aggregate scores in two states, $s$ and $s'$ that differ only at the value of one context parameter, $C_i$, is bounded, if the two values of $C_i$ are similar. This indicates that the relative order of the results in states $s$ and $s'$ is rather similar.

**Property 1.** Let $t_1$, $t_2$ be two tuples that have aggregate scores $d_1$, $d_2$ in a context state $s$ and $d'_1$, $d'_2$ in a context state $s'$ respectively. If $s$, $s'$ differ only in the values of one context parameter, $C_i$, and these two values of $C_i$ are similar up to $nt_i$, then if $|d_1 - d_2| \leq \varepsilon$, $|d'_1 - d'_2| \leq \varepsilon + 2 * w_1 * nt$, where $w_i$ is the weight of the context parameter $C_i$.

Property 1 is easily generalized for the case in which two states differ in more than one similar up to $nt_i$ context parameter. In particular:

**Property 2.** Let $t_1$, $t_2$ be two tuples that have aggregate scores $d_1$, $d_2$ in a context state $s$ and $d'_1$, $d'_2$ in a context state $s'$ respectively. If $s$, $s'$ differ only in the value of $m$ context parameters, $C_{j_k}$, $1 \leq k \leq m$, and these two values of $C_{j_k}$ are similar up to $nt_{j_k}$, then if $|d_1 - d_2| \leq \varepsilon$, then, $|d'_1 - d'_2| \leq \varepsilon + 2 * (w_{j_1} * nt_{j_1} + w_{j_2} * nt_{j_2} \ldots + w_{j_m} * nt_{j_m})$, where $w_{j_k}$ is the weight of a context parameter $C_{j_k}$.

## 5   Performance Evaluation

In this section, we evaluate the expected size of the context tree as well as the accuracy of the two approximation methods. We divide the input parameters into three categories: *context parameters*, *query workload parameters*, and *query approximation parameters*. In particular, we use three context parameters and thus, the context tree has three levels (plus one for the *top − k* lists). There are two different types regarding the *cardinalities* of the domains of the context parameters: the *small* domain with 10 values and the *large* one with 50 values.

We performed our experiments with various numbers of queries stored at the context tree varying from 50 to 200, while the number of tuples is 10000. 10% of the values in the queries are '*'. The other 90% are either selected *uniformly* from the domain of the corresponding context parameter, or follow a *zipf* data distribution. The *coverage approximation threshold* $ct$ refers to the percentage of values that need to be stored for a context parameter, to compute the $top-k$ list by combining their corresponding $top-k$ lists when there is the '*' value at the corresponding level in a new query. The *neighborhood approximation threshold* $nt$ refers to how similar are the scores for two "similar" values of a context parameter. Our input parameters are summarized in Table 1.

## 5.1 Size of the Context Tree

In the first set of experiments, we study how the mapping of the context parameters to the levels of the context tree affects its size. In particular, we count the total number of cells in the tree as a function of the number of stored queries, taking into consideration the different orderings of the parameters. For a context tree with three parameters, we call *ordering 1* the ordering of the context parameters in which the parameter whose domain has 10 values is assigned to the first level, the parameter with 10 to the second one, and the parameter with 50 values to the last one. *Ordering 2* is the ordering when the domains have 10, 50, 10 values respectively, and for the *ordering 3* the domains have 50, 10, 10 values. As discussed in Section 3, the mapping of the context parameters to levels that is expected to result in a smaller sized tree, is the one that places the context parameters with the large domains lower in the tree.

In our experiments, 10% of the query values are selected to be the *any* value. The rest 90% of the values are selected from the corresponding domain, either using a *uniform* data distribution, or a *zipf* data distribution with $a = 1.5$. In both cases, as shown in Fig. 7, the total storage space is minimized when the parameter with the large domain (50 values) is assigned to the last level of the tree (ordering 3). Also, for the *zipf* distribution (Fig. 7 (right)), the total number of cells is smaller than for the *uniform* distribution, (Fig. 7 (left)), because using the *zipf* distribution "hot" values appear more frequently in queries, i.e., more context values are the same.

However, the best way of assigning parameters to levels depends also on the query workload, that is, on the percentage of values from the domain of each parameter that *actually* appears in the queries. Thus, if a parameter has a *very* skewed data distribution, it may be more space efficient to map it higher in the tree, even if its domain is large. This is shown with the next experiment (Fig. 8). We performed this experiment 50 times with 200 queries. The values of the context parameters with *small* domains are selected using a *uniform* data distribution and the values of the context parameter with the *large* domain are selected using a *zipf* data distribution with various values for the parameter $a$, varying from 0 (corresponding to the *uniform* distribution) to 3.5 (corresponding to a very high skew).

**Table 1.** Input Parameters

| Context Parameters | Default Value | Range |
|---|---|---|
| Number of Context Parameters | 3 | |
| Cardinality of the Context Parameters Domains | | |
|     *Small* | 10 | |
|     *Large* | 50 | |
| **Query Workload** | | |
| Number of Tuples | 10000 | |
| Number of Stored Queries | | 50-200 |
| Percentage of '*' values | 10% | |
| Data Distributions | *uniform* | |
| | *zipf* - a $= 1.5$ | a $= 0.0$ - $3.5$ |
| Top-k results | 10 | |
| **Query Approximation** | | |
| Coverage Approximation Threshold ($ct$) | $\geq 40\%, 60\%, 80\%$ | |
| Neighborhood Approximation Threshold ($nt_i$) | 0.08 | 0.04, 0.08, 0.12 |
| Weights | 0.5, 0.3, 0.2 | |

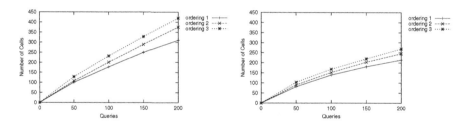

**Fig. 7.** Uniform (left) and zipf data distribution with $a = 1.5$ (right)

## 5.2    Accuracy of the Approximations

In this set of experiments, we evaluate the accuracy of the approximation when using the coverage and the neighborhood approximation thresholds. In both cases, we report how many of the *top-k* tuples computed using the results stored in the tree actually belong to the *top-k* results.

**Using the Coverage Approximation Threshold.** A *coverage approximation threshold* of $ct\%$ means that at least $ct\%$ of the required values are available, i.e., are already computed and stored in the context tree. We use three values for $ct$, namely, 40%, 60%, and 80%. All weights take the value 0.33. In Fig. 9, we present the percentage of different results in the *top-k* list for each $ct$ value, when a '*' value is given for a parameter with a small domain or a large domain, respectively. To compute the actual aggregate preference scores, we use

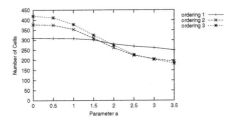

**Fig. 8.** Combined *uniform* and *zipf* data distributions

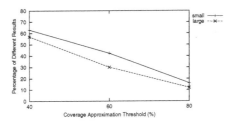

**Fig. 9.** Different results when the *ct* has values 40%, 60%, 80%

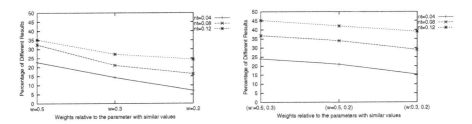

**Fig. 10.** Different results between two similar queries when $nt = 0.04, 0.08, 0.12$

the second of the two approaches presented in Section 2.2. The approximation is better when '*' refers to the context parameter with the large domain. This happens because in this case, more related paths of the context tree are available, and so, more *top-k* lists of results are merged to produce the new *top-k* list.

**Using the Neighborhood Approximation Threshold.** We consider first that a query is similar with another one, when they have the same values for all the context parameters except one, and the values of this parameter are similar up to *nt*. We use three values for the parameter *nt*: 0.04, 0.08, and 0.12. The weights have the values 0.5, 0.3, and 0.2. We count first, the number of different results between two similar queries that differ at the value of one context parameter, as a function of the weight of this parameter, taking into consideration the different values of *nt*. The results are depicted in Fig. 10 (left). Then, we examine the case in which the values of two context parameters are different (Fig. 10 (right)). In this case, the accuracy of the results depens on both the weights that correspond to the context parameters whose values are similar. As expected, the smaller the value of the parameter $nt$, the smaller the difference between the results in the *top-k* list of two similar queries. Note further, that the value of the weight that corresponds to the similar context parameter also affects the number of different results: the smaller the value of the weight, the smaller the number of different results.

## 6   Related Work

Although there has been a lot of work on developing a variety of context infrastructures and context-aware middleware and applications (such as, the Context Toolkit [6] and the Dartmouth Solar System [7]), there has been only little work on the integration of context into databases. Next, we discuss work related to context-aware queries and preference queries. A preliminary version of the model without the context tree and the performance evaluation part appears in [8].

*Context and Queries.* Although, there is much research on location-aware query processing in the area of spatio-temporal databases, integrating other forms of context in query processing is less explored. In the context-aware querying processing framework of [9], there is no notion of preferences, instead context attributes are treated as normal attributes of relations. Storing context data using data cubes, called context cubes, is proposed in [5] for developing context-aware applications that archive sensor data. In this work, data cubes are used to store historical context data and to extract interesting knowledge from large collections of context data. In our work, we use data cubes for storing context-dependent preferences and answering queries. The Context Relational Model (CR) [10] is an extended relational model that allows attributes to exist under some contexts or to have different values under different contexts. CR treats context as a first-class citizen at the level of data models, whereas in our approach, we use the traditional relational model to capture context as well as context-dependent preferences. Context as a set of dimensions (e.g., context parameters) is also considered in [11] where the problem of representing context-dependent semistructured data is studied. A similar context model is also deployed in [12] for enhancing web service discovery with contextual parameters.

*Preferences in Databases.* In this paper, we use context to confine database querying by selecting as results the best matching tuples based on the user preferences. The research literature on preferences is extensive. In particular, in the context of database queries, there are two different approaches for expressing preferences: a quantitative and a qualitative one. With the *quantitative approach*, preferences are expressed indirectly by using scoring functions that associate a numeric score with every tuple of the query answer. In our work, we have adapted the general quantitative framework of [13], since it is more easy for users to employ. In the quantitative framework of [1], user preferences are stored as degrees of interest in *atomic query elements* (such as individual selection or join conditions) instead of interests in specific attribute values. Our approach can be generalized for this framework as well, either by including contextual parameters in the atomic query elements or by making the degree of interest for each atomic query element depend on context. In the *qualitative approach* (for example, [14]), the preferences between the tuples in the answer to a query are specified directly, typically using binary preference relations. This framework can also be readily extended to include context.

## 7   Summary

The use of context allows users to receive only relevant information. In this paper, we consider integrating context in expressing preferences, so that when a user poses a preference query in a database, the result also depends on context. In particular, each user indicates preferences on specific attribute values of a relation. Such preferences depend on context and are stored in data cubes. To allow re-using results of previously computed preference queries, we introduce a hierarchical data structure, called context tree. This tree can be used further to produce approximate results, using similar stored results. Our future work includes exploring context information in answering additional queries, not just preference ones.

## References

1. Koutrika, G., Ioannidis, Y.: Personalization of Queries in Database Systems. In: Proc. of ICDE. (2004)
2. Dey, A.K.: Understanding and Using Context. Personal and Ubiquitous Computing **5** (2001)
3. Chen, G., Kotz, D.: A Survey of Context-Aware Mobile Computing Research. Dartmouth Computer Science Technical Report TR2000-381 (2000)
4. Stefanidis, K., Pitoura, E., Vassiliadis, P.: Modeling and Storing Context-Aware Preferences (extended version). University of Ioannina, Computer Science Departement, TR 2006-06 (2006)
5. Harvel, L., Liu, L., Abowd, G.D., Lim, Y.X., Scheibe, C., Chathamr, C.: Flexible and Effective Manipulation of Sensed Contex. In: Proc. of the 2nd Intl. Conf. on Pervasive Computing. (2004)
6. Salber, D., Dey, A.K., Abowd, G.D.: The Context Toolkit: Aiding the Development of Context-Enabled Applications. CHI Conference on Human Factors in Computing Systems (1999)
7. Chen, G., Li, M., Kotz, D.: Design and implementation of a large-scale context fusion network. International Conference on Mobile and Ubiquitous Systems: Networking and Services (2004)
8. Stefanidis, K., Pitoura, E., Vassiliadis, P.: On Supporting Context-Aware Preferences in Relational Database Systems. International Workshop on Managing Context Information in Mobile and Pervasive Environments (2005) (extended version to appear in JPCC).
9. Feng, L., Apers, P., Jonker, W.: Towards Context-Aware Data Management for Ambient Intelligence. In: Proc. of the 15th Intl. Conf. on Database and Expert Systems Applications (DEXA). (2004)

10. Roussos, Y., Stavrakas, Y., Pavlaki, V.: Towards a Context-Aware Relational Model. In the proceedings of the International Workshop on Context Representation and Reasoning (CRR'05) (2005)
11. Stavrakas, Y., Gergatsoulis, M.: Multidimensional Semistructured Data: Representing Context-Dependent Information on the Web. International Conference on Advanced Information Systems Engineering (CAiSE 2002) (2002)
12. Doulkeridis, C., Vazirgiannis, M.: Querying and Updating a Context-Aware Service Directory in Mobile Environments. Web Intelligence (2004) 562–565
13. Agrawal, R., Wimmers, E.L.: A Framework for Expressing and Combining Preferences. In: Proc. of SIGMOD. (2000)
14. Chomicki, J.: Preference Formulas in Relational Queries. TODS **28** (2003)

# An Integrated Framework for Meta Modeling

Mauri Leppänen

Department of Computer Science and Information Systems
P.O. Box 35 (Agora), FI-40014 University of Jyväskylä, Finland
mauri@cs.jyu.fi

**Abstract.** Meta modeling is an essential means to systematize, formalize, standardize, integrate, analyze and compare models, techniques, methods and tools. Numerous fields, such as databases, software engineering, software architectures, semantic web, computer-aided tools and method engineering, have benefited from it. The importance of meta modeling is ever increasing along with the emergence of novel approaches, architectures, techniques and languages based on UML and MDA. This paper presents a framework to integrate and compare divergent conceptions of meta modeling in databases, software engineering, and information systems development. The framework is applied to analyze and compare conceptions of meta levels in the literature.

## 1 Introduction

Meta modeling has been an important research topic and practical means since the 1980's. Database Architecture Framework Task Group (DAFTG) of the ANSI/X3/SPARC [1], for instance, engineered a reference model in which the intension-extension dimension was based on meta levels. Nowadays, numerous disciplines benefit from modeling on meta levels: e.g. business process engineering [42, 33], schema and data integration [5, 9], software process modeling [38, 14, 21], software maintenance [31, 39], software architectures [32], ontology engineering [11], method engineering [34, 8, 36], and computer–aided engineering [26, 30, 20, 19].

Meta modeling means basically a process which takes place on one level of abstraction higher than modeling (cf. [16]). Although there is a common agreement on generic characterizations such as this, there is a wide divergence of conceptions of meta modeling and ways it is applied, on a more detailed level. Meta modeling is seen to involve data (e.g. [25]) or processes (e.g. [42]). The root level in meta modeling may concern phenomena in business systems, information systems (IS) (e.g. [4, 7]), or IS development (e.g. [22, 26]). Meta modeling may be applied to stories (e.g. [15]), models (e.g. [37, 26]) or languages (e.g. [41, 35]). The importance of meta modeling is still growing. For instance, to specify UML in a more unambiguous fashion, OMG has used UML itself as the meta language to define the semantics of UML [37]. OMG has also established the Model-Driven Architecture in which transformations between models on different levels can be specified based on the meta models of source and target languages [32, 6]. UML and MDA are commonly seen to play a central role in the integration of different languages, architectures and computer-aided design environments in software engineering and information systems development. There

Y. Manolopoulos, J. Pokorný, and T. Sellis (Eds.): ADBIS 2006, LNCS 4152, pp. 141 – 154, 2006.

are, however, some deficiencies in how meta modeling is dealt with in UML and MDA, which hampers their use for the intended purposes [2, 17].

The purpose of this study is to derive a coherent and consistent framework, a kind of ontology [18], in order to obtain an integrated view on meta modeling. The framework specifies fundamental concepts, constructs and principles for meta levels and meta modeling. The framework recognizes two major approaches to meta modeling, a model-based approach and a language-based approach, and integrates them. It also connects meta levels to processing layers and thus provides a basis for the consideration of root levels in meta modeling. To demonstrate the applicability of the framework, we deploy it to analyze and compare divergent conceptions of meta levels presented in the literature.

The rest of the article is structured as follows. First, we define the basic concepts and categories related to model and modeling. Second, we derive the notion of meta level through the discussion about concepts and meta concepts, and apply this to establish the framework composed of levels of models and languages. Third, we discuss meta modeling approaches and present a comparative analysis of meta levels defined in the literature. The article ends with a summary and conclusions.

## 2   Systems of Levels

The purpose of this section is to derive a conceptual framework which can be used to specify and analyze systems of meta levels in databases (DB), software engineering (SE) and information systems development (ISD). First, we specify a system of model levels (Section 2.1) and a system of language levels (Section 2.2), and then we integrate them with one another (Section 2.3). In Section 2.4 we associate a system of model levels with information processing layers.

### 2.1   Model Levels

According to a common understanding, a model is to serve as a means to gain relevant knowledge about things in reality. To elaborate this generic conception, we apply three viewpoints (i.e. teleological, semantic and semiotic) and define the notion in three parts. A *model* is a thing that is used to help or enable the understanding, communication, analysis, design, and/or implementation of some other thing(s) to which the model refers (Teleological viewpoint). It may help the users better understand reality, design options for changes, foresee consequences of changes, reason on information and knowledge carried by the model, etc. (cf. [29]). Second, a *model* is a perception and an abstraction of relevant things in reality (Semantic viewpoint). Third, a *model* appears in one of three forms, namely as a conceptual construct, as a linguistic expression, or as a physical construct (Semiotic viewpoint).

Implied from the semiotic viewpoint, we distinguish between three kinds of models: a concept model, a model denotation and a physical model (cf. [12]). A *concept model* is composed of concepts and conceptual constructs referring to relevant things in reality. To enable communication a concept model has to be represented in some language. A precise and unambiguous representation of a concept model in a language is called a *model denotation* (cf. [13]). A *physical model* consists of physical parts, which, as an organized whole, resemble some other thing(s). In this study we are only interested in concept models and model denotations.

Based on which kinds of concepts and conceptual constructs models are composed of, we distinguish between instance models, type models and meta models. An *instance model* is a model which mainly comprise concepts that are instances of the concepts of some other model, called a *type model*. Likewise, a type model comprises concepts that are instances of the concepts of some other model, called a *meta model*. A meta model is a thing that is used to help or enable the understanding, communication, analysis, design and / or implementation of models. Models with the instanceOf relationships between their concepts constitute a hierarchy of levels, which we call a *system of model levels*. A *model level* is composed of models that comprise concepts on the same concept level. We distinguish between four model levels: instance level, type level, meta level, and meta meta level. Besides the instanceOf relationships, the model levels are also related to each other in another way: a model on a higher level describes / prescribes models on the next lower level.

## 2.2  Language Levels

A *language* is an abstract thing that is used in communication among people, between people and computers, or between computers. A language is composed of syntax and semantics. Syntax consists of two parts, an abstract syntax and a concrete syntax. An *abstract syntax* gives the conceptual components of a language and rules for connecting them, leaving out representational details [23]. A *concrete syntax* gives notational elements, called the symbols in the vocabulary of a language, and rules for connecting them with one another and with the concepts (cf. signification rules). *Semantics* of a language defines meaning of the symbols. A *vocabulary* of a language is a non-empty and finite set of symbols [13]. A *symbol* is a special sign used as an undividable part of an expression [13].

To specify and communicate about a language some other language, called a *meta language,* is used. A language representation is referred to as a *language denotation*. A meta language, in turn, is represented in a *meta meta language*, and so on. Hence, we have a system of language levels which are related to one another through the representedIn relationships. The hierarchy of language levels continues upward until, on some level, a self-descriptive language is used, i.e. a language is reached that is sufficiently expressive to be used to formulate its own rules [13].

## 2.3  Integration of Levels

After having derived the systems of levels for models and languages, we next relate them to one another through a framework presented in Figure 1. The framework is composed of four levels (L0 – L3). Two lowest levels correspond to relevant phenomena in reality (L0) and models about them (L1), correspondingly. The models (e.g. an ER schema) appear either as conceptual structures, or as denotations. The next higher level (L2) contains meta models of which the models on the lower level are instances (e.g. the ER model [10]). In addition, the level contains languages, in the form of conceptual constructs and denotations, which are used to represent model denotations. On the highest level (L3) there are meta meta models of which meta models are instances, as well as meta languages which are used to represent meta model denotations and languages. A meta language denotation is expressed by using the language itself.

The key point in relating the levels of models and languages to one another is abstract syntax: a model is represented as a model denotation based on a certain language with a conceptual foundation that consists of basic concepts, constructs and rules. These basic concepts and constructs constitute the abstract syntax of the language that is the same as the meta model of the model (see Figure 1).

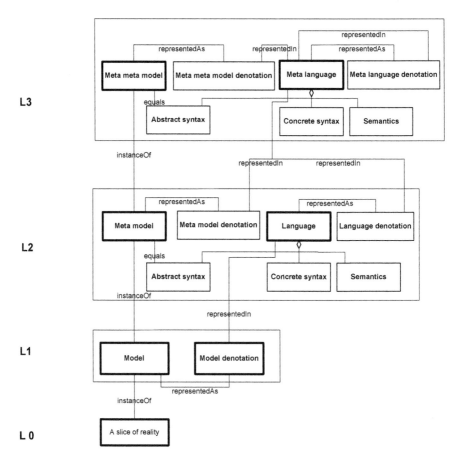

**Fig. 1.** Levels of models and languages

## 2.4  Levels and Processing Layers

Up till now, the models have been considered irrespective of phenomena they are describing and prescribing. Based on what object systems the models have, we recognize four information processing layers: information system (IS) layer, information system development (ISD) layer, method engineering (ME) layer, and research work (RW) layer (see Figure 2). The bottom layer stands for daily information processing actions (e.g. inventory control, order processing), with or without computers, in the organizations. The next higher layer means all those development actions by which information systems are analyzed, design, implemented, tested and taken into use. The ME layer means engineering actions through which procedures, techniques and methods for ISD are developed, selected, configured and customized. The RW layer involves research and development actions which aim to produce better conceptual and methodical means for ME work.

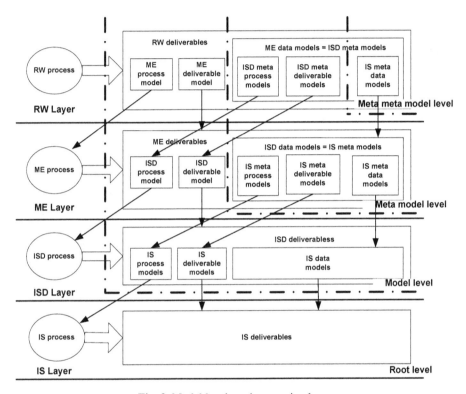

**Fig. 2.** Model levels and processing layers

With attaching models, meta models and meta meta models to the four processing layers, we can show how the model levels and the processing layers are interrelated and which kinds of models there actually are. On each layer we distinguish between three kinds of models, process models, deliverable models, and data models[1]. The process models describe/prescribe what actions are carried out, in which order and how. The deliverable models describe/prescribe purposes, structures and representations of deliverables. The data models describe/prescribe the conceptual

---

[1] Actually, each layer represents a context which can be modeled through nine kinds of models: purpose models, actor models, process or action models, deliverable models, data models, facility models, location models, time models, and inter-domain models [36]. Here, we consider only three of them.

contents of deliverables. Respectively, there are meta process models, meta deliverable models, and meta data models. The arrows between the meta models and the models, as well as between the models and the phenomena in reality, stand for the instanceOf relationships and the describes/prescribes relationships in Figure 2.

The processing layers and the model levels are not orthogonal to one another. For instance, on the ME layer there are models on two levels, and the RW layer contains models on three different levels. We have attached the root level to the IS layer in Figure 2, but it is equally possible to regard the ISD layer as the root layer, as it is done in [22] and [26].

# 3  Meta Modeling Approaches

There is a wide divergence of conceptions of meta modeling and systems of levels in the DB, SE and ISD literature. We make an in-dept analysis of these conceptions in the next section. Here, we discuss, on a general level, meta modeling approaches, based on the framework constructed above.

Concluded from the literature analysis, we can distinguish between three different approaches to define a system of meta levels: (a) a model-based approach, (b) a language-based approach, and (c) a technique-based approach (or a method-based approach). In the model-based approach the levels in the system are derived through the instanceOf relationships between the concepts within the models on two adjacent levels in the hierarchy (e.g. [4, 26, 37]). In the language-based approach a system of meta levels is established for the languages such that a language used to present another language is called a meta language [41, 35]. In the technique-based approach a meta model is a model of a modeling technique (e.g. [43, 7]). The purpose of this approach is commonly to produce a structural framework for an information base of method knowledge [20] or project knowledge [26].

Jarke, Klamma and Lyytinen [27] discuss interoperability and adaptability of meta model based environments and distinguish between "ontology based meta modeling", "notation oriented meta modeling" and "process oriented meta modeling". This categorization is based on the diamond model [28] which describes a possible space of choices when adapting or interrelating models. Ontology based meta modeling deals with representations of domain-related concepts and vocabularies. Notation based meta modeling concerns specifications of notations and notational systems. Process oriented meta modeling involves specifications of processes and process structures. Compared to our framework, ontology based meta modeling means meta data modeling, in other words making models of concepts and conceptual constructs of (type) models. Notation oriented meta modeling corresponds to meta deliverable modeling. Process oriented meta modeling means producing models about process models. As concluded from the above, the approaches in [27] are not orthogonal to one another.

Atkinson and Kühne [3] distinguish between linguistic meta modeling and ontological meta modeling. This categorization is based on what kinds of instanceOf relationships there are between the concerned entities. Linguistic instanceOf relationships are, for instance, those connecting 'Lassie' and 'Object', and 'Object' and 'Class' (in UML) [3]. Examples of ontological instanceOf relationships are those relating 'Lassie' and 'Collie', and 'Collie' and 'Breed'. Compared to this dichotomy we can say that our instanceOf relationships are linguistic ones. We assume that ontological instanceOf relationships are specified within the models, not between the models on different meta levels.

## 4  Comparative Analysis of Related Work

In this section we describe and analyze presentations for systems of levels given in the literature. Our aim is to find out viewpoints from which meta levels have been established, approaches applied to meta modeling, and systems of levels built up in the presentations. For the analysis we have selected twelve well-known presentations [4, 25, 7, 16, 43, 22, 26, 40, 20, 24, 13, 37] in the fields of DB, SE and ISD. With the selection of this variety we want to advance the achievement of a shared understanding of meta modeling in these fields. The results of the analysis are summarized in Appendix 1. Next, we first describe the selected presentations one by one, in the temporal order, and then summarize the results from the comparative analysis.

Bergheim et al. [4] present a taxonomy of concepts of the science of information systems to distinguish between four meta levels: ω-level, α-level, β-level, and γ – level. The lowest level, the operational level, concerns the changes of states in the application. The next meta level, also known as the application level, contains descriptions about a specific application (e.g. a data flow diagram or a Java program). The β-level is about how to make instances on the α-level (e.g. a DFD model or the language Java itself). The highest level is about how to make instances on the β-level, that is, about the ways to make different formalisms. For each level, a universe, constructs, a theory, an interpretation, valuations, a model, a description, and a method are considered. The discussion about the levels is comprehensive in [4], and considering when it was published, it was in advance of one's time. It is a pure representative of the model-based approach to establishing a system of meta levels.

ISO [25] launched the Information Resource Dictionary Standard (IRDS), which is composed of four levels: application data, IRD level, IRD Definition level, and IRD Definition Schema level. The first level includes data and program execution (i.e. computerized IS). The next level stands for a data base schema and application programs. The IRD Definition level specifies the models and languages by which schemata and programs are described. The IRD Definition Schema level specifies a meta meta model, according to which things on the ISD Definition level are associated and described. The IRDS is an outcome of the model-based approach, although a language as a means of description is recognized.

Brinkkemper [7] distinguishes between three levels: a system to be modeled, a modeling technique, and a meta modeling technique. In the hierarchy of levels, "the system of concepts of a modeling technique is considered as a concrete system on an abstraction level higher than the application of modeling in the development of an IS" ([7] p. 28). The levels are mentioned to be resulted from "type abstraction". The approach is clearly technique-based. Brinkkemper [7] provides a figure showing the unnamed relationships between the aforementioned concepts and between the notions of modeling notation and meta modeling notation. The figure does not make clear the semantics of the relationships. The models are missing in the hierarchy.

Van Gigch [16] categorizes the knowledge needed to solve a problem into three levels of inquiry. The level of implementation or intervention contains e.g. citizens, clients and practitioners participating in activities involving real world problems. On the modeling level understanding and solving problems requires formulation of models. On the meta level or meta modeling level people are involved in the design of methods and approaches to be used on the other levels of inquiry. A meta model is considered to be a model of the modeling process. Hence, although the approach in [16] is mainly model-based, it also covers a modeling process.

Wijers [43] divides the knowledge needed in modeling into three levels: application level, meta level, and theory level. On the application level actual ISD processes and products (ISD models) are dealt with. Modeling knowledge concerning the ways of working and modeling, as well as the acquisition of modeling knowledge are included on the meta level. The theory level is concerned with a theory applicable on the meta level. A meta model is defined to encompass a concept structure (for a way of modeling) and a task structure (for a way of working) as well as constructs interrelating those two. Wijers [43] apply the model-based approach. However, the scope also contains the process of modeling. This should not, however, be situated on the same meta levels as models.

Heym et al. [22] suggest a methodology reference model that is based on three levels of abstraction in which each level applies the notation or specification model from the next higher level. This means that an object type on the higher level is instantiated on the next lower level. The levels are: methodology level, method level and project level. The methodology level describes a methodology reference model, which contains all the object types and relationships necessary to describe ISD methods. The method level specifies an ISD method by a number of description objects of object types defined on the higher level. The project level describes a particular project to which a certain method is applied, by creating instances of special method description objects from the method level. The scope in [22] is very broad, covering the whole ISD knowledge. The levels of abstraction are not pure model levels, because on the method level, for instance, part of knowledge concerns ISD processes which should not be on the meta level (cf. Figure 2).

Jarke [26] uses Telos' metaclass hierarchy in ConceptBase to document data of projects on three levels: instance level, class level, and metaclass level. The instance level consists of concrete development projects within their environments. The class level defines the basic structure for development processes. The metaclass level describes the development environment. The metaclass hierarchy of [26] applies the model-based approach.

Saeki et al. [40] defines a meta model as a data model for representing design methods. To specify the structural relationships among a meta model, formal representations of design methods, and actual specification processes, Saeki et al. [40] distinguish between three levels: instance level, object level and meta level. The instance level corresponds to actual products and design activities. The object level stands for the formal representations of a design method. The meta level contains a model for the representations on one level lower, as well as the relationships between the representations of design methods. The hierarchy of levels in [40] applies the method-based approach on a general level.

Harmsen [20] allocates methodological knowledge onto three levels: method engineering level (ME), IS engineering methods level (ISEM), and IS engineering level. The ME level describes classes of ISEM concepts, that is to say, concepts of any ISD method. The IS engineering methods level describes instances of concepts on the method engineering level. The IS engineering level addresses the actual models, reports, steps and tools used in an ISD project. There are the type/instance relationships between the levels. Meta modeling is carried out on the ISEM level, and meta meta models belong to the method engineering level. Harmsen [20] applies the method-based approach, and typically for the adherents of this approach he leaves the specification of the system of levels rather general.

ter Hofstede et al. [24] distinguish between three levels of abstraction on which method knowledge can be viewed. The levels are: method level, application level, and operational level. The method level concerns knowledge which enables to control the ways how information modeling process may be performed and to define which products may result from those processes. The application level is concerned with information which results from projects for specific organizations and applications. It is an instantiation of the method level. The operational level is an instantiation of the application level and as such it consists of concrete entities, relationships, process traces, etc. ter Hofstede et al. [24] apply the method-based approach. Unfortunately, the elements on, and the relationships between, the levels are considered on quite a general level.

The Frisco Report [13] recognizes three meta levels: meta-level 0, meta-level 1, and meta-level 2. On each meta level, a model and a model denotation are specified. The models are: a base model (meta-level 0), a language used to represent the base model (meta-level 1), and a meta-language used to represent the language (meta-level 2). A base model may be a particular model consisting of states and transitions, and a base model denotation is its graphical representation. The representing relationships relate the meta levels to one another. The Frisco applies a mixed approach, considering the relationships between the languages and between the models, although the latter ones are only implicitly specified.

OMG [37, 32] presents a four-layered architecture to be used as a basis of standards. In the OMG terminology these layers are known as M0, M1, M2, and M3. On the M0 layer there is a (computerized) running system (CIS) in which the actual instances exist. The M1 layer contains models of the system. The M2 layer contains meta models (e.g. the UML meta model and the CWM). On the M3 layer there are meta meta models (e.g. MOF) that are used to define meta models. Every meta model is an instance of some meta meta model, and every model must be an instance of some meta model. The architecture has clearly been built following the model-based approach.

The descriptions above concretely show that there is a large variety of terms and meanings with which models and languages on different levels are specified in the literature. The systems of levels are also considered from different viewpoints, e.g. from the viewpoint of the science of information systems [4], of meta modeling [3, 43, 13], of method engineering [22, 40, 20, 24], of problem solving [16], of metadata management systems [26], and of standardization of development environments [25, 37]. The root level is considered to be either the IS [4, 7, 13], the CIS [25, 37], ISD work [22, 26, 40, 20, 24], or part of ISD (IS modeling [43]). In the latter cases, the aim is to specify and structure ISD method knowledge into a method base. Van Gigch [16] advocates yet another approach and applies a general view of problem solving to IS's, ISD or any other human action. This diversity of viewpoints largely explains the differences between the systems of levels. Our analysis revealed several deficiencies and inconsistencies in the systems of levels presented in the literature. In many presentations the systems of levels are specified in too a general manner. The most common inconsistence results from mixing the levels and the processing layers. As a consequence, ISD process models, for instance, are considered to be on the same model level as IS meta process models, just because they are on the ME layer. This is typical for presentations applying the technique-based or method-based approach [7, 16, 43, 22, 40, 20, 24]. In addition, some of the levels are not explicitly specified in some presentations (e.g. Level 1 in [7] and Level 0 in [13]).

## 5  Summary and Conclusions

Meta modeling is of high importance in several disciplines. There are, however, quite divergent conceptions of its approaches, focal points and outcomes in the literature. We have derived an integrated conceptual framework to analyze, compare and elaborate these conceptions. The framework is composed of two hierarchical systems of levels, the system of model levels and the system of language levels, structured onto four levels. The systems are integrated with one another and associated with four processing layers.

The framework has been applied to categorize, analyze and compare meta modeling approaches presented in the literature. In addition, an extensive analysis of twelve presentations for the systems of levels has been carried out. The analyses showed, in a concrete manner, how diversified conceptions of meta modeling are in the DB, SE and ISD literature. Some deficiencies and inconsistencies were also revealed. In another study [36] the framework has been deployed to build a comprehensive ontological framework, called OntoFrame, for IS, ISD, and method engineering. Both of these efforts demonstrated the usability of our framework for the consideration of meta modeling.

In future, our aim is to elaborate the framework, for instance, to recognize more explicitly contextual features of the domains on each layer. We are also committed to examine more deeply various suggestions to improve the levels in the MOF specification [37]. These suggestions include, among others, deep instantiation based meta modeling [3] and power type-based meta modeling [17].

The importance of meta modeling is still growing in the future. Novel artifacts are emerging necessitating compatible approaches to, foundations for, and outcomes from, meta modeling in the environments which integrate data bases, software architectures, and IS engineering tools. We believe that our framework can benefit a search for a shared understanding of meta modeling and provide a common conceptual groundwork for these efforts.

# References

1. ANSI/X3/SPARC 1986. Reference model for DBMS standardization. Database Architecture Framework Task Group (DAFTG) of the ANSI/X3/SPARC Database System Study Group, SIGMOD Record, Vol. 15, No. 1, 19-58.
2. Atkinson, C. & Kühne, T. 2002. Rearchitecting the UML infrastructure. ACM Trans. On Modeling and Computer Simulation, Vol. 12, No. 4, 290-321.
3. Atkinson, C. & Kühne, T. 2003. Model-driven development: a metamodeling foundation, IEEE Software, Vol. 20, No. 5, 36-41.
4. Bergheim, G., Sanders, E. & Sölvberg A. 1989. A taxonomy of concepts for the science of information systems. In E. Falkenberg & P. Lindgren (Eds.) Proc. of the IFIP TC8/WG8.1 Working Conference on Information Systems Concepts: an In-Depth Analysis. Amsterdam: North-Holland, 269-321.
5. Bernstein, P. 2001. Generic model management - a database infrastructure for schema management. In Proceedings of Ninth International Conference on Cooperative Information Systems (CoopIS'01), Trento, Italy, LNCS 2172, Springer, 1-6.
6. Bezivin, J. & Gerbe O. 2001. Towards a precise definition of the OMG/MDA framework. In Proc. of the 16th Annual International Conference on Automated Software Engineering (ASE 2001), Los Alamitos, California: IEEE Computer Society, 273-280.
7. Brinkkemper, S. 1990. Formalization of information systems modeling. University of Nijmegen, Amsterdam: Thesis Publishers, Dissertation Thesis.
8. Brinkkemper S. 1996. Method engineering: engineering of information systems development methods and tools. Information and Software Technology, 38 (6), 275-280.
9. Calvanese, D., De Giacomo, G., Lenzerini, M., Nardi, D. & Rosati, R. 2001. Data integration in data warehousing. In Proceedings of Ninth International Cooperative Information Systems (CoopIS'01), Trento, Italy, LNCS 2172, Springer, 237-272.
10. Chen, P. 1976. The entity-relationship model – toward a unified view of data. ACM Trans. on Database Systems. Vol. 1, No. 3, 9-36.
11. Davies I., Green P., Milton S., Rosemann M. 2004. Analyzing and comparing ontologies with meta-models. In J. Krogstie, T. A. Halpin & K. Siau (Eds.), Advanced Topics of Database Research: Information Modeling Methods and Methodologies, Idea Group Publishing, 1-16.
12. Dietz, J. 1987. Modelling and specification of information systems (In Dutch: Modelleren en specificeren van informatiesystemen). Technical University of Eindhoven, Dissertation Thesis.
13. Falkenberg, E, Hesse, W., Lindgreen, P., Nilsson, B., Oei, J. L. H., Rolland, C., Stamper, R., van Asche, F., Verrijn-Stuart, A. & Voss, K. 1998. A framework of information system concepts, The FRISCO Report (Web edition), IFIP.
14. Firesmith, D. & Henderson-Sellers, B. 2002. The OPEN Process Framework: An Introduction. Addison-Wesley, Harlow,
15. Gaarder, J. 1994. Sophie's world. Farrar, Straus and Giroux Inc.
16. Gigch van, J. 1991. System design modeling and metamodeling. New York: Plenum Press.
17. Gonzales-Perez, C. & Henderson-Sellers, B. 2005. A powertype-based metamodeling framework. Software and Systems Modeling, November, online.
18. Gruber, T. 1993. A translation approach to portable ontology specification. Knowledge Acquisition, Vol. 5, No. 2, 119-220.
19. Gupta, D. & Prakash, N. 2001. Engineering methods from method requirements specifications. Requirements Engineering, Vol. 6, No. 3, 135-160.

20. Harmsen, F. 1997. Situational method engineering. University of Twente, Moret Ernst & Young Management Consultants, The Netherlands, Dissertation Thesis.
21. Henderson-Sellers, B. & Gonzalez-Perez, C. 2005. A comparison of four process metamodels and the creation of a new generic standard. Information and Software Technology, Vol. 47, No. 1, 49-65.
22. Heym, M. & Österle, H. 1992. A reference model for information systems development. In K. Kendall, K. Lyytinen & J. DeGross (Eds.) Proc. of the IFIP WG 8.2 Working Conference on the Impacts on Computer Supported Technologies on Information Systems Development. Amsterdam: North-Holland, 215-240.
23. Hofstede ter, A. & Proper, H. 1998. How to formalize it? Formalization principles for information system development methods. Information and Software Technology, Vol. 40, No. 10, 519-540.
24. Hofstede ter, A. & Verhoef, T. 1997. On the feasibility of situational method engineering. Information Systems, Vol. 22, No. 6/7, 401-422.
25. ISO 1990. International Standard. Information Resource Dictionary System (IRDS) – Framework ISO/IEC 10027.
26. Jarke, M. 1992. Strategies for integrating CASE environments. IEEE Software, Vol. 9, No. 2, 54-61.
27. Jarke, M., Klamma, R. & Lyytinen, K. 2005, Meta modeling. Unpublished manuscript, 2005.
28. Jarke, M., Pohl, K., Weidenhaupt, K., Lyytinen, K., Marttiin, P., Tolvanen, J.-P. & Papazoglou M. 1998. Meta modeling: a formal basis for interoperability and adaptability. In M. Krämer & P. Papazoglou (Eds.) `Information Systems Interoperability, Wiley & Sons, 1997, 229-263.
29. Kangassalo, H. 2002. Foreword., In S. Spaccapietra, S. March & Y. Kambayaski (Eds.) Proc. of 21st Intern. Conf. on Conceptual Modeling (ER 2002). Berlin: Springer, V-VI.
30. Kelly, S., Lyytinen, K. & Rossi, M. 1996. MetaEdit+: a fully configurable multi-user and multi-tool CASE and CAME environment. In Y. Vassiliou & J. Mylopoulos (Eds.) Proc. of the 8th Conf. on Advanced Information Systems Engineering (CAiSE'96). Berlin: Springer, 1-21.
31. Kitchenham, B., Travassos, H., von Mayrhauser, A., Nielssink, F., Schneiderwind, N., Singer, J., Takada, S., Vehvilainen, R. & Yang, H. 1999. Towards an ontology of software maintenance. Journal of Software Maintenance: Research and Practice, Vol. 11, No. 6, 365-389.
32. Kleppe, A., Warmer, J. & Bast, W. 2003. MDA explained: the Model Driven Architecture: practice and promise. Reading: Addison Wesley Professional.
33. Koubarakis, M., Plexousakis, D. 2002. A formal framework for business process modelling and design. Information Systems, Vol. 27, No. 5, 299-320.
34. Kumar, K. & Welke, R. 1992. Methodology engineering: a proposal for situation specific methodology construction. In W. Kottermann & J. Senn (Eds.) Challenges and Strategies for Research in Systems Development. Chichester: John Wiley & Sons, 257-269.
35. Laine, H., Maanavilja, O. & Peltola, E. 1979. Grammatical database model. Information Systems, Vol. 4, 257-267.
36. Leppänen, M. 2005. An ontological framework and a methodical skeleton for method engineering. Ph.D thesis, Jyväskylä Studies in Computing 52, University of Jyväskylä, Finland.
37. OMG 2002. Meta-Object Facility (MOF) Specification, v. 1.4, April [Referred on 12.1.2003]. Available at URL: <http://www.omg.org/cgi-bin/doc?formal /2002-04-03>

38. OMG 2005. Software Process Engineering Metamodel Specification, Version 1.1, Object Management Group, formal/05-01-06
39. Ruiz, F., Vizcaino, A., Piattini, M. & Garcia, F. 2004. An ontology for the management of software maintenance projects. International Journal of Software Engineering and Knowledge Engineering, Vol. 14, No. 3, 323-349.
40. Saeki, M., Iguchi, K., Wen-yin, K. & Shinokara M. 1993. A meta-model for representing software specification & design methods. In N. Prakash, C. Rolland & B. Pernici (Eds.) Proc. of the IFIP WG8.1 Working Conf. on Information Systems Development Process. Amsterdam: North-Holland, 149-166.
41. Smith, B.C. 1984. Reflection and the semantics of Lisp. In: Proceedings of the 12th Annual Conf. on Principles of Programming Languages (POPL), Salt Lake City, 23-35.
42. Söderström, E., Andersson, B., Johannesson, P., Perjons, E. & Wangler, B. 2002. Towards a framework for comparing process modeling languages. In A. Banks Pidduck, J. Mylopoulos, C. Woo & T. Ozsu (Eds.) Proc. of the 14th Intern Conf on Advanced Information Systems Engineering (CAiSE'2002). Berlin: Springer-Verlag, 600-611.
43. Wijers, G. 1991. Modelling support in information systems development. Delft University of Technology, Amsterdam: Thesis Publishers, Dissertation Thesis.

**Appendix 1.**    Comparative analysis of the systems of levels

| Reference | Object System | L0 | L1 | L2 | L3 |
|---|---|---|---|---|---|
| Bergheim et al. [4] | Application | ω-level | α-level | β-level | γ-level |
| ISO [25] | CIS | Application data | IRD level | IRD Definition level | IRD Definition Schema level |
| Brinkkemper [7] | IS | System to be modeled | - | Modeling technique | Meta modeling technique |
| van Gigch [16] | Problem solving | Implementation level | Modeling level | Meta level | |
| Wijers [43] | IS modeling | Application level | Meta level | Theory level | |
| Heym et al. [22] | ISD | Project level | Method level | Methodology level | |
| Jarke [26] | ISD project | Instance level | Class level | Metaclass level | |
| Saeki et al. [41] | ISD | Instance level | Object level | Metalevel | |
| Harmsen [20] | ISD | IS engineering level | IS engineering methods level | Method engineering level | |
| ter Hofstede et al. [24] | ISD | Operational level | Application level | Method level | |
| Falkenberg et al. [13] | IS | - | Meta-level 0 | Meta-level 1 | Meta-level 2 |
| OMG [37] | CIS | M0 | M1 | M2 | M3 |

# Implementation of UNIDOOR, a Deductive Object-Oriented Database System

Mohammed K. Jaber and Andrei Voronkov

School of Computer Science, The University of Manchester
316 Oxford Road, Manchester, M13 9PL, United Kingdom

**Abstract.** This paper proposes the *DJR* approach for implementing deductive object-oriented database systems(DOOD). This technique is based on classifying DOOD features into three abstract implementation levels. The classified features are then delegated to the *DJR suite*, which is built around the *Data Model, Java* and *Relational* components. The use of the Java virtual machine (JVM) provides essential object-oriented features that were hard to implement and maintain. The implementation of many critical database management features is delegated to the relational back-end. As a result, only a minimal implementation effort is needed to build a very complex system. The *DJR* approach was used to implement our DOOD system *UNIDOOR*. The system was successfully and rapidly built and it supports essential object-oriented features along with the major database management features which were hard to implement in previous DOOD prototypes.

## 1 Introduction

It has long been recognised that the principal benefits provided by the deductive and the object-oriented paradigms to database systems are complementary. Deductive databases (DDBs) are logically well-founded and offer a declarative query language and a rule-based programming environment but they lack real-world data modelling capabilities. Object-oriented databases (OODBs), on the other hand, support rich data modelling constructs but lack formal semantics and declarative query languages. Any database system which smoothly integrates the two paradigms, without sacrificing the principal features of either, will provide significant opportunities for conventional and novel application areas such as building database middle-ware for distributed information systems [21], managing and querying the Web [8], and for building advanced decision support and knowledge discovery systems [7].

Research on deductive object-oriented databases (*DOOD*) started in the late 1980s. It seeks to provide the combined support for the modelling features of OODBs and the declarative query languages of DDBs. But unlike the relational database systems, DOOD systems were engineered without an agreed notion of a standard object data model and without an ample understanding of what appropriate query model for DOOD is. Consequently, a variety of language constructs,

Y. Manolopoulos, J. Pokorný, and T. Sellis (Eds.): ADBIS 2006, LNCS 4152, pp. 155–170, 2006.

architectures, and query processing methodologies have been developed [9]. However, due to implementation limitations, DOOD systems were often monolithic, lack certain services provided by the commercial DBMS, thus discouraging users that could benefit from a deductive query language but are not inclined to migrate their data and programs to non-mainstream DBMS.

In this paper, we describe a technique called the *DJR* approach for implementing DOOD systems. *DJR* is based on the implementation suite (*Data model,Java,Relational back-end*). The rationale behind this technique is to classify the features of a DOOD system into an abstract hierarchy of features depending on their dependency on each other and on the underlying data model of the DOOD system. These features are then distributed among the suite components in a way that optimally utilise the services of Java Virtual Machine (JVM) and the relational database system. Thus, *DJR* shifts the main implementation efforts into (1) those high-level features strongly dependent on the data model and (2) maintaining the communication between the suite components.

The *DJR* approach was used in the implementation process of the current prototype of *UNIDOOR*, a DOOD system based on the data model proposed in [23]. The impact of the *DJR* approach in implementing *UNIDOOR* was great in both effort and time. Many essential database management features such as persistent store, transaction control and database administration, that were missing from many other DOOD systems, were successfully implemented. Moreover, only a minimum effort was needed to implement complex OO features such as inheritance, overriding, overloading and encapsulation. So, the deductive part of *UNIDOOR* is significantly freed from the burden of manipulating the database persistent objects and their associated complexity and behaviour. As a result, the implementation of the deductive side is now focused on optimising and evaluating declarative queries and can smoothly incorporate in addition to the traditional techniques, any novel techniques with a great flexibility.

This paper is structured as follows. Section 2 presents a brief coverage of DOOD research focusing on their implementation limitations. Section 3 introduces the *DJR* approach and explains the rationale of feature abstraction and the *DJR* suite. Section 4 illustrates how the *DJR* approach was used in the implementation of the *UNIDOOR* system. Section 5 concludes the paper with the summary and outline of some future work.

## 2   DOOD Systems

A DOOD system encompasses a deductive, object-oriented and database managements components. Some of these components have conflicting features. For example, Deduction is based primarily on predicates while OO favours functional methods. Database updates are mainly imperative while a deductive language is logical. As a result, an integration may requires sacrificing certain conflicting features. There have been a number of attempts to design DOOD systems since late 1980s [13,11,1,3]. A wave of DOOD implementation started in early 1990s based on the assumption that DOOD systems can be implemented by integrating working systems and languages rather than building the systems from scratch. But the possible combinations of systems and languages were noticeably many. For example, $CORAL++$ [19] extended the deductive database system $CORAL$ [16] with the C++ type system. $Chimera$ [5] combined the imperative and declarative features into a single language over an OO data model. $Noodle$ [15] introduced a declarative query language over the OODB system $SWORD$ [14], $ROCK\&ROLL$ [2] was based on a formally defined semantic object data model from which an imperative language $ROCK$ and a declarative language $ROLL$ were derived and integrated. $Validity$ [7] was based on the language $DEL$, which contains declarative and imperative constructs. A formal treatment of many other DOOD systems can be found in [9,18,6].

## 2.1 A Glance at a DOOD System

In this subsection, we intend to give a glance at DOOD systems by presenting the *bill of materials* problem described in [4] into $UNIDOOR$. We would like to compute a *bill of materials* presenting information about parts, their number and suppliers, corresponding to a cheapest purchase. The formalisation is as follows. We assume that the device, components and parts mentioned above informally belong to a class Part:

```
class Part {
  components : Set(<part : Part,quantity : int>)
  suppliers : Set(<supplier : Supplier, price : int>)
  ...}
```

Here Supplier is a class. We define a function bill giving, for each part, the best price and the corresponding bill of materials.

```
bill: Part => <price:int,
  components:Set(<part:Part, quantity:int, supplier:Supplier>)>
```

Note that the return value of bill has a complex type.

We want to define the best price for a part if it is ordered directly from a supplier. To do this we will introduce some definitions. These definitions illustrate many features underpinning the design of $UNIDOOR$. The first definition

```
has_supplier(_part) :- isNonEmpty(_part.suppliers).
```

is a typical Prolog-style rule that can be read as follows: "For all parts, a part has a supplier if the set of suppliers of this part is non-empty". Variables in the rule begin with the underscore character. Even for this very simple rule there are several features bringing it well beyond logic programming:

1. the *path expression* _part.suppliers uses the attribute suppliers in the class Part;
2. the (built-in) relation isNonEmpty is a relation on sets;
3. the variable _part ranges over complex values, structured as tuples, which have a set as a component.

In addition, the operational semantics of the language will treat this rule in a special way (roughly speaking, it can only be used with _part instantiated to a concrete set), but the operational semantics of the rule language is beyond the scope of this paper. The next rule

```
best_price(_part)= min {_supplier.price|_supplier in _part.suppliers}.
```

illustrates the following concepts of the language

1. The use of set comprehension to form sets.
2. The use of functions in addition to relations.
3. Iteration over set elements logically using the membership relation in.
4. A completely logical view of aggregates as functions from sets (or multisets).

Unlike many other deductive query languages (e.g., [22]) *UNIDOOR*'s grouping operations are also defined in a logical way using a function definition and set comprehension. For example, using the function definition of best_price, one can define the best prices for all parts as follows:

```
  best_prices = {(_part,best_price(_part)) |  _part in Part}.
```

Finally, the last definition demonstrates the use of tuple values in the language

```
best_direct_order(_part,_supplier,_price) :-
   has_supplier(_part), _price= best_price(_part),
   <supplier=_supplier,price=_price> in _part.suppliers.
```

An implementation of a system able to cope with such definitions and have features of a full-fledged database system poses a highly non-trivial challenge.

## 2.2   Implementation Limitations

In early 1990s, object-oriented database systems products started to appear. From a competition point of view, it was an important step for DOOD research to go beyond the theory to the practise. Because DOOD research was immature at that time, this step was done by paying a high price. Many essential database and OO features were compromised or sacrificed. These features are listed below.

**Data Persistence.** In most DOOD implementations, the persistence store was designed and implemented from scratch, as in [10,3,15]. Other DOOD systems were designed as deductive layer over a persistent OODB system, as with [17]. Some DOOD implementations provided persistence by interfacing with experimental object stores, as it was with [2,19]. Meanwhile other implementations compromised the persistent store by using primitive data storage techniques such as the UNIX file system in [12], or simply ignoring data persistence as in [1].

**Concurrency.** Current DOOD implementations are single-user. Multi-users environment requires additional functionalities (such as locks) on top of the persistent store.

**Transaction Control.** Most DOOD implementations do not provide transaction management for their updates.

**Database Administration.** Because most DOOD implementations were single-user, there was no concern for a database administrator (DBA). In general, users are granted all privileges by default. However, if a DOOD system is interfaced with a DBMS, then privileges are controlled by the DBA of this particular DBMS and it is done in isolation from the DOOD system.

**Crash Recovery.** Most DOOD implementations do not support crash recovery. However, for DOOD systems that are interfaced with a DBMS back-end, this facility is supported if the back-end supports it.

**Object-Orientation.** Many implementation have ignored many basic OO features such as encapsulation, method expression and invocation, public/private access specifiers and class members (i.e. static attribute and method). Some of these features were sacrificed because including them into the data model and the query language will significantly complicate their semantics.

Meanwhile, other database management features, in addition to several OO features were implemented inefficiently. This is due to the following reasons

**Implementation Tools.** Many DOOD systems were implemented using programming languages that have not been extensively tested in terms of their efficiency, specially for implementing large-scale products such as DOOD systems. For example, languages such as O++ and E, which are extensions of C++, where used in the implementation of [15] and [2] respectively. Moreover, the lack of important features such as automatic garbage collection or meta-access to some built-in facilities means that these facilities must be implemented from scratch. Similarly, database systems are much more than centralised repositories of passive data. Thus implementing persistence from scratch requires far more facilities than a passive persistence. If a back-end is used, then its limitations will also affect the final product, for example, [17] does not support methods and method invocation because it is not supported by its OODBMS back-end.

**Implementation Strategies.** Most implementations do not provide detailed explanation of their algorithms and techniques, such as how data types are mapped into the implementation language type system, how types are resolved, how unification of complex terms in deductive rules is performed and how schema queries are evaluated. Some implementation strategies are extremely expensive. For example, in [2], when an object is deleted, the system must scan a huge list of object-references and null each object attribute referencing the deleted object to avoid dangling references.

# 3   The DJR Approach

If we abstract the DOOD features, under the implementation criteria, we will get the following three abstract feature levels

1. *low-level* features: in which their implementation is not affected by the implementation of other features;

2. *middle-level* features: in which their implementation depends on the the implementation of the low level features, but the implementation of some other features depend on their implementation;
3. *high-level* features: in which their implementation strongly depends on the middle-level and low-level features;

Low-level features such as transaction control, crash recovery and concurrency are in the kernel of this abstraction. Their implementation is totally independent from the implementation of other features. Implementation of the middle-level features such as updates, encapsulation, inheritance, late binding, object identity, access specifiers, overriding and overloading depends on the low-level features. Finally, implementation of high-level features such as query evaluation and optimisation, the type system and type resolution are mainly built on top of the other features. Note that having low level does not imply being simple. A feature has a low level if its implementation is independent of other features. Implementation of higher level feature depends on the lower level features.

### 3.1   The DJR Suite

We can notice that the abstraction of features implicitly suggests the following:

1. low level features are already provided by most commercial database management systems. Thus, we can rely on one of them to handle these features.
2. middle level features are integral parts of many OO programming languages such as Java and C++. The choice of the programming language should also consider the fact that these features are built on top of the low level features. Thus, it is necessary that the chosen language provides additional interfacing facilities to link these features to the back-end.

So, we can reduce the implementation effort by delegating as many features as possible to the programming language and the back-end DBMS. However, high level features mainly depend on the data model. Thus, they need to be implemented from scratch. But because they also depend on the features of the middle and low levels, additional interfacing effort is needed. The selection of the programming language and the back-end is a crucial step in this approach.

For an implementation programming language, Java turned out to be indispensable as a candidate choice for the following reasons

- Java is an OO programming language with an extensible type system. It has meta-programming facilities for handling classes, attributes and methods. It also provides a persistent object facility through object serialisation;

- Java is a good choice for rapid prototyping. It has a huge library of utility packages for services and application program interfaces (APIs). Java is also backed by a variety of third party development tools provided by major system vendors for interfacing relational DBMSs (JDBC) and OODBs (JDO). In addition, Java is web friendly and it has a phenomenal popularity within the Internet community and Web APIs (i.e JDOM and SAX);

- Java applications are portable. Applications are executed inside a runtime instance of the abstract specification of JVM. This facility provides several runtime utilities such as run-time compilation/linking/loading of classes, an automatic garbage collection, an advanced memory management, a distinguished exception handler and an automatic initialisation of variables. Java has an optimised and secured compiler.

On the other hand, we believe that a relational database systems (RDBMS) is the best candidate to serve as a back-end due to the following reasons

- RDBMS products have been available for a long time, undergone extensive development and are highly reliable in terms of database integrity and crash recovery. Moreover, RDBMSs are scalable and they provide extensive proved optimisation techniques at both software and hardware levels;

- RDBMS products are widely available with reasonable prices compared to products from other database paradigms. Moreover, most relational database vendors provide a standard API for the major programming languages.

- In a DOOD context, a relational back-end is appealing because relations are an integral part of the DOOD data model. If properly interfaced, a DOOD system can directly access and query the relational legacy data with no need for any data transformation. Moreover, if successfully engineered, a DOOD system can integrate and query several databases simultaneously;

In our approach, Java will be used to implement the data model specific features of the high level, while middle level features will be delegated to JVM. Low level features are delegated to the relational back-end. The result of applying those tools over the feature abstraction divides the conceptual world into three overlapping parts. This is called the *DJR suite*. This term stands for the *Data model, Java* and the *Relational back-end*. Figure 1 depicts the *DJR* suite as the result of applying Java and a relational back-end over the feature abstraction.

*DJR* also indicates several important properties. For example, low-level features are handled in the *R* area. Middle-level features are handled in the *DJ, DR, JR* and *J* areas. High-level features are in the *D* area. We can identify the necessary skills needed in each area. For example, any intersection areas containing *J* require Java API skills (such as JDBC in the area *JR*), while any area involving *R* requires a considerable knowledge of relational database. Any area involving *D* requires a considerable knowledge of the DOOD system data model and its query language. The *DJR* area requires all skills.

The contribution of feature abstraction also suggest a collaboration between the different levels to achieve some goals such as efficient computation or optimisation. Consider for example the following query

{_x in Part |_x.partNo < 8800 & _x.componentsCount() > 15 }

This query simply returns the set of all parts which have a part number less than 8800 and which contains more than 15 components. However, if the extension of class Part is huge, there will be a significant overhead in evaluating the extension expression, and consequently the invocation of *componentCount()* method. But with *DJR* a collaboration between Java and the back-end can evaluate this query more efficiently. The effective extension expression of class *Part* can be minimised by selecting only the objects that satisfy the condition < 8800 using the back-end query language. The method invocation expression can be evaluated by calling a stored procedure in the back-end.

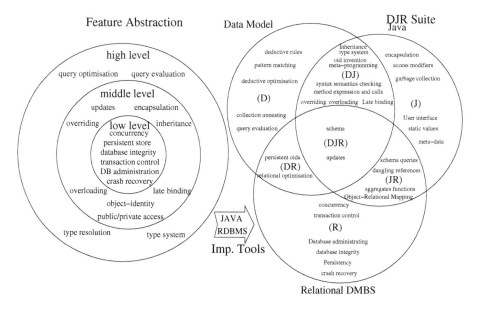

**Fig. 1.** Feature abstraction + Implementation tools = DJR Suite

Java applications run slower than their C++ counterpart. But, when it comes to databases, the ability to manipulate large amount of data efficiently is more important than the speed of the application execution. Moreover, Java has a huge advantage over C++ due to its meta-programming facilities and garbage collection.

An OO back-end looks more appealing than a relational one. However, object-oriented databases are more expensive and their legacy data are far too small than their relational counterpart. This is almost certainly requires a transformation of the relational legacy data into the OODBMS. Moreover, the OODBMS technology is relatively younger and far more complex than the relational technology. Their products are relatively immature and their management and optimisation facilities are still under development.

Object-relational databases (ORDBMS) are not a better choice for a back-end. The reason is that the DOOD object model is different than the OR model. This means that we still need to build an additional mapping layer on top of the mapping layer provided by the OR vendor. Nevertheless, if a DOOD data model is generally accepted, its additional constructs can be added to the original mapping layer.

# 4   DJR in Action

In this section, we illustrate how the *DJR* tools (i.e. Java and the relational back-end) contributed in the implementation of the DOOD system *UNIDOOR*. We focus on the implementation techniques for the object-oriented and database management features. The deductive features, however, are presented briefly because they are data-model specific. We show how *DJR* paves the ground to incorporate in addition to the traditional techniques, any novel techniques with a great level of flexibility and orthogonality with the underlying complexity of OO and database management.

## 4.1   The Contribution of Java

The main programming effort will be centred around the interfacing areas (i.e. *DJ,DR, DJR* and *JR*). Luckily, the facilities in the *J* area are automatically supported by JVM. The implementation in the *D* area (i.e. the query language) will be illustrated later.

*UNIDOOR* has an extensible type system hierarchy. Types can be either atomic, such as `Integer, Real`, classes or constructed from other types using collections and tuple type constructors. The *DJR* approach suggests the following technique for implementing similar type systems.

• An atomic type is compiled into the corresponding atomic Java class.

• A collection type is compiled into a uniform Java class that extends a generic collection class with basic utility methods (such as union, membership, . . .etc).

• A tuple type is compiled into a Java class consisting of the same set of attributes but with additional set/get methods.

• A user-defined class is compiled into a corresponding Java class. This class mirrors the inheritance hierarchy, and the attributes static/non-static and public/private access specifiers of the corresponding *UNIDOOR* class definition.

In general, *UNIDOOR* types are compiled into Java classes with the necessary private components and a corresponding public set/get methods for the type components.

Methods are handled differently. Each method is compiled into a corresponding Java method definition. This definition mirrors the original interface part of the method but its implementation part depends on the query expression involved. The set of expressions depends on the proposed data model, and thus will not be covered here. Nevertheless, simple method expressions can easily be compiled to Java. For example, if class `Part` contains the method

```
complex():Boolean= count(components) >9;
```

then the following definition will be included in the `Part` Java class

```
public Boolean complex(){return new Boolean(components.count()>9);}
```

We can now identify the advantages of the implementation approach of the type system. The inheritance hierarchy will be respected by the type Java classes. Method overloading, overriding, late binding and invocation will be handled automatically at runtime by JVM. Aggregate functions (such as `count`) are compiled into calls for some inherited methods in the generic collection class.

One may argue that the above compilation of *UNIDOOR* type system into Java is natural and straightforward. However, it is important to know that it is an essential step in the implementation of a highly complex system. This step is an integral part of the whole implementation process and thus is related not only to Java but also to both the deductive side and the back-end side.

The static analysis of a DOOD query expressions depends on the query language semantics of the data model. Nevertheless, the *DJR* approach provides guidelines that can be adapted to handle data-model specific expressions. In *UNIDOOR*, *syntax* checking is done mainly by the parser, while *semantic* checking of *UNIDOOR* query expressions is handled in the following way. *UNIDOOR* has rich collection of expressions. *UNIDOOR* defines special class for every kind of expression. For example, we have a class for binary expressions, a class for set comprehension expressions, a class for quantified expression, ... etc. Expression classes are defined with a set of utility methods for type resolution, expression evaluation and error handling. These classes are arranged in a hierarchical order. When *UNIDOOR* parser encounters an expression, it generates the corresponding expression tree in a bottom-up fashion from simple expression up to the full expression. Each node of the expression tree is an instance of the corresponding expression class. Tree generation breaks if a syntax error is encountered. *UNIDOOR* semantic checking then starts by calling the utility method `resolveType`. This method has different behaviour according to the underlying expression class. For example, in the `IntExpr` class, it simply returns the type `Integer`, while in `BinExpr` class, the type of the expression is determined by considering, the binary operator domain, and the types of the left and right hand side expressions. Generally speaking, an expression type is determined by calling the `resolveType` method of the root of the expression tree, which (recursively) calls `resolveType` methods of its subexpression and so on down to the expression tree terminals. In case of type conflicts, the compiler produce an error. Since *UNIDOOR* does not have polymorphic types, type resolution is relatively unsophisticated.

The evaluation of an expression is done by recursively calling the (overloaded) utility method `Object evaluate()` on the root of the expression tree. The behaviour of this method depends on the expression it self.

It proved to be crucial to use Java runtime facilities in some critical cases. Consider for example that a new type is introduced at runtime in following query expression

`_x in {{1,2,3},{4,5}} & 5 in _x`

here the type of the subexpression `{{1,2,3},{4,5}}` is `Set(Set(Integer))`. If this type was first introduced at run-time, then there is no corresponding Java class definition yet in JVM. Java will throw an exception stating the absence of that Java class. In our approach, this can be solved using the following technique. First, a special exception handler catches the exception and then calls the Java code-generating method to generate the required class file. It then compiles it, loads it to the main memory and finally links it to the running database session. This can be done by using the JVM compile/load/link facilities. If the new type is deeply constructed from types in which their Java class are yet not linked in JVM, the process is recursively repeated until all type references have their corresponding Java class linked in JVM. Run-time types are available as long as the session is running. This means that there will be no need for regenerating any type if it is referenced again during the same session. If one could not load new class definitions, many functions would have required several implementations for both compile-time and run-time generated classes.

Path expressions are also handled automatically by JVM. For example, if we have the following static method definition in class `Supplier`:

`static riskySup():Set(Supplier)={_x in Supplier|_x.man.age<20};`

This static method returns the set of suppliers that are managed by young managers. The path expression $\_x.man.age$ navigates from a `Supplier` object, then via an `Employee` object and then to the attribute `age`. In our approach, Java automatically handles the necessary path expressions and inheritance.

In the update language, when we create a new instance of a *UNIDOOR* class, a corresponding new instance must be created in its corresponding Java class. In our implementation, we can create a new instance by calling **new** followed by the class name with a named tuple argument. The attributes of this named tuple must be a subset of the *UNIDOOR* class attribute list. *UNIDOOR* first creates an instance using the empty constructor of that class. Then, it iterates over the tuple attributes and calls the corresponding **set** method to assign each value to the specified attribute. If a particular attribute was not defined in the class, then an exception is thrown. *UNIDOOR* catches this exception and reports a type error. Invoking the constructor and the set methods is done using Java meta-programming facilities for run-time method invocation. JVM will automatically handle any inherited fields from their superclasses. Noticeably, the created object will automatically be assigned a unique object identity by Java. Deleting and modifying object values is handled by the relational back-end to insure the database integrity. This will be explained in the next subsection.

Java provides an interesting feature called the *object serialisation*. Java takes an object's state and converts it to a stream of data thus making object persistence easy. This feature is utilised in our approach to store the values of static attributes across the sessions. It is also used to pass the generated *UNIDOOR*/Java schema mapping from the compilation stage to the querying stage.

## 4.2   The Contribution of the Relational DBMS

When *UNIDOOR* compiles an input schema into a collection of Java classes, it also create a relational schema at the back-end. This schema defines a collection of tables with the necessary integrity constraints. The relational schema is defined in a special way to maintain objects persistence and database integrity.

Mapping between *UNIDOOR* data model and the relational model is performed using the well-known *object-relational (OR) mapping* technique [20]. The technique is slightly modified to incorporate the deductive side. We create a table for each class. Each table includes the attributes implemented by the class and excludes the inherited attributes. There is an additional key column OID with an AUTO_INCREMENT modifier to guarantee a unique persistent object identity. The types of the columns depend on the types of the corresponding attributes in the class. The root class UNIDOORObject is mapped into a table with two columns, a key column and a string-valued column storing the principal class of that particular OID's value. This table is important for two reasons. First, it is used to synchronise between the in-memory object instances and the persistent objects. Second, foreign keys will reference one table only instead of several tables (for each referenced class table). Attributes of atomic types are mapped into columns of the corresponding relational atomic type. For example, an String attribute is mapped into a column of type CHAR(256). But if an attribute was of a class type, a tuple type or a collection type (i.e. a set or a Multiset), then it is mapped into a column of type INT. In general, key columns (OID) and references columns (OID_REF) are of type INT. These columns will store the persistent key value of the referenced type table.

Tuple types are handled similar to objects, but with an additional foreign key column (OID_REF) to reference the key value of the value (or object) that contains this tuple value. Finally, a collection type is mapped into a table with three columns, a key column (OID) to uniquely identify each member in the collection, a foreign key column (OID_REF) to store the key value of the referencing value, and a VALUE column of the corresponding collection type, to store the actual value of a collection member. In this respect, collection values are mutable.

One of the important features in this OR mapping mechanism is that we need not care about dangling references. This is done in the following way. For each column of a class type, we create an integrity constraint that will set the value of that column to null if the referenced column was deleted. Thus, for the the manager attribute (man) of the Supplier class, the schema of the Supplier table will contain the following integrity constraint

```
FOREIGN KEY(man) REFERENCES Employee(OID) ON DELETE SET NULL;
```

so, if an Employee object is deleted, then all manager attributes referencing that particular Employee object will be automatically set to NULL by the backend. For tuple and collection attributes, we have two integrity constraints. The First one is to ensure that the tuple or the collection entry that refers to that particular object is deleted once the object that references them is deleted. For example, schema of the tuple type Set(<part: Part, quantity: int> table will contain the integrity constraint

```
FOREIGN KEY(OID_REF) REFERENCES Part(OID) ON DELETE CASCADE;
```

so, if a Part object is deleted, then all entries in that set table that reference this particular object (that is its components values) will automatically be deleted by the back-end. The CASCADE modifier ensures that the deletion will cascade down the nested tables. The second integrity constraint is used for class collection types to insure the deletion of a collection object member if that object was deleted. For example, if for a particular Part instance, one if its components object member was deleted. Then we need to ensure that this particular subpart is removed from that part *components* collection. This can be maintained by adding the following constraint

```
FOREIGN KEY(VALUE) REFERENCES Part(OID) ON DELETE CASCADE;
```

into the set of components table.

During a query session, when a particular object of some class is referenced, the OR mapping mechanism creates an empty object instance and then sets its attributes using the data stored in the relational back-end. It also build a synchronisation list so that any changes in any active (i.e. in memory) object is mirrored in the persistent copy of that object. The OR mapping mechanism uses the *UNIDOOR*-Java schema created during the compilation of the original *UNIDOOR* schema to determine the necessary tables for initiating that object. If we retrieve an object of a class with some inherited attributes, the OR mapping mechanism will perform the necessary joins between the tables that build up the inheritance hierarchy up to the base class. OR mapping mechanism uses the JDBC API to execute the necessary SQL commands for both data definition and object initialisation.

Class extension is an important expression in the *UNIDOOR* query language (and also in nearly all DOOD systems). A class extension is simply the set of all object instances of that class. Whenever a class extension is referenced, it is better not to initiate the whole set of objects instances of that class to perform a query. Queries that involve class extension expressions are prone to huge optimisation by the back-end. Consider the following query:

```
{_x in Part | _x.partNo < 8800 & ...};
```

*UNIDOOR* query optimiser notices that it is better to initiate the class extension expression with only persistent objects that had an `partNo` column with value less than 8800. Thus, the optimiser indexes the `Part` table on the `partNo` column and access only those entires with `partNo<8800`. The query evaluator can then proceeds with the remaining portion of the query. Another clear example is the following query:

```
count(PART);
```

in the non-optimised version, the above query will be evaluated in the following way. An empty instance of the type `Set(Part)` is created. It is then populated with the `Part` objects using the back-end. Finally, the `count` method associated with the `Set(Part)` is called and its result is returned as the query answer. However, an optimised version of the query evaluator will recognise the fact that this query can be evaluated entirely by the back-end by invoking the following *SQL* command

```
SELECT COUNT(*) FROM PART;
```

This sort of collaboration between Java and the back-end is the backbone for deductive query evaluation and optimisation. Deductive rules are compiled into static methods defined in a special class. A static EDB predicate can be stored using Java persistent object facility while a dynamic EDB predicate can be stored as a static multiset of some tuple type. *UNIDOOR* monitors many important information such as class extension sizes and potential indexing attributes at compile-time and at run-time. These information are used for potential optimisation. To illustrate this consider the following rule

```
payroll(_supplier, _manager, _salary):-
 _manager=_supplier.man, _salary=_manager.salary + supplier.bonus.
```

Suppose that the predicate `payroll` is called with all its arguments free. In this case both extensions (i.e. `Suppliers`, `Employee`) need to be computed. If *UNIDOOR* finds that the `Employee` extension is larger than the `Supplier` extension, then it evaluates the extension of the `Supplier` first then proceed with evaluation using path expressions. When an argument is bound, *UNIDOOR* checks if it can use this value as an index for a faster access to some class extension. Details of the techniques behind such decisions are beyond the scope of this paper.

Because a DOOD model is mapped into the relational back-end, all basic database facilities are provided directly. For example, the crash recovery feature of the relational back-end means that DOOD has a crash recovery feature too. Database administration can be maintained by using the DBA facilities of the relational back-end. This is done first by providing an administrator privilege to some user. Then all administration features are provided by building an interface that simply connects to the relational database server and then these commands are provided as a layer by the DOOD interface. The interface simply executes the necessary administration commands using the JDBC API. Users can be added and their respective privileges can be modified by the administrator. If a user violates his/her privileges, an a exception is thrown and the interface layer should deal with that properly without leaving the query session. The DBA interface layer can be incorporated within the complier so that only the administrator has the power to compile a schema. Concurrent access to the database is also controlled by the locking mechanism provided by the relational back-end. Nevertheless, the logical treatment for concurrent access relies heavily on the proposed DOOD system.

Updates are handled in the following way. An update layer is built between Java and the relational back-end. This interface layer provides the facilities to load/store object from/to main memory and to/from relational back-end. When a new object is created, a *storeObject* method inside that layer is called which receives this object, retrieve its non-null attributes using Java meta-classes, and then executes the corresponding SQL commands to insert that instance. If a particular object is deleted, its persistent OID is retrieved using the synchronisation list and then an SQL delete statement is executed. Updates are handled similarly but we need to consider only the modified attributes.

Transaction can be performed using the transaction control service provided by the back-end. A transaction block is automatically mapped into a relational transaction block. Whenever a `start transaction` command is encountered, a corresponding `START TRANSACTION` is also executed. When *UNIDOOR* encounters a `commit/rollback` command, a corresponding `COMMIT/ROLLBACK` command is executed in the back-end. The transaction logic in *UNIDOOR* will determine when roll-back or commit command are executed.

## 5 Conclusion

The *DJR* approach is a new technique for implementing DOOD systems. It proposes an abstraction of the DOOD features. It then defines the *DJR* implementation suite consisting of Java as the implementation programming language and a relational DBMS as a back-end. It also provides many useful guidelines on how to use the built-in facilities of the implementation tools to implement many important but hard-to-implement DOOD features. The power of *DJR* for rapid implementation highly complex systems (such as *UNIDOOR*) lies heavily on the cumulative contribution and collaboration between Java and the back-end.

The consistency of the *DJR* approach was verified when we successfully built the DOOD system *UNIDOOR*. The *UNIDOOR* prototype successfully maintains the integrity of its data and it supports most of the database facilities such as the transaction control, updates, persistence store, crash recovery mechanism and database administration facilities. The *DJR* approach can also help in the management of the implementation process. Basically, it cuts away a great deal of the implementation effort by identifying the implementation areas along with the necessary programming skills. Thus, the implementation of a DOOD system can easily be distributed among a group of programmers. We argue that the *DJR* approach can also be used on implementing any system that requires a persistence store such as deductive databases.

In the future, we will investigate further optimisation techniques over the *DJR* suite. We shall also extend *UNIDOOR* to work in a distributed database environment and to interface with the Web. We believe that the *DJR* tools has the potential for these added functionality. But this will require a revision for the feature abstraction.

## References

1. S. Abiteboul. Towards a deductive object-oriented database language. In *Deductive and Object-Oriented Databases*, pages 453–472, 1989.
2. M. L. Barja, A. A. A. Fernandes, N. W. Paton, M. H. Williams, A. Dinn, and A. I. Abdelmoty. Design and implementation of ROCK & ROLL: a deductive object-oriented database system. *Information Systems*, 20(3):185–211, 1995.
3. F. Cacace, S. Ceri, S. Crespi-Reghizzi, L. Tanca, and R. Zicari. Integrating object-oriented data modelling with a rule-based programming paradigm. In *Proceedings of the 1990 ACM SIGMOD international conference on Management of data*, pages 225–236. ACM Press, 1990.
4. S. Ceri, G. Gottlob, and L. Tanka. *Logic Programming and Databases*. Surveys in Computer Science. 1990.
5. S. Ceri and R. Manthey. Chimera: A model and language for active DOOD systems. In *East/West Database Workshop*, pages 3–16, 1994.

6. A. A. A. Fernandes, N. W. Paton, M. H. Williams, and A. Bowles. Approaches to Deductive Object-Oriented Databases. *Information and Software Technology*, 34(12):787–803, December 1992.
7. O. Friesen, A. Lefebvre, and L. Vieille. Validity: Applications of a DOOD system. In P. M. G. Apers, M. Bouzeghoub, and G. Gardarin, editors, *Advances in Database Technology - EDBT''96,5 th International Conference on Extending Database Technology, Avignon, France, March25 -29,1996 , Proceedings*, volume 1057 of *Lecture Notes in Computer Science*, pages 131–134. Springer, 1996.
8. R. Himmeröder, d Lausen, B. Ludäscher, and S. Schlepphorst. Florid: A DOOD-system for querying the web, 1998.
9. M. K. Jaber and A. Voronkov. Deductive object-oriented database systems: from an evolutionary perspective, draft, 2005.
10. M. Jarke, R. Gallersdorfer, M. Jeusfeld, M. Staudt, and S. Eherer. Conceptbase - a deductive object base for meta data management. *Journal on Intelligent Information Systems*, 4(2):167–192, 1995.
11. M. Kifer and G. Lausen. F-logic: a higher-order language for reasoning about objects, inheritance, and scheme. In *Proceedings of the 1989 ACM SIGMOD international conference on Management of data*, pages 134–146. ACM Press, 1989.
12. X. Li and M. Liu. Design and implementation of the OLOG deductive object-oriented database management system. In *Database and Expert Systems Applications*, pages 764–773, 2000.
13. D. Maier. A logic for objects. Technical Report CS/E-86-012, 11 1986.
14. I. Mumick, K. Ross, and S. Sudershan. Design and implementation of the sword declarative object-oriented database system, 1993.
15. I. S. Mumick and K. A. Ross. Noodle: A language for declarative querying in an object-oriented database. In *Deductive and Object-Oriented Databases*, pages 360–378, 1993.
16. R. Ramakrishnan, D. Srivastava, S. Sudarshan, and P. Seshadri. The CORAL deductive system. *The VLDB Journal:The International Journal on Very Large Data Bases*, 3(2):161–210, 1994.
17. P. Sampaio and N. Paton. Deductive queries in ODMG databases: the DOQL approach. In *In Proc. of the 5th Intl. Conference on Object-Oriented Information Systems OOIS*, pages 57–74. Springer-Verlag., 1998.
18. P. R. F. Sampaio and N. W. Paton. Deductive Object-Oriented Database Systems: A Survey. In *Rules in Database Systems*, pages 1–19, 1997.
19. D. Srivastava, R. Ramakrishnan, P. Seshadri, and S. Sudarshan. CORAL++: Adding object-orientation to a logic database language. In R. Agrawal, S. Baker, and D. A. Bell, editors, *19th International Conference on Very Large Data Bases, August 24-27, 1993 , Dublin, Ireland, Proceedings*, pages 158–170. Morgan Kaufmann, 1993.
20. M. Stonebraker and P. Brown. *Object-Relational DBMSs, Traking the next great wave*. Morgan Kaufmann, 1999.
21. J. D. Ullman. Information integration using logical views. *Theoretical Computer Science*, 239(2):189–210, 2000.
22. J. Vaghani, K. Ramamohanarao, D. B. Kemp, Z. Somogyi, P. J. Stuckey, T. S. Leask, and J. Harland. The Aditi deductive database system. *The VLDB Journal: The International Journal on Very Large Data Bases*, 3(2):245–288, 1994.
23. A. Voronkov. Unidoor, a deductive object oriented data model, submitted, 2005.

# Preloading Browsers for Optimizing Automatic Access to Hidden Web: A Ranking-Based Repository Solution

Justo Hidalgo[1], Alberto Pan[2,*], José Losada[1], and Manuel Álvarez[2]

[1] Denodo Technologies, Inc.
Madrid, Spain
{jhidalgo, jlosada}@denodo.com
[2] Department of Information and Communications Technologies,
University of A Coruña, Spain
{apan, mad}@udc.es

**Abstract.** As Web applications grow in terms of quantity and quality, different vertical solutions could make use of them as an important source of information. Nevertheless, obtaining information from web sources becomes a challenging issue because of their complex access due to the hypertext browsing paradigm, and HTML's semistructured format. Web Automation middleware navigates through web links and fills web forms in an automatic way, so to extract information from the Hidden Web. The main optimization parameter is the time required to navigate through the intermediate pages that lead to the desired results. This work proposes a technique which focuses on improving the browsing time by storing information from previous queries, and using it to preload an adequate subset of the navigational sequence on a specific browser, before the next sequence is launched. It also takes into account the most commonly used sequences, being the ones to be preloaded more often.

## 1 Introduction

The world wide web is the most important source of information for many types of knowledge areas, like competitive intelligence, product search and comparison, operational business intelligence, and so on. Most of the information stored in the web is hidden behind forms (authentication, information-filling, etc.), navigational links with JavaScript, session maintenance, and so on. These web sites, generically known as Deep Web or Hidden Web, are estimated to keep more than five hundred times the information which resides in web pages accessible through a static URL [2].

In the last years some research groups and industrial companies have been focusing on automatic browsing and extraction of information from Deep Web sources. Basically, obtaining information from web sources is divided into two main steps: firstly, being able to browse through the access pages up to the first page of results; secondly, extracting information from the result web pages, in either a structured or unstructured way. Some of the research groups (e.g. [11]) deepen into how to browse through

---

* Alberto Pan's work was partially supported by the "Ramón y Cajal" programme of the Spanish Ministry of Education and Science.

Y. Manolopoulos, J. Pokorný, and T. Sellis (Eds.): ADBIS 2006, LNCS 4152, pp. 171–183, 2006.

the different access pages for the system to get to the result page. Other works focus on the extraction step ([1], [6], [7] and [8] for a survey) and how to obtain structured or indexed information from the web. Both steps (browsing and structuring) are intertwined since after browsing to the first result page, it must be parsed as to know its internal structure, and also to know how to access possible detail and "more result" pages.

When building web automation systems or information integration applications with access to web sources, it is critical to optimize the web access efficiency. Web sources are slower than traditional corporate and local sources, such as relational databases, because of: (1) their inherent distributed structure, (2) http, WWW's communication protocol, and (3) the way web sources structure their information in pages, so that a "virtual table" might imply browsing through tenths, hundreds or even thousands of web pages (mainly "more results" pages and "detail" pages).

There are complex web sources which require long navigation sequences before arriving at the real query form, due to session maintenance. For example, in many real sources it is necessary to introduce login/password information, after what the user must navigate through one or more pages until arriving at a certain query form. This fact can cause that a query take a very long time to execute.

The different flows of navigation of several queries have "common denominators", that is, sequence elements that are repeated such as the login/password access, or the different options by which the site can be browsed before arriving at a concrete page. Much processing time is lost because the system does not consider that from a query to another, it would only be necessary one step back and a new selection; instead, it repeats the complete navigation access path from the beginning.

The optimization of the process flow can provide many considerable improvements as far as the access time to the remote information of each source is concerned, sometimes in orders of magnitude - mainly in sources which reside in servers with small bandwidth, or in sources with many intermediate steps -. This work describes a series of techniques which allow to optimize access to web sources in a mediator-wrapper architecture [14], even though this approach is valid for a stand-alone web extraction system.

This paper shows a novel approach with regards to web source browsing optimization, based on browser reutilization and use of a cost repository. The structure of this work is as follows: Section 2 and Section 3 introduce the web browsing optimization challenge by characterizing its main components. Section 4 shows the Cost Repository Parameters, while Section 5 describes how to obtain an adequate sequence prefix; Section 6 explains how the browser pool can select which sequences must be preloaded at execution time. Section 7 explains the two sequence ranking algorithms proposed. Finally, Section 8 takes care or other important issues, and Section 9 summarizes on conclusions. A previous phase of this work was presented in [4].

## 2   Using a Browser Pool to Browse Web Sources

The web automation system proposed in this work uses browsers as basic elements which are able to access information stored or dynamically generated by web applications, and that might require prior authentication, and/or link traversing. The use of a browser instead of an HTTP client improves the quality and quantity of web applications which can be browsed since it emulates a user's behaviour, so many issues such as session maintenance, javascript, etc., are taken care by the browser internals.

The approach followed in this paper is focused on the component known as Browser Pool. This module is responsible for receiving the requests, each of which is associated with a specific web navigation, and selecting one of its set of browsers to be executed. This request is called "Navigational Sequence", and it is composed of a set of actions which must be performed by the browser. The language to describe these sequences is known as NSEQL –Navigational Sequence Language, thoroughly described in [9]-, and has been designed for executing them on the Internet browser interface (Microsoft Internet Explorer and Netscape Firefox). Table 1 shows an example of an NSEQL program, which guides a browser from the home page of a hypothetical electronic bookshop to a query result page, after the user is authenticated, the search terms are inserted and the query form is submitted.

As it can be observed, the syntax is very simple to understand. The first line commands the browser to access the initial page. Lines 3 to 6 show how the browser must fill the authentication form and click on a button in order to submit the information. "@LOGIN" and "@PASSWORD" are NSEQL attributes which can be used to parameterize the sequence (for example, by telling the system the specific login and password values). Finally, after the browser receives the page after the authentication process, lines 8 to 11 are executed so that the page's "searchBrick" form is found and its search field "field-keywords" is filled with information provided by attribute "@QUERY". Finally, the form information is submitted, and the result page is returned. The browser will return information about the status of each of the sequence steps, plus the HTML code of the last page.

When this query must be executed several times with the same of different attributes, one can observe that the most important optimization parameter is the "browse time" spent by the system to access the information stored in the pages hidden behind links, authentication and query forms. How the Browser Pool decides which browser is assigned to a specific request, and how to optimize the execution of these sequences, are the main purposes and value propositions of this paper.

**Table 1.** NSEQL Description

```
1.  Navigate(http://www.ebookshop.com,0)
2.  WaitPages(1)
3.  FindFormByName(implogin,0)
4.  SetInputValue(imapuser,0,^EncodeSeq(@LOGIN))
5.  SetInputValue(pass,0,^EncodeSeq(@PASSWORD))
6.  ClickOnElement(button,INPUT,0)
7.  WaitPages(1)
8.  FindFormByName(searchBrick,0)
9.  SetInputValue(field-keywords,0,^EncodeSeq(@QUERY))
10. FindElementByAttribute(INPUT,NAME,Go,0,true)
11. ClickOnSelectedElement()
12. WaitPages(1)
```

A browser pool receives the different petitions from the web automation system, each of which is related with an NSEQL program. The browser pool uses the browsers already opened and in a passive state to execute each of the programs. If a petition arrives and a browser is not available, the browser would open one if the number of browsers is below the maximum number of open browsers, or queue the petition until one is available. Fig. 1 shows an example of these steps, in which a browser pool is configured to have at most three active browsers at a time. Three different types of browsing sequences are sent to the browser pool, each of them with specific number of elements. Two premises in this example are that: (1) each sequence element takes exactly the same time (something not very real in internet environments, but which help us to better understand how this architecture works), and (2) the browsing petitions arrive at the same time, so that browsers have no gap time between requests.

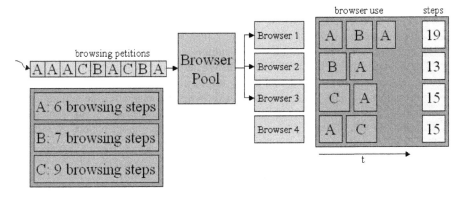

**Fig. 1.** Browser Pool Steps without Optimization

Here we can see how each the browser pool assigns each browsing petition to a free browser (according to a specific ordering). After each browser finished a petition, it starts a new one if it exists.

The following sections show the different optimization techniques required to decrease the number of browsing steps.

## 3   Optimizing Navigational Sequences

The proposed solution in this article is an extension of the pool of browsers, so that for each browser, the sequence of navigation actions which took it to its present state is stored. When a new sequence is received by the browser pool to be executed, it is verified whether there is any browser that it has some sequence with a common prefix with the recently received sequence. In that case, the system will evaluate whether it is better to reuse the browser's present state or to start from the beginning. Thus, in the previously commented case, when the new sequence arrives, the pool would realize that there is a browser which is a single step from the desired state, and would reuse it.

In addition, to avoid the problem of the initialization cost –that is, the time required to start the browser, and navigate through different pages until arriving at a concrete result page-, the pool of browsers starts up a preconfigured number of browsers already initialized, that is, pointing to the pages which, according to the cost repository, are more suitable to respond to the queries, anticipating themselves to the future needs. This is obtained by means of a historical ranking of sources and states, so that we can construct a heuristic model.

The browser pool must make use of both status information and cost statistics –or, more precisely, access cost statistics-.

Status information will be used by the pool to control where its browsers are in each moment. Currently, information managed is the set of navigational sequences, where the path followed by each browser is defined sequentially. Every element from this sequence is actually a state of a particular deterministic finite automata. This information is required by the pool to determine, when a new query arrives, which of its elements has a minor distance with respect to the target –the element of the new sequence to execute-.

Access information will allow the pool to initialize its browsers so that, statistically, the following sequences' starting nodes are as close to the first ones' finishing nodes as possible. The associated cost will be lower when sequences are closer.

In the case that the browser selected for the following sequence had previously executed that same one, the system must decide whether the browser's current state is the optimal, or whether it must browse to a later or earlier state. When the optimal state is at a previous step, a "back sequence" must be executed. This special sequence has a series of implications that will be commented in section 8.

## 4   Web Automation Optimization Cost Parameters

A cost repository is used to store information about the browsers, such as the complete access route for parameterised query (query type) to a web source and the utilization ranking, which will allow for the pool of browsers to select the appropriate access route to initialize the new navigators.

An important characteristic in the cost repository is the storage of information by each access route and time section. In our preliminary studies we have observed great existing differences of web source performance in different time sections. The use of a navigational sequence or another also depends on the time section in which the request is made.

The required general parameters for an adequate physical access optimization are the following for each query type:

a)   information about its related navigational sequence (the one which allows the browser to access the desired results), written in NSEQL.

b)   each query will increase by one the number of queries per time section on this query type. This will be used to generate the sequence ranking.

c)   finally, the last attribute stored is the route subset, the navigational sequence prefix that the browser should navigate automatically so that the user query is optimized regarding the access to the web source. Initially, it is assigned the complete NSEQL sequence. The browser reuse algorithm can be used so that when it finds the "back sequence", that prefix (the difference between the whole NSEQL sequence and the back sequence) is the value stored at the cost repository.

An aggregate method will compute the number of ocurrences per time section for each navigation sequence, thus obtaining a relative ordering with respect to their frequence of utilization.

On a frequency basis (so as not to disturb the runtime execution of the optimizer), an update thread will take care of taking these occurrences and generating the relative ordering of each query type per time section with respect to the rest of them, according to their frequency of utilization. This processing can make use of a typical mean average $M(k) = \Sigma \eta_i(k) v_i$, i=1..k, where $\eta_i(k) = 1/k$, or more appropriate probability functions. This ordering will be stored in a "position" attribute on the cost repository, for every query type and time section.

## 5 Selecting a Reutilization Prefix for a Specific Sequence

One of the optimization techniques described in this work is related to selecting the most appropriate subset of the NSEQL navigational sequence (a "prefix") to preload a browser so that, when a web automation query is executed on the system, the browser is already positioned on the best possible sequence element. This way, web browsing performance can improve even orders of magnitude, since HTTP connection is the parameter which affects the most to efficiency overall. A conservative approach takes as prefix the sequence elements counting from the home page to the first page with variables. For example, the sequence elements required to access the authentication or the query form. This technique is not error-prone, but might not be optimal in the case there are more than one form, and the changing variables between queries do not take part on the first n-m forms (where m=0 would mean the worst case possible, in which no variable changes among queries, so that the browser could just stay at the first result list page).

In our case we propose the following: for every query type and time section (in case the behaviour differs depending on the time), we keep information about whether there are any value changes in each attribute of the sequence. These changes take the last "m" sample queries (which value has been heuristically determined as 5). This way, the system can choose at runtime whether the prefix should "stop" at the first query form, or, in case its variables have not changed, it can use some more sequence elements.

This is implemented with a 2xN matrix, where n is the number of attributes per query type and time section, in the following way: {{attribute$_1$, boolean$_1$}, {attribute$_2$, boolean$_2$}, ..., {attribute$_n$, boolean$_n$}}, where boolean$_i$ indicates whether that attribute has changed in the previous i executions or not.

This method, although more computationally intensive (requiring $O(N*m)$), it is very flexible with regards to the use of the variables. For example, the prefix will take into account whether an attribute used in an authentication form stores always the same values or not; in the first case, it will be considered that the attribute has, actually, a constant value.

As an example we will use the NSEQL program from Table 1, in which a bookshop web application access is automated. We can observe that there are two pages in which attributes are used: the authentication page and the query page. A conservative optimization technique would select the sequence prefix defined from the home page to the authentication page (that is, the sequence `Navigate(http://www.ebookshop.com,0); WaitPages(1)`), and would use it from then on.

However, the technique proposed in this work does not create a prefix *a priori*. Instead, it will depend on the queries performed by the system on that specific query type. Let us take a look at a set of sample queries for the previously mentioned electronic bookshop in Table 2. Let us also imagine that the configuration attribute "m" equals to 3, which is the number of sample queries checked for each attribute in order to find any change of values. With this information, in each iteration the 2xN matrix is generated, indicating the attributes which value has changed in the previous "m" iterations.

**Table 2.** Sample Queries for the Electronic Bookshop Web Application

| N | LOGIN | PASSWORD | QUERY | N | LOGIN | PASSWORD | QUERY |
|---|---|---|---|---|---|---|---|
| 1 | Joe | Joe | Java | 8 | Joe | Joe | CORBA communication |
| 2 | Joe | Joe | Java | 9 | Christie | Christie | Java |
| 3 | Joe | Joe | Relational Databases | 10 | Christie | Christie | Java |
| 4 | Joe | Joe | UML | 11 | Christie | Christie | Java |
| 5 | Christie | Christie | UML | 12 | Christie | Christie | Java |
| 6 | Christie | Christie | Mediators Web | 13 | Joe | Joe | Java |
| 7 | Joe | Joe | ActiveX | | | | |

Using the information on that matrix, the system generates the sequence prefix before each query. For the first query, as there is no previous information, the conservative technique is used in which the browser is positioned in the first page in which any attribute is required –in this case, the authentication page-. Since "m" equals to 3, the first three queries use this technique strictly. In the fourth query, since the login and password values have kept the same value in the last "m" queries, the prefix is modified so that it positions the browser in the query form page. This allows this fourth query to save a few page browsings. Again, for the fifth query the browser is position in the query form page, but a different pair login/password is provided. In this case, if a "back page" sequence is provided by the user, the appropriate subset of this sequence is provided in order to go back to the authentication page; if no sequence is given, it is very dangerous to try the Back button in session maintenance web applications, so, if it is not explicitly configured to try it –because the administrator has decided that this web application behaves correctly with the Back option-, it is better to open a new browser (in order to clean any session information) or reuse an existing one, and perform the whole sequence. As the sample queries are being executed, this technique works as depicted. The last issue we want to show here is that, before executing the twelfth query, since both the pair login/password and query attributes have not changed in the previous "m" queries, then the prefix used is actually the whole sequence, so that, since the twelfth query repeats all the attributes, the response will be the same as in the previous query.

This last behaviour must be described a little bit more carefully. In some cases, re-using the browser results absolutely can be a better-than-good idea, since web data might have been updated since the last query (p.e. in highly-variable values in financial web applications, or because the last query was executed a long time ago). There-fore, in these cases it might be better that, even if all attribute values have not changed, to repeat the last query form so that the browser is forced to query the server for new results. This, too, can be configured.

Obviously, the prefix sequence for the fourteenth query execution goes back to the authentication form, since, even though the QUERY attribute has not changed, so have the LOGIN and PASSWORD attributes done.

The value of the "m" attribute can be chosen heuristically, but must be carefully se-lected. If we choose a very low "m" (p.e. 1), this means that the algorithm will react by taking only the last query executed. When attributes vary in a frequent way, the prefix will not be very useful, and "back page" sequences will have to be executed many ways. If m takes a big value, this means that the conservative technique will be used unless fixed attribute values are used most of the times.

## 6  Browser Pool Run-Time Optimization

The previous technique allows the system to choose a promising prefix sequence which avoids automatic browsing of the whole web flow. This section complements it by allowing the browser pool to preload the most promising sequences, that is, the ones which will be executed with the most probability.

Every time a query is executed with a predefined navigational sequence, the cost repository must store that fact, so that a "sequence ranking" per time frame is created. A time frame is a division of the 24-hour period, for example 00:00-07:59. Thus, the browser pool will start up the preconfigured number of browsers. Each one of these browsers will directly access, without a query having been made, the set of better positioned sequences in the ranking –this does not mean one sequence per browser: if one sequence is much better positioned than the rest, this could mean than two or more browsers navigate to it-. These browsers will stop right in the state of the se-quence in which it is necessary to insert execution-time data –user data, login, pass-word, etc.- by using the technique from section 5; thus, the system is optimizing their utilization.

When a new browser is launched, the optimizer must take into account two types of information: the one provided by the cost repository, plus that provided by the pool about the rest of the browsers which are already active –so that, for instance, if the active browsers are already coping with the first two sequences in the ranking, the new browser is taken to the third one-.

If a new query arrives which implies the use of a browser, the pool will check whether there are already some of the already active-but-idle ones with the same se-quence required. If more than one browser responds, the pool will decide which one to use by measuring which one has to use a lesser number of navigational events to get to the step in which execution-time data must be inserted. This is achieved by using the concept of "distance".

The other possibility is that no active-but-idle browser is in that required sequence (i.e. no browser is currently in any page belonging to that sequence). This situation can lead to the following choices: (1) If the probability that this sequence is invoked again in a future query is much lower –a configurable parameter- than the probability of the sequences already involved in the current executable queries, a new browser can be started even if some of the rest are not in use, in order to avoid that arriving queries which make use of the more typical sequences can not take advantage of the optimizer, because they have to either wait for a browser to finish, or start up another browser. (2) It also can happen that the pool does not accept the creation of a new browser –p.e. there is a maximum number of allowed instances-. In this case, the pool will use the active-but-idle browser with owns the sequence with the lowest ranking number.

The following section explains the ranking algorithm in more detail.

## 7   Ranking Phase

The browser pool is responsible for creating a ranking with the set of navigational sequences used by the system in real time. The issue in creating this ranking relates to how will the topmost sequences be mapped to the browsers which are currently available (NUM_BROWSERS).

We offer two possibilities: the first one is to map these browsers with the top $x\%$, while the second one is to use the NUM_BROWSERS/n top sequences. Let us see one example for each choice.

### 7.1   Mapping Browsers with Query Types in the Top X%

Table 3 shows the sample query type utilization used in the following examples. We have nine sources (from "A" to "F"), each of which has a percentage value of use as shown in the table. This value has been obtained as described in sections 4 and 6.

**Table 3.** Sequence Utilization Example

| SEQUENCE | % | SEQUENCE | % |
|----------|-----|----------|-----|
| A | 8% | F | 2% |
| B | 6% | G | 2% |
| C | 6% | H | 1% |
| D | 4% | I | 1% |
| E | 2% | | |

If NUM_BROWSERS = 10, and X%=20 (that is, the user wants to map the topmost 20% of the sequences to the browsers):

a)   20% is achieved by the first three sequences: A, B and C (8% + 6% + 6%).
b)   8%*10 browsers / 20% = 4 browsers for sequence A
c)   6%*10 browsers / 20% = 3 browsers for sequences B and C

This means that the first four browsers will be started and preloaded with sequence A's prefix, other three will have B's prefix, and the other three, C's prefix.

"X" is a parameter configurable by the user, and its value will depend on the type of application for which is being used. If the solution mostly accesses a concrete and limited set of sources, and there are not many browsers available (due, for instance, to hardware constraints), X could be a low percentage of the total use to improve the use of the browsers. Nevertheless, if the use distribution of the sources is lineal, X should be big enough to, basically, distribute the browsers as much as possible.

## 7.2 Mapping Browsers with a Maximum Number of Query Types

A parameter $n = 5$ means  that the user wishes the first five sequences to be adequately distributed along the available browsers.

In the previous table, this means that sequences A, B, C, D and E will be used, which stands for $8\% + 6\% + 6\% + 4\% + 2\% = 26\%$

a) $8\%*10$ browsers$/26\% = 40/13 = 3$ browsers for sequence A
b) $6\%*10$ browsers$/26\% = 30/13 = 2.5$ browsers for sequence B and C (3 and 2)
c) $4\%*10$ browsers$/26\% = 20/13 = 1$ browser for sequence D
d) $2\%*10$ browsers$/26\% = 20/26 = 1$ browser for sequence E

# 8   Other Issues

Some issues must be taken into consideration when considering the implementation of these techniques.

## 8.1  "Back Navigation" to a Common Page

If a browser can be reused so that the same sequence previously executed is called again, one would wish that it would navigate back to the most adequate sequence element (i.e. web page) so that this new query does not have to take the whole path back from the beginning; unluckily, this is not possible in most of the times: (1) in some occasions, this is due to web redirections which do not allows us to exactly know how many "back steps" the system must perform; (2) in other ones, when a web application does not allow to open more than one session with the same login/password values, the system might not be able to find the correct back sequence; (3) finally, in some stateful web applications, the back sequence does not work (this is also true in some AJAX-based web applications [3]). Therefore, the system will not browse back, but will start from the beginning of the sequence to achieve the correct state.

This is not always a feasible solution. When session maintenance is kept by the browser, the navigational sequence might change (usually because this second time, the authentication form page is not shown, leading the user from the home page directly to the search form page, thus disabling the usefulness of the sequence). In those cases, the user should explicitly provide a "back sequence" to lead the browser to the correct sequence element (for example, by pressing the "Disconnect" button and browsing to the most interesting page in terms of optimization).

## 8.2  Browser Session Maintenance

A problem that arises here is that the browser session can expire before an appropriate query arrives. In order to avoid the error produced if this browser is tried to be used, there are a few options: one is to make browsers navigate randomly through a link and repeating this same sequence at certain intervals. Another one is to restart the sequence whenever it fails. The chosen option is the configuration of session timeout for each source - with a default value -, so that the pool of browsers acts before the session expires.

## 8.3  Pay-per-Access Web Sites

This approach can be expensive if a pay is realized per access, since the system will automatically access web sources which might not be actually used. Thus, in these cases, this optimization must not be taken into account.

## 8.4  Changes in Web Sources

Web sites are autonomous sources with regards to the Web Automation middleware, that is, they do not inform the system about their possible changes with respect to format or navigational sequences. One issue to take into account is how the Automation system must behave if after a sequence prefix has been generated, the source changes so that the sequence navigation is no longer valid. This leads us to the problem of automatically detecting those changes and regenerating the sequences to adjust them to the new situation.

The wrapper maintenance approaches presented to date are based on wrapper induction techniques [8]. In this approach, wrappers are generated by providing the system with user-labeled examples which are used to induce the underlying structure of the target HTML pages. The main idea in our automatic maintenance implementation system [12][13] is to collect results from valid queries against the web connector and, when the source changes, use them to generate new examples to bootstrap the wrapper induction process again.

When the maintenance system starts regenerating the program, the information stored in the cost repository about this specific navigational sequence must be deleted so not to cause future inconsistences.

## 9  Conclusions

Fig. 2 shows how applying the previously detailed optimization techniques causes a very important decrease in the number of navigational steps required to answer all the browsing requests made to a Web Automation system. Compare this with Fig. 1, and you can see a reduction from 62 to 30 steps. That means that, if each step takes approximately the same time to execute, we would be saving more than half the time.

And this with the premise used in this example, in which all browsing requests come at the same time; if some of the requests had delayed a little bit (p.e. the second "B", and the second "C"), the number of steps would decrease down to 10 steps (having B and C the same number of steps in their back sequences than A), obtaining a gain of 6-to-1 (Fig. 3).

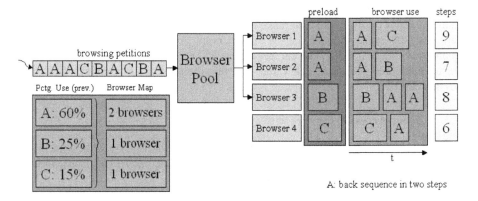

**Fig. 2.** Browser Pool Steps with Optimization

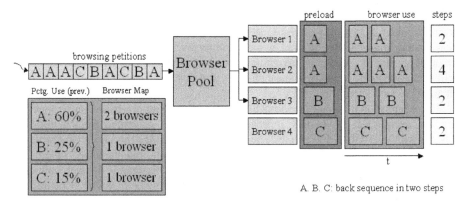

**Fig. 3.** Browser Pool Steps with B and C delays

This paper has described and explained a set of techniques and algorithms which optimize how web automation and extraction systems access transactional web applications. These systems are critical in mediator applications which make use of web data for solutions such as Competitive Intelligence or Single Customer View, and, thus, must behave with a high performance and efficiency. Use of cache is not always the best solution, since web application usually store real-time, highly changing information. We show an innovative way of accessing data from Hidden Web, by storing historical information from previous queries to the different query types, and applying a set of techniques to obtain the best sequence element that each browser should point to. These techniques have been developed as part of the physical layer optimization of a mediator/wrapper environment for web sources [5][10].

# References

1. Arasu, A. and Garcia-Molina, H. Extracting Structured Data from Web Pages. Proceedings of the ACM SIGMOD international conference on Management of data. 2003.
2. Bergman M.K. The Deep Web. Surfacing Hidden Value. http://www.brightplanet. com/technology/deepweb.asp
3. Garret, J. J. Ajax: A New Approach to Web Applications. http://www.adaptivepath.com/ publications/ essays/archives/000385print.php
4. Hidalgo, J., Pan, A., Losada, J., Álvarez, M. Adding Physical Optimization to Cost Models in Information Mediators. 2005 IEEE Conference on e-Business Engineering. 2005.
5. Hidalgo, J., Pan, A., Losada, J., Álvarez, M., Viña, A. Building the Architecture of a Statistics-based Query Optimization Solution for Heterogeneous Mediators. 6th International Conference on Information Integration and Web-based Applications & Services. 2004.1.
6. Knoblock, C.A., Lerman, K., Minton, S. and Muslea, I. Accurately and Reliably Extracting Data from the Web: A Machine Learning Approach. Bulletin of the IEEE Computer Society Technical Committee on Data Enginnering. 1999.
7. Kushmerick, N., Weld, D.S. and Doorembos, R. Wrapper induction for information extraction. Proceedings of the fifteenth International Joint Conference on Artificial Intelligence. 1997.
8. Laender, A. H. F., Ribeiro-Neto, B. A., Soares da Silva, A. and Teixeira, J. S. A Brief Survey of Web Data Extraction Tools. ACM SIGMOD Record 31(2). 2002.
9. Pan A., et al, 2002. Semi-Automatic Wrapper Generation for Commercial Web Sources. Proceedings of IFIP WG8.1 Working Conference on Engineering Information Systems in the Internet Context. 2002.
10. Pan, A., Raposo, J., Álvarez, M., Montoto, P., Orjales, V., Hidalgo, J., Ardao, L., Molano, A., Viña, A. The DENODO Data Integration Platform. 28th International Conference on Very Large Databases. 2002.
11. Raghavan S. and García-Molina H., Crawling the Hidden Web. Proceedings of the 27th International Conference on Very Large Databases. 2001.
12. Raposo, J., Pan, A., Álvarez, M., Hidalgo, J. Automatically Generating Labeled Examples for Web Wrapper Maintenance. Proceedings of the 2005 IEEE/WIC/ACM International Conference on Web Intelligence. 2005.
13. Raposo, J., Pan, A., Álvarez, M., Viña, A. Automatic Wrapper Maintenance for Semi-Structured Web Sources Using Results from Previous Queries. Proceedings of the 2005 ACM Symposium on Applied Computing. 2005.
14. Wiederhold, G. Mediators in the Architecture of Future Information Systems. IEEE Computer, March 1992.

# A Middleware-Based Approach to Database Caching

Andreas Bühmann, Theo Härder, and Christian Merker

Department of Computer Science, University of Kaiserslautern,
P. O. Box 3049, D-67653 Kaiserslautern, Germany
{buehmann, haerder, merker}@informatik.uni-kl.de

**Abstract.** Database caching supports declarative query processing close to the application. Using a full-fledged DBMS as cache manager, it enables the evaluation of specific project-select-join queries in the cache. In this paper, we propose significant improvements and optimizations – as compared to the well-known DBCache approach – that make our caching concept truly adaptive. Furthermore, we describe an adaptive constraint-based cache system (ACCache) relying on middleware components as a DBMS-independent realization of this approach.

## 1 Motivation

While Web caching is concerned with reducing response time and bandwidth consumption for service requests in the user-to-server path, *database (DB) caching* focuses on request optimization in the remaining path from the Web server to the *backend* database, which keeps the dynamic up-to-date data used by transactional programs to derive user query results. In contrast to Web caching, which can only answer identifier-based cache requests, DB caching provides declarative query processing, which makes it much more powerful but also more complex.

To accelerate service requests of Web users and, at the same time, to improve scalability of applications accessing the backend DB, application servers frequently migrate to data centers closer to the user "at the edge of the Internet". Special algorithms enable Web clients to select one of the replicated servers close to them thereby minimizing response times of Web services. However, this is only true if locality of data reference can be provided by such application servers – often achieved through geographical contexts of these services. Otherwise, frequent round-trips to the remote backend DB may degrade the performance of DB-based services to a level much worse than without application server migration. Therefore, it is vital for the entire migration approach to keep prevalently used data close to the application in database *caches* (also called *frontend* DB servers).

In Sect. 2, we present an adaptive constraint-based caching concept supporting the evaluation of project-select-join (PSJ) queries. This mechanism must be entirely transparent to application programs such that turning caching on or off only affects query performance. Because (any type of) caching always has inherent trade-offs as far as cache consistency and maintenance is concerned, only DB contents exhibiting high locality of reference should be kept in the cache. Therefore, only a few tables containing selected records are maintained in a typical cache, arranged into *cache groups*, although the backend DB may consist of hundreds of tables. Moreover, caching is always kind of

Y. Manolopoulos, J. Pokorný, and T. Sellis (Eds.): ADBIS 2006, LNCS 4152, pp. 184–199, 2006.
© Springer-Verlag Berlin Heidelberg 2006

speculative, because it should anticipate changing workload needs in the future. Thus, caching adaptivity is of utmost importance. As compared to [1], we propose a much more flexible mechanism enabling orthogonality of parameter specification (by candidate values) and cache filling as well as evaluation of more query types.

Section 3 describes an implementation of this mechanism based on middleware concepts. While cache management is rather straightforward for simple cache groups (e. g., *Director → Movie*), query processing power is limited in such cases. Thus, to reveal the strengths and weaknesses of ACCache, we have chosen a rather complex running example (Fig. 1). Section 4 summarizes our results and identifies future work.

## 2    Constraint-Based Database Caching

*Constraint-based database caching* promises a new quality for the placement of data close to their application. The key idea is to accomplish *predicate completeness* in the cache for some given types of query predicates $P$ such that all queries matching $P$ can be evaluated correctly.

A database cache is a database consisting of cache tables. Cache tables represent selected backend tables in the cache and contain subsets of their records[1]. All records (of various types) in the backend DB that are needed to evaluate a predicate $P$ are called the *predicate extension* of $P$. If a collection of cache tables contains the predicate extension of a predicate $P$, it is said to be *predicate complete* with respect to $P$. Note that a predicate extension in the sense used here consists of all records from the backend tables needed to reconstruct the query result. For an aggregate query, the predicate extension would not be the aggregate (as the query result) but all records to be aggregated.

*Cache constraints* enable cache loading in a constructive way and guarantee the presence of their respective predicate extensions in the cache. This technique does not rely on static predicates: Parameterized constraints make the specification adaptive; it is completed when specific values instantiate the parameters: An "instantiated constraint" then corresponds to a predicate and, once the constraint is satisfied (i. e., all related records have been loaded), it delivers correct answers to eligible queries. Note, the set of all present predicate extensions flexibly allows combined evaluation of their predicates in the cache.

Given suitable cache constraints, there are no or only simple difficulties in deciding whether certain predicates can be evaluated. At run time, only simple existence queries are required to determine whether suitable predicate extensions are available.

The primary task of this constraint-based caching approach is to support local processing of queries that typically contain simple projection and selection operations as well as equi-joins (PSJ). Because all columns of the corresponding backend tables are kept, all *project* operations possible in the backend DB can also be performed in the cache. Other operations like *selection* and *join* depend on specific cache constraints. Furthermore, since full DB functionality is available, the results of these PSJ queries can be subjected to further arbitrary selections and transformations.

---

[1] In the present state of our model, we deal with whole records only and do not consider projections of certain sets of columns, as DBProxy [2] does, for example.

## 2.1  Completeness

For predicates we would like to evaluate in the cache, we must guarantee predicate completeness. Considering a cache table $S$, we denote by $S_B$ its corresponding backend table, by $S.c$ a column $c$ of $S$.

Let us begin with single cache tables. For simple equality predicates like $S.c = v$, where $v$ is a value, the predicate completeness takes the shape of *value completeness*.

**Definition 1 (Value completeness).** *A value[2] $v$ is said to be value complete (or complete for short) in a column $S.c$ if and only if all records of $\sigma_{c=v} S_B$ are in $S$.*

Obviously, *if* we know that a value $v$ is value complete in a column $S.c$, we can correctly evaluate $S.c = v$ in the cache, because all records from table $S_B$ that carry this value are there. Determining which values actually are complete is the task of *probing*, which will be introduced in Sect. 2.2.

To obtain the predicate extensions of PSJ queries we use *referential cache constraints* (RCCs) between cache columns to specify all records needed to satisfy specific equi-join predicates.

**Definition 2 (Referential cache constraint).** *A referential cache constraint $S.a \rightarrow T.b$ from a source column $S.a$ to a target column $T.b$ is satisfied if and only if all values $v$ in $S.a$ are value complete in $T.b$.*

An RCC $S.a \rightarrow T.b$ guarantees, whenever we find a record $s$ in cache table $S$, that all join partners of $s$ with respect to $S.a = T.b$ are in $T$, too. Note, the RCC alone does not allow us to correctly perform this join in the cache: Many records of $S_B$ that have join partners in $T_B$ may be missing from $S$. But using an equality predicate with a complete value in column $S.c$ as an *anchor*, we can restrict this join to pairs of records that are present in the cache: The RCC $S.a \rightarrow T.b$ expands the predicate extension of $S.c = x$ to the predicate extension of $S.c = x \wedge S.a = T.b$. In this way, a column with a complete value can serve as an *entry point* for a query into the cache; it allows us to start reasoning about predicates evaluable in the cache: Once the cache has been entered in this sense, reachable RCCs show us where joins can correctly be performed. Of course, the application of RCCs can be chained: A second RCC $T.d \rightarrow U.e$ could expand the predicate extension to $S.c = x \wedge S.a = T.b \wedge T.d = U.e$.

Figure 1 shows a cache setup for a movie database, including many RCCs used to connect the selected cache tables. Let us assume we know that the name 'Bond' is complete in $A.name$[3], which means that *all* actors named 'Bond' are in the cache. We can then safely evaluate the predicate $A.name = $ 'Bond' in the cache, because it is predicate complete with respect to this predicate. Furthermore, since we guarantee that all specified RCCs hold at any time, we are allowed to evaluate

$$A.name = \text{'Bond'} \wedge A.id = P.aid \wedge P.mid = M.id \wedge M.zip = C.zip$$

in the cache, too. Of course, this is only a skeleton of a possible query and could be enriched with further selection predicates such as $M.title = $ 'Dr. No'.

---

[2] As SQL's *null* indicates the absence of a value, we do not regard *null* in itself as a value.

[3] In formulas like this one, we like to abbreviate the table names.

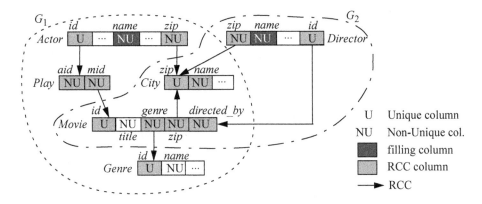

**Fig. 1.** Cache groups $G_1$ and $G_2$

Using RCCs we implicitly introduce a value-based table model intended to support queries. Despite similarities to the relational model, RCCs are not identical to the primary-key/foreign-key (PK/FK) relationships contained in the backend schema. A PK/FK relationship can be processed symmetrically, whereas our RCCs can be used for join processing only in the specified direction. Considering that we have unique (U) and non-unique (NU) columns, there are other important differences: $n : m$ RCCs (NU → NU) have no counterparts in the backend DB, and a column may be the source of $n$ and the target of $m$ RCCs. In contrast, a column in the role of a primary key may be the starting point of $k$, but in the role of a foreign key the ending point of only one (meaningful) PK/FK relationship.

## 2.2 Probing for Entry Points

RCCs allow us to draw conclusions about predicate extensions that are in the cache, but only if we can rely on some value being complete and serving as an entry point. Considering some column $S.c$, how do we know that a value $v$ is complete there? Obviously, our goal ought to be to provide simple and efficient means for deciding about the completeness of values in the cache: The process of using simple (existence) queries on the cache to decide about completeness is called *probing*; the queries used are called *probe queries* accordingly.

In contrast to DBCache [1], we use a new probing approach [3], which does not require new constraints and thus does not load extra records into the cache (as DBCache's cache keys do). The fundamental insight is that RCCs already provide guarantees about complete values in the cache: The source column $S.a$ of an RCC $S.a \rightarrow T.b$ (or more precisely, the values therein) controls which values are complete in its target column $T.b$. We therefore call $S.a$ a *control column* of $T.b$.

In general, any given column $S.c$ can have zero or more control columns. Whenever a column $S.c$ we would like to use as an entry point for a predicate $S.c = v$ has at least one control column, we can probe (i. e., check for the existence of value $v$) in the control columns of $S.c$. If we find $v$ in one of these columns, we know that it is value complete in $S.c$ and that we can correctly evaluate the predicate in the cache.

In our example in Fig. 1 the following five columns possess control columns and could thus serve as entry points: *P.aid*, *M.id*, *M.directed_by*, and *G.id* have one control column each, *C.zip* even three (*A.zip*, *D.zip*, and *M.zip*), which would require – in the worst case – to probe in all the three columns for a value.

Probing can be optimized if we can deduce that, at all times, a column can contain complete values only.

**Definition 3 (Column completeness).** *A cache column S.c is said to be column complete (or complete for short) if and only if all values v in S.c are value complete.*

Given a complete column *S.c*, if a probe query confirms that value *v* is present in *S.c* (a single record suffices), we can be sure that *v* is value complete and thus evaluate *S.c* = *v* in the cache. Unique columns of a cache table are complete per definition. In contrast, non-unique columns are only complete under special conditions (or if completeness is enforced through additional cache constraints[4]).

You can show that a column *T.c* is complete (at all times) if

 – it is a U column,
 – it is a column with an (self-)RCC *T.c* → *T.c*, or
 – it is the only column in table *T* with incoming RCCs.

In our example, we have five U columns and one additional complete NU column, namely *P.aid*. Column *M.directed_by* is not complete, because table *M* is reached by another incoming RCC on column *M.id*.

The set of possible entry points is directly dependent on the cache group design. If an additional NU columns *c* seems to be beneficial as an entry point, because many queries refer to this column *c*, we may have to rethink our design and, for example, make *c* a filling column or add an RCC to *c*.[5]

**Probing Strategies.** When looking for an entry point for a predicate *S.c* = *v*, we have two kinds of probing operations at our disposal:

 – If *S.c* is column complete, we can probe directly in *S.c*.
 – If *S.c* has at least one incoming RCC, we can probe in a control column of *S.c*.

We may choose between these two, based on the probing costs (e. g., is there an index on the probed column?). We may even apply a number of successive probing operations for a single entry point, thereby forming probing strategies. In this case, the order of the probing operations and their probabilities of success determine the average costs of the whole probing strategy.

### 2.3  Loading Predicate Extensions

To be able to evaluate a predicate *Q* in the cache, the cache manager must guarantee predicate completeness for *Q* by loading all required records into the cache tables.

---

[4] For example, DBCache's cache key columns are forcibly complete.
[5] Whether such a change really pays off has to be determined by cost models and measurements; cf. Sect. 3.6.

Following the RCCs, the cache manager can construct predicate extensions using only simple loading steps based on equality of values.

Obviously, there must be some way to tell the cache manager which predicate extensions to load. In essence, this means placing single values into specific cache columns, from where the cache manager will fill the cache, guided by the cache constraints.

**Candidate Values in Filling Columns.** Besides RCCs, a second type of cache object is needed in order to establish a parameterized loading mechanism: Attached to selected *filling columns* are sets of *candidate values* (CVs), which alone initiate the loading of predicate extensions when they are referenced by user queries.

The set of all candidate values of a filling column $S.f$ is denoted by $C_{S.f}$ and is always a subset of $S_B.f$'s domain. Whenever a candidate value $v$ in $C_{S.f}$ occurs in an equality predicate of a query ($S.f = v$), the cache manager probes the respective cache table as usual to see whether this value is present: A successful probe query (the value $v$ is found) implies that the predicate extension for the given equality query is in the cache and that this query can be evaluated locally. Otherwise, the query is sent to the backend to continue processing.

As a further consequence of this cache miss attributed to $v$, the cache manager satisfies the value completeness for $v$ asynchronously by fetching all required records from the backend and loading them into the respective cache table. It then proceeds to restore the validity of all RCCs by loading the necessary records into the remaining tables. Hence, the cache is ready to answer the corresponding equality query locally from then on as well as all queries anchored by it.

Apparently, a reference to a candidate value $v$ serves as a kind of indicator that, in the immediate future, locality of reference is expected on the predicate extension determined by $v$. Candidate values therefore carry information about the future workload and sensitively influence caching performance. Hence, candidate values must be selected carefully. In a straightforward case, the database administrator (DBA) specifies the set of candidate values (e. g., as the domain itself, an enumeration, a range, or as other predicates) positively or negatively (stop-words). Which candidate values are actually placed into the cache depends on the query load, which makes this caching scheme adaptive. In an advanced scheme, the cache manager itself takes care, by monitoring the query load, that only those values with high re-reference probability become and stay candidate values: This adds a second level of adaptivity.

**Master Control Columns.** The subset of candidate values of a filling column $S.f$ that have already been referenced and therefore actually are in the cache controls which values are complete in $S.f$ and, hence, behaves similar to the contents of a control column. To allow uniform treatment of all cache columns with regard to probing and filling, we introduce an *artificial* control column $\text{ctrl}(f)$ for each filling column $f$.

This *master control column* $\text{ctrl}(f)$ is a U column of a separate, anonymous (master control) table with an RCC $\text{ctrl}(f) \rightarrow f$ pointing to the filling column $f$.

Having made this step, we can simply regard the domain of $\text{ctrl}(f)$ as the set of candidate values of $f$, whereas the actual contents of column $\text{ctrl}(f)$ (i. e., some of the candidate values) determines which predicate extensions are in the cache. When looking for an entry point for a predicate $f = v$, we can use our regular probing strategies (and

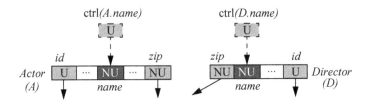

**Fig. 2.** Master control columns of filling columns

probe in the control column $ctrl(f)$, for instance); in case of a cache miss, the value $v$ is inserted into the master control column $ctrl(f)$ from where the cache manager will start its loading steps to reestablish the validity of all cache constraints.

Now the only special thing about filling columns is their sensitivity to references of values in equality predicates, which leads to new values in their artificial control columns. With respect to probing, query evaluation, and even filling via RCCs they behave exactly like any other column.

Figure 2 shows the master control columns $ctrl(A.name)$ and $ctrl(D.name)$ for the two filling columns $A.name$ and $D.name$ (dark gray) of our example. Assume $A.name =$ 'Bond' is part of a predicate. Hence, the filling column $A.name$ is our potential entry point. We can now probe for 'Bond' in the control column of $A.name$, which happens to be the master control column $ctrl(A.name)$. If we find the value there, we can evaluate the predicate in the cache. If we do not, we must pass the predicate on to the backend, but can prepare for subsequent cache-based evaluations of the predicate by inserting 'Bond' into $ctrl(A.name)$.

With the master control columns in place, we can add the NU columns $A.name$ and $D.name$ to our set of potential entry points gathered in Sect. 2.2, which yields a total count of nine.

### 2.4 Cache Groups and Federations

In general, our caching mechanism supports PSJ queries that are characterized by predicate types of the form $(EP_1 \vee \ldots \vee EP_n) \wedge EJ_1 \wedge \ldots \wedge EJ_m$, where the $EP_i$, $1 \leq i \leq n$, are equality predicates on filling columns of a specific cache table called *root table* and the $EJ_j$, $1 \leq j \leq m$, correspond to RCCs that (transitively) connect the root table with the remaining cache tables involved. The resulting structure is called *cache group*, which is our unit of design to support a specific predicate type in the cache.

**Definition 4 (Cache group).** *A cache group is a collection of cache tables linked by a set of RCCs. A distinguished cache table is called the root table R of the cache group and holds one or more filling columns. The remaining cache tables are called member tables and must be reachable from R via RCCs.*

Whenever more than one basic predicate type should be supported in a cache, we have to consider the *federation* of cache groups overlapping in some tables. On the one hand, memory space may be saved in shared cache tables, but, on the other hand, implicit extension of one cache group by RCCs of another one may lead to the loading of many unwanted records into the cache.

In our example, cache group $G_1$ and $G_2$ are designed for the two predicate types

$$(A.name = v_1) \wedge A.id = P.aid \wedge P.mid = M.id \wedge M.genre = G.id \wedge A.zip = C.zip$$
$$(D.name = v_2) \wedge D.zip = C.zip \wedge D.id = M.directed\_by \wedge M.zip = C.zip$$

and share the member tables $C$ and $M$ in the federation (see Fig. 1).

### 2.5   Related Approaches

At first sight, DBCache [1,4] uses similar concepts to perform database caching with cache groups: The concept RCC and the basic method of determining predicates evaluable in the cache are the same. But DBCache does not use the concept of predicate extensions or predicate completeness to explain why the cache is structured as it is. It has no notion of master control columns or of probing in control columns in general and is restricted to complete columns (DBCache term: domain-complete columns) as potential entry points. To make at least filling columns complete, further constraints called cache keys are employed – they fail to separate values referenced and wanted to be complete in the cache (contents of our master control columns) from values that are in the cache because of other constraints and may thus lead to unwanted cache loading.

Our master control columns have been inspired by the *control tables* in the MTCache project [5,6], which are used in quite a similar way: There a set of stacked materialized views is used to describe the cache contents, each dependent on the contents of another view (which resembles RCCs) or ultimately on the contents of a control table.

## 3   Architecture of ACCache

The key idea of DB caching is to provide – close to the application server – a query processing facility, which must be transparent for the transaction programs requesting DBMS services. For developing an adequate architecture, it is reasonable to strive for a solution which is independent of a specific DBMS and exclusively rests on the availability of some SQL engine. Hence, it became obvious that we should go for a flexible solution based on middleware concepts. In this way, our work does not rely on the goodwill of a single manufacturer (which would require to massively modify and expand the code of an existing DBMS) and gains flexibility and openness thereby enabling the use of different DBMS engines at minimal porting costs. Furthermore, we have the opportunity to avoid the trade-offs and to combine – based on our concepts described in Sect. 2 – the advantages of different existing systems [1,5].

### 3.1   Component Architecture

Figure 3 illustrates the main tasks of our adaptive constraint-based caching system by its components providing the required services and their interaction. Cache transparency for the user is achieved through the JDBC interface, which accepts SQL statements and delivers results in the way the application program expects. All requests are passed on to some Query Worker, which analyzes them, regarding the cache's configuration and its current contents, and – if processing in the cache is possible – transforms them

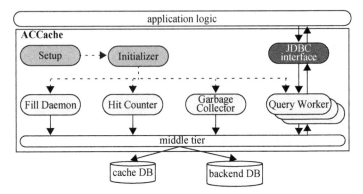

**Fig. 3.** Constraint-based caching system: Overview

such that references to cache and backend tables can be separated. Hence, the native federated query facility of the DBMS used [7] can distribute (appropriate parts of) the query statement to the cache DB and backend DB. Sending DB requests and receiving their results are handled by the middle tier thereby providing a uniform interface (to all ACCache components) and controlling all accesses to the underlying DBMSs.

The Setup and Initializer components perform the initial cache creation using a configuration file and possibly some initial cache filling. Cache maintenance and adaptivity is primarily accomplished by the Fill Daemon and the Garbage Collector whereas the Hit Counter is responsible for collecting reference statistics to enable accurate load/unload decisions.

### 3.2 Initializing DB Cache Processing

The Setup and Initializer components provide an administrator interface to ACCache. They enable the setup of a specific cache DB configuration and, for each operating session, the creation and initialization of appropriate data structures within ACCache. These data structures are used for keeping meta-data for the cache tables (table and column names, column types, RCCs, filling columns, etc.) as well as statistics for cache operation control.

The kernel part of the ACCache-internal data structure contains the object types illustrated in a UML class diagram in Fig. 4. A table object represents a pair of associated backend and cache table. For a column, the kind of information recorded is dependent on the role it plays: For example, if a filling column is specified, two additional table objects are created and referenced by this column object. The first one is a master control table carrying information about cached values in a filling column (value, loading time stamp, most recent reference, etc.), whereas the second one keeps all candidate values for the filling column (filling value table).

Cache DB setup requires the following essential steps:

– allocation of the specified cache tables and their related control tables: They can be created in any sequence, because foreign-key relationships are not maintained in the cache (but only RCCs)

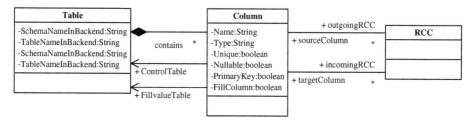

**Fig. 4.** Meta-data of the cache-related object types

- specification of filling value tables
- creation of appropriate indexes (on source columns of RCCs and on U columns) to speed up probe queries.

An important optimization feature is the use of prepared statements for probing, filling, and other housekeeping operations on the cache. Because of their frequency, these SQL operations should be highly optimized and ready for running when needed. Because all possible operations are known in advance – once a cache DB configuration is fixed –, they can be prepared in the form of query execution plans (QEPs) and kept ready as soon as the cache DB is set up. The ACCache components accessing the cache DB via the middle tier require four different types of SQL statements:

- existence queries, primarily used by the Query Workers for probing
- insert statements used by the Fill Daemon to load new records into cache tables
- update queries to modify information in control tables
- delete statements to unload records from cache tables.

### 3.3 Query Worker

The Query Worker component (QW) is responsible for the processing of user queries and therefore provides the key ACCache functionality. As shown in Fig. 3, several QW instances are managed in a pool at run time; a free QW is assigned to an arriving query and put back in the pool when finished. At first, a QW validates the request against a grammar of a subset of SQL. If no match is obtained, the query is passed on to the back-end DB. Otherwise, local processing is initiated which is only sketched in its essential steps. Assume the following query is a potential candidate for cache processing (see Fig. 1):

```
SELECT d.name, m.title, g.name
FROM Director d, Movie m, Genre g
WHERE d.id = m.directed_by AND m.genre = g.id AND d.id = '711'
ORDER BY g.name ASC
```

After checking for correct SQL syntax, the query is decomposed into its different clauses. At first, all table (and alias) names from the FROM clause are extracted. Then the WHERE clause is analyzed. For predicates of the form $column_i = column_j$ (equi-join predicate), QW checks whether an RCC exists between these columns. The data structure illustrated in Fig. 4 greatly supports the analysis. When an RCC is identified, QW

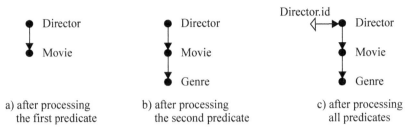

a) after processing          b) after processing          c) after processing
the first predicate          the second predicate         all predicates

**Fig. 5.** Anchoring of cache tables

creates/expands a directed graph – the so-called cache group evaluation graph (CEG) –, which receives the table names of the related columns as vertices. These table vertices are connected by a directed edge representing the direction of the RCC.

Figure 5 shows the result of the analysis process for our example. After two join predicates, QW extracts a predicate of the form $column_k = value$ which is considered as a potential entry point. Hence, QW initiates a probing process. If $column_k$ is a U column (like $d.id$), a probing query is sent to the cache DB. Otherwise, probing is performed on the source columns of incoming RCCs (see Sect. 2.2). The related existence queries probing potential entry points have the form

```
SELECT 1 FROM TABLE (VALUES 1) AS tmp
WHERE EXISTS (SELECT * FROM ⟨cache table⟩ WHERE ⟨column⟩ = ?)
```

As soon as a complete value is determined (assume, $d.id = $ '711' is in the cache), the probing process stops successfully. In this case, the column can be used as an entry point for the query: It is taken as an anchor for the related table and added/connected to the CEG. Depending on the query analyzed, several entry points attached to table vertices may exist. Obviously, all table vertices reachable from an entry point are automatically anchored. Hence, the CEG enables the generation of modified queries that are to be (partially) evaluated in the cache DB. For our example, the original query is rewritten to read

```
SELECT d.name, m.title, g.name
FROM CA_Director d, CA_Movie m, CA_Genre g
WHERE d.id = m.directed_by AND m.genre = g.id AND d.id = '711'
ORDER BY g.name ASC
```

where the prefix CA_ indicates a reference to a cache table. When the middle-tier component forwards the transformed query to the federated query facility, the entire query evaluation is performed in the cache DB in this case.

If probing fails, the value looked up is not complete in the cache. QW then checks whether the related column is a filling column and whether the value belongs to the candidate values. If so, a message is sent to the Fill Daemon to load this value into the cache.

### 3.4   Fill Daemon

Loading of records must be accomplished very carefully, that is, caching of duplicate records must be prevented and – after the filling process as a consequence of a CV reference is finished – all cache constraints must be satisfied by the state of the cache. The principal approach to loading predicate extensions has been discussed in Sect. 2.3. Here we outline its implementation.

Assume Actor name 'Bond' is included in the list of CVs, was referenced in a query, and was not found in the cache (see Fig. 1). Hence, the Fill Daemon will receive a message to make Actor name 'Bond' complete thereby loading the resp. predicate extension. Inserting 'Bond' into the control table implies loading the related Actor records which force Play and City records into the cache. The inserted Play records require the filling of Movie records and these, in turn, Genre and City records.

We have already mentioned that the insert statements for such a filling process are prepared by the Initializer component. However, these statements necessarily carry so-called markers (for actual parameters values) instead of concrete values. Hence, starting with the control table, we insert value 'Bond' and request all Actor records with name 'Bond' from the backend DB. These records are then inserted into the Actor table in the cache (bewaring of duplicates). Furthermore, they deliver the values replacing the markers in the prepare statements for Play and City, and so on.

**Top-Down Filling.** The filling process sketched so far iteratively loads a sequence of cache tables starting with the control table. This table sequence can be computed by recursively following the outgoing RCCs of each table visited. As an example, we list the insert statement for the Actor table:

```
INSERT INTO CA_Actor
SELECT * FROM Actor a
WHERE a.name = 'Bond'
AND a.name NOT IN (SELECT name FROM CA_Actor)
```

The entire filling process must be executed by a transaction whose insertions have to be protected by locks. Otherwise, parallel QWs could see inconsistent cache states which could lead to wrong query evaluations. For example, when inserting Actor record having $a.id =$ '007', the corresponding records are not present in cache table Play. Hence, "long" X locks must be kept until the filling process is successfully finished which, in turn, may block reader transactions for long time spans.

**Bottom-Up Filling.** A more sophisticated filling mechanism may avoid such situations. The key observation is that loading the cache tables bottom-up, we can fill each table in a separate transaction thereby providing cache consistency and only need to lock until the resp. cache table is loaded. More precisely, we have to define so-called atomic zones which can be loaded independently. In the simplest case, if no cycles are present, every cache table is an atomic zone. Due to space limitations, we cannot discuss cycle issues in detail and refer to [8]; suffice it to say that all tables belonging to an allowed cycle end up in the same atomic zone.

Figure 6 illustrates the atomic zones for the filling process of cache group $G_1$. The loading sequence of these zones can be determined by topological sorting which results for our example in: (Genre, City), Movie, Play, Actor, and finally the control table for *A.name*. Hence, after having finished loading of, say, cache table Genre, we can release the locks on Genre and let concurrent QWs run reader transactions on this table, and

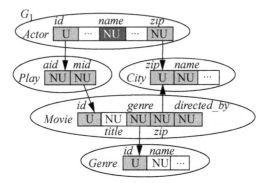

**Fig. 6.** Loading cache tables bottom-up

so on. However, to start the filling process with table Genre, we need to determine the records to be inserted. Therefore, we need to travel along the reverse RCC path from Genre up to Actor to select the Genre records depending on a CV to be filled in.

In the general case, the reverse RCC path be $R_n, R_{n-1}, \ldots, R_1$ where the target table of $R_n$ is the cache table to be filled and the source table of $R_1$ is the root table. Then, the prepared insert statements have the following generic form:

```
INSERT INTO ⟨cache table⟩ (
    SELECT * FROM ⟨corresponding backend table⟩ WHERE ⟨Rn target col.⟩ IN (
        SELECT ⟨Rn source col.⟩ FROM ⟨Rn source table⟩ WHERE ⟨Rn−1 target col.⟩ IN (
        ... SELECT ⟨R1 source col.⟩ FROM ⟨R1 source table⟩ WHERE ⟨filling col.⟩ = ?
        )
    )
)
```

If a cache table is reachable by several RCC paths, it may receive records via all these paths. Therefore, prepared insertion statements are generated for all these paths – done in a stereotypical way, as shown below.

Again, we illustrate the insertion statement for the first table to be loaded. The only marker to be replaced is 'Bond'.

```
INSERT INTO CA_Genre SELECT * FROM Genre g WHERE g.id IN (
    SELECT m.genre FROM Movie m WHERE m.id IN (
        SELECT p.mid FROM Play p WHERE p.aid IN (
            SELECT a.id FROM Actor a WHERE a.name = 'Bond'
        )
    )
) AND g.id NOT IN (SELECT id FROM CA_Genre)
```

Hence, bottom-up filling provides a trade-off between potentially higher concurrency during the filling process and the need for more complex queries to be evaluated in the backend DB.

## 3.5  Hit Counter and Garbage Collector

The Hit Counter (HC) is responsible for recording statistical data used by the Garbage Collector (GC) for its cache replacement strategy. It is implemented as a separate process owning a queue continuously monitored and emptied. QWs fill this queue with messages recording each entry point found while a query was analyzed. In all control tables, HC maintains statistical information on the (candidate) values which triggered the load of those values identified as potential entry points for a query. In particular, the columns *hitcounter* and *lastaccess* are incremented or modified.

GC is responsible for controlling the size of the cached data by periodically checking whether or not a pre-specified cache filling level (high-water mark) is observed. If this level is reached, GC initiates one or more deletions of cache instances by removing a CV from a control table. As a consequence, the entire predicate extension for the removed CV has to be deleted from the cache thereby preserving the cache constraints. Thus, records belonging to multiple predicate extensions must not be deleted. In such cases, records can leave the cache only if the last predicate extension they belong to is removed from the cache.

Again, the prepared statements for delete operations are generated by the Initializer. The concrete CVs to be replaced, however, are chosen by means of an LRU algorithm. As a victim, GC selects the entry from a control table which has the least recent time stamp in the *lastaccess* column. This CV replaces the marker in the prepared statement.

Deletion starts from the control table removing the selected LRU CV and proceeds to all connected cache tables via outgoing RCCs. As in case of cache loading, we exclude the discussion of cycles. Assume, we want to remove the predicate extension for $D.name = $ 'Spielberg' in cache group $G_2$ (see Fig. 1). After 'Spielberg' is not in master control table, say $K_1$, anymore, the records in cache table Director are removed by:

```
DELETE FROM CA_Director
WHERE (name IS NOT IN (SELECT name FROM K1))
```

The deletion procedure has to follow all RCC paths starting from the root table. The prepared statements to be applied have the following generic form where corresponding expressions have to be generated and ANDed for each incoming RCC of a cache table. Hence, the base template is

```
DELETE FROM ⟨cache table⟩
WHERE (⟨RCC target column⟩ IS NOT IN (
  SELECT ⟨RCC source column⟩ FROM ⟨RCC source table⟩)
)
```

which can easily applied to cache table Movie. Removing records from City with two incoming RCCs requires the following statement:

```
DELETE FROM CA_City
WHERE (zip IS NOT IN (SELECT zip FROM CA_Movie))
  AND (zip IS NOT IN (SELECT zip FROM Director))
```

At this point, you might wonder whether or not the deletion procedure is complete. What happens to RCC-dependent records in table Genre?

### 3.6   Savings and Penalties in Cache Group Federations

So far, we have discussed the management of single cache groups. As our running example in Fig. 1 reveals, it may be sometimes beneficial to allocate multiple overlapping cache groups in a federation. This design was influenced by the transparency requirements for cache tables which demand that each table (logically) appears only once in the cache.

For example, $G_1$ and $G_2$ share the tables Movie and City, which may save multiple representations of the same records. However, loading of records intended for one cache group may unintentionally cause records to be loaded in other cache groups. For example, table Genre only belongs to $G_1$. However, it is RCC-connected to table Movie to be loaded in $G_1$ and $G_2$. Hence, to preserve the RCC constraint, Genre may have to be filled whenever new records appear in table Movie. Therefore, loading a new predicate extension in $G_2$ may enforce records into Genre (in $G_1$) – only to satisfy all cache constraints.

Hence, if we load a new predicate extension into $G_2$, ACCache may have to insert Genre records, too, that is, new records in Movie may imply via RCC $M.genre \rightarrow G.id$ the insertion of (unwanted) Genre records. Symmetrically, deletion of a predicate extension in $G_2$ may remove records from Movie. To keep the cache consistent, Genre records may have to be deleted, too. Thus, deletion statements must cover all cache tables reachable by RCC paths starting from the root table of $G_2$.

The penalty each group in a federation must pay can be considered as a "membership fee". Separate allocation of cache groups, however, does not offer a perfect solution either. In such cases, we necessarily create copies in the cache which have to be kept consistent. For these reasons, savings and penalties of different solutions should be quantified, before a specific cache group design is chosen. Such an approach requires quantitative models for loading and unloading cache tables depending on specific workloads. A so-called cache group adviser could be a valuable tool for such design decisions. First steps in this direction are proposed by the authors in [9].

## 4   Summary

In this paper, we have primarily discussed the design and implementation issues of a middleware-based solution for database caching. For this reason, we have sketched our model for adaptive constraint-based caching and have emphasized the benefits and added value of this model as compared to the DBCache approach. The main part of our work has addressed our ACCache system which provides a database caching solution kept independent from specific DBMSs.

Our future work concentrates on optimization in ACCache. This includes the design of a suitable benchmark enabling representative performance measurements with comparable results and providing a refined exploration of federation issues. Moreover, these results could empower an adviser to support the specification of adequate configurations for cache groups and federations.

# References

1. Altinel, M., Bornhövd, C., Krishnamurthy, S., Mohan, C., Pirahesh, H., Reinwald, B.: Cache tables: Paving the way for an adaptive database cache. In: VLDB Conference. (2003) 718–729
2. Amiri, K., Park, S., Tewari, R., Padmanabhan, S.: DBProxy: A dynamic data cache for web applications. In: ICDE Conference. (2003) 821–831
3. Bühmann, A.: Einen Schritt zurück zum negativen Datenbank-Caching (A step back towards negative database caching). In: BTW Conference, Karlsruhe (2005) 107–124
4. Bornhövd, C., Altinel, M., Mohan, C., Pirahesh, H., Reinwald, B.: Adaptive database caching with DBCache. Data Engineering Bulletin **27**(2) (2004) 11–18
5. Larson, P., Goldstein, J., Zhou, J.: MTCache: Transparent mid-tier database caching in SQL server. In: ICDE Conference, IEEE Computer Society (2004) 177–189
6. Zhou, J., Larson, P., Goldstein, J.: Partially materialized views. Technical Report MSR-TR-2005-77, Microsoft Research (2005)
7. IBM: DB2 Universal Database (V 8.2) (2005)
8. Merker, C.: Konzeption und Realisierung eines Constraint-basierten Datenbank-Cache. Master's thesis, TU Kaiserslautern (2005)
9. Härder, T., Bühmann, A.: Database caching – Towards a cost model for populating cache groups. In: ADBIS Conference. Volume 3255 of LNCS., Budapest, Springer (2004) 215–229

# Integrating Caching Techniques on a Content Distribution Network

Konstantinos Stamos, George Pallis, and Athena Vakali

Department of Informatics
Aristotle University of Thessaloniki,
54124, Thessaloniki, Greece
kstamos@csd.auth.gr, gpallis@ccf.auth.gr, avakali@csd.auth.gr

**Abstract.** Web caching and replication tune capacity with performance and they have become essential components of the Web. In practice, caching and replication techniques have been applied in proxy servers and Content Distribution Networks (CDNs) respectively. In this paper, we investigate the benefits of integrating caching policies on a CDN' s infrastructure. Using a simulation testbed, our results indicate that there is much room for performance improvement in terms of perceived latency, hit ratio and byte hit ratio. Moreover, we show that the combination of caching with replication fortifies CDNs against flash crowd events.

## 1 Introduction

The rapid evolution of the Internet along with the increasing interest of the end-user for Web services has lead to the development of a wide variety of on-line applications (video-on-demand (VOD), e-commerce, information retrieval (IR), on-line gaming). Web sites (i.e. news sites), offering those services, have to deal with the increasing number of requests, whereas, on the server side, this results in increasing demand for processing time and overloading. On the end-user side, noticeable latency, connection interrupts and Denial of Service (DoS) are perceived due to network traffic and server overloading. For instance, in an application which gets real-time data from the NAS-DAQ Stock Market and makes buying decisions, delayed (stale) data will lead to misleading actions. In order to deal with such situations caching and replication have been proposed.

**The Caching Approach.** The key idea behind caching [10,22] is to keep content close to the end-user according to a cache replacement policy. Specifically, the end-user's request for an object is posed to a proxy server, which may contain a cached version of the object. If the proxy server contains a "fresh copy" of the requested object (cache hit) then the end-user receives it directly from the proxy cache, elsewhere (cache miss) the end-user is redirected to the origin server (where the Web site is located). Therefore both the bandwidth consumption and the network traffic are reduced [11,2]. Additionally, network availability is significantly improved since the end-user may receive a copy even if the origin server is unavailable. Another advantage of caching is that fresh content is added into the caches leading to better storage usage.

Y. Manolopoulos, J. Pokorný, and T. Sellis (Eds.): ADBIS 2006, LNCS 4152, pp. 200–215, 2006.

A complementary to caching technique is prefetching [14]. Prefetching is proposed to find meaningful object access patterns in order to predict future requests. Therefore, objects may be transferred to the proxy server a priori (before they are even requested).

**The Replication Approach.** The main idea is to bring static content replicas close to the end-user. This is currently applied in the Content Distribution Networks [16,23]. A CDN consists of a set of surrogate servers geographically distributed in the Web, which contain copies (replicas) of content belonging to the origin server (according to a specific storage capacity). Therefore, CDNs act as a network layer between the origin server and the end-users, for handling their requests. With this approach, content is located near to the end-user yielding low response times and high content availability since many replicas are distributed. The origin server is "relieved" from requests since the majority of them is handled by the CDN, whereas, Quality of Service (QoS) and efficiency are guaranteed in a scalable way. Finally an important characteristic of the CDNs is the efficiency against flash crowd events [25]. Specifically, a flash crowd event occurs when unpredictably numerous users access a Web site. Events that affect global communities (i.e. Sept. 11th, Tsunamis etc) lead to flash crowd events affecting popular news Web sites. The side effects are significant: DoS, increased network latency and Web servers overloading. Therefore it is important to enhance content delivery management especially in unpredictable crisis situations.

Caching and replication deals with situation as separate approaches. While caching is mainly addressed to proxy servers, replication is the main technology of CDNs. However, implementing caching techniques over a CDN may improve performance by allowing fresh content to be replicated. In this paper, we focus on adapting representative cache replacement policies over a CDN along with replication. We explore the potential performance benefit in terms of perceived latency, hit ratio and byte hit ratio by using surrogate servers both as replicators and proxy caches. Caching and replication may benefit if used together, shown by our extensive experimentation using a detailed simulation model. Moreover, we demonstrate the robustness of the integrated approach in a CDN during a flash crowd event since it is a crucial issue.

The rest of this paper is organized as follows. In Sect. 2 we discuss the motivation of this work and present some previous related work. Section 3 formally presents the problem of content management in CDNs when using replication and caching. In Sect. 4 a brief description of the developed simulation model is given which has been used in order to perform the experiments presented in Sect. 5. Finally, the conclusion of this work and potential future work are given in Sect. 6.

## 2    Previous Work and Motivation

### 2.1    Previous Work

The performance of CDNs is affected by three main issues:

- **Surrogate servers placement over the network:** The optimal selection of proper spots over the network [12,19,20] where the surrogate servers should be placed yielding optimized performance. Algorithms that proposed to solve this problem are investigated in [19].

- **Content outsourcing:** The detection of the proper content for outsourcing[6]. Full mirroring is a naive approach because even if disk prices are continuously dropping, the sizes of Web objects increase and updating such a huge amount of Web objects is a cumbersome task.
- **Object replicas' placement:** Placing object replicas on surrogate servers [7,17,18,8] in a way that leads to optimized performance. Benchmarks of algorithms that manage this issue can be found in [7].

In this paper, we address the problems of object replicas selection and placement by applying caching policies integrated with the existing replication scheme. The problem of optimal content placement is proved to be NP-complete and therefore only heuristic approaches are feasible [7] such as Greedy Global algorithm. Greedy global recursively, for all objects and surrogate servers, detects the object that if placed at a specific surrogate server leads to optimized performance. Although Greedy Global seems to be the choice, its complexity is too high for applying a per-object placement on a large set of surrogate servers and objects. An alternative self-adaptive algorithm (lat-cdn) has been proposed in [17] that requires no other knowledge (such as recorded access logs) besides the network topology. The il2p algorithm [18] is proposed which takes into account the servers' load. Specifically, il2p using recursively two phases selects which object should be placed and where. During the first phase for each object the appropriate surrogate is selected minimizing network latency. Given the candidate pairs of (object, surrogate server), at the second phase, the one that yields the maximum utility value (depended on server's load) is selected.

Since CDNs have to deal with large amounts of data it is crucial to apply several data and communication management policies. Up to now, the uncooperative pull-based [23,26], cooperative pull-based [1], cooperative push-based and uncooperative push-based are the basic approaches, as reported in [16].

## 2.2  Motivation

The motivation of this work originates from the idea of improving a cooperative push based CDN by solving problems arising from pure replication. More specifically:

- Due to replication and distribution cost, a replicas' placement should be static for a large amount of time. This leads to unoptimized storage capacity usage since the surrogate servers would contain redundant content. If the end-users' access patterns change the replicas will no longer cover a large percentage of the requests. Besides replication no other action, such as replacement of unpopular objects by other currently popular, is performed.
- The placement of surrogate servers on the network is static reducing the flexibility of the CDN.

A possible brute-force solution to fight these drawbacks is to upgrade the Web servers and the network infrastructure. Faster Web servers and increased bandwidth solves the problem of fast data transfer and handling large amount of requests. However, this is a temporary solution. It includes increasing economic cost, since more and more resource-demanding services would emerge flooding again the network. Furthermore, it is not scalable since upgrading the hardware infrastructure is not always practically and economically feasible.

In order to deal with the static nature of the information stored on the surrogate servers we propose the integration of caching and replication. If replication and caching cooperate they may be beneficial since both deal with the same problem but from a different approach. Although caching may suffer from low hit ratio and byte hit ratio [11] (typically below 50%) the performance gain from static replication along with caching in terms of response time (as we will show in the experiments) is significant. An evaluation of caching and replication as seperate approaches in CDNs is covered in [9], where caching outperforms but replication is still preferred for content availability and reliability of service. In [3] authors proved that integrating a simple LRU with replication, on a CDN, via a hybrid greedy algorithm yields performance outperforming a pure caching or replication scheme. Specifically, in each iteration a benefit value for every server-object pair is assigned and the one that produces the best benefit is selected for replication. At the end of the algorithm a percentage of the available storage capacity is reserved by static content and the rest is available for LRU. However, the possibility of using various representative cache replacement policies is not examined and the proposed approach is not tested during flash crowd events.

To the best of our knowledge, in the past the possibility of using caching along with replication on CDNs has not been studied in more extend. Therefore, the challenge is to improve the performance by using caching and replication together. In the context of integrating caching policies on a CDN's infrastructure our primary contributions are:

- Extend the policies of content selection and placement on CDNs by adopting representative cache replacement techniques. We select the LRU, LFU and SIZE as representatives of the main categories of cache replacement algorithms namely *Recency, Frequency* and *Size based* [24].
- Develop a detailed trace-driven simulation environment to test the efficiency of the proposed integrated scheme. The development of such an environment is crucial since we can capture the behavior of a realistic CDN infrastructure. Moreover, we avoid the oversimplified approach of a hop-based implementation that may give misleading results.
- Provide extensive experimentation covering all the possible combinations with real and artificial datasets, using representative cache replacement policies and replication at different levels of integration showing that pure caching or replication cannot meet the performance benefit of the integrated method.
- Demonstrate results proving that the integration has superior performance during flash crowd events and address several considerations and future road maps for such an integrated approach.

## 3   Integrating Caching in a Cooperative Push-Based CDN

Here we formally propose the problem of content management on cooperative push-based CDNs using replication integrated with caching policies. We choose the cooperative push-based scheme since it has been proved in [7] that is optimal. According to this approach, replicas are selected and placed at the surrogates servers a priori. Then the surrogate servers cooperate with each other in order to reduce the response times and replication cost. Specifically, the end-users' requests are directed to the closest surrogate server. If the surrogate server contains the requested object then it is satisfied without causing traffic to the network backbone. Otherwise, the request is redirected to another server. The CDN may redirect the request to a surrogate server which contains the requested object or to the origin server, if the object is not outsourced at all. The bandwidth is shared among the surrogate servers and the objects replication redundancy is reduced.

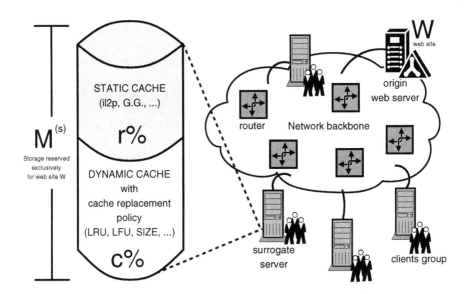

**Fig. 1.** CDN infrastructure

Here, we propose a modification of the cooperative push based scheme. Specifically, we consider the surrogate servers to operate both as static caches and proxy caches by partitioning the available storage capacity into two parts. The first one is used for replicating statically content and the second one for running a caching policy replicating content dynamically (Fig. 1). Assigning such a "dual" role to surrogate servers is feasible due to their increasing capacities and capabilities. When a surrogate server receives a request for an object a check to the static cache is performed. If it is a hit the request is served, else another check to the dynamic cache is performed. In case the object is in the dynamic cache, it is served and the cache is updated according to the cache replacement policy. If the requested object is not outsourced either in the dynamic cache, it is pulled from another server (selected based on proximity measures) and stored into the dynamic cache according to the current cache replacement policy and then the end-user receives the cached object. Therefore the end-user deals only with the nearest surrogate server and is not redirected elsewhere. Cached objects will be available in cache for future requests as long as they are allowed by the current cache replacement policy. The content of a surrogate server adapts to the current needs for objects and the static nature of replication is overcome. The surrogate server plays a more active role and performs content management deciding which object should remain or not. Furthermore, besides the static cache, the content selection and placement is automated and it fits to the current objects' access pattern. The reason to keep the static part of the cache, as we will prove in the experiments, is to maintain content availability by distributing a large number of replicas to the network.

**Table 1.** Variables description

| Variable | Description |
|---|---|
| $W$ | The Web site |
| $N$ | Number of objects of $W$ |
| $W^{(\text{s})}$ | Web site's size |
| $U_k^{(\text{s})}$ | Size of $k^{\text{th}}$ object |
| $M$ | Number of surrogate servers |
| $M_i$ | The $i^{\text{th}}$ surrogate server |
| $M_i^{(\text{s})}$ | Storage capacity of the $i^{\text{th}}$ surrogate server |
| $M^{(\text{s})}$ | Storage capacity of each surrogate server |
| $f_{ik}$ | Function indicating whether the $k^{\text{th}}$ object is placed at the $i^{\text{th}}$ surrogate server or not |
| $r$ | Percentage of the $M^{(\text{s})}$ for replication |
| $c$ | Percentage of the $M^{(\text{s})}$ for caching |

Therefore, consider a Web server representative who has signed a contract with the described CDN for outsourcing content of a Web site $W$. The Web site contains $N$ objects initially located only at the origin Web server (outside of the CDN). The total size of $W$ is $W^{(\text{s})}$ and is given by the following equation:

$$W^{(\text{s})} = \sum_{k=1}^{N} U_k^{(\text{s})} \tag{1}$$

where $U_k^{(\text{s})}$ is the size of the $k^{\text{th}}$ ($1 \leq k \leq N$) object.

Let $M$ be the number of surrogate servers consisting the CDN. Each surrogate server $M_i(1 \leq i \leq M)$ has a total cache size $M_i^{(\text{s})}$ dedicated (hired) for $W$. However, the surrogate servers may contain content from other Web sites without interfering with $M_i^{(\text{s})}$. The $M_i^{(\text{s})}$ is exclusively reserved for replicating content of $W$, of which the original copies are located in the origin Web server. For simplicity, we consider that the surrogate servers are homogeneous (same storage capacity $M_i^{(\text{s})} = M^{(\text{s})}(1 \leq i \leq M)$).

In order to apply replication and caching techniques the available storage capacity is split into two parts (Fig. 1):

- **Static cache:** Dedicated for replicating content statically. Its size is a percentage $r, (r \in [0..1])$ of $M^{(\text{s})}$. Therefore, the replicated objects, in static cache, obey the following constrain:

$$\sum_{k=1}^{N}(f_{ik}U_k^{(s)}) \leq rM^{(s)} \tag{2}$$

where $f_{ik}$ is a function denoting if an object exists (outsourced) in cache or not. Specifically, $f_{ik} = 1$ if the $k^{th}$ object is placed at the $i^{th}$ surrogate server and $f_{ik} = 0$ otherwise. The content of the static cache is defined by applying a replication algorithm like il2p.

- **Dynamic cache:** Reserved for applying cache replacement policies. The size reserved for dynamic caching is a percentage $c, (c \in [0..1])$ of $M^{(s)}$. More specifically, the stored objects respect the following storage capacity constrain:

$$\sum_{k=1}^{N}(f_{ik}U_k^{(s)}) \leq cM^{(s)} \tag{3}$$

Initially, the dynamic cache is empty since it is filled with content at run-time according to the selected cache replacement policy (upon misses).

Given the above cache segmentation scheme, the percentages $(r, c)$ and must obey the following:

$$r + c = 1 \tag{4}$$

If $c = 0$ the cooperative push-based scheme is applied where the pulled objects are not stored for future use (pure replication). If we set $r = 0$ the surrogate servers turns into cooperative proxy caches (dynamic caching only). For $c > 0$ and $r > 0$ we get the integrated approach where replication is used along with caching. Here the problem addressed is to select the optimal values for $r$ and $c$, given a replica placement and caching algorithm, which improves the performance of the CDN.

## 4   CDNsim: The Simulation Testbed

For the experimentation needs, we have implemented a complete simulation environment, called CDNsim. CDNsim simulates a main CDN infrastructure and is implemented in the C programming language. It is based on the ParaSol library[1] which provides a parallel and discrete event simulation environment. Further details about CDNsim along with the source code can be found at http://oswinds.csd.auth.gr/~cdnsim/. Due to space limitations, only the basic characteristics of the simulator are presented here.

CDNsim uses a network graph generated by the GT-ITM internetwork topology generator [27] in order to build the network backbone with a realistic TCP/IP protocol implementation. This includes packets routing, retransmissions on errors or DoS, finite bandwidth links, bottlenecks, etc. Packets routing is performed by following the shortest paths generated by the Dijkstra algorithm. The nodes of the generated network topology are assigned to specific network elements which include the following a) routers, b) surrogate servers, c) origins servers and d) client groups (clients grouped according to their domains). Communication via routers causes the main network traffic and

---

[1] http://www.cs.purdue.edu/research/PaCS/parasol.html

perceived delays. Therefore, requests that lead to cache misses and must be pulled are "expensive" in order to be satisfied. We avoid the oversimplified approach of network latency depended only by the number of network-hops since we simulate a realistic network.

There are several clients' log files on the Web[2] but we do not have the respective Web sites' structure, and vice versa. Moreover, the CDN providers do not offer their log files. Therefore, we use articial workloads and Web sites. For that reason, we used the R-MAT Web site generator [5] and we assigned sizes to the objects according to the log-t distribution as described in [13]. For each of the generated sites we have produced a set of object requests using the generator presented in [14].

An issue that may affect the performance of a simulation is cache consistency. Since there is a certain amount of literature that deals with the problem of cache consistency we assume that there is implemented an appropriate mechanism like Web server invalidation [4] that ensures the freshness of the objects. Moreover the probability of requesting for a stale object is low because according to [15] the duration between two modifications in the same object is up to 24 hours.

## 5   Performance Evaluation and Experimentation

In this section we present results demonstrating the behavior of the integrated scheme in terms of mean response time, hit ratio and byte hit ratio. Section 5.1 summarizes the performance parameters evaluated in the experiments. In Sect. 5.2 the simulations' setup and the used datasets are described while Sect. 5.3 presents the experimentation.

### 5.1   Parameters

Here we briefly present the performance criteria used in the experiments, namely the a) mean response time, b) response time CDF, c) hit ratio and d) byte hit ratio. These criteria have been used since they are the most indicative ones for performance evaluation.

- **Mean response time.** This is the expected time for a request to be satisfied. It is the summation of all request times divided by their quantity. Low values denote that content is close to the end-user.
- **Response time CDF.** The Cumulative Distribution Function (CDF) in our experiments denotes the probability of having a response times lower or equal to a given response time. The goal of a CDN is to increase the probability of having response times around the lower bound of response times.
- **Hit ratio.** It is defined as the fraction of cache hits to the total number of requests. A high hit ratio indicates an effective cache replacement policy and defines an increased user servicing, reducing the average latency.
- **Byte hit ratio.** It is the hit ratio expressed in bytes. It is defined as the fraction of the total number of bytes that were requested and existed in cache to the number of bytes that were requested. A high byte hit ratio improves the network performance (i.e. bandwidth savings, low congestion etc.).

---

[2] Traces available in the Internet Traffic Archive: http://ita.ee.lbl.gov/html/traces.html

## 5.2 Simulation Configuration

**Network and CDN Topology.** Using the GT-ITM we have indicatively created an AS network topology with a total of 3037 nodes. Given a standard link speed of 1MB per second we have generated the shortest paths of all nodes to all nodes for optimal packets routing. A set of 20 surrogate servers is randomly attached in the existing network backbone.

For the experimentation needs we express $M^{(s)}$ as a percentage $p$ of the origin server's Web site size $W^{(s)}$ (i.e. $M^{(s)} = pW^{(s)}$). For the static cache, we have used the il2p algorithm since its complexity is acceptable on a per-object replication. Specifically, we follow the following steps to initialize and run the surrogate servers caches:

1. Initially the surrogate servers are empty. We set the $(r, c)$.
2. We fill the static cache specified by the $r$ by running the il2p algorithm.
3. We set the cache replacement policy for the dynamic cache specified by $c$. In our experiments the caching policy may be LRU, LFU or SIZE.

The $(r, c)$ pairs that we used for the simulator are i) (1,0) for pure replication, ii) (0.8,0.2), iii) (0.5, 0.5), iv) (0.2, 0.8) and v) (0, 1) for pure caching. Additionally for setting the upper and lower bound of performance we have configured CDNsim for full mirroring of the Web sites and then to have empty disks (caches) without possible addition of objects into the cache.

**Datasets.** With the above described configuration we present three experiments using three datasets. The first dataset concerns an artificial Web site of 2994 objects, size 746.86 MBs and set of 1969114 requests. We set $p = 0.15$ leading to a cache size of 112.03 MBs. As mentioned before, we had to use synthetic datasets due to the lack of real CDN traces. The second dataset includes the same Web site but it runs under a flash crowd event. We have shrunk the time window of the requests in order to increase their density and rate. This leads to greater network traffic since more packets travel simultaneously and the surrogate servers' load is increased because of the greater number of simultaneously active sessions. The final dataset is a real Web site. We have used the Standford's Web site [3] which contains 281904 objects and its size is 8.66 GBs. The number of requests is 3744460 and the $p = 0.015$, since it is much larger than the artificial Web sites, leading to storage capacity of 133,15 MBs. Table 2 summarizes the overall experimentation configuration.

## 5.3 Simulation Results

In this section we present the results and we compare the performance parameters of pure replication, pure caching and integration of replication with LRU, LFU and SIZE (representatives of *Recency, Frequency* and *Size based* policies [24]).

**Experiments Without Flash Crowd Event**
**Artificial Data.** The resulting mean response times are depicted in Fig. 2. The $x$ axis represents the integration level of replication and caching (the $(r, c)$ values) while the

---

[3] http://www.stanford.edu/~sdkamvar/research.html

**Table 2.** Experimentation configuration summary

| | |
|---|---|
| Network topology | AS 3037 nodes |
| Link speed | 1MB/s |
| $N$ | 20 |
| $(r, c)$ | (1, 0), (0.8, 0.2), (0.5, 0.5), (0.2, 0.8), (0, 1), full mirroring, empty disks |
| Rep. alg. | il2p |
| Caching policies | LRU, LFU, SIZE |
| Dataset 1 | Artificial, 2994 objects, 746.86 MBs, 1969114 reqs., $p = 0.15$ |
| Dataset 2 | Artificial, 2994 objects, 746.86 MBs, 1969114 reqs., $p = 0.15$, flash c.e. |
| Dataset 3 | Real, 281904 objects, 8.66 GB, 3744460 reqs., $p = 0.015$ |

$y$ axis is the resulting mean response times of the requests. The performance limits are bounded by the cases of full mirroring and empty disks. By using pure replication the mean response time is reduced significantly denoting that the existence of replicas on the network participates to the improvement of performance setting the limits of pure replication. However, there is still room for optimization. For the integration level where $(r, c) = (0.5, 0.5)$ the mean response times are reduced up to 40% compared to pure replication and 15% compared to pure caching, for all caching schemes. Reducing $c$ the results are gradually worsen for values of $c > 0.8$ meaning that there is still need for static replicas to exist. This behavior is presented also in Fig. 3 which shows the hit ratio at the $y$ axis and the integration level at $x$ axis. The combination of replication with SIZE outperforms all the other combinations in terms of hit ratio. The hit ratio gain may reach 70% compared to pure replication and around 10% compared to pure caching. Examining the byte hit ratio ($y$ axis) at Fig. 4 at different pairs of $(r, c)$ ($x$ axis), we can conclude that the performance gain in terms of byte hit ratio is not signifi-cant, however a gain around 10% is still possible with all cache replacement algorithms demonstrating the same behavior. Another illustration of the situaton is shown in Fig. 5. The $x$ axis contains the response times of all requests ascending while the $y$ represents the portion of requests that their response time is lower than a given value. The CDFs of the intergrated approach tend to fit the ideal situation of full mirroring with SIZE as the leading algorithm.

In this experiment we can conclude that LRU, LFU and SIZE has similar behavior in terms of mean response time, byte hit ratio and CDFs. The leading algorithm, in the hit ratio case, is SIZE which can be explained by the fact that SIZE favors smaller objects leading to increased number of objects in cache.

**Real Data.** The second experiment, given the same execution environment, is run with the Standfors's Web site. Figure 6 illustrates the mean response time. As we can see the pure replication is unable to offer considerable performance benefit. This can be explained by the fact that $W^{(s)} \gg M^{(s)}$, therefore a relatively small set of replicas cannot cover a large enough percentage of the requests. However, for $(r, c) = (0.8, 0.2)$ we get a 70% which is peak for all caching policies. Pure caching seems to be the choice here because the average object size is too small (around 33 Kb). Although the pure caching outperforms the use of integration is preferred because it has comparable results to the pure caching and distributes a number of replicas over the network increasing

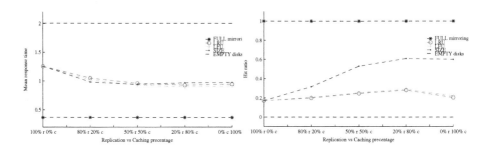

**Fig. 2.** Artificial Web site - Mean response time     **Fig. 3.** Artificial Web site - Hit ratio

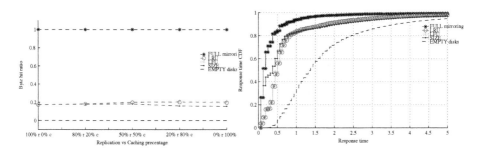

**Fig. 4.** Artificial Web site - Byte hit ratio     **Fig. 5.** Artificial Web site - CDF (r, c) = (0.5, 0.5)

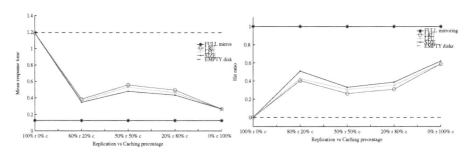

**Fig. 6.** Real Web site - Mean response time     **Fig. 7.** Real Web site - Hit ratio

content availability. Both in hit ratio Fig. 7 and byte hit ratio Fig. 8 the peak occurs at the same integration level $((r, c) = (0.8, 0.2))$ with SIZE slightly better in terms of hit ratio and worse in terms of byte hit ratio. At $(r, c) = (1.0, 0.0)$ the estimated values are quite low since the available storage capacity is too limiting and therefore the replica placement algorithm does not perform well. The reasons we have selected this storage capacity constrain $(p = 0.015)$ are: a) the il2p execution time for the real dataset was restricting and b) we would like to monitor the system performance with low cache sizes. It is clear that in low cache sizes caching is preferred since it updates the content

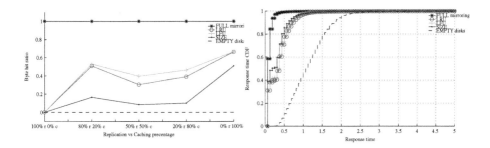

**Fig. 8.** Real Web site - Byte hit ratio

**Fig. 9.** Real Web site - CDF (r, c) = (0.8, 0.2)

while replication is not recommended since the static replicas cannot cover a satsifying portion of the requests. In Fig. 9 for $(r, c) = (0.8, 0.2)$ can the intergrated approach fits to the upper bound performance limit.

As a conclusion for this experiment, pure caching outperforms in case the objects have small sizes. However, at the integration level where $(r, c) = (0.8, 0.2)$, the results are comparable. As expected, LRU and LFU has similar behavior while SIZE is leading in terms of hit ratio and it is not recommended for optimizing byte hit ratio.

**Experiments with Flash Crowd Event**
As mentioned in the Introduction, it is crucial to enhance content delivery during flash crowd events. Therefore the integration of caching with replication should be tested appropriately.

**Artificial Data.** In this experiment we record the behavior of the CDN during a flash crowd event in the considered logs. The CDN's operation is intensive since a large amount of requests is served simultaneously. Figure 10 depicts the mean response times. The situation where the disks are empty leads to an unstable state where, as expected, increased response times are observed. In the case of full mirroring the performance is similar to the no flash crowd event case (Fig. 2) since the entire network backbone is skipped. Using pure replication an important performance benefit exists, however, now the response times are 100% larger than the no flash crowd event operation. For $(r, c) = (0.8, 0.2)$ the percieved mean response times are comparable to the ones depicted in Fig. 2 during no flash crowd event, meaning that the CDN copes with the flash crowd event efficiently. For LRU and LFU the performance of the model is the same as the no flash crowd event but for SIZE at $c > 0.2$ it is worse but still better than pure replication or caching. In terms of hit ratio (Fig. 11) the combination of SIZE with replication for $(r, c) = (0.2, 0.8)$ yields performance 60% greater than replication and around 8% better than caching. For this integration level, all caching policies reach peak in their performance. The expected byte hit ratio Fig. 12 seems to follow the same behavior just like the no flash crowd event case. Looking the model from the perspective of CDF Fig. 13 for $(r, c) = (0.8, 0.2)$ we notice that in the case of empty disks the distribution is uniform explained by the flash crowd event. For the inergated approach the choice algorithm is the SIZE.

Summarizing this experiment, during a flash crowd event the absence of a caching or replication mechanism leads to unacceptable response times. However, pure replication, as applied currently in CDNs, improves the performance. The performance may be significantly ameliorated using replication with caching showing the robustness of the integrated approach.

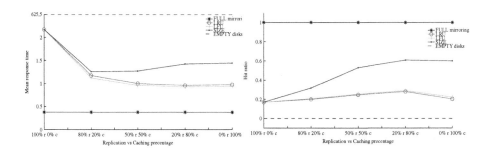

**Fig. 10.** Artificial Web site - Mean response time at flash crowd event

**Fig. 11.** Artificial Web site - Hit ratio at flash crowd event

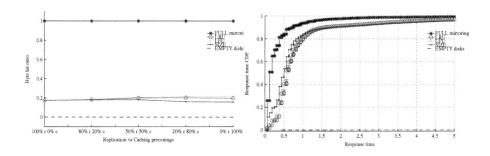

**Fig. 12.** Artificial Web site - Byte hit ratio at flash crowd event

**Fig. 13.** Artificial Web site - CDF (r, c) = (0.8, 0.2) at flash crow event

### Summary of Experiments

To summarize the experiments, we can conclude that the integration of replication with caching leads to improved performance in terms of perceived network latency, hit ratio and byte hit ratio. The results reinforce the initial intuition that replicating replicas statically for content availability along with caching policies improves the performance. Our experimentation has shown that:

– The integrated approach demonstrates mean response times up to 40% better than pure replication.

- A performance benefit of 15% may be achieved when compared with pure caching in terms of mean response time.
- Pure replication yields poor performance, 70% worse than the integrated approach, in terms of hit ratio.
- Pure caching demonstrates performance in hit ratio which may be 10% worse than the caching-replication combination.
- It can be observed in the experiments that there is not a fixed pair of $(r, s)$ that gives us the peak of performance.
- As presented in the experimentation , CDNs using the integrated approach, demonstrate improved performance during a flash crowd event, comparable to the case of a no flash crowd event.
- The performance peak appears to be independent from the selected cache replacement policy.

## 6   Conclusion and Future Work

This paper investigates the potential performance gain occurring by replication and caching if used together in a CDN. We offered an extensive set of experiments exploring the performance limitations. For the purposes of the experiments a detailed simulation environment has been developed. It has been shown that caching outperforms static content replication. Moreover, a possible integrated scheme outperforms the pure replication or caching scheme as separate implementations. CDNs may take advantage of the dynamic nature of cache replacement policies while maintaining static object replicas for availability, reliability and bounded update propagation cost. Finally our experiments shown that CDNs are effectively fortified against flash crowd events.

The integrated approach should be tested and applied on several network topologies such as ad-hoc mobile wireless networks [21]. Currently we are working on the extension of the replicas placement in terms of dynamic data and various dynamic parameters of QoS, since it is an open issue in this work. Moreover, the development of an automated mechanism for detecting the appropriate level of integration (i.e. $(r, c)$ pair) which leads to performance peak is crucial. Finally, another consideration is the implementation of a mechanism that dynamically recalculates the $(r, c)$ at run-time adapting to the varying needs.

## References

1. Annapureddy, S., Freedman, M.J., Mazières, D.: Shark: Scaling file servers via cooperative caching. In: 2nd Symposium on Networked Systems Design and Implementation, USENIX, ACM SIGCOMM, ACM SIGOPS (2005)
2. Arlitt, M., Friedrich, R., Jin, T.: Performance evaluation of Web proxy cache replacement policies. Lecture Notes in Computer Science **39** (2000) 149–164
3. Bakiras, S., Loukopoulos, T.: Increasing the performance of CDNs using replication and caching: A hybrid approach. In: 19th International Parallel and Distributed Processing Symposium, IEEE Computer Society (2005)
4. Cao, P., Liu, C.: Maintaining strong cache consistency in the world wide web. IEEE Transactions on Computers **47**(4) (1998) 445–457

5. Chakrabarti, D., Zhan, Y., Faloutsos, C.: R-MAT: A recursive model for graph mining. In: 4th SIAM International Conference on Data Mining, SIAM (2004)

6. Chen, Y., Qiu, L., Chen, W., Nguyen, L., Katz, R.H.: Clustering web content for efficient replication. In: 10th IEEE International Conference on Network Protocols, IEEE Computer Society (2002) 165–174

7. Jin, S., Wang, L.: Content and service replication strategies in multi-hop wireless mesh networks. In: 8th ACM International Symposium on Modeling, analysis and simulation of wireless and mobile systems, ACM Press (2005) 79–86

8. Karlsson, M., Karamanolis, C.: Choosing replica placement heuristics for wide-area systems. In: 24th International Conference on Distributed Computing Systems, IEEE Computer Society (2004) 350–359

9. Karlsson, M., Mahalingam, M.: Do we need replica placement algorithms in content delivery networks? In: 7th International Workshop on Web Content Caching and Distribution, IWCW (2002) 117–128

10. Katsaros, D., Manolopoulos, Y.: Caching in web memory hierarchies. In: 19th Annual ACM Symposium on Applied Computing, ACM Press (2004) 1109–1113

11. Kroeger, T.M., Long, D.D.E., Mogul, J.C.: Exploring the bounds of web latency reduction from caching and prefetching. In: USENIX Symposium on Internet Technologies and Systems, USENIX (1997)

12. Li, B., Deng, X., Golin, M.J., Sohraby, K.: On the optimal placement of web proxies in the internet: The linear topology. In: 8th International Conference on High Performance Networking, Kluwer, B.V. (1998) 485–495

13. Mitzenmacher, M., Tworetzky, B.: New models and methods for file size distributions. In: 41st Annual Allerton Conference on Communication, Control, and Computing. (2003) 603–612

14. Nanopoulos, A., Katsaros, D., Manolopoulos, Y.: A data mining algorithm for generalized web prefetching. IEEE Transactions on Knowledge and Data Engineering **15**(5) (2003) 1155–1169

15. Padmanabhan, V.N., Qiu, L.: The content and access dynamics of a busy web site: ndings and implications. In: ACM SIGCOMM Conference on Applications, Technologies, Architectures, and Protocols for Computer Communication, ACM Press (2000) 111–123

16. Pallis, G., Vakali, A.: Insight and perspectives for content delivery networks. Communications of the ACM **49**(1) (2006) 101–106

17. Pallis, G., Vakali, A., Stamos, K., Sidiropoulos, A., Katsaros, D., Manolopoulos, Y.: A latency-based object placement approach in content distribution networks. In: 3rd Latin American Web Congress, IEEE Computer Society (2005) 140–147

18. Pallis, G., Stamos, K., Vakali, A., Katsaros, D., Sidiropoulos, A., Manolopoulos, Y.: Replication based on objects load under a content distribution network. In: 22nd International Conference on Data Engineering Workshops, IEEE Computer Society (2006)

19. Tang, X., Xu, J.: QoS-aware replica placement for content distribution. IEEE Transactions on Parallel and Distributed Systems. **16**(10) (2005) 921–932

20. Szymaniak, M., Pierre, G., van Steen, M.: Latency-driven replica placement. In: International Symposium on Applications and the Internet, IEEE Computer Society (2005) 399–405

21. Tseng, Y.C., Ni, S.Y., Shih, E.Y.: Adaptive approaches to relieving broadcast storms in a wireless multihop mobile ad hoc network. In: 21st International Conference on Distributed Computing Systems, IEEE Computer Society (2001) 481–488

22. Vakali, A.: LRU-based algorithms for web cache replacement. In: 1st International Conference on Electronic Commerce and Web Technologies, Springer-Verlag (2000) 409–418

23. Vakali, A., Pallis, G.: Content delivery networks: Status and trends. IEEE Internet Computing **7**(6) (2003) 68–74

24. Wang, J.: A survey of web caching schemes for the internet. Computer Communication Review **29**(5) (1999) 36–46
25. Wang, L., Pai, V., Peterson, L.: The effectiveness of request redirection on cdn robustness. In: 5th Symposium on Operating System Design and Implementation, USENIX (2002) 345–360
26. Yu, H., Vahdat, A.: Minimal replication cost for availability. In: 21st Annual Symposium on Principles of Distributed Computing, ACM Press (2002) 98–107
27. Zegura, E.W., Calvert, K.L., Bhattacharjee, S.: How to model an internetwork. In: Conference on Computer Communications, Fifteenth Annual Joint Conference of the IEEE Computer and Communications Societies, Networking the Next Generation, IEEE (1996) 594–602

# Interactive Discovery and Composition of Complex Web Services

Sergey Stupnikov[1], Leonid Kalinichenko[1], and Stephane Bressan[2]

[1] Institute of Informatics Problems, Russian Academy of Science
{ssa, leonidk}@synth.ipi.ac.ru
[2] National University of Singapore
steph@nus.edu.sg

**Abstract.** Among the most important expected benefits of a global service oriented architecture leveraging web service standards is an increased level of automation in the discovery, composition, verification, monitoring and recovery of services for the realization of complex processes. Most existing works addressing this issue are based on the Ontology Web Language for Services (OWL-S) and founded on description logic. Because the discovery and composition tasks are designed to be fully automatic, the solutions are limited to the realization of rather simple processes. To overcome this deficiency, this paper proposes an approach in which service capability descriptions are based on full first order predicate logic and enable an interactive discovery and composition of services for the realization of complex processes. The proposed approach is well suited when automatic service discovery does not constitute an absolute requirement and the discovery can be done interactively (semi-automatically) with human expert intervention. Such applications are, for instance, often met in e-science. The proposed approach is an extension and adaptation of the compositional information systems development (CISD) method based on the SYNTHESIS language and previously proposed by some of the authors. The resulting method offers a canonical extensible object model with its formal automatic semantic interpretation in the Abstract Machine Notation (AMN) as well as reasoning capabilities applying AMN interactively to the discovery and composition of web services.

## 1 Introduction

The current Web service infrastructure offers syntactic interoperability by means of widely accepted standards such as the Web Services Description Language (WSDL1.1 [27]), the Universal Description, Discovery and Integration language (UDDI [26]) and the Simple Object Access Protocol (SOAP [21]).

Yet semantic interoperability is one of the most important expected features of a global service oriented architecture. In order to reach the necessary level of automation of service discovery, composition, verification, monitoring and recovery, a large body of research works aims at devising richer specifications providing for semantically well-founded reasoning about services. Many such approaches

Y. Manolopoulos, J. Pokorný, and T. Sellis (Eds.): ADBIS 2006, LNCS 4152, pp. 216–231, 2006.
© Springer-Verlag Berlin Heidelberg 2006

are based on OWL-S [17], a language for the semantic specification of services building upon OWL [16], the Ontology Web Language proposed by W3C. In OWL-S each service is provided with an advertisement containing three descriptions: *service profile* ("what the service does"), *service model* ("how the service works"), and *service grounding* ("how to access the service"). OWL-S and other similar languages assume mechanisms for their combined use with existing Web service standards such as UDDI and WSDL. The solutions proposed realize simple "on the fly" dynamic discovery – usually referred to as service matchmaking – and composition of services based on the service's capability descriptions, i.e. inputs, outputs, pre-conditions and effects (IOPEs) of a service [20].

Because of the limitations of the OWL description and of the reasoning mechanism based on description logic, and because the discovery and composition tasks are designed to be fully automatic, the solutions are limited to the realization of rather simple processes. Indeed, full automation applies to tractable problems (checking credit, simple procurement, etc.). Most importantly, such approaches do not apply to the problems of discovery and composition of services for the realization of complex processes that are in use in numerous application domains such as e-science.

In order to overcome this deficiency, this paper[1] proposes an approach in which IOPEs service capability descriptions based on full first order predicate logic that enable an interactive discovery and composition of services for the realization of complex processes. The proposed approach is well suited when automatic service discovery does not constitute an absolute requirement and the discovery can be done interactively (semi-automatically) with human expert intervention. The proposed approach extends and adapts the Compositional information systems Development (CISD) method [4] devised and proposed by some of the authors.

CISD is a method for the semantically correct composition of software components into coherent application. The CISD method is originally designed for object- oriented platforms such as CORBA, RMI and J2EE. CISD leverages an ontological model and a canonical object model, both based on the SYNTHESIS language [10], to offer a unified representation of both the new application (specification of requirement) and pre-existing components. Discovery and composition of components relevant to the application is realized in the framework offered by the domain ontology and the canonical object model.

In order to apply the CISD method to Web services, we have preliminarily defined in [5] a mapping of WSDL specifications into the canonical model. The basic steps for composing Web services by refining a specification of requirement were also demonstrated in [5].

In this paper, we concentrate on the discovery based on the IOPEs capabilities of services, putting aside other service properties (e.g., non functional properties) defined by other metadata facilities of the augmented UDDI. We use the canonical extensible object model of SYNTHESIS [10], its formal automatic

---

[1] This research has been partially supported by the grants 05-07-90413, 06-07-89188-a of the Russian Foundation for Basic Research and by NUS Eastern Europe Research Scientists & Students Exchange & Collaboration Programme (EERSS).

semantic interpretation in the Abstract Machine Notation (AMN) [2] and reasoning mechanisms obtained by applying AMN interactively. If a service is defined in WSDL or UDDI augmented with OWL-S, such definition is also assumed to be mapped into the canonical model. How to do such mapping for OWL is considered in detail in [12,15].

The paper is structured as follows. In Section 2 we give a brief introduction to the canonical model. We define the operations of the type composition calculus based on the *refinement*[2] relation. We show the need for a formal proof of the refinement relation between type specifications. B-Technology that implements AMN [1] is used for that purpose. We give a short characterization of AMN as well as of the program facilities that have been recently developed [24] for the automatic mapping of the canonical model specifications into AMN.

In Section 3, we present an example with two Web services. The first Web service is specified in OWL-S and WSDL. Pre-conditions and effects in this service are defined using Semantic Web Rule Language (SWRL) [25] which is tractable. The second Web service is described with formulae expressed in the canonical model to describe pre-conditions and effects. Such formulae are generally not tractable (as they make use of full first order predicate logic). Appropriate composition of services is realized by using the type specification calculus [11]. To show that the discovery of Web services is correct, we prove that a relevant type of specification of requirements is refined by the composition of Web services obtained. In Section 4, we illustrate an approach to the formal proof of this condition showing also some details of the mapping of the canonical model into AMN. In section 5, we survey the related work. In the conclusion section, we summarize the contribution of the paper.

## 2    Complex Service Discovery for Compositional IS Development

In CISD, the SYNTHESIS language is intended to provide a uniform (canonical) representation of heterogeneous data, programs and processes for their use as interoperable entities. Strongly typed, object-oriented subset of the language (as required in this paper) contains a universal constructor of arbitrary abstract data types, a comprehensive collection of the built-in types, as well as type expressions based on the operations of type calculus.

All operations over typed data in the SYNTHESIS language are represented by functions. Functions are given by predicative specifications expressed by mixed pre- and post-conditions formulae of typed first order predicate logic.

In the SYNTHESIS language the type specifications are syntactically represented by frames, their attributes by slots of the frames. Frames are embraced by figure brackets { and }, slots are represented as pairs ⟨*slot name*⟩ : ⟨*slot value*⟩ (a frame can be used as a slot value). Slots in a frame are separated by semi-colons.

---

[2] A non-formal definition of refinement is as follows. Type $A$ *refines* type $B$ if $A$ can be substituted instead of $B$ so that a user does not notice the difference.

Compositional development is a process of systematic manipulation and transformation of specifications. Type specifications of the SYNTHESIS language are chosen as the basic units for such manipulation. The manipulations required include decomposition of type specifications into consistent fragments, identification of reusable fragments, composition of identified fragments into specifications refining [2] the requirements, justification of the refinement relation reached. The compositional specification calculus [11], designed for such manipulations, uses the following concepts and operations.

**Definition 1.** *A* **signature** $\Sigma_T$ *of a type specification* $T = \langle V_T, O_T, I_T \rangle$ *includes a set of operation symbols* $O_T$ *indicating operation arguments and result types and a set of predicate symbols* $I_T$ *for invariants. Conjunction of all invariants in* $I_T$ *constitutes the type invariant* $Inv_T$. $O_T$ *is a union of type state attributes* $Att_T$ *and type methods* $Meth_T$. *Extent* $V_T$ *of the type* $T$ *(carrier of the type) is modeled by a set of admissible instances of the type. Each instance of the type is a tuple of pairs* $\langle a, v \rangle$ *such that* $a$ *is a state attribute of the type* $(a \in Att_T)$ *and* $v$ *is a value of the attribute. Every instance must satisfy the invariant* $Inv_T$.

**Definition 2.** *A* **type reduct** $R_T$ *is a subspecification of an abstract data type* $T$ *specification. A signature* $\Sigma'_T$ *of* $R_T$ *is a subsignature of* $\Sigma_T$ *including the extent* $V_T$, *a set of operation symbols* $O'_T \subseteq O_T$, *a set of symbols of invariants* $I'_T \subseteq I_T$.

The identification of a fragment of an existing component type that may be reused in the implementation of another type requires a *most common reduct* of these types to be constructed.

**Definition 3.** **Most common reduct** $R_{MC}(T_1, T_2)$ *for types* $T_1$ *and* $T_2$ *is a reduct* $R_{T_1}$ *of* $T_1$ *such that there exists a reduct* $R_{T_2}$ *of* $T_2$ *such that* $R_{T_2}$ *refines* $R_{T_1}$ *and there can be no other reduct* $R'_{T_1}$ *such that* $R_{MC}(T_1, T_2)$ *is a reduct of* $R'_{T_1}$, $R'_{T_1}$ *is not equal to* $R_{MC}(T_1, T_2)$ *and there exists* $R'_{T_2}$ *of* $T_2$ *that refines* $R'_{T_1}$.

**Definition 4.** *Type* $C$ *is a* **refinement** *of type* $R$ *iff:*

- *there exists an injective mapping* $Ops : O_R \to O_C$;
- *there exists a total abstraction function* $Abs : V_C \to V_R$;
- *for all* $v \in V_C$, $Inv_C(v)$ *implies* $Inv_R(Abs(v))$;
- *for all* $m \in Meth_R$, $m$ *is refined by* $Ops(m)$.

To establish a method refinement $m_1$ *refines* $m_2$ it is required that method pre-condition $pre(m_2)$ implies pre-condition $pre(m_1)$ and post-condition $post(m_1)$ implies post-condition $post(m_2)$.

The type calculus operations (such as *meet* and *join*) are used for the composition of identified reusable fragments into specification refining the specification of requirements. The *meet* operation $T_1 \sqcap T_2$ produces a type $T$ as an "intersection" of specifications of the operand types. The *join* operation $T_1 \sqcup T_2$ produces a type $T$ as a "join" of specifications of the operand types [11]. To save space, we provide a complete definition only for *join* operation.

**Definition 5.** *Generally type $T$ – a result of an operation $T_1 \sqcup T_2$ – includes a merge of specifications of $T_1$ and $T_2$. Common elements of specifications of $T_1$ and $T_2$ are included into the merge (resulting type) only once. Common elements of the types are defined by most common reducts $R_{MC}(T_1, T_2)$ and $R_{MC}(T_2, T_1)$. More formally $O_{T_1 \sqcup T_2}$ is defined as*

$$O_{T_1 \sqcup T_2} = (O_{T_1} \setminus O_{R_{MC}(T_1, T_2)}) \cup (O_{T_2} \setminus O_{R_{MC}(T_2, T_1)})$$

*Type invariant of $T$ is defined as a conjunction of operand types invariants $Inv_{T_1} \& Inv_{T_2}$.*

The most important stage of CISD is the proof of the refinement relation between requirement type $R$ and component composition of type $C$. Since predicative specifications of functions in the SYNTHESIS language are based on an undecidable first order logic, special methods and tools should be used for establishing of the refinement. In CISD for this purpose B-Technology [1] is used. B-Technology provides an implementation for formal specification language – Abstract Machine Notation (AMN) as well as tools (B-Toolkit[28]) for automatic/interactive proof of the refinement.

AMN [2] is based on the first order predicate logic and Zermelo-Frenkel set theory and enables to consider state space specifications and behavior specifications in an integrated way. The system state is specified by means of state variables and invariants over these variables, system behavior is specified by means of operations defined as generalized substitutions – a sort of predicate transformers. Refinement of AMN specifications is formalized as a set of refinement proof obligations – theorems of first order logic. Generally speaking in terms of pre- and post-conditions of operations, refinement of AMN machines means weakening pre-conditions and strengthening post-conditions of corresponding operations included in these constructions. Proof requests are automatically generated by B-Toolkit and should be proven with the help of B-Toolkit theorem prover.

To reduce refinement of SYNTHESIS type specifications to refinement of AMN specifications, specific program facilities were recently developed for automatic mapping of the canonical model (SYNTHESIS) specifications into AMN. These facilities were developed as a part of CISD tool [4] [5] and include a graphical user interface enabling an expert to select an appropriate type from the meta-information repository to map into AMN and a translator of the SYNTHESIS specifications into AMN. The paper introduces the principles of the canonical model into AMN mapping (section 4) and demonstrates their use for formal verification of complex services discovery and composition.

## 3   Specifications of Requirement and Web Services

Compositional development includes several stages mentioned on Fig. 1. In this paper we concentrate on the stage of formal verification of the refinement assuming the previous stages to be done and results obtained. The stage of formal verification is marked in grey on Fig. 1. Some details about the stages omitted including ontological relevance check can be found in [4][5].

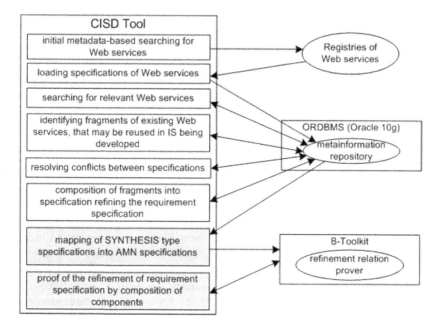

**Fig. 1.** CISD Tool structure

We shall consider formal verification of compositional development of a part of *Funding Agency* system managing finances aimed at support of research projects. A group of researchers prepares a proposal and registers it at the Funding Agency to obtain a grant. The funding Agency nominates experts to review proposals and decides whether to support a proposal or not.

As a example of a requirement specification consider the type `Secretary` of a Funding Agency system. A secretary of the agency identifies a set of available experts (`obtainExperts` method), searches for relevant experts and reports the number of relevant experts (`searchForExperts` method). An expert is considered to be relevant if her or his research area is `computer science`. The secretary selects some relevant experts to review a proposal (`dispatch` method). An expert can be selected to review a proposal if and only if her or his area of expertise is the same as the research area of the proposal. The area of expertise of an expert can be more specific than the research area of the expert, for example data mining can be an area of expertise.

`Secretary` type specification in the SYNTHESIS language is as follows.

```
{ Secretary; in: type;
  availableExperts: {set; type_of_element: Expert;};
  obtainExperts:  { in: function;
   params: {+exprts/{set; type_of_element: Expert;}};
   {{ this.availableExperts' = exprts }};
  };
  searchForExperts: { in: function; params: {-numberOfExperts/integer};
```

```
    {{ this.availableExperts' = {exp/Expert | in(exp, availableExperts) &
                                exp.researchArea = "computer sci"} &
       numberOfExperts = card(this.availableExperts')  }};
  };
  dispatch: { in: function; params: { +revi/Review };
    {{ ^isempty(this.availableExperts) &
         ex exp/Expert (in(exp, this.availableExperts) &
           exp.area_of_expertise = revi.forProposal.area &
           revi.byExpert' = exp)  }};
  };
}
```

Input and output parameters of methods are marked by + and − respectively, term `this` denotes a reference to an instance of a type for which a method is called. Terms marked by apostrophe refer to the post-state of the system, built-in boolean function `in` checks whether an item belongs to a set, `card` function returns a cardinality of a set, `isempty` function checks whether a set is empty, ˆ denotes logical not, `ex` denotes existential quantifier.

We can assume that, as a result of the primary stages of compositional development, two Web services have been chosen to be relevant to `Secretary` type (requirement).

A first service is `Dispatcher` service specified in OWL-S with grounding in WSDL. Pre-conditions and effects in this service are defined using SWRL [12]. To save space the `Dispatcher` service XML code is omitted:

```
<wsdl:portType name="Dispatcher">
  <wsdl:operation name="getExperts" ... </wsdl:operation>
  <wsdl:operation name="checkExpert" ... </wsdl:operation>
  <wsdl:operation name="countExperts"  </wsdl:operation>
</wsdl:portType>
```

`Dispatcher` looks for all the specialists which are potential experts (operation `getExperts`). After that `Dispatcher` considers potential experts one by one and chooses relevant experts such that their research field is `computer science` (`checkExpert` method) and reports the number of relevant experts (`countExperts` method). Semantics of `Dispatcher` service is provided by the OWL-S service profile specification. To save space this XML code is omitted.

A second service is the `Executive` service specified in the SYNTHESIS language and uses for pre-conditions and effects the formulae of the canonical model that is not tractable (as it uses full first order predicate logic). A specialist can be appointed to review a submission if and only if his/her field of expertise is the same as research field of submission, specialists with PhD degree are preferred (`appoint` method).

```
{ Executive; in: type;
  relevantExperts: {set; type_of_element: Specialist;};
  expertsChecked: boolean;
  appoint: {in: function; params: { +revi/Evaluation };
```

```
    {{ this.expertsChecked = true & ^isempty(this.relevantExperts) &
       ( ex exp/Specialist(in(exp, this.relevantExperts) &
            exp.fieldOfExpertise = ev.submRef.field &
            exp.degree = "PhD" & revi.bySpecialist' = exp)  |
       ( all exp/(Specialist)((in(exp, this.relevantExperts) &
            exp.fieldOfExpertise = revi.submRef.field) ->
                exp.degree <> "PhD") &
            ex exp/(Specialist)(in(exp, this.relevantExperts) &
            exp.fieldOfExpertise = revi.submRef.field &
            revi.bySpecialist' = exp) ) ) }};
    };
}
```

To satisfy the requirement specified by type `Secretary` it is required to create an appropriate composition of `Dispatcher` and `Executive` components. For this purpose WSDL+OWL-S specification of `Dispatcher` should be mapped into the `Dispatcher` type of the canonical model:

```
{ Dispatcher; in: type;
  experts: {set; type_of_element: Specialist;};
  expertsGot: boolean;
  relevantExperts: {set; type_of_element: Specialist;};
  expertsChecked: boolean;

  getExperts: { in: function; ... };
  checkExpert: { in: function; ... };
  countExperts: {in: function; params: {-numberOfExperts/integer};
   {{ isempty(this.experts) & this.expertsGot = true &
      numberOfExperts = card(this.relevantExperts) &
      this.expertsChecked' = true
   }};
  };
}
```

The required composition intended to refine `Secretary` type is the join of `Dispatcher` and `Executive` types that is `DispatcherJOINExecutive` type:

```
{ DispatcherJOINExecutive; in: type;
  experts: {set; type_of_element: Specialist;};
  expertsGot: boolean;
  relevantExperts: {set; type_of_element: Specialist;};
  expertsChecked: boolean;

  getExperts: { in: function; ... };
  checkExpert: { in: function; ... };
  countExperts: {in: function; ... };
  appoint: {in: function; ... };
}
```

Discovery of relevant services includes also the establishment of ontological relevance of structure and methods of requirement and component types.

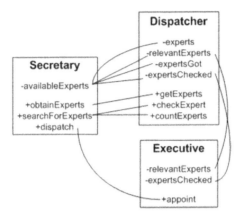

**Fig. 2.** Ontological relevance diagram

Specifications of requirement and pre-existing components must be associated with ontological contexts defining concepts of the respective subject areas. Here we assume that ontological concepts are described with their verbal definitions similarly to definitions of words in a dictionary. Fuzzy relationships between concepts of different contexts are established by calculating correlation coefficients between concepts on the basis of their verbal definitions. The correlation coefficients are calculated using the vector-space model [4]. This can be done with the help of CISD tool [4][5]. In this paper only the final picture of ontological relevance is presented on Fig. 2. Arcs on the figure denotes a relation of ontological relevance. For example, method `appoint` of type `Executive`, a pair of methods `checkExpert` and `countExpert`, four state attributes of type `Dispatcher` were established to be relevant to method `dispatch` of type `Secretary`, method `searchForExperts`, attribute `availableExperts` of type `Secretaty` respectively. Note that ontological relevance should be established also for types used in specification of requirement type `Secretary` (`Proposal`, `Expert`, `Review` types) and types used in composition of components type `Dispatcher` ⊔ `Executive` (`Submission`, `Specialist`, `Evaluation` types). In the example considered type `Proposal` was established to be relevant to the type `Submission`, type `Expert` – to the type `Specialist`, type `Review` – to the type `Evaluation`.

## 4   Formal Verification of Web Service Discovery

To show that the discovery of Web services is correct, we need to prove that a relevant type of specification of requirements `Secretary` is refined by the composition of Web services obtained (`Dispatcher` ⊔ `Executive`). To use automatic/interactive tools of B-technology for proving the refinement it is required to map `Secretary` and `Dispatcher` ⊔ `Executive` types into AMN.

In this section general principles underlying the mapping of the SYNTHESIS language into AMN is demonstrated by the example of mapping the `Secretary` type into AMN. Mapping of abstract types into AMN is based on extensional principle: every type is represented by its extent – a constant set of possible instances of the type. For a set of interrelated types a special AMN construction is provided, so-called *context machine*.

MACHINE *FundingAgency_structureContext*
SETS *AVAL*; ...
CONSTANTS *Obj*, ..., *ext_Review*, *ext_Secretary*, *ext_Expert*, ...
PROPERTIES $Obj \in POW(AVAL) \land ext\_Review \in POW(Obj) \land$
  $ext\_Secretary \in POW(Obj) \land ext\_Expert \in POW(Obj) ...$
END

It contains a definition of the extent of all object types – *Obj* which is a subset of the set of all abstract values (*AVAL*) expressible in the language and definitions of extents of all types required (*ext_Secretary*, *ext_Expert*, etc.). An extent of every type (for example, **Secretary**) is a subset of *Obj*: $ext\_Secretary \in POW(Obj)$. $POW(Obj)$ denotes a set of all subsets of the set *Obj*.

An abstract type is represented in AMN by a separate construction:

REFINEMENT *Secretary*
INCLUDES *Review*
SEES *String_TYPE*, *Bool_TYPE*, *Expert*, *FundingAgency_structureContext*, ...
VARIABLES *available_experts*
INVARIANT $available\_experts \in ext\_Secretary \rightarrow POW(ext\_Expert)$
OPERATIONS ...

REFINEMENT is the most universal AMN construction, since it can be used both as refined and as refining machine in the hierarchy of refinement. Therefore this construction is most preferable for homogeneous representation of abstract types in AMN. This construction is composed with context machine, with machines corresponding to other types used (**Expert**, **Review**, etc.) and to auxiliary constructions (*String_TYPE*, *Bool_TYPE*) with the help of AMN composition facilities (SEES, INCLUDES [2]).

State attributes of a type is represented in AMN by variables. Variables are appropriately typed as total functions from extent of the type into a type of the attribute in the INVARIANT section. Methods of a type are represented in AMN as operations defined as generalized substitutions [2]. Every operation is of sort

$$op = S$$

Here *op* is an operation signature, *S* is a substitution, defining the effect of the operation on the state space. The Generalized Substitution Language (GSL [2]) provides for description of transitions between system states. Each generalized substitution *S* defines a predicate transformer, linking some post-condition *R* with its *weakest* pre-condition $[S]R$. This guarantees preservation of *R* after the operation execution. In such case we say that *S* *establishes* *R*. We shall use substitutions given in the table 1.

Here $S$, $T$ stand for substitutions, $x, y, t$ are variables, $E, F$ denote expressions, $G$, $P$ are predicates, $P\{x \rightarrow E\}$ denotes predicate $P$ having all free occurrences of variable $x$ replaced by $E$.

**Table 1.** The Generalized substitutions and their semantics

| The generalized substitution $S$ | $[S]P$ |
|---|---|
| $x := E$ | $P\{x \rightarrow E\}$ |
| $x := E \parallel y := F$ | $[x, y := E, F]P$ |
| ANY $t$ WHERE $G$ THEN $T$ END | $\forall t \bullet (G \Rightarrow [T]P)$ |
| $S$ ; $T$ | $[S][T]P$ |

To save space full representation of a method by AMN operation is provided only for the method `searchForExperts` of the type `Secretary`.

$receiveExperts(av, expts) = \ldots$
$dispatch(av, revi) = \ldots$
$numberOfExperts \leftarrow searchForExperts(av) =$
PRE $av \in ext\_Secretary$ THEN
    ANY $v1, numberOfExperts1$ WHERE
        $v1 \in POW(ext\_Expert) \wedge numberOfExperts1 \in NAT \wedge$
        $\exists(exprts).(exprts \in POW(ext\_Expert) \wedge$
            $(exprts = \{exp \mid exp \in ext\_Expert \wedge exp \in availableExperts(av) \wedge$
                $researchArea(exp) = "computer \; sci"\} \wedge$
                $v1 = exprts \wedge numberOfExperts1 = \text{card}(exprts)))$
    THEN
        $availableExperts(av) := v1;$
        $numberOfExperts := numberOfExperts1$
    END
END

This example demonstrates some principles of mapping SYNTHESIS specifications of mixed pre and post-conditions of methods (formulae of typed first order logic) into AMN generalized substitutions. The general idea is to extract terms referring to the system post-state from a formula and replace them by auxiliary variables. In case of `searchForExperts` method these terms are `this.availableExperts`' and output parameter `numberOfExperts`. Auxiliary variables are $v1$ and $numberOfExperts1$. After that the formula should be transformed into AMN predicate: every term, built-in operation or logical operation of the formula should be transformed into AMN expression, built-in operation or logical operation. Note that every operation has an obligatory input parameter $av$ that denotes an instance of the type for which a method is called (parameter $av$ is a representation of `this` reference).

In the same way the composition type `Dispatcher` ⊔ `Executive` is mapped into AMN construction $DispatcherJOINExecutive$.

REFINEMENT *DispatcherJOINExecutive*
INCLUDES *Evaluation*
SEES *String_TYPE, Bool_TYPE, Submission, Expert, Specialist,*
   *FundingAgency_structureContext*
VARIABLES *dispatcher, relevantExperts, expertsGot, experts*
INVARIANT
   $dispatcher \in POW(ext\_Dispatcher) \wedge$
   $relevantExperts \in ext\_Dispatcher \rightarrow POW(ext\_Specialist) \wedge$
   $expertsGot \in ext\_Dispatcher \rightarrow BOOL \wedge$
   $experts \in ext\_Dispatcher \rightarrow POW(ext\_Specialist) \wedge \ldots$
OPERATIONS
$getExperts(av) = \ldots$
$numberOfExperts \leftarrow countExperts(av) =$
PRE $av \in ext\_Dispatcher$
THEN
   ANY $v1, numberOfExperts1$ WHERE
      $v1 \in BOOL \wedge numberOfExperts1 \in NAT \wedge experts(av) = \varnothing \wedge$
      $v1 = TRUE \wedge numberOfExperts1 = \text{card}(relevantExperts(av))$
   THEN
      $expertsGot(av) := v1; \ numberOfExperts := numberOfExperts1$
   END
END ;
$checkExpert(av) =$
PRE $av \in ext\_Dispatcher$
THEN
   ANY $v2, v1$ WHERE
      $v2 \in POW(ext\_Specialist) \wedge v1 \in POW(ext\_Specialist) \wedge \neg(experts(av) = \varnothing) \wedge$
      $\exists(exp).(exp \in ext\_Specialist \wedge exp \in experts(av) \wedge$
         $(researchField(exp) = "computer \ sci" \wedge v1 = \{exp\} \cup relevantExperts(av) \vee$
         $researchField(exp) \neq "computer \ sci" \wedge v1 = relevantExperts(av)) \wedge$
         $v2 = experts(av) \setminus \{exp\})$
   THEN
      $experts(av) := v2; \ relevantExperts(av) := v1$
   END
END ;
$appoint(av, revi) = \ldots$
END .

Mapping of services presented in the SYNTHESIS language into AMN is done automatically by means of mapping facilities developed as a part of CISD tool. These facilities implement principles introduced above.

The last stage of the proof consists in applying the automation facilities of B-Technology to prove that construction *Secretary* is refined by construction *DispatcherJOINExecutive*. Complex proofs are carried out with human expert intervention. We use B-Toolkit 5.4.1. In the example at hand, it automatically

formulated 20 theorems, expressing the fact that construction *Secretary* is refined by construction *DispatcherJOINExecutive*. Large number of theorems is
explained by automatically subdividing complex theorems by the tool into simpler ones to prove them independently. In the table 2 total number of theorems
formulated and number of theorems automatically proved are shown.

**Table 2.** The number of theorems

| | Number of theorems | Number of automatically proved theorems |
|---|---|---|
| Theorems of the initialisation refinement | 6 | 1 |
| Theorems of refinement for operation *getExperts* | 3 | 2 |
| Theorems of refinement for operation *checkExpert* | 4 | 3 |
| Theorems of refinement for operation *searchForExperts* | 2 | 1 |
| Theorems of refinement for operation *dispatch* | 5 | 3 |
| Total number of theorems | 20 | 10 |

Complete proof of all the refinement theorems make us sure that discovered
services and their proper composition implement the requirement specification.

## 5   Related Work

In order to enhance Web service descriptions, existing approaches extend UDDI
or WSDL. For instance, [23] combines OWL-S and UDDI by embedding an
OWL-S profile description into a UDDI data structure. The UDDI registry is
augmented with an OWL-S matchmaking component. [8] uses OWL-S profile
elements with no corresponding UDDI. It defines specialized UDDI T-Models
for each unmapped elements in the OWL-S Profile. Mechanisms for augmenting
WSDL to provide semantic descriptions and for enhancing UDDI to provide
semantic discovery are defined in [20]. Extensions to Web service description are
presented as annotated WSDL 1.1 files. The internal organization of UDDI data
structures are modified to act as place holders of semantic information [18]. In
the SYNTHESIS CISD we combine the canonical model and UDDI similarly to
[23].

A number of capability matching algorithms have been proposed for OWL-
S. They use the service descriptions in the Service Profiles and the ontologies
that are available to decide whether there is a match between service requests
and advertisements. A first family of approaches relies on an extensive ontology
where OWL ontological classes in request and advertisements are compared.
The matching process [13] is reduced to subsumption between the classes in the
ontology. Different degrees of matching can be detected.

A second family represents capabilities in terms of the state transformation.
The respective matchmakers [14][19][3][22] compare the state transformation described in each advertisement to the one described in the request. They compare

both outputs and inputs of the IOPEs. If the output required by the requester subsumes that of the advertisement, then the inputs are checked. If the inputs requested are subsumed by the input acceptable to the service, then the service is a candidate.

Distinctively, our approach uses a full first-order predicate language, which is more powerful than description logic as used in OWL-S. In our approach, it is possible to interactively prove a refinement relation between type specifications. Type specifications are used as ontological concept definitions as well as abstract specifications of services.

A Service aggregation matchmaking (SAM) [7] can be used to match queries with service registries enriched with OWL-S ontologies. SAM provides more flexible matching with respect to matchmakers of the entire services. It performs a fine-grained matching at the level of atomic processes and sub-services. It can return (when no full match is possible) a list of partial matches.

The service discovery approach proposed in our work is a significant Generalization of the SAM capabilities. According to the compositional calculus used, we discover the most common reduct (fragment) of request and advertisement services and try to construct a composition of such common reducts developed for existing advertisements that should refine the request [4].

## 6   Conclusion

In this paper we reported the latest results that we obtained extending the CISD method for compositional information systems development to the semantic composition of Web services. The CISD method has been developed for correct composition of software components. It was originally designed [4] for object-oriented platforms (like CORBA, RMI, J2EE). In CISD, an ontological model and a canonical object model (both based on the SYNTHESIS language) are used for the unified representation of the new application (specification of requirement) and of the pre-existing components. Discovering of components relevant to the application and producing their compositions are provided in frame of the domain ontology and the canonical object model. In 2003, we started to investigate the application of the CISD method to the composition of Web services. We studied the mapping of WSDL specifications into the canonical model and we defined the basic steps in the composition of Web services [5].

Meanwhile, the lack of semantic interoperability of Web service infrastructure motivated researchers to develop rich specifications catering for semantically well-founded reasoning about services. Focusing on the realization of complex processes and considering an interactive active approach that allows harnessing the intractability of full first order logic, we now present a novel approach extending and adapting CISD to web service composition. The approach leverages a mapping of the SYNTHESIS language into the Abstract Machine Notation (AMN). AMN is a formal method providing for interactive proof of a refinement relation between type specifications.

The paper shows by example how the CISD method extended with such mapping can be applied for interactive provable discovery of the application relevant complex Web services to develop their composition refining a specification of requirement. We are convinced that such approach can co-exist with approaches based on OWL-S or similar ideas for applications where automatic service discovery does not constitute the absolute requirement and can be done interactively (semi-automatic) with human expert intervention. We are currently applying the approach that we have presented to the composition of services in the e-science framework of the Virtual Observatory in astronomy [6] project.

# References

1. Abrial J.-R. B-Technology. Technical overview. – BP International Ltd., 1992.
2. Abrial. J.-R. The B-Book. – Cambridge University Press, 1996.
3. T. Andrews, et. al. Business Process Execution Language for Web Services // http://www-106.ibm.com/developerworks/webservices/library/ws-bpel/ – 2003.
4. Briukhov D.O., Kalinichenko L.A. Component-based information systems development tool supporting the SYNTHESIS design method // Advances in Databases and Information Systems: Proc. of the Second East European Conference. – Berlin-Heidelberg: Springer-Verlag, 1998. – P. 305-327.
5. Briukhov D.O., Kalinichenko L.A., Tyurin I.N. Extension of Compositional Information Systems Development for the Web Services Platform // Advances in Databases and Information Systems: Proc. of the Second East European Conference. – Berlin-Heidelberg: Springer-Verlag, 2003. – P. 16-29.
6. Briukhov D.O., Kalinichenko L.A. et. al. Information Infrastructure of the Russian Virtual Observatory (RVO). – http://synthesis.ipi.ac.ru/synthesis/publications/rvoii/rvoii.pdf – Moscow: IPI RAN, 2005. – 173 p.
7. A. Brogi, S. Corfini, R. Popescu. Composition-oriented Service Discovery // Department of Computer Science, University of Pisa.
8. Colgrave et. al. Using WSDL in a UDDI Registry // UDDI TC Note. – 2003.
9. D.Fensel, C. Bussler. Web Services Modeling Framework // Electronic Commerce: Research and Applications. – http://www.wsmo.org/papers/publications/wsmf.paper.pdf – 2002.
10. Kalinichenko L.A. SYNTHESIS: the language for description, design and programming of the heterogeneous interoperable information resource environment. – Moscow, 1995.
11. Kalinichenko L.A. Compositional Specification Calculus for Information Systems Development // Advances in Databases and Information Systems: Proc. of the 3rd East European Conference. – Berlin-Heidelberg: Springer-Verlag, 1999. – P. 317-331.
12. Kalinichenko L.A., Skvortsov N.A. Extensible ontological modeling framework for subject mediation // Proc. of the Fourth Russian Scientific Conference "DIGITAL LIBRARIES: Advanced Methods and Technologies, Digital Collections. – Dubna, 2002.
13. L. Li, I. Horrocks. A Software Framework for Matchmaking Based on Semantic Web Technology // Proc. 12th Internationall World Wide Web Conf. – 2003.
14. D. Martin, et. al. Bringing Semantics to Web Services: The OWL-S Approach // J. Cardoso and A. Sheth (Eds.): Proc. SWSWPC 2004, LNCS 3387. – Springer, 2005.
15. Kalinichenko L.A., Skvortsov N.A. Ontology reconciliation in terms of type refinement // Proc. of the Sixth Russian Conference on Digital Libraries RCDL2004. – Pushchino, 2004.

16. OWL Web Ontology Language Reference // http://www.w3.org/TR/owl-ref/
17. OWL-S Coalition. OWL-S 1.0 Release // http://www.daml.org/services/owl-s/ 1.0/
18. M. Paolucci, T. Kawamura, T. Payne, K. Sycara. Importing the Semantic Web in UDDI // Proc. of Web Services, E-Business and Semantic Web Workshop, CAiSE. – 2002.
19. M. Paolucci et al. Semantic Matching of Web Services Capabilities // The Semantic WebISWC 2002: First International Semantic Web Conf., LNCS 2342. - - Springer-Verlag, 2002.
20. P. Rajasekaran, J. Miller, K. Verma, A. Sheth. Enhancing Web Services Description and Discovery to Facilitate Composition // LSDIS Lab, Computer Science Department, University of Georgia. – Athens, 2004.
21. Simple Object Access Protocol (SOAP) 1.1 // W3C Note 08 May 2000. – http://www.w3.org/TR/SOAP/
22. E. Sirin, B. Parsia, J. Hendler. Filtering and Selecting Semantic Web Services with Interactive Composition Techniques // IEEE Intelligent Systems. – July/August 2004.
23. N. Srinivasan, M. Paolucci, K. Sycara. Adding OWL-S to UDDI, implementation and throughput // Robotics Institute, Carnegie Mellon University. – 2003.
24. S.A. Stupnikov. Automation of refinement verification in information systems compositional design// The Systems and Means of Informatics: Special Issue *Formal Methods and Models for Compositional Infrastructures of Distributed Information Systems.*— Moscow: IPI RAN, 2005. – P. 96-119. (In Russian)
25. SWRL: A Semantic Web Rule Language: Combining OWL and RuleML // W3C Member Submission 21 May 2004. – http://www.w3.org/Submission/SWRL/
26. UDDI Version 3.0 Specification // http://uddi.org/pubs/uddi_v3.htm
27. Web services description language (wsdl) 1.1 // W3C note 15 March 2001. – http://www.w3.org/tr/wsdl/
28. http://www.b-core.com/ONLINEDOC/BToolkit.html

# Efficient Processing SAPE Queries Using the Dynamic Labelling Structural Indexes[*]

Attila Kiss and Vu Le Anh

Department of Information Systems, Eötvös Loránd University, Hungary
kiss@ullman.inf.elte.hu, leanhvu@inf.elte.hu

**Abstract.** There are a variety of structural indexes which have been proposed to speed up path expression queries over XML data. They usually work by partitioning nodes in the data graph into equivalence classes and storing equivalence classes as index nodes. In most of current structural indexes, the nodes in the same partition have the same label. They are not flexible with queries containing the wild- or alternation cards, and sometimes their size is bigger than the necessity.

In this paper, we introduce the *dynamic labelling* structural indexes. These structural indexes only support a set of frequently used simple alternation path expressions (*SAPE* for short), where expressions may contain wild- or alternation cards. The labels of data nodes in the same partition may be different. The dynamic labelling not only decreases the size of the structural index, but also supports *SAPE's* better. Every static labelling structural index can be improved by using dynamic labelling. Because of the limitation, in this paper we just study the *DL-1*-index improved from the 1-index, and the *DL-A\*(k)*-index improved from the $A(k)$-index. The construction and refinement of these indexes are based on our results from the properties of partitions and the *split* operation. Our experiments show that the size of the improved dynamic labelling structural indexes is smaller and the query processing on these indexes is more efficient comparing to the naive ones.

## 1 Introduction

In recent years, the XML has become the dominant standard for exchanging and querying documents over the Internet. XML data is graph structured and self describing. There are a variety of query languages proposed to query XML [1,2,3,4]. *Path expressions* are the basic building blocks of XML queries. To summarize the structure of XML data and speed up path expression evaluation, the structural indexes have been proposed [5,6,7,8,9,10]. The query is processed on the index graph first, the answer is validated on the data graph if it is necessary. Usually, a structural index is a graph defined by an equivalence relation on the nodes of the data graph. Each index node corresponds to an equivalence class of data nodes. The equivalence relation used in structural indexes can be static

---

[*] The authors thank the (partial) support of the Hungarian National Office for Research and Technology under grant no.: RET14/2005.

Y. Manolopoulos, J. Pokorný, and T. Sellis (Eds.): ADBIS 2006, LNCS 4152, pp. 232–247, 2006.
© Springer-Verlag Berlin Heidelberg 2006

[5,6,9], which depends only on the data graph, or dynamic [7,8], which depends on the data graph and the query load (*a set of frequently used queries*). The most popular structural indexes are the 1-index [5], the $A(k)$-index [6] (static structural indexes), the $D(k)$-index [7], the $M(k)$-index and the $M^*(k)$-index [8] (adaptive structural indexes).

The 1-index is based on the notion of bisimulation. All nodes in the same index node have the same set of incoming label paths. Hence, we can evaluate accurately any path expression on the 1-index without validating on the data graph. However, the size of 1-index can be quite large. The $A(k)$-index is based on the notion of $k$-bisimilarity, which can be considered as weakening of the bisimulation. All nodes in the same index node have the same set of incoming label paths not longer than $k$. Thus with the $A(k)$-index all path expressions not longer than $k$ can be evaluated accurately. In the case the path expression is longer than $k$ we have to validate the answer on the data graph. The equivalence relation in $A(k)$-index is weaker than in the 1-index and the length of queries is often short in practice, so the size of the $A(k)$-index is also smaller than the 1-index's, and the queries evaluation is more efficient.

With the static nature, the 1-index and the $A(k)$-index treat all data nodes uniformly and do not support the query load, in which all structures do not have the same significance. The $D(k)$-, the $M(k)$- and the $M^*(k)$-indexes are based on the notion of the dynamic local similarity, which means different index nodes have different local similarity requirements that can be tailored to support a given set of frequently used path expressions. The values of $k$ depend on the length of the path expressions and they can be adjusted dynamically to adapt changing query load. The adaptive nature makes these indexes flexible and more effective and smaller than the static ones.

In above structural indexes, data nodes in the same index node must have the same label. They are static label structural indexes, in which the labels are uniform. When the query load is considered, specially if the queries contain the wild card or alternation card, the significance of labels are different. For example, let us see the Benchmark data set [13] with the path expression $//regions/*$ $/item$. The wild card ($*$) is matched by 6 data nodes, whose labels are *asia*, *africa*, *europe*, *namerica*, *samerica*, *australia*. They have similar meaning and structure but they are stored in 6 different index nodes because of the difference of their labels. Grouping them in a same index node not only decreases the cost of the query evaluation, but also decreases the size of the index graph. Moreover the labels, which do not occur in queries, should be grouped as an unique unused-label.

To overcome the above limitations, we introduce the dynamic labelling structural indexes. Not like previous adaptive indexes, in our scenario the frequently used path expressions may contain the wild or alternation cards, which are called *simple alternation path expressions* (or *SAPE* for short). In the same index node data nodes may have different label. Every static labelling structural indexes can be improved by using dynamic labelling. The construction and refinement of the improved indexes are based on our new results of studying *split* operation over partitions. Because the limitation of this paper, we just study the *DL-1*-index improved from the 1-index, and the *DL-A\*(k)*-index improved from the *A(k)*-index. However, most of dynamic labelling technics and spirits using for the improvement of other structural indexes can be found in two samples introduced in this paper, the *DL-1*-index and the *DL-A\*(k)*-index.

We introduce and study the *stable structural indexes*. The 1-index is a special stable structural index, which supports any *SAPE*. The *DL-1*-index is also a stable structural index, but supports only a finite set of *SAPE*'s. Our refinement and construction algorithms guarantee that the 1-index is a refinement of the *DL-1*-index, and the size of the *DL-1*-index is bound by the size of the 1-index.

The *DL-A\*(k)*-index supports a finite set of *SAPE*'s, which are not longer than $k$. The *DL-A\*(k)*-index does not contain only the $k$ similarity index graph like the *A(k)*-index, but also stores ancestor bisimilarity layers. In literature, the *A(k)*-index is determined by only one equivalence relation and the *DL-A\*(k)*-index is determined by $k$ equivalence relations. Astonishingly, the cost of query processing on the *DL-A\*(k)*-index is quite more efficient than on the *A(k)*-index. The $i$-th layer of the *DL-A\*(k)*-index is a $i$-bisimilarity and it is a refinement of $(i-1)$-th layer. Our refinement and construction algorithms guarantee that the *A(i)*-index is a refinement of the $i$-th layer, and the size of the $i$-th layer is bound by the size of the *A(i)*-index.

The remainder of the paper is organized as follows. Section 2 is the preliminary. In section 3, we study partitions and the *split* operation. In section 4, we introduce and study the *DL-1*-index. In section 5, we introduce and study the *DL-A\*(k)*-index. In section 6, we present our experiments. Section 7 concludes the paper.

## 2    Preliminaries

### 2.1    Data Model and Simple Alternation Path Expressions

We model XML or other semi structured data as a finite rooted directed labelled graph $\mathcal{G} = (V, E, \Sigma, r)$. $V$ is the finite set of data nodes. Each node $u \in V$ has a label $l = Label(u) \in \Sigma$. $E$ is the set of edges. $r$ is the single root of the graph, with no incoming edges and distinguished label, ROOT. We define $Succ(u) = \{v \in V | (u, v) \in E\}$, $Succ(W) = \bigcup_{u \in W} Succ(u)$ and $Label(W) = \bigcup_{u \in W} \{Label(u)\}$ $(W \subseteq V)$. An example data graph is shown in Figure 1. The dotted lines represent reference edges.

$Label^{-1}(S)$ $(S \subseteq \Sigma)$ denotes the set of data nodes $u$, in which $Label(u) \in S$. A *node path*, $p$, in the data graph $\mathcal{G}$ is a sequence of nodes, $u_0 u_1 ... u_l$, such that there exists an edge from $u_i$ to $u_{i+1}$ for each $0 \leq i \leq l - 1$. A *SAPE*, $R$, is a sequence of non-empty subsets of $\Sigma$, $S_0 S_1 ... S_l$, where $S_i \neq \varnothing$ and $S_i \subseteq \Sigma$ for each $0 \leq i \leq l$. A node path, $p$, *matches a SAPE*, $R$, if $Label(u_i) \in S_i$ for each $0 \leq i \leq l$. $l$ is the length of $p$ and $R$. $T_{\mathcal{G}}^i(R)$ denotes the set of the $i$-th data nodes $u_i$ of the node paths on $\mathcal{G}$ matching $R$. The *target set* of $R$ on $\mathcal{G}$ is the set of the end data nodes $u_l$ of the node paths on $\mathcal{G}$ matching $R$ $(T_{\mathcal{G}}^l(R))$, and it is also denoted by $T_{\mathcal{G}}(R)$. For example, in XPath syntax [4], the path expression

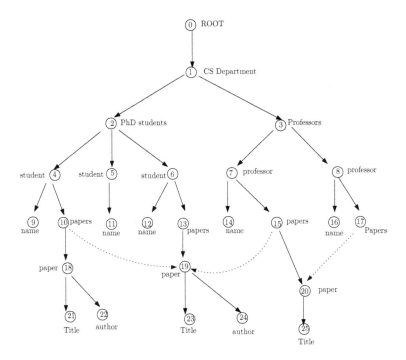

**Fig. 1.** An Example of Graph Structured Data

$/CSDepartment/*/*/name$ returns the target set $\{9, 11, 12, 14, 16\}$. In this paper, we focus on simple alternation path expressions.

## 2.2   Structural Indexes

In general, a structural index of the data graph $\mathcal{G}$ is a labelled directed graph $I(\mathcal{G}) = (V_I, E_I, \Sigma, r_I)$, which is built by the following general procedure: (1) partitioning the data nodes into classes according to some equivalence relation, (2) making an index node for each equivalence class, with all data nodes in this class being its extent, and (3) adding an index edge from index node $I$ to index node $J$ if there exists an edge from data node $u$ to data node $v$, where $u$ is an element of $I$ and $v$ is an element of $J$ . The root of the index graph is $r_I$, that contains only the root of data graph. In most of the previously introduced structural indexes data nodes in the same index node have the same label, and the label of an index node is defined as the label of data nodes in its extent. In our scenario the labels of the data nodes in the same index node may be different. An index node $U$ is labelled by $Label(U)$. In the case a dynamic labelling structural index is determined by several equivalence relations, each equivalence relation determines a data node partition and two different index nodes of two different partitions may have common element.

An *index node path* of the index graph $I_\mathcal{G}$, $U_0 U_1 \ldots U_l$, *matches* a *SAPE*, $R = S_0 S_1 \ldots S_l$, if $Label(U_i) \cap S_i \neq \emptyset$ for each $0 \leq i \leq l$. Similarly, we define

$T_{I_\mathcal{G}}(R)$ the *target set* of $R$ on $I_\mathcal{G}$, as the set of the end nodes of the node paths in $I_\mathcal{G}$ matching $R$. We say an index graph, $I_\mathcal{G}$, is *safe* with a *SAPE*, $R$, if for each data node, $u$, of the target set of $R$ on $\mathcal{G}$, $U$ is also an element of the target set of $R$ on $I_\mathcal{G}$, where $U$ is the index node containing $u$.

An index graph, $I_\mathcal{G}$, is *sound* with a *SAPE*, $R = S_0 S_1 \ldots S_l$, if for each index node, $U$, of the target set of $R$ on $I_\mathcal{G}$, all data nodes in its extent are also elements of the target set of $R$ on $\mathcal{G}$. A target index node $U$ of $R$ is *sound*, if there exists an index node path $U_0 U_1 \ldots U_l$ such that $U_l = U$ and $Label(U_i) \subseteq S_i$ for each $i = 0, \ldots, l$.

**Proposition 1.** *Let $U_0 U_1 \ldots U_l$ be an index node path, $u_0 u_1 \ldots u_l$ be a node path, in which $u_i \in U_i$ for each $i = 0, \ldots, l$; $R = S_0 S_1 \ldots S_l$ be a SAPE.*

*1. If $u_0 u_1 \ldots u_l$ matches $R$ then $U_0 U_1 \ldots U_l$ also matches $R$.*

*2. If $U_{i+1} \subseteq Succ(U_i)$ for each $i = 0, \ldots, l-1$ and $Label(U_i) \subseteq S_i$ for each $i = 0, \ldots, l$ then all data nodes in $U_l$ are elements of the target set of $R$.*

*Proof.* 1. $u_0 u_1 \ldots u_l$ matches $R$, so $Label(u_i) \in S_i$ and $Label(U_i) \cap S_i \neq \emptyset$ $(Label(u_i) \in Label(U_i) \cap S_i)$. Thus $U_0 U_1 \ldots U_l$ also matches $R$.

2. $U_{i+1} \subseteq Succ(U_i)$ implies that for each $u_{i+1} \in U_{i+1}$ there exists $u_i \in U_i$ such that $u_i u_{i+1}$ is an edge. Therefore, for each $u_l \in U_l$ there exists a node path $u_0 \ldots u_l$ such that $u_i \in U_i$. $Label(U_i) \subseteq S_i$ implies $Label(u_i) \in S_i$. Thus $u_l$ is an element of the target set of $R$.

Proposition 1 implies two following claims about the sufficient conditions for the *soundness* and the *safeness* of structural indexes.

**Claim 1.** $I_\mathcal{G}$ *is safe with any SAPE if the following condition is satisfied:*

*(i) For each index node $U$, data node $u \in U$ and edge $(u', u)$ there exists an index node $U'$ such that $U'$ contains $u$ and $(U', U)$ is an index edge.*

**Claim 2.** $I_\mathcal{G}$ *is sound with $R$ if two following conditions are satisfied:*

*(i) For each index edge $(U', U)$, we have $U \subseteq Succ(U')$ and*

*(ii) All target index nodes $U$ of $R$ on $I_\mathcal{G}$ are sound.*

# 3   Partitions and the *Split* Operation

## 3.1   Partitions

**Definition 1.** *We say $\mathcal{B} = \{B_i | i \in I, B_i \subseteq V(\mathcal{G}), B_i \neq \emptyset\}$ a **partition** over $V(\mathcal{G})$ if $V(\mathcal{G}) = \bigcup_{i \in I} B_i$ and for all $i, j \in I, i \neq j : B_i \cap B_j = \emptyset$.*

**Definition 2.** *Let $\mathcal{C}$ be a set of subsets of $V(\mathcal{G})$, $\mathcal{B}$ be a partition over $V(\mathcal{G})$. We say $\mathcal{B}$ is a **refinement** of $\mathcal{C}$ if for all $C \in \mathcal{C}, B \in \mathcal{B} : B \subseteq C$ or $B \cap C = \emptyset$.*

Clearly, $\mathcal{B}^* = \bigcup_{u \in V(\mathcal{G})} \{u\}$ is a refinement of any set of subsets of $V(\mathcal{G})$. As a special case of the refinement relation, we define the $\succeq$ relation over the set of partitions as follows.

**Definition 3.** $\mathcal{B}$ *and $\mathcal{B}'$ are partitions. $\mathcal{B}' \succeq \mathcal{B}$ if $\mathcal{B}'$ is a refinement of $\mathcal{B}$.*

*Remark 1.* 1. $\succeq$ is reflexive, transitive and antisymmetric relation.

2. $\mathcal{B}' \succeq \mathcal{B} \Leftrightarrow$ for all $B \in \mathcal{B}$, $B$ is the union of some elements of $\mathcal{B}'$.

**Definition 4.** *Let $\mathcal{C}$ be a set of subsets of $V(\mathcal{G})$. $\mathcal{B}$ is called **the coarsest refinement** of $\mathcal{C}$, if $\mathcal{B}$ is a refinement of $\mathcal{C}$ and for all partition $\mathcal{B}'$ being a refinement of $\mathcal{C}$ holds $\mathcal{B}' \succeq \mathcal{B}$. $CRF(\mathcal{C})$ denotes the coarsest refinement of $\mathcal{C}$.*

The following proposition shows the existence and the recursive construction of the coarsest refinement.

**Proposition 2.** *Let $\mathcal{B}$ be a partition, $C$ be a subset of $V(\mathcal{G})$, $\mathcal{C}$, $\mathcal{C}'$ be set of subsets of $V(\mathcal{G})$. Moreover, we assume that there exists $CRF(\mathcal{C}')$. We have:*

1. $CRF(\{C\}) = \{C, V(\mathcal{G}) \setminus C\} \setminus \{\emptyset\}$.
2. $CRF(\mathcal{B} \cup \{C\}) = \bigcup_{B \in \mathcal{B}} \{B \setminus C, B \cap C\} \setminus \{\emptyset\}$.
3. $CRF(\mathcal{C}' \cup \mathcal{C}) = CRF(CRF(\mathcal{C}') \cup \mathcal{C})$.

The definitions of the coarsest refinement and the partitions imply (1) and (2). The proof of (3) can be found at [16].

As a simple case, $CRF(\{\emptyset\}) = CRF(\{V(\mathcal{G})\}) = \{V(\mathcal{G})\}$. If $V(\mathcal{G}) = \{1, 2, 3, 4, 5, 6\}$ then $CRF(\{1, 2\}, \{2, 3\}, \{3, 4, 5\}) = \{\{1\}, \{2\}, \{3\}, \{4, 5\}, \{6\}\}$. Several trivial properties of the $CRF$ function are shown below.

*Remark 2.* 1. $CRF(\mathcal{C}) = \mathcal{C} \Leftrightarrow \mathcal{C}$ is a partition over $V(\mathcal{G})$.

2. If $\mathcal{C} \subseteq \mathcal{C}'$ then $CRF(\mathcal{C}') \succeq CRF(\mathcal{C})$.

3. $CRF(\mathcal{C}' \cup \mathcal{C}) = CRF(CRF(\mathcal{C}') \cup CRF(\mathcal{C}))$.

4. If $CRF(\mathcal{C}') \succeq CRF(\mathcal{C})$ then $CRF(\mathcal{C}' \cup \mathcal{C}'') \succeq CRF(\mathcal{C} \cup \mathcal{C}'')$.

## 3.2   The *Split* Operation

**Definition 5.** *Let $C$ be a subset of $V(\mathcal{G})$ and $\mathcal{C}$ be a set of subsets of $V(\mathcal{G})$. We define $Succ^0(C) = C$, $Succ^{k+1}(C) = Succ(Succ^k(C))$ and $Succ^k(\mathcal{C}) = \{C' | \exists C \in \mathcal{C} : C' = Succ^k(C)\}$ $(k \in \mathbb{N})$.*

**Definition 6.** *We define*

1. $split(\mathcal{C}) = CRF(\mathcal{C} \cup Succ(CRF(\mathcal{C})))$.
2. $split_0(\mathcal{C}) = CRF(\mathcal{C})$ and $split_{k+1}(\mathcal{C}) = split(split_k(\mathcal{C}))$ $(k \in \mathbb{N})$.
3. *We say partition $\mathcal{B}$ is **stable**, iff $split(\mathcal{P}) = \mathcal{B}$.*
4. *If there exists $k_0 \in \mathbb{N}$ such that for all $k \in \mathbb{N}$, $k \geq k_0$: $split_k(\mathcal{C}) = split_{k_0}(\mathcal{C})$ then let $split_\infty(\mathcal{C}) = split_{k_0}(\mathcal{C})$.*

The existence of $k_0$ in the definition of $split_\infty$ follows by the fact that $split_{k+1}(\mathcal{C})$ is a refinement of $split_k(\mathcal{C})$ and $V(\mathcal{G})$ is finite.

**Proposition 3.** *Let $\mathcal{B}$, $\mathcal{B}'$ be partitions and $\mathcal{B}' \succeq \mathcal{B}$. We have:*

1. *If $\mathcal{B}' \succeq split(\mathcal{B})$ then for all $B' \in \mathcal{B}'$ and $B \in \mathcal{B}$: $B' \cap Succ(B) = \emptyset$ or $B' \subseteq Succ(B)$.*
2. $split_k(\mathcal{B}') \succeq split_k(\mathcal{B})$ $(k \in \mathbb{N})$.
3. $split_\infty(\mathcal{B}') \succeq split_\infty(\mathcal{B})$.
4. *If $\mathcal{B}'$ is stable then $\mathcal{B}' \succeq split_\infty(\mathcal{B}) \succeq \mathcal{B}$.*

*Proof.* Because $\mathcal{B}' \succeq split(\mathcal{B}) \succeq CRF(Succ(\mathcal{B}))$ (Remark 2.2) so (1) is true.
(2) is proved by using induction. The full proof can be found at [16].
(2) implies (3) and (3) implies (4) directly.

Let $m$ be the number of edges and $n$ be the number of nodes of the data graph. The $split(\mathcal{C})$ can be computed with the complexity $O(m + n)$ by scanning only one time all edges and nodes. The $split_\infty(\mathcal{C})$ can be computed by using PT algorithm [11] with the complexity $O(m \, log \, n)$.

## 4    The *DL-1*-Index

### 4.1    The 1-Index and the Stable Structural Indexes

The equivalence relations in the 1-index [5] are *bisimilarity* relations, which are defined as follows:

**Definition 7.** *Two data nodes $u$ and $v$ are bisimilar ($u \approx v$), if*
*(1) they have the same label, and*
*(2) if $(u', u)$ is an edge, then there exists $v'$ such that $u' \approx v'$ and $(v', v)$ is also an edge, and vice versa.*

$\mathcal{P}_c$ is the partition determined by the equivalence $\approx_c$, where $u \approx_c v \Leftrightarrow Label(u) = Label(v)$. $\mathcal{P}$ is a partition determined by a bisimilarity relation. The first condition in definition 7 implies that $\mathcal{P} \succeq \mathcal{P}_c$, the second condition follows that $\mathcal{P}$ is *stable*. Proposition 3 implies that $\mathcal{P} \succeq split_\infty(\mathcal{P})$. Generally, $\mathcal{P}$ is a stable refinement of $split_\infty(\mathcal{P}_c)$, iff the associated equivalence relation is bisimilarity.

The set of index nodes of the 1-index is $split_\infty(\mathcal{P}_c)$. The 1-index is a special case of the stable structural indexes, which are defined as follows.

**Definition 8.** $I_\mathcal{G}$ *is a* **stable structural index**, *iff the set of index nodes is a stable partition and there is an index edge $(U', U)$ if there exists a data edge $(u', u)$ such that $u' \in U'$ and $u \in U$.*

All stable structural indexes satisfy the condition in Claim 1. Because the set of index nodes is a stable partition so Proposition 3 implies that for all index nodes $U$, $U'$: $U \cap Succ(U') = \emptyset$ or $U \subseteq Succ(U')$. Therefore all stable structural indexes also satisfy the first condition in Claim 2 for any *SAPE*. We say a stable structural index $I_\mathcal{G}$ *supports* a *SAPE R*, if it satisfies the second condition in Claim 2. Clearly, if $I_\mathcal{G}$ supports a *SAPE R* then it is safe and sound with $R$.

With the 1-index for each index node $U_i$, we have $|Label(U_i)| = 1$ so if $Label(U_i) \cap S_i \neq \emptyset$ then $Label(U_i) \subseteq S_i$. Therefore the 1-index satisfies the second condition in Claim 2 for any *SAPE*. Hence *the 1-index is safe and sound with any* SAPE.

A stable structural index graph $I_\mathcal{G}$ is a *refinement* of the stable structural index graph $I'_\mathcal{G}$, if the data node partition of $I_\mathcal{G}$ is a refinement of the data node partition of $I'_\mathcal{G}$. We study the inheritance of the support of a *SAPE* between a stable structural index and its stable refinements in following proposition.

**Proposition 4.** *Let $I_\mathcal{G}$, $I'_\mathcal{G}$ be stable structural index graphes, in which $I_\mathcal{G}$ is a refinement of $I'_\mathcal{G}$, and $R = S_0 \ldots S_l$ be a SAPE. We have:*

*1. If $U_0 \ldots U_l$ is an index node path of $I_\mathcal{G}$ matching $R$ and $U'_0, \ldots, U'_l \in V(I'_\mathcal{G})$ such that $U_i \subseteq U'_i$, $0 \leq i \leq l$, then $U'_0 \ldots U'_l$ is also an index node path of $I'_\mathcal{G}$ matching $R$.*

*2. If $I'_\mathcal{G}$ supports $R$ then $I_\mathcal{G}$ supports $R$, too.*

The proof of Proposition 4 can be found at [16].

## 4.2   The *DL-1*-Index

*DL-1*-indexes are stable structural indexes, which support a given query finite set of *SAPE*'s. A *DL-1*-index is constructed as follows: (1) The set of index nodes of the initial *DL-1*-index is $split_\infty(\mathcal{P}_u)$, where $\mathcal{P}_u = \{V(\mathcal{G})\}$. (2) Using DL1-REFINE algorithm we refine the index step by step so that it supports a given finite set of *SAPE*'s. $\mathcal{P}_u$ is the coarsest partition so every stable structural index is a refinement of the initial structural index. The DL1-REFINE algorithm refines the index graph $I_\mathcal{G}$ to support a *SAPE* $R = S_0 \ldots S_l$.

> DL1-REFINE($I_\mathcal{G}$,$R$)
> **begin**
> 1.   $\mathcal{C} \leftarrow \{T_\mathcal{G}(R)\}$
> 2.   **for** $i \leftarrow 0$ **to** $l - 1$ **do**
> 3.       $\mathcal{C} \leftarrow \mathcal{C} \cup \{Extent(T^i_\mathcal{G}(R)) \cap Label^{-1}(S_i)\}$
> 4.   DL1-TOTALSPLIT($I_\mathcal{G}$, $\mathcal{C}$)
> 5.   $\mathcal{C} \leftarrow \emptyset$
> 6.   **for each** $U_0 \ldots U_l$ index node path matching $R$, and $U_l \cap T_\mathcal{G}(R) = \emptyset$ **do**
> 7.       **for** $i \leftarrow 0$ **to** $l - 1$ **do**
> 8.           $\mathcal{C} \leftarrow \mathcal{C} \cup \{U_i \cap Label^{-1}(S_i)\}$
> 9.   DL1-TOTALSPLIT($I_\mathcal{G}$, $\mathcal{C}$)
> **end**

> DL1-TOTALSPLIT($I_\mathcal{G}$, $\mathcal{C}$)
> **begin**
> 1.   $\mathcal{P}$ is the partition over data nodes
> 2.   $\mathcal{P} \leftarrow split_\infty(\mathcal{P} \cup \mathcal{C})$
> 3.   **for each** edge $(u', u)$ **do**
> 4.       $U$, $U'$ are index nodes such that $u \in U$ and $u' \in U'$
> 5.       **if** $\nexists$ an index edge from $U'$ to $U$ **then**
> 6.           Add an index edge from $U$ to $U'$
> **end**

The refinement algorithm has two phases. After the first phase (step 1-4.), *if $U$ is a target index node of $R$ on $I_\mathcal{G}$ and $U \cap T_\mathcal{G}(R) \neq \emptyset$ then $U$ is sound* . After the second phase (step 5-9.), *there is no false target index node*. It means: *there does not exist an index node $U$ of $I_\mathcal{G}$, such that $U$ is a target index node of $R$ and $U \cap T_\mathcal{G}(R) = \emptyset$*. Thus $I_\mathcal{G}$ supports $R$ after applying the DL1-REFINE algorithm.

Let us see the illustration for the *DL-1*-index and the DL1-REFINE algorithm which is shown in Figure 2. The data graph is represented in Figure 2(a) The

1-index and the data graph coincide. The initial *DL-1*-index is represented in Figure 2(b). The *DL-1*-index, which is constructed by refining the initial *DL-1*-index to support $R_1 = //(K|L)$ is represented in Figure 2(c). The *DL-1*-index, which is constructed by refining the *DL-1*-index in Figure 2(c) to support $R_2 = //(B|C)/E$ is represented in Figure 2(d). In the refinement to support $R_1$, we refine the index graph by using $\mathcal{C} = \{\{1,2\}\}$ at the first phase, the second phase is not necessary as there is no false target index node. In the refinement to support $R_2$, we refine the index graph by using $\mathcal{C} = \{\{5,6\},\{9,10\}\}$ at the first phase, but only the second phase changes the index graph to exclude the false target index node by using $\mathcal{C} = \{\{7\}\}$.

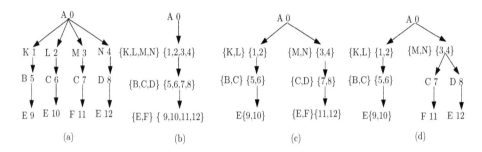

**Fig. 2.** An example of *DL-1*-indexes

**Proposition 5.** *$I_{\mathcal{G}}$ supports $R$ after applying the* DL1-REFINE *algorithm and if at the beginning the 1-index is a refinement of $I_{\mathcal{G}}$ then at the end the 1-index is still a refinement of $I_{\mathcal{G}}$.*

The proof of Proposition 5 can be found at [16]. The 1-index is a refinement of the initial *DL-1*-index so the 1-index is a refinement of all *DL-1*-indexes. The algorithms for evaluating a *SAPE* on index graph are quite similar to the algorithms for evaluating an simple path expression which are introduced and studied in [5,6,7].

## 5    The *DL-A\*(k)*-Index

### 5.1    The *A(k)*-Index, the *k*-Stable Structural Indexes

The equivalence relations in the *A(k)*-indexes [6] are *k-similarity* relations, which are defines inductively as follows:

**Definition 9.** *1. Two data nodes $u$ and $v$ are 0-bisimilar ($u \approx^0 v$), if they have the same label.*

*2. Two data nodes $u$ and $v$ are k-bisimilar ($u \approx^k v$) if*

*i. $u \approx^{k-1} v$ and*

*ii. for each edge $(u',u)$ there exists $v'$ such that $u' \approx^{k-1} v'$ and $(v',v)$ is also and edge, and vice versa.*

They shown that the partition created by the $k$-*similarity* is equal to $split_k(P_c)$ [6], which is defined as the set of index nodes of the $A(k)$-index. An index edge is added from index node $U'$ to index node $U$, iff there is exists an edge from $u' \in U'$ to $u \in U$. They also show that the $A(k)$-index is safe and sound with any *SAPE* not longer than $k$.

However the $A(k)$-index does not satisfies the first condition of Claim 2 as if $(U', U)$ is an index edge then $U$ may not be a subset of $Succ(U')$. We introduce and study the $k$-stable structural indexes, in which the first condition in Claim 2 is hold.

**Definition 10.** *A $k$-stable structural index is determined by* $(\mathcal{P}_0, \mathcal{P}_1, \ldots, \mathcal{P}_k)$ *partitions in which* $\mathcal{P}_{i+1} \preceq split(\mathcal{P}_i)$ *for each* $i = 0, \ldots, k - 1$. *The set of index nodes is* $V_I = \bigcup_{i=0}^{k} \mathcal{P}_i$. *An index edge is added from* $U'$ *to* $U$ *if there exists an edge from* $u' \in U'$ *to* $u \in U$ *and there exists* $i_0 \in \{0, 1, \ldots, k - 1\}$ *such that* $U' \in P_{i_0}$ *and* $U \in P_{i_0+1}$.

$\mathcal{P}_0, \mathcal{P}_1, \ldots, \mathcal{P}_{k-1}$ are called *ancestor partitions*. The condition $P_{i+1} \preceq split(P_i)$ and the definition of the index implies that if $(U', U)$ is an index edge then $U \subseteq Succ(U')$ (Proposition 3.1). Hence the $k$-stable structural indexes satisfy the first condition of Claim 2.

The $A(k)$-index stores information of all data node paths not longer than $k$, and only the $k$-bisimilarity partition is used for the query evaluation. With the $k$-stable structural indexes we store information of the most important data node paths not longer than $k$ determined by the set of given queries. By using the ancestor bisimilarity partitions the complexity of query evaluation is reduced. To avoid refining the ancestor bisimilarity partitions, we modify the definition of target index node of a SAPE $R = S_0 S_1 \ldots S_l$ ($l \leq k$) on a $k$-stable structural index by a plus condition that the target index node must be an element of $\mathcal{P}_k$. It implies that if $U_0 U_1 \ldots U_l$ matches $R$ and $U_l$ is a target node then $U_i \in \mathcal{P}_{k-l+i}$ for each $i = 0, \ldots, l$.

Similar to the *DL-1*-index, we say a $k$-stable structural index $A_{\mathcal{G}}$ supports a not longer than $k$ SAPE $R$, if the second condition in Claim 2 is satisfied. Clearly, if $A_{\mathcal{G}}$ supports a SAPE $R$ not longer than $k$ then it is safe and sound with $R$.

A $k$-stable structural index graph $A_{\mathcal{G}}$ determined by $(\mathcal{P}_0, \ldots, \mathcal{P}_k)$ is a refinement of the $k$-stable structural index graph $A'_{\mathcal{G}}$ determined by $(\mathcal{P}'_0, \ldots, \mathcal{P}'_k)$, if $\mathcal{P}_i$ is a refinement $\mathcal{P}'_i$ for each $i = 0, \ldots, k$. Similar to Proposition 4, the following proposition describes the inheritance of the support of a SAPE between a stable structural index and its stable refinements.

**Proposition 6.** *Let $A'_{\mathcal{G}}$ be $k$-stable structural index graphes, $A_{\mathcal{G}}$ be a refinement of $A'_{\mathcal{G}}$ and $R = S_0 \ldots S_l$ ($l \leq k$) be a SAPE. We have:*

*1. If $U_0 \ldots U_l$ is an index node path of $A_{\mathcal{G}}$ matching $R$ and $U'_0, \ldots, U'_l \in V(A'_{\mathcal{G}})$ such that $U_i \subseteq U'_i$, $0 \leq i \leq l$, then $U'_0 \ldots U'_l$ is also an index node path of $A'_{\mathcal{G}}$ matching $R$.*

*2. If $A'_{\mathcal{G}}$ supports $R$ then $A_{\mathcal{G}}$ supports $R$, too.*

The proof of Proposition 6 is quite similar to the proof of Proposition 4.

## 5.2  The *DL-A\*(k)*-Index

*DL-A\*(k)*-indexes are *k*-stable structural indexes, which support a given finite set of *SAPE*'s not longer than *k*. A *DL-A\*(k)*-index is constructed as follows:(1) The initial *DL-A\*(k)*-index is determined by $(\mathcal{P}_u, split(\mathcal{P}_u), \ldots, split_k(\mathcal{P}_u))$ (2) Using AK-REFINE algorithm we refine the index step by step so that it supports a given finite set of *SAPE*'s. We define $Extent_i(W) = \bigcup_{u \in W, U \in P_i, u \in U} U$. The AK-REFINE algorithm refining $A_{\mathcal{G}}$ to support $R = S_0 S_1 \ldots S_l$ ($l \leq k$) is shown as follows.

AK-REFINE($A_{\mathcal{G}}$,$R$)
**begin**
1.  $T_l \leftarrow T_{\mathcal{G}}(R)$
2.  **for** $i \leftarrow 0$ **to** $l - 1$ **do**
3.      $T_i \leftarrow \{Extent_{k-l+i}(T_{\mathcal{G}}^i(R)) \cap Label^{-1}(S_i)\}$
4.  **for** $i \leftarrow 0$ **to** $l$ **do**
5.      AK-SPLIT($A_{\mathcal{G}}$,$\{T_i\}$,$k - l + i$)
6.  AK-EDGE-CONSTRUCT($A_{\mathcal{G}}$)
7.  $T_i \leftarrow \emptyset$ ($i = 0, \ldots, l - 1$)
8.  **for each** $U_0 \ldots U_l$ index node path matching $R$, and $U_l \cap T_{\mathcal{G}}(R) = \emptyset$ **do**
9.      **for** $i \leftarrow 0$ **to** $l - 1$ **do**
10.         $T_i \leftarrow T_i \cup (U_i \cap Label^{-1}(S_i))$
11. **for** $i \leftarrow 0$ **to** $l - 1$ **do**
12.     AK-SPLIT($A_{\mathcal{G}}$,$\{T_i\}$,$k - l + i$)
13. AK-EDGE-CONSTRUCT($A_{\mathcal{G}}$)
**end**

AK-SPLIT($A_{\mathcal{G}}$,$\mathcal{C}$,$i$)
**begin**
1.  $\mathcal{P}_i \leftarrow CRF(\mathcal{P}_i \cup \mathcal{C})$
2.  **if** $i < k$ **then**
3.      AK-SPLIT($A_{\mathcal{G}}$,$\mathcal{P}_i \cup Succ(\mathcal{P}_i)$,$i + 1$)
**end**

AK-EDGE-CONSTRUCT($A_{\mathcal{G}}$)
**begin**
1.  **for each** edge $(u', u)$ **do**
2.      **for** $i = 0$ **to** $k - 1$ **do**
3.          Let $U' \in P_i$, $U \in P_{i+1}$ be index nodes such that $u \in U$ and $u' \in U'$
4.              **if** $\nexists$ an index edge from $U'$ to $U$ **then**
5.                  Add an index edge from $U$ to $U'$
**end**

Similar to the DL1-REFINE algorithm, the AK-REFINE algorithm also has two phases. After the first phase (step 1-6.), *if U is a target index node of R on* $I_{\mathcal{G}}$ *and* $U \cap T_{\mathcal{G}}(R) \neq \emptyset$ *then U is sound with R*. After the second phase (step 7-13.), *there is no false target index node*, thus $A_{\mathcal{G}}$ supports $R$.

Let us see the illustration for the *DL-A\*(k)*-index and the AK-REFINE algorithm which is shown in Figure 3. The data graph is represented in Figure 2(a). The *A(1)*-index and the data graph coincide. There are three *DL-*

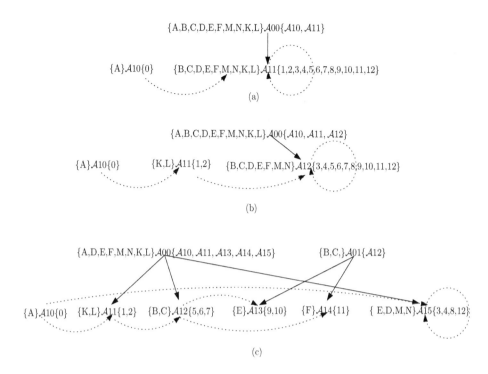

**Fig. 3.** An example of the $DL\text{-}A^*(1)$-index

$A^*(1)$-indexes. Each $DL\text{-}A^*(1)$-index is determined by two partitions $\mathcal{P}_0 = \{\mathcal{A}_{0i}\}$ and $\mathcal{P}_1 = \{\mathcal{A}_{1i}\}$. Because of $\mathcal{P}_1 \succeq \mathcal{P}_0$, for each index node $\mathcal{A}_{0i} \in \mathcal{P}_0$ we enumerate on the right the index nodes $\mathcal{A}_{1j} \in \mathcal{P}_1$, which are subsets of $\mathcal{A}_{0i}$, and for each index node $\mathcal{A}_{1i} \in \mathcal{P}_1$ we enumerate on the right the data nodes in its extent. The label of each index node is enumerated in the left. Index edges are solid lines. The $DL\text{-}A^*(1)$-index in Figure 3(b) is the result when we refine the initial $DL\text{-}A^*(1)$ in Figure 3(a) to support $R_1 = //(K|L)$, and the $DL\text{-}A^*(1)$-index in Figure 3(c) is the result when we refine the $DL\text{-}A^*(1)$-index in Figure 3(b) to support $R_2 = //(B|C)/E$.

Let $A^*(k)$-index be the $k$-stable structural index determined by $(\mathcal{P}_c, \ldots, split_k(\mathcal{P}_c))$.

**Proposition 7.** $\mathcal{A}_\mathcal{G}$ *supports $R$ after applying the* AK-REFINE *algorithm. If at the beginning the* $A^*(k)$ *is a refinement of* $\mathcal{A}_\mathcal{G}$ *then after refinement the* $A^*(k)$ *is still a refinement of* $\mathcal{A}_\mathcal{G}$.

The proof of Proposition 7 is similar to the proof of Proposition 5, and the full version can be found at [16]. The $A^*(k)$ is a refinement of the initial $DL\text{-}A(k)$-index so the $A^*(k)$ is a refinement of all $DL\text{-}A(k)$-indexes.

In the case the length of the path expression is longer than $k$, the information supplied by index edges of the $DL\text{-}A^*(k)$-index is not enough since they are planned just for $SAPE$ queries not longer than $k$. We suggest the $DL\text{-}A^*(k)$-index should be extended by adding *extended index edges* between index nodes in $k$-layer (the dotted lines in Figure 3). We add a extended index edge from $U' \in P_k$ to $U \in P_k$ iff there exists a data edge from $u' \in U'$ to $u \in U$. In summary, when the path expression is not longer than k the evaluation is calculated on *"origin"* index edges, in the case the path expression is longer than $k$, the "origin" index edges are used to find the first $k$ index edges of the matching index node paths, the extended index edges are used to find the remainder.

## 6     Experiments

We compared the performance of the *DL-1*-index vs. the 1-index, the *DL-A\*(k)*-index vs. the $A(k)$-index on the same large data sets with different finite sets of *SAPE*'s. The experiments were performed on Celeron R (2.4 G.hz), platform with MS-Windows XP and 512 MBytes of main memory. The Xerces Java SAX parser 1 [15] was used to parse XML data. We implemented the algorithms in C++. The data sets and the sets of frequently used *SAPE*'s were chosen as follows.

*Data Sets.* We used two data sets: the *XMark* data set(100 Mb) and the *TreeBank* data set (82M). The *XMark* data set containing the activities of an auction Web site is generated by using the Benchmark Data Generator [13]. The *TreeBank* data set is the collection of English sentences, tagged with parts of speech [14]. The properties of the data sets are as below:

| Data set | Number of Nodes | Number of Edges | Number of Labels |
|----------|-----------------|-----------------|------------------|
| XMark    | 1.681.342       | 1.987.929       | 76               |
| TreeBank | 2.437.667       | 2.437.666       | 251              |

*Query Loads.* For the simplicity, we assumed that in our *SAPE* queries $S_i$ is a wild card or unique label value ($S_i = \Sigma$ or $|S_i| = 1$). For each data set, we generated 4 query loads randomly. Each query load contained 100 *SAPE* queries. The length of each query was less than 5. In the $i$-th query load the probability of $S_i$ is a wild card was equal to $(i-1) * 20\%$ (In the query load 1, there did not exist wild card, and in the query load 2 the probability of $S_i$ be wild card was 20%, etc...).

The sizes of index graphs and the average of the evaluation cost of the queries in the query loads were focused in the performance of the *DL-1*-indexes vs. the 1-index, the *DL-A\*(k)*-index vs. the $A(k)$-index. We measured the size of the index graph by the number of index nodes. Similar to [6,7,8] we adopted the same main-memory cost metric for query evaluation. The cost was the number of the visited index nodes. The validation was not necessary because each query load was supported by the corresponding dynamic labelling index graphs.

### 6.1     The *DL-1*-Index vs. the 1-Index

The results of the *DL-1*-index vs. the 1-index experiments are shown in Figure 4 (A, B, C and D). In each chart, we represent the results of 4 tests

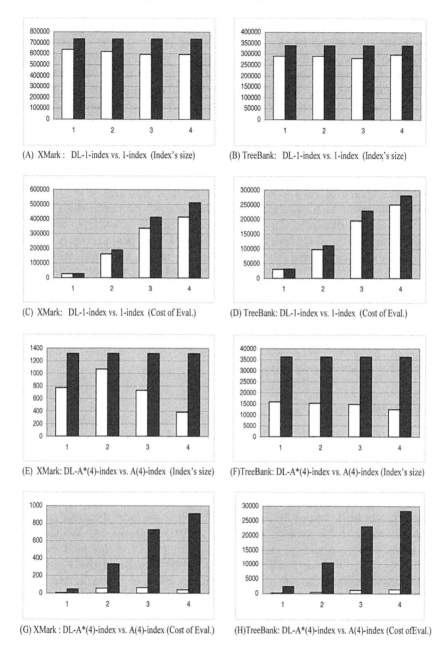

(A) XMark :  DL-1-index vs. 1-index  (Index's size)    (B) TreeBank:  DL-1-index vs. 1-index  (Index's size)

(C) XMark:  DL-1-index vs. 1-index  (Cost of Eval.)    (D) TreeBank: DL-1-index vs. 1-index  (Cost of Eval.)

(E)  XMark: DL-A*(4)-index vs. A(4)-index  (Index's size)    (F)TreeBank: DL-A*(4)-index vs. A(4)-index  (Index's size)

(G) XMark : DL-A*(4)-index vs. A(4)-index (Cost of Eval.)    (H)TreeBank: DL-A*(4)-index vs. A(4)-index (Cost ofEval.)

**Fig. 4.** The results of the experiments

corresponding with 4 query loads. Black color corresponds to the 1-index, and
white color corresponds with to *DL-1*-index. Comparing with the 1-index, the
sizes of the *DL-1*-indexes are smaller and the average cost of the query evaluation

of the *DL-1*-index is lower, since the 1-index is a refinement of the *DL-1*-indexes. However, the sizes of the *DL-1*-indexes increased very fast after each refinement and converge to the size of the 1-index since they must fulfill to be stable structural indexes. In test 3 the proportions of the index size the *DL-1*-index vs. the 1-index were $80, 70\%$ (XMark) and $83, 41\%$ (TreeBank). As a result the efficiency of the *DL-1*-indexes decreased quickly after each refinement. In test 3 the proportions of the average cost of the query evaluation the *DL-1*-index vs. the 1-index were $81, 55\%$ (XMark) and $84, 87\%$ (TreeBank).

## 6.2   The *DL-A\*(k)*-Index vs. the *A(k)*-Index

Because the length of each query was less than 5, we chose $k = 4$. Not like the *DL-1*-indexes, which were limited by the "stable" property, the *DL-A\*(k)*-index were almost dynamic. The results were impressive. Although storing the ancestor bisimilarity layers but the sizes of the *DL-A\*(k)*-indexes in our tests were smaller comparing with the *A(k)*-index. In test 3, the proportions of the index size between the *DL-A\*(k)*-index vs. the *A(k)*-index were $53, 58\%$ (XMark) and $40, 87\%$ (TreeBank). By using ancestor bisimilarity layers the cost of query evaluation on the *DL-A\*(k)*-index was quite cheaper than on the *A(k)*-index. In test 3, the proportions of the average cost of the query evaluation the *DL-A\*(k)*-index vs. the *A(k)*-index were $8, 46\%$ (XMark) and $4, 97\%$ (TreeBank). Because of the above results we believe that the *DL-A\*(k)*-index is one of the most efficient adaptive structural indexes.

## 7   Conclusion

The dynamic label similarity not only makes the size of a index graph be smaller, but also supports the queries, which contain wild- or alternation cards, better. The labels of data nodes in the same index node may be different. They depend on the set of frequently used queries. Every static label structural index can be improved so that it supports dynamic label similarity.

The *DL-1*-index is improved from the 1-index to support dynamic label similarity. We study stable structural indexes and their properties. We show that the 1-index is only a special case of stable structural indexes, and guarantee that the sizes of the weak 1-indexes are bound by the size of the 1-index. Our experiments show that the size of a weak 1-index is not only smaller but the cost of the query evaluation is also cheaper than the 1-index.

The *DL-A\*(k)*-index is improved from the *A(k)*-index. By storing ancestor bisimilarity layers we reduce the cost of the query evaluation on the *DL-A\*(k)*-index. With the results of our experiments we believe that the weak *DL-A\*(k)*-index is one of the most efficient adaptive structural indexes.

In future, we continue our work to improve the $D(k)$-index, $M(k)$-index to support dynamic label similarity. We will also investigate adaptive structural indexes, which support more complex queries (tree-structured, branching).

# References

1. P. Buneman, M. Fernandez, and D. Suciu 2000. UNQL: A query language and algebra for semi-structured data based on structural recursion. In VLDB J.9, 1, 76-110.
2. J. McHugh, S. Abiteboul,R. Goldman, D. Quass and J. Widom 1997. The Lorel query language for semi-structured data. In International Journal on Digital Libraries, 68-88.
3. A. Deutsch, M. Fernandez, D. Florescu, A. Levy, and D. Suciu 1999. A query language for XML. In Proceedings of the Eights International World Wide Web Conference (WWW8), Toronto.
4. A. Berglund, S. Boag, D. Chamberlin, M. F. Fernandez, M. Kay, J. Robie, and J. Simeon. XML path language (xpath) 2.0. In http://www.w3.org/TR/xpath20, August 2002.
5. T. Milo and D.Suciu 1999. Index Structures for Path Expressions. In ICDT, 1999.
6. R. Kaushik, P. Shenoy, P. Bohannon and Ehud Gudes 2002. Exploiting Local Similarity for Efficient Indexing of Paths in Graph Structured Data. In ICDE,2002.
7. Q. Chen, A. Lim, K. W. Ong 2003. D(K)-Index: An Adaptive structural Summary for Graph-Structured Data. In ACM SIGMOD 2003, June 9-12.
8. Hao He, Jun Yang 2004. Multiresolution Indexing of XML for Frequent Queries. In Proceedings of the 20th International Conference on Data Engineering.
9. H. Wu, Q. Wang, J. X. Yu, A. Zhou, and S. Zhou 2003. Ud(k,l)- index: An efficient approximate index for XML data. In Proc. of the 2003 Intl. Conf. on Web-Age Information Management, August 2003.
10. C. Chung, J. Min, and K. Shim 2002. Apex: An adaptive path index for XML data. In Proc. of the 2002 ACM SIGMOD Intl. Conf. on Management of Data, June 2002.
11. R.Paige and R.Tarjan 1987. Three Partition Refinement Algorithms. In SIAM Journal of Computing, 16:973-988.
12. Peter Buneman, Susan B. Davidson, Mary F. Fernandez, Dan Suciu 1997. Adding Structure to Unstructured Data. In Proceedings of the 6th International Conference on Database Theory, p. 336-350.
13. XMark: The XML benchmark project. http://monetdb.cwi.nl/xml/index.html.
14. Treebank dataset. http://www.cs.washington.edu/research/xmldatasets/.
15. The apache XML project - Xerces Java Parsers. http://xml.apache.org/xerces-j/.
16. The Extended Version of this paper. http://people.inf.elte.hu/leanhvu/papers/DLIndexes(extend version).pdf

# ICB-Index: A New Indexing Technique for Continuous Time Sequences

Dmitry V. Maslov and Andrew A. Sidorov

Sensors Modules Systems, Research and Innovation Company
Section 3, 25 Minskaya St.,
443035 Samara, Russia
{dmaslov, ac}@industrialauto.ru

**Abstract.** Various application domains require databases to store time sequences. Very often time sequences describe some continuous processes at discrete time points. Many applications require queries to take into consideration not only explicit values of time sequences, but also the values of the processes represented by them (these values can be derived from explicit values by user-defined interpolation functions). For example, a user of industrial process control system may ask the following query: "Find those time intervals during which specified physical value, represented by a series of measurements, was greater than given limit value". We show that conventional secondary indexes are not suitable to support such queries. We also investigate the properties of IP-index – the first index structure supporting queries on time sequences taking into account the interpolation (so-called "queries on continuous time sequences"). We show that IP-index improves the performance of such queries, but its size is enormously big for many real-life sequences. This fact makes it nearly impossible to use IP-index in some application domains. In this paper we present a new indexing technique to support queries on continuous time sequences – ICB-index. ICB-index makes the performance of such queries as high as IP-index does, but it requires substantially less space than IP-index. The effectiveness of ICB-index is verified by experiments on sensor-generated time sequences from a power plant.

## 1 Introduction

Data ordered over time – time sequences (TS) – can be found in many diverse application domains – financial, medical, industrial, scientific, and so on. That is why lots of database research papers address the problems of time sequences modeling and querying. There have been proposed many specialized data models for time sequences, as well as query languages and query evaluation and optimization techniques (see, for example, [1, 3, 4, 5, 7, 15, 16, 17, 18, 20, 21, 22, 23, 24, 25]).

Most of the work was done to meet the requirements of *financial applications* and was focused mainly on statistical analysis and similarity search. But, as [11] pointed out, "in many applications individual values are at least as important as shapes of time sequences". This is especially the case for *industrial applications*.

Y. Manolopoulos, J. Pokorný, and T. Sellis (Eds.): ADBIS 2006, LNCS 4152, pp. 248–265, 2006.

For example, process control system of hydroelectric power station "Zhigulevskaya" generates some 5000 time sequences with cardinality 0.25 – 2.5 million. A user of this system is interested in individual value queries and range queries rather than in shape queries. Fig. 1.1 shows a fragment of hydroelectric generator active power time sequence. Typical queries on this time sequence are: 1) "When did the generator work normally with full load?" ("When was the power greater than 100 but less than 120 MW?"); 2) "When did the generator work with ultimate load?" ("When was the power greater than 120 MW?"); 3) "When did generator loading/unloading take place?" ("When did the power value cross the limit of 50 MW?"). In [11] such queries were termed as *value queries* (in contrast to shape queries). It is difficult to answer such queries because we should take into consideration not only explicit values of TS, but also the values of the process represented by it (these values can be derived from explicit values by user-defined interpolation functions).

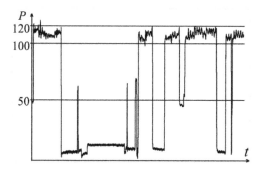

**Fig. 1.1.** Generator active power time sequence in megawatts (MW)

We shall say that time sequence is *continuous* if it requires queries to consider *interpolation assumptions* (in some research papers some other terms are used to describe the same object, e.g. "interpolated time series", but we use the term "continuous time sequence" because this term is used in paper [11], which is, in some sense, the prototype of this paper). Many applications (including the above example) require time sequences to be seen as continuous.

Conventional secondary indexes are not suitable to support queries on continuous TSs, because they allow finding only those values that are explicitly stored in the database, while the answer to the query on continuous TS may contain implicit values. That is why most of the systems which support value queries on continuous TSs use full scan of TS to answer the query. As a result, the response time of the system may be inadequate (recall the number and the cardinality of TSs in above example and notice that these values are typical for industrial process control systems).

The first index structure supporting value queries on continuous TSs is IP-index [10, 11, 12]. It dramatically improves the performance of such queries, but it has a serious drawback – its size is enormously big for many real-life TSs (in section 5 we show that the size of IP-index can be many times greater than the size of TS). This fact makes it nearly impossible to use IP-index in some application domains.

In this paper we present a new indexing technique to support value queries on one-dimensional continuous time sequences – *ICB-index*. ICB-index is based on the idea of IP-index and makes the performance of the queries as high as IP-index does, but it requires substantially less space than IP-index. The effectiveness of ICB-index is verified by experiments on 2180 sensor-generated time sequences from hydroelectric power station "Zhigulevskaya".

The rest of this paper is organized as following. In section 2 we discuss existing research work that focuses on the support of interpolation in databases. In section 3 we formulate mathematical definition of the problem of supporting queries on TSs considering interpolation assumptions. In section 4 we show that conventional secondary indexes are unsuitable to solve this problem. In section 5 we describe the idea of IP-index (because ICB-index is based on it) and give the experimental results showing that the size of IP-index is enormously big. Section 6 presents ICB-index and experimental results made with it. Section 7 concludes the paper.

## 2  Related Research Work

There are not so many research papers that consider the problem of supporting interpolation in databases. One of the first of them was [6], but it considered only *stepwise-constant interpolation*. Some research papers address the problem of supporting interpolation in databases *on the logical level* (they investigate, how we can formulate the queries that consider interpolated data). The model proposed in [20, 21] supports different types of interpolation by introducing different types of TSs: stepwise constant, continuous, discrete and user-defined. It also introduces an operator for selecting data by specifying the set of time points of interest. Paper [2] proposes another approach. It suggests any relational query on a database DB to be viewed as a query on database DB$^*$ which consists of all the data of DB and is supplemented by all the data that can be derived from explicit data of DB using interpolation assumptions.

Even fewer research papers are dedicated to the effective evaluation of the queries supporting the interpolation. Neugebauer [14] proposed to supplement the original time sequence with the values at the specified equidistant time points before evaluating the query (these values can be derived from explicit ones using specified interpolation function). But this approach does not allow us to answer the query "When was the value of continuous time sequence equal to a given value?" Grumbach et al. [8, 9] concerned the problem of efficient manipulation of interpolated data. They proposed a novel optimization technique for the queries supporting the interpolation. But anyway, their approach requires the full scan of the table to answer the query.

L. Lin et al. [10, 11, 12] proposed specialized indexing technique – IP-index, which supports queries on the time sequences that take into consideration the interpolation assumptions. IP-index was the first indexing technique supporting such queries. A. Nanopoulos and Y. Manolopoulos [13] proposed an improvement of IP-index – SIQ-index that is based on the R*-tree and deals with the problem of the size of IP-index. In this paper we propose another improvement of IP-index – ICB-index. It also deals with the problem of the size of IP-index, but it takes another approach.

# 3  Mathematical Definition of the Problem

This section contains the definitions of terms and notations that we use in this paper and the definition of the problem of supporting value queries on continuous time sequences. We try to use the same notations as in papers [10, 11, 12], because our indexing technique is an extension of the approach proposed there.

*One-dimensional time sequence* is a sequence of pairs $(t_i, v_i)$, $i = "1...n"$, where each $t_i$ is a time point, each $v_i$ is a numeric value corresponding to this time point, and these pairs are ordered, i.e. $\forall i, j : i > j \rightarrow t_i > t_j$. In this paper we consider time sequences only of this sort. We term each pair $(t_i, v_i)$ as *state*, denoted by $S_i$.

In this paper we assume that each time sequence describes some continuous process $v(t)$ (i.e. each value $v_i$ of the time sequence equals to the value of this process at time point $t_i$, and we do not know the values of this process at time points not included into the time sequence). To derive the values of this process at time points that are not included into the time sequence some continuous piecewise interpolation function $v^*(t)$ is used. We denote by $\sigma^*_\Theta (TS)$ the operator that is used to formulate value queries on the time sequence $TS$ that is seen as continuous. This operator returns the set of time points (or time intervals) at which the value of $v^*(t)$ satisfies the condition $\Theta$ (note that we do not know at which points the value of the process $v(t)$ satisfies the condition, we can only determine at which points the value of interpolation function satisfies it). We allow the following types of conditions for this operator: 1) $v = x$ (for finding time points at which $v^*(t)$ is equal to $x$); 2) $v > x$ (for finding time intervals during which $v^*(t)$ is greater than $x$); 3) $v < x$; 4) their combinations.

Our definitions are independent of the data model. In practice time sequence can be modeled as a relation, as an attribute of abstract data type or as an object, and $\sigma^*_\Theta$ operator can be implemented as an additional operator of relational algebra or as a method accordingly.

Now we can formulate the problem we concerned like following: "*How can $\sigma^*_\Theta$ operator be efficiently executed (without linear scan of time sequence)?*" Obviously, the beginnings and the ends of time intervals included into the result of $\sigma^*_{v>x}$ (or $\sigma^*_{v<x}$) operator could be retrieved by $\sigma^*_{v=x}$ operator (see Fig. 3.1). So, the problem of supporting $\sigma^*_\Theta$ operator is reduced to the problem of supporting $\sigma^*_{v=x}$ operator.

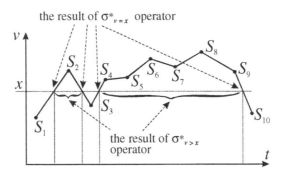

**Fig. 3.1.** $\sigma^*_{v>x}$ and $\sigma^*_{v=x}$ operators

This problem can be further reduced. Let us denote by $v^*_i(t)$ the piece of interpolation function $v^*(t)$ that is defined between time points $t_i$ and $t_{i+1}$ and is used to derive the values of $v(t)$ between them. The most practical interpolation functions have the following property: to construct $v^*_i(t)$ we need the states $S_i$ and $S_{i+1}$ and sometimes several states around them. For example, if the interpolation is piecewise-linear we need only $S_i$ and $S_{i+1}$ in order to find the coefficients of linear function $v^*_i(t)$. That is why we can find the result of $\sigma^*_{v=x}$ operator in the following three steps.

1.  Determine all the states $S_i = (t_i, v_i)$ with the following property:

$$\min_{t_i \le t \le t_{i+1}} v^*_i(t) \le x \le \max_{t_i \le t \le t_{i+1}} v^*_i(t) . \tag{3.1}$$

Note, that in case of piecewise-linear interpolation the above condition is equivalent to the following:

$$\min(v_i, v_{i+1}) \le x \le \max(v_i, v_{i+1}) . \tag{3.2}$$

2.  Read out all the states found in the previous step as well as their surrounding states needed to find the coefficients of corresponding pieces $v^*_i(t)$ of the interpolation function.
3.  For each $v^*_i(t)$ that we have found coefficients for in the previous step solve the equation $v^*_i(t) = x$.

The third step involves only main memory operations with the states that have already been read out, so its performance is not very critical. The performance of the second step depends only on the number of the states returned by the first step and on the type of interpolation function, so it cannot be optimized. In contrast, performance of the first step is critical and is subject to optimization. If we do not have any specialized index, we have to scan the whole time sequence in order to complete this step. Thus, we have reduced the problem of supporting value queries on continuous time sequences to the problem of finding all the states satisfying the condition (3.1) if the value of $x$ is given.

## 4   Why Conventional Secondary Indexes are Unsuitable to Solve the Problem?

At the first glance it seems that if we have certain additional information about some time sequence then conventional secondary indexes can be used to support value queries on this time sequence considering interpolation assumptions. For example, assume that a time sequence is regular (i.e. the distance $\Delta t$ between its time points is always the same) and describes some continuous process $v(t)$. Assume that the first derivative of this process is bounded: $|v'(t)| \le M$, and that piecewise-linear interpolation is used to derive the values of $v(t)$ at time points that are not included into the time sequence. If we need to find time points at which the value of the process $v(t)$ (to be more correct, the value of interpolation function) was equal to a given value $x$, we should find all the states which satisfy the condition (3.2). With the assumptions we made above we can use standard relational selection operator to find them:

$$\sigma_{x-M \cdot \Delta t \le V \le x+M \cdot \Delta t}(R) \tag{4.1}$$

(we assume here that the time sequence is modeled as the relation $R$ with attributes "$T$" – timestamp and "$V$" – value). Obviously, the result of this operator will contain all the states satisfying the condition (3.2). Operator (4.1) is efficiently supported by conventional secondary indexes and seems to solve the problem.

But there are at least two reasons why this solution is not very good. First, the assumption that TS is regular seems unrealistic (many applications work with irregular TSs). Second, even if the above assumptions hold, operator (4.1) returns *all* the states satisfying the condition (3.2), *but not only* such states. Fig. 4.1 illustrates this fact. In this example operator (4.1) will return the following states: $(t_7, v_7)$, $(t_8, v_8)$, $(t_9, v_9)$, $(t_{10}, v_{10})$, $(t_{11}, v_{11})$, $(t_{12}, v_{12})$ and $(t_{14}, v_{14})$. The states $(t_7, v_7)$, $(t_9, v_9)$ and $(t_{11}, v_{11})$ satisfy the condition (3.2) (they are marked by bold dots in the figure), while the states $(t_8, v_8)$, $(t_{10}, v_{10})$, $(t_{12}, v_{12})$ and $(t_{14}, v_{14})$ are "*unwanted*" because they do not satisfy this condition. So, the problem is that the operator (4.1) returns a number of unwanted states. It causes unnecessary disk operations.

We have made an experiment on the real-life TS shown in Fig. 1.1 to determine how many unwanted states are returned by operator (4.1). For different values of $x$ (the value we search for) we determined the number of states satisfying the condition (3.2) and the total number of states returned by operator (4.1). The results of this experiment (see Fig. 4.2) show that the number of unwanted states is great. The total number of the states returned by operator (4.1) is on average 50 times greater than the number of states satisfying the condition (3.2). It means that we have to read out much more information than we need and to sort it out afterwards. So, conventional

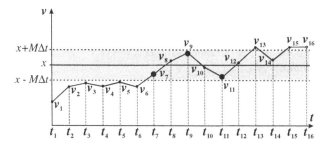

**Fig. 4.1.** Using relational selection operator for querying continuous time sequence

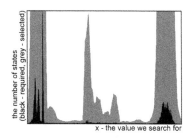

**Fig. 4.2.** The number of states satisfying the condition (3.2) (*black area*) and the total number of states returned by operator (4.1) (*grey area*)

secondary indexes are unsuitable to solve our problem. We need some specialized indexing structure allowing us to find all the states satisfying the condition (3.1) (or (3.2) in case of piecewise-linear interpolation) without reading any unwanted states.

## 5  IP-Index: Advantages and Drawbacks

IP-index (Interpolation-index) [10, 11, 12] was developed by Ling Lin et al. to support value queries on continuous TSs. It allows efficient finding of time sequence states satisfying the condition (3.2) (IP-index supports only piecewise-linear interpolation).

### 5.1  The Idea of IP-Index

Each state $S_i$ of a time sequence can be viewed as a point in two-dimensional plane $t$-$v$. Let us denote by $Sg_i$ the segment that starts with $S_i$ and ends with $S_{i+1}$. IP-index is built like following.

1.  All the states $S_i$ are projected on the $v$-axis. As a result the $v$-axis is partitioned into non-overlapping intervals $[k_j, k_{j+1}]$, $j = "1...m-1"$, where $m$ is a number of distinct values of time sequence.
2.  Obviously, each interval $[k_j, k_{j+1}]$ has the following property: for all the values $x$ between $k_j$ and $k_{j+1}$ the sequence of segments $Sg_i$ intersecting the line $v = x$ is the same (see Fig. 5.1) and consequently the sequence of states satisfying the condition (3.2) is also the same. The sequence of such states is associated with each interval $[k_j, k_{j+1}]$ building up the IP-index.
3.  Each interval $[k_j, k_{j+1}]$ is identified by its starting point $k_j$ in IP-index (interval $[k_j, k_{j+1}]$ can be uniquely identified by its starting point because its ending point is the starting point for the next interval). The values $k_j$, $j = "1...m"$, are called *the keys of IP-index*.

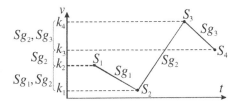

**Fig. 5.1.** The idea of IP-index

The IP-index for the time sequence shown in Fig. 5.1 looks like following:

$k_1$: $S_1$, $S_2$;   $k_2$: $S_2$;   $k_3$: $S_2$, $S_3$;   $k_4$: $-$ .

In order to find the result of $\sigma^*_{v=x}$ operator we should find TS states satisfying the condition (3.2). To do this we should find such key $k_j$ in IP-index that $x \in [k_j, k_{j+1}]$ and then just read out the state sequence associated with it. To allow for the fast finding of the keys of IP-index any conventional indexing technique can be used.

The main advantage of IP-index is that we do not have to read out any unwanted states of time sequence. We read out only those states that are needed to calculate the result of $\sigma^*_{v=x}$ operator. Thus, IP-index makes the performance of $\sigma^*_{v=x}$ operator as high as possible. Its effectiveness is verified by the experiments made by Ling Lin.

## 5.2  IP-Index: Experimental Results

We have made a series of experiments on real-life TSs from hydroelectric power station "Zhigulevskaya" to determine the space requirements of IP-index. Fig. 5.2 shows the TSs we used in the experiments. Two of these TSs describe slow processes (temperature), four of them describe fast processes (electrical and hydromechanical processes). All of these TSs are regular and their cardinality is 300 thousand states.

For each time sequence we calculated the size of IP-index and IP-index size/TS size ratio (see Table 1). All the time sequences were generated by 15-bit analog-to-digital converter, that is why 2 bytes are enough to represent each state of these time sequences (it is not necessary to store timestamps, because TSs are regular). So, the size of each TS is 300 000·2/1024 ≈ 586 Kb. The size of IP-index has two components: 1) 3 bytes multiplied by the total number of the states in all the state sequences associated with the keys of IP-index (3 bytes are enough to address 16 million states); 2) 6 bytes multiplied by the number of the keys (2 bytes to store the value of the key and 4 bytes for the pointer to the state sequence associated with the key).

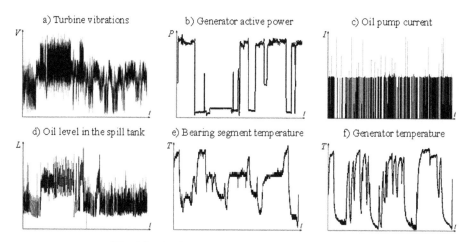

**Fig. 5.2.** The time sequences used in the experiments

**Table 1.** IP-index size and IP-index size/TS size ratio

| Time sequence | IP-index size, Kb | IP-index size / TS size ratio |
|---|---|---|
| Turbine vibrations | 609 050 | 1041.1 |
| Generator active power | 10 989 | 18.8 |
| Oil pump current | 56 455 | 96.5 |
| Oil level in the spill tank | 5 006 | 8.6 |
| Bearing segment temperature | 310 | 0.5 |
| Generator temperature | 650 | 1.1 |

Table 1 shows that the size of IP-index for time sequences that describe fast processes can be enormously big. This fact made it impossible to use IP-index at hydroelectric power station "Zhigulevskaya".

# 6  ICB-Index

ICB-index (Interpolation Compressed Block index) is an extension of IP-index and is the main contribution of this paper. ICB-index efficiently supports the value queries on continuous time sequences by allowing the fast finding of time sequence states satisfying the condition (3.1) if the value of $x$ is given. This index is suitable for any type of interpolation. It makes the performance of queries as high as IP-index does, but it requires substantially less space than IP-index.

ICB-index is based on the idea of IP-index and the following two ideas that allowed to reduce its space requirements.

1.  We replace the state sequences associated with each key of IP-index by the sequences of disk blocks that contain the states of these state sequences.
2.  We use an additional level of index to eliminate the redundancy that exists in IP-index (very often a state sequence associated with a key of IP-index is very similar to the state sequences associated with its neighbor keys).

In the next subsection we discuss these ideas in more detail.

## 6.1  The Ideas of ICB-Index

For large time sequences the size of IP-index becomes great because state sequences corresponding to each key have large cardinality. The first idea of ICB-index is based on the fact that usually each of these state sequences contains lots of the states stored *in the same disk block*. To reduce the cardinality of state sequences it makes sense to store pointers to the blocks containing the states of this sequence instead of the pointers to the states. This change will not decrease the performance of the queries because even if we have the pointers to the states that should be read we always read the whole blocks from the disk. For example, suppose that the following state sequence is associated with some key $k_j$ of IP-index:

$$S_1, S_2, S_6, S_{15}, S_{18} \ . \tag{6.1}$$

It means that all the states $S_1, S_2, S_6, S_{15}, S_{18}$ satisfy the condition (3.2) for all the values contained in the interval $[k_j, k_{j+1}]$. If we know that the states $S_1 - S_{10}$ are contained in block $B_1$ and the states $S_{11} - S_{20}$ are contained in block $B_2$, we can replace the state sequence (6.1) with the following sequence of blocks: $B_1, B_2$. If such sequence is associated with the key $k_j$, it means that to get all the states that satisfy the condition (3.2) for all the values contained in the interval $[k_j, k_{j+1}]$ we have to read out the blocks $B_1$ and $B_2$. We then should check all the states we've read whether they satisfy the condition (3.2) or not. But this check involves only main memory operations, while the number of disk operations remains the same. Thus, we can reduce the size of the sequences associated with the keys of IP-index.

The second idea is based on the fact that very often a state sequence associated with a key of IP-index is very similar to the state sequences associated with its neighbor keys. The naive way to eliminate such redundancy is to use differential encoding [19]. Each state sequence can be stored as the list of differences from the state sequence associated with the previous key or with the first key of some group. But with this approach we shall either loose the ability of random access to the index or face the difficulties with adding a new key to the index. Thus, differential encoding will reduce either the performance of index search or index update speed; both are undesirable. We propose a better solution – we introduce an additional level of the index. Its keys $k'_l$, $l =$ "$0...K-1$" (where $K$ is some constant), partition the $v$-axis into the intervals that are larger than the intervals $[k_j, k_{j+1}]$, $j =$ "$1...m-1$" (intervals into which the keys of IP-index partition the $v$-axis). Then suppose, that amongst intervals $I_j = [k_j, k_{j+1}]$, $j =$ "$1...m-1$", those (and only those) intervals whose indexes fall into the range "$j_1...j_2$", are contained in the interval $[k'_l, k'_{l+1}]$, and suppose that state sequences associated with the keys $k_j$, $j =$ "$j_1...j_2$", have the same subsequence. Then we can remove this subsequence from these state sequences and associate it with the key $k'_l$ of the additional level of the index (see Fig. 6.1). Thus, we do not lose any information contained in the IP-index, but reduce the size of the index. Our approach does not have the drawbacks of differential encoding we've mentioned above.

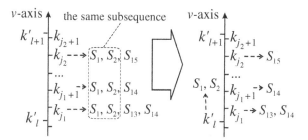

**Fig. 6.1.** An additional level for IP-index

These are two ideas ICB-index is based on. Note, that these are *only the ideas*, we give the precise description of the ICB-index structure in the next subsection.

## 6.2   The Structure of ICB-Index

Before building ICB-index the TS itself should be a little bit reorganized on the disk. TS should be stored in such a way that allows to find the coefficients for each piece

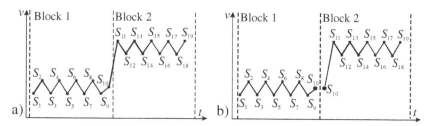

**Fig. 6.2.** Time sequence that does not fulfill the requirement of ICB-index (a) and reorganized time sequence that fulfills the requirement of ICB-index (b)

$v^*_i(t)$ of interpolation function $v^*(t)$ using time sequence states *from only one disk block*. We can easily fulfill this requirement by adding duplicate states to TS. Fig. 6.2 (a) shows an example of TS for which piecewise-linear interpolation is used. To find the coefficients of the piece of interpolation function defined on the interval $[t_{10}, t_{11}]$ we need the states $S_{10}$ and $S_{11}$ that are stored in the different blocks. So, the above requirement is not fulfilled. To fulfill it we can reorganize the time sequence by duplicating the state $S_{10}$, see Fig. 6.2 (b). Now the requirement is fulfilled.

Let us now describe the structure of ICB-index. In this section we use the notations from the section 3 and introduce some new notations. Let us denote by $B$ the disk block containing several sequential states of TS. Assume that $v^*_i(t)$, $i = "n_1...n_2"$, are the pieces of the interpolation function $v^*(t)$ for which we can find the coefficients having only the states from the block $B$. We shall use the following notations:

$$B_{min} = \min_{t \in [t_{n_1}, t_{n_2+1}]} (v^*(t)); \quad B_{max} = \max_{t \in [t_{n_1}, t_{n_2+1}]} (v^*(t)).$$

So, $B_{min}$ and $B_{max}$ are the minimum and the maximum value of the interpolation function on the interval where it can be constructed using the TS states from the block $B$.

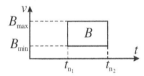

**Fig. 6.3.** Visual representation of the time sequence block

Then disk block $B$ can be represented as a rectangle in two-dimensional plane $t$-$v$ (see Fig. 6.3), and the whole time sequence can be represented as a series of such rectangles (see Fig. 6.4). We shall use such visual representation to illustrate the structure of ICB-index.

ICB-index consists of two parts: *the auxiliary index* and *the main index*.

The auxiliary index (see Fig. 6.4) is built like following. Let $v_{min}$ and $v_{max}$ be the minimum and the maximum value of the process $v(t)$. We partition the interval $[v_{min}, v_{max}]$ into $K$ equal intervals: $[k'_l, k'_{l+1}]$, $l = "0...K-1"$. With each interval $[k'_l, k'_{l+1}]$ we associate the sequence of pointers to such blocks $B$, that $[k'_l, k'_{l+1}] \subseteq [B_{min}, B_{max}]$. Each interval $[k'_l, k'_{l+1}]$ is uniquely identified by its starting point $k'_l$ in the index. The values $k'_l$, $l = "0...K"$, are called *the keys of the auxiliary index*.

The main index (see Fig. 6.4) is built like following.

1.  The values $B_{min}$ and $B_{max}$ of all the blocks of TS are projected on the $v$-axis. As a result the interval $[v_{min}, v_{max}]$ is partitioned into non-overlapping intervals $[k_j, k_{j+1}]$, $j = "1...m-1"$, where $m$ is a number of distinct $B_{min}$ and $B_{max}$ values.
2.  Each interval $[k_j, k_{j+1}]$ has the following property: for all the values $x$ between $k_j$ and $k_{j+1}$ the sequence of such blocks $B$ that $x \in [B_{min}, B_{max}]$ is the same. Please note, that if for some block $B$ the following property holds: $x \in [B_{min}, B_{max}]$, then there exists at least one state $S$ satisfying the condition (3.1) in the block $B$. It means that for all the values $x$ between $k_j$ and $k_{j+1}$ the states satisfying the condi-

tion (3.1) are contained in the same sequence of blocks. These blocks can be determined by checking the condition $[k_j, k_{j+1}] \subseteq [B_{min}, B_{max}]$. We associate the sequence of pointers to such blocks with each interval $[k_j, k_{j+1}]$.

3.  Each interval $[k_j, k_{j+1}]$ is identified by its starting point $k_j$ in the index. The values $k_j$, $j = "1...m"$, are called *the keys of the main index*.

4.  If there exists such key $k'_l$ in the auxiliary index that

$$[k_j, k_{j+1}] \subseteq [k'_l, k'_{l+1}] , \tag{6.2}$$

we remove all the block pointers associated with the key $k'_l$ in the auxiliary index from the sequence of block pointers associated with the key $k_j$ in the main index. We can do this for the following reason. Associating a pointer to the block $B$ with a key $k_j$ in the main index means that for all values $x$ belonging to the interval $[k_j, k_{j+1}]$ there exists at least one state $S$ in the block $B$, for which the condition (3.1) is satisfied. But if the block $B$ is already associated with a key $k'_l$ in the auxiliary index, then $[k'_l, k'_{l+1}] \subseteq [B_{min}, B_{max}]$. It means that for all values $x$ belonging to the interval $[k'_l, k'_{l+1}]$ (and, according to (6.2), for all values belonging to the interval $[k_j, k_{j+1}]$) there exists at least one state $S$ in the block $B$, for which the condition (3.1) is satisfied. So, we already have this information in the auxiliary index and do not have to duplicate it in the main index.

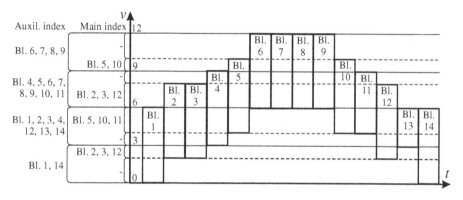

**Fig. 6.4.** Schematic representation of a time sequence and ICB-index structure (here "Bl." means "Block")

**Table 2.** The structure of ICB-index

| | The auxiliary index | The main index |
|---|---|---|
| The keys of the index | $k'_l = v_{min} + l \cdot \dfrac{v_{max} - v_{min}}{K}$, <br> $l = "0...K"$ <br> (where $K$ is a parameter) | Distinct values $B_{min}$ and $B_{max}$ of all the blocks containing the states of time sequence, <br> denoted by $k_j$, $j = "1...m"$ |
| Block pointers associated with the keys | Pointers to such blocks $B$ that <br> $[k'_l, k'_{l+1}] \subseteq [B_{min}, B_{max}]$ <br> are associated with the key $k'_l$ | Pointers to such blocks $B$ that <br> $[k_j, k_{j+1}] \subseteq [B_{min}, B_{max}]$ and <br> $\nexists l \, (0 \le l \le K\text{-}1): [k'_l, k'_{l+1}] \subseteq [B_{min}, B_{max}]$ <br> & $[k_j, k_{j+1}] \subseteq [k'_l, k'_{l+1}]$ <br> are associated with the key $k_j$ |

**Table 3.** The effectiveness of the auxiliary index

(a) The main index for TS shown in Fig. 6.4 (without auxiliary index)

(b) ICB-index for the time sequence shown in Fig. 6.4

| Key values | Blocks associated with the keys |
|---|---|
| 0 | 1, 14 |
| 2 | 1, 2, 3, 12, 14 |
| 3 | 1, 2, 3, 4, 12, 13, 14 |
| 4 | 1, 2, 3, 4, 5, 10, 11, 12, 13, 14 |
| 6 | 2, 3, 4, 5, 6, 7, 8, 9, 10, 11, 12 |
| 8 | 4, 5, 6, 7, 8, 9, 10, 11 |
| 9 | 5, 6, 7, 8, 9, 10 |
| 10 | 6, 7, 8, 9 |
| 12 | - |

| The auxiliary index | | The main index | |
|---|---|---|---|
| Key values | Blocks associated with the keys | Key values | Blocks associated with the keys |
| 0 | 1, 14 | 0 | - |
| 3 | 1, 2, 3, 4, 12, 13, 14 | 2 | 2, 3, 12 |
| | | 3 | - |
| 6 | 4, 5, 6, 7, 8, 9, 10, 11 | 4 | 5, 10, 11 |
| | | 6 | 2, 3, 12 |
| 9 | 6, 7, 8, 9 | 8 | - |
| 12 | - | 9 | 5, 10 |
| | | 10 | - |
| | | 12 | - |

The above indexing technique is applied only to the blocks that satisfy the condition $B_{max} > B_{min}$. Blocks for which $B_{max} = B_{min}$ can be indexed separately using any conventional indexing technique (using the values $B_{max}$ as the keys).

Table 2 contains an overview of what are the keys of the main and the auxiliary index and which blocks are associated with them.

The auxiliary index allows to reduce the overall size of ICB-index. Table 3 (a) shows the main index for the time sequence shown in the Fig. 6.4 for the case when the auxiliary index is not created; Table 3 (b) shows ICB-index consisting of the auxiliary and the main index for the same time sequence. The number of block pointers contained in the index shown in Table 3 (a) is less than the overall number of block pointers contained in the auxiliary and the main index shown in Table 3 (b).

Let us now describe how ICB-index is used to support value queries on continuous TSs. In order to find the result of $\sigma^*_{\nu=x}$ operator we should find TS states satisfying the condition (3.1). To do this we should accomplish the following steps.

1.  Find such key $k_j$ in the main index that $x \in [k_j, k_{j+1}]$ and read out all the blocks associated with it (if $x$ is equal to some key of the index there may exist two keys satisfying the above condition and in this case we should read out the blocks associated with both of them).
2.  Find such key $k'_l$ in the auxiliary index that $x \in [k'_l, k'_{l+1}]$ and read out all the blocks associated with it.
3.  In the blocks that were read out in steps 1 and 2 find the states that satisfy the condition (3.1).

To allow the fast finding of the keys of the main index any conventional indexing technique can be used. The keys of the auxiliary index can be accessed even faster – we can compute the address of the key $k'_l$ satisfying the condition $x \in [k'_l, k'_{l+1}]$ using the following formula:

$$key\ address = first + key\ size \cdot \left( \left\lceil \frac{(x - v_{min}) \cdot K}{v_{max} - v_{min}} \right\rceil - 1 \right),$$

where *first* is the address of the first key of the auxiliary index, *key size* is the size needed to store one key of the auxiliary index, $K$ is a parameter used in the auxiliary index definition, $\lceil \cdot \rceil$ is the ceiling operation.

To find the result of $\sigma^*_{v\,=\,x}$ operator using ICB-index we should read out only those blocks of time sequence that certainly contain the states satisfying the condition (3.1) (i.e. the states we search for). That is why ICB-index makes the performance of value queries on continuous TSs nearly as high as IP-index does (we say "*nearly*" because ICB-index requires one additional disk operation to read the sequence of block pointers associated with a key of the auxiliary index). But ICB-index has an important advantage – it requires substantially less space than IP-index. Subsection 6.4 contains the results of experiments verifying the effectiveness of ICB-index.

### 6.3 ICB-Index Size Optimization

While describing the structure of the auxiliary index in the previous subsection we used a parameter $K$. Obviously, the value of this parameter influences the overall size of ICB-index. It can easily be seen that the function *ICBSize(K)* (ICB-index size as a function of $K$) is unimodal (it has the only minimum). For example, Fig. 6.5 shows the function graph of *ICBSize(K)* for the time sequence shown in Fig. 1.1.

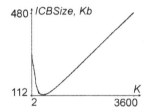

**Fig. 6.5.** The function graph of *ICBSize(K)* (in kilobytes) for TS shown in Fig. 1.1

So, for each time sequence there is exactly one optimal value of $K$ that minimizes the overall size of ICB-index. We can calculate the value of *ICBSize(K)* function at any point by building the ICB-index in the main memory for some part of the time sequence, that is why the task of finding optimal value of $K$ can be viewed as one-dimensional optimization problem of finding the minimum of *ICBSize(K)* in the interval $[2, (v_{max} - v_{min}) \cdot 10^p]$, where $p$ is the precision of time sequence values (the number of digits after the decimal point). We can solve this problem using any existing optimization approach, e.g. golden section search or Fibonacci search (in our implementation we use golden section search).

### 6.4 ICB-Index: Experimental Results

To compare ICB-index size with IP-index size we've made a series of experiments on the real-life TSs from hydroelectric power station that we used to determine the space requirements of IP-index. For each TS we determined the optimal value of $K$ parameter, the size of ICB-index and ICB-index size/TS size ratio. Obviously, the size of ICB-index depends on the number of the states of one time sequence contained in one disk block (let us denote this number by $N_{DB}$). In practice $N_{DB}$ is not very large, because each disk block usually contains the states of several time sequences (in order to optimize TSs update speed). In our experiments we considered 3 different values of $N_{DB}$: 80, 120 and 160 (these values are typical for process control systems for which we plan to use ICB-index). Table 4 contains the results of the experiments.

**Table 4.** ICB-index size and ICB-index size/TS size ratio for different values of $N_{DB}$

| Time sequence | Optimal value of $K$ parameter for $N_{DB}$ = 80, 120 and 160 | | | ICB-index size, Kb, for $N_{DB}$ = 80, 120 and 160 | | | ICB-index size / TS size ratio for $N_{DB}$ = 80, 120 and 160 | | |
|---|---|---|---|---|---|---|---|---|---|
| | 80 | 120 | 160 | 80 | 120 | 160 | 80 | 120 | 160 |
| Turbine vibrations | 93 | 80 | 80 | 1 864 | 1 130 | 788 | 3.2 | 1.9 | 1.3 |
| Generator active power | 538 | 432 | 429 | 562 | 418 | 331 | 1.0 | 0.7 | 0.6 |
| Oil pump current | 112 | 102 | 121 | 984 | 817 | 695 | 1.7 | 1.4 | 1.2 |
| Oil level in the spill tank | 99 | 77 | 66 | 617 | 476 | 392 | 1.1 | 0.8 | 0.7 |
| Bearing segment temp. | 13 | 13 | 13 | 40 | 31 | 30 | 0.1 | 0.1 | 0.1 |
| Generator temperature | 26 | 16 | 16 | 102 | 81 | 78 | 0.2 | 0.1 | 0.1 |

Table 4 shows that if $N_{DB}$ = 160 (or greater) then the size of ICB-index is not more than 1.3 times greater than the size of time sequence (recall that the size of IP-index is adequate only for those TSs that describe temperature processes, for the others the size of IP-index is 8–1000 times greater than the size of time sequence).

We have made further experiments on 2180 sensor-generated time sequences from hydroelectric power station "Zhigulevskaya" that describe temperature, electrical and hydromechanical processes. The cardinality of these TSs varied from 0.25 to 2.5 million, for all time sequences $N_{DB}$ = 160. We achieved the following results.

1.  For all time sequences the size of ICB-index is not more than 1.5 times greater than the size of time sequence.
2.  ICB-index makes the performance of value queries on continuous time sequences as high as IP-index does.
3.  ICB-index (as well as IP-index) improves the performance of value queries on continuous time sequences compared to conventional secondary indexes.

Table 5 shows how ICB-index (as well as IP-index) improves the average performance of value queries on continuous time sequences that belong to different groups compared to conventional secondary indexes.

**Table 5.** The performance increase of value queries on continuous time sequences due to the use of ICB-index compared to conventional secondary indexes

| The group of time sequences (depending on the type of the processes described by time sequences) | The number of time sequences in the group | Performance increase (averaged by the value we search for) | | |
|---|---|---|---|---|
| | | Minimum performance increase within the group | Average performance increase within the group | Maximum performance increase within the group |
| Electrical | 500 | 2.1 times | 2.62 times | 2.7 times |
| Hydromechanical | 440 | 2.1 times | 2.58 times | 2.7 times |
| Temperature | 1240 | 1.4 times | 1.55 times | 1.9 times |

Please note, that we achieved performance increase shown in Table 5 for real-life time sequences that conform to assumptions made in section 4, i.e. they are regular and describe continuous processes $v(t)$ such that $|v'(t)| \leq M$. If any of these assumptions doesn't hold, we cannot use relational operator (4.1) to find all the states satisfying the condition (3.2), because in this case the difference between $v_i$ and $v_{i+1}$ can be unpredictably great and, therefore, there is no such $M$ that the result of (4.1) operator contains all the states satisfying the condition (3.2). In this case the only way to support $\sigma^*_\Theta$ operator is to use ICB-index (we do not mention linear scan of TS and IP-index that, as we have shown in this paper, is enormously big).

# 7   Conclusions and Future Work

In this paper we presented a new indexing technique that supports value queries on continuous time sequences – the queries, which consider not only explicit values of the time sequence, but also the values that can be derived by interpolation functions. We formulated the mathematical definition of the problem of supporting such queries and showed that although in some cases the conventional secondary indexes can be used to support such queries, their use is an ineffective solution.

We also investigated the properties of IP-index – the first index structure supporting value queries on continuous time sequences. We showed that IP index can significantly speed up such queries (as its authors promised). But for some real-life time sequences the size of IP-index becomes enormously big. It makes it impossible to use IP-index in some application domains, e.g. in process control systems.

We proposed a new index structure supporting value queries on continuous time sequences – ICB-index. ICB-index is based on the idea of IP-index and on the two ideas of how we can reduce the size of IP-index: 1) replacing the state pointers (i.e. record pointers) by the block pointers in the index; 2) introducing the additional level of the index that allows to reduce the redundancy in IP-index. ICB-index makes the performance of the queries as high as IP-index does, but it requires substantially less space than IP-index.

The effectiveness of ICB-index is verified by the experiments on 2180 different sensor-generated time sequences from the hydroelectric power station "Zhigulevskaya". We gained the following results: 1) for all the time sequences the size of ICB-index is not more than 1.5 times greater than the size of time sequence, while the size of IP-index is up to 1000 times greater than the size of time sequence; 2) the performance of value queries of continuous time sequences is the same when using ICB-index and IP-index; 3) ICB-index (as well as IP-index) makes the response time of value queries on continuous time sequences, averaged by the value we search for, $1.4 - 2.7$ times shorter compared to the conventional secondary indexes, if time sequences are regular; ICB-index (or another index based on the idea of IP-index) is the only way to support such queries, if time sequences are irregular.

We consider the following directions for the future work.

1. Comparison of ICB-index with another improvement of IP-index – SIQ-index that was proposed in [13], in order to determine their difference both in query performance and size of the index structure.

2. Optimization of ICB-index, e.g. we can partition the $v$-axis into unequal intervals while building the auxiliary index (it can further reduce the size of ICB-index).
3. The development of the data structure that allows to build and update ICB-index for the time sequences that are dynamically updated in real-time mode.
4. The integration of ICB-index into some well-known extensible database management system.

# References

1. Andre-Jönsson, H.: Indexing Strategies for Time Series Data. Linköping University Dissertation No 757 (2002)
2. Bettini, C., Wang, X.S., Bertino, E., Jajodia, S.: Semantic Assumptions and Query Evaluation in Temporal Databases. In: Proceedings of ACM SIGMOD International Conference on Management of Data (1995) 257–268
3. Bonnet, P., Gehrke, J., Seshadri, P.: Towards Sensor Database Systems. In: Proceedings of the Second International Conference on Mobile Data Management (2001) 3–14
4. Bonnet, P., Seshadri, P.: Device Database Systems. In: Proceedings of the 16th International Conference on Data Engineering (2000) 194
5. Chandra, R., Segev, A.: Managing Temporal Financial Data in an Extensible Database. In: Proceedings of 19th VLDB Conference (1993) 302–313
6. Clifford, J., Warren, D.S.: Formal Semantics for Time in Databases. ACM Transactions on Database Systems, Vol. 8, No. 2 (1983) 214–254
7. Faloutsos, C., Ranganathan, M., Manolopoulos, Y.: Fast Subsequence Matching in Time-Series Databases. In: Proceedings of ACM SIGMOD International Conference on Management of Data (1994) 419–429
8. Grumbach, S., Rigaux, P., Segoufin, L.: Manipulating Interpolated Data is Easier than You Thought. In: Proceedings of 26th VLDB Conference (2000) 156–165
9. Grumbach, S., Rigaux, P., Segoufin, L.: Modeling and Querying Interpolated Spatial Data. In: Proceedings of 15th "Journees Bases de Donnees Avancees" (BDA) (1999) 469–487
10. Lin, L.: Management of 1-D Sequence Data – from Discrete to Continuous. Linköping University Dissertation No 561 (1999)
11. Lin, L., Risch, T.: Quering Continuous Time Sequences. In: Proceedings of 24th VLDB Conference (1998) 170–181
12. Lin, L., Risch, T., Sköld, M., Badal, D.: Indexing Values of Time Sequences. In: Proceedings of the 5th International Conference on Information and Knowledge Management (1996) 223–232
13. Nanopoulos, A., Manolopoulos, Y.: Indexing Time-Series Databases for Inverse Queries. In: Proceedings of the 9th International Conference on Database and Expert Systems Applications, LNCS 1460 (1998) 551–560
14. Neugebauer, L.: Optimization and Evaluation of Database Queries Including Embedded Interpolation Procedures. In: Proceedings of ACM SIGMOD International Conference on Management of Data (1991) 118–127
15. Perng, C.-S., Wang, H., Zhang, S.R., Parker, D.S.: Landmarks: A New Model for Similarity-Based Pattern Querying in Time Series Databases. In: Proceedings of the 16th International Conirence on Data Engineering (2000) 33–42
16. Pratt, K.B., Fink, E.: Search for Patterns in Compressed Time Series. International Journal of Image and Graphics, Vol. 2, No. 1 (2002) 89–106

17. Ramakrishnan, R., Donjerkovic, D., Ranganathan, A., Beyer, K.S., Krishnaprasad, M.: SRQL: Sorted Relational Query Language. In: Proceedings of the 10th International Conference on Scientific and Statistical Database Management (1998) 84–95
18. Richardson, J.: Supporting Lists in a Data Model (A Timely Approach). In: Proceedings of 18th VLDB Conference (1992) 127–138
19. Sayood, K.: Introduction to data compression. The Morgan Kaufmann Publishers Inc., ISBN 1-55860-346-8 (1996)
20. Segev, A., Shoshani, A.: A Temporal Data Model Based on Time Sequences. In: Tansel A.U. et al. (Eds.): Temporal Databases – Theory, Design and Implementation. The Benjamin/Cummings Publishing Company, ISBN 0-8053-2413-5 (1993) 248–269
21. Segev, A., Shoshani, A.: Logical Modeling of Temporal Data. In: Proceedings of ACM SIGMOD International Conference on Management of Data (1987) 454–466
22. Seshadri, P.: Management of Sequence Data. Ph.D. Thesis, University of Wisconsin, Computer Science Department (1996)
23. Seshadri, P., Livny, M., Ramakrishnan, R.: The Design and Implementation of a Sequence Database System. In: Proceedings of 22nd VLDB Conference (1996) 99–110
24. Shasha, D.: Tuning Time Series Queries in Finance: Case Studies and Recommendations. Data Engineering Bulletin, Vol. 22, No. 2 (1999) 40–46
25. Wolski, A., Kuha, J., Luukkanen, T., Pesonen, A.: Design of RapidBase – An Active Measurement Database System. In: Proceedings of International Database Engineering and Applications Symposium (2000) 75–82

# Multiple $k$ Nearest Neighbor Query Processing in Spatial Network Databases

Xuegang Huang, Christian S. Jensen, and Simonas Šaltenis

Department of Computer Science, Aalborg University
Fredrik Bajers Vej 7E, DK-9220 Aalborg Øst, Denmark
{xghuang, csj, simas}@cs.aau.dk

**Abstract.** This paper concerns the efficient processing of multiple $k$ nearest neighbor queries in a road-network setting. The assumed setting covers a range of scenarios such as the one where a large population of mobile service users that are constrained to a road network issue nearest-neighbor queries for points of interest that are accessible via the road network. Given multiple $k$ nearest neighbor queries, the paper proposes progressive techniques that selectively cache query results in main memory and subsequently reuse these for query processing. The paper initially proposes techniques for the case where an upper bound on $k$ is known a priori and then extends the techniques to the case where this is not so. Based on empirical studies with real-world data, the paper offers insight into the circumstances under which the different proposed techniques can be used with advantage for multiple $k$ nearest neighbor query processing.

## 1 Introduction

A variety of location-based services for travelers such as tourists, visitors, and commuters are currently expected to be among the mobile services that have the highest likelihood of being used widely as the use of data services takes off.

An infrastructure is emerging that enables such services. In particular, vehicles are increasingly being equipped with general-purpose computing devices, e.g., in-board devices and aftermarket PDAs and dedicated navigation devices, and cellular data connections, e.g., GSM/GPRS and UMTS. Mobile users may thus request services from a central server, and these services will involve the processing of spatial queries, among which $k$ nearest neighbor ($k$NN) queries are expected to be frequent.

This general scenario underlies a number of recent contributions to spatial query processing. In particular, it is reasonable to assume that the service users are constrained to a road network and that points of interest located in the road network are of interest to the services. Contributions exist that consider a variety of spatial queries in this setting, including range queries, closest-pair queries, distance joins, and also $k$NN queries. However, existing contributions focus on efficient means of answering a single query.

In contrast, it is reasonable to expect that the central server will at times receive many query requests, making it important to not simply consider the efficient processing of each query in isolation, but to process multiple queries efficiently, thus obtaining improved throughput. This paper does exactly that. The idea underlying multiple spatial query processing is to re-use cached results of recently computed, nearby queries

Y. Manolopoulos, J. Pokorný, and T. Sellis (Eds.): ADBIS 2006, LNCS 4152, pp. 266–281, 2006.

for computing a location-dependent query. The restriction of the mobile users and the points of interest to a road network contributes to making such re-use effective.

This paper thus considers the efficient processing of multiple $k$NN queries. More specifically, it presents a range of approaches for the main-memory caching and re-use of previously computed queries; and it reports on empirical studies of its proposals that utilize real-world road network and points of interest data. The caching approaches proposed are relatively easy to implement. Since it is also easy to switch from one approach to another, it is possible to combine the approaches so that the currently best approach is always utilized. The empirical studies suggest that the paper's proposals yield better performance than the existing single-query processing approach.

We believe that the contributions made by the paper are applicable to other $k$NN algorithms than the one considered, and we believe that they are applicable also to other types of spatial queries than $k$NN queries.

Query processing in the context of spatial networks as well as $k$NN query processing have recently attracted significant attention, and several papers are available that concern $k$NN and related queries for spatial networks [2,5,6,7,8,11]. One approach, the INE algorithm [11], uses variation of Dijkstra's algorithm for incremental network expansion, in that way computing a $k$NN query. In contrast, other approaches [2,5,6,8] pre-compute local distances to data objects or $k$NNs and store these on disk, so that subsequent $k$NN queries can be processed more efficiently. These approaches all consider the processing of queries one at a time, and they use disk-based structures. In contrast, our focus is on the efficient processing of multiple $k$NN queries by using main-memory caching strategies. This paper's proposal uses a modified INE algorithm.

Past proposals have utilized different storage structures for spatial networks. This paper adopts the data structures proposed along with the INE and Islands approaches [5,11], which are also similar to the CCAM [13] structure. Among the existing spatial network models [4,12], we adopt the link-node representation of a road network.

Within spatial databases, existing papers [9,10,14] discuss the processing of multiple queries by assuming that objects move in Euclidean space. Specifically, techniques [10] have been proposed for processing multiple range queries with the idea of ordering the queries so that "similar" queries are close and can be executed together. For continuously answering a collection of concurrent continuous $k$NN queries, the SEA-CNN approach [14] groups similar queries in a query table so that these continuous $k$NN queries are reduced to a spatial join between the objects and queries. The conceptual partitioning monitoring (CPM) algorithm [9] partitions the space around each query with a 2-dimensional grid and improves the nearest neighbor search on the grid by organizing the cells into conceptual rectangles for each query. In contrast, we consider the processing of multiple static $k$ nearest neighbor queries in spatial networks. This functionality is novel and also essential for continuous $k$NN query processing in spatial networks where static $k$NN queries have to be computed several times during a single continuous query.

The paper is outlined as follows. Section 2 presents the background of this paper. Section 3 introduces the multiple query processing approaches and their extensions. The performance of these approaches is studied in Section 4. Finally, Section 5 summarizes the paper and offers directions for future research.

## 2 Background

In the prototypical usage scenario for this paper's contribution, a population of on-line users move in a road network (e.g., by foot, bicycle, bus, or car) while issuing requests to a central server for location-based services. The services involve $k$NN queries for points of interest (e.g., gas stations or attractions) that are located within the road network. The objective is now for the server to be able to process as many queries as possible. Terming the users *query points* and the points of interest *data points*, we proceed to consider the modeling of this scenario in more detail.

### 2.1 The Road Network Model

A *road network* is defined as a two-tuple $RN = (G, co\mathcal{E})$, where $G$ is a directed, labeled graph and $co\mathcal{E}$ is a binary, so-called co-edge, relationship on edges. The graph $G$ is itself a two-tuple $(V, E)$, where $V$ is a set of vertices and $E$ is a set of edges. Vertices model intersections and starts and ends of roads. An edge $e$ models the road in-between an ordered pair of vertices and is a three-tuple $e = (v_s, v_e, l)$, where $v_s, v_e \in V$ are, respectively, the start and end vertex of the edge. The edge can be traversed only from $v_s$ to $v_e$. The element $l$ captures the travel length of the edge. A pair of edges $(e_i, e_j)$ belong to $co\mathcal{E}$, if and only if they represent the same bi-directional part of a road and a u-turn is allowed from $e_i$ to $e_j$.

Next, a *location loc* in the road network is a two-tuple $(e, pos)$ where $e$ is the edge where the location is located and $pos$ represents the length from the start vertex of the edge to *loc*. Then, a *data point* is modeled as a non-empty set of locations, i.e., $dp = \{loc_1, \cdots, loc_k\}$.

A *query point qp* is modeled as a two-tuple $(e, pos)$ where $e$ is the edge on which the query point is located and $pos$ represents the length from the start vertex of the edge to $qp$. Given a query point and a value $k$, the $k$NN query returns $k$ data points for which no other data points are closer to the query point in terms of road-network distance. The distance between a query point and a data point is the length of a shortest path between the query point and the location of the data point that is closest to the query point.

An edge with start and end vertices $v_i$ and $v_j$ is denoted by $e_{i,j}$. Figure 1 illustrates the concepts defined above, e.g., edge $e_{3,4} = (v_3, v_4, 6)$, data point $dp_1 = \{(e_{3,4}, 5),$ $(e_{4,3}, 1)\}$, and query point $qp = (e_{8,9}, 2)$.

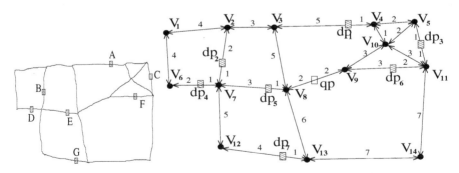

**Fig. 1.** Road Network Model

For the simplicity of our discussion, we assume that each edge in the road network has a corresponding co-edge connecting the two vertices in the opposite direction. Each data point then has two positions—one on each edge that models the road along which the data point is located. Note that in figures (as in Figure 1) we draw the two co-edges as one edge with two arrows.

## 2.2 INE Revisited

The INE algorithm is an adaptation of Dijkstra's shortest-path algorithm to use a disk-based network data structure [11]. It incrementally expands its search for data points through a network, starting at a query point. At each step, it reads the closest vertex $w$ from a priority queue, $Q_v$, which stores yet-to-be-visited vertices in the order of their network distance from the query point. Then it puts all non-visited adjacent vertices of $w$ into $Q_v$ and inserts the data points found on the adjacent edges of $w$ into a queue $Q_{dp}$ that stores the data points found so far. Let $d_k$ denote the network distance from the query point to the $k$th nearest neighbor in $Q_{dp}$. The search terminates when $k$ nearest neighbors are found and the distance from the query point to the next vertex to be explored is larger than $d_k$. For the example road network in Figure 1, Figure 2 illustrates the steps of the INE algorithm for a 3NN query at $qp = (e_{8,9}, 2)$.

| Step | $Q_v$ | $Q_{dp}$ | $d_k$ |
|---|---|---|---|
| 1 | $\langle (v_8, 2), (v_9, 2) \rangle$ | $\emptyset$ | $\infty$ |
| 2 | $\langle (v_9, 2), (v_7, 6), (v_3, 7), (v_{13}, 8) \rangle$ | $\langle (dp_5, 3) \rangle$ | $\infty$ |
| 3 | $\langle (v_{10}, 5), (v_7, 6), (v_3, 7), (v_{11}, 7), (v_{13}, 8) \rangle$ | $\langle (dp_5, 3), (dp_6, 5) \rangle$ | $\infty$ |
| 4 | $\langle (v_4, 6), (v_7, 6), (v_3, 7), (v_{11}, 7), (v_5, 7), (v_{13}, 8) \rangle$ | $\langle (dp_5, 3), (dp_6, 5) \rangle$ | $\infty$ |
| 5 | $\langle (v_7, 6), (v_3, 7), (v_{11}, 7), (v_5, 7), (v_{13}, 8) \rangle$ | $\langle (dp_5, 3), (dp_6, 5), (dp_1, 7) \rangle$ | 7 |
| 6 | $\langle (v_3, 7), (v_{11}, 7), (v_5, 7), (v_{13}, 8),$ $(v_2, 9), (v_6, 9), (v_{12}, 11) \rangle$ | $\langle (dp_5, 3), (dp_6, 5), (dp_1, 7),$ $(dp_2, 7), (dp_4, 7) \rangle$ | 7 |

**Fig. 2.** Steps for 3NN Using the INE Algorithm

## 2.3 System Architecture

We assume a client-server architecture: mobile users issue requests that involve $k$NN queries from their mobile devices to a central server that perform the processing. If, during a short time span, more queries arrive than the server can process, they are queued. As answering a $k$NN query entails accessing a certain amount of road network data, only some of which can be cached in main memory, the focus of this paper is to minimize the number of disk accesses to the road network data needed for answering multiple queries. Queries are put in a queue based on their arrival order. The road network model and the points of interest are also managed by the server. In each iteration, the query processor takes one query request from the queue and processes it by accessing these data sets. We omit the description of the detailed structures used for the network model and points of interest, as we simply re-use those described for the INE and Islands approaches [5,11].

# 3   Multiple $k$NN Processing Algorithms

By caching results of previously answered $k$NN queries in main memory, it becomes possible for a new query to experience a reduction of accesses to disk-resident road network data if it is able to re-use cached data. We denote the conventional algorithm that simply processes the multiple queries as they arrive using the INE approach as *Conv_kNN*. We proceed to introduce three approaches that improve the multiple $k$NN query processing when an upper-bound on $k$ is known, and then we extend the algorithms to the general case.

## 3.1   The Case of Known Upper Bound on $k$

We assume an upper bound $k_{\max}$ on the $k$ in the multiple $k$NN queries, i.e., $k \leq k_{\max}$. Such a bound may be realistic in real-world applications, as it can either be pre-defined by LBS vendors or be obtained by observing historical records.

**Basic Observation**

**Lemma 1.** Let $qp$ be a query point, $v$ a network vertex, and $dp$ a data point. If $dp$ is one of the $k$ nearest neighbors of $qp$ and the shortest path from $qp$ to $dp$ passes through $v$, then $dp$ is also one of the $k$ nearest neighbor data points of $v$.

Based on this lemma, during the $k$NN expansion process from a query point $qp$, if a network vertex $v$ is visited and the $k$ nearest neighbor data points of $v$ are already known, the expansion process reuses these $k$ nearest neighbors of $v$ and avoids visiting adjacent vertices of $v$. This is possible because the INE algorithm guarantees that when $v$ is visited (removed from the queue of vertices), the shortest path from $qp$ to $v$ has already been found. This, combined with Lemma 1, guarantees that all $qp$'s $k$ nearest neighbors, which have the shortest paths from $qp$ passing through $v$, can be found among the $k$ nearest neighbor data points of $v$.

With this observation, if we cache a certain amount of network vertices together with their $k$ nearest data points, a newly-started $k$NN expansion process will be able to re-use the cached data and save computation.

We extend the INE algorithm with the capability of using the cached data. The extended algorithm, $INE^*$, takes three parameters: the query point $qp$, the value $k$, and a list $L$ of cached results. Entries in the list $L$ have the form $(v, QP^v)$, where $v$ is a vertex and $QP^v$ is the set of the $k$ nearest data points of $v$ (including corresponding distance values). Similar to the INE approach, during the network expansion process, the $INE^*$ algorithm uses two priority queues, $Q_{dp}$ and $Q_v$, to record, respectively, data points and vertices together with their distance to the query point, denoted as $d(qp, dp)$ and $d(qp, v)$. Both queues sort elements by the distance value and do not allow duplicate data points or vertices. The size of $Q_{dp}$ is limited to $k$ elements. We introduce *update* and *deque* operations for the two queues. The *update*($dp/v$, *dist*) operation inserts a new data point or vertex and the corresponding distance into the queue. If this data point or vertex is already in the queue then, if *dist* is smaller than the distance stored in the queue, the distance value in the queue is updated to *dist*. The *deque* operation removes a vertex with the smallest distance and returns it. The pseudo code is listed next. Queues $Q_v$ and $Q_{dp}$ are assumed to be empty initially.

(1)  **procedure** $INE^*(qp, k, L)$
(2)  **for each** data point $dp$ on edge $qp.e$: $Q_{dp}.update(dp, d(qp, dp))$
(3)  $Q_v.update(qp.e.v_s, d(qp, qp.e.v_s)), Q_v.update(qp.e.v_e, d(qp, qp.e.v_e))$
(4)  **if** $\exists a$ such that $(a, qp.e) \in co\mathcal{E}$,do lines (2)–(3) assuming $qp = (a, a.l - qp.pos)$
(5)  Let $dp_k$ denote the $k$-th element in $Q_{dp}$, or $dp_k = \perp$ if there is no such element
(6)  $d_k \leftarrow d(qp, dp_k)$ // $d_k \leftarrow \infty$ if $dp_k = \perp$
(7)  $v_x \leftarrow Q_v.deque$, mark $v_x$ visited
(8)  **while** $d(qp, v_x) < d_k \wedge Q_v \neq \emptyset$
(9)    **if** $(v_x, QP^{v_x}) \in L$
(10)      **for each** $dp \in QP^{v_x}$: $Q_{dp}.update(dp, d(qp, v_x) + d(v_x, dp))$
(11)    **else**
(12)      **for each** non-visited adjacent vertex $v_y$ of $v_x$
(13)        **for each** $dp$ on edge $e_{x,y}$ (and edge $e_{y,x}$ if $(e_{x,y}, e_{y,x}) \in co\mathcal{E}$)
(14)          $Q_{dp}.update(dp, d(qp, v_x) + d(v_x, dp))$
(15)          $Q_v.update(v_y, d(qp, v_x) + e_{x,y}.l)$
(16)    $d_k \leftarrow d(qp, dp_k)$
(17)    $v_x \leftarrow Q_v.deque$, mark $v_x$ visited
(18) **return** $Q_{dp}$

During the $INE^*$ expansion process, whenever a vertex $v_x$ in the list $L$ is visited, the algorithm updates the queue $Q_{dp}$ with the $k$NNs of $v_x$ (line 10) and proceeds to visit the next vertex in the queue $Q_v$ (line 17). It can be observed that the algorithm still works if the list $L$ keeps more than $k$ nearest neighbors to corresponding query points. Then line 10 only uses the first $k$ data points of $v_x$. With this algorithm as a basis, we introduce three approaches for multiple $k$ nearest neighbor query processing.

**The Sharing Approach.** A basic approach to improving the efficiency of multiple query processing is to re-use the results of finished $k$NN queries for new queries. Since these finished query points can be treated as extra vertices on the road network, Lemma 1 applies, and the $INE^*$ algorithm can be used. To control the size of the list of cached query results (list $L$), we define a threshold $\mathcal{D}$ and add this threshold as an additional parameter to the $INE^*$ algorithm. For a query started at $qp$, if a cached query point $qp'$ is discovered in the network expansion process within a network distance $\mathcal{D}$ from $qp$, the result of the query at $qp$ is not saved in $L$. Otherwise, it is saved in the list for future queries.

Assuming a sequence of queries $\mathcal{S} = \langle \ldots, (qp_i, k_i), \ldots \rangle$, where $qp_i$ is a query point and $k_i$ is the number of nearest neighbors $(0 < k_i \leq k_{\max})$, we describe the sharing approach in the following.

**Approach 1.** (The $S\_kNN(\mathcal{S}, \mathcal{D}, k_{\max})$ algorithm)

1. Retrieve query request $(qp_i, k_i)$ from $\mathcal{S}$
2. Execute $INE^*(qp_i, k_i, L, \mathcal{D})$; in the expansion process, if $k_i$ neighbors are found within $\mathcal{D}$ while no cached query points are discovered, continue the expansion to distance range $\mathcal{D}$ or until a cached query point is reached; If there are no cached query points found within $\mathcal{D}$, continue the expansion until $k_{\max}$ neighbors are found and save the query result $(qp_i, QP^{qp_i})$ in $L$
3. Go to step 1 until $\mathcal{S} = \emptyset$                                       □

Step 2 of the approach guarantees that no two cached queries are closer to each other than $\mathcal{D}$ and that all of the cached results contain $k_{\max}$ neighbors. If $k$ nearest neighbors are found within the distance threshold $\mathcal{D}$ from the query, the algorithm continues the expansion to distance $\mathcal{D}$ to check if the query has to be cached.

An alternative policy is to cache a query point if its $k$ nearest neighbors are found within $\mathcal{D}$ and no other cached query points are reached in the process. With this policy, parts of the road network with a high density of data points will obtain many cached queries. This, in turn, may result in queries from other areas of the road network being purged from the cache due to its limited size. In this way, areas dense with data points are favored in the cache, and this may not be desirable because, even without caching, queries run fast in these areas due to small expansion ranges. Thus, we choose to enforce the threshold $\mathcal{D}$ strictly, which results in a uniform distribution of cached queries in the road network.

**The Clustering Approach.** Intuitively, if a number of queries are clustered in a small area of the road network, most of them will benefit from queries cached near the cluster. In the following, we explore a approach that finds the clusters of queries in order to obtain maximum reuse of cached query results within the clusters.

We divide the road network into "sub-networks" generated by the clusters of query points (details will follow). Consider Figure 3. The network inside the big rectangle R is a sub-network of the example road network in Figure 1. We denote this sub-network $R$. A network vertex belongs to $R$ if, based on coordinates of this vertex, it is inside the rectangle R. We divide all vertices belonging to $R$ into two types. First, those vertices whose adjacent vertices also belong to $R$ are called *internal vertices* of $R$. Second, those vertices that have at least one adjacent vertices not belonging to $R$ are defined as *border vertices*. In Figure 3, vertex $v_{10}$ is an internal vertex while vertices $v_4$, $v_9$, and $v_{11}$ are border vertices. A network edge belongs to $R$ if both its vertices belong to $R$, e.g., edges $e_{4,5}$ and $e_{9,11}$ belong to $R$ in Figure 3. A data point or a query point belongs to a sub-network $R$ if its edge belongs to $R$. As shown in Figure 3, data point $dp_6$ and query point $qp_2$ belong to $R$ while $dp_1$ and $qp_1$ do not.

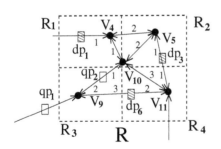

**Fig. 3.** The Clustering Approach

The clustering approach is based on the following observation. In Figure 3, suppose a 3NN query is issued from query point $qp_2$ in $R$. We can answer the query in two steps. First, we run the $INE^*$ algorithm to find 3NNs to all border vertices of $R$: $v_4, v_9, v_{11}$. Second, we run the $INE^*$ at $qp_2$, but during the incremental expansion process, when a border vertex is visited, we treat it as a cached query—its corresponding 3NNs (computed in the first step) are added into queue $Q_{dp}$ and the expansion process does not proceed to the adjacent vertices. Since 3NNs of all border vertices are pre-computed, the network expansion process is constrained inside $R$. The 3NNs of $qp_2$ are data points found either by the expansion process inside $R$ or by reading nearest neighbors of border vertices. Based on Lemma 1, the result of such a two-step execution is correct.

Although this procedure restricts the expansion scope of a $k$NN query to a sub-network, it is expensive to answer a single $k$NN query in such a way due to the cost of pre-computing $k$NNs of border vertices. However, since the pre-computed data can be used for all the query points inside the same sub-network, sharing of the pre-computed border vertices may be beneficial if a substantial amount of queries are running in the same sub-network. In addition, we "pre-compute" the border vertices in a lazy fashion—a $k$NN query on a border vertex is run and the result is cached only when we first encounter this vertex during the processing of some query.

To generate sub-networks, we assume that a spatio-temporal histogram $\mathcal{H}$ is available. It is a uniform two-dimensional $m \times m$ grid covering the MBR (Minimum Bounding Rectangle) of the whole road network. Each histogram cell records the number of query points located in this cell in a short history. We use the $DBSCAN$ algorithm [3] to cluster the histogram cells based on the recorded numbers of query points. A cluster's ID is then recorded with each cell of the cluster. Cells that are not assigned to any cluster by $DBSCAN$ are assigned to the "cluster" of outliers.

The modified $INE^*$ algorithm gets $\mathcal{H}$ as an extra parameter and uses the cluster IDs of grid cells to determine border vertices in the network expansion process. When examining a vertex, the algorithm uses the coordinates of the vertex to find its histogram cell and the corresponding cluster ID. By comparing the cluster IDs of the vertex and all its adjacent vertices, the algorithm determines if the vertex is a border vertex. For example, suppose the four small rectangles in Figure 3 are histogram cells and are assigned the same cluster ID while their neighboring rectangles (not shown in the figure) have different cluster IDs. Vertex $v_9$ is a border vertex because it is inside the cluster while one of its adjacent vertex is in a cell of a different cluster.

The clustering approaches takes the following parameters: a sequence of queries $\mathcal{S}$, the histogram $\mathcal{H} = \{c_1, c_2, \ldots, c_m\}$, the upper-bound $k_{\max}$, and the $DBSCAN$ parameters $Eps$ and $MinPts$ [3]. Briefly, $Eps$ defines a distance scope for searching neighborhood points and $MinPts$ defines the minimum number of points in a neighborhood to a "center" point. We proceed to consider the clustering approach in more detail.

**Approach 2.** (The $C\_kNN(\mathcal{S}, \mathcal{H}, k_{\max}, Eps, MinPts)$ algorithm)

1. Execute $DBSCAN(\mathcal{H}, Eps, MinPts)$ saving cluster IDs with each cell in $\mathcal{H}$
2. Retrieve $(qp_i, k_i)$ from $\mathcal{S}$
3. Execute $INE^*(qp_i, k_i, L, \mathcal{H})$; in the expansion process, if a border vertex $v$ is visited, do not consider its adjacent vertices (lines 12–15 in $INE^*$). If $v$ is in $L$, update $Q_{dp}$ with $k_i$NNs of $v$ (line 10). If $v$ is not in $L$, execute $INE^*(v, k_{\max}, L)$, placing the result $(v, QP^v)$ into $L$ and update $Q_{dp}$.
4. Go to step 2 until $\mathcal{S} = \emptyset$ □

As discussed, the cached list $L$, which is used to record border vertices of clusters and their $k$NNs, is populated in a lazy fashion. When enough border vertices of a cluster are computed, network expansions starting inside the cluster will have a reduced scope.

For an example of the running of this algorithm, consider the sub-network covered by rectangle $R$ in Figure 3 as a sub-network of the whole network in Figure 1. Assume that a number of queries were already processed in this sub-network, so that 3NNs to the border vertices are computed (shown in Figure 4(a)). Then, Figure 4(b) demonstrates the running steps of $INE^*(qp_2, 3, L, \mathcal{H})$ at $qp_2 = (e_{9,10}, 2)$.

| Border Vertex | 3NNs |
|:---:|:---:|
| $v_4$ | $\langle (dp_1, 1), (dp_3, 3), (dp_6, 6) \rangle$ |
| $v_9$ | $\langle (dp_6, 3), (dp_1, 5), (dp_5, 5) \rangle$ |
| $v_{11}$ | $\langle (dp_3, 1), (dp_6, 2), (dp_1, 5) \rangle$ |

(a) List $L$

| Step | $Q_v$ | $Q_{dp}$ | $d_k$ |
|:---:|:---|:---|:---:|
| 1 | $\langle (v_{10}, 1), (v_9, 2) \rangle$ | $\emptyset$ | $\infty$ |
| 2 | $\langle (v_9, 2), (v_4, 2), (v_5, 3), (v_{11}, 4) \rangle$ | $\emptyset$ | $\infty$ |
| 3 | $\langle (v_4, 2), (v_5, 3), (v_{11}, 4) \rangle$ | $\langle (dp_6, 5), (dp_1, 7), (dp_5, 7) \rangle$ | 7 |
| 4 | $\langle (v_5, 3), (v_{11}, 4) \rangle$ | $\langle (dp_1, 3), (dp_3, 5), (dp_6, 5) \rangle$ | 5 |
| 5 | $\langle (v_{11}, 4) \rangle$ | $\langle (dp_1, 3), (dp_3, 4), (dp_6, 5) \rangle$ | 5 |
| 6 | $\emptyset$ | $\langle (dp_1, 3), (dp_3, 4), (dp_6, 5) \rangle$ | 5 |

(b) Steps for 3NN from $qp_2$

**Fig. 4.** Running Example of $INE^*$ in $C\_kNN$

**The Combined Approach.** In an attempt to combine the benefits of the sharing and clustering approaches, we combine step 3 of the $C\_kNN$ algorithm with step 2 of the $S\_kNN$ algorithm. The combined approach takes six parameters: the sequence of queries $\mathcal{S}$, the histogram $\mathcal{H}$, the upper bound $k_{\max}$, clustering parameters $Eps$, $MinPts$, and the threshold $\mathcal{D}$. We describe the approach in the following.

**Approach 3.** (The $SC\_kNN(\mathcal{S}, \mathcal{H}, k_{\max}, Eps, MinPts, \mathcal{D})$ algorithm)

Execute $C\_kNN(\mathcal{S}, \mathcal{H}, k_{\max}, Eps, MinPts)$ with the following modifications: In step 3, execute $INE^*(qp_i, k_i, L, \mathcal{H})$; in the expansion process, if a border vertex $v$ is visited, do not consider its adjacent vertices (lines 12–15 in $INE^*$). If $v$ is in $L$, update $Q_{dp}$ with the $k_i$NNs of $v$ (line 10). If $v$ is not in $L$, run $INE^*(v, k_{\max}, L)$, put the result $(v, QP^v)$ into $L$, and update $Q_{dp}$. If $k_i$ neighbors are found within $\mathcal{D}$ while no cached query points are discovered, continue the expansion to distance range $\mathcal{D}$ or until a cached query point is reached; if there are no cached query points found within $\mathcal{D}$, continue the expansion until $k_{\max}$ neighbors are found and save the query result $(qp_i, QP^{qp_i})$ in $L$. $\qquad \square$

Here, list $L$ contains two types of cached results—results of previous queries and for border vertices. We assign equal weight to both types and use LRU cache-replacement.

### 3.2 The Case of Unknown Upper Bound on $k$

As described, the $S\_kNN$, $C\_kNN$, and $SC\_kNN$ algorithms assume a have fixed upper-bound on $k$. Such an assumption, although is applicable in real LBS applications, limits the flexibility of these applications. Thus, we proceed to extend the algorithms to process queries with arbitrary $k$ values.

To see how the $S\_kNN$ algorithm can be extended, suppose a $k_1$NN query at query point $qp_1$ in Figure 5 is processed and cached. When the $k_2$NN query at $qp_2$ visits $qp_1$, if $k_2 \leq k_1$, based on Lemma 1, the network expansion process can update the result with the first $k_2$ nearest data points of $qp_1$ and stop visiting neighbor vertices of $qp_1$. If

$k_2 > k_1$, the network expansion can also use the $k_1$ nearest data points of $qp_1$, but it has to continue visiting adjacent vertices of $qp_1$. The bigger the sizes ($k$'s) of the cached query results, the better such a strategy works.

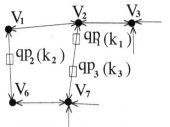

**Fig. 5.** Extension to $LS\_kNN$

To achieve high $k$'s of the cached query results, we exchange a cached query point with a new query point with a higher $k$, whenever such a new query is issued on the same edge or co-edge. For example in Figure 5, when another $k_3$NN query at $qp_3$ is issued and $qp_3$ is on the same edge as $qp_1$, after processing of $qp_3$, if $k_3 > k_1$, we replace the cached $qp_1$ with $qp_3$ and corresponding nearest neighbors. This way, the sizes ($k$'s) of the cached query results is increased lazily, as queries with high $k$'s arrive.

We summarize the "lazy-update" sharing approach in the following. The parameters for the algorithm are the same as for $S\_kNN$, except for the upper bound of $k$.

**Approach 4.** (The $LS\_kNN(\mathcal{S}, \mathcal{D})$ algorithm)

Execute the $S\_kNN$ algorithm with the following modifications. In step 2, in the expansion process of $INE^*(qp_i, k_i, L, \mathcal{D})$, when a cached query point is encountered and $L$ is updated with its nearest neighbors, if its $k$ value is smaller than $k_i$, continue visiting its adjacent vertices. Before step 3, if there is another query point on the same edge as $qp_i$ with a smaller $k$ value than $k_i$, replace that query point and its corresponding nearest neighbors with $qp_i$ and its nearest neighbors. □

With this "lazy-update" strategy, the $LS\_kNN$ algorithm is able to process multiple $kNN$ queries without setting the upper bound of $k$. Notice that the efficiency of the strategy largely depends on the distribution of $k$ values in the query stream. The worst case for the algorithm is when $k$ values are small at the beginning of a query stream and increase with time. Also notice that, by replacing cached query points with new ones on the same edge, the enforcement of the precise threshold $\mathcal{D}$ is compromised.

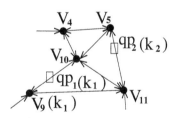

**Fig. 6.** Extension to $LC\_kNN$

We can also apply the lazy-update strategy to the $C\_kNN$ algorithm. As shown in Figure 6, let the border vertices of the sub-network be $v_4, v_5, v_9$, and $v_{11}$. Suppose also that after processing the $k_1$NN query at $qp_1$, border vertex $v_9$ is cached with $k_1$ nearest neighbors. Then, when a $k_2$NN query at $qp_2$ visits its border vertex $v_9$, if $k_2 \leq k_1$, the expansion process updates the query result with the first $k_2$NNs of $v_9$ and avoids visiting its adjacent vertices.

If $k_2 > k_1$, the network expansion is paused and a new $k_2$NN query is fired at $v_9$ to find $k_2$ nearest neighbors. Then the query uses these NNs of $v_9$ to update the query result and continues expanding in other directions. The cached $k_1$NNs of $v_9$ are replaced with its $k_2$NNs.

The pseudo code for this lazy-update clustering approach follows. It uses the same parameters as the $C\_kNN$ algorithm, except from the upper bound of $k$.

**Approach 5.** (The $LC\_kNN(\mathcal{S}, \mathcal{H}, Eps, MinPts)$ algorithm)

Execute the $C\_kNN$ algorithm with the following modification. In step 3, in the expansion process of $INE^*(qp_i, k_i, L, \mathcal{H})$, when a border vertex $v$ is visited, if $v$ is in $L$ and has no less than $k_i$ cached NNs, update $Q_{dp}$ with the $k_i$NNs of $v$. If $v$ is not in $L$ or it has less than $k_i$ cached NNs, run $INE^*(v, k_i, L)$, place the result $(v, QP^v)$ in $L$, and update $Q_{dp}$. □

We can also extend the $SC\_kNN$ algorithm by applying the above-described strategies. We omit the presentation of the "Lazy-Combined Approach" (denoted as **Approach 6**) and denote the algorithm as the $LSC\_kNN$ algorithm. It has the same parameters as the $SC\_kNN$ algorithm, but is able to handle multiple nearest neighbor queries with arbitrary $k$ values.

### 3.3  Discussion

As pointed out in the coverage of the VN3 and Island approaches [5,8], for an online-processing system, it is necessary to consider updates to the road network as well as points of interest during query processing. For the algorithms proposed in this paper, updates to both the network and data points will cause the cached list $L$ to be truncated and re-filled by new queries. In addition, since the Islands approach uses a similar network expansion algorithm as the INE algorithm, the approaches proposed here can be directly applied with the Islands approach. It will be an interesting direction to consider how to accommodate updates to the network and points of interest data while, at the same time, improve the efficiency of processing multiple queries.

As we have proposed a total of 6 approaches, we believe that, since the different approaches may perform best in different situations, it is possible to design query execution strategies that, based on given situations, automatically switch among these approaches to always achieve the best performance. The switching among the six approaches is straightforward since one only needs to replace the network expansion strategy in the $INE^*$ algorithm. In the next section, we focus on experimentally exploring the settings for which each of the approaches excels.

## 4   Evaluation

We use two data sets for examining the performance properties of the caching approaches. The first consists of a real-world road network and associated points of interest for Aalborg (AAL), Denmark, containing $11,300$ vertices, $13,375$ bi-directional edges, and $279$ data points. The second data set is a representation of the road network of San Francisco (SF) [1]. It contains $175,343$ vertices as well as $223,140$ bi-directional edges. The road network and points of interest data are arranged into disk pages based on the data structures described for the INE and Islands approaches [5,11]. We set the page size to 4k and use an LRU buffer for caching the disk pages read by the algorithms. While the $Conv\_kNN$ algorithm uses the whole main-memory buffer for the LRU buffer of disk pages, the algorithms proposed in the paper also use an in-memory list $L$ that occupies part of the main-memory buffer. We also apply the LRU strategy to $L$. The total size of the buffer is 15% of the network data. The AAL and SF datasets contain 129 and 4,023 pages. We study the performance of these approaches in terms of the average disk accesses. The approaches are implemented in C++ (the *DBSCAN* algorithm is based on the source code kindly provided to us by its authors [3]).

Values for parameters used in the experiments are listed in Figure 7 (the values in bold are defaults). Briefly, they are the number of query points, the range of $k$, the size of the cached list $L$, the distance threshold $\mathcal{D}$, the number of histogram cells, and parameters $Eps$ and $MinPts$ for the clustering algorithm. We define the maximum Euclidean distance between any two vertices of the road network as $D_{\max}$. The

| Query Points | 200, 500, 2000, **5000**, 20000 |
|---|---|
| Range of $k$ | $[1,5], [1,10], [\mathbf{1,20}], [1,50], [1,80]$ |
| Size of List $L$ | $0.1, 0.15, \mathbf{0.2}, 0.25, 0.3, 0.35, 0.4$ of the buffer size |
| Threshold $\mathcal{D}$ | $0.001, 0.005, \mathbf{0.01}, 0.05, 0.1$ of $D_{\max}$ |
| Histogram Cells | $5 \times 5, 8 \times 8, \mathbf{10 \times 10}, 15 \times 15, 20 \times 20$ |
| $Eps$ | $\mathbf{2 * C_l}$ |
| $MinPts$ | $\mathbf{0.5 * C_{ave}}$ |

**Fig. 7.** Parameter Values

distance threshold $\mathcal{D}$ is represented as a fraction of $D_{\max}$. The histogram is a uniform $m \times m$ grid exactly covering the MBR of the whole road network. We define $C_l$ as the length of the diagonal of a histogram cell, and $C_{ave}$ as the average number of query points inside an "occupied" cell, i.e., a cell containing at least one query point. The parameter $Eps$ is represented as a function of $C_l$, and $MinPts$ as a function of $C_{ave}$.

We use the real data points in the AAL data set and introduce synthetic data points for the SF data set in our evaluations. The synthetic data points are generated randomly at a density of 0.1%, where the density is defined as the number of data points versus the number of bi-directional edges in the network. The query points and $k$ values (within a given range) are generated randomly.

In the experiments, we first explore the differences among the **sharing, clustering**, and **combined** approaches. As described, updates to network data cause the cached list $L$ to be invalidated for all approaches. Depending on the frequency of such updates, the average number of queries issued in-between two resettings of the cached list $L$ may vary. In the first set of experiments, we explore the average query performance for varying amount of queries. The average number of disk accesses per query is measured, and the experiments are run on both the AAL and SF data sets, for both cases with and without a known upper bound on $k$. The parts of the curves to the right in Figure 8 describe the performance when updates are infrequent, while the parts of the curves towards the left represent the performance when updates are increasingly frequent.

For the **clustering** approach, at the beginning of each experiment, all the query points to be executed are clustered. Assuming that the query distribution does not change with time, the resulting sub-networks should be similar to the sub-networks generated by clustering a history of past queries as described in Section 3. Figure 8 shows that the **sharing** approach is competitive with the conventional algorithm in the AAL network, but has worse performance in the SF network. The results also demonstrate that the **clustering** and the **combined** approaches have high costs for very small amounts of query points. Thus, when the cached list $L$ is invalidated too often, which happens when updates occur, the approaches are worse than *Conv_kNN*.

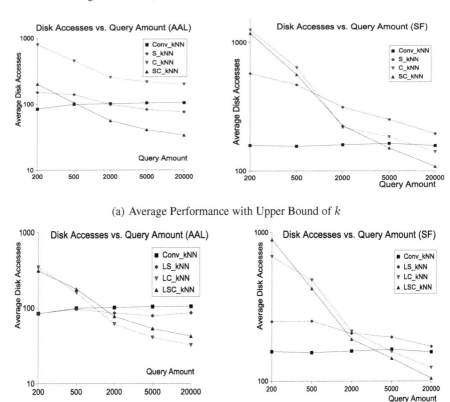

(a) Average Performance with Upper Bound of $k$

(b) Average Performance without Upper Bound of $k$

**Fig. 8.** Accumulated Query Performance

To study in detail how the cached data influence query efficiency, we perform $5,000$ queries (on the AAL data set) and measure the average disk accesses for every $100$ queries. We define the "steady state" for the cached list $L$ as the first time it becomes full. As illustrated in Figure 9, the performances of the **sharing** approaches are very close to that of the conventional algorithm, but exhibit slightly better performance than $Conv\_kNN$ after the "steady state."

The **clustering** and **combined** approaches both show substantially improved query performance after the steady state. An interesting observation is that the **clustering** algorithm with an upper bound of $k$ ($C\_kNN$) has the worst performance of all (see Figure 9(a)), while the variant without an upper bound of $k$, $LC\_kNN$, is the best one (see Figure 9(b)). This is because the upper bound of $k$ in the first case is used by $k$NN queries at border vertices. Depending on the value of $k_{max}$, each such query has a substantial cost and the corresponding cached result occupies substantial space in the list $L$. On the other hand, the $LC\_kNN$ algorithm incurs smaller cost for the queries at border vertices and uses less caching space to save the results of these queries, which, in turn, enables more items to be cached in $L$.

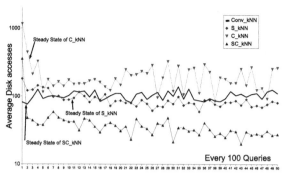

(a) Disk Accesses with Upper Bound of $k$

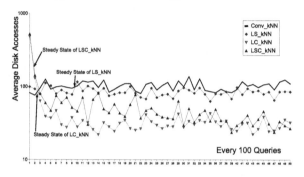

(b) Disk Accesses without Upper Bound of $k$

**Fig. 9.** Evolution of Performance on AAL Network

Figures 9(b) and 8(b) show that the $LC\_kNN$ algorithm is slightly better than $LSC\_kNN$ for the AAL data set, while the same experiment on the SF data set shows that $LSC\_kNN$ outperforms $LC\_kNN$. To further study the differences between these two approaches, experiments were performed varying other parameters: the size of the cached list $L$, the amount of cells in a histogram of queries, and the distance threshold $\mathcal{D}$ used by the $LSC\_kNN$ approach. Figure 10 shows the results for the AAL data set. It can be observed that the $LSC\_kNN$ algorithm performs better than the $LC\_kNN$ algorithm when the cache size is small, but it is outperformed by $LC\_kNN$ when the cache size grows. With more histogram cells, the $LC\_kNN$ algorithm seems to get worse and worse as the number of border vertices becomes too large compared to the given cache size. As expected, when the distance threshold $\mathcal{D}$ increases, less and less results of queries from non-border vertices are saved in the cache, and the performance of $LSC\_kNN$ becomes closer to $LC\_kNN$. The difference between the $LC\_kNN$ and $LSC\_kNN$ algorithms is also affected by the network topology, the density and distribution of data

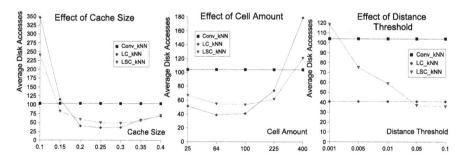

**Fig. 10.** Comparison of $LC\_kNN$ and $LSC\_kNN$ on Other Parameters (AAL)

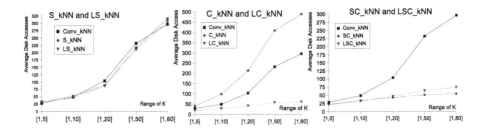

**Fig. 11.** Comparison of Approaches With or Without $k_{\max}$ (AAL)

points (the AAL data set includes real data points with a density of $2\%$ and the SF data set has synthetic, uniformly distributed data points with a density of $0.1\%$), as well as the effect of the clustering functions.

Based on the described experiments, we conclude that with a tight upper bound on $k$ that is not far from the average $k$ value of the queries, the **combined** approach is the best suited approach. For the case where there is no such upper bound, both the **clustering** and the **combined** approaches have similar performance. The **clustering** approach may then be preferable because it is simpler than the **combined** approach.

To explore further the difference among the approaches when the upper bound of $k$ is fixed or not, we execute $5,000$ queries for different ranges of $k$ values. The parameter $k_{\max}$ is used in the $S\_kNN$, $C\_kNN$, $and SC\_kNN$ algorithms, while the "lazy" variants of these algorithms use actual $k$ values as described in Section 3. As shown in Figure 11, the performances of the $S\_kNN$ and $LS\_kNN$ algorithms are quite close even with a very big upper bound of $k$. The **combined** approaches exhibit similar behavior. In contrast, the difference between the performances of $C\_kNN$ and $LC\_kNN$ is substantial. Comparing the performances of $LC\_kNN$ and $SC\_kNN$, we conclude that the "lazy" **clustering** approach ($LC\_kNN$) is the most suitable, independently of whether the upper bound of $k$ is known or not.

Experiments were also performed to check how the performance of these algorithms is influenced by other parameters, i.e., density of data points and the clustering parameters $Eps$ and $MinPts$. The results of these experiments, not covered in detail here, are quite consistent to those reported and thus provide a further validation of our findings.

Summarizing the performance evaluation, we can conclude that when the amount of successive queries between adjacent updates in a workload exceeds one thousand, the proposed approaches have better performance than the conventional approach, which uses the main-memory buffer solely as a disk-page buffer. Next, the "lazy" **clustering** approach ($LC\_kNN$) is the most competitive of the proposed approaches under a broad variety of settings.

## 5  Summary and Research Directions

With focus on the use of main-memory caching strategies for improving the efficiency of multiple $k$ nearest neighbor query processing, this paper presents a total of six caching algorithms. The paper first presents three basic approaches that assume that an upper bound on $k$ is known a priori. Then it extends these approaches to contend with the general case where the upper bound is unknown.

Empirical performance studies demonstrate that the algorithms excel over the conventional algorithm in a variety of circumstances. The algorithms termed the "lazy" **clustering** approach is the best in most settings. In addition, these algorithms are easy to implement and can be used in combination to achieve multiple $k$ nearest neighbor query processing that outperforms existing proposals.

Future work can be explored in several directions. First, as discussed in the paper, it is relevant to consider updates to the network as well as the points of interest when processing multiple queries. Second, it is of interest to conduct a theoretical analysis of the relationships among parameters such as the cache size, the range of $k$, the query throughput, the data point density, and the performance of multiple queries. Third, it is of interest to investigate approaches that off-load the server side by delegating processing to the mobile devices.

**Acknowledgments.** C. S. Jensen is also an adjunct professor in Department of Technology, Agder University College, Norway.

# References

1. T. Brinkhoff. Network-based Generator of Moving Objects. http://www.fh-oldenburg.de/iapg/personen/brinkhof/generator/
2. H. -J. Cho, C. -W. Chung. An Efficient and Scalable Approach to CNN Queries in a Road Network. In *Proc. VLDB*, pp. 865–876, 2005.
3. M. Ester, H. P. Kriegel, J. Sander, X. Xu. A Density-Based Algorithm for Discovering Clusters in Large Spatial Databases with Noise. In *Proc. KDD*, pp. 226–231, 1996.
4. R. H. Güting, V. T. de Almeida, and Z. Ding. Modeling and Querying Moving Objects in Networks. In *VLDB J.*, 2006, to appear.
5. X. Huang, C. S. Jensen, S. Šaltenis. The Islands Approach to Nearest Neighbor Querying in Spatial Networks. In *Proc. SSTD*, pp. 73–90, 2005.
6. H. Hu, D. L. Lee, J. Xu. Fast Nearest Neighbor Search on Road Networks. In *Proc. EDBT*, pp. 186–203, 2006.
7. C. S. Jensen, J. Kolář, T. B. Pedersen, I. Timko. Nearest Neighbor Queries in Road Networks. In *Proc. ACMGIS*, pp. 1–8, 2003.
8. M. Kolahdouzan, C. Shahabi. Voronoi-Based Nearest Neighbor Search for Spatial Network Databases. In *Proc. VLDB*, pp. 840–851, 2004.
9. K. Mouratidis, M. Hadjieleftheriou, D. Papadias. Conceptual Partitioning: An Efficient Method for Continuous Nearest Neighbor Monitoring. In *Proc. SIGMOD*, pp. 634–645, 2005.
10. A. Papadopoulos, Y. Manolopoulos. Multiple Range Query Optimization in Spatial Databases. In *Proc. ADBIS*, pp. 71–82, 1998.
11. D. Papadias, J. Zhang, N. Mamoulis, Y. Tao. Query Processing in Spatial Network Databases. In *Proc. VLDB*, pp. 802–813, 2003.
12. L. Speičys, C. S. Jensen, A. Kligys. Computational Data Modeling for Network Constrained Moving Objects. In *Proc. ACMGIS*, pp. 118–125, 2003.
13. S. Shekhar, D. Liu. CCAM: A Connectivity-Clustered Access Method for Networks and Network Computations. In *IEEE TKDE*, 19(1): 102–119, 1997.
14. X. Xiong, M. F. Mokbel, W. G. Aref. SEA-CNN: Scalable Processing of Continuous K-Nearest Neighbor Queries in Spatio-Temporal Databases. In *Proc. ICDE*, pp. 643–654, 2005.

# Searching for Similar Trajectories on Road Networks Using Spatio-temporal Similarity

Jung-Rae Hwang[1], Hye-Young Kang[2], and Ki-Joune Li[2]

[1] Department of Geographic Information Systems, Pusan National University, Korea
[2] Department of Computer Science, Pusan National University, Korea
{jrhwang, hykang}@isel.cs.pusan.ac.kr, lik@pnu.edu

**Abstract.** In order to search similar moving object trajectories, the previously used methods focused on Euclidean distance and considered only spatial similarity. Euclidean distance is not appropriate for road network space, where the distance is limited to the space adjacent to the roads. In this paper, we consider the properties of moving objects in road network space and define temporal similarity as well as spatio-temporal similarity between trajectories based on POI (Points of Interest) and TOI (Times of Interest) on road networks. Based on these definitions, we propose methods for searching for similar trajectories in road network space. Experimental results show the accuracy of our methods and the average search time in query processing.

**Keywords:** Trajectories, Road Network Space, Spatio-Temporal Similarity.

## 1 Introduction

In the real world, most moving objects exist in road network space rather than in Euclidean space. Nevertheless, most previous studies on moving object trajectories have been based on Euclidean distance. Euclidean distance is not appropriate for road network space in query processing or measuring similarity between moving object trajectories.

The previously used methods related to searching for similar moving object trajectories have several problems. First, the previous methods were based on Euclidean space. This is not suitable for road network space with the distance defined along a road. That is, it is difficult to apply the distance of Euclidean space to road network space. Second, the previous methods considered only spatial similarity without considering temporal similarity to search for similar moving object trajectories. For example, if two moving objects pass through the same points at different time intervals, we can know that they are similar to each other spatially, but not spatiotemporally.

In order to solve the problems of the previous methods, we investigate the properties of moving objects on road networks and consider spatial similarity as well as temporal and spatio-temporal similarity. In terms of real applications, we are not interested in meaningless locations or times. We consider interesting

Y. Manolopoulos, J. Pokorný, and T. Sellis (Eds.): ADBIS 2006, LNCS 4152, pp. 282–295, 2006.
© Springer-Verlag Berlin Heidelberg 2006

points on road networks. We also interest in the time interval of moving objects on road networks. In this paper, we define temporal similarity as well as spatio-temporal similarity between moving object trajectories based on POI (Points of Interest) and TOI(Times of Interest). Based on these definitions, we propose methods for searching for similar trajectories of moving objects on road networks.

This paper is organized as follows. In section 2, we introduce the related work and the problems of the previously used methods and propose the motivations of this paper. In section 3, we propose methods in order to search for similar trajectories on road networks based on POI and TOI. Experimental results are given in section 4. Finally, we conclude and suggest future work in section 5.

## 2    Related Work and Motivation

In this section, we introduce related work with moving object trajectories on road networks. We discuss the problem of previous methods and propose the motivations of this paper.

### 2.1    Related Work

In order to analyze the behavior of moving objects, we must first define a similarity measure between moving object trajectories. To define this similarity, research representing the trajectory of moving objects in road network space is required. There has been some research representing moving object trajectories. Models for representing and querying moving objects on road networks were presented in [1][2] and approaches for representing and reasoning moving objects in constrained environments moving along a road network were introduced in [3][4].

In previous studies, the similarity measure between trajectories was based on Euclidean space and considered only spatial similarity without considering temporal and spatio-temporal similarity. In particular, some methods searching for similar trajectories were introduced in [5][6]. The method proposed in [6] searched for the most similar trajectory with a given query trajectory. However, it is not suitable for road networks because this method is based on Euclidean space. The similarity retrieval for the trajectory of mobile objects was presented in [7], which determined the similarity between trajectories based on shape. Contrary to other existing studies, this considered the spatio-temporal similarity but has the problem of Euclidean distance. Methods searching for similar trajectories using the distance function based on OWD (one way distance) or Time Warping Distance were proposed in [8][9]. These methods also considered only spatial similarity without considering temporal and spatio-temporal similarity and it is difficult to apply these to road network space because of the problem of Euclidean distance and Time Warping Distance.

### 2.2    Motivation

In order to search moving object trajectories, some methods of existing research have been proposed in Euclidean space. However, Euclidean distance is not appropriate for road network space defined along a road. We investigate several differences between Euclidean space and road network space. First, while moving object trajectories in Euclidean space are expressed to a sequence of points in $(x,y,t)$ space, those of road networks are represented as a set of $(SegID, offset, t)$, where *SegID* is a road sector identifier, and *offset* is the offset from the starting point of the road sector. Therefore, the distance between two points is calculated more easily on road networks defined along road sectors than Euclidean space. Second, moving object trajectories in Euclidean space have a linear interpolation problem.

Figure 1 shows the difference in linear interpolation between Euclidean space and road network space. In figure 1, the moving object trajectory $TR_A$ passes $a$ and $c$. For example, suppose that find an intermediate point between $a$ and $c$. Then, we can find point $b$ in road network space using $(SegID, offset, t)$, but find point $b$' in Euclidean space. This means that Euclidean distance is not suitable for road network space.

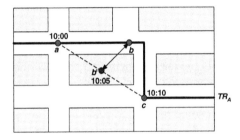

**Fig. 1.** Linear interpolation between Euclidean space and road network space

Based on these properties, figure 2 shows another example of the difference between Euclidean space and road network space. In figure 2, suppose that find the nearest two gas stations from a moving vehicle. If we find them by Euclidean distance, they are $a$ and $d$. However, if we find them along a road, they are $e$ and $f$. Consequently, we can know that $a$ and $d$ are meaningless gas stations from a given vehicle.

Most previous methods considered only spatial similarity in measuring the similarity between moving object trajectories. For example, if two trajectories pass through the same points at different time intervals on road networks, we understand by spatio-temporal intuition that they are not similar to each other. However, previous methods asserted that two trajectories are similar to each other.

To solve these problems concerning previous methods, we define spatial and temporal similarity based on road networks. In general, moving objects on road networks are represented as locations and times obtained by GPS. In real applications, however, we are not interested in these meaningless locations or times. We consider POI (Points Of Interest) on road networks and TOI (Times Of interest) of moving objects. In this paper, we define similarity between moving object trajectories based on POI and TOI and search for similar trajectories

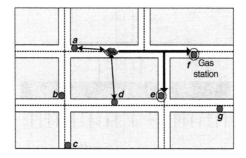

**Fig. 2.** Difference between Euclidean distance and road network distance

based on this similarity. For example, if two trajectories passed the same POI and TOI, we assert that they are similar to each other.

Figure 3 shows an example of how to define similarity of trajectories based on POI and TOI. For example, suppose that compare the similarity $Sim(TR_A,TR_B)$ between two trajectories $TR_A$ and $TR_B$ and the similarity $Sim(TR_B,TR_C)$ between two trajectories $TR_B$ and $TR_C$. In figure 3, while $TR_A$ and $TR_B$ have a few temporal differences because they pass the same POIs at different time intervals, $TR_B$ and $TR_C$ do not fully pass the same POIs but pass at an almost similar time interval. In figure 3, it is hard to distinguish the differences between $Sim(TR_A,TR_B)$ and $Sim(TR_B,TR_C)$. Therefore, we define not only temporal similarity and spatio-temporal similarity but also spatial distance and spatio-temporal distance based on POI and TOI. We propose methods for searching for similar trajectories using these definitions.

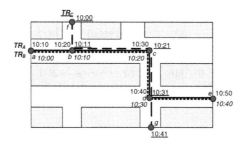

**Fig. 3.** How to define similarity of trajectories

## 3   Methods for Searching for Similar Trajectories on Road Networks

It is difficult to search directly for similar trajectories from a number of trajectories on road networks. To search for similar trajectories on road networks, therefore, we need a filtering step. In this paper, we use spatial filtering and temporal filtering because we search for similar trajectories based on spatial and

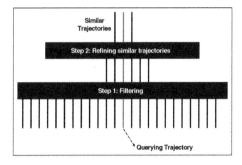

**Fig. 4.** Process of searching for similar trajectories

temporal similarity. Spatial filtering is considered by spatial similarity, which is based on POI. The spatial similarity was proposed in our previous research[10]. Temporal filtering is considered by temporal similarity, which is based on TOI. For example, if two trajectories passed by the same TOI, it is regarded that they are similar to each other temporally.

After performing the filtering step based on the spatial or temporal similarity, we need a refinement step in order to search for similar trajectories. In this paper, we use the refinement step in order to search for similar trajectories from the trajectories selected by the filtering step. Figure 4 shows the process of searching for similar trajectories by using the filtering step and the refinement step.

We introduced the following three methods in our previous research in order to search for similar trajectories on road networks[10]. Among three methods, we proposed the method for searching for similar trajectories in [10], which consists of two steps; the filtering step based on spatial similarity and the refinement step based on temporal distance. We also investigated problems related to the remaining methods. In this paper, we present methods in order to search for similar trajectories by solving the problems of our previous research.

- Method 1: Searching for similar trajectories based on spatial filtering and temporal distance.
- Method 2: Searching for similar trajectories based on temporal filtering and spatial distance.
- Method 3: Searching for similar trajectories based on spatio-temporal filtering and spatio-temporal distance.

In this section, we investigate each method in detail.

### 3.1   Searching for Similar Trajectories Based on Spatial Filtering and Temporal Distance

We proposed method 1 in our previous research. We briefly introduce method 1 in this subsection. Method 1 filters trajectories based on spatial similarity and refines similar trajectories based on temporal distance. We defined the spatial similarity between trajectories based on POI in method 1.

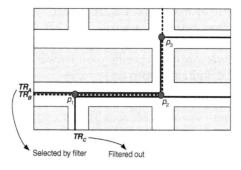

**Fig. 5.** Spatial Filter by POIs

Figure 5 shows an example of filtering based on the spatial similarity for POIs $(p_1,p_2,p_3)$ of a given query. As shown in figure 5, $TR_A$ and $TR_B$ were selected by filtering and $TR_C$ was filtered out.

In [10], we defined spatial similarity as well as the temporal distance between trajectories so as to apply method 1. Figure 6 shows an example of temporal distance between two trajectories. In this figure, the temporal distance between two trajectories $TR_A$ and $TR_B$ is calculated as follows:

$$dist_T(TR_A, TR_B, P) = 10 + 10 + 10 + 20 + 15 = 65$$

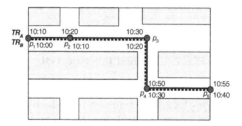

**Fig. 6.** An example of temporal distance

The advantage of this method is that a lot of trajectories are removed from trajectory data by spatial filtering. The disadvantage is that a long period of time is required in spatial filtering because the time complexity for the comparison between POIs of the query trajectory and those of trajectory data is $O(n^2)$.

## 3.2 Searching for Similar Trajectories Based on Temporal Filtering and Spatial Distance

In terms of practical application, the meaning of distance between two time intervals can rarely be found. Thus, our previous research introduced that method 2 was not appropriate for searching for similar trajectories. However, we are interested in time intervals of moving objects. TOI (Times of interest) is an important characteristic of road networks. If trajectories pass the same points at the same TOI on road networks, we consider that they are similar to each other. Therefore, we define temporal similarity based on TOI. For example, the heaviest traffic time intervals on a specific road network can be TOI. We filter trajectories using this definition. If two trajectories pass through the same TOI, they are considered similarity by the following definition:

**Definition 1.** *Temporal Similarity between Trajectories on Road Networks. Suppose that $T$ is a set of TOIs on a given road networks. Then, temporal similarity between two trajectories $TR_A$ and $TR_B$ is defined as*

$$Sim_{TOI}(TR_A, TR_B, T) = \begin{cases} 1, & if \forall t \in T, \\ & t \in [t_s(TR_A), t_e(TR_A)] \;\&\&\; t \in [t_s(TR_B), t_e(TR_B)] \\ 0, & otherwise \end{cases}$$

Figure 7 shows an example of filtering based on temporal similarity. Suppose that TOI of a given query trajectory is $[8:00 \sim 9:00]$. Then, $TR_C$, $TR_D$ and $TR_E$ are selected according to temporal similarity.

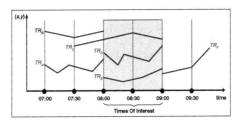

**Fig. 7.** Temporal Filter by TOI

With filtered trajectories based on temporal similarity, we define spatial distance and refine similar trajectories based on this. Spatial distance can be defined as the difference between the locations of two objects passing the same TOI as follows:

**Definition 2.** *Spatial Distance between Trajectories. Suppose that $t \in T$, and $T$ is the set of TOIs. Then the spatial distance between two trajectories $TR_A$ and $TR_B$ is defined as*

$$dist_S(TR_A, TR_B, T) = \sum dist_S(p(TR_A, t_i), p(TR_B, t_i))$$

Figure 8 shows an example of the spatial distance between two trajectories $TR_A$ and $TR_B$. Their spatial distance is calculated as follows:

$$dist_S(TR_A, TR_B, T) = 3 + 4 + 2 + 2.5 + 3.5 = 15$$

Consequently, method 2 searches for similar trajectories using filtering based on temporal similarity and refining based on spatial distance. However, the disadvantage of this method is that many trajectories are selected from trajectory

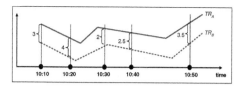

**Fig. 8.** An example of spatial distance

---

**Algorithm 1.** Searching on based Temporal Filter and Spatial Distance

---

Input.    input trajectories $TR_{IN}$, threshold $\delta$, query trajectory $tr_Q$, TOI set $T$,
          time interval $t$
Output.   similar trajectories $TR_{OUT}$
**Begin**
  $TR_{Candidate} \leftarrow \phi$
  $TR_{OUT} \leftarrow \phi$
  **For** each $tr \in TR_{IN}$
    **If** $tr.t \supseteq tr_Q.t$
    **then** $TR_{Candidate} \leftarrow TR_{Candidate} \cup \{tr\}$
  **For** each $tr \in TR_{Candidate}$
    **If** $dist_S(tr_Q, tr, T) < \delta$
    **then** $TR_{OUT} \leftarrow TR_{OUT} \cup \{tr\}$
  **return** $TR_{OUT}$
**End**

---

data by temporal filtering. For example, if the time interval of a query trajectory is much shorter than the total time interval for all moving objects, most trajectories are selected from trajectory data; nevertheless, the advantage is that little time is required in temporal filtering because the comparison between the time interval of a query trajectory and that of the trajectory data can be calculated simply and quickly.

Algorithm 1 summarizes the search procedure of method 2 explained in this subsection. It consists of two steps; the filtering step based on temporal similarity and the refinement step used in order to search for similar trajectories based on spatial distance.

## 3.3  Searching for Similar Trajectories Based on Spatio-temporal Filtering and Spatio-temporal Distance

There is a possibility that we search more efficiently for similar trajectories, if spatio-temporal similarity is considered in searching for similar trajectories on road networks. Therefore, method 3 considers both methods 1 and 2. That is, method 3 uses spatial and temporal similarity together in the filtering step.

Afterwards, we refine similar trajectories using spatio-temporal distance based on POI and TOI. In order to apply this method, we need a definition for measuring spatio-temporal distance. However, we stated in section 2 that it is difficult to define similarity between trajectories by spatio-temporal distance directly. In this paper, we regard spatio-temporal distance as the sum of temporal distance and spatial distance, which is defined as follows:

**Definition 3.** *Spatio-Temporal Distance between Trajectories. Suppose that* $TR_A$ *and* $TR_B$ *are two trajectories. Then the spatio-temporal distance between* $TR_A$ *and* $TR_B$ *is*

$$dist_{ST}(TR_A, TR_B) = dist_T(TR_A, TR_B) + dist_S(TR_A, TR_B)$$

To use this definition, the equivalence between temporal distance and spatial distance is defined so that 1 second = $\alpha$ meters. Moving objects on road networks move with various speeds. With this observation, we solve the equivalence problem between temporal distance and spatial distance using the speed of moving objects. That is, the equivalence problem between temporal distance and spatial distance is solved by the following formula:

$$Convt_S(TR_A, TR_B) = |(V_{TR_A}) - V_{TR_B}| \times dist_T(TR_A, TR_B)$$

The above formula converts temporal distance into spatial distance. Applying this formula to definition 3, the spatio-temporal distance between two trajectories is defined as follows:

$$dist_{ST}(TR_A, TR_B) = Convt_S(TR_A, TR_B) + dist_S(TR_A, TR_B)$$

By solving the equivalence problem, it is possible to represent the spatio-temporal distance as the spatial distance. Consequently, we search for similar trajectories based on spatiotemporal similarity and spatiotemporal distance. Figure 9 shows an example of the spatiotemporal distance between a query trajectory $TR_{Query}$ and the other trajectory $TR_A$. In this figure, suppose that the distance from $p_1$ to $p_4$ is 30 km and that between each POIs is 10 km, with each speed of $TR_{Query}$ and $TR_A$ during the blocks being 60 km/h and 30 km/h. Then, a query trajectory passes through four POIs($p_1, p_2, p_3, p_4$) during the time interval [10:00~10:30].

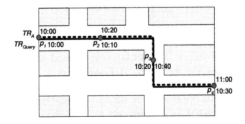

**Fig. 9.** An example of spatio-temporal distance

As shown in figure 9, $TR_A$ satisfied the condition of $TR_{Query}$. Thus, the spatio-temporal distance between $TR_{Query}$ and $TR_A$ is calculated as follows by the above formula and definition:

$$
\begin{aligned}
dist_{ST}(TR_{Query}, TR_A) &= dist_T(TR_{Query}, TR_A) + dist_S(TR_{Query}, TR_A) \\
&= |(V_{Query} - V_A)| \times dist_T(TR_{Query}, TR_A) + dist_S(TR_{Query}, TR_A) \\
&= |(60km/h - 30km/h)| \times 60 \text{ minutes} + 30 \text{ km} = 60 \text{ km}
\end{aligned}
$$

The advantage of this method is that the similar trajectories with a query trajectory are selected by spatial and temporal filtering, but the disadvantage is that more similar trajectories than the selected trajectories are included among the trajectories removed by the filtering step. For example, figure 10 shows another example of the spatio-temporal distance between the query trajectory $TR_{Query}$ and the trajectory $TR_B$ removed by the filtering step. In this example, we follow the assumptions of figure 9. We just suppose that the speeds of two trajectories $TR_{Query}$ and $TR_B$ are 60 km/h and 75 km/h.

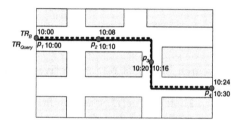

**Fig. 10.** Another example of spatio-temporal distance

When apply equally with the example of figure 9, the spatio-temporal distance between two trajectories is calculated as follows:

$$
\begin{aligned}
dist_{ST}(TR_{Query}, TR_B) &= dist_T(TR_{Query}, TR_B) + dist_S(TR_{Query}, TR_B) \\
&= |(V_{Query} - V_B)| \times dist_T(TR_{Query}, TR_B) + dist_S(TR_{Query}, TR_B) \\
&= |(60km/h - 75km/h)| \times 12 \text{ minutes} + 15 \text{ km} = 18 \text{ km}
\end{aligned}
$$

With $dist_{ST}(TR_{Query}, TR_A)$ and $dist_{ST}(TR_{Query}, TR_B)$ of the above examples, we know that $TR_B$ is more similar than $TR_A$ to the query trajectory $TR_{Query}$. However, method 3 does not compare $TR_B$ with $TR_{Query}$ because $TR_B$ is a trajectory removed by the filtering step based on temporal similarity.

Algorithm 2 summarizes the search procedure of method 3 explained in this subsection.

## 4   Experimental Results

In order to examine the feasibility of methods proposed in this paper, we performed experiments that compare the accuracy and the performance of our

**Algorithm 2.** Searching on based Spatio-Temporal Filter and Spatio-
Temporal Distance

Input.    input trajectories $TR_{IN}$, threshold $\delta$ and $\varepsilon$, query trajectory $tr_Q$,
POI set $P$, TOI set $T$, time interval $t$
Output.    similar trajectories $TR_{OUT}$
**Begin**
$TR_{Candidate} \leftarrow \phi$
$TR_{OUT} \leftarrow \phi$
**For** each $tr \in TR_{IN}$
**If** $(\forall p \in P,$ p is on $tr)$ && $(tr.t \supseteq tr_Q.t)$
**then** $TR_{Candidate} \leftarrow TR_{Candidate} \cup \{tr\}$
**For** each $tr \in TR_{Candidate}$
**If** $(dist_T(tr_Q, tr, P) < \delta)$ && $(dist_S(tr_Q, tr, T) < \varepsilon)$
**then** $TR_{OUT} \leftarrow TR_{OUT} \cup \{tr\}$
**return** $TR_{OUT}$
**End**

methods. In previous research, the most representative moving object generator based on road networks was T.Brinkhoff's moving object data generator[11][12]. Data generated by T.Brinkhoff's generator is not fit to real data because its movement is uniform and acceleration and deceleration are unexpressed. Thus, We experimented with a moving object generator based on real road networks in Pusan. This generator reflects the real road information and the traffic information and generates a near real moving object data by adding the various speeds of moving objects.

Figure 11 shows the generator of moving object data used in this paper. We defined 10,000 POIs on road networks in Pusan. We generated 100,000 moving object trajectories using this generator and 5,000 query trajectories from the moving object trajectories.

In our experiments, we compared our methods proposed in this paper. Figure 12 shows the consistency rate when searching for the same trajectory between method 1 and method 3. As shown in this figure, method 1 and method 3 show a high consistency rate. Here, we regarded the search result of the same trajectory by using these two methods as having been in agreement. For example, suppose that find the most similar trajectory with a query trajectory. As shown in this figure, the consistency rate between method 1 and method 3 is 100 % because they found the same trajectory.

We excluded method 2 from this experiment because method 2 searched for so many trajectories and they included meaningless trajectories. These meaningless trajectories are trajectories that pass different POIs with a query trajectory. This means that most trajectories are selected by temporal filtering because the time interval of a query trajectory is smaller than the total life span for all moving objects.

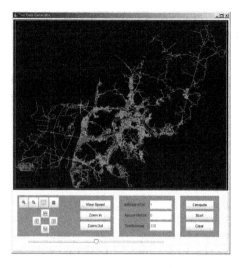

**Fig. 11.** Generator of moving object trajectories based on road networks

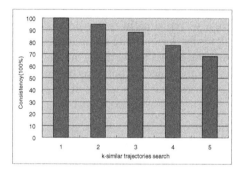

**Fig. 12.** Consistency rate between method 1 and method 3

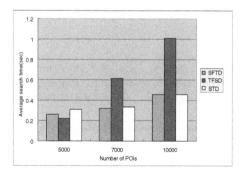

**Fig. 13.** Average search time in query processing

Figure 13 shows the average search time in query processing for our methods by changing the number of POIs. As stated above, method 2 searched for so many trajectories including meaningless trajectories. As shown in this figure, however, method 2 required the least search time. Contrary to our expectations, this means that method 1 is more necessary the search time than method 2. Because the time complexity of the spatial distance and the temporal distance is $O(N)$, those of the spatial filtering and the temporal filtering are $O(n^2)$ and a constant.

## 5   Conclusion and Future Work

The previously used methods related to searching for similar moving object trajectories were based on Euclidean space. A few studies introduced a similarity measure between moving object trajectories in road network space, but most studies considered only the spatial similarity between trajectories. In this paper, we defined the temporal similarity and the spatio-temporal similarity as well as the spatial distance and the spatio-temporal distance based on POI and TOI. Based on these definitions, we proposed methods for searching for similar trajectories on road networks. Our experimental results showed the accuracy of our methods and the average search time in query processing.

In the future, we will apply data mining techniques such as pattern analysis or clustering method to moving object trajectories on road networks. By using these mining techniques, detection of specific patterns of moving object trajectories or clusters of similar trajectories may be possible in the future.

## Acknowledgements

This research was supported by the Internet information Retrieval Research Center(IRC) in Hankuk Aviation University. IRC is a Regional Research Center of Kyounggi Province, designated by ITEP and Ministry of Commerce, Industry and Energy.

## References

1. Michalis Vazirgiannis and Ouri Wolfson. A Spatiotemporal Model and Language for Moving Objects on Road Networks. In *Proceedings of the Seventh International Symposium on Spatial and Temporal Databases*, pages 20–35. Springer-Verlag, 2001.
2. Laurynas Speicys, Christian S. Jensen, and Augustas Kligys. Computational Data Modeling for Network-constrained Moving Objects. In *Proceedings of the Eleventh ACM International Symposium on Advances in Geographic Information Systems*, pages 118–125, 2003.
3. Nico Van de Weghe, Anthony G. Cohn, Peter Bogaert, and Philippe De Maeyer. Representation of Moving Objects along a Road Network. In *Proceedings of the twelfth International Conference on Geoinformatics*.

4. Nirvana. Meratnia and Rolf A. de By. Representation in Location-based Services: Problems & Solution. In *Proceedings of the Third International Workshop on Web and Wireless Geographical Information Systems*.

5. Michail Vlachos, Dimitrios Gunopulos, and George Kollios. Robust Similarity Measures for Mobile Object Trajectories. In *Proceedings of the Thirteenth International Workshop on Database and Expert Systems Applications*, pages 721–728. IEEE Computer Society, 2002.

6. Michail Vlachos, George Kollios, and Dimitrios Gunopulos. Discovering Similar Multidimensional Trajectories. In *Proceedings of the Eighteenth International Conference on Data Engineering*, pages 673–684. IEEE Computer Society, 2002.

7. Yutaka Yanagisawa, Jun ichi Akahani, and Tetsuji Satoh. Shape-Based Similarity Query for Trajectory of Mobile Objects. In *Proceedings of the Fourth International Conference on Mobile Data Management*, pages 63–77. Springer-Verlag, 2003.

8. Bin Lin and Jianwen Su. Shapes based Trajectory Queries for Moving Objects. In *Proceedings of the Thirteenth ACM International Workshop on Geographic Information Systems*, pages 21–30, 2005.

9. Choon-Bo Shim and Jae-Woo Chang. Similar Sub-Trajectory Retrieval for Moving Objects in Spatio-temporal Databases. In *Proceedings of the Seventh East-European Conference on Advances in Databases and Informations Systems*, pages 308–322. Springer-Verlag, 2003.

10. Jung-Rae Hwang, Hye-Young Kang, and Ki-Joune Li. Spatio-temporal Similarity Analysis between Trajectories on Road Networks. In *Perspectives in Conceptual Modeling, ER Workshop on CoMoGIS*, pages 280–289. Springer, 2005.

11. Thomas Brinkhoff. Generating Network-Based Moving Objects. In *Proceedings of the twelfth International Conference on Scientific and Statistical Database Management*, pages 253–255, 2000.

12. Thomas Brinkhoff. A Framework for Generation Network-Based Moving Objects. *GeoInformatica*, 6(2).

# Efficient and Coordinated Checkpointing for Reliable Distributed Data Stream Management[*]

Gert Brettlecker[1], Heiko Schuldt[1], and Hans-Jörg Schek[2]

[1] University of Basel, Department of Computer Science, Basel, Switzerland
[2] University of Konstanz, Department of Computer & Information Science,
Konstanz, Germany
{gert.brettlecker, heiko.schuldt}@unibas.ch, schek@inf.ethz.ch

**Abstract.** Data Stream Management (DSM) addresses the continuous processing of sensor data. DSM requires the combination of stream operators, which may run on different distributed devices, into stream processes. Due to the recent advantages in sensor technologies and wireless communication, DSM is increasingly gaining importance in various application domains. Especially in healthcare, the continuous monitoring of patients at home (telemonitoring) can significantly benefit from DSM. A vital requirement in telemonitoring is however that DSM provides a high degree of reliability. In this paper, we present a novel approach to efficient and coordinated stream operator checkpointing supporting reliable DSM while maintaining the high result quality needed for healthcare applications. Furthermore, we present evaluation results of our checkpointing approach implemented within our process and data stream management infrastructure OSIRIS-SE. OSIRIS-SE supports flexible failure handling and efficient and coordinated checkpointing by means of consistent operator migration. This ensures complete and consistent continuous data stream processing even in the case of failures.

## 1 Introduction

*Data Stream Management* (DSM) addresses the continuous processing of sensor data. This is done by combining dedicated stream operators into *stream processes*. These operators might run on different distributed devices (e.g., sensor signal filtering at a PDA while sophisticated analysis and correlation operators are hosted by a more powerful server). Recent advantages in wireless communication standards, powerful mobile devices, and wearable computers proliferate ubiquitous and pervasive computing. At the same time, new sensor technologies are emerging and producing vast amounts of data. These trends are fostering distributed DSM. Especially in healthcare, the continuous monitoring of patients at home (telemonitoring) is becoming more and more important, mainly due to the progression of chronic ailments in an aging society. A vital requirement in

---

[*] The work presented in this paper has been done while all authors had been with the University of Health Sciences, Medical Informatics and Technology (UMIT) in Tyrol, Austria.

Y. Manolopoulos, J. Pokorný, and T. Sellis (Eds.): ADBIS 2006, LNCS 4152, pp. 296–312, 2006.

telemonitoring is that the infrastructure for distributed DSM provides a high degree of reliability and availability, since it can potentially be life-saving.

Consider, as an example, a patient being equipped with a wearable telemonitoring system consisting of ECG and blood pressure sensors attached to the body. Quality of life and disease treatment can greatly benefit from reliable and correct interpretation of the patient's physiological signs. Dedicated operators (e.g., for detection of pathological heartbeats) are shared among a wearable device (e.g., smartphone or PDA), a PC at the patient's home and servers at the caregiver side. Sensor information is reliably processed by a telemonitoring infrastructure. A telemonitoring infrastructure offers distributed DSM, supports the analysis of the data accumulated, and allows extracting and forwarding relevant information to the healthcare provider in charge. Reliability is of utmost importance in this scenario. Therefore no data stream elements are allowed to be omitted from processing since the infrastructure is in charge of detecting critical situations or even anticipating them.

In this paper, we present coordinated and efficient checkpointing of various operators within a stream process in order to reduce runtime and recovery overhead by maintaining result quality even in case of multiple failures. We consider a passive standby reliability approach [1] based on checkpointing as promising to the medical application scenario, where result quality is of utmost importance. Furthermore, we apply reliability in a fine grained way at the level of operators, rather than considering the whole stream processing engine running on the affected node. Hence in case of failures or overload situations, each running operator instance can be individually restarted at the best available node. The incident of restarting an operator instance on an alternative node is called *operator migration*. Based on operator migration, we propose and evaluate a new reliability protocol, called *Efficient and Coordinated Operator Checkpointing* (ECOC), to reduce the drawbacks of passive standby, i.e., high runtime and recovery overhead. Similar high demands on result quality may also arise in different stream processing applications, e.g., traffic control or scientific sensor networks.

The ECOC approach is incorporated into *OSIRIS-SE* [2,3], our infrastructure for distributed DSM. In particular, OSIRIS-SE provides an infrastructure that is able to efficiently combine, process, and manage continuous streams of data coming from different sensors across a loosely coupled network of nodes.

This paper is organized as follows: The basics of our data stream model and an overview of failures are presented in Section 2. In Section 3, we describe our ECOC approach to efficient and coordinated checkpointing in order to achieve a high degree of reliability for data stream management. Section 4 describes the implementation within OSIRIS-SE and gives experimental results on our reliability strategies. Section 5 surveys related work and Section 6 concludes.

## 2   Data Stream Model and Supported Failures

The basis of our ECOC approach on data streams is the operator and failure model we present in this section. A *data stream* is defined as a continuous

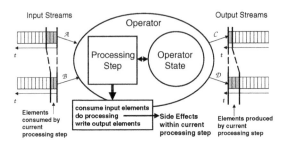

**Fig. 1.** Operator Model

transmission of sequentially ordered data elements. Each data element contains several data items as payload information and has a time context. For the illustration of timing issues (as used in Fig. 4), we apply two timelines to data stream elements: Each stream element has a logical time context (e.g., sequence number), which is called *stream-time*. On the other hand, each stream element has a physical time context, which corresponds to the time of execution by the consuming operator instance and is called *execution-time*. Stream elements which are pipelined through multiple operator instances have consequently one execution-time per operator. The latency between the execution-times of two subsequent operators is caused by processing and transmission delays and is only visible at execution-time scale. The stream-time is not showing these delays. If delays were neglected, stream-time and execution-time coincide.

### 2.1 Operators

*Operators* (Fig. 1) perform the *processing steps* as atomic units of execution of DSM by consuming input elements and producing output elements (marked in grey color in Fig. 1), while performing a state transition. Produced output elements are stored in output queues for downstream operators. In the remainder of the paper, the term 'operator' is used as short notation for an operator instance. A node in the DSM infrastructure hosting a running operator is also called *provider*. With respect to the investigated application scenario, we consider operators as stateful and deterministic machines. This means that every operator produces the same output stream and result into the same operator state when provided with the same input stream starting from the same operator state without regarding the execution-time. Optionally, the processing step may produce a *side effect*, e.g., performing a backup of the current operator state. A processing step has a stream-time context tuple according to the last consumed and last produced stream elements (shown grey in Fig. 1). In the following, we describe the state information accumulated during the execution of an operator instance, which is called *operator state*:

*Stream-Time Context:* The stream-time context refers to the last processing step executed by the operator with respect to input and output streams.

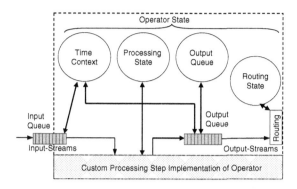

**Fig. 2.** Operator State

*Processing State:* Operators may aggregate a processing state. For example, a windowed average calculation requires to sum all data stream elements within the time window.

*Output Queue:* Output queues contain processed data stream elements for downstream operators. Data stream elements are allowed to be removed from the output queue only if no downstream operator relies on them. This mechanism is described in detail in Section 3.1. The content of input queue shown in Fig. 2 is not considered as part of the operator state. The purpose of the input queue is solely to decouple transport from execution and assure FIFO order of stream elements. The elements are immediately removed after processing.

*Routing State:* The destination of outgoing data streams, which is also stored within the operator state. This state changes very infrequently. The destination of an outgoing data stream only changes when the provider of the subsequent operator has changed, due to either a failure or an overload situation.

*Sensor operators* are operators without input data streams in our model. Sensor operators acquire their input directly from senor data sources. Our deterministic ECOC approach for reliability is not valid for these sensors, because regardless they are restarted from a given state, the acquired physical sensor data will be different and thus the output stream is not consistent. Reliability for sensor operators demands additional effort, e.g., establishing active standby sensor operators. Details on this are out of scope of this paper. *Output operators* are operators without output data streams. These operators store or transmit the result of stream processing to external systems.

## 2.2 Stream Processes

A *stream process* is a well defined set of logically linked operators continuously processing the selected input data streams, thereby producing results and having side effects. Figure 3 illustrates a stream process which continuously monitors ECG and blood pressure of a patient. Each box in Fig. 3 contains a full-fledged

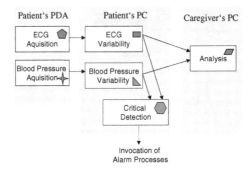

**Fig. 3.** Stream Process for Telemonitoring

operator of Fig. 2. *Quality of service parameters* attached to a process definition specify time-constraints for reliability. For example, a timeout-constraint indicates a maximum tolerable delay $d_{max}$ between stream-time and execution-time. After exceeding the threshold, the failure has to be handled by operator migration to ensure proper continuation of DSM. Fig. 4 illustrates this scenario within the given telemonitoring stream process by using the two timelines of DSM we introduced. After exceeding $d_{max}$ the infrastructure starts to seamlessly migrate the operator instance to another node. After $t_{migrate}$ the operator is migrated and after $t_{catch-up}$ the new operator instance has reduced its delay to normal.

### 2.3   Reliable DSM and Supported Failures

In general, reliable and fault-tolerant DSM implies that stream processes have to be executed in a way that the process specification is met, even in case of failures, i.e., to correctly execute all operators in proper order without generating gaps, duplicates, or wrong elements in the result stream. The definition based on our deterministic operator model reads as follows: Reliable DSM produces

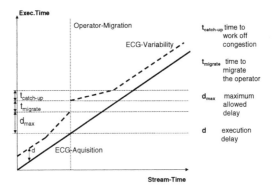

**Fig. 4.** Timelines of an Operator Migration

a result stream and side effects, which are equal to the result stream and side effects produced by an ideal, faultless DSM system.

In this work, our approach supports the following failure scenarios for reliable DSM: single or multiple fail-stop failures of operator instances or their providers and single or multiple network failures. Multiple failures are a sequence of single failures within the recovery time. With respect to failure handling, we apply the following failure classification:

*Temporary failures*, e.g., a temporary network disconnection (loss of messages) or a temporary failure of a provider which is able to recover within the maximum allowed delay time $d_{max}$, are compensated by the output buffers of the upstream provider. For recovery, the upstream provider resends the data stream elements and receives an acknowledge message. Failures exceeding $d_{max}$ become permanent failures.

*Permanent failures*, e.g., a permanent network disconnection or failure of a provider, require *to migrate* the operator instance with its aggregated operator state from the affected provider to another suitable provider. *Operator migration* implies the continuation of an operator instance from a recent checkpoint on a new provider in order to allow for seamless continuation of DSM, and eventually the stopping of an old running operator instance. Details on handling of permanent failures are described in Section 3.

Consequences of a failure in distributed DSM usually affect more than one node of the infrastructure because upstream and downstream operators may be on different nodes. Therefore, it is vital for proper failure handling of OSIRIS-SE that all affected nodes detect the failure or have to be informed about the failure. Further details on OSIRIS-SE can be found in [3].

# 3   Reliable Operator Checkpointing

In what follows, we present our proposed efficient and coordinated checkpointing (ECOC) approach in order to provide reliable DSM as needed for example in healthcare applications.

## 3.1   Operator Checkpoints

An *operator checkpoint* implies the reliable storage of the current operator state at a suitable backup node. The checkpoint contains the processing state, e.g., the hash table of a hash join or the current sum value for an aggregated sum operator. Additionally, the current stream-time of each input and output operator is part of the checkpoint and forms together the time-context tuple, i.e., for a checkpoint of operator B by $(t_B^{in}, t_B^{out})$, and for a checkpoint of operator A by $(t_A^{out})$, see Fig. 5. The superscript of the timestamp indicates the data stream, we refer the timestamp to. For simplification, we have only one input and one output stream named 'in' and 'out'. The time-context tuple of a checkpoint of operator A has only one value because A has only one output stream.

Output queues exist for each outgoing data stream, which allow for retransmission of data stream elements between producer and consumer operators in

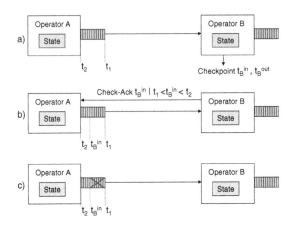

**Fig. 5.** Acknowledge Checkpointing Example

case of failures. The time-context of an output queue is characterized by an time-interval of the oldest and the youngest data stream element in the queue. This time-interval is given in square brackets, e.g., $[t_1, t_2]$ describes an output queue with the oldest stream-timestamp $t_1$ and the youngest stream-timestamp $t_2$. Within this work the backup node is considered as always available. Nevertheless, a failure of the backup node may be compensated by using multiple backup nodes, which could be seamlessly integrated in the approach presented in this paper.

As described in Section 2.1, the output queue elements are part of the operator state. Output stream elements may be sent to multiple downstream neighbors. After sending the elements, the sent elements still remain in this output queue. Whenever an operator is performing a checkpoint, a *checkpoint-acknowledge message (Check-Ack)* to the upstream operator indicates the stream-time of the youngest stream element that has contributed to this checkpoint. Until then, the downstream operator was able to rely on having the input elements before this timestamp buffered by the upstream operator. Figure 5 illustrates that by performing the checkpoint (see Fig. 5a), operator B can be sure that stream elements already contributing to this checkpoint are no longer needed for possibly necessary recovery. When all downstream operators have given a Check-Ack for certain output elements (illustrated in Fig. 5b), the output queue of operator A is trimmed and these elements are discarded (see Fig. 5c).

## 3.2   On the Coherence of Operator Checkpoints

Considering operator checkpoints of consecutive operators in the data stream process flow, we can identify some important time-dependencies which are leveraged by our ECOC approach. For illustration and experimental studies, we consider a simple stream process consisting of three operators (ECG, DF, and QRS) as shown in Figure 6. In here, 'EGC' is reading a sensor gathering an ECG sig-

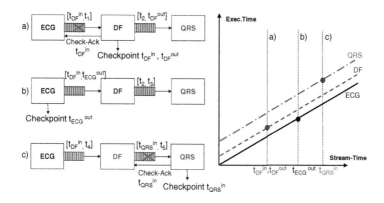

**Fig. 6.** Checkpointing in an Example Stream Process

nal, 'DF' is performing digital filtering in order to remove noise, and 'QRS' is analyzing the filtered ECG for detection and evaluation of the QRS complex, which is an important characteristic of heart activity.

In the following example, we analyze temporal relations between checkpoints of subsequent operators in the stream process flow. Firstly, DF is performing a checkpoint and the output queue of ECG is trimmed (illustrated in Fig. 6a). Secondly, ECG is performing a checkpoint later in time (see Fig. 6b). Since the time of the ECG checkpoint is later, some elements have accumulated in the output queue of ECG $[t_{DF}^{in}, t_{ECG}^{out}]$ and need to be saved within the checkpoint. Thirdly, QRS accomplishes its checkpoint at last and DF can trim its output queue accordingly (illustrated in Fig. 6c). The right hand side of Fig. 6 illustrates the corresponding timelines of checkpointing as introduced in Section 2.2.

In case of a single failure, e.g., the provider hosting the DF operator fails, the DSM infrastructure is able to migrate the operator instance. A new DF operator instance is restarted from the checkpoint $(t_{DF}^{in}, t_{DF}^{out})$ (see Fig. 6a). Since operator ECG keeps unacknowledged output elements, operator ECG is able to replay the data stream to the DF operator. Due to our deterministic operator model, duplicate data stream elements can be transparently dropped by the DSM infrastructure. In this failure scenario, the recovery of the output queue of the failed operator DF is not needed.

We further investigate the failure of two consecutive operators in the process control flow, e.g., both operators DF and QRS fail, illustrated in Fig. 7. The DSM infrastructure migrates the operator instances and restarts both operators from their recent checkpoints $(t_{DF}^{in}, t_{DF}^{out}; t_{QRS}^{in})$. Fig. 7 illustrates different cases dependent of the relative stream-time between the checkpoint of DF and QRS. Firstly, both checkpoints of DF and QRS are synchronous with respect to stream-time $(t_{DF}^{out} = t_{QRS}^{in})$. In this case, the recovered DF seamlessly feeds the recovered QRS. Secondly, we are moving the checkpoint of QRS after the checkpoint of DF $(t_{QRS}^{in} > t_{DF}^{out})$. This results in unnecessary duplicates produced by

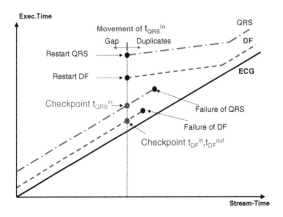

**Fig. 7.** Timelines of two consecutive operator failures

DF, because DF has recovered from an older checkpoint than QRS and replays elements already processed by QRS. Thirdly, the checkpoint of QRS is moved before the checkpoint of DF ($t_{QRS}^{in} < t_{DF}^{out}$). In this case, QRS expects elements before the checkpoint of DF. Since operator DF keeps unacknowledged output elements (starting from the time of the checkpoint of QRS), DF is able to replay the elements from the recovered output queue and fill the gap. These three failure scenarios are equivalent to scenarios where multiple consecutive operators fail.

Concluding the investigations so far, we see that the checkpointing and recovery of the output queue is not necessary for the single failure scenario. In the single failure scenario, the recovered operator starts from a checkpoint, which is before the current state of any subsequent operator. If a subsequent operator does not fail in the meantime, it will never need to process older stream elements again. Furthermore, the investigation of the multiple failure scenario has shown that the recovery of the output queue is not always needed. In the following, we guarantee that the most recent checkpoint of a subsequent operator is later or equal than the most recent checkpoint of its predecessor (e.g., $t_{QRS}^{in} \geq t_{DF}^{out}$). In this case, a recovered subsequent operator expects only elements, which are not yet produced by the recovered predecessor, and the checkpoints does not need to include the output queue.

Omitting the output queue from checkpointing is beneficial because usually many stream elements enter the output queue between two consecutive checkpoints. For the example of our stream process (Fig. 6), 100 ECG elements are arriving at the DF operator per second, the processing state of the digital filter consists of 4 values, and checkpoints are scheduled every 250 elements. In this case, the processing state is negligible compared to the average size of the output queue. Since checkpoint messages have to be transferred across network connections, the size of checkpoint messages has to be reduced by ensuring cases where no output queues are needed (see Section 4).

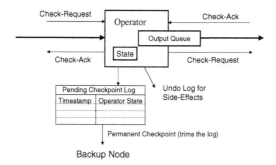

**Fig. 8.** Efficient Coordinated Operator Checkpointing

## 3.3   Efficient Coordinated Operator Checkpointing

*Efficient coordinated operator checkpointing* (ECOC) describes an algorithm that applies to the planning of checkpoints in order to guarantee that the input check-point timestamp of an operator is equal to the output checkpoint timestamp of the preceding operator. In this case, output queue content can be safely omitted from checkpoint messages because the output queue is empty at the time of sav-ing the checkpoint. This strategy describes a protocol between neighboring op-erators in the process control flow and controls the times of checkpoints. For this reason, an additional *checkpoint-request message (Check-Request)* is introduced.

Figure 8 illustrates the messages needed for checkpoint coordination and the internal logs. Figure 9 describes the algorithm in pseudocode. In order to delay a scheduled checkpoint for acknowledgment, a two-phase protocol is needed. In the first phase (*planning phase*), a checkpoint is scheduled locally and stored in the *pending checkpoint list*. Additionally, subsequent operators are informed by Check-Request messages. In the second phase (*backup phase*), subsequent operators confirm the pending checkpoint by Check-Ack messages. If all subse-quent operators have acknowledged the pending checkpoint is send as permanent checkpoint to the backup node. The pending checkpoint list is a data structure in the local memory assigned to an operator instance holding a list of check-points ordered by their corresponding timestamps. Contrary to the standard uncoordinated checkpointing, this data structure is additionally needed in order to perform ECOC. Due to the coordination of the checkpoints, the checkpoints in the pending checkpoint list are waiting for their acknowledgement from all subsequent operators. If all acknowledgements are received, it is guaranteed that permanent checkpoints of downstream operators have the acknowledged stream-timestamp.

A drawback of the ECOC approach is the delay of permanent checkpoints in the planning phase with respect to execution time. This delay is not blocking the stream processing and has no affect on time constraints in stream time. Assuming the case of a failure in the planning phase, the affected operator is recovered from the most recent permanent checkpoint before. In this case, correct data stream processing is still guaranteed, but duplicates are produced because

```
1   while (true)
2       wait to receive message or for local scheduler event;
3       if (message = Check-Request) or (local scheduler event) then
4           //planning phase if outputs available
5           if outputs.length > 0 then
6               do pending checkpoint;
7               add to PendingCheckpointList;
8               send Check-Request downstream;
9           else
10              do permanent checkpoint at backup node;
11              send Check-Ack upstream;
12          endif
13      endif
14      if (message = Check-Ack) then
15          //backup phase if pending checkpoint available
16          trim ouput queue;
17          if PendingCheckpointList.length>0 then
18              select last pending checkpoint;
19              save pending checkpoint permanently at backup node;
20              trim PendingCheckpointList;
21              send Check-Ack upstream;
22          endif
23      endif
24  endwhile
```

**Fig. 9.** Pseudocode of the ECOC Algorithm

of recovering from the older checkpoint. Therefore, we consider this drawback as acceptable.

Checkpoints may be triggered by a *local operator scheduler* or by a Check-Request message from an upstream operator. The local scheduler can follow different strategies for checkpoint planning, e.g., every 50 data stream elements or triggered by side-effects during operator processing.

Figure 10 illustrates the life cycle of pending checkpoints. Firstly, DF receives a Check-Request message (1.) and adds a pending checkpoint at stream-time 650 into the pending backup list (planning phase). After execution of the pending checkpoint a Check-Request message (2.) containing the corresponding stream-time is send to all downstream operators (only QRS in this example). Output operators, like QRS, have no output queues to consider for ECOC and are allowed to immediately perform a permanent checkpoint (3.). In the backup phase, DF receives the corresponding Check-Ack message (4.) from the downstream neighbor (QRS), indicating the execution of the requested checkpoint at QRS. In the meantime DF has received a new Check-Request (5.) for 700, which triggered a new pending checkpoint and is treated in the same way as the former request. Only if appropriate acknowledge messages of all downstream operators are received, the output queues are trimmed and the last recently pending checkpoint before or equal the acknowledgement is send as permanent checkpoint (6.) to the backup node (the one with stream-time 650). The selected pending checkpoint and all pending checkpoints before are removed from the pending checkpoint list whereas the newer pending checkpoints are kept in the list. After the permanent checkpoint of stream-time 650 a corresponding Check-Ack message (7.) is sent upstream.

Considering side-effects, the local operator scheduler normally plans a checkpoint after the execution of a side-effect. Due to the pending checkpoints in

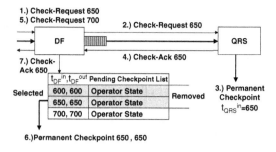

**Fig. 10.** Pending Checkpoints for ECOC

our approach, consistency of side-effects needs additional treatment. This can be done by an undo log for side-effects, which is immediately propagated to the backup node because a pending checkpoint may not become permanent in case of a failure during the planning phase. Considering the following example, in which a heart analysis operator is increasing a counter of pathological heartbeats as side effect. Given the case that the heart analysis operator has to be restarted from a recent checkpoint, the number of pathological heartbeats may be incorrect if pending checkpoints have not become permanent due to a failure. In this case, the side-effect may be executed too often. Applying the undo log would correct this failure.

Revisiting our example stream process again (see Fig. 6), we illustrate this checkpoint strategy according to Figure 11. In this scenario, ECOC is applied to the three operators ECG, DF, and QRS. In the following, we describe how the DSM infrastructure performs a checkpoint of ECG, which is synchronous to the checkpoint of DF. Operator ECG performs a pending checkpoint and sends a Check-Request message for timestamp $t_{ECG}^{out}$ to node hosting DF. Operator DF performs also a pending checkpoint and sends a Check-Request for timestamp $t_{DF}^{out}$ to the QRS operator. Finally, the QRS operator performs a permanent checkpoint sends a Check-Ack Message for timestamp $t_{DF}^{out}$ to DF. Operator DF is now able store the pending backup permanently at the backup node and sends a Check-Ack message for timestamp $t_{DF}^{in} = t_{ECG}^{out}$ to operator ECG. Operator ECG has now acknowledgments from all downstream neighbors (only operator DF) and is allowed to save the checkpoint of operator ECG permanently.

As the previous example has shown, ECOC can be cascaded to chains of arbitrary length, because Check-Request messages trigger the planning phase at

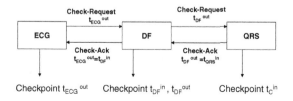

**Fig. 11.** ECOC of the Example Stream Process

the downstream neighbors and Check-Ack messages allow to move to the backup phase (see pseudocode in Fig. 9). Also splits in the stream process are supported by ECOC since Check-Request messages are send to all downstream neighbors and the pending checkpoint has to wait for all acknowledgements. Join operators are also supported by ECOC since Check-Request messages are obeyed from all upstream operators. Loops in the data flow of stream processes are currently not supported but topic of future work.

## 4    Evaluation

In this section, we present evaluation results of the different checkpointing strategies presented in Section 3. Our reliable DSM is implemented within our information management infrastructure *OSIRIS-SE* (Open Service Infrastructure for Reliable and Integrated process Support - Stream Enabled) [2,3]. In particular, we focus on network transport overhead and memory overhead during the runtime of a stream-process. Network transport overhead is the additional amount of communication data due to our reliability strategies. Memory overhead is the additional amount of main memory of a node imposed by our reliability measures. Furthermore, we evaluate the performance of the recovery phase by measuring the restart delays for operator recovery (see $t_{migrate}$ of Fig. 4).

OSIRIS-SE is an extended version of the predecessor OSIRIS [4,5,6,7] which offers an infrastructure for reliable P2P process execution. OSIRIS-SE, in addition, allows for the P2P execution of stream-processes in a distributed environment. OSIRIS-SE is programmed in Java and runs on various platforms, including also PDAs with MS Windows Mobile 2003. The experimental setup consists of a network of three Intel Xeon based Windows PCs as providers of operators and as backup nodes. Hence, these providers are equipped with a local OSIRIS-SE software layer hosted by a J2SE1.5 JVM and thus are able to run stream processes. In this experimental setup one node is an operator provider and a backup node for another provider at the same time. For this reason, also costs at the backup node are included in the evaluations.

The runtime evaluations cover the network overhead of checkpointing and the average JVM memory consumption. For the experiments, the sample stream process depicted in Figure 6 is used to process real world ECG data. The stream process is running at a rate of 400 ECG samples per second. Throughout the experiments, we compare three different checkpointing settings. The first setting (*Unsafe*) performs no operator checkpointing. This setting is used for overhead comparison. In the second setting (*Uncoordinated*), we have investigated uncoordinated locally scheduled checkpoints every *check-interval* elements. The third setting (*Coordinated*) considers our ECOC checkpointing approach triggered by the ECG operator every *check-interval* elements.

Figure 12 illustrates the network overhead caused by checkpointing based on the Unsafe setting, where no checkpointing is performed. The Uncoordinated setting shows the expected high network overhead since output stream elements are sent in checkpointing messages. The overhead of 100 % results from the fact that data stream elements are sent a second time within a checkpoint message.

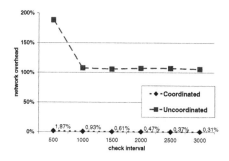

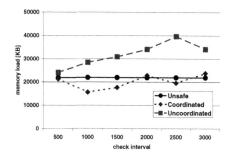

**Fig. 12.** Network Overhead          **Fig. 13.** Memory Consumption

For the shortest check-interval some elements are even sent a third time within a second checkpoint message resulting in an overhead of far more than 100 %. The ECOC approach used in the Coordinated setting shows only minor network overhead since the output elements are not part of checkpoint messages. Even more beneficial, ECOC shows a further reduction of network overhead when the check-interval is extended. Figure 13 illustrates the average memory consumption of the JVMs of the three settings. Coordinated shows about the same memory consumption as the Unsafe setting. Some deviations occur due to the heuristics of the JVM's garbage collector. The Uncoordinated setting shows higher memory consumption because of long output queues as part of checkpoint messages.

For the recovery evaluation the same setup as for the runtime evaluations is used. In the recovery case only Coordinated and Uncoordinated settings are evaluated because the Unsafe setting is not able to perform proper recovery needed in our medical scenario. The DF operator is deactivated at random times to simulate a failure scenario. The provider of the ECG operator detects the failure because of missing acknowledgments. If the maximum allowed timeout (see $d_{max}$ of Fig . 4) is reached the backup node of DF is assigned to activate a new DF operator instance from its recent checkpoint. The backup node needs $t_{migrate}$ to recover a new operator instance from the checkpoint. During $d_{max}$ and $t_{migrate}$ the ECG operator has to continuously acquire ECG readings from the sensor in order to avoid a dangerous gap in monitoring.

Fig. 14 illustrates the recovery times. Both settings perform about equal in this measurement. Uncoordinated needs slightly more time because of the recovery of output queues, which is not needed in the Coordinated setting.

The evaluations have shown that the ECOC approach performs significantly better than the Uncoordinated setting, which uses the standard passive standby approach. In particular, ECOC dramatically reduces the network overhead, which is a major drawback of the uncoordinated passive standby approach. Additional measurements demonstrate that ECOC does not result in higher memory consumption than the uncoordinated checkpointing approach. In the recovery phase, ECOC shows about the same performance as the uncoordinated approach.

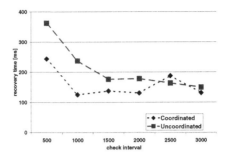

**Fig. 14.** Recovery Times

# 5   Related Work

Various approaches in the distributed database area address process-pairs [8], which describe a model of primary and backup processes. The primary process checkpoints all requests to the backup process, so the backup has all information necessary to take over control in case the primary fails. This approach has been adopted in the Tandem architecture [9] and combined with transaction checkpoints. Elonazhy et al. [10] have presented a survey of work on rollback recovery protocols in message-passing systems. Distributed DSM systems are a special kind of message-passing systems, therefore many of these protocols can be applied to DSM as well. Nevertheless, our DSM model that also follows the process-pairs idea extends this general approach. For example the domino effect does not appear in our approach because consistency between checkpoints is guaranteed by ECOC.

Although data stream management has received an increasing popularity among researchers in the recent years, only few work is focusing on aspects of availability and reliability.

*Aurora* [11] allows for user defined continuous query processing by placing and connecting operators in a query plan. Queries are based on a set of well-defined operators. QoS definitions specify performance requirements. Algorithms for high available DSM in the context of Aurora are discussed in [1]. In contrast to our work, this work addresses reliability at the level of the whole stream processing engine running on the affected node whereas we focus on reliability at the level of operator execution. We extended the well-know idea of process-pairs and checkpointing by leveraging the nature of operator states and their correlation between neighboring operators in a stream-process. Contrary to upstream backups and passive standby of Aurora, we apply coordinated checkpoints, which we state as more beneficial for our interested application area. Further work [12] presented in the context of *Borealis* [11], an extension of Aurora, allows for reduced result quality which is not applicable considering our indented healthcare application scenario.

*TelegraphCQ* [13] is a DSM project with special focus on adaptive query processing. *Fjords* allows for inter-module communication between an extensible set of operators enabling static and streaming data sources. *Eddies* supports adaptive query processing. Sets of operators are connected to the Eddy, and Eddy routes each tuple individually. *Flux* [14] provides load balancing and fault tolerance [15] by providing adaptive partitioning of operator execution over multiple network nodes. This is realized by placing Flux between producer/consumer pairs. Therefore, contrarily to our approach, Flux describes an active process-pairs approach, where parts of stream processing are partitioned to be reliably executed in parallel. This active approach is not applicable to our intended healthcare monitoring scenario, where hardware resources at the patient homes are limited.

# 6   Conclusion

In this paper, we have presented a novel approach to reliability for data stream management in a distributed environment. By implementing ECOC for efficient and coordinated operator checkpointing, the degree of reliability to be achieved in DSM can be significantly increased with affordable overhead. The presented reliability approach is implemented in OSIRIS-SE, a stream-enabled information management infrastructure. Additionally to reliability at operator level as presented in this paper, OSIRIS-SE addresses reliability also at network and application level [3]. Compared to other approaches in this field, our approach is particularly suited to be used in healthcare applications where a high degree of reliability is a vital requirement. A major contribution of this paper is the detailed presentation and experimental evaluation of coordinated checkpointing for transparent failure handling and state backup at the operator level. Operators are executed reliably by applying the process pairs approach.

In a first series of experiments with the OSIRIS-SE system, we have shown that coordinated checkpointing not only provide a higher degree of consistency in the system but also impose significantly less overhead compared to uncoordinated checkpointing. In particular, the high network overhead of uncoordinated checkpointing is significantly reduced by applying coordinated and efficient checkpointing. Especially, with respect to the intended medical application scenario including mobile devices and wireless connections energy consumption caused by network traffic is crucial.

In future work, we will emphasize also on the performance of complex stream processes with intra-process parallelism, i.e., on data stream processes containing join and split operators, and stream processes with cyclic data stream processing flows.

# References

1. Hwang, J., Balazinska, M., Rasin, A., Cetintemel, U., Stonebraker, M., Zdonik, S.: High Availability Algorithms for Distributed Stream Processing. In: Proc. of ICDE Conf. (2005)
2. Brettlecker, G., Schuldt, H., Schatz, R.: Hyperdatabases for Peer–to–Peer Data Stream Processing. In: Proc. of ICWS Conf., San Diego, CA, USA (2004) 358–366

3. Brettlecker, G., Schuldt, H., Schek, H.J.: Towards Reliable Data Stream Processing with OSIRIS-SE. In: Proc. of BTW Conf., Karlsruhe, Germany (2005) 405–414
4. Schuler, C., Schuldt, H., Türker, C., Weber, R., Schek, H.J.: Peer-to-Peer Execution of (Transactional) Processes. International Journal of Cooperative Information Systems (IJCIS) **14** (2005) 377–405
5. Schuler, C., Weber, R., Schuldt, H., Schek, H.J.: Peer–to–Peer Process Execution with OSIRIS. In: Proc. of ICSOC Conf., Trento, Italy (2003) 483–498
6. Weber, R., Schuler, C., Neukomm, P., Schuldt, H., Schek, H.J.: Web Service Composition with OGrape and OSIRIS. In: Proc. of VLDB Conf., Berlin, Germany (2003)
7. Schuler, C., Weber, R., Schuldt, H., Schek, H.J.: Scalable Peer–to–Peer Process Management – The OSIRIS Approach. In: Proc. of ICWS Conf., San Diego, CA, USA (2004) 26–34
8. Bartlett, J.: A NonStop Kernel. In: Proc. of ACM Symposium on Operating Systems Principles, Asilomar, CA, USA (1981) 22–29
9. Bartlett, J., Gray, J., Horst, B.: Fault Tolerance in Tandem Computer Systems. Technical Report TR 86.2, Tandem (1986)
10. Elnozahy, E., Alvisi, L., Wang, Y., Johnson, D.: A survey of rollback-recovery protocols in message-passing systems. ACM Comput. Surv. **34** (2002) 375–408
11. Balakrishnan, H., et al.: Retrospective on Aurora. VLDB Journal (2004)
12. Balazinska, M., Balakrishnan, H., Madden, S., Stonebraker, M.: Fault-Tolerance in the Borealis Distributed Stream Processing System. In: Proc. of ACM SIGMOD Conf., Baltimore, MD, USA (2005) 13–24
13. Chandrasekaran, S., et al.: TelegraphCQ: Continuous Dataflow Processing for an Uncertain World. In: Proc. of CIDR Conf., Asilomar, USA (2003)
14. Shah, M., Hellerstein, J., Chandrasekaran, S., Franklin, M.: Flux: An adaptive partitioning operator for continuous query systems. In: Proc. of ICDE Conf., Bangalore, India (2003)
15. Shah, M., Hellerstein, J., Brewer, E.: High Available, Fault-Tolerant, Parallel Dataflows. In: Proc. of ACM SIGMOD Conf. (2004) 827–838

# Towards Automatic *Eps* Calculation in Density-Based Clustering

Marcin Gorawski and Rafal Malczok

Silesian University of Technology,
Institute of Computer Science,
Akademicka 16,
44-100 Gliwice, Poland
{Marcin.Gorawski, Rafal.Malczok}@polsl.pl

**Abstract.** Many real-life applications use various kinds of clustering algorithms. Very popular and interesting are applications dealing with spatial data, like on-line map services or traffic tracking systems. A very important branch of spatial systems is telemetry. Our current research is focused on providing an efficient caching structure that will accelerate spatial queries evaluation and improve the ways of storing and processing aggregates. We use a density-based clustering algorithm to create the structure levels. The used clustering algorithm is fast and efficient but it requires a user-defined *Eps* parameter. As we cannot get the *Eps* parameter from the user for every level of the structure, we propose an Automatic *Eps* Calculation (AEC) algorithm which, based on the points distribution characteristics, is able to estimate the *Eps* parameter value. The algorithm is not limited to the telemetry-specific data and can be applied to any set of points located in a two-dimensional space. We describe in detail the algorithm operation, test results and possible algorithm improvements.

## 1 Introduction

Recent years have seen a rapid evolution in the spatial information systems. The systems are extremely useful and find their application in many aspects of everyday life. There are on-line services providing very precise and high-quality maps created from satellite images [1,2]. Another example is traffic-tracking systems monitoring car traffic in big cities. A very important branch of spatial systems is telemetry. Our team is doing research in spatial data warehousing. As a motivating example we use a telemetric system of integrated meter readings. The system consist of utility meters, collecting nodes and telemetric servers. The meters are located in blocks of flats, housing developments etc. They meter water, natural gas and electrical energy usage. The readings are sent to the telemetric server via radio. The ETL process extracts the readings and loads them to the data warehouse database. Apart from meter readings, the database stores information about the meters' geographical location and their attributes.

The most typical use for the data warehouse is to investigate utilities consumption. Our current research is focused on providing fast and accurate answers to

Y. Manolopoulos, J. Pokorný, and T. Sellis (Eds.): ADBIS 2006, LNCS 4152, pp. 313–328, 2006.

spatial aggregate queries. We are in the process of designing and implementing a caching structure dedicated to telemetry-specific data. We named the structure a Clustered Hybrid aR-Tree (CHR-Tree) because we intend to use clustering to create the structure nodes, and, like in the aR-Tree [5], the structure nodes store aggregates.

We already have a solution to the problem of storing and processing aggregates in the CHR-Tree nodes (please refer to [4]). Currently we are trying to employ density-based clustering to group telemetry objects and, consequently, construct the hierarchical structure of the CHR-Tree. The used clustering algorithm, although fast and efficient, requires a user-defined *Eps* parameter. We cannot assume getting the *Eps* parameter from the user for every level of the structure. In this paper we present the results of our research on finding a way to automatically calculate the *Eps* parameter. We propose an Automatic *Eps* Calculation (AEC) algorithm, which based on the points distribution characteristics is able to properly estimate the *Eps* parameter value. The reminder of the paper is organized as follows. In the next section we present more details of the problem we intend to solve. We then provide an extensive description of the AEC algorithm, its operation, input parameters and outcome. We also present tests results proving that the AEC algorithm is applicable to sets of two-dimensional points of a wide variety. Lastly, we conclude the paper presenting our future plans and possible algorithm improvements.

## 2    Problem Description

Constructing the caching structure for telemetry-specific data we have to take into consideration the telemetry objects distribution. A natural, although specific feature of the telemetric spatial data is that the meters are gathered in bigger or smaller groups (blocks of flats, housing developments). Also, in some regions the density of the meters is much higher than in other regions (the straightforward consequence of the natural distribution of housing developments in the cities, suburbs and uninhabited areas). Using density-based clustering we reflect the distribution of the meters in the hierarchical structure of the CHR-Tree. Figure 1 presents an example of a very simple CHR-tree created for a few meters located along roads. The tree leaves (spotted-line rectangles) are clusters of meters located by the same street. Intermediate level nodes (dotted-line rectangles) contain groups of neighboring leaves. The tree root (solid-line rectangle) contains all meters located in the region.

### 2.1    Clustering

Henceforth, we will use points and meters interchangeably. We know the geographical location of every meter. The meters are clustered (merged into groups) according to their location. The most similar are those points with the shortest distance between them. For our research we decided to use the density-based clustering algorithms. The well-known algorithms from this group are DBScan [3]

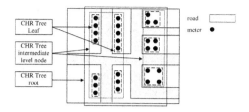

**Fig. 1.** A hypothetic CHR-Tree structure

and DBRS [6]. To start the clustering process the algorithms require two configuration parameters:

- *Eps* – a parameter that defines a half of the range query square side. The side length is used by the clustering algorithm to evaluate range queries when searching for neighboring points,
- *MinPts* – a parameter defining the minimal number of objects (points) required to create a cluster. If in the point neighborhood (area of which is defined by *Eps*) there are less than *MinPts* points, the point is marked as *noise*.

Motivated by the fact that to the best of our knowledge there is no automatic method for calculating or even estimating the *Eps* parameter for the density-based clustering [1], we decided to study the problem and try to propose a solution. In the following section we present an Automatic *Eps* Calculation (AEC) algorithm which, basing on the points distribution characteristics, is able to estimate the *Eps* parameter value. The algorithm application is not limited to the telemetry-specific data. It can be applied to any set of two-dimensional points. We do not address the problem of estimating the *MinPts* parameter, as we always set $MinPts = 1$ (we mark no utility meters as *noise*).

## 3    AEC Algorithm

To estimate the *Eps* parameter we have to investigate the distribution of the points in a given dataset. Datasets may be large, hence in some way we have to limit the amount of analyzed data. In such a situation using a random sampling approach is justified and can give good results in acceptable time.

The AEC algorithm uses three sets of data, whose usage is explained in the following subsections.

1. Set of all points $P$. The points in the set $P$ are located in an abstract region, in two-dimensional space.
2. Set $N$. The set contains points randomly chosen from the set $P$. There is a function $VNC$ that is used for creating the $N$ set. The function takes one optional parameter $r$, that defines the region from which the points are being

---

[1]  Authors of [3] proposed a simple heuristics to determine the *Eps* and *MinPts*. However, the heuristics cannot be considered automatic as it requires user interaction.

picked. When the $r$ parameter is present during the $N$ set generation, we mark the set with an appropriate subscript: $N_r$.

3. Set $H$. Like the $N$ set, the $H$ set contains points randomly picked from the $P$ set. The $H$ sets are created for points $n_i \in N$. In the case of the $H$ set, the function creating the set is named $VHC$. Next to the $r$ optional parameter, whose meaning is identical as for the $N$ set, the $VHC$ function takes another parameter defining the point $n_i$ that is skipped during random points drawing. The notation $H_{r,n_i}$ means that the $H$ set was created for the point $n_i \in N$; the point $n_i$ was skipped during random points drawing and the points in $H$ are located in a region $r$.

The cardinalities of $N$ and $H$ sets are the AEC algorithm parameters. Thanks to the parametrization of those values we can easily control the precision and the algorithm operation time. The cardinality of the $N$ set is defined as the percent of the whole $P$ set. The cardinality of the $H$ set is defined directly by the number of points creating the set.

### 3.1 Distance-Only Method

We start with the distance-only method which though not giving the proper results, is a good introduction to subsequent subsections. Our first observation was, that some knowledge about clusters distribution in a given region can be gained by analyzing the distances between points. To analyze the distances we utilize the $N$ and $H$ sets. The beginning of the AEC algorithm operation is as follows: from the set $P$ pick randomly points creating the set $N$. In the next step, for each point $n_i \in N$ create set $H_{n_i}$ (figure 2). The distance analysis is based on calculating the Euclidean distances between the point $n_i$ and all the points in the related $H_{n_i}$ set. The distances are calculated for all points in the $N$ set and all related $H$ sets. In the next step we sort all the distances in ascending order. The sorted distances $(dist_1, dist_2, \ldots, dist_k)$ are then analyzed; the algorithm searches for the biggest difference (the biggest delta: $\triangle_i = dist_i - dist_{i-1}$) between two distances.

Let's consider the example shown in figure 3. We have a set $P$ of 16 points grouped in 3 clusters. Of course the algorithm does not know anything about the

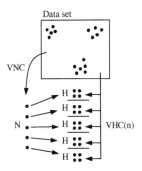

**Fig. 2.** $N$ and $H$ sets creation process

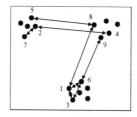

**Fig. 3.** An example of the distance-only based method

**Table 1.** Hypothetical $N$ and $H$ sets, and distances between the points

| $n_i$ | $H$ set | distances |
|---|---|---|
| 1 | 6, 3 | dist(1,6) = 45.7; dist(1,3) = 37.2 |
| 2 | 4, 7 | dist(2,4) = 342.4; dist(2,7) = 52.2 |
| 6 | 9, 8 | dist(6,9) = 222.4; dist(6,3) = 79.2 |
| 8 | 5, 1 | dist(8,5) = 302.1; dist(8,1) = 325.0 |

clusters. For this example, to make the N and H sets small for better presentation, we set the N cardinality to 25%, and the H cardinality to 2 points. We randomly pick 25% of the points from the $P$ set and we get the points marked: 1, 2, 6, 8. For each of the points we randomly choose 2 points to create the $H$ sets.

When we sort the distances in ascending order and look for the greatest delta we see that it is for $dist(6,3)$ and $dist(6,9)$. The first distance, between point $p_6$ and point $p_3$ is the greatest distance inside a cluster, while the distance between $p_6$ and point $p_9$ is the least distance between clusters. It may seem that having such a result is enough for determining the *Eps* parameter for density-based clustering, because we can simply choose the greatest distance inside a cluster as an *Eps* and we can expect the clustering algorithm to discover all the clusters and to merge none of them.

This is true, but only for very simple sets of clusters. There are many cases which cannot be correctly analyzed by simply checking the distances between clusters. Below we mentioned only a selection of them:

- there are many clusters. Some of them are close to each other, but there are also distant ones. The greatest distance delta will be between the close clusters and between the distance ones, not between points inside clusters and close clusters. One may want to analyze the series of measurements to find the *first biggest delta*, but we found it extremely complicated,
- the density of points in clusters is different. There are very dense clusters and also sparse clusters. It may happen that dense clusters are closer to each other than the points in sparse clusters.

### 3.2 Stripe Density

From the above we see that knowing only the distance between points $p_i$ and $p_j$ is not enough to calculate the *Eps* parameter. Missing is the knowledge about the neighborhood of the analyzed points, specifically the points in the region between the investigated points $p_i$ and $p_j$. We decided to introduce a new coefficient $PIS$ (*Points In Stripe*). The $PIS(p_i, p_j)$ is the number of points located in a *stripe* connecting the points $p_i$ and $p_j$.

To evaluate the $PIS$ coefficient value for a pair of points we use one spatial query and four straight lines. Having the $p_i$ and $p_j$ points coordinates we can easily calculate the parameters $a$ and $b$ of the straight line $L$ equation $y = ax + b$. The line $L$ contains the points $p_i$ and $p_j$. In the next step we calculate equations of the lines perpendicular to $L$ in points $p_i$ and $p_j$, respectively $L_{p_i}$ and $L_{p_j}$ (we do not include the equations because of the complicated notation and straightforward computation). The final step is to calculate two lines parallel to $L$, first above line $L - L_a$ and the second below line $L - L_b$. The distance between the parallel lines and the $L$ line (the difference in the $b$ line equation coefficient) is defined as a fraction of the distance between points $p_i$ and $p_j$. The fraction is the AEC algorithm parameter named *stripeWidth*; *stripeWidth* $\in (0, 1)$. The lines create a *stripe* between the points, and the *stripe* encompasses some number of points.

Having the lines equations we can easily calculate whether or not an arbitrary point from the set $P$ is located inside the stripe between points $p_i$ and $p_j$ or not. In order to reduce the number of points being analyzed we evaluate a rectangle encompassing the whole stripe. The rectangle vertexes coordinates are set by calculating the coordinates of the points where the stripe-constructing lines ($L_a$, $L_b$, $L_{p_i}$ and $L_{p_j}$) cross, and then choosing the extreme crossing points coordinates. Using the stripe-encompassing rectangle we execute the range query to choose the points which can possibly be located within the stripe between $p_i$ and $p_j$. In the next step, only the points chosen by the range query are examined if they are located within the stripe.

After calculation of the $PIS$ coefficient we are equipped with two values that provide interesting knowledge not only about distance between points $p_i$ and $p_j$ but also about their neighborhood. Basing on the distance between points: $dist(p_i, p_j)$ and the number of points in a stripe between points $PIS(p_i, p_j)$ we can calculate another coefficient, which is a density of the stripe between $p_i$ and $p_j$: $dens(p_i, p_j) = \frac{PIS(p_i, p_j)}{dist(p_i, p_j)^2 \cdot stripeWidth}$.

Figure 4 presents an example of a stripe between two points. The *stripeWidth* parameter was set to 0.98. In this example we are checking two pairs of points: $p_5$, $p_8$ and $p_3$, $p_6$. We used a dashed line to indicate the line linking two points. Solid lines depict the parallel and perpendicular lines. Rectangles drawn with spotted lines describe the regions encompassing the stripes. From the picture we see, that there is one point between points $p_5$, $p_8$ and there are 3 points between points $p_3$, $p_6$. The density for $p_5$, $p_8$: $dens(p_5, p_8) = \frac{1}{302.1^2 \cdot 0.98} = 0.11 \cdot 10^{-4}$ and for $p_3$, $p_6$: $dens(p_3, p_6) = \frac{3}{79.2^2 \cdot 0.98} = 4.88 \cdot 10^{-4}$. From the example we see that the density inside the cluster is much greater than outside the cluster. The density coupled with the distance between points brings much more knowledge than the distance only.

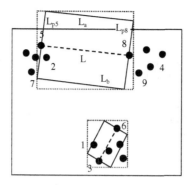

**Fig. 4.** Illustration of the stripe between two Points

Now we are able to ascertain whether two points are relatively close to each other, and whether they are located in a dense neighborhood or, on the other hand, if the points are relatively distant and there are almost no points in the stripe between them. After analyzing the operation of the density-based algorithms, that are executing a series of range queries, we decided to search not for a distance between points in clusters or for the thinnest cluster diameter, but rather for a minimal distance between clusters. The distance, or at least a value based on the distance, can be used as the *Eps* parameter in the density-based clustering algorithm. Using a minimal distance between clusters as the *Eps* parameter should result in grouping all the points whose distances to their closest neighbors are shorter than the minimal distance between clusters (they are in one cluster) and not grouping points when the distance between them is greater than the minimal distance between clusters.

### 3.3   Algorithm Operation

Our first approach utilizing the *PIS* coefficient was as follows:

1. Calculate an average density $dens_{avg}$ of the region where the points from the set $P$ are located.
2. Create the $N$ set and related $H$ sets. The creation process is analogical to the presented in 3.1.
3. For every analyzed pair of points calculate: distance, *PIS* and density of the stripe between the points.
4. From all the results choose the shortest distance, for which the $PIS > 0$ and the density of the stripe between the points is less than $dens_{avg}$.

The algorithm operation was much better in comparison to the distance-only method, but it was very unstable (the algorithm often returned very different values for the same input data). Moreover, the algorithm was very sensitive to the cluster distribution characteristics, especially for small cardinalities of $N$ and $H$.

To improve the algorithm operation we decided to apply an iterative approach. Iterative approaches are often applied in many data analyzing and data mining tasks. Coupled with random sampling, the iterative approach can improve the results and make them more precise.

In the case of the AEC algorithm, in every iteration we are try to minimize the possible minimum distance between clusters. The iterative version of the AEC algorithm performs the following steps:

1. Evaluate an initial average distance between clusters $dist_{init}$ and initial density $dens_{init}$. Details of this process are described later. At this moment it is enough to mention that this fragment is not iterative.
2. The iterative section:
    (a) If the current iteration is the first iteration, assume that the current minimum distance between clusters $dist_{cur} = dist_{init}$, and the respective current density is $dens_{cur} = dens_{init}$.
    (b) Create a new $N$ set, analogically as described in 3.1.
    (c) For every point $n_i \in N$ create a rectangle $r_{n_i}$, which vertexes coordinates are given by the following equation:
    $r_{n_i}(left, top, right, bottom) = r_{n_i}(n_i.x - dist_{cur}, n_i.y + dist_{cur}, n_i.x + dist_{cur}, n_i.y - dist_{cur})$.
    (d) For every point $n_i \in N$ create a set $H_{r_{n_i},n_i}$ skipping the point $n_i$ (the $VHC$ function).
    (e) Evaluate an average density of the $r_{n_i}$ rectangle.
    (f) For every point $n_i$, and points from the related $H_{n_i}$ set calculate a set of quantities: distance, $PIS$ and density of the stripe.
    (g) From all the results choose the shortest distance, for which the $PIS > 0$ and the density is less than the average density of the $r_{n_i}$. If there is no such result, do not return anything.
    (h) Compare the result obtained for the point $n_i$ with the current values of $dist_{cur}$ and $dens_{cur}$. If $dist_i < dist_{cur}$ and $dens_i <= dens_{cur}$ then update the current values of minimal distance and minimal density between clusters: $dist_{cur} := dist_i$ and $dens_{cur} := dens_i$. If only the first part of the condition holds ($dist_i < dist_{cur}$), then check a *suspected region* defined by using the coordinates of points for which the $dist_i$ was calculated. Details of this operation are described below. The *suspected region* checking operation can possibly return a pair of results: the distance $dist_s$ and related density $dens_s$. The returned pair is compared with the iteration results and if $dist_s < dist_{cur}$ and $dens_s <= dens_{cur}$ then the result of the iteration results are updated: $dist_{cur} := dist_s$ and $dens_{cur} := dens_s$.
    (i) Check the iteration breaking condition. The iterations can be broken in two cases: (1) the number of performed iterations is greater than the allowed number of iterations (which is another AEC algorithm parameter), and (2) if the result returned from consecutive iterations was repeated a fixed number of times. Breaking the iteration because of the second condition is more desirable, because we can expect that the algorithm found a minimal distance between clusters that cannot be replaced by any other distance.

**Initialization.** In order to start the iterative algorithm operation, the initial minimal distance between clusters $dist_{init}$ and initial density $dens_{init}$ must be properly set. The initial values should be set in a way that they reduce the number of iterations, but on the other hand, the initial values cannot narrow down the set of possible solutions.

We use the average distance between randomly selected points, and average density related to the distance as the initial values.

**Suspected Regions.** The case of a *suspected region* is considered for points $p_i$, $p_j$ when only the distance condition $(dist(p_i, p_j) < dist_{cur}))$ holds, the density condition $(dens(p_i, p_j) <= dens_{cur}))$ does not. Our experiments showed that there are two possible scenarios resulting in examining the *suspected region*:

1. the points $p_i$, $p_j$ are located close to each other inside a cluster. Then the distance then is short, but the density of the stripe between the points is high.
2. the points $p_i$, $p_j$ are located in separate clusters but they are not border points. The density of the stripe between the points is increased by the presence of the border points of both clusters.

Of considerable interest is the second case. The AEC algorithm does not analyze distances with the zero $PIS$ coefficient. There are many cases when the clusters' shapes make it difficult to randomly pick two points so that one of them is a border point of the first cluster and the second is located near the border of the second cluster. The analysis is performed as follows:

1. define the *suspected region*. The rectangle $r_s$ for the *suspected region* has its center directly between the points $p_i$ and $p_j$. In the next step calculate the density $dens_{r_s}$ of the $r_s$.
2. create a set of points $N_{r_s}$.
3. for each point $n_i \in N_{r_s}$ create a set $H_{n_i, r_s}$, then calculate distances and densities of the stripe between points $n_i$ and the related points $h_i \in H_{n_i, r_s}$. As the result choose the minimal distance with the minimal density.

In the event that the calculated result density is less than the average density of the $r_s$ region, the *suspected region* analysis results are compared with the results of the analysis in the iterative section of the AEC algorithm. For a pair of points located inside a cluster the *suspected region* analysis does not influence the results because the density condition is not satisfied (the density is high inside a cluster). But for the points located in two different clusters the analysis often gives important results.

The amount of points checked during *suspected regions* analysis depends on the number of points in the $r_s$ rectangle. If the number is less than the $N$ set cardinality, then all the points are checked. But if the number is greater, the cardinality of the $N_{r_s}$ set equals the cardinality of the $N$ set created in the iterative section of the algorithm. The situation is identical for the $H$ sets.

### 3.4   Results Interpretation

The interpretation of the result obtained from the analysis is as follows:

- if the density of all clusters of points in the set $P$ is similar, then the result of the AEC algorithm is the distance between a pair of closest clusters. By *similar density* we understand that the distances between neighboring points in all clusters are always less than the distances between border points of the closest clusters. We can define the *Eps* parameter for the density-based clustering as 85% – 90% of the obtained distance. Decreasing the value of the distance we prevent merging of the closest clusters during the clustering process.
- if the points from the set $P$ are grouped in clusters of significantly different density, then, depending on density of the sparse clusters, the result of the AEC algorithm is one of the following:
  - if the distance between dense clusters is less than the distance between neighboring points in the sparse clusters, then the AEC algorithm outcome is the distance between the dense clusters. Performing the clustering results in creating the dense clusters and merging points located close to each other in sparse clusters. The sparse clusters will be represented as a set of smaller clusters.
  - if the distance between border points in dense clusters is greater than the distance between neighboring points in sparse clusters, then the AEC algorithm outcome is the distance between points in the most sparse clusters. Clustering results in creating dense clusters and most of the sparse clusters. Depending on the points distribution in the most-sparse clusters, some of the most-sparse clusters can be divided into a few smaller clusters.
  - if distances between neighboring points in all kinds of clusters (both dense and sparse) are greater than the minimal distance between border points of the closest clusters, then the AEC algorithm outcome is the minimal distance between clusters. Performing clustering results in creating both dense and sparse clusters.

## 4   Test Results

In this section we present the results obtained for a set of five various datasets. For each dataset we performed a set of experiments with the following parameters:

- the cardinality of the $N$ set was 5, 15, 25 and 35% of the input dataset cardinality,
- the cardinality of the $H$ set was 10, 20, 30 and 40 points for each value of the $N$ set cardinality,
- the number of iterations was set to 10, 20 and 30 for each combination of $N$ and $H$ sets cardinality.

As can be easily calculated, a single test set contained $4 \times 4 \times 3 = 48$ tests. The test sets were run for the *stripeWidth* parameter set to 0.98 and 0.6. The iterations were broken if the result of the consecutive iterations was repeated more than 4 times. It never happened for all the test sets that the number of iterations exceeded the maximum. The iteration breaking was always caused by the number of repeated consecutive results. Thus we can treat the tests for identical cardinality of $N$ and $H$ sets as three repeated tests, which is useful in the presence of the random factor. All the experiments were run on a machine equipped with Pentium IV 2.8 GHz and 512 MB RAM. The software environment was Windows XP Professional, Java Sun 1.5 and Oracle 10g.

The main purpose of the experiments was to verify the AEC algorithm operation against various datasets. The AEC algorithm was run with a given set of parameters. The calculated *Eps* parameter was passed to the DBRS clustering algorithm, which was returning the number of created clusters. If the number of clusters declared for a given dataset equaled the number of clusters found by the DBRS, we marked the experiment as a success. If the number of clusters were not equal, we marked the experiment as a failure.

In figure 5 we present five datasets used for the experiments. Preparing the datasets we tried to provide the clusters and datasets with as much variety as possible. In the presented test datasets we included both dense and sparse clusters; and also clusters strongly varying in shapes and sizes. We also included clusters located inside other clusters. The purpose of such datasets was to check the AEC algorithm operation for datasets that might exist in real-life applications. Below we present the results obtained for the test datasets. Each table cell contains AEC algorithm operation times in milliseconds; in the braces we placed the number of performed iterations. The blank table cell represents a failure.

The first dataset (about 650 points) contained 10 small, dense clusters; densities of all clusters were very similar. The results for this dataset (fig. 6) show that

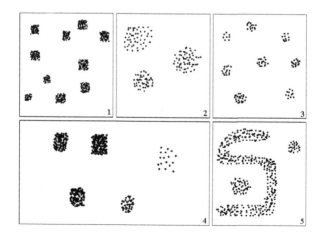

**Fig. 5.** Five datasets used for the experiments

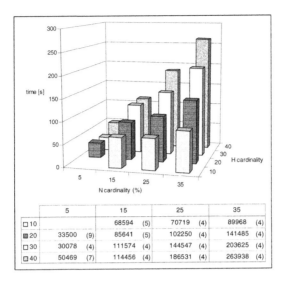

| | 5 | | 15 | | 25 | | 35 | |
|---|---|---|---|---|---|---|---|---|
| □ 10 | | | 68594 | (5) | 70719 | (4) | 89968 | (4) |
| ▣ 20 | 33500 | (9) | 85641 | (5) | 102250 | (4) | 141485 | (4) |
| □ 30 | 30078 | (4) | 111574 | (4) | 144547 | (4) | 203625 | (4) |
| □ 40 | 50469 | (7) | 114456 | (4) | 186531 | (4) | 263938 | (4) |

**Fig. 6.** Results for the first dataset

only for the least cardinality of $N$ and $H$ sets the algorithm could not estimate the proper $Eps$ value. For the remaining cases the four iterations were enough to properly estimate the parameter.

The second dataset contained about 200 points grouped in three relatively sparse clusters, densities of all clusters were similar. The clusters were located close to each other (relating the distance to the cluster sizes). Alike in the first dataset, the AEC algorithm rarely performed more than four iterations (fig. 7).

The third dataset contained only about 120 points grouped in eight small clusters. A big number of small, relatively sparse clusters caused the AEC algorithm to not work well for the low cardinalities of the $N$ and $H$ sets. The algorithm needed to check more than 25% of the whole dataset to provide proper results. Also, the number of iterations is greater than for other datasets (fig. 8).

The next, fourth dataset containing 400 points was an example of a dataset with clusters of different density. There are three dense clusters, one less dense cluster, and one sparse cluster. Despite differences between the clusters' densities the algorithm gave proper results for all tested cardinalities of $N$ and $H$ sets. Only once, for the lowest $N$ and $H$ sets cardinalities, the algorithm performed more than four iterations (fig. 9).

The last dataset contained over 420 points in three clusters of similar density but different shapes. Small clusters located inside the big ones were intended to disrupt the AEC algorithm when calculating the $PIS$ coefficient. For this dataset the AEC algorithm gave proper results for greater numbers of analyzed points. Also the number of performed iterations is greater (when compared with the results for other datasets). However, for the cardinality of the set $N$ equal 35%, the algorithm gave proper results for all cardinalities of the set $H$ (fig. 10).

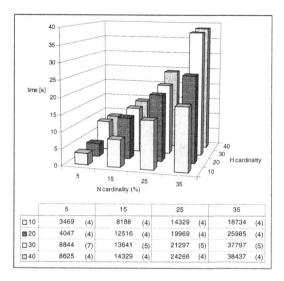

| | 5 | | 15 | | 25 | | 35 | |
|---|---|---|---|---|---|---|---|---|
| ☐ 10 | 3469 | (4) | 8188 | (4) | 14329 | (4) | 18734 | (4) |
| ▣ 20 | 4047 | (4) | 12516 | (4) | 19969 | (4) | 25985 | (4) |
| ☐ 30 | 8844 | (7) | 13641 | (5) | 21297 | (5) | 37797 | (5) |
| ☐ 40 | 8625 | (4) | 14329 | (4) | 24266 | (4) | 38437 | (4) |

**Fig. 7.** Results for the second dataset

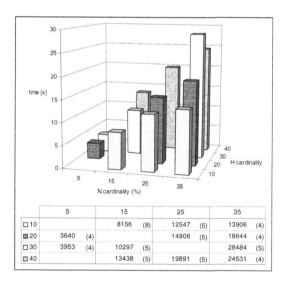

| | 5 | | 15 | | 25 | | 35 | |
|---|---|---|---|---|---|---|---|---|
| ☐ 10 | | | 8156 | (8) | 12547 | (5) | 13906 | (4) |
| ▣ 20 | 3640 | (4) | | | 14906 | (5) | 18844 | (4) |
| ☐ 30 | 3953 | (4) | 10297 | (5) | | | 28484 | (5) |
| ▣ 40 | | | 13438 | (5) | 19891 | (5) | 24531 | (4) |

**Fig. 8.** Results for the third dataset

Summarizing the tests result we can say that for all tested datasets the algorithm gave proper results. There are *easy* datasets like the second or the fourth, for which it is enough to test only 5% of the whole dataset but there are also more *difficult* ones, for which a proper estimation of the *Eps* parameter requires testing more than 25% of the whole dataset.

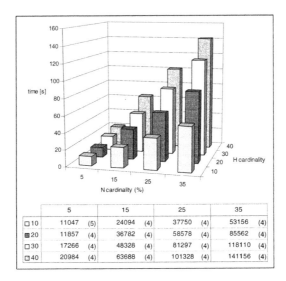

| | 5 | | 15 | | 25 | | 35 | |
|---|---|---|---|---|---|---|---|---|
| ☐ 10 | 11047 | (5) | 24094 | (4) | 37750 | (4) | 53156 | (4) |
| ▣ 20 | 11857 | (4) | 36782 | (4) | 58578 | (4) | 85562 | (4) |
| ☐ 30 | 17266 | (4) | 48328 | (4) | 81297 | (4) | 118110 | (4) |
| ☐ 40 | 20984 | (4) | 63688 | (4) | 101328 | (4) | 141156 | (4) |

**Fig. 9.** Results for the fourth dataset

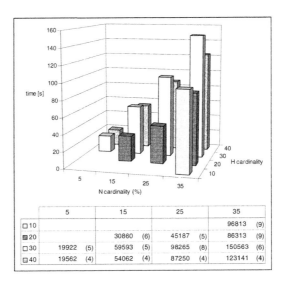

| | 5 | | 15 | | 25 | | 35 | |
|---|---|---|---|---|---|---|---|---|
| ☐ 10 | | | | | | | 96813 | (9) |
| ▣ 20 | | | 30860 | (6) | 45187 | (5) | 86313 | (9) |
| ☐ 30 | 19922 | (5) | 59593 | (5) | 98265 | (8) | 150563 | (6) |
| ☐ 40 | 19562 | (4) | 54062 | (4) | 87250 | (4) | 123141 | (4) |

**Fig. 10.** Results for the fifth dataset

In general, when a given dataset contains a big number of small, sparse clusters the AEC algorithm needs to analyze relatively big numbers of points to properly estimate the *Eps* parameter. This results from the fact that the more sparse clusters in the dataset, the lower is the probability of checking the distance and the *PIS* coefficient for a pair of points located inside one cluster.

The *stripeWidth* parameter had little influence on the algorithm results, at least for the tested datasets. In most cases the 0.98 value gave better results; for the third dataset narrow stripe (0.6) only were results better.

The accuracy of the AEC algorithm is determined by the algorithm parameters. The bigger the $N$ and $H$ sets cardinalities (the more pairs of points the algorithm investigates) and the more iterations performed, the more accurate the results. However, every investigated pair of points has its influence on the algorithm operation time. The parameters should be set according to the tested dataset. If the dataset characteristics are not known in advance (as with the presented test scenario) the obtained results show that investigating 25% of a dataset always gives accurate results.

## 5   Future Plans

The current implementation of the AEC algorithm is time-intensive. Executing spatial queries and calculating lines equations for many pairs of points causes the whole process of estimating the *Eps* parameter to be long-lasting in comparison to the clustering process. In figure 11 we can see the percentage participation of the AEC algorithm components in the total algorithm execution time. The most time-intensive fragment of the algorithm is calculating the value of the *PIS* coefficient. This fragment consists of two operations (marked as merged in the figure): executing range queries (19%) and checking the relation between points and lines (39%). We want to use distributed processing to achieve better algorithm efficiency and scalability. The set of points can be distributed over the computers and then each machine can separately calculate the *Eps* parameter. Finally one computer will choose the best result utilizing the standard distance and density condition.

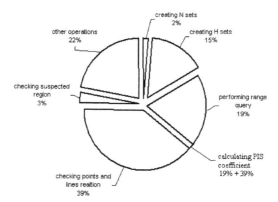

**Fig. 11.** Percentage participation of the AEC algorithm components in the total algorithm execution time

## 6   Conclusions

In this paper we proposed an empirical approach to a problem of automatic calculation of *Eps* parameter for density-based clustering algorithms like DBRS and DBScan. The AEC algorithm, working iteratively, chooses randomly a fixed number of sets of points and calculates three coefficients: distance between the points, number of points located in a stripe between the points and density of the stripe. Then the algorithm chooses the best possible result, which is the minimal distance between clusters. The calculated result has an influence on the sets of points created in the next iteration. If the result is repeated a few times, the iteration is broken and the shortest distance is passed as the *Eps* parameter to the density-based clustering algorithm.

We presented test results for a set of five different sets of points. With a suitably high number of checked points the algorithm was able to estimate the proper *Eps* parameter for all tested datasets. We also presented the algorithm drawbacks and suggested possible improvements.

## References

1. Barclay T., Slutz D.R., Gray J.: TerraServer: A Spatial Data Warehouse, Proc. ACM SIGMOD 2000, pp: 307-318, June 2000
2. http://www.lsgi.polyu.edu.hk/sTAFF/zl.li/vol_2_2/02_chen.pdf
3. Ester M., Kriegel H.-P., Sander J., Wimmer M.: A Density-Based Algorithm for Discovering Clusters in Large Spatial Databases with Noise. In proc. of $2^{nd}$ International Conference on Knowledge Discovery and Data Mining, 1996
4. Gorawski, M., Malczok, R.: On Efficient Storing and Processing of Long Aggregate Lists. DaWaK, Copenhagen, Denmark 2005.
5. Papadias D., Kalnis P., Zhang J., Tao Y.: Effcient OLAP Operations in Spatial Data Warehouses. Spinger Verlag, LNCS 2001
6. Wang X., Hamilton H.J.: DBRS: A Density-Based Spatial Clustering Method with Random Sampling. In proceedings of the $7^{th}$ PAKDD, Seoul, Korea, 2003

# Symbolic Music Genre Classification Based on Note Pitch and Duration*

Ioannis Karydis

Aristotle University of Thessaloniki, Thessaloniki 54124, Greece
karydis@delab.csd.auth.gr

**Abstract.** This paper presents a music genre classification system that relies on note pitch and duration features, derived from their respective histograms. Feature histograms provide a simple but yet effective classifier for the purposes of genre classification in intra-classical genres such as sonatas, fugues, mazurkas, etc. Detailed experimental results illustrate the significant performance gains due to the proposed features, compared to existing baseline features.

**Keywords:** Music genre classification, music features, histograms, pitch, duration, content-based information retrieval.

## 1 Introduction

Digitised music exists in broadly two categories depending on whether its recording contains directions of what to be played by a performer or a particular audio-recorded performance of a piece. The former representation of music is the symbolic, while the latter is the acoustic. Music Information Retrieval (MIR) is accordingly divided into two categories depending on the representation of music that is under examination.

Although young a field, MIR and especially Content-Based MIR (CBMIR) mainly orientate towards acoustic data, a fact that can easily be partially explained by the popularity of acoustic recordings. Though, the two representations are interconnected with acoustic music being, improvisation set aside, up to a great degree the product of symbolic music. Thus, taking into consideration the relationship between the two representations of music and the existence of very large acoustic databases (for both commercial and not purposes) one can imagine not only the existence of large analogous collections of symbolic music but also the significance of MIR on symbolic data, especially for music distribution.

One of the necessities that prevails in MIR is genre classification. Apart from the obvious significance to numerous occupations (retailers, librarians, musicologists, e.t.c.) as a means for music organisation, genre classification is additionally important as research indicates that liking a music piece can adhere to the performance style instead of the actual piece itself [4]. Since predefined metadata in

* This research is supported by the *ΗΡΑΚΛΕΙΤΟΣ* and *ΠΥΘΑΓΟΡΑΣ II* national programs funded by *ΕΠΕΑΕΚ*.

Y. Manolopoulos, J. Pokorný, and T. Sellis (Eds.): ADBIS 2006, LNCS 4152, pp. 329–338, 2006.

symbolic music data are rare and their manual appointment inhibits difficulties and potential inconsistencies, the need for an effective automatic means of music classification unfolds as the collections of symbolic digital music files increase at a rapid rate. Moreover, genre classification is of great assistance to the wide public accessing musical archives, offering increased ease in identifying types of music.

As aforementioned, musical pieces in symbolic format represent the intention of the composer towards the performer. Thus, the symbolic representation engulfs an excess of information, that may not always be perceivable in the respective acoustic piece. In order to process all the information included in the music files, one can rely on perceptual criteria (features) related to pitch, rhythm, timbre, etc of the music in order to characterise a musical genre. The key to success is the choice of features to be based upon, while the effectiveness of the classifier, although still important, remains secondary as is limited by the feature selectivity. In this paper, we focus on the note pitch and duration information of the musical data.

### 1.1 Contribution and Paper Organisation

This paper examines the problem of determining the musical genre of a musical piece, provided in symbolic representation. Based on prior work on symbolic music genre classification, we focus on note pitch and duration information of the musical data.

Current research on music genre classification based on musical feature histograms [5], has been isolated on the pitch information of notes solely. Although pitch is described in the literature as one of the predominant musical characteristics [2], rhythm, one of the main dimensions of which is note durations, is also given high credit and current research is not considering it.

Moreover, current research examines broad categories that, although up to a degree overlapping and vague, present far more distinctive characteristics than the sub-categories of any category.

To address these issues, this paper proposes the following:

- Re-examination of the selectivity of pitch features in different music categories that present more similarities,
- Introduction of duration and pitch-duration combination features that are based on pitch and duration information of the notes,
- A differentiated approach to pitch feature as described by current research.

The rest of the paper is organised as follows. Section 2 is devoted in background information and related research as far as symbolic music genre classification is concerned. Moreover, a baseline approach is reviewed therein and the motivating factors that led to this research are summarised. Extending the idea proposed in Section 2.1, Section 3 provides a complete account of the features proposed in this paper. Subsequently, Section 4 presents and discusses the experimentation results obtained. Finally, the paper is concluded by a summary and the intended future work in Section 5.

## 2    Background and Related Work

Musical genre classification is one of the key areas MIR researchers are interested in. Although, as already mentioned, genre classification research is mainly oriented towards acoustic data, approaches for symbolic data do exist and have interesting results to demonstrate.

Tzanetakis et al. [5] presented pitch histograms as a way to represent the pitch content of music signals both in symbolic and acoustic form. Based on features extracted from these histograms the authors of [5] managed a 50% accuracy for 5 genres (for more details see Section 2.1).

Following the participation success of the International Symposium on Music Information Retrieval (ISMIR) conference on 2005, the MIREX competition was held. The goal of the contest was to classify symbolic recordings into genre categories. The best ranking results were presented by [3] with 77.17% and 65.28% mean hierarchical and raw classification accuracy, respectively.

In [3] a short account of a system that extracts 109 musical features from symbolic recordings and uses them to classify the recordings by genre is presented. The features used are based on instrumentation, texture, rhythm, dynamics, pitch statistics, melody and chords. The achieved reported classification reaches 90% for intra-category subcategories and 98% for categories. Though, this approach has an increased execution time while the space reduction is limited. The execution times (as seen from the results of the MIREX contest) are prohibitive for applications that require responses in real time, especially when frequent content update is potential. Additionally, the increased execution times were for a small database of 950 songs. Overall, the required methods need focus on a small selection of features which deliver increased selectivity performance. Moreover, the approach described in [3] additionally requires training for the "fittest" set of features.

Finally, Basili et al. [1] presented five features based on melody, timbre and rhythm for the purposes of symbolic music genre classification. Though, their investigation was oriented towards the comparison of different machine learning algorithms in genre classification.

### 2.1    Pitch Histograms

The authors of [5] introduced pitch histograms as a means to represent the pitch content of the notes of both symbolic and acoustic musical data. MIDI data files were used to extract note pitches, the frequency of occurrence of which constitutes the pitch histogram. As MIDI specification allows only for 128 discrete notes, each pitch histogram is an array of 128 values, indexed by the note number, representing the frequency of appearance of each note.

Tzanetakis et al. considered two versions of the pitch histogram according to whether the octave discrimination of notes is taken into consideration or not. Thus, the unfolded version does consider octaves in pitches of the notes leading to two C notes, being one octave apart, to be considered as, two different notes. In the folded version, all note pitches are transposed into a single octave, that is the two C notes of the previous example would be the same note, and then are mapped to a circle of fifths, so that adjacent histogram bins are spaced a fifth apart, rather than a semitone.

The rationale these choices rely on is that unfolded histograms can capture the pitch range of a piece, folding supports octave independency and the mapping to the circle of fifths ameliorates the expression of tonal music.

In order to minimise the search space, four one-dimensional features were extracted from the two histograms (folding and non-folding), namely PITCH-Fold, AMPL-Fold, PITCH-Unfold & DIST-Fold. The first is the bin number of the maximum peak of the folded histogram. The second is the amplitude of the maximum peak of the folded histogram. PITCH-Unfold is period of the maximum peak of the unfolded histogram, while DIST-Fold is the interval (in bins) between the two highest peaks of the folded histogram.

## 2.2  Motivation

Although the work of Tzanetakis et al. is rather intuitive, easy to perform, fast to calculate and the results reported are 1.6 times better than random classification, the accuracy still remains at levels that allow further amelioration. This is especially true, considering that each note carries additional information to pitch, its duration, that can equivalently easily be extracted and would not burden the dimensionality of the search space, at least to the point of recompensation by increasing the accuracy.

The use of the note duration is intuitively supported by the connection of note duration with rhythm. In a simplistic point of view, rhythm can be perceived as the number of notes within a bar, played at a specific tempo. As the total duration of notes within a bar is explicitly defined, smaller duration values lead to more notes within a bar, thus making the rhythm faster. The effect of the

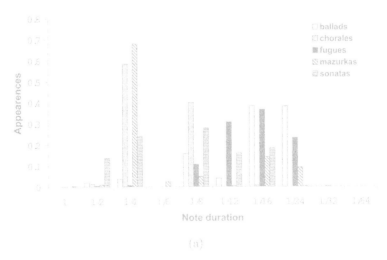

**Fig. 1.** Normalised duration histogram

note durations on rhythm is rather important, as the music genres, generally, abide to rhythmic patterns.

The aforementioned arguments broadly appear in Figure 1 where it can be seen that different musical genres have different frequencies of appearance for each note duration.

# 3    The Proposed Method

This work's key proposal is the utilisation of the duration histograms for the purposes of symbolic music genre classification.

This section presents three features that are based on the note duration dimension of a musical piece, as well as a differentiated, with respect to [5], approach in the extraction of features from the note pitch information of a piece.

A duration histogram is an array of 25 integer values (the eight standard durations, their dotted and double dotted augmentations and the breve duration) indexed by duration size that represents the frequency of occurrence of each note duration in a musical piece. Intuitively, duration histograms offer a means to capture the structure and rhythmic part of a piece. This is especially true in classical music where musical genres were created and evolved based on rules. For example, it is quite common for fugues to have several parts where the durations of the notes therein are significantly shorter than the other parts, in order to convey a sense of tenseness, since the original theme of fugues was an escape. On the other hand, sonatas are known to be structured to be more slow especially in their second parts.

As already discussed, the feature selection process is of great importance for all information retrieval purposes. This work proposes the extraction of three one-dimensional features from the duration histograms, namely the duration that has the greater frequency of appearance in a piece, the number of appearances of the duration with the highest frequency and the distance between the two highest frequency durations in terms of relative temporal duration.

The selection of the feature set is highly important, since the performance of the classifier mainly depends on the selectivity capability of the features to filter out statistical properties of the histogram that are irrelevant while retaining information that describe genre differences and thus assist the classification.

Accordingly, the proposed selection of features was based on the specific characteristics required to retain such as the note duration that appears more often as well as the second (indirectly through the distance) and the appearances of the most often duration. Additionally, features of the same style have successfully been employed in the literature for the purposes of symbolic genre classification, although on differentiated characteristic of the musical data.

## 3.1    The Proposed Features

**Non-folding Pitch.** In non-folding pitch features, the effect of folding is not taken into consideration. Accordingly, the four one-dimensional feature vectors described in Section 2.1 are extracted based solely on unfolded his-

tograms. This is done in order to establish the effect of folding in the classical
works examined herein.

**Duration.** In duration features, all features (as described in Section 3) are
derived solely from duration histograms in order to determine the selectivity
of the feature vectors produced by the duration histograms.

**Pitch & Duration.** This feature is the combination of the feature vectors of
the pitch information of the notes combined with the feature vectors produced by the duration information. Thus, each musical piece is represented
by seven feature vectors, four from the pitch histogram and three from the
duration histogram. As, pitch histogram can exist in two versions, the pitch
& duration (or combination) feature vectors come in two flavours as well,
the folding and non-folding.

**Weighted Pitch & Duration.** The last feature proposed in this paper is a
modified version of the combination feature previously described. The modification consists of a weighting scheme that allows the prediction of the genre
to be more or less affected by one of the two features, in order to determine
their contribution.

## 4   Performance Evaluation

In support of the efficiency of the proposed features, this section presents the
experiments that have been performed. A concise description of the experimentation platform and data sets is also given followed by a performance analysis
based on experimental comparison of the baseline and proposed features.

### 4.1   Experimental Set-Up

All algorithms described have been implemented and performed on a personal
computer with 3,06GHz Intel Pentium IV processor, 1 GByte RAM, MS Windows XP operating system while the developing package utilised was MS Visual C++. The performance measure was the precision accuracy of the k-NN
classifier.

The data sets employed for the experiments include real music objects, that
originated from **kern Humdrum files acquired from the Humdrum website [6].
Each **kern file was stripped in order to retain only the note pitch and duration
information. All the music objects pertain to classical works. The following five
sub-categories were selected: ballads, chorales, fugues, mazurkas & sonatas and
50 songs were randomly selected by each category, adding up to a total corpus
of 250 pieces.

After the vector extraction is completed (as described in Section 3), the distinguishing capability of the feature vectors is examined by means of the k-NN
classifier, using the "leave one out" method. That is, one musical piece in the
database is assumed to be of unknown genre and the rest of the pieces are considered as training data. Of the k nearest neighbour genres to the unknown piece,
the genre with majority of appearances is predicted to be the genre of the piece
assumed to be unknown. The process is repeated for all pieces in the database
leading to the accuracy of the features.

## 4.2   Results

Initially, pitch, duration and combination were considered separately for both folding (pitch and combination) and non-folding features and the accuracy results are illustrated in Figure 2a and Figure 2b, respectively.

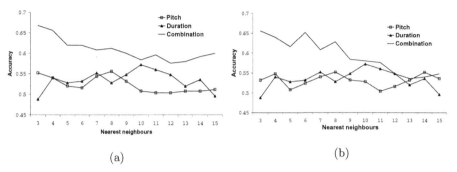

(a)                                                      (b)

**Fig. 2.** Accuracy of all approaches (a) folding and (b) non-folding

Although pitch and duration have quite similar performances, duration is slightly better, while the combination features clearly outperform both. In addition, the changes in accuracy of the folding affected features seem to be rather marginal.

The next experimentation refers to the combination weighted approaches. Figure 3a and Figure 3b, provide four of the most characteristic weighting selections for both folding and non-folding. The legent titles imply the percentage of duration - pitch that participated.

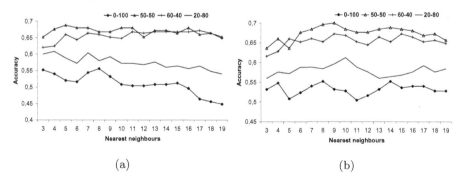

(a)                                                      (b)

**Fig. 3.** Accuracy of weighted combination (a) folding and (b) non-folding

Once again, the "0-100" combination, in which duration is not participating, presents the worse accuracy, while even 20% of duration contribution offers 9% increase in accuracy. The best performance is produced by the equally balanced participation of both duration and pitch ("50-50"). It should be noted that the performances between folding and non-folding are again quite similar. From this point on, folding features have not been considered further and all results imply non-folding features, where applicable.

Next, we experimented (Figure 4) on the size of the musical piece regarded as unknown (L). The size was adjusted by means of the number of notes within, while for the pitch features, cropping occurred at the ending of the piece, retaining, thus, the first L notes. For the pieces that had less a number of notes than L, the full piece was selected.

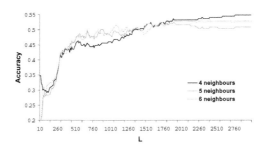

**Fig. 4.** Pitch accuracy for varying query size

An obvious trend towards better accuracy is clearly depicted in Figure 4, while for very small L the accuracy is equivalent to random (for five categories) since the note number is not enough for an accurate prediction.

In the following experiment, the size of the musical piece regarded as unknown (L) was examined against the accuracy for the duration features. In this experiment we additionally tested the offset the L notes are taken from. Figure 5 depicts the accuracy for L notes of the unknown genre piece taken from the middle part of the datum.

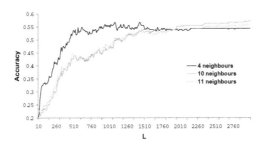

**Fig. 5.** Duration accuracy for varying query size taken from the middle of a file

A slightly better performance in accuracy for the duration features is apparent in comparison to pitch features (Figure 4). The results for different offsets of the L notes proved identical making clear that the offset from which the part of the musical piece regarded of unknown genre is taken has no significant effect in the accuracy.

Following, is the experiment of the combination feature against the size of the musical piece regarded as unknown (Figure 6). Once again the performance of the combination approach is clearly better, in comparison to the accuracy results gathered for both pitch and duration separately.

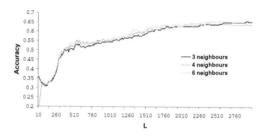

**Fig. 6.** Combination accuracy for varying query size

Finally, the last experiment performed a pairwise comparison between different genres. In this case, herein are presented two of the most representative results, the comparison between fugues - mazurkas (Figure 7a) & ballads - mazurkas (Figure 7b).

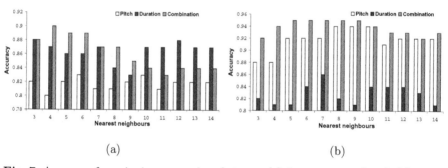

|  (a)  |  (b)  |

**Fig. 7.** Accuracy for pairwise comparison between (a) fugues - mazurkas & (b) ballads - mazurkas

In Figure 7a, we observe the domination of the duration features over the pitch features, while in Figure 7b pitch features perform far better than duration features, though, the combination features are overall better.

## 5  Conclusions

This paper proposes the use of note pitch and duration histograms for the purposes of symbolic music genre classification. Note information histograms have a great capability in capturing a fair amount of information regarding harmonic as well as rhythmic features of different musical genres and pieces.

This paper proposes the incorporation of the note duration information during the feature extraction process. The duration dimension of a note is highly capable of supporting genre classification, though its weighted use with the pitch information proves even better.

This is verified through extensive experimental results, which illustrate the suitability of the proposed feature, reaching an accuracy level of 70%, that is a gain of 40% from the baseline approach.

Future work includes plans to examine broader ranges of musical categories, in order to establish the suitability of the proposed features, as well as the incorporation of the notion of patterns in genre classification. Patterns have played a significant role in the indexing of music even since the very first attempts of the creation of musical dictionaries.

# References

1. R. Basili, A. Serafini, and A. Stellato. Classification of musical genre: a machine learning approach. In *Proceedings of ISMIR*, 2004.
2. D. Byrd and T. Crawford. Problems of music information retrieval in the real world. *Information Processing and Management*, 38(2):249–272, 2002.
3. C. McKay and I. Fujinaga. Automatic genre classification using large high-level musical feature sets. In *Proceedings of ISMIR*, pages 31–38, 2004.
4. A. C. North and D. J. Hargreaves. Liking for musical styles. *Musicae Scientiae*, 1:109–128, 1997.
5. G. Tzanetakis, A. Ermolinskyi, and P. Cook. Pitch histograms in audio and symbolic music information retrieval. In *Proceedings of ISMIR*, pages 31–38, 2002.
6. The Humdrum website. A library of virtual musical scores in the humdrum **kern data format. http://kern.humdrum.net.

# PPPA: Push and Pull Pedigree Analyzer for Large and Complex Pedigree Databases

Arturas Mazeika, Janis Petersons, and Michael H. Böhlen

Department of Computer Science
Free University of Bozen-Bolzano
Dominikanerplatz-3, I-39100, Bozen, Italy
arturas@inf.unibz.it, jpetersons@unibz.it, boehlen@inf.unibz.it

**Abstract.** In this paper we introduce a novel push and pull technique to analyze pedigree data. We present the Push and Pull Pedigree Analyzer (PPPA) to organize large and complex pedigrees and investigate the development of genetic diseases. PPPA receives as input a pedigree (ancestry information) of different families. For each person the pedigree contains information about the occurrence of a specific genetic disease. We propose a new solution to arrange and visualize the individuals of the pedigree based on the relationships between individuals and information about the disease. PPPA starts with random positions of the individuals, and iteratively pushes apart non-relatives with opposite diseases patterns and pulls together relatives with identical disease patterns. The goal is a visualization that groups families with homogeneous disease patterns.

We investigate our solution experimentally with genetic data from peoples from South Tyrol, Italy. We show that the algorithm converges independent of the number of individuals $n$ and the complexity of the relationships. The runtime of the algorithm is super-linear wrt $n$. The space complexity of the algorithm is linear wrt $n$. The visual analysis of the method confirms that our push and pull technique successfully deals with large and complex pedigrees.

**Keywords:** pedigree data mining, visual data mining, pedigree visualization.

## 1   Introduction

The pedigree of an individual shows the family and ancestors of the individual. Typically, a pedigree is shown as a diagram with symbols representing people and lines representing genetic relationships. Figure 1(a) shows a typical pedigree of an individual. Squares represent males and circles represent females. Lines connecting a male and female represent mating. Vertical lines that extend downward link parents to their children. Therefore, the youngest individuals are at the bottom of the diagram and the oldest individuals are at the top. The purpose of pedigrees is to show relationships between the family members and investigate genetic diseases of closed populations. Individuals that suffer from the disease of interest are colored black.

Y. Manolopoulos, J. Pokorný, and T. Sellis (Eds.): ADBIS 2006, LNCS 4152, pp. 339–352, 2006.

Figure 1(b) shows an example of a relational representation of a pedigree. The ID attribute uniquely identifies the individual, the mother and father attributes are the IDs of the parents, Sex denotes the gender of the individual, and Sick denotes whether the individual suffers from the disease of interest.

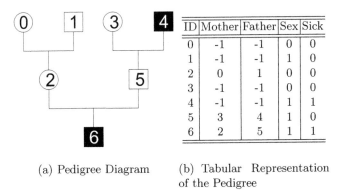

| ID | Mother | Father | Sex | Sick |
|----|--------|--------|-----|------|
| 0  | -1     | -1     | 0   | 0    |
| 1  | -1     | -1     | 1   | 0    |
| 2  | 0      | 1      | 0   | 0    |
| 3  | -1     | -1     | 0   | 0    |
| 4  | -1     | -1     | 1   | 1    |
| 5  | 3      | 4      | 1   | 0    |
| 6  | 2      | 5      | 1   | 1    |

(a) Pedigree Diagram         (b) Tabular Representation of the Pedigree

**Fig. 1.** An Example of the Pedigree Data

Mining pedigree data is a complicated task. A genetic disease of an individual might be the result of a cross-over of ancestors many generations ago. To support the investigation of the causes of the disease one needs a good arrangement and visualization of the individuals of a pedigree. First, the whole pedigree should be visualized to reveal all correlations between both female and male individuals of the family. Second, the relatives (parents and children) of the individual should be visualized closer to the individual allowing efficient identification of individuals that are related to the disease. Finally, the relatives of sick individuals should be visualized closer to the sick person indicating the potential cause of the disease for other members of the family.

This paper introduces the Push and Pull Pedigree Analyzer (PPPA) that arranges and visualizes pedigree data. The idea of the solution comes from closed physical systems with few opposing forces. In such systems particles start with an initial chaotic state and are subjected to opposing forces. After some time an equilibrium state is reached with a stable arrangement of particles. Similar to this the PPPA method starts with random positions of individuals in space (cf. Figure 2(a)), and then pushes non-relatives with opposite disease patterns from each other and pulls relatives with identical disease patterns towards each other. The equilibrium state yields a graph with an arrangement between the individuals of the pedigree: relatives are arranged to be close to each other and non-relatives to be far away from each other (cf. Figure 2(b)).

The motivation for our solution comes from a genetic research project of isolated populations in South Tirol, Italy [1]. South Tirol is naturally divided into four valleys that are separated by mountain ranges. Because of the physical setting the inhabitants of the valleys form closed societies and almost full pedigrees

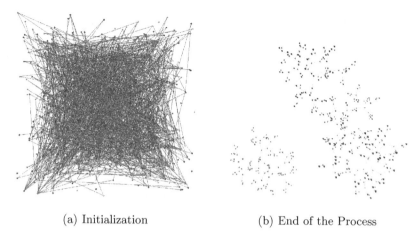

(a) Initialization                    (b) End of the Process

**Fig. 2.** Illustration of the PPPA Algorithm

of up to 15 generations are available. The investigation of these pedigrees and associated diseases requires novel techniques. Existing solutions work for small pedigrees only and attempts to generalize them to larger settings failed.

The organization of the paper is as follows. We review related work in Section 2. We describe the PPPA method in Section 3. Section 4 experimentally evaluates our solution. Finally, Section 5 draws conclusions and offers future work.

## 2    Related Work

Tulip [2] and graph visualization tools of the Tulip framework [3,4,5,6,7,8] is the closest related work to our method. The tools allow to draw and manipulate very large graphs (up to a million of nodes). The algorithms of the framework implement different graph visualizations including, clustering, different metrics, and mapping of visual attributes. U. Brandes [7] investigates the graph drawing methods based on the physical analogies using different forces between the nodes (spring forces, energy based placement). These systems have a layout component and aim to optimize the overall visualization of the graph.

Visual Technologies [9], Cyrillic [10,11], Progeny [12], aiSee [13], Pedigree visualizer [14,15], offers a broad range of tools to investigate and visualize pedigree data. Typically, the visualizations are limited to pedigree diagrams (cf. Figures 1(a), 3(a)) and do not focus on the arrangement of the members.

Lineage [16] computes different statistics of the pedigrees and allows to visualize the pedigrees. The pedigrees are visualized in layers starting with the oldest generation at the top, and younger generations towards the bottom (cf. Figure 3(b)). The tool allows to visually analyze the individual members and the properties of the individual members of the tree. However, an analysis of the families and classification of the members of families is complicated, since the individuals are visualized equidistant on the layers.

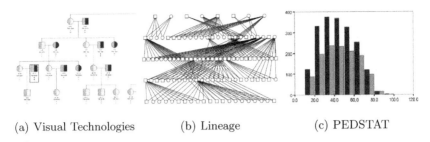

(a) Visual Technologies        (b) Lineage              (c) PEDSTAT

**Fig. 3.** Pedigree Visualizations of Different Tools

PEDSTATS [17] allows to compute and visualize summary structures including statistics about the family, the founders of the family, sex of the family, distribution of specific genes and alleles of the family, and pair wise investigation of different variables of the population. The tool investigates relationships between individual members of the pedigree and classifies the relationships (for example number of family member, number of founders of the family). Statistical information is reported. In this paper we focus on the relationships between individual and aim to arrange the individuals of the pedigree based of the relationships of between the members of the pedigree.

Research on pedigree data includes linkage analysis, likelihood tests of pedigree relationships, allele sharing, etc [18,17,19,20]. The work typically focuses on a very specific problem. Histograms and Scatter plots are used to illustrate the result (cf. Figure 3(c)).

There's a large body of research papers in the area of graph visualization [2,21]. The research papers focus on the optimal and esthetic visualization of general graphs including identification of hierarchies, reduction of the number of both non-edge and edge crossings, overlappings of sub-graphs [8], zoom-in/out and fold/unfold functionality [22], organization of nodes into layouts [23] in the graphs. In this paper we focus on informative but not necessarily nice visualizations of pedigree data. For example, assymetric and visually not nice graphs might indicate individuals that potentially could have genetic diseases.

## 3   The PPPA Method

The PPPA method inputs pedigree data of a population and assigns a point in space to each individual of the pedigree. In subsequent iterations the algorithm pushes points that are not related away from each other and pulls points that are related towards each other. We use a kd-tree to efficiently implement the push and pull step. We stop the iterative process once the average distance of moving points is below $\varepsilon$.

The organization of the Section is the following. First we describe the push-pull functions in Section 3.1. The stop criteria is described in Section 3.2. Finally, Section 3.3 presents the algorithm of the method.

### 3.1   Push and Pull Functions

Below we define a class of push and pull function between two individuals of a pedigree. The meaning of the constants is the following. $c_{push}^{dmax}$ and $c_{pull}^{dmax}$ determine the maximal strength of push and pull. $c_{push}^{sick}$ and $c_{pull}^{sick}$ quantify the push and pull force of sick individuals. $c_{push}^{skew}$ determines the skew of the function: a large constant means that close points are pushed more and far away points are pushed less. $c_{pull}^{close}$ quantifies the pull force of close relatives. $c_{pull}^{adjust}$ guarantees the convergence of the method, i.e., $f_{pull}(0) = 0$.

**Definition 1 (Push function).** *Let $p$ be a point representing an individual of the given pedigree. Let $q$ be an individual of the pedigree such that $q$ is neither a child nor a parent of $p$. Then $p$ and $q$ push away from each other by $\delta$:*

$$p \leftarrow p - \delta \frac{p - q}{\|p - q\|} \tag{1}$$

$$q \leftarrow q + \delta \frac{p - q}{\|p - q\|}, \tag{2}$$

$$\tag{3}$$

*where*

$$\delta = f_{push}(\|p - q\|, sick) = \frac{c_{push}^{dmax}}{1 + (1 + sick) \cdot e^{c_{push}^{skew} \cdot (1 + c_{push}^{sick} \cdot sick) \cdot \|p - q\|}}, \tag{4}$$

*and sick is 1 if either $p$ or $q$ are sick (but not both), and 0 otherwise.*

**Definition 2 (Pull function).** *Let $p$ be a point representing an individual of the given pedigree. Let $q$ be an individual of the pedigree such that $q$ is either a child or a parent of $p$. Then $p$ and $q$ pull towards each other by $\delta$:*

$$p \leftarrow p + \delta \frac{p - q}{\|p - q\|} \tag{5}$$

$$q \leftarrow q - \delta \frac{p - q}{\|p - q\|}, \tag{6}$$

$$\tag{7}$$

*where*

$$\delta = f_{pull}(\|p - q\|, sick) = \frac{c_{pull}^{dmax}}{1 + e^{1/(c_{pull}^{close} \cdot (1 + c_{pull}^{sick} \cdot sick) \cdot \|p - q\| + c_{pull}^{adjust})}} \tag{8}$$

*and sick is 1 if either $p$ or $q$ are sick (but not both), and 0 otherwise.*

Figure 4 illustrates the push and pull functions as the distance between points $p$ and $q$ increases. First, the push function pushes non-relatives almost twice further if either $p$ or $q$ suffers from the disease. The pull function pulls a child and a parent towards each other if one of them suffers from the disease. Second, the strength of the push function decreases exponentially as the distance between the points increases and is almost 0 for distances more than 0.2–0.4. Intuitively, this is because such individuals are neither in a parent nor child relationship. In contrast, the strength of the pull function is high for relatives that are far away (0.2–0.4) and decreases very rapidly as the parent approaches the child.

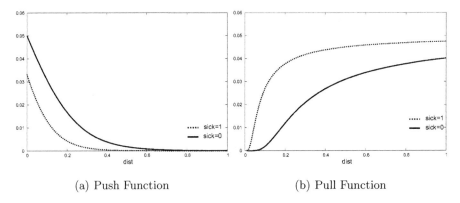

(a) Push Function                          (b) Pull Function

**Fig. 4.** Push and Pull Functions

We experimented with different values of the constants in Equations (4) and (8) and different datasets. We chose the following values, because they guaranteed best convergence rate: $c_{push}^{dmax} = c_{pull}^{dmax} = 0.1$, $c_{push}^{sick} = 1.5$, $c_{pull}^{sick} = 3.0$, $c_{push}^{skew} = 8.0$, $c_{pull}^{close} = 2.5$, $c_{pull}^{adjust} = 0.0001$.

*Example 1 (Push and Pull functions for a 3D case.).* Let $p = (0.0, 0.0, 0.0)$ and $q = (0.1, 0.0, 0.1)$, neither $p$ nor $q$ is sick, and $p$ is neither child nor parent of $q$. Then $p$ and $q$ push each other away. The distance between the points is:

$$d(p, q) = \sqrt{0.1^2 + 0.0^2 + 0.1^2} = 0.14$$

The push distance is

$$\delta = f_{push}(0.14, 0) = \frac{0.1}{1 + e^{20 \cdot 0.14}} = 0.006$$

and therefore point $p$ and $q$ are pushed away from each other by 0.006. The new coordinates for $p$ are:

$$(0.0, 0.0, 0.0) - \frac{(0.1, 0.0, 0.1)}{0.14} 0.006 = (-0.004, 0.000, -0.004).$$

The new coordinates for $q$ are:

$$(0.1, 0.0, 0.1) + \frac{(0.1, 0.0, 0.1)}{0.14} 0.006 = (0.104, 0.000, 0.104).$$

Now consider $p = (0.0, 0.0, 0.0)$ and $q = (0.1, 0.0, 0.1)$, $p$ is a father of $q$ and $q$ suffers from the disease. Then $p$ and $q$ pull towards each other and the pull distance is

$$\delta = f_{pull}(0.14, 1) = \frac{0.1}{1 + e^{1/(2.5 \cdot 4 \cdot 0.14 + 0.0001)}} = 0.032$$

and therefore point $p$ and $q$ are pulled towards each other. The new coordinates for $p$ are:

$$(0.0, 0.0, 0.0) + \frac{(0.1, 0.0, 0.1)}{0.14} 0.032 = (0.023, 0.000, 0.023).$$

The new coordinates for $q$ are:

$$\bar{q} = (0.1, 0.0, 0.1) - \frac{(0.1, 0.0, 0.1)}{0.14} 0.032 = (0.977, 0.000, 0.977).$$

The PPPA method scans the database and for each data point $p$ pushes and pulls the other database points. The complexity of the straightforward implementation of this step is $O(n^2)$ and is prohibitively expensive. Instead we query for data points in the $\varepsilon$ neighborhood and use a kd-tree to improve the performance of look-ups of points that are the nearest to the given point $p$. At the beginning of each iteration we build a kd-tree ($O(n \log^2 n)$ complexity) and then query the tree for neighborhoods. In contrast the pull function pulls only points $q$ that are either the parents or the children of $p$. We pre-compute the parents and the children for every data point. Therefore the complexity of the pull step is constant, and the overall complexity of the method is to $O(n \log^2 n) \cdot N$, where $N$ is the average size of the neighborhood per iteration.

## 3.2   Stop Criteria

The PPPA method starts with a uniform distribution of the data points, and pushes non-relatives away from each other and pulls relatives towards each other. The stop criteria determines when the iterative process is stable and the points do no longer move significantly with respect to each other. Let $\varepsilon$ be the given error. Let $p_b^1, p_b^2, \ldots, p_b^n$ be the positions of the individuals in space before the iteration, and $p_a^1, p_a^2, \ldots, p_a^n$ be the positions of the individuals after the iteration. Let

$$average\_movement = \frac{1}{n} \sum_{i=1}^{n} \|p_b^i - p_a^i\| \qquad (9)$$

be the average movement of points during the iteration. Then we stop when the $average\_movement$ is less than $\varepsilon$.

## 3.3   The PPPA Algorithm

Figure 5 presents the PPPA algorithm. First, the algorithm assigns random positions for all individuals in the pedigree (cf. Line 1 in Figure 5). Then it starts the iterative process (cf. block 2). For each iteration it scans the database, builds the kd-tree, and pushes and pulls the relevant points. It stops if the average movement of points is less than $\varepsilon$ (cf. Line 2.3).

```
Input:
    p[i].{id, mother, father, sex, sick}: an array of individuals, i = 1,...,n
    ε: precision of the estimation
Output:
    p.x[i], p.y[i], p.z[i]: 3D positions of the individuals of the pedigree
Body:
    1. Initialize the positions of the individuals
```
$p[i].\{x, y, z\} \leftarrow \{UNIFORM(0.0, 1.0), UNIFORM(0.0, 1.0), UNIFORM(0.0, 1.0)\}$;
$average\_movement = \infty$
```
    Compute the diameter of the neighborhood that correspond to ε error level:
```
$diam = f_{push}^{-1}(\varepsilon)$
```
    2. WHILE average_movement > ε DO
        2.1 Build the kd-tree K
        2.2 Scan database. FOR EACH i = 1,...,n DO
            2.2.1 Identify the points that are within diam from p[i]:
                  ε_neigh = K.ε_neighborhood(p[i], diam)
            2.2.2 FOR EACH q[j] ∈ ε_neigh DO
                2.2.2.1 Push p[i] and q[j] outwards each other:
```
$$\delta = f_{pull}(d(p[i], q[j]), \ p[i].sick \ XOR \ q[i].sick)$$
$$p = p - \delta(p - q)/(\|p - q\|)$$
$$q = q + \delta(p - q)/(\|p - q\|)$$
```
            2.2.3 Identify the set PC(p[i]) of parents and children of p[i]
                  FOR EACH q[j] ∈ PC(p[i]) DO
                2.2.3.1 Pull p[i] and q[j] towards each other:
```
$$\delta = f_{push}(d(p[i], q[j]), \ p[i].sick \ XOR \ q[i].sick)$$
$$p = p + \delta(p - q)/(\|p - q\|)$$
$$q = q - \delta(p - q)/(\|p - q\|)$$
```
        2.3 Compute average_movement
```

**Fig. 5.** The PPPA Algorithm

## 4   Experimental Investigation

We organize the experiments in three sub-sections. First we evaluate the stop criteria and investigate the convergence of the method as the number of iterations of the method increases (cf. Section 4.1). Then we investigate the time complexity as the number of individuals in the database increases (cf. Section 4.2). Finally, we give a visual evaluation of the method for different datasets (cf. Section 4.3).

The algorithms were implemented in C++ and integrated into the 3DVDM system [24,25]. The experiments were run on Intel Mobile P4 1.7GHZ machine with 512MB of RAM.

### 4.1   Convergence of the Method and Stop Criteria

We varied the complexity of the relationships of families and generated the following three datasets: a dataset with four independent non-intersecting families

(5 generations in each family, 63 persons per family), a dataset with one family and no cycles (7 generations in the family, 255 persons in the family), and a dataset with one family and cycles (7 generations in the family, 255 persons in the family, 8 individuals of the last generation of the same family were married to each other). The number of individuals per dataset is around 250.

Figure 6 illustrates the typical convergence of the method for the datasets. At the end of the process the individual families are clearly separated: close relatives of the family are placed close to each other and far relatives are placed far apart (cf. Figure 6(a)).

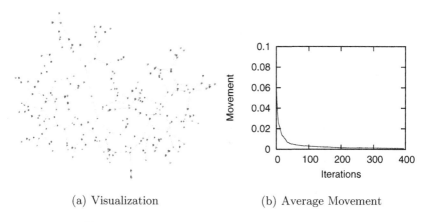

(a) Visualization                    (b) Average Movement

**Fig. 6.** Typical Visualization and Average Movement

Figure 6(b) shows the average movement of individual points of the database as the number of iterations increases. During the first iterations (cf. number of iterations 0–50 in Figure 6(b)) the method experience an exponential convergence rate. During the first iterations the families are separated in space, and the distribution of the individuals of the families is close to uniform. During the last iterations (cf. number of iterations 50–400 in Figure 6(b)) the convergence rate is linear and the positions of the individuals of the families are stable. Since we update the visualization as the number of iterations increase, we can investigate and mine the pedigrees after the first few seconds of the runtime of the PPPA method (cf. Section 4.2).

Figure 7 illustrates the number of active points (points that move further than threshold $\varepsilon$) as the number of iterations increase. The decrease of the active points is less pronounced for the case of the four independent families (cf. Figure 7(a)), since the members of the families should separate from the non-members of the family and the internal structure of each of the family must be constructed. The decrease of the active points of one large family is more pronounced (cf. Figure 7(b)), since there are no individuals of other families that should be pushed away, and only the internal structure of the family must be built. Figure 7(c) shows the decrease of the active points for one family with

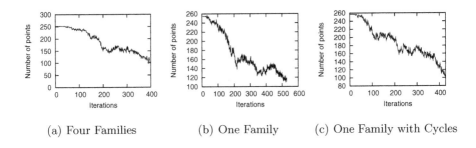

(a) Four Families          (b) One Family          (c) One Family with Cycles

**Fig. 7.** Active Points

several cycles. Since the structure of the family is more complicated compared to the one family case, the decrease of the number of active points is less pronounced.

### 4.2   Numerical Evaluation

Figure 8 shows the computational time as the number of individuals in the pedigree increases. Figures 8(a) and 8(b) show that the computational time is super-linear wrt the number of families (the number of individuals per family is fixed to 15) and wrt the number of individuals (the number of families is fixed to 1). This is due to the usage of the kd-tree.

In general, the computational time increases only slightly as the number of cycles increases averaging around 20 seconds (cf. Figure 8(c)). However, due to random positioning of the initial points the variance of the computational time in this case is high.

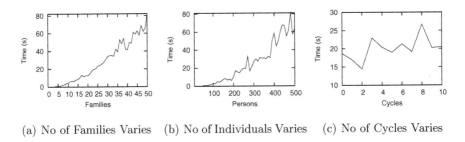

(a) No of Families Varies   (b) No of Individuals Varies   (c) No of Cycles Varies

**Fig. 8.** Computational Time

### 4.3   Visual Evaluation

In this section we investigate a number of case studies and present screen shots of the 3DVDM system. We organize the experiments such that the experiments of pedigrees of only healthy individuals and similar pedigrees with some unhealthy individuals can be compared. Note that the figures use colors to identify healthy and sick individuals, respectively.

*Many small families.* Figure 9 illustrates the screen shot of one thousand individual families. Each family consists of the parents (father, mother) and a child.

The families form compact graphs clearly separated from each other when the family members are all healthy individuals (cf. Figure 9(a)) In contrast, families with the disease (cf. Figure 9(b)) push away healthy families twice stronger than healthy ones. Therefore healthy families are placed in the center of the Figure while sick families are pushed away from the center.

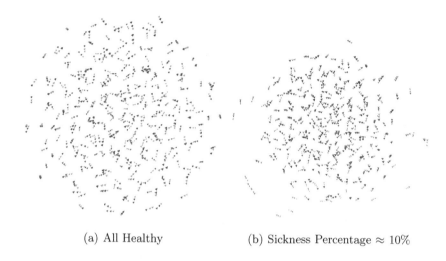

(a) All Healthy                    (b) Sickness Percentage ≈ 10%

**Fig. 9.** 333 Families of One Child and Parents

*Few big families.* Figure 10 illustrates a visualization of four families (127 individuals each). Figure 10(a) illustrates the case of all healthy individuals, while Figure 10(b) illustrates a case of three healthy and one sick family. In case of the healthy pedigree all families are clearly separated from each other (cf. Figure 10(a)). In case of a sick family the three healthy families form a compact structure. The sick family is pushed away from the healthy ones.

*Partly sick families.* In contrast to the previous experiments where families were either completely sick or not sick at all (this is not uncommon for genetic diseases), this paragraph experiments with families with sick and healthy persons.

Figure 11(a) illustrates 6 families with ancestors up to the 5th generation. Half of the individuals of the families are sick. In this case the sick population does not form a separate cluster from the healthy one, but the visualization forms typical patterns: sick and healthy individuals form small sub-clusters inside the families.

Figure 11(b) illustrates four big families (one of them is completely healthy) and 50 small families. Every second generation contains around 70% of sick people. As one can expect, the healthy family stays in the middle of the Figure

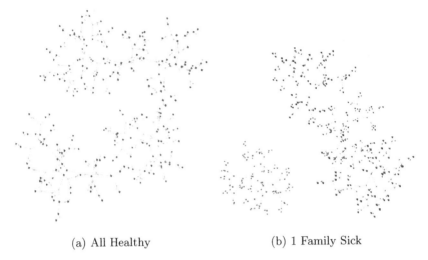

(a) All Healthy                    (b) 1 Family Sick

**Fig. 10.** 4 Families with Ancestors Till 6th Generation

and the families with sick members are pushed away from the healthy one. In contrast to Figure 10(b) sick individuals do not form clear clusters.

In summary our PPPA method produces good results and makes it easy to identify individuals who are potential carriers of a genetic defect. Note that the PPPA algorithm does not include an explicit layout component that, e.g., attempts to avoid intersecting edges. Only the push and pull mechanism is used to arrange individuals. Despite this approach the edges of graphs rarely intersect

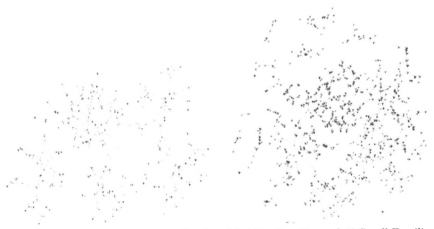

(a) 6 Families with Ancestors Till 5th    (b) 4 Big Families and 50 Small Families
Generation

**Fig. 11.** Families with Sick and Healthy Individuals Mixed

and graphs are divided into clearly visible sub-graphs if the pedigree consists of independent families.

## 5 Conclusion and Future Work

This paper introduces the PPPA method to mine large and complex pedigree databases. The PPPA method organizes the individuals of a given pedigree: close relatives are visualized close to each other while non-related individuals are visualized far away from each other. The arrangement of the pedigree allows to mine large and complex pedigrees and focuses on the relationships between individuals. We evaluate the PPPA method experimentally. We show that the method converges to a stable arrangement of the pedigree independent of the initial distribution of the data. The time complexity of the method is slightly worse than linear wrt the number of individuals of the pedigree. The visual evaluation of the method shows that it is possible to mine large and complex pedigree databases with the help of the PPPA method.

There are two interesting directions for future work. First, we will evaluate the method analytically. This will establish conditions for the convergence of the method as the number of iterations increases. Second, we want to progress the mining of real world pedigree data of South Tirol. This will allow to understand the complex structures of pedigrees of isolated populations and come up with better identification and treatment methods of genome diseases.

## Acknowledgments

We thank the European Academy in Bozen-Bolzano and especially Christian Fuchsberger for the introduction to pedigree data and extensive discussions.

## References

1. Marroni, F., Pichler, I., Grandi, A.D., Volpato, C.B., Vogl, F.D., Pinggera, G.K., Bailey-Wilson, J.E., Pramstaller, P.P.: Population isolates in south tyrol and their value for genetic dissection of complex diseases. In: Ann. Hum. Gen. (2006)
2. Auber, D.: Tulip. In Mutzel, P., Jünger, M., Leipert, S., eds.: 9th Symp. Graph Drawing. Volume 2265 of Lecture Notes in Computer Science., Springer-Verlag (2001) 335–337
3. Auber, D.: Tulip : A huge graph visualisation framework. In Mutzel, P., Jünger, M., eds.: Graph Drawing Softwares. Mathematics and Visualization. Springer-Verlag (2003) 105–126
4. Reingold, E.M., Tilford, J.S.: Tidier drawing of trees. IEEE Transactions on Software Engineering **SE-7**(2) (1981) 223–228
5. Robertson, G.G., Mackinlay, J.D., Card, S.K.: Cone trees: animated 3d visualizations of hierarchical information. In: CHI '91: Proceedings of the SIGCHI conference on Human factors in computing systems, New York, NY, USA, ACM Press (1991) 189–194

6. Sugiyama, K., Tagawa, S., Toda, M.: Methods for visual understanding of hierar-chical system structures. IEEE Transactions on Systems, Man, and Cybernetics **SMC-11**(2) (1981) 109–125

7. Brandes, U.: Drawing on physical analogies. In Kaufmann, M., Wagner, D., eds.: Drawing Graphs: Methods and Models. Number 2025. Springer-Verlag, Berlin, Germany (2001) 71–86

8. Archambault, D., Munzner, T., Auber, D.: Topolayout: Graph layout by topolog-ical features. In: INFOVIS '05: Poster Track of the IEEE Symposium on Informa-tion Visualization (INFOVIS'05), Washington, DC, USA, IEEE Computer Society (2005) 3–4

9. Visual Technologies. http://www.visualizeinc.com/ (2006) [Online; accessed 09-June-2006].

10. Chapman, C.: Cyrillic 2.1. Oxford: Cherwell (1997)

11. Cyrillic Software. http://www.cyrillicsoftware.com/ (2006) [Online; accessed 09-June-2006].

12. Progeny Software. http://www.progeny.com/ (2006) [Online; accessed 09-June-2006].

13. aiSee Graph Layout Software. http://www.aisee.com (2006) [Online; accessed 09-June-2006].

14. Wong, L.: Visualization and manipulation of pedigree diagrams. Genome Infor-matics **11** (2000) 63–72

15. Tores, F., Barillot, E.: Optimizing pedigree drawing using interval graph theory. Currents in Computational Molecular Biology (2000) 194–195

16. Lineage. http://www.ansci.cornell.edu/lineage/index.html (2006) [Online; ac-cessed 09-June-2006].

17. Wigginton, J.E., Abecasis, G.R.: PEDSTATS: descriptive statistics, graphics and quality assessment for gene mapping data. Bioinformatics **21**(16) (2005) 3445–3447

18. Abecasis, G.R., Cherny, S.S., Cookson, W.O.C., Cardon, L.R.: GRR: graphical representation of relationship errors. Bioinformatics **17**(8) (2001) 742–742

19. Tools of Linkage Analysis. http://linkage.rockefeller.edu/soft/ (2006)

20. Pixton, B., G.-Carrier, C.: MAL4:6 - Using Data Mining for Record Linkage. In: the 5th Annual Workshop on Technology for Family History and Genealogical Research. (2005)

21. Gansner, E.R., North, S.C.: An open graph visualization system and its applica-tions to software engineering. Software — Practice and Experience **30**(11) (2000) 1203–1233

22. Gansner, E., Koren, Y., North, S.: Topological fisheye views for visualizing large graphs. infovis **00** (2004) 175–182

23. Dynagraph. http://www.dynagraph.net/ (2006) [Online; accessed 09-June-2006].

24. Böhlen, M.H., Bukauskas, L., Eriksen, P.S., Lauritzen, S.L., Mazeika, A., Musaeus, P., Mylov, P.: 3d visual data mining: Goals and experiences. Computational Statistics & Data Analysis **43**(4) (August 2004)

25. Mazeika, A., Boehlen, M.H., Taliun, A.: Adaptive density estimation, demo. In: VLDB, 32nd International Conference on Very Large Data Bases. (2006)

# Discovering Emerging Topics in Unlabelled Text Collections

Rene Schult and Myra Spiliopoulou

Otto-von-Guericke-University Magdeburg, Germany
Institute of Technical and Business Information Systems
{schult, myra}@iti.cs.uni-magdeburg.de

**Abstract.** As document collections accummulate over time, some of the discussion subjects in them become outfashioned, while new ones emerge. Then, old classification schemes should be updated. In this paper, we address the challenge of finding emerging *and persistent* "themes", i.e. subjects that live long enough to be incorporated into a taxonomy or ontology describing the document collection. We focus on the identification of cluster labels that "survive" changes in the constitution of the underlying population of documents, including changes in the feature space of dominant words, because the terminology of the document archive also changes over time. We have conducted a set of promising experiments on the identification of themes that manifested themselves in section H2.8 of the ACM digital library and juxtapose them with the classes foreseen in the ACM taxonomy for this section.

## 1 Introduction

Document archives are usually organized by some rather rigid categorization scheme, often a taxonomy of subjects. If no full text retrieval is permitted, these taxonomy subjects are the sole means of search in it. Even by full text retrieval, they are still a major indicator of the documents' contents. However, the usability of taxonomies towards old documents is limited: There is a time lag between the emergence of a new subject and the expansion of the taxonomy to include it. This time lag may be quite large, since taxonomies are usually expanded to include *persistent*, long-lived subjects rather than short-lived hypes. This implies that old documents may become invisible because they are characterized by too generic subjects, although new ones would be more appropriate for them.

As an example, consider the ACM archive[1] , which uses the ACM taxonomy for keyword assignment, categorization and browsing. The taxonomy has been extended with themes like "data mining" and "image databases" to cover documents on these subjects. However, two particularities must be considered here. First, there is some elapsed time between the insertion of the first document on e.g. data mining and the addition of the new class in the categorization scheme; in this time period, documents on the new subject are assigned to the generic parent class. If a knowledge seeker is interested on early advances on data mining, she must go through the whole subarchive on database

---

[1] http://portal.acm.org/ccs.cfm

Y. Manolopoulos, J. Pokorný, and T. Sellis (Eds.): ADBIS 2006, LNCS 4152, pp. 353–366, 2006.

applications. Although keyword-based search is available, the appropriate keywords for search on data mining in the early nineties are likely to be different from those of to-day. Second, a concept added in the taxonomy may be too generic or too specific with respect to the name of the class. For example, a dominant concept among the early documents on data mining is "association rules", while the "image databases" class seems to be dominated by the concept "image retrieval" (this is further discussed in the section on our experiments). In such cases, it is necessary to perform a retrospective *re-categorization* of the documents or at least discover the keywords characterizing the emerging themes.

To address this issue, we propose the monitoring of evolving *themes* from the ac-cummulating document collection and the actualization of the categorization scheme with emerging and persistent ones. We define a "theme" as a topic that (a) describes an adequately large cluster of documents, (b) persists over several timeslots during the period of observation and (c) is described by the same words, at least to a cer-tain extend, although the terminology of the document collection may change with time. We are further interested in connecting themes that may refer to the same sub-ject but use different terminology or are subordinate to an a priori unknown new broad subject.

Our "Theme-Monitor" builds upon our previous work [SS06] for the identification of short-term trends. In [SS06], we have studied the appearance and decay of themes from one timeslot to another, by clustering the documents inserted in the collection at each timeslot and then comparing the themes found at adjacent timeslots. In this study, we concentrate on themes found in the document collection as it accummulates, i.e. under the constraint that old documents should be further represented in the model. This deviates from the conventions pursued in Topic Discovery and Tracking (for TDT see [All02]), where newer documents are assigned higher weights than old ones, but is more appropriate for re-categorization in document collections, where old documents must still be assigned to an appropriate category and be accessible, even if the theme they represent has stagnated in the meanwhile.

Our Theme-Monitor takes feature space evolution into account. Although we expect that dominant features in an accummulating collection are not changing often, we do take account of the emergence of new words by reconsidering the feature space when-ever it does not return satisfactory text clustering results.

In the next section, we discuss relevant research. The Theme-Monitor is described in section 3, starting with a conceptual model for clusters and themes over an accummu-lating collection and continuing with the monitoring algorithm itself. In section 4 we describe our experiments with the H2.8 section of the ACM archive. The last section concludes and gives an outlook on theme and terminology evolution.

## 2   Related Work

The subjects of Topic Detection and Topic Tracking are defined in [All02], where the five tasks of TDT are enlisted. As stated in that book, TDT concentrates on the de-tection and tracking of *stories* (a "topic" is a story) and encompasses the tasks of (1) story segmentation, (2) first story detection, (3) cluster detection, (4) tracking and (5) story link detection. There is a conceptual similarity to our problem specification, in the sense that the emerging classes to be discovered are "topics". However, these classes are not stories in the TDT sense: For our problem specification, the documents in the stream are distinct, none of them refering to older documents - hence task (5) does not apply. It is not of interest to detect a story and then track it across documents, as in tasks (2) and (4), but rather identify documents across different time periods, which, when taken together contribute to the same, a priori unknown but statistically important "topic". This separation has been first elaborated in the survey of [KGP+03], where the new task of topic trend discovery was introduced. However, the methods presented under this task in [KGP+03] rely on cross-references among documents, i.e. on task (5) of the original TDT agenda and thus do not transfer to our problem specification.

Moringa and Yamanishi use a finite mixture model to detect emerging topic trends in a document stream and adapt the model describing the stream [MY04]. As stressed in the introduction, adaptation of the model is not appropriate in our case, because old documents should still be present and accessible in the categorization scheme. Moreover, their soft clustering algorithm allows a document to contribute in multiple topics. Documents may indeed adhere to multiple categories and some libraries do allow the assignment of a document to more than one classes. However, before extending an existing categorization scheme by a new category, one needs proof that this category is needed, i.e. there is an adequate number of documents that are characterized by this category *and* cannot be accommodated properly elsewhere.

The same shortcoming pertains to the work of Mei and Zhai [MZ05], where mixture models are used to cluster documents, derive themes from them and study the evolution of those themes. The authors model the time span in which a topic is traced and propose an "evolution graph", in which transitions of one theme to another can be identified. The emphasis of that study is on modeling and tracing semantically connected themes, i.e. themes that are partially described by the same words. Our Theme-Monitor also expresses a theme as a set of words that describe a cluster. However, our clusters are crisp and are built over an evolving feature space where new words may be added and old ones may become obsolete. Moreover, Theme-Monitor is more restrictive in its definition of "theme", thus skipping changes that may be simply due to the instability of the underlying clusters.

There is a relevance between theme evolution and cluster evolution, since themes are essentially cluster descriptors. Cluster evolution is addressed in the context of "spatiotemporal clustering", including the studies of [Agg05, NMSD05], and in the context of finding differences between datasets and between models over datasets, as pursued by the FOCUS framework [GGR99]. Spatiotemporal clustering is not applicable to theme monitoring though, because the feature space over which clusters are built may change; when the feature space changes, the trajectory of the old clusters becomes obsolete and cannot be used to compare old and new clusters. Although cluster comparison in general may be applicable for theme monitoring, we should keep in mind that not all cluster changes correspond to changes of themes. Therefore, in our experiments we use FOCUS as reference to show that Theme-Monitor locates theme changes only and ignores the evolution of many unstable clusters.

# 3    Theme-Monitor on an Accummulating Document Collection

Our algorithm Theme-Monitor takes as input a document collection, typically a bibliographical archive, thematically categorized according to a taxonomy. It monitors this archive over a series of time periods and tries to discover *persistent thematic subcollections* and assign labels to them. These labels are meant as themes that should become new classes in the original taxonomy.

We first present the model of documents and themes used by Theme-Monitor and then describe the cluster matching and cluster quality evaluation mechanism as parts of the monitoring algorithm. A more extensive version of this model has appeared in [SS06] for the ThemeFinder algorithm that operates on non-accummulated document sets.

## 3.1    Modeling Clusters, Labels and Themes

The archive $\mathcal{A}$ monitoring by Theme-Monitor is a homogeneous, accummulating document collection corresponding to one node of the categorization hierarchy and its children. We observe $\mathcal{A}$ over a series of $T$ time periods $t_1, \ldots, t_T$, whereupon each period $t_i$ encompasses a subset of documents $D_i$ such that $D_i \subseteq D_j, \forall i < j$.

In an archive that accummulates over a long period of time, old documents are likely to have been described differently than more recent ones. In our running example of the H2.8 section of the ACM digital library, many early documents do not have abstracts. In such a case, considering *all* information available for each document would lead to the suppression of old documents or of those belonging to specific, possibly stagnating categories. To alleviate this problem, we consider the same set of information pieces for all documents, for example title and keywords. In the following, this "view over the document" is considered as "the document" itself, since all further information is filtered out.

A document in $D_i, \forall i$ is a vector of words derived from a feature space. There are many sophisticated methods for the selection of a feature space. In our preliminary experiments with several clustering algorithms and feature space selection schemes, it turned out that conventional methods that consider all words perform poorly – most likely because the texts are small and highly diverse. The best performance was achieved when limiting the number of features to the "best" $n$ ones according to two criteria: (a) the features with the highest TF×IDF values or (b) the features with the highest scores in the entropy-based measure proposed in [BN04]. In our experiments, we opted for the former on reasons of computational simplicity.

For a given document subset $D$ and feature space $fs$, we cluster the documents on semantic similarity. Typically, not all clusters are of the same quality. We concentrate on clusters that can be described by a representative label – a "theme" as follows:

**Definition 1.** *Let $D$ be a collection of documents and $fs$ be a feature space. Let $\zeta(D, fs) = \{C_1, \ldots, C_k\}$ be a clustering, i.e. a set of clusters that partition $D$ into $k$ non-overlapping groups of similar document vectors over the feature space $fs$.*

*A cluster $C \in \zeta(D, fs)$ is a "thematic cluster" if the following set is not empty:*

$$L_C = \{w \in fs | support(w, C) \geq \tau_{wordsupport}\} \tag{1}$$

*This set constitutes the "label" of $C$, denoted as $label(C)$.*

In this definition, $support(w, C)$ returns the fraction of documents in cluster $C$ that contain the word $w$, divided by the number of documents in $C$, $card(C)$. The threshold $\tau_{wordsupport}$ restricts the set $L_C$ to the words of the feature space that are frequent in $C$, i.e. those that characterize the documents in $C$.

Cluster labels are candidates for themes. A theme is a persistent label, i.e. one that appears for several, possibly consecutive periods:

**Definition 2.** *Let $t_1, \ldots, t_T$ be the series of $T$ periods of observation over the accumulating archive. Let $l \equiv label(C)$ be a the label of some detected thematic cluster $C$. Then the label $l$ is a "theme" if there are at least $m$ periods $t_{i_1}, t_{i_2}, \ldots, t_{i_m}$ such that: $\forall j = i_1, i_2, \ldots, i_m \exists C^j \in \zeta(D_j, fs_j) : |l \backslash label(C^j)| \leq \tau_{deviation}$ where the threshold $\tau_{deviation}$ allows for (a) differences among the feature spaces used in different periods and (b) variations in the cluster's dominant words.*

This definition specifies that a label is a theme if some of its words appear in at least $m$ arbitrary, not necessarily consecutive periods. The threshold $\tau_{deviation}$ determines how many of the words may deviate. By setting $\tau_{deviation} := 0$ and $m := T$, we demand that a label is a theme only if it appears in all periods. In [MZ05], such a label would be called a "trans-collection theme", with the difference that their clusters may overlap, so that these themes cannot be used for the separation of documents into future classes.

## 3.2  Label Monitoring and Cluster Tracing

The Theme-Monitor starts with an initial clustering of the documents in the first period. In each subsequent period, the accummulating document set is re-clustered using the original feature space and the new clustering is evaluated on quality. If the clustering is of poor quality, it is rejected, the feature space is computed anew over the whole accummulated document set and clustering is performed again. Then, the labels of the new clusters are matched to the old labels. Matched labels (or fragments of labels, subject to $\tau_{deviation}$) are retained as theme candidates. Candidates surviving for more than $m$ periods (cf. Def. 2) are declared as themes.

**Assessing the Quality of Clusterings.** The quality of clusters and of clusterings can be assessed according to different criteria, usually a combination of cluster homogeneity and separability, combined with stability of the clustering scheme. For Theme-Monitor, clustering quality refers rather to the existence of thematic clusters that may result in themes:

**Definition 3.** *Let $D$ be a documentset, $fs$ be a feature space and $\zeta(D, fs)$ be the clustering of $D$ using $fs$. This clustering is good iff the number of thematic clusters in it is no less than a threshold $\tau_{clustering}$.*

While this seems oversimplifying at first glance, the existence of thematic clusters *presupposes* cluster homogeneity. We use this criterion to decide whether the feature space should be rebuild to accommodate words that are more representative of the newly inserted documents.

**Finding the Best Match for a Thematic Cluster.** Once a clustering is built, the thematic clusters in it are juxtaposed to those of the previous clustering. The simplest case of a match for a thematic cluster $C \in \zeta_{i-1}$ would be a cluster $C' \in \zeta_i$ such that $label(C) = label(C')$. As pointed out in Def. 2, we allow for a deviation between two labels. This deviation is realized in the heuristic algorithm $best\_match(\cdot)$ shown in Table 1.

**Table 1.** The heuristic $best\_match$

| Step Action in $best\_match(C, \xi)$ |
| --- |
| 1 $candidates \leftarrow \emptyset$ |
| 2 for each $X \in \xi$ do |
| 3    if $label(X) == label(C)$ then |
| 4       return $X$ |
| 5    endif |
| 6    if $label(X) \cap label(C) \neq \{e\}$ then |
| 7       $candidates \leftarrow candidates \cup \{X\}$ |
| 8    endif |
| 9 endfor |
| 10 if $candidates == \emptyset$ then |
| 11    return $\emptyset$ |
| 12 endif |
| 13 $L \leftarrow ordering(label(C), MFWF)$ |
| 14 for each $w \in L$ do |
| 15    $wL \leftarrow \{X \in candidates | w \in label(X)\&$ |
|         $support(w, X) \approx support(w, C)\}$ |
| 16    if $wL \neq \emptyset$ then |
| 17       $candidates \leftarrow wL$ |
| 18    endif |
| 19 endfor |
| 20 $L \leftarrow ordering(candidates, MCWF)$ |
| 21 return $firstOf(L)$ |
| $MFWF = Most\_Frequent\_Word\_First$ |
| $MCWF = Most\_Common\_Words\_First$ |

The heuristic $best\_match(C, \xi)$ is actually a series of heuristics applied upon the set of clusters $\xi$. In step 3 it is checked whether there is a cluster with the same label as $C$. If this is the case, this cluster is returned. Otherwise, a list of candidates is built, consisting of the thematic clusters having at least one common word with the label of $C$ (Steps 6, 7). If there are no such candidates, the empty set is returned in step 11. If there are candidates, then they are filtered on the basis of the frequency of the words in their labels (Steps 13-19).

The motivation of ordering the words in the label of $C$ by frequency is that frequent words inside the cluster are likely to be more important. Then, starting with the most frequent word in step 14, a subset of candidates is identified in step 15: These are the clusters, where the word appears in the label *and* has a similar support as in the cluster $C$. If this set is not empty, it replaces the original set of candidates (steps 16-17). In any case, the next most frequent word is processed in the next iteration (step 14).

Steps 10 and 16 guarantee that the set of candidates considered in step 20 is not empty. In this step, the candidates are ordered by number of common words between their label and the label of $C$. Then, in step 21, the cluster with the most common words is returned as best match.

**Cluster Monitoring *vs* Theme Discovery.** In each iteration, the Theme-Monitor builds a clustering, eventually after re-constructing the feature space and then matches each thematic cluster of the old clustering to the best candidate in the new clustering. Labels that pertain to more than $m$ periods are reported as themes, i.e. as candidates for an extension of the library's original taxonomy.

By virtue of Def. 2, a theme does not correspond to one label but to a set of similar but not necessarily identical labels supported by clusters of different periods. Moreover, themes are not exclusive to clusters: Depending on the $\tau_{support}$ threshold for labels, two clusters may have the same label. This is quite likely for poorly separated clusters that may occur if the information in the vector space is not adequate for a better separation.

To deal with those cases, the Theme-Monitor constructs themes in two steps: First, clusters of the same clustering but sharing *exactly* the same label are taken together. Second, all clusters contributing to the same theme are considered together and a new label is constructed as the most frequent subset of words – subject to either a length limit (the $n$ most frequent words) or a frequency limit (all words that appear in at least $N$ documents).

## 4    Experimenting with the ACM Digital Library

We tested our Theme-Monitor on section H2.8 of the ACM digital library. This section, named "database applications" contains documents on several subcategories that have been gradually added. Once made available to the authors, those topics have been used as keywords. The topic "image databases" appears already in the first period of observations ($\leq 1994$), the topic "data mining" first appears in 1995, "spatial databases and GIS" in 1996, while "scientific databases" and "statistical databases" are used since 1997. The ACM categories are listed in Table 2, together with the acronyms we have assigned to them for brevity.

**Table 2.** The ACM categories in section H2.8

| Data mining | DM |
|---|---|
| Spatial databases & GIS | SpatDB |
| Image databases | ImgDB |
| Statistical Databases | StatDB |
| Scientific Databases | SciDB |

For our experiments, we have downloaded the documents from 1996 to 2004, distributed as shown in Table 3 including the original distribution of the five subcategories. Our objective was the a posteriori discovery of the five subcategories by juxtaposing them to the themes that emerged in the collection. For our vectorization, we have used titles and keywords but no abstracts, since some documents did not contain abstracts. We have built a feature space of the 30 features with the highest TF×IDF and set the

**Table 3.** Number of documents in the ACM subarchive "database applications" and the subgroups

| Period | 1996 | 1997 | 1998 | 1999 | 2000 | 2001 | 2002 | 2003 | 2004 |
|--------|------|------|------|------|------|------|------|------|------|
| numbers | 89 | 150 | 369 | 675 | 1155 | 1634 | 2338 | 3371 | 4434 |
| DM | 16 | 56 | 148 | 315 | 580 | 872 | 1330 | 1984 | 2577 |
| SpatDB | 40 | 53 | 124 | 188 | 316 | 388 | 517 | 662 | 851 |
| ImgDB | 16 | 22 | 70 | 135 | 208 | 287 | 340 | 429 | 571 |
| StatDB | 17 | 19 | 21 | 25 | 33 | 44 | 66 | 84 | 89 |
| SciDB | 0 | 0 | 6 | 12 | 18 | 43 | 85 | 212 | 346 |

number of target clusters to 5. We have experimented with different algorithms and then decided for bisecting K-means that delivered the best results.

### 4.1 Indicator of New Themes

For the theme discovery, we have set $\tau_{wordsupport} = 0.6$ and $\tau_{thematic} = k - 2$.

The new ACM topics in the subarchive indicate that the ACM taxonomy designers have responded to emerging research threads. These threads are associated with a drift in the frequent terms in the documents: new research areas use new terms. A simple way of detecting such a drift is by clustering the documents and check whether the thematic clusters degenerate. So, we first have checked whether the anticipated themes could be found without using Theme-Monitor.

A high number of feature space changes is not desirable, because it is apt to features of short-term popularity and prohibits a long-term observation of the clusters. For $\tau_{matches} = \tau_{thematic} - 2$, a change in the feature space is needed only for 2 periods. The same holds for $\tau_{matches} = \tau_{thematic} - 3$, which is less restrictive. Although the value of $\tau_{thematic}$ is too small (4 thematic clusters) for generalization, this experiment indicates that the value $\tau_{thematic} - 2$ is appropriate for $\tau_{matches}$.

### 4.2 Cluster Evolution Tracking vs Theme Discovery

Theme discovery and evolution, as pursued by Theme-Monitor, is narrowly coupled with cluster evolution. However, the appearance of a theme may be independent of cluster changes. For example:

- One or more old clusters may be absorbed by a new one. Nonetheless, the new cluster may retain the label of one of the old clusters.
- themes are not exclusive to clusters: Depending on the $\tau_{support}$ threshold for labels, two clusters may have the same label. This is quite likely, if clusters are poorly separated.
- A label may "migrate" from one cluster to another, especially if clusters are unstable and noisy but contain a homogeneous subgroup of documents.

To study the difference between cluster evolution and theme discovery, we have invoked next to Theme-Monitor a method that tracks cluster evolution and have compared their findings. In [SNTS06], we present the method MONIC for the detection of cluster transitions, such as survivals, absorptions and splits. Here, we have used a more restricted version of MONIC, concentrating only on cluster survivals. For survival detection, we have then used an adapted version of FOCUS [GGR99].

As described in [SNTS06], we assume that a cluster $C$ has survived into a cluster $C'$ if the portion of $C$ contained in $C'$ exceeds a threshold $\tau_{overlap}$, i.e. $overlap(C, C') :=$ $\frac{|C \cap C'|}{|C|} \geq \tau_{overlap}$. If $\tau_{overlap}$ is set to a value larger than 0.5, then an old cluster may survive in at most one new cluster. For smaller values, the contents of an old cluster may survive in more than one new clusters.

### 4.3 Themes vs ACM Categories

We have applied bisecting K-means upon the vectorized ACM documents accummulated up to each timepoint, setting $k = 5$ and $\tau_{wordsupport} = 0.6$. For experiments with different values of $k$, the reader is referred to [SNTS06]. Our experimental results are shown in Table 4 and discussed below.

The first column in Table 4 shows the time period under observation. In the second column, we see the feature space used by Theme-Monitor for the clustering. For 1997, the old feature space of 1996 has been replaced by the period-specific feature space. Differently from our experiments on non-accummulated data, this feature space has turned out to be adequate for all subsequent periods.

The labels found by Theme-Monitor are shown in the third column. Next to each word, we see its support inside the cluster. We can see that there is a gap in the support of the words in the label: If $\tau_{wordsupport}$ were set to any value larger than 0.6, only words appearing in all documents would have qualified. This would have lead to shorter labels but also to the disappearance of some thematic clusters, like the cluster labelled "datum" which refers to data mining (this label is discussed below).

The third column shows that there are no collection themes according to Def. 2, since no label persists across all periods. However, there are several, quite interesting themes: When we set the number of periods $m$ to 4 and insist that no word from a label may disappear $(u = 0)$, the label {datum, mine} qualifies as theme, while the label {retrieval, image, base} persists in 4 non-consecutive periods. If we allow that a label may change by at most one word $(u = 1)$, then {retrieval, image} with the additional word "base" becomes a very stable theme, appearing for the last 5 time periods. This theme refers obviously to "image retrieval", a subcategory of image databases that emerges in 1997, disappears for a short time and then becomes stable from 2000 on.

The emergence and evolution of labels associated to data mining is also very interesting. The first cluster of period 1996 contains the words "discovery", "knowledge" and "datum" (data) in all documents, the word "pattern" is also very frequent. With the period-specific feature space of 1997, the cluster on data mining becomes separated under the label {datum, discovery}. The words "knowledge" and "discovery" persist in the next three periods. For $m = 3$, the label {datum, discovery, knowledge} would have become a theme, the "knowledge discovery [from] data". Starting from 1998, the label {datum, mining} becomes present; the two sibling labels {datum, mine} and {datum, mining} finally absorb the older label {datum, discovery, knowledge} and the new theme for "data mining" becomes a very stable label.

An explanation of the sibling labels {datum, mine} and {datum, mining} is due here. They are an artefact of the linguistic preprocessor, which (correctly) distinguishes

**Table 4.** Thematic clusters and corresponding ACM categories for each period

| Time period | Feature space of | Words in the label $\tau_{wordsupport} \geq 0,6$ | ACM topic name | correctness | coverage |
|---|---|---|---|---|---|
| 1996 | 1996 | discovery (1), knowledge (1), datum (1), gis (0.67), pattern (0.67), spatial (0.67) | DM | 0.67 | 0.25 |
| | | ... COVERS ALSO | SpatDB | 0.33 | 0.5 |
| | | database (1), datum (1) | DM | 0.53 | 0.5 |
| | | database (1) | – | – | – |
| 1997 | 1997 | datum (1), discovery (1) | DM | 0.9 | 0.5 |
| | | image (1), content (1), base (1), retrieval (0.67) | ImgDB | 0.83 | 0.23 |
| | | statistical (1), database (1), security (1) | StatDB | 0.93 | 0.68 |
| 1998 | same | datum (1), discovery (1), knowledge (1) | DM | 0.89 | 0.26 |
| | | datum (1), mining (0.64) | DM | 0.9 | 0.5 |
| | | database (1) | – | – | – |
| 1999 | same | datum (1), discovery (1), knowledge (1) | DM | 0.92 | 0.22 |
| | | system (1), computer (1) | ImgDB | 0.67 | 0.01 |
| | | system (1), geographical (1), information (0.69) | SpatDB | 0.9 | 0.23 |
| 2000 | same | datum (1), mine (1) | DM | 0.91 | 0.22 |
| | | discovery (1), knowledge (1), datum (0.62) | DM | 0.92 | 0.22 |
| | | retrieval (1), image (1), base (0.69) | ImgDB | 0.92 | 0.27 |
| 2001 | same | datum (1), mine (1) | DM | 0.91 | 0.21 |
| | | datum (1), mining (1) | DM | 0.87 | 0.33 |
| | | retrieval (1), image (1), base (1) | ImgDB | 0.93 | 0.36 |
| 2002 | same | datum (0.65) | DM | 0.69 | 0.44 |
| | | datum (1), mine (1) | DM | 0.92 | 0.23 |
| | | retrieval (1), image (1), base (1) | ImgDB | 0.91 | 0.35 |
| | | system (1) | – | – | – |
| 2003 | same | datum (0.63) | DM | 0.7 | 0.44 |
| | | datum (1), mine (1) | DM | 0.92 | 0.22 |
| | | retrieval (1), image (1) | ImgDB | 0.91 | 0.41 |
| | | database (1) | – | – | – |
| 2004 | same | datum (0.6) | DM | 0.64 | 0.46 |
| | | datum (1), mine (1) | DM | 0.92 | 0.21 |
| | | retrieval (1), image (1), base (1) | ImgDB | 0.87 | 0.34 |
| | | image (1) | ImgDB | 0.78 | 0.30 |

between "mining" and "mine". Since the documents of the ACM subarchive though are quite unlikely to refer to explosives, though, we can assume that all appearances of "mine" refer to data mining. We intend to remove the artefact in future implementations. For the time being, however, the artefact causes either distinct clusters (as in 2001) or cannibalization – none of the two words is adequately frequent to appear in a label. We suspect that this is the cause of the uninformative label "datum" that appears in the last three periods. This is further indicated by the juxtaposition of the cluster labelled "datum" to the ACM categories: 64% of its members refer to data mining.

For the fifth and sixth column of Table 4 we introduce two measures, emanating from the conventional measures of correctness and coverage for two-class prediction.

For any ACM category $cat$ and for any cluster $C$ we define the correctness of the cluster towards the category as the ratio of cluster members belonging to this category:

$$correctness(cat, C) = \frac{|\{x \in C | x \in cat\}|}{|C|}$$

We similarly define the coverage of the cluster towards the category as the ratio of category members that appear in this cluster:

$$coverage(cat, C) = \frac{|\{x \in cat | x \in C\}|}{|cat|}$$

Then, in the last two columns of Table 4, we show the correctness and coverage of each cluster $C$ towards its "dominant" category, i.e. the category in which most of its members belong. This corresponds to the category $cat$ with the maximum correctness. We use the value 0.5 for this measure, to enforce cluster homogeneity.

The forth column of the Table shows the dominant category. For labels like "database" and "system" we did not assess a dominant category. For the other labels, we see in the fifth column that the correctness is rather low at first (1996). As soon as the new feature space of 1997 is introduced, though, there is a good mapping of clusters to the individual categories, reaching a correctness of 0.92 for data mining in some periods. For the first cluster in period 1996, we also show the second category present in the cluster: We see that the cluster consists of documents on data mining and on spatial databases in a 2/3 to 1/3 relation.

We can see from Table 4 that more than one cluster may be mapped to the same category. This is reflected in the last column, where the coverage towards the dominant category only once exceeds 0.5. This is natural: Categories like DM or ImgDB are very broad and we find some subtopics of this categories. Since we trace only stable themes, the coverage cannot reach 1. This is best reflected in the theme "image retrieval", which is a clear subcategory of image databases. We find no subtopics at the small categories, the "scientific database" and "statistical database" category.

Our analysis of the accummulating subcollection can identify stable *and popular* themes. Some stable themes with lower support, e.g. subtopics of the themes we find here, can be better traced by the analysis of the non-accummulating subcollections [SS06]. In comparison to the experiments in [SS06] we have identified some themes like "association, mine, rule", a popular subarea of data mining and we have found the themes "discovery knowledge" and "Mine" as two different themes at the non-accumulated subcollections. Here we have seen both themes as part of an evolution of the main collection theme "datum".

**Coverage of the ACM Section H2.8.** It can be seen in Table 4 that the coverage towards the ACM subarchive is rather low and that some clusters reflect subtopics rather than whole categories.

We first checked whether the low coverage can be attributed to the clustering algorithm. As already mentioned, we have experimented with different clustering algorithms. In [SNTS06], we have also considered $k = 10$ and discovered that this larger value finds more informative subtopics (obviously) but still does not allow for the identification of all classes. Hence, we performed a series of classification experiments, i.e. used the document labels, and searched for features/keywords with high predictive power.

Similarly to many clustering algorithms, classification algorithms like C4.5 and Naive Bayes require special tuning to deal with highly skewed data. Therefore, we have first attempted a separation of the dominant class "Data Mining" from the rest of the collection and then tried to build a classifier for the remaining classes. We concentrated on data from one period, 2001. The separation of the "Data Mining" class from the others was achieved with an accuracy of more than 80%. This reflects that the identification of this class in the data is easy - a fact that is apparent in our clustering results as well. However, the classification accuracy for the other four categories was low. One of the most remarkable results was that the SVM and the J4.8 classifiers assigned the documents of the category "scientific databases" to the class "spatial databases", while Naive Bayes assigned a large portion of documents on spatial, statistical and image databases to the class "scientific databases". Hence, we came to the conclusion that the categories cannot be properly separated, most likely because of the existence of subcategories. The subtopics found by Theme-Monitor (association rules, image retrieval) are indicatory of such subcategories.

**Comparing Themes to Evolving Clusters.** The comparison of cluster evolution and theme discovery is shown in Fig. 1. We can see that some clusters of one period merged together into one cluster at the next period. One example are the clusters 3 and 4 at period 1997 which merged at period 1998 into cluster 3, which also merged with cluster 2 at period 1998, and into cluster 2 at period 1999. An other interesting point, that after a merge new clusters exist and sometimes they also are merged later.

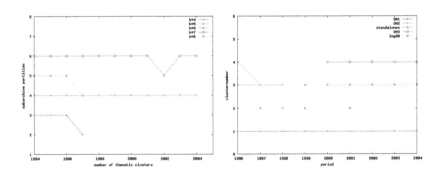

**Fig. 1.** followed cluster at bisecting k-means (left) and Theme-Monitor (right)

The right diagram of figure 1 show the results of our Theme-Monitor, after the cluster matching described at sec. 3.2. As we can see, the Theme-Monitor follows nearly the same clusters like the adapted FOCUS framework. One important difference of the results between the Theme-Monitor and the adapted FOCUS is that the Theme-Monitor follows only the labelled clusters and not all clusters of the clustering. So we see at the right diagram a smaller number of clusters.

An other difference of the Theme-Monitor is that we normally not detect merges and splits of a cluster, because our *best_match* algorithm only find one cluster as best match to an other cluster. One exception exist for merges detection, this is possible with the Theme-Monitor. If the *best_match* algorithm has as result the same cluster at $t_{i+1}$ for two different clusters at $t_i$. Then we can say that both clusters at $t_i$ merge together to the best match cluster at $t_{i+1}$. At the diagram we see such point at cluster 3 and 4 at period 1996, which merge together to cluster 3 at period 1997. We see that the label "discovery knowledge datum" at period 1996 change over time to the label "datum mining" at period 2001 and "datum" at the following periods. Here we see that our assumption is correct that the terminology of this document archive change over this long time.

## 5   Conclusions and Outlook

We have expanded the Theme-Monitor algorithm for the discovery of persistent "themes" and detection of their evolution over time at an accummulating document collection and studied its behaviour upon the ACM subarchive on "database applications". Theme-Monitor identifies emerging and persistent "themes", i.e. labels of stable clusters that survive re-clustering in each period and occasional changes in the feature space with minimal changes of the feature space. Our text documents are very short and so we have not a typical text collection. So we have used the bisecting k-means algorithm for clustering and the vector space model for document representation. For other experiments with larger text documents we will try other algorithms for clustering which are better for text clustering and try digrams for document representation. Since our algorithm considers occurring words rather than abstract concepts, it could not extract the concrete ACM topics from the reference archive but did discover the subjects that gave raise to the inclusion of these topics in the ACM taxonomy.

We intend to enhance Theme-Monitor with a more sophisticated clustering core that exploits cluster homogenity metrics. We also envisage a mechanism that varies the expected number of themes over time, possibly by replacing the bisecting k-means with a Nearst-Neighbor- algorithm. Finally, we want to cross-check the performance of the Theme-Monitor against a fully labeled archive, e.g. by the retrospective re-assignment of the ACM topics to the subarchive documents.

**Acknowledgement.** We would like to cordialy thank Dirk Dreschel for the classification experiments on the ACM digital library.

## References

[Agg05]   Charu Aggarwal.  On change diagnosis in evolving data streams.  *IEEE TKDE*, 17(5):587–600, May 2005.

[All02]   J. Allan. *Introduction to Topic Detection and Tracking*. Kluwer Academic Publishers, 2002.

[BN04]   Christian Borgelt and Andreas Nürnberger.  Experiments in Document Clustering using Cluster Specific Term Weights. In *Proc. Workshop Machine Learning and Interaction for Text-based Information Retrieval (TIR 2004)*, pages 55–68, University of Ulm, Germany 2004, 2004.

[GGR99]     Venkatesh Ganti, Johannes Gehrke, and Raghu Ramakrishnan. A Framework for Measuring Changes in Data Characteristics. In *Proceedings of the 18th ACM SIGACT-SIGMOD-SIGART Symposium on Principles of Database Systems*, pages 126–137, Philadelphia, Pennsylvania, May 1999. ACM Press.

[KGP+03]   A. Kontostathis, L. Galitsky, W.M. Pottenger, S. Roy, and D.J. Phelps. *A Survey of Emerging Trend Detection in Textual Data Mining*. Springer Verlag, 2003.

[MY04]      Satoshi Moringa and Kenji Yamanishi. Tracking Dynamics of Topic Trends Using a Finite Mixture Model. In Ronny Kohavi, Johannes Gehrke, William DuMouchel, and Joydeep Ghosh, editors, *Proceedings of the 2004 ACM SIGKDD international conference on Knowledge discovery and data mining*, pages 811–816. ACM Press New York, NY, USA, August 2004.

[MZ05]      Qiaizhu Mei and ChengXiang Zhai. Discovering Evolutionary Theme Patterns from Text - An Exploration of Temporal Text Mining. In *Proceeding of the eleventh ACM SIGKDD international conference on Knowledge discovery in data mining*, pages 198–207, Chicago, Illinois, USA, August 2005. ACM Press.

[NMSD05]   Daniel Neill, Andrew Moore, Maheshkumar Sabhnani, and Kenny Daniel. Detection of emerging space-time clusters. In *Proc. of KDD 2005*, pages 218–227, Chicago, IL, Aug. 2005.

[SNTS06]   Myra Spiliopoulou, Irene Ntoutsi, Yannis Theodoridis, and Rene Schult. Monic – modeling and monitoring cluster transitions. In *Proc. of 12th ACM SIGKDD Int. Conf. on Knowledge Discovery and Data Mining (KDD'06)*, page (6 pages total), Philadelphia, USA, Aug. 2006. ACM. poster paper, to appear (acceptance quote: 23%).

[SS06]       Rene Schult and Myra Spiliopoulou. Expanding the Taxonomies of Bibliographic Archives with Persistent Long-Term Themes. In *Procedings of the 21th Annual ACM Symposium on Applied Computing (SAC'06)*. ACM, ACM Press, April 2006.

# Computational Database Technology Applied to Option Pricing Via Finite Differences

Jöns Åkerlund, Krister Åhlander, and Kjell Orsborn

Department of Information Technology, Uppsala University, Uppsala, Sweden
jons.akerlund@asia.apple.com,
krister.ahlander@it.uu.se,kjell.orsborn@it.uu.se

**Abstract.** Computational database technology spans the two research fields data-base technology and scientific computing. It involves development of data-base capabilities that support computational-intensive applications found in science and engineering. This includes support for representing and processing of mathematical models within the database environment without any significant performance loss compared to conventional implementations.

This paper describes how an existing database management system, AMOS II, is extended with capabilities to solve the Black–Scholes equation commonly used in option pricing. The numerical method used is finite differences, and a flexible database framework that can deal with complex mathematical objects and numerical methods is created. We describe how computational data representations and operations are adapted to the database management system and the approach is evaluated with respect to performance, extensibility, and ease of use.

## 1 Introduction

The numerical solution of partial differential equations (PDEs) is an important area of scientific computing, since there are so many processes in e.g. engineering, physics, biology, and even economics, that can be modeled by PDEs, but there are so few PDEs that are solvable analytically. This kind of applications usually require a very high performance, and a wish to solve PDEs numerically has often been an important force in the development of high performance hardware, such as the Earth Simulator [1]. Finding a suitable, general environment for numerical computations is also an ongoing concern in the field of scientific computing. Historically, the scientific computing community developed successful Fortran libraries for numerical linear algebra such as Linpack [8] and Lapack [9]. With the advent of object-oriented (OO) methods came better modeling tools for supporting complex data structures. Examples of OO projects are Cogito [36,35], Overture [10], and Diffpack [11]. OO frameworks have also been developed and Compose [3] presents a quite general PDE solver design, implemented on top of Overture. Pantazopoulos [26] presents Finanzia as an OO framework for financial modeling. Generally, we find that program packages are either optimized for speed, often written in C or Fortran, or developed in a high-level language such as Matlab to allow for fast development and more readable code. Most of these solutions miss out on one or some of the aspects of performance, maintenance, ease of use, and ability to analyze data.

Y. Manolopoulos, J. Pokorný, and T. Sellis (Eds.): ADBIS 2006, LNCS 4152, pp. 367–382, 2006.

The approach of using computational databases for numerical methods in engineering has been explored by Orsborn [24], where a FEM application has been integrated with the AMOS database management system (DBMS). The general idea with this approach is to make database technology with efficient data management and query capabilities accessible to computational-intensive applications. However, this will put new demands on the DBMS itself including support for new types of mathematical data and operations. If these requirements can be resolved, future database tools can be used for developing computational database applications found in advanced scientific and engineering applications and furthermore to extend their functionality with facilities like ad hoc query capabilities.

In this paper, a problem solving environment for PDEs is created by extending AMOS II [5] with suitable numerical mechanisms [4]. Specifically, support for finite difference approximations and methods for solving the resulting linear systems of equations are developed. We use the framework to develop a financial modeling application. We solve the Black–Scholes (BS) equation in one and two dimensions. The BS equation describes how the prices of options and financial instruments vary over a certain designated time. This application is very important in today financial markets. The issue to construct general software for modeling it has also been addressed by Skavhaug using Diffpack [32], and by the already mentioned project Finanzia.

We think, however, that a full-fledged computational environment for financial modeling must employ a database for evaluating simulations and for monitoring the market. We argue that a computational database is the appropriate way to design a useful software environment for this kind of applications, in the same way as OO analysis and design stress the importance of data before algorithms. While the computational problem chosen has been the BS equation, it should be emphasized that the overall objective is on providing a framework for scientific computing that is both effective and easy to use, rather than focusing on some specific equation or type of problem.

## 2   Database Technology for Computational Applications

Database systems have traditionally been positioned for administrative systems development. However, the current trend broadens this perspective to incorporate support for more advanced and complex data sets and applications. These advanced applications are often found in science and engineering where many applications involve large data sets of high complexity. Furthermore, many of these complex data sets originate from some mathematical model where data are generated by applying mathematical operators and algorithms of various complexity.

This work focus on this interdisciplinary research area of database technology and scientific computing that we term *computational database technology* earlier discussed in [24] and [23] that studies how to provide database support for computational-intensive database applications. A central idea is here to provide query-based computations and analysis of complex models within the DBMS while withholding computational performance competitive with conventional codes for scientific computing. To support these computational-intensive applications, a computational database management system (CDBMS) must be extensible on all levels [12] [24] that include:

- *Storage and access extensions* - it should be possible to create new storage structures and operations on them. Computational-intensive applications normally involve tailored and optimized data structures such as numerical matrix and vector representations. These tailored data representations also require specialized indexes and operators such as indexing of numerical matrices and numerical operations such as matrix multiplication and decomposition operations.
- *Query language extensions* - the possibility to create abstract data types and define operations on them, or overloading existing operations. Furthermore, the storage and access extensions should be transparently integrated into the query language to become accessible in query expressions.
- *Query processing extensions* - changing execution strategies should be an option, so that the database can choose between different operations. For instance, the most efficient execution plan for a set of complex arithmetical operations of a matrix expression. Here, the query processor needs to understand specialized indexes, cost models and possibly optimization algorithms.

Extensibility, have mainly been promoted for the object-relational class of database management systems [31] and by the release of the SQL:99 standard. Besides extensibility, also embeddable [29] and main-memory [16] database management systems are important enabling technologies for supporting computational database systems. The ability to embed, extend, compose and configure a DBMS into a tailored system for developing advanced scientific applications can really have the capability to leverage development of scientific software as well as scientific data management. Main-memory database technology is also critical since computational performance must compete with that of conventional implementations in C or Fortran. Earlier work have compared differences between secondary and primary memory storage techniques, especially with regard to speed and results indicates that this approach is feasible [24]. A more thorough discussion on the requirements on computational database systems is given in [24] and several authors have been discussing the need to develop database technology to support advanced applications [30] [6] [2] [17] [18].

The AMOS II DBMS [27] [5], used in this work, is an object-relational DBMS that combines object-oriented modeling with powerful query capabilities. AMOS II is a fully extensible system, covering all levels of extensibility discussed in the previous section, and can be composed and configured for specific needs. The AMOSQL database language of AMOS II can be extended by transparently integrating foreign functions implemented in a conventional programming language such as C/C++, Java or Lisp. Furthermore, AMOS II has a small footprint and can be embeddable into applications providing access to full DBMS capabilities within conventional applications. The final characteristic that makes AMOS II most suitable for developing computational database systems is that it is a main-memory DBMS making it possible to achieve computational performance on par with corresponding C or Fortran implementations.

## 3  Financial Derivatives and Finite Differences

As mentioned in the introduction, the Black–Scholes (BS) equation is commonly used in the financial field to value financial instruments, such as option pricing of financial derivatives. These instruments usually depend on the more or less random fluctuation of an underlying value or asset. It is beyond the scope of this paper to discuss finance modeling in depth and we refer to standard financial textbooks for more details [21,38].

In Section 3.2, we mention a few numerical methods for the BS equation. In particular, we recall some basic ideas regarding the finite difference method, and we highlight some requirements on the software that this method imposes. For a thorough treatment on finite differences we refer to e.g. [19], and for a good description of how to solve the BS equation with finite differences we refer to Tavella [34].

### 3.1 Financial Derivatives and the Black–Scholes Equation

There are many variants of financial derivatives. Among the simplest are Europeran call and put options. A call option is an agreement between two parties that the option holder has the right but not the obligation to buy a specified asset for a fixed price at a future date—i.e., to *exercise* the option. The asset is often a stock, but may be anything from gold to cattle. A put option instead gives the right to sell the asset. There are also American options with the difference that, while a European option can only be exercised at a specified future date, an American option can be exercised at any time prior to the expiry date.

Options can be used for mere speculation—if you think that the price of a stock will increase drastically at the open market, it might be a good idea to buy call options for this stock. If the stock is worth more at the market than the exercise price, you make a profit. Otherwise, it is no gain in exercising the option and you have lost worth the option cost. Another common use of options is to limit various risks for a company, i.e., *hedging*. The bottom-line is that it is important to have appropriate models for the pricing of options, whether you sell or buy them and whatever your purpose is.

In order to model financial markets, it is often assumed that the *Efficient Market Hypothesis* holds. Its weak form states that no excess returns can be earned by analyzing historical data, and the only factor that affects stock prices is the introduction of news, and the market responds immediately to it. Under various assumptions, see e.g. [21,38], the BS equation for the value $V$ of an option based upon a single stock with price $S$ is derived:

$$\frac{\partial V}{\partial t} + \frac{1}{2}\sigma^2 S^2 \frac{\partial^2 V}{\partial S^2} + rS\frac{\partial V}{\partial S} - rV = 0. \tag{1}$$

This PDE states how the time derivative of the value ($\partial V/\partial t$) depends upon the volatility $\sigma$, the interest-free rate $r$, and on the first and second derivatives of the option value with respect to the underlying stock, $\partial V/\partial S$ and $\partial^2 V/\partial S^2$, respectively. At termination time, the value of the option as a function of the underlying stock price is known. For example, a European call option is worth nothing if the actual stock price $S$ is less than the exercise price $V$, and it is worth $V - S$ if $V > S$. The PDE described by (1) can then be used to compute backwards in time, in order to obtain an estimate of what the option is worth today.

The model is quite sensitive to the underlying data, and the parameter $\sigma$ is very hard to estimate. The partial derivatives of $V$ are important to consider when analyzing the computations. In financial modeling, they are often referred to as the "Greeks". They are delta, gamma, rho, theta and vega (which is not actually a Greek letter):

$$\Delta = \frac{\partial V}{\partial S}, \; \Gamma = \frac{\partial^2 V}{\partial S^2}, \; \rho = \frac{\partial V}{\partial r}, \; \Theta = \frac{\partial V}{\partial t}, \; \mathcal{V} = \frac{\partial V}{\partial \sigma}. \tag{2}$$

Options may be based upon more than one asset, so called *basket options*. When modeling basket options on $d$ underlying assets, BS equation in $d$ dimensions are used. The value $V$ now depends on the coefficiency matrix $\sigma\sigma^T$, where the individual components represent volatilities or connection between different volatilities, as well as on partial derivatives with respect to each of the underlying assets:

$$\frac{\partial V}{\partial t} + \frac{1}{2} \sum_{i,j=1}^{d} [\sigma\sigma^T]_{ij} S_i S_j \frac{\partial^2 V}{\partial S_i \partial S_j} + \sum_{i=1}^{d} r S_i \frac{\partial V}{\partial S_i} - rV = 0 \tag{3}$$

The "multi-dimensional" BS equation (3) is difficult to solve when $d$ becomes large.

## 3.2 Finite Differences

There are many different ways to numerically solve PDEs. Finite elements, finite differences, and finite volume methods are well-known general purpose methods. For the BS equation, Monte-Carlo methods are often used, particularly when the number of dimensions grow large. Another standard method is based upon trees; see e.g. Hull for an introduction to so-called *lattice methods* [21]. Finite elements are applied to the BS equation in [32]. A thorough description on finite differences for the BS equation is found in Tavella [34].

Ideally, a CDBMS for the BS equation should support a variety of numerical methods. To start with, we have chosen to use finite differences, because it is a fairly simple method to implement and because it is generally applicable. In this section, we recall the basics of finite differences. We also discuss how to solve the resulting linear system of equations by means of iterative methods.

When using the finite difference method, a solution to a certain equation is approximated over a number of discrete points, generally referred to as a grid or mesh, which might be in any number of dimensions depending on the equation. For some problems it is useful to have non-uniform grids, with individual points more densely placed in areas that require higher precision.

In the finite difference method, all partial derivates in the PDE are approximated by finite difference operators. As an example, the partial derivative $\partial u/\partial t$ is defined as follows:

$$\frac{\partial u}{\partial t}(x,t) = \lim_{\delta t \to 0} \frac{u(x, t + \delta t) - u(x, t)}{\delta t} \tag{4}$$

The discretization is now made by setting $\delta t$ to a small but nonzero number:

$$\frac{\partial u}{\partial t}(x,t) \approx \frac{u(x, t + \delta t) - u(x, t)}{\delta t} \tag{5}$$

It is this step, which involves a number of small differences that are not infinitesimal, that is referred to as a *finite difference*. The example given above makes a forward step in time and is for this reason called a *forward difference*, often denoted $D_{+,t} u(x,t)$. Similarly,

$$\frac{\partial u}{\partial t}(x,t) \approx D_{-,t} u(x,y) = \frac{u(x,t) - u(x, t - \delta t)}{\delta t}, \tag{6}$$

is referred to as a *backward step*. These approximations are of first order, which means that the error is proportional to the time step $\delta t$. A more accurate approximation is

$$\frac{\partial u}{\partial t}(x, t) \approx D_{0,t} u(x, y) = \frac{u(x, t + \delta t) - u(x, t - \delta t)}{2\delta t}, \tag{7}$$

which is a second order approximation. Combinations of these and other finite differences are used for approximating other partial derivatives. For example,

$$\frac{\partial^2 u}{\partial x^2}(x, t) \approx D_{+,x} D_{-,x} u(x, t) \tag{8}$$

which is also a second order approximation.

For our application, we have chosen the following interior discretization of the BS equation. In one dimension,

$$D_{+,t} V(S, t) + \frac{1}{2}\sigma^2 S^2 D_{+,S} D_{-,S} \frac{1}{2} \left(V(S, t) + V(S, t + \delta t)\right) +$$

$$rS D_{0,S} \frac{1}{2} \left(V(S, t) + V(S, t + \delta t)\right) - rV(S, t) = \frac{1}{2} \left(V(S, t) + V(S, t + \delta t)\right), \tag{9}$$

with obvious generalizations to higher dimensions, see Tavella [34]. Tavella also presents the boundary conditions that we use.

A seen above, finite differences may be applied in both space and time, leading to a discrete approximation of the PDE in every interior space point. This approximation is often referred to as a *stencil*. If the time discretization is a forward difference, the values at each time level can be calculated from the values at the previous level—i.e., the method is *explicit*. With a backward difference, the values at a new time level are dependent on each other. The method is *implicit*, which implies that a sparse linear system of equations must be solved at each time level. The implications for a general-purpose software that should support finite differences, is that there should be an easy interface to construct different finite difference stencils, and it should be possible to use them both in explicit and implicit settings. However, since (9) is implicit, we have here focussed on this case.

In order to solve linear systems of equations, we can basically choose between direct methods and iterative methods. Iterative methods are often advantageous for sparse systems. We have chosen to implement the generalized minimal residual (GMRES) iterative method, which is a well-known and robust method for this application. There are also several sparse matrix formats to choose from, such as the Compressed Sparse Row (CRS) format and the Ellpack-Eispack format [28]. Initially, we have chosen to support the Ellpack-Eispack format. Even though it is less flexible than CRS, it is appropriate for our application.

## 4   Implementation

Constructing a suitable database environment for a finite difference solver requires that the suitable numerical methods described are implemented. While these different parts have all been referred to as extensions, they are regarded as a whole, and all contribute to the solution.

An important part of modelling has been to construct a general storage format for sparse matrices that commonly occur in finite difference computations. The general framework for the matrix extension is first described followed by a description of the scientific computing extension.

## 4.1  The Matrix Extension

In order to extend the database query language with matrix and vector functionality, a foreign data source must be created that creates numerical objects and methods that can be used with them. Such an extension has been written in C, thereby enabling the external code to use the same physical storage as the database.

The most important points that the extended query language can do is listed in [24], notably the following:

– Make queries involving matrix types in combination with other types of heterogenous data.
– Express more complex matrix operations in terms of simpler ones.
– Understand domain-specific operators and thereby choose algorithms based on cost measures. This is important in conjunction with solving the BS equation where different solvers for equation systems will be considered based on matrix size and dimension of the problem.
– Enables specific algorithms to be written for specific combinations of matrices and vectors.

As a basis for the matrix extension used in this package, a new version of the same basic representation that is described in [24] has been used. It builds upon the object hierarchy shown in Fig. 1. Part of this hierarchy has been implemented previously by Orsborn [24].

While a full-fledged implementation should contain all different matrix types, the implementation focuses on the core types that are needed for most PDE solvers - sparse matrices and dense vectors. The row type has been implemented due to its similarity with the column type, and dense matrices have been included as a proof of concept (partly of how different algorithms can be chosen for different types of matrices).

The matrix package also distinguishes what sort of numerical representation is used, by keeping the types `imatrix`, `dmatrix` and `fmatrix`, where $i$, $d$ and $f$ stands for int, double and float, respectively. It should be noted that in the implementation described here, only the double type is supported.

The basic operations that the query language must be able to perform on the matrices include the following matrix and vector operations: (this is a combination of a subset of the operations required by sparse matrix kits as described in [33], with vector operations)

– sparse matrix times dense vector
– sparse matrix plus sparse matrix
– sparse matrix minus sparse matrix
– sparse times constant
– sparse matrix times diagonal matrix (C = AD) and vice versa (C = DA)

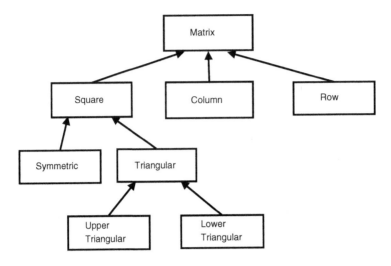

**Fig. 1.** Type taxonomy for the matrix package

- vector plus vector
- vector minus vector
- vector times constant
- cross product
- dot product
- Euclidean norm

As can be seen from the above, the polymorphism employed in the database allow users to choose many kinds of different operations depending on the chosen formats.

### 4.2   The Scientific Computing Extension

The scientific computing extension contains a few useful tools commonly used in general PDE solvers. In the present project, capabilities for easily constructing a typical finite difference coefficient matrix as well as two different solution methods, have been added.

*Stencil to Matrix.* As many computational problems require setting up some sort of banded matrix, especially when stencils are concerned, the function stencil_to_matrix has been designed to do that It takes as argument two AMOS vectors, where the first vector describes positions relative to the main diagonal, and the other the coefficients the respective diagonals should have.

For example, to construct the matrix

$$
\begin{pmatrix}
1. & -2. & 0. & 0. & 0. & 0. \\
-2. & 1. & -2. & 0. & 0. & 0. \\
0. & -2. & 1. & -2. & 0. & 0. \\
0. & 0. & -2 & 1. & -2 & 0. \\
0. & 0. & 0. & -2. & 1. & -2. \\
0. & 0. & 0. & 0. & -2. & 1.
\end{pmatrix}
$$

one could simply type:

```
set :s = square_sparse_dmatrix(6, 3);
stencil_to_matrix(:s, {-1,0,1}, {-2.0, 1.0, -2.0});
```

*Numerical Solvers.* The ability to solve linear systems of equations is important in most PDE solvers. Generally, there are two approaches: direct solution methods such as Gaussian elimination (LU decomposition) or iterative solution methods. We have implemented a direct tridiagonal solver, which is often useful for one-dimensional problems [38], as well as GMRES, an iterative solver, since this usually is a better approach for PDEs in higher dimensions [28]. Both solvers are optimized for the present application.

## 5  Performance

For the database to be a viable alternative to other applications and problem solving environments, it is not only important that it is easy to use but performance is critical as well. Since most of the time is spent in the time-marching process, the speed of the solvers becomes one of the most important measures. Three factors are important in this case: the time it takes to add and subtract sparse matrices and vectors, the speed of the solvers and the overhead of the database operations. The speed of the solvers have been tested with both the tridiagonal solver and GMRES (which is not the native Matlab GMRES but the same version implemented in the database).

In both tests dummy problems with tridiagonal matrices were used. Both solvers were given sparse matrices with 1.0 on the main diagonal. In the tridiagonal case, the side diagonals had the value 0.000001, and for GMRES, the value of 0.0001 was used.

As can be seen in Fig. 2, the differences between a pure C implementation and the database are too slight to be noticeable. Further, the database system is around 4 times faster than Matlab. In the example with GMRES, Fig. 3, the difference is even more emphasized, the database implementation being around 8 times faster. This should not be seen as saying that Matlab is really that much slower, since an interpreted function for GMRES is used. The time difference between the tridiagonal solver, which is an atomic function in Matlab, says more about real temporal differences.

It is safe to say, however, that the database implementation can provide quite competitive performance in comparison to the native C implementation which is a most promising result for the computational database approach.

In the case with the complete solvers for the BS equation, the difference needs some extra interpretation, as can be seen from Fig. 4, in which the database is around 9 times faster. The combination of the fact that Matlab is an interpreted language, and that both the inner and the other loop is in the foreign function *threediag_solve*, gives an explanation for the big difference.

In the case with the two-dimensional solver differences are much smaller, even though the database is faster, see Fig. 5. Since GMRES has been shown to be around 4 times faster in the database, and care has been taken to see that they achieve the same results, either the overhead of the database or the large number of sparse additions and multiplications in the database plays a role. For such operations it is most probable that

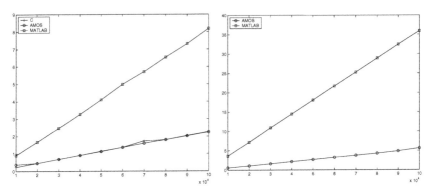

**Fig. 2.** Comparison between tridiagonal solver in C, AMOS and MATLAB

**Fig. 3.** Comparison between GMRES solver in AMOS and MATLAB

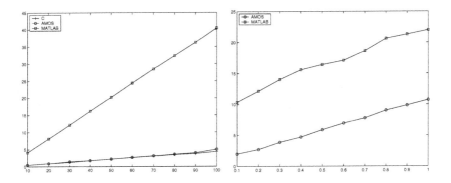

**Fig. 4.** Comparison of one-dimensional solver in AMOS and MATLAB

**Fig. 5.** Comparison of two-dimensional solver in AMOS and MATLAB

Matlab and the database have the same performance. It should further be noted that the two-dimensional database operations do not currently have an optimal implementation and should be exchanged with improved representations in future work.

For the one-dimensional solver, the values used were $S = 120$, $K = 20.0$, $r = 0.555555$, number of grid points = 48, $dt = 0.00005$, $\sigma = 0.3$.

For the two-dimensional solver, $S_1 = 120.0$, $S_2 = 120.0$, $K = 20.0$, $r = 0.555555$, number of grid points = $31 * 31$, $dt = 0.00005$, $\sigma_1 = 0.3$, $\sigma_2 = 0.3$, $\sigma_c = 0.05$ (where $\sigma_c$ is the relation between the two volatilities).

## 6   Use Cases

As has been seen earlier on, PDE problems generally involve finding a problem domain, selecting initial values and then time-marching to a specific solution. In any case, regardless of dimensions, this amounts to the following:

1. Create the contract function as initial values.
2. Create the system matrix that is used for solving the system of linear equations.
3. Use a solver for the time-marching.

Both the 1d and 2d solvers are functions that already exist in the database, with predefined functions for the boundary values in 1d and 2d.

This section first gives an account of how the one- and two-dimensional cases work, followed by examples of queries a user might want to perform, including determining some of the Greeks in Eqs. (2).

## 6.1   1d Solver

While the contract function always looks the same, the system matrix used in this particular implementation consists of finite difference operators for the first- and second-order derivatives in the equation, as well as the time derivative and the $r$ value. While the latter two only affects the main diagonal of the matrix, the operators for the other two (called $D_0$ and $D_+D_-$, respectively) use stencils that require information in directly adjacent gridpoints.

The boundary conditions used in both the 1d and the 2d solvers enforce the second derivative to zero (as described in [34]). In the one-dimensional case, this means that the $D_+D_-$-operator is not used in the first and the last point of the domain. The first-order derivative also looks slightly different in the end points.

The one-dimensional operators have been set up in a sparse matrix by using the *stencil_to_matrix* function described in Section 4.2. Either defined through a function or typed directly at the command line, the user can create the $D_+D_-$ operator by the following set of commands, where *:s* is an instance of a sparse matrix, and c1 and c2 are the different values in the stencil:

```
stencil_to_matrix(:s, {-1,0,1}, {c1, c2, c1}, 1, size-2);
```

This says that the matrix should be filled in all places except on the first and the last position (i.e. the first and the last rows in the matrix) However, if a user choosed to fill the whole matrix by these values and wants to change to the boundary condition described above, the following will suffice:

```
stencil_to_matrix(:s, {0, 1}, {0.0, 0.0}, 0);
stencil_to_matrix(:s, {-1,0}, {0.0, 0.0}, size-1);
```

The values in the first and the last rows in the matrix are now replaced by zero values.

When the difference operators have been created (this has been stored in the current implementation of the database as the *d0* and the *dpdm* functions, respectively), the system matrix can be expressed as follows:

```
sysmatrix = i(n) -    (diag(x) * d0 * r2 +
                       diag(x2) * dpdm * pow(sigma, 2.0) -
                       i(n) * r2) * dt_scaled;
```

Here, $i(n)$ creates an identity matrix, $x2$ is computed as $pow(x, 2.0)$, $n$ is the size of the computed matrix, $dt = \frac{\sigma^2}{2}$, $dt\_scaled = dt * 0.5 * pow(sigma, 2.0)$ and $r2$ is the r value multiplied by 2. All the computations involved use the sparse functionality.

The Matlab command for the same expression would be:

```
sysmatrix = eye(n) - (sparse(diag(x)) * d0 * r2 +
                      sparse(diag(x.*x)) * dpdm * sigma^2
                      - eye(n) * r2) * dt_scaled;
```

As can be seen from this example, the complexity of the matrix and vector expressions in the database system can be at least as simple as the corresponding Matlab expression. There is no additional complexity introduced in using the database and numerical data can be freely combined with any other data in the database.

Finally, since the resulting system matrix is tridiagonal, that solver can be used. An example of calling the one-dimensional solver function is the following:

```
set :c = bs_solve_1d(120.0, 20.0, 0.555555, 50, 0.00005,
                     0.3, 0.2)
```

where the parameters given is $S_{max}$, $E$ (exercise price), $r$, number of grid points, $dt$, volatility and the time step the user is interested in. The $:c$ object is a vector containing the answer.

## 6.2   2d Solver

The specific equation for the two-dimensional problem is obtained from (3). The contract function used is:

$$max(\frac{S_1 + S_2}{2} - K, 0) \tag{10}$$

The main difference between the one-dimensional and two-dimensional solvers is that the latter require a two-dimensional mesh and have more complicated boundary values. As there is still no specific mesh object available in this implementation (an issue that will be addressed in future), extra functionality must be added to treat a one-dimensional vector that is used in the solution process as two-dimensional.

For this purpose, the structure $size\_2d$ is created:

```
create type size_2d properties (y_size integer,
                                x_size integer);
```

This structure is then used as a basis for performing two-dimensional operations. The function $abs\_pos$ calculates the corresponding one-dimensional position of a two-dimensional position:

```
create function abs_pos(size_2d c, integer y,
                        integer x) -> integer as
                select y * y_size(c) + x;
```

The derived function $stencil\_to\_matrix\_2d$ uses this functionality to set boundary conditions in the correct rows in the system matrix. For the stencils used in the two-dimensional case, there are eight boundary conditions (four for the corners, and four for the upper, lower, left and right boundaries, respectively).

In order to specify that only the inner part of the square should be filled with stencil coefficients for the $D_+D_-$ operator in the x dimension (as stated above, the second-order derivatives are zero), the following is sufficient. In this example, $:s$ is the system matrix, $:s2d$ is a $size\_2d$ structure, $c1$ and $c2$ are constants, and $y\_size2$ and $x\_size2$ are the sizes in the x and y dimensions minus 2, respectively:

```
stencil_to_matrix_2d(:s, :s2d, 1, y_size2, 1, x_size2,
                     {-1,0,1}, {c1, c2, c1});
```

To add or remove a certain boundary condition, one expression like the above is needed. That makes testing different boundary conditions a rather simple task.

Since the stencils used in the two-dimensional case are more complicated than in the one-dimensional problem, the tridiagonal solver can no longer be used. Instead, GMRES is used for the solution.

An example of calling the two-dimensional solver function is

```
set :c = bs_solve_2d(120.0, 120.0, 20.0, 0.555555,
                     30, 0.00005, 0.3, 0.3, 0.05, 0.01);
```

As before, $:c$ is the vector containing the solution, and the parameters are $S^1_{max}$, $S^2_{max}$, $E$ (exercise price), $r$, number of grid points (the function currently only handles quadratic grids), $dt$, volatilities for the two underlying assets, the relation between the two volatilities, and the time amount.

### 6.3    Query Examples

One specific feature of the database that sets it apart from other systems with a similar aim is the ability to perform ad hoc queries, i.e. finding new information from previously calculated data (or computing new data) that it was not specifically designed for. Queries provide a simple way to find numerical information.

As an example of the latter, the following query is used to get the values of the most commonly used Greek, namely Delta (where $:c$ is the result of the one-dimensional solver).

```
select r from real r, gridpoint_1d g,
            integer size, integer pos
  where size = size(:c) - 1
    and g = unload(:c, 1, size)
    and pos = pos(g) - 1
    and r = (val(g) - val(unload_pos(:c, pos))) / 2.0;
```

The *unload* and *unload_pos* are functions that return a vector as a collection of gridpoints, or as a similar gridpoint for one position.

For Gamma, the expression is only slightly more complicated:

```
select r from real r, gridpoint_1d g, integer size,
            integer pos1, integer pos2
  where size = size(:c) - 2
```

```
and g = unload(:c, 1, size)
and pos1 = pos(g) - 1 and pos2 = pos(g) + 1
and r = val(unload_pos(:c, pos1)) +
        val(unload_pos(:c, pos2)) - 2.0 * val(g);
```

While the Greeks are an important use of queries, there are other examples that really show their capabilities. This example, in two dimensions, show how to get all values in the final solution that are above 1.0 (:s is a result from the two-dimensional solver, and :s2d is a size_2d structure):

```
select yp, xp, r from real r, gridpoint_2d g,
                integer xp, integer yp
  where g = unload(:s, :s2d) and r = val(g) and r > 1.0
    and xp = xpos(g)
    and yp = ypos(g);
```

Here, by explicitly including x and y positions in the select statement, the result will show not only the requested values but also their positions.

As another example, say that a user wants to get the numerical values at the upper boundary. This is simply done by asking for the values at the upper gridpoints:

```
select r from real r, gridpoint_2d g
  where g = unload(:c,:s2d)
    and ypos(g) = 0 and r = val(g);
```

## 7  Concluding Remarks

We have developed an extension to an existing database system, AMOS II, that can handle complex numerical models. The extension transparently handles sparse matrices and corresponding operations including numerical solvers, and we demonstrate how a PDE solver for the Black–Scholes equation is developed and used within the extension.

The computational database approach integrates advanced numerical capabilities within a database environment that can avoid unnecessary data duplication and transformation while making queries and other database facilities accessible to computational applications. Using a call-out interface with precompiled database functions and foreign functions allows a user to approach a problem with the same ease of use as for example using the Matlab system. Furthermore, these capabilities can be provided without any significant performance loss making the computational performance comparable with native C implementations. This combination of core functionality written as foreign functions, combined with the high-level efficiency and ease of use of the query language, shows that this approach has the capabilitity to perform as well as other problem solving environments.

The ability to pose queries over numerical results is one of the most attractive features of our computational database environment and one that also distinguishes it from other environments. Future work include improved representations of some financial and mathematical concepts and operations and extending the approach to other application areas. Related work studies visualization of numerical data and, to address huge data sets and high performance, we are currently developing support for parallel algorithms on distributed platforms.

# References

1. The Earth Simulator web site: `http://www.es.jamstec.go.jp/esc/eng/`. Jun 2006.
2. S Abiteboul et al: *The Lowell database research self-assessment.* Commun. ACM, 48(5), May 2005, 111–118.
3. K Åhlander: *An Object-Oriented Framework for PDE Solvers*, PhD Thesis, Thesis No. 423, Uppsala University, Uppsala 1999.
4. J Åkerlund: *A Computational Database for Black-Scholes Equation*, MSc Thesis, Department of Information Technology, Uppsala University, Uppsala, June 2005.
5. The Amos II web site: `http://user.it.uu.se/~udbl/amos/`, Mar 2006.
6. P Bernstein et al: *The Asilomar report on database research.* SIGMOD Record, 27(4), Dec 1998, 74–80.
7. T Björk: *Arbitrage Theory in Continuous Time.* Oxford University Press, 1998.
8. The Linpack web site at NetLib: `http://www.netlib.org/linpack/`, Jun 2006.
9. The Lapack web site at NetLib: `http://www.netlib.org/lapack/`, Jun 2006.
10. D Brown et al: *Overture: An object-oriented framework for solving partial differential equations on overlapping grids.* In M E Henderson, C R Anderson, S L Lyons (eds), Object-oriented Methods for Interoperable Scientific and Engineering Computing, SIAM Philadelphia, 1999.
11. A M Bruaset, H P Langtangen: *Object-oriented design of preconditioned iterative methods in Diffpack.* ACM Transactions on Mathematical Software, 23, 1997, 50–80.
12. M Carey, L Haas: *Extensible Database Management Systems*, SIGMOD Record, 19(4), Dec 1990, 54–60.
13. T Conolly, C Begg: *Database Systems - A Practical Approach to Design, Implementation and Management,* 3rd ed, Addison-Wesley 2002.
14. V Eijkhout: *LAPACK working note 50 - distributed sparse data structures for linear algebra operations.* 1992. Available from `http://www.cs.utk.edu/~library/TechReports/1992/ut-cs-92-169.ps.Z`, 10 Feb 2005.
15. R Eggermont: *Sparse Matrix Compression Formats.* Available from `http://ce.et.tudelft.nl/~robbert/sparse_matrix_compression.html`, 10 Feb 2005.
16. H Garcia-Molina, K Salem: *Main memory database systems: an overview.* IEEE Transactions on Knowledge and Data Engineering, 4(6), 1992, 509–516.
17. J Gray, M Compton: *A call to arms.* Queue, 3(3), Apr 2005, 30–38.
18. J Gray et al: *Scientific data management in the coming decade.* SIGMOD Record, 34(4), Dec 2005, 34–41.
19. B Gustafsson et al: *Time Dependent Problems and Difference Methods.* John Wiley & Sons, Inc., 1995.
20. M T Heath: *Scientific Computing - An Introductory Survey,* 2nd ed, McGraw Hill, 2002.
21. J C Hull: *Options, Futures and other Derivatives,* 4th ed, Prentice-Hall International, Inc., 2000.
22. H Löf: *Parallelizing the method of conjugate gradients for shared memory architectures,* Uppsala University, Department of Information Technology, Uppsala 2004.
23. M Nyström, K Orsborn: *Computational Database Technology for Component Mode Synthesis.* Advances in Engineering Software, 35(10-11), Oct-Nov 2003, 735–745.

24. K Orsborn: *On Extensible and Object-Relational Database Technology for Finite Element Analysis Applications.* PhD Thesis, Thesis No. 452, Linköping University, Linköping 1996.

25. K Orsborn et al: *Representing matrices using multi-directional foreign functions.* In The Functional Approach to Data Management: Modeling, Analyzing and Integrating Heterogeneous Data. P M D Gray, L Kerschberg, P J H King, A Poulovassilis (eds), Springer-Verlag, 2004.

26. K N Pantazopoulos, E N Houstos: *Modern software techniques in computational finance.* In E Arge, A M Bruaset and H P Langtangen (eds): Modern Software Tools for Scientific Computing, Birkhäuser, 1997, 227–246.

27. T Risch et al: *Functional data Integration in a distributed mediator system,* In The Functional Approach to Data Management: Modeling, Analyzing and Integrating Heterogeneous Data. P M D Gray, L Kerschberg, P J H King, A Poulovassilis (eds), Springer-Verlag, 2004.

28. Y Saad: *Iterative Methods for Sparse Linear Systems,* 2nd ed, 2000. Available from `ftp://ftp.cd.umn.edu/dept/users/saad/ITBOOK.tar.gz`

29. M Seltzer: *Beyond relational databases.* Queue 3(3), Apr 2005, 50–58.

30. A Silberschatz, S Zdonik: *Strategic directions in database systems – breaking out of the box.* ACM Computing Surveys, 28(4), Dec 1996, 764–778.

31. M Stonebraker, P Brown: *Object-Relational DBMSs: Tracking the Next Great Wave.* Morgan Kaufmann Publishers, Inc., 1999.

32. O Skavhaug: *Numerical Methods and Software with Applications in Computational Finance.* PhD Thesis, Thesis No. 338, University of Oslo, Oslo 2004.

33. Y Saad: *SPARSKIT: a basic tool kit for sparse matrix computations, version 2,* 1994. Available from `http://www-users.cs.umn.edu/~saad/software/SPARSKIT/paper.ps`, 10 Feb 2005.

34. D Tavella and C Randall: *Pricing Financial Instruments - The Finite Difference Method,* John Wiley & Sons, Inc., 2000.

35. M Thuné et al: *Object-oriented modeling of parallel PDE solvers.* In R F Boisvert and P T P Tang (eds), The Architecture of Scientific Software, Kluwer Academic Publishers, Boston, 2001, 159–174.

36. M Thuné, et al: *Object-oriented construction of parallel PDE solvers.* In E Arge, A M Bruaset, and H P Langtangen (eds), Modern Software Tools for Scientific Computing, Birkhäuser, 1997, 203–226.

37. G Wiederhold: *Information systems that really support decision-making,* Journal of Intelligent Information Systems, 14, 2000, 85–94.

38. P Willmott, J Dewynne and S Howison: *Option pricing - mathematical models and computation,* Oxford Financial Press, 2000.

# A Framework for Merging, Repairing and Querying Inconsistent Databases

Luciano Caroprese and Ester Zumpano

DEIS
Università della Calabria
87030 Rende, Italy
{caroprese, zumpano}@deis.unical.it

**Abstract.** This paper presents a framework for merging, repairing and querying inconsistent databases in the presence of functional dependencies and foreign key constraints and investigates the problem related to the satisfaction of general integrity constraints in the presence of null values. In more details, the approach consists in i) merging the source databases to reduce the set of tuples inconsistent with respect to the constraints defined by the primary keys, ii) repairing the integrated database with respect to functional dependencies and foreign key constraints, and iii) computing consistent answers over repaired database. This paper presents a system prototype, RAINBOW, developed at the University of Calabria, implementing the proposed framework. The system receives in input an integration operator and a query and outputs the answer to the query. The system currently implements many of the integration operators proposed in the literature.

## 1 Introduction

Data integration aims to provide a uniform integrated access to multiple heterogeneous information sources, designed independently and having strictly related contents. However the integrated view, constructed by integrating the information provided by the different data sources, by means of a specified integration strategy, could potentially contain inconsistent data, i.e. it can violate some of the constraints defined on the data.

*Example 1.* Consider the database consisting of the relation $Employee(Name, Age, Salary)$ where the attribute *Name* is a key for the relation. Assume there are two different instances for the relations *Employee*: $\mathcal{DB}_1 = \{Employee(Mary, 28, 20), Employee(Peter, 47, 50)\}$ and $\mathcal{DB}_2 = \{Employee(Mary, 31, 30), Employee(Peter, 47, 50)\}$. The merging of the two databases, performed by using as integration strategy the union operator (i.e. by considering the union of the tuples in both the relations), produces the following integrated database : $\mathcal{DB} = \{Employee(Mary, 28, 20), Employee(Mary, 31, 30), Employee(Peter, 47, 50)\}$ which does not anymore satisfy the key constraint. ☐

In the presence of an inconsistent integrated database, i.e. a database that does not satisfy some integrity constraints two possible solutions have been investigated in the literature [2,3,6,7,8,9,10,11,13,14,15]: repairing the database or computing consistent answers over the inconsistent database. Intuitively, a repair of the database consists in

Y. Manolopoulos, J. Pokorný, and T. Sellis (Eds.): ADBIS 2006, LNCS 4152, pp. 383–398, 2006.

deleting or inserting a minimal number of tuples so that the resulting database is consistent, whereas the computation of the consistent answer consists in selecting the set of *certain tuples* (i.e. those belonging to all repaired databases) and the set of *uncertain tuples* (i.e. those belonging to a proper subset of repaired databases).

*Example 2.* Consider the integrated database $\mathcal{DB}$ reported in Example 1. There are two possible repaired databases each obtained by deleting one of the two tuples whose value of the attribute $Name$ is $Mary$. The answer to the query asking for *the age of Peter*, this is constituted by the set of certain tuples $\{\langle 47 \rangle\}$, whereas the answer to the query asking for *the age of Mary* produces the set of uncertain values $\{\langle 28 \rangle, \langle 31 \rangle\}$.    □

The paper proposes a framework for merging, repairing and querying inconsistent databases. To this aim the problem of the satisfaction of integrity constraints in the presence of null values is investigated and a new semantics for constraints satisfaction, inspired by the approach presented in [5], is proposed. The present work focuses on the inconsistencies of a database instance w.r.t. particular types of integrity constraints, implemented and maintained in commercial DBMS, such as primary keys, general functional dependencies and foreign key constraints. The motivation to consider general functional dependencies, and special forms of functional dependencies such as primary keys, is that primary keys are used in the merging phase, whereas functional dependencies and foreign key constraints are used to repair the database.

More specifically, the task of merging data provided by various sources is performed using an integrator operator [17,13,12], which often reduces the set of tuples inconsistent w.r.t. the primary key; the task of repairing an inconsistent database, so that achieving a consistent state, is obtained by removing or inserting some tuples in the database in order to satisfy functional dependencies and foreign key constraints. Finally, the consistent answer to a query $Q$ is computed by evaluating the set of set of *certain* tuples, i.e. those tuples satisfying the query and belonging to all repaired database, and the set of *uncertain* tuples, i.e. those tuples satisfying the query and belonging to some, but not all, repaired databases. The framework for merging, repairing and querying inconsistent databases with functional dependencies, restricted to primary key constraints, and foreign key constraints has been implemented in a system prototype, developed at the University of Calabria. The system, called RAINBOW, receives in input an integrator operator, a flag $F$ specifying how to manage the inconsistent database, i.e. by repairing it or by consistently answering queries. More specifically, the integration operator is used in order to perform the merging phase, so that obtained an integrated, possibly inconsistent database, $\mathcal{DB}^I$. Then the system performs the management of $\mathcal{DB}^I$ by allowing, coherently with the solutions provided in the literature, either to compute the repairs ($F$ =0) or to consistently answer to a given query ($F$=1). In the first case the system outputs the repaired database, in the latter case the system receives in input a query and outputs the answer to the query.

## 2    Preliminaries on Relational Databases

Before formally introducing the problems related to the merging, repairing and querying of inconsistent databases let us introduce some basic definitions and notations. For additional material see [1,18].

A *relational schema* $\mathcal{DS}$ is a pair $\mathcal{DS} = \langle Rs, \mathcal{IC} \rangle$ where $Rs$ is a set of relational symbols and $\mathcal{IC}$ is a set of *integrity constraints*, i.e. assertion that have to be satisfied by a generic database instance.

Given a database schema $\mathcal{DS} = \langle Rs, \mathcal{IC} \rangle$ and a database instance $\mathcal{DB}$ over $Rs$, we say that $\mathcal{DB}$ is *consistent* if $\mathcal{DB} \models \mathcal{IC}$, i.e. if all integrity constraints in $\mathcal{IC}$ are satisfied by $\mathcal{DB}$, otherwise it is *inconsistent*.

A *relational query* (or simply a *query*) over $Rs$ is a function from the database to a relation. In the following we assume queries over $\mathcal{DS} = \langle Rs, \mathcal{IC} \rangle$ are conjunctive queries, i.e. first order relational formulas with existential quantification and conjunction of the form: $Q(y_1, ...y_n) \equiv \exists x_1, ...\exists x_m \Phi(x_1, ...x_m, y_1, ...y_n)$ where $\Phi$ is a conjunction of atoms whose predicate symbols are in $Rs$ and each $x_i$ with $i \in [1..n]$ and $y_j$ with $j \in [1..m]$ is either a variable or a constant.

We will denote with $Dom$ the database domain, i.e. the set of values an attribute can assume, consisting of a possibly infinite set of constants and assume $\bot \in Dom$, where $\bot$ denotes the null value.

## 3  Databases Merging

This section investigates the problem of database merging. Let us introduce some simple definitions in order to simplify the description of our approach. Let $R$ be a relation name, then we denote by: i) *attr(R)* the set of attributes of $R$; ii) *key(R)* the set of attributes in the primary key of $R$; iii) *fd(R)* the set of functional dependencies defined on *attr(R)*. Given a tuple $t \in R$, *key(t)* denotes the values of the key attributes of $t$. The absence of information for an attribute is indicated by $\bot$ (the null value).

Once the logical conflicts owing to the schema heterogeneity have been resolved, conflicts may arise, during the integration process, among data provided by different sources. In particular, the same real-world object may correspond to many tuples, that may have the same value for the key attributes but different values for some non-key attribute.

The database integration problem consists in the merging of $n$ databases $\mathcal{DB}_1 = \{R_{1,1}, ...R_{1,n_1}\}, ..., \mathcal{DB}_k = \{R_{k,1}, ...R_{k,n_k}\}$. In the following we assume that relations corresponding to the same concept and furnished by different sources are homogenized with respect to a common ontology, so that attributes denoting the same property have the same name [17]. We say that two homogenized relations $R$ and $S$, associated to the same concept, are *overlapping* if $key(R) = key(S)$. Given a set of overlapping relations an important feature of the integration process is related to the way conflicting tuples are combined.

Before performing the database integration the relations to be merged, i.e. the set of overlapping relations, must be first *reconciled* so that they have the same schema.

**Definition 1.** Given a set of overlapping relations $\{S_1, ..., S_n\}$, a *reconciled* relation $R$ is s.t.: i) $attr(R) = \bigcup_{i=1}^{n} attr(S_i) \cup \{Src\}$, ii) $R$ contains all tuples $t \in S_i, 1 \le i \le n$ completed as follows: all attributes belonging to $attr(R) - attr(S_i)$ are fixed to $\bot$; $R[Src] = i$, where $i$ is the unique index of the source database.                              □

*Example 3.* Consider the following two overlapping relations $S_1$ and $S_2$:

| K | Title | Author |
|---|---|---|
| 1 | Moon | Greg |
| 2 | Money | Jones |
| 3 | Sky | Jones |

$S_1$

| K | Title | Author | Year |
|---|---|---|---|
| 3 | Flowers | Smith | 1965 |
| 4 | Sea | Taylor | 1971 |
| 7 | Sun | Steven | 1980 |

$S_2$

The reconciled relation $R$ is the following:

| K | Title | Author | Year | Src |
|---|---|---|---|---|
| 1 | Moon | Greg | $\perp$ | 1 |
| 2 | Money | Jones | $\perp$ | 1 |
| 3 | Sky | Jones | $\perp$ | 1 |
| 3 | Flowers | Smith | 1965 | 2 |
| 4 | Sea | Taylor | 1971 | 2 |
| 7 | Sun | Steven | 1980 | 2 |

$R$

Given a database $\mathcal{DB}$ consisting of a set of reconciled relations $\{R_1, ..., R_n\}$ the *integrated database*, $\mathcal{DB}^I$ consists of a set of $n$ integrated relations $\{R_1^I, ..., R_n^I\}$, where each $R_j^I$ ($j \in [1..n]$) is obtained by applying an *integration operator*, denoted as $\diamond$, to the reconciled relation $R_j$, i.e. computes $R_j^I = \diamond(R_j)$.

In order to perform the database integration task several integration operators have been proposed in the literature, we recall here: the match join operator [17], the merging by majority operator [13], the merge operator and the prioritized merge operator [12].

Before presenting, in an informal way, these operators we introduce some preliminary definition and define desirable properties of integration operators.

**Definition 2.** Given two relations $R$ and $S$ such that $attr(R) = attr(S)$ and two tuples $t_1 \in R$ and $t_2 \in S$, we say that $t_1$ is *less informative* than $t_2$ ($t_1 \ll t_2$) if for each attribute $A$ in $attr(R)$, $t_1[A] = t_2[A]$ or $t_1[A] = \perp$. Moreover, we say that $R \ll S$ if $\forall t_1 \in R, \exists t_2 \in S$ s.t. $t_1 \ll t_2$. □

In the following given a set of overlapping relations $\{S_1, \ldots, S_n\}$ and the corresponding reconciled relation $R$ we will denote as $R|_i$ the set of tuples in $R$ obtained by extending tuples in $S_i$ with $\perp$ value for each attribute $A \notin attr(S_i)$. Thus $R|_i$ contains those tuples in $R$ having $Src = i$ ($R|_i = \Pi_{attr(R)-\{Src\}}(\sigma_{Src=i}(R))$).

**Definition 3.** Let $\{S_1, ..., S_n\}$ be a set of overlapping relations and $R$ the corresponding *reconciled* relation, then an integration operator, $\diamond$, is said to be (i) *complete* (or *lossless*), if $R|_i \ll \diamond(R)$, for $i \in [1..n]$; (ii) *dependency preserving*, if $\diamond(R) \models fd(S_i)$; (iii) *correct* if $\forall t \in \diamond(R) \exists t' \in \Pi_{attr(R)-\{Src\}}(R)$ s.t. $t' \ll t$. □

Informally, if an integration operator is both correct and complete it preserves the information provided by the sources. In fact, it could modify some input tuples by replacing null values with not null ones, but all the associations of not null values which were contained in the source relations will be inserted into the result (completeness) and no association of not null values which was not contained in the source relations will be inserted into the result (correctness).

In the rest of this section we will briefly describe some integration operators proposed in the literature. We suppose the database source $\mathcal{DB}_i$ is preferred by the user over each database $\mathcal{DB}_j$, with $j > i$.

The integration strategy performed by different integration operators, proposed in the literature, will be described by evaluating the integrated relation, $R^I$, obtained by applying them to the reconciled relation $R$ in Example 3. Moreover, we suppose the functional dependency $Title \rightarrow Author$ is defined over $R$, i.e. the attribute $Author$ is functionally dependent on the attribute $Title$. We recall that inconsistencies taken into account by these integration operators only derive from primary keys violations.

**The Mach Join Operator,** proposed in [17], manufactures tuples in the integrated relation by performing the outer-join of the $ValSet$ of each attribute, where the $ValSet$ of an attribute $A$ is the projections of the reconciled relation on $\{K, A\}$.

*Example 4.* The integrated relation $R^I$ is the following:

| K | Title | Author | Year |
|---|-------|--------|------|
| 1 | Moon | Greg | $\perp$ |
| 2 | Money | Jones | $\perp$ |
| 3 | Sky | Jones | 1965 |
| 3 | Sky | Smith | 1965 |
| 3 | Flowers | Smith | 1965 |
| 3 | Flowers | Jones | 1965 |
| 4 | Sea | Taylor | 1971 |
| 7 | Sun | Steven | 1980 |

$R^I$

The Match Join operator is complete, but it is not correct, since it mixes values coming from different tuples with the same key in all possible ways. As a consequence, when applying the Match Join operator to the relation $R$ in Example 3 we obtain an integrated view $R^I$ violating the functional dependency $Title \rightarrow Author$. Thus the Match Join operator produces tuples containing associations of values that may be not present in any original relation and the integration process may generate a relation which is not anymore consistent w.r.t. the functional dependencies.

**The Merging by Majority Operator,** proposed in [13], tries to remove conflicts taking into account the majority view of the databases, i.e. it maintains the (not null) value which is present in the majority of the databases. Thus the operator constructs an integrated relation containing *generalized* tuples, i.e. tuples where each attribute value is a simple value, if the information respects the majority criteria, or a set, if the operator does not resolve the conflict.

*Example 5.* The merging by majority operator is not able to solve the conflict present in $R$ between the two tuples $t_1$ and $t_2$ having $key(t_1) = key(t_2) = 3$. Thus $R^I$ will contain also the generalized tuple $\{3, \{Sky, Flowers\}, \{Jones, Smith\}, 1965\}$. □

**The Prioritized Merge operator,** introduced in [12], is an operator which, if conflicting tuples are detected, gives preference to those belonging to the source on which the user expressed preference: a tuple coming from a preferred relation is always maintained, and if it has some null values it is completed with not null values provided by less preferred relations.

*Example 6.* The integrated relation $R^I$ is:

| K | Title | Author | Year |
|---|-------|--------|------|
| 1 | Moon | Greg | $\perp$ |
| 2 | Money | Jones | $\perp$ |
| 3 | Sky | Jones | 1965 |
| 4 | Sea | Taylor | 1971 |
| 7 | Sun | Steven | 1980 |

$$R^I$$

Obviously, the prioritized merge operator is correct, but it is not complete as in the presence of conflicting tuples it maintains the not null values coming from the first relation holding it, following the preference ordering.

**Fact 1.** *The complexity of constructing the merged database by means of an integration strategy is polynomial time.*    □

## 4    Repairing and Querying Inconsistent Databases in the Presence of Null Values

In this section we propose a semantics for constraint satisfaction in the presence of null values, inspired by the approach presented in [5]. Bertossi et al. in [5] investigate the problem related to the satisfaction of integrity constraints in an incomplete database, i.e. a database in which incomplete information is represented by null values. The authors consider general constraint of the form[1]:

$$(\forall X)[ \bigwedge_{j=1}^{m} b_j(X_j), \varphi(X_0) \supset \bigvee_{j=m+1}^{n} (\exists Z_j) b_j(X_j, Z_j) ] \tag{1}$$

where $b_j$, for $j \in [1..n]$, are predicate symbols, $\varphi(X_0)$ denotes a conjunction of built-in atoms, $X = \bigcup_{j=1}^{m} X_j$, $X_i \subseteq X$ for $i \in [0..n]$ and all existentially quantified variables appear once. The notion of relevance of attributes w.r.t. the occurrence of null values in constraints is defined: the *relevant attributes* for a constraint of the form (1) are those involved in joins, those appearing in both the body and the head of (1), and those appearing in $\varphi$. Thus, a constraint is satisfied if any of the relevant attributes has a null value or the constraint is satisfied in the standard way (no null value involved).

*Example 7.* Consider the constraint $ic : \forall(X, Y, Z)[p(X, Y), p(X, Z) \supset Y = Z]$ and the database $\mathcal{DB} = \{p(a, \perp), p(a, b)\}$. The set of relevant attributes is $\{X, Y, Z\}$. When checking the satisfaction of $ic$ for $X = a$, $Y = b$ and $Z = \perp$, a null value is present in a relevant attribute, thus the constraint $ic$ is satisfied and the database $\mathcal{DB}$ is consistent w.r.t. the semantics proposed in [5].

Observe that the database of previous example is inconsistent w.r.t. the semantics adopted by commercial DBMS as two different tuples with the same value for primary key attributes belong to the database. In order to capture the behavior of commercial DBMS

---

[1] The order of literals in a conjunction or in a disjunction is immaterial. A literal can appear in a conjunction or in a disjunction at most once. The meaning of the symbols '$\wedge$' and ',' is the same.

semantics, in the following we provide an alternative notion of satisfaction for integrity constraints. Our semantics can be thought of as a refinement of the one in [5] as is obtained from the one in [5] by modifying as follows the definition of relevant attributes: the *relevant attributes* for a constraint of the form (1) are those involved in joins, those appearing in both body and head of (1), and those appearing in $\varphi$ that are not involved in equality conditions in the head of (1) or in inequality conditions in the body of (1).

*Example 8.* Consider the constraint and the database of Example 7. The set of relevant attributes is $\{X\}$; $ic$ is not satisfied for $X = a, Y = b$ and $Z = \perp$, therefore the database $\mathcal{DB}$ is inconsistent.

In the following we will provide further details on the satisfaction of functional dependencies and foreign key constraints in the presence of null values and will show how to handle a violation for these kinds of constraint. The motivation for considering only these limited form of constraints, relies in the fact they can be defined and maintained in commercial DBMS and are the types of constraints we manage in the system prototype for integrating, repairing and querying inconsistent databases.

**Definition 4.** *(Functional Dependency Satisfaction)* Given a functional dependency $fd$ of the form

$$\forall(X,Y,Z)[p(X,Y), p(X,Z) \supset Y = Z] \tag{2}$$

a database $\mathcal{DB}$ satisfies $fd$ if for each $p(x,y) \in \mathcal{DB}$ and, $p(x,z) \in \mathcal{DB}$ then $y = z$ or $x = \perp$. If a violation of $fd$ occurs, i.e. there exists $p(x,y) \in \mathcal{DB}$ and $p(x,z) \in \mathcal{DB}$ with $x \neq \perp$ and $y \neq z$, then the constraint can be satisfied by deleting either $p(x,y)$ or $p(x,z)$. □

**Definition 5.** *(Foreign Key Satisfaction)* Given a foreign key constraint $fk$ of the form

$$\forall(X,Y)[p(X,Y) \supset \exists Z q(X,Z)], \tag{3}$$

where $X, Y, Z$ are lists of variables and $Y, Z$ may be empty lists, then a database $\mathcal{DB}$ satisfies $fk$ if for each $p(x,y) \in \mathcal{DB}$, there exists $q(x,z) \in \mathcal{DB}$ or $x = \perp$. If a violation of $fk$ occurs, i.e. there exists $p(x,y) \in \mathcal{DB}$ with $x \neq \perp$ and there does not exist $q(x,z) \in \mathcal{DB}$, then the constraint can be satisfied by either deleting the tuple $p(x,y)$ or inserting a tuple $q(x, \perp)$. □

Before formally introducing the notion of repair in the presence of null values some preliminaries are provided.

An update atom is in the form $+a(X)$ or $-a(X)$. A ground atom $+a(t)$ states that $a(t)$ will be inserted into the database, whereas a ground atom $-a(t)$ states that $a(t)$ will be deleted from the database. Given a set $\mathcal{U}$ of ground update atoms we define the sets $\mathcal{U}^+ = \{a(t) \mid + a(t) \in \mathcal{U}\}, \mathcal{U}^- = \{a(t) \mid - a(t) \in \mathcal{U}\}$. We say that $\mathcal{U}$ is *consistent* if does not contain two update atom $+a(t)$ and $-a(t)$ (i.e. if $\mathcal{U}^+ \cap \mathcal{U}^- = \emptyset$). Given a database $\mathcal{DB}$ and a consistent set of update atoms $\mathcal{U}$, we denote as $\mathcal{U}(\mathcal{DB})$ the updated database $\mathcal{DB} \cup \mathcal{U}^+ - \mathcal{U}^-$. In the following we will use $\mathcal{IC}$ to denote a set of constraints including functional dependencies and foreign key constraints, i.e. $\mathcal{IC} = \mathcal{FD} \cup \mathcal{FK}$. Moreover, we denote with $\mathcal{PK}$ the subset of the functional dependencies defining primary keys.

**Definition 6.** Given a database $DB$ and a set of integrity constraints $IC$, a *repair* for $\langle DB, IC \rangle$ is a consistent set $R$ of update atoms such that

1. $R(DB) \models IC$ and
2. there is no consistent set $U$ of update atoms such that $U \subset R$ and $U(DB) \models IC$ and
3. there is no update atom $+a(x) \in R$ s.t. there exists $+a(x')$ with $+a(x') \ll +a(x)$ and, let $R' = R \cup \{+a(x')\} - \{+a(x)\}$, $R'(DB) \models IC$. $\qquad \square$

The third condition in the previous definition ensures that for each database $DB$ and set of integrity constraints $IC$ there is a finite number of repairs.

Observe that if $\bot \notin Dom$, the notion of repair here provided coincides with the one given in [11].

*Example 9.* Consider the following set of integrity constraints $IC$ :

- $\forall(X, Y, Z)[p(X, Y), p(X, Z) \supset Y = Z]$
- $\forall(X, Y, Z)[q(X, Y), q(X, Z) \supset Y = Z]$
- $\forall(X, Y)[p(X, Y) \supset \exists Z \, q(Y, Z)]$

and the database $DB = \{p(a, \bot), p(a, b)\}$. $DB$ is inconsistent w.r.t. $IC$ and the repairs for $\langle DB, IC \rangle$ are: $R_1 = \{-p(a, b)\}$ and $R_2 = \{-p(a, \bot), +q(b, \bot)\}$. Observe that each set $U = \{-p(a, \bot), +q(b, X)\}$ of update atoms with $X$ a constant different from $\bot$ is not a repair as it does not satisfy the third condition in Definition 6.

In the rest of the section we investigate the problem of querying an inconsistent database by considering the computation of consistent answers. The set of tuples present in the database, i.e. those implied by the constraints or originally present may be either *true*, *false* or *undefined*.

**Definition 7.** Given a database schema $DS = \langle Rs, IC \rangle$ and a database $DB$ over $Rs$, an atom $A$ is *true* (resp. *false*) with respect to $\langle DB, IC \rangle$ if $A$ belongs to all repaired databases (resp. there is no repaired database containing $A$). The set of atoms which are neither *true* nor false are *undefined*. $\qquad \square$

Thus, true atoms appear in all repaired databases [3], whereas undefined atoms appear in a proper subset of repaired databases.

**Definition 8.** Given a database schema $DS = \langle Rs, IC \rangle$ and a database $DB$ over $Rs$, the application of $IC$ to $DB$, denoted by $IC(DB)$, defines three distinct sets of atoms: the set of *true tuples* $IC(DB)^+$, the set of *undefined tuples* $IC(DB)^u$ and the set of *false tuples* $IC(DB)^-$. $\qquad \square$

**Definition 9.** Given a database schema $DS = \langle Rs, IC \rangle$, a database $DB$ over $Rs$ and a query $Q$, the *consistent answer* of the query $Q$ on the database $DB$, denoted as $Q(DB, IC)$, consists of three sets, denoted $Q(DB, IC)^+$, $Q(DB, IC)^-$ and $Q(DB, IC)^u$, containing, respectively, the sets of tuples which are *true* (i.e. belonging to $Q(DB')$ for all repaired databases $DB'$), *false* (i.e. not belonging to $Q(DB')$ for all repaired databases $DB'$) and *undefined* (i.e. set of tuples which are neither *true* nor *false*). $\qquad \square$

*Example 10.* Consider the set of constraints in Example 9 and the database $\mathcal{DB} = \{p(a, \perp), p(a, b), p(c, d), q(d, e)\}$. There are two repairs $\mathcal{R}_1$ and $\mathcal{R}_2$ that coincide with those reported in Example 9 and produce respectively the repaired databases : $\mathcal{DB}_1 = \{p(a, \perp), p(c, d), q(d, e)\}$ and $\mathcal{DB}_2 = \{p(a, b), p(c, d), q(d, e), q(b, \perp)\}$. Given the query $Q_1 :\ p(X, Y)$, the set of true tuples is $\{\langle d, e \rangle\}$, whereas the set of undefined tuples is $\{\langle a, \perp \rangle, \langle a, b \rangle\}$. For the query $Q_2 :\ s(X, Z) \leftarrow p(X, Y), q(Y, Z)$, the set of true tuples is $\{\langle c, e \rangle\}$, whereas the set of undefined tuples is $\{\langle a, \perp \rangle\}$.

## 5  RAINBOW: A System for Merging, Repairing and Querying Inconsistent Databases

RAINBOW (RepAiring INconsistent dataBases fOr query answWering) is a system prototype for merging, repairing and querying inconsistent databases with functional and foreign key constraints implemented at the University of Calabria. The system, which currently works for foreign key constraints and functional dependencies defining primary key constraints, has been implemented by using Java 2 Platform and all the experimentations have been performed on databases managed by MySQL. The overall architecture of the system prototype is reported in Figure 1.

RAINBOW receives in input an integrator operator - $\mathcal{IO}$ that specify how to construct the integrated database $\mathcal{DB}^I$, a flag $F \in \{0, 1\}$ and i) if $F=0$ returns the repaired databases that can be obtained from the possibly inconsistent database $\mathcal{DB}^I$, ii) if $F=1$ the system receives in input a query $Q$ and outputs the answer - *Ans*. It performs this task by i) merging of the set of overlapping relations, contained in the Source Database - $\mathcal{SDB}$ - ii) constructing the integrated database - $\mathcal{DB}^I$ - as specified by $\mathcal{IO}$ and iii) if ($F=0$) building a repaired database $\mathcal{DB}^R$ that maintains information on the set of repairs associated with $\mathcal{DB}^I$, i.e. the set of databases obtained from $\mathcal{DB}$ which are consistent w.r.t. the set of constraints; or iii) if ($F=1$) answering the query $Q$ by returning the answer *Ans* partitioned into two parts: certain answer (set of tuples which are *true* in all repaired database) and uncertain answer (set of tuples which are *true* in just in some repaired database).

The system can be used by means of a User Interface - $\mathcal{UI}$ - that allows to specify the integration operator, selected among those defined in the literature, the flag $F$ and, eventually, the user query $Q$. The user interface module interacts with the integration module - $\mathcal{IM}$ - the repairing module - $\mathcal{RM}$ - and the query evaluation module - $\mathcal{QEM}$ - and outputs either a repaired database $\mathcal{DB}^R$ that maintains information on the set of repairs associated with $\mathcal{DB}^I$ or the answer *Ans*. In the rest of this section the main features of the modules that constitute the system will be detailed.

### 5.1  Integration Module

The integration module receives in input the source database, the integration operator and constructs the corresponding integrated database. It is in charge of computing the integration of the reconciled relations, belonging to the source database, by using a specified integration strategy as described in Section 3. The integration module implements many of the integration operators, proposed in the literature, such as the match

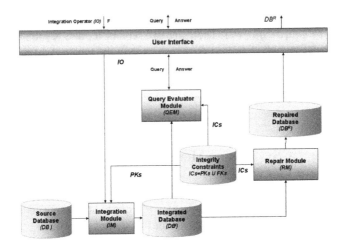

**Fig. 1.** System architecture

join [17], the merging by majority [13], the merge and the prioritized merge operator [12]. The implementation of these operators is obtained by means of SQL statements.

In the following, for the sake of brevity, the notation $R.X$ will be used either in the case $X$ is a single attribute or a list of attributes of $R$. Moreover, a condition $\theta$ expressed over a list of attributes $X = \{X_1, \ldots, X_n\}$ is intended to be expressed over each attribute in $X$, as an example X IS NULL denotes the conjunction $X_1$ IS NULL AND... AND $X_n$ IS NULL; and $R_1.X = R_2.X$ denotes the equality condition $R.X_1 = R_2.X_1$ AND... AND $R_1.X_m = R_2.X_n$; whereas $R_1.X <> R_2.X$ denotes the inequality condition $R.X_1 <> R_2.X_1$ OR ... OR $R_1.X_m <> R_2.X_n$.

Examples of different integration operators will be described in the following, by referring to the reconciled relation $R = \{K, X_1, .., X_n, Src\}$.

***The Match Join Operator.*** The Match Join operator can be easily expressed by means of the following SQL statement:

```
for each  X_i ∈ attr(R) − {K, Src}
    CREATE VIEW  T_i(K, X_i) AS
        SELECT  K, X_i    FROM  R
        WHERE  X_i IS NOT NULL

CREATE VIEW  R^I(K, X_1, ..., X_n) AS
SELECT  T_1.K,  T_1.X_1,  ...,  T_n.X_n
FROM  T_1, ..., T_n
WHERE  T_1.K = T_2.K    AND ...
        AND  T_{n-1}.K = T_n.K ;
```

***The Merging by Majority Operator.*** The SQL statement expressing the Merging by Majority operator is the following:

```
for each  X_i ∈ attr(R) − {K, Src}  {
   CREATE VIEW  W_i(K, X_i, Counter)  AS
      SELECT  K, X_i, COUNT(∗)    FROM  R
      GROUP BY  (K, X_i) ;

   CREATE VIEW  T_i(K, X_i)  AS
      SELECT  K, X_i   FROM  W_i
      WHERE NOT EXISTS(
         SELECT ∗    FROM  W_i  AS  W'_i
         WHERE  W_i.K = W'_i.K  AND
               W_i.Counter < W'_i.Counter) ;  }

CREATE VIEW  R^I(K, X_1, ..., X_n)  AS
SELECT  T_1.K,  T_1.X_1,  ...,  T_n.X_n
FROM  T_1, ..., T_n
WHERE  T_1.K = T_2.K   AND ...
      AND  T_{n−1}.K = T_n.K ;
```

***The Prioritized Merge Operator.*** The Prioritized Merge operation can be easily expressed by means of an SQL statement, as follows:

```
for each  X_i ∈ attr(R) − {K, Src}  {
   CREATE VIEW  T_i(K, X_i)  AS
      SELECT  K, X_i  FROM  R
      WHERE NOT EXISTS(
         SELECT ∗ FROM  R  R'
         WHERE  R.K = R'.K  AND
         R'.X_i  IS NOT NULL AND
         ((R.X_i  IS NOT NULL AND  R.Src > R'.Src)  OR
         (R.X_i  IS NULL))) }

CREATE VIEW  R^I(K, X_1, ..., X_n)  AS
SELECT  T_1.K,  T_1.X_1,  ...,  T_n.X_n
FROM  T_1, ..., T_n
WHERE  T_1.K = T_2.K   AND ...
      AND  T_{n−1}.K = T_n.K ;
```

## 5.2   Repairing Module

The Repairing Module - $\mathcal{RM}$ - is responsible for solving $PKs$ and $FKs$ inconsistencies and implements the strategy reported in Section 4. It receives in input the Integrated Database $\mathcal{DB}^I$ and produces a repaired database $\mathcal{DB}^R$ in which each tuple $t$ has an additional attribute ($Truth$) reporting its truth value (i.e. *undefined*, *true*) in a deterministic semantics.

$\mathcal{RM}$ first creates a copy of the integrated database $\mathcal{DB}^I$ into a database $\mathcal{DB}^R$ in which each relation $R^R$ is constructed as follows: its schema is obtained by adding the attribute $(Truth)$ to the schema of the corresponding relation $R^I \in \mathcal{DB}^I$, and its instance is obtained from the corresponding instance by setting to *true* the value of each tuple. Obviously each constraint defined over $\mathcal{DB}^I$ can be considered valid over $\mathcal{DB}^R$.

The - $\mathcal{RM}$ - then works as follows:

- *Test on FKs satisfaction.* For each $FK$ constraint $\forall (X, Y)[p(X, Y) \supset \exists Z q(X, Z)]$ and $\forall t = p^R(x, \_, true) \in \mathcal{DB}^R$,
  - if $\nexists q^R(x, \_, true) \in \mathcal{DB}^R$, then $t[Truth]$ is updated to $undefined$ and
  - if $\nexists q^R(x, \_, \_) \in \mathcal{DB}^R$, the tuple $q(x, \bot, undefined)$ will be inserted in $\mathcal{DB}^R$;
- *Test on PKs satisfaction.* For each relation $R^R$ with key $K$ and for each tuple $t \in R^R$, $t[Truth]$ is updated to $undefined$ if $\exists t' \in R^R$ s.t. $t \neq t'$ and $t[K] = t'[K]$.

Given a relational schema $R(K, X)$, where $K$ denotes the list of attributes belonging to the primary key, and $X$ denotes the remaining attribute in $R$, we denote the key constraint with $K \rightarrow X$. Given two relational schema $R(X)$ and $Q(Y)$ a foreign key constraint will be expressed by using the syntax $R[C] \subseteq Q[D]$, where $C \subseteq X$ and $D \subseteq Y$ (its primary key).

In the following, we suppose the relation $R^R$, obtained from $R^I$ by adding to its schema the attribute $Truth$, has been already constructed as previously specified.

The repair module first verifies $FK$s satisfaction and updates the repaired database $\mathcal{DB}^R$ by executing the following SQL statements:

---

```
UPDATE R^R SET Truth = 'undefined'
WHERE R^R.X IS NOT NULL AND NOT EXISTS(
    SELECT * FROM Q^R
    WHERE Q^R.Y = R^R.X AND Q^R.Truth = 'true');

INSERT INTO Q^R
    SELECT X,NULL,'undefined' FROM R^R
    WHERE R^R.X IS NOT NULL AND NOT EXISTS(
        SELECT * FROM Q^R
        WHERE Q^R.Y = R^R.X);
```

---

Then, in order to check the satisfaction of primary key constraints the $\mathcal{RM}$ executes the following SQL statement for each relation $R(K, X)$.

---

```
UPDATE R^R, R^R AS R' SET R^R.Truth = 'undefined'
WHERE R^R.K = R'.K AND R^R.X <> R'.X
```

---

*Example 11.* Consider the relations $Employee(Name, City, Age, Level)$ and $Level$ $(Id, Salary)$. Suppose to have the constraints:

- $Name \rightarrow City, Age, Level$;
- $Id \rightarrow Salary$
- $Employee[Level] \subseteq Level[Id]$

and assume the following instances of the integrated relations:

$Employee^I = \{\langle Mary, Venice, 28, A\rangle, \langle Mary, Venice, 31, A\rangle, \langle Peter, Rome, 47, B\rangle, \langle Peter, Rome, 40, B\rangle, \langle David, Naples, 40, A\rangle, \langle David, Florence, 40, B\rangle\}$ and $Level^R = \{\langle A, 20\rangle\}$.

The repaired relations, computed by $\mathcal{RM}$ are the following:

$Employee^R = \{\langle Mary, Venice, 28, A, undefined\rangle, \langle Mary, Venice, 31, A, undefined\rangle, \langle Peter, Rome, 47, B, undefined\rangle, \langle Peter, Rome, 40, B, undefined\rangle, \langle David, Naples, 40, A, undefined\rangle, \langle David, Florence, 40, B, undefined\rangle\}$ and $Level^R = \{\langle A, 20, true\rangle, \langle B, \bot, undefined\rangle\}$.

The value of $Truth$ attribute states that the relation $Employee$ of a repaired database cannot contain both tuples $\langle Mary, Venice, 28, A\rangle$ and $\langle Mary, Venice, 31, A\rangle$, both tuples $\langle Peter, Rome, 47, B\rangle$ and $\langle Peter, Rome, 40, B\rangle$ and both tuples $\langle David, Naples, 40, A, true\rangle$ and $\langle David, Florence, 40, B, true\rangle$.    □

### 5.3   Query Evaluator Module

The Query Evaluator Module - $\mathcal{QEM}$ - receives the query $Q$ and returns, to the user interface, the answer $Ans$ partitioned into the sets of certain and uncertain tuples. The computation of the answer is performed over a database $\mathcal{DB}^Q$ computed from $\mathcal{DB}^I$ by applying the technique presented in the section 4 using the set of constraints that directly or even indirectly are meaningful for the query.

Before presenting a complete example that illustrates the main feature of the $\mathcal{QEM}$ we introduce some preliminary concepts.

**Definition 10.** Given a database $\mathcal{DB}$, a set $FK$ of foreign key constraints and a conjunctive query $Q$, involving the relations $\{R_1, ..., R_n\}$, the *dependency graph* $G(\mathcal{DB}, FK)$ is the graph $\langle N, A\rangle$, with $N$ the set of nodes and $A$ the set of arcs, obtained as follows: for each relation $R \in \mathcal{DB}$, $N$ contains a node identified with the same name of the relation and for each foreign key constraint $R[X] \subseteq Q[Y] \in FK$, $A$ contains an arc $(R, Q)$.

The query graph $G(\mathcal{DB}, FK, Q)$ is the subgraph of $G(\mathcal{DB}, FK)$ containing each node *reachable from* or *from which is reachable* a node in $\{R_1, ..., R_n\}$.    □

*Example 12.* Consider the database $\mathcal{DB}$ containing the relations $Employee(Name, City, Age, Level)$, $Level(Id, Salary)$ and $Product(Id, Description)$. Suppose to have the set of foreign key constraints $FK = \{Employeee[Level] \subseteq Level[Id]\}$ and the query $Q : g(Name, Age) \leftarrow Employee(Name, \_Age, \_)$, asking for *name and age of each employee*. The query graph $G(\mathcal{DB}, FK, Q)$ contains the nodes $Employee$ and $Level$.    □

The $\mathcal{QEM}$ receives in input a query $Q$ and works as follows:

*Step 1* - It executes a process similar to the one performed by the repairing module $\mathcal{RM}$, in order to compute the database $\mathcal{DB}^Q$ in which each relation $R^Q$ has an additional attribute $Truth$;

*Step 2* - It executes the query $Q$ on $\mathcal{DB}^Q$ and returns the answer $Ans$ partitioned in two sets: the set of *true* tuples and the set of *undefined* tuples.

In more details, in the *Step 1* for each relation $R$, corresponding to a node in $G(\mathcal{DB}, FK, Q)$, the $\mathcal{QEM}$ computes the relation $R^Q$. The attribute $Truth$ of each tuple $t \in R^Q$ is fixed by checking the satisfaction of $FK$ constraints involving $R$ (corresponding to arcs of $G(\mathcal{DB}, FK, Q)$), and the satisfaction of functional dependencies in the form $K \rightarrow X$, where $K$ denotes the key attribute and $X$ is an attribute involved in $Q$. The SQL statements that allows to perform *Step 1* are analogous to the one reported in previous subsection. Finally, in the *Step 2* the $\mathcal{QEM}$ evaluates the query $Q$ over the database $\mathcal{DB}^Q$.

*Example 13.* Consider the Example 11 and the query $Q : g(Name, City, Level) \leftarrow$ *Employee* $(Name, City, \_, Level)$ asking for *name, city and level of employees*. The information holds in the repaired relations $Employee^R$ and $Level^R$ states that i) all the repaired databases agree that *Mary has an A level and lives in Venice* because in each of them the relation $Employee$ contains a tuple of the form $\langle Mary, Venice, \_, A \rangle$ and the relation $Level$ contains the tuple $\langle A, 20 \rangle$; ii) the information that *Peter has a B level and lives in Rome* is not confirmed by all repaired databases because a tuple $\langle B, \_ \rangle$ is not present in the relation $Level$ and a way to repair the original database (in order to satisfy the foreign key constraint) is to delete both tuples $\langle Peter, Rome, 47, B \rangle$ and $\langle Peter, Rome, 40, B \rangle$ from $Employee$; iii) finally some repaired database holds the information that *David has an A level and lives in Naples* and some other stores the information that *David has a B level and lives in Florence*.

The database $\mathcal{DB}^Q$, computed by $\mathcal{QEM}$ is the following: $Employee^Q = \{\langle Mary, Venice, 28, A, true \rangle, \langle Mary, Venice, 31, A, true \rangle, \langle Peter, Rome, 47, B, undefined \rangle, \langle Peter, Rome, 40, B, undefined \rangle, \langle David, Naples, 40, A, undefined \rangle, \langle David, Florence, 40, B, undefined \rangle\}$ and $Level^Q = \{\langle A, 20, true \rangle, \langle B, \bot, undefined \rangle\}$. Therefore, the answer to the query $Q$ has to return the certain tuple $\{\langle Mary, Venice, A \rangle\}$ and the uncertain tuples $\{\langle Peter, Rome, B \rangle, \langle David, Naples, A \rangle, \langle David, Florence, B \rangle\}$.

The SQL statement allowing to answering the query $Q$ by computing the relation $Ans$ is the following:

```
CREATE VIEW Ans AS
  SELECT Name, City, Level, Truth
  FROM Employee^Q
```

Obviously, in order to partition the answer $Ans$ into certain and undefined tuples, we have just to select from $Ans$ the set of tuples having truth value equal to *true* and *undefined*, respectively. □

Another peculiarity of the $\mathcal{QEM}$ that is important to point out is that, in order to correctly answering queries, each undefined tuple $t \in Ans$ (i.e. $t[Truth] = undefined$) is obtained from tuples that could be present in the same repaired database (i.e. their simultaneous presence does not violate any $PK$s).

The following example should make this crystal clear.

*Example 14.* Consider the database of previous example and suppose to have the query $Q : g(City_1, City_2) \leftarrow Employee(\_, City_1, Age, \_), Employee(\_, City_2, Age, \_),$ $City_2 \neq City_1$ asking for *pairs of different cities in which live employees having the same age.* The SQL statement allowing to answering the query $Q$ is the following:

---

```
CREATE VIEW Ans AS
    SELECT E₁.City, E₂.City, Eval({E₁.Truth, E₂.Truth})
    FROM Employeeᵠ AS E₁, Employeeᵠ AS E₂
    WHERE E₁.Age = E₂.Age AND E₁.City ≠ E₂.City
    AND NOT (E₁.Name IS NOT NULL AND E₁.Name = E₂.Name AND
       (E₁.City <> E₂.City OR E₁.Age <> E₂.Age OR E₁.Level <> E₂.Level))
```

---

where the function $Eval$ receives a list of truth values and returns *true* if all the values are *true* and *undefined* otherwise.

In this case $Employee^Q = \{\langle Mary, Venice, 28, A, undefined\rangle, \langle Mary, Venice,$ $31, A, undefined\rangle, \langle Peter, Rome, 47, B, undefined\rangle, \langle Peter, Rome, 40, B,$ $undefined\rangle, \langle David, Naples, 40, A, undefined\rangle, \langle David, Florence, 40, B,$ $undefined\rangle\}$.

Previous statement ensures that tuples that cannot be simultaneously present in the same repaired database are not joined (note that these tuples have *undefined* as truth value): e.g. the tuples $\langle David, Naples, 40, A, undefined\rangle$ and $\langle David, Florence,$ $40, B, undefined\rangle\}$ are not joined. The answer $Ans$ to the query $Q$ contains the uncertain tuples $\{\langle Rome, Naples\rangle, \langle Naples, Rome\rangle, \langle Rome, Florence\rangle, \langle Florence,$ $Rome\rangle\}$.    □

# 6   Conclusion

In this paper a framework for merging, repairing and querying inconsistent databases has been presented. The framework considers integrity constraints defining primary keys, foreign keys and general functional dependencies. The approach consists of three steps: i) merging of the source databases, by means of integration operators or general SQL queries, to reduce the set of tuples coming from the source databases which are inconsistent with respect to the constraints defined by the primary keys, ii) repairing the integrated database which may be inconsistent with respect to functional dependencies and foreign keys constraints and iii) computing the consistent answers over the repaired database. Finally, the architecture of a system prototype, developed at the University of Calabria, implementing the proposed approach, has been presented.

# References

1. Abiteboul, S., Hull, R., Vianu, V. *Foundations of Databases.* Addison-Wesley, 1994.
2. Agarwal, S., Keller, A. M., Wiederhold, G., Saraswat, K., Flexible Relation: an Approach for Integrating Data from Multiple, Possibly Inconsistent Databases. *ICDE*, 1995.
3. Arenas, M., Bertossi, L., Chomicki, J., Consistent Query Answers in Inconsistent Databases. *Proc. PODS 1999*, pp. 68–79, 1999.

4. Baral, C., Kraus, S., Minker, J., Combining Multiple Knowledge Bases. *IEEE-TKDE*, 3(2): 208-220 (1991)

5. Bravo, L., Bertossi, L., Semantically Correct Query Answers in the Presence of Null Values. To appear in Proc. EDBT WS on Inconsistency and Incompleteness in Databases (IIDB), 2006.

6. Bry, F., Query Answering in Information System with Integrity Constraints,*IICIS*, pp. 113-130, 1997.

7. Cali, A., Calvanese, D., De Giacomo, G., Lenzerini, M., Data Integration under Integrity Constraints. *CAiSE*, pp. 262-279, 2002.

8. Dung, P. M. ,Integrating Data from Possibly Inconsistent Databases. *COOPIS*, pp. 58-65, 1996.

9. Grant, J., Subrahmanian, V. S., Reasoning in Inconsistent Knowledge Bases. *IEEE-TKDE*, 7(1): 177-189, 1995.

10. Greco, S., Zumpano, E., Querying Inconsistent Database *LPAR*, pp. 308-325, 2000.

11. Greco, G., Greco, S., Zumpano, E., A Logic Programming Approach to the Integration, Repairing and Querying of Inconsistent Databases. *ICLP* pp. 348-364, 2001.

12. Greco, S., Pontieri, L., Zumpano, E., Integrating and Managing Conflicting Data. *Ershov Memorial Conference* pp. 349-362, 2001.

13. Lin, J., Mendelzon, A. O., Knowledge Base Merging by Majority, in R. Pareschi and B. Fronhoefer (eds.), *Dynamic Worlds*, Kluwer, 1999. Kluwer, 1999.

14. Lin, J., A Semantics for Reasoning Consistently in the Presence of Inconsistency. *AI*, 86(1), pp. 75-95, 1996.

15. Lin, J., Integration of Weighted Knowledge Bases. *Artificial Intelligence*, Vol. 83, No. 2, pages 363-378, 1996.

16. Subrahmanian, V. S., Amalgamating Knowledge Bases. *ACM-TODS*, Vol. 19, No. 2, pp. 291-331, 1994.

17. Yan, L.L., Ozsu, M. T., Conflict Tolerant Queries in Aurora *Coopis*, pp. 279-290, 1999.

18. Ullman, J. D., *Principles of Database and Knowledge-Base Systems*, Vol. 1, Computer Science Pressingness, 1989.

# An On-Line Reorganization Framework for SAN File Systems

Shahram Ghandeharizadeh[1], Shan Gao[1], Chris Gahagan[2], and Russ Krauss[2]

[1] Department of Computer Science, University of Southern California,
Los Angeles, CA 90089, USA
[2] BMC Software Inc., 2101 CityWest Blvd., Houston, TX 77042, USA

**Abstract.** While the cost per megabyte of magnetic disk storage is economical, organizations are alarmed by the increasing cost of managing storage. Storage Area Network (SAN) architectures strive to minimize this cost by consolidating storage devices. A SAN is a special-purpose network that interconnects different data storage devices with servers. While there are many definitions for a SAN, there is a general consensus that it provides access at the granularity of a block and is typically used for database applications.

In this study, we focus on SAN switches that include an embedded storage management software in support of virtualization. We describe an On-line Re-organization Environment, ORE, that controls the placement of data to improve the average response time of the system. ORE is designed for a heterogeneous collection of storage devices. Its key novel feature is its use of "time" to quantify the benefit and cost of a migration. It migrates a fragment only when its net benefit exceeds a pre-specified threshold. We describe a taxonomy of techniques for fragment migration and employ a trace driven simulation study to quantify their tradeoff. Our performance results demonstrate a significant improvement in response time (order of magnitude) for those algorithms that employ ORE's cost/benefit feature. Moreover, a technique that employs bandwidth of all devices intelligently is superior to one that simply migrates data to the fastest devices.

## 1   Introduction

Organizations are alarmed by the increasing cost of *managing* storage [31]. These costs include expenses associated with the human operators who manage disk storage, and the lost productivity when data is unavailable. Data might be unavailable for several reasons. Failure of the disk subsystem containing the referenced data is one. Another might be the load imposed on the system which results in formation of hot spots and bottlenecks, preventing it from responding in a timely manner, causing the user to perceive the data as being unavailable.

Storage Area Network (SAN) architectures strive to minimize the cost of managing storage by consolidating storage devices in a centralized place. They also promise to increase the productivity and effectiveness of human operators by providing detailed information about the system, advanced notification of when

Y. Manolopoulos, J. Pokorný, and T. Sellis (Eds.): ADBIS 2006, LNCS 4152, pp. 399–414, 2006.

the storage subsystem is not meeting the performance requirements of an application (or filling up), suggestions on how to improve system performance, etc. A SAN is a special-purpose network that interconnects different kinds of data storage devices with servers. It may consist of multi-vendor storage systems, storage management software and network hardware. It provides block-level access to the data[1]. This is important for database management systems that implement the concept of a transaction and its ACID properties: Atomic, Consistent, Isolation, and Durable [22]. The commercial arena offers SAN solutions in a variety of hardware configurations, e.g., Fibre Channel, iSCSI, Intel's Infiniband, etc.

The focus of this study is on SANs that include an embedded storage management software in support of virtualization. This software includes a file system that separates storage of a device from the physical device, i.e., physical data independence. Virtualization is important because it enables a file to grow beyond the capacity of one disk (or disk array). Such embedded file systems constitute the focus of this study. We investigate ORE, a framework that enables these embedded devices to incorporate new devices and populate them intelligently. Moreover, ORE migrates fragments from one device to another with the objective to minimize the average response time of the system. It incorporates the availability requirements of data and controls its placement to meet this objective.

ORE consists of three steps: monitor, predict, and migrate. The first step gathers data about the environment. The second predicts what data to migrate (if any) to which node. Finally, migrate schedules and performs the data migration. Its novel feature is its use of "time" to quantify the benefit and cost of a migration. It migrates a fragment only when its net benefit exceeds a pre-specified threshold, zero in this study. We describe a taxonomy of techniques with and without this feature. Our performance results indicate that this feature enhances average response time significantly. This is because it (a) migrates those fragments that impose the highest load to the fastest disks, and (b) assigns fragments that are referenced together to different devices, minimizing the formation of queues.

In order to realize acceptable throughput, we assume the distribution of blocks is based on a large striping unit [21,28,35,7,18,6]. This means (a) the fraction of a file assigned to a disk is larger than a block size and (b) a block is almost always assigned to a single device. The focus of our framework is to improve average response time with inter-block (instead of intra-block) parallelism.

We use a trace-driven performance evaluation study to compare this framework with alternative re-organization algorithms. Our performance results demonstrate the superiority of the proposed algorithm. The rest of this paper is organized as follows. Section 2 details related work and how this study is novel. Section 3 details our target environment. Based on this, we details our re-organization framework in Sections 4 and 5. Section 6 contains a comparison of this algorithm with its alternatives and different parameter settings. Brief conclusions and future research directions are described in Section 7.

---

[1] A SAN may also provide the key element of a Network Attached Storage (NAS) system, namely, manage data at the granularity of a file.

## 2   Related Work

The Petal [25] file system is one of the early studies to describe virtual disks. While it does not explicitly describe a SAN or an embedded file system, it employs the concept of "storage servers" that resemble a SAN embedded file system. It outlines an addressing scheme for these servers to map logical block references to physical disk address spaces. It employs chain-declustering [23,18] for high availability and dynamic load balancing. We adapt their concept to a SAN embedded file system and describe ORE as a novel extension that decides what fragment to migrate to improve response time.

On-line data re-organization has been studied by the COMFORT [28,29,33] and SNOWBALL [32] projects. Our work is novel for several reasons. First, there is a conceptual difference: We assume magnetic disks are inexpensive and small enough to justify their presence in an embedded device for SAN switches. This enables our framework to collect and maintain trace data on how requests utilize disks in order to make decisions that improve average response time dramatically. A key assumption here is that past request patterns resemble future access patterns. Second, we focus on how to migrate fragments amongst a *heterogeneous* collection of disks. Our performance results demonstrate that a simple extension[2] of the algorithms described in either COMFORT or SNOWBALL does **not** result in the best possible performance.

## 3   Target Environment

In our assumed environment, there are $K$ storage devices. Each storage device $d_i$ has a fixed storage capacity, $C(d_i)$, and an average bandwidth, $BW(d_i)$. With one or more applications that consume $B_{total}$ bandwidth during a fixed amount of time, ideally, each disk must contribute a bandwidth proportional to its $BW(d_i)$:

$$Fairshare(d_i) = B_{total} \times \frac{BW(d_i)}{\sum_{i=1}^{K} BW(d_i)} \tag{1}$$

The bandwidth of a disk is a function of the average requested block size ($\beta$) and its physical characteristics [19,6]: seek time, rotational latency, and transfer rate (tfr). It is defined as:

$$BW(d_i) = tfr \times \frac{\beta}{\beta + (tfr \times (seek\ time + rotational\ latency))} \tag{2}$$

Given a fixed seek time and rotational latency, $BW(d_i)$ approaches disk transfer rate with larger block sizes ($\beta$).

There are $F$ files stored on the underlying storage. The number of files might change over times, causing the value of $F$ to change. A file $f_i$ might be partitioned into two or more fragments. Its number of fragments is independent of

---

[2] This simple extension would be the EVEN policy of Section 5.1 that is several orders of magnitude slower than either $EVEN_{C/B}$ or $PYRAMID_{BW,C/B}$ proposed in this study.

the number of storage devices, i.e., $K$. Fragments of a file may have different sizes. Fragment $j$ of file $f_i$ is denoted as $f_{i,j}$. In our assumed environment, two or more fragments of a file might be assigned to the same disk drive[3].

# 4    ORE: A Three Step Framework

ORE consists of 3 logical steps: monitor, predict, and migrate. It partitions time into fixed intervals, termed *time slices*. During **monitor**, it constructs a profile of the load imposed by each file fragments per time slice. During **predict**, it performs two tasks. First, it computes what fragments to migrate from one disk to another in order to enhance system performance. Second, it identifies when in the future the migration should be performed so that it does not interfere with the current system load. Once an idle time arrives and there are candidates to migrate, ORE enters the **migrate** phase and changes the placement of these fragments. Below, we detail each of these steps.

**Monitor:** During each time slice, ORE constructs a profile of the load imposed on each disk drive and the average response time of each disk $d_i$. The load imposed on disk drive $d_i$ is quantified as the bandwidth required from disk $d_i$. It is the total number of bytes retrieved from $d_i$ during a time slice divided by the duration of the time slice. The average response time of $d_i$ is the average response time of the requests it processes during the time interval.

This process produces two tables, FragProfiler and DiskProfiler, that are used by the other two steps. FragProfiler table maintains the average block request size, heat, and load imposed by each fragment $f_{i,j}$ per time slice. DiskProfiler table maintains the following metadata for each disk drive $d_i$ per time slice: its heat, load, standard deviation in system load, average response time, average queue length, and utilization.

**Predict:** During this stage, ORE predicts what fragments to migrate to enhance response time. Section 5 describes a taxonomy of algorithms that can be employed for this step. In Section 6, we quantify the tradeoff associated with these alternatives.

**Migrate:** Fragment migration might be performed in two possible ways. With the first, the fragment is locked in exclusive mode while it is migrated from $d_{src}$ to $d_{dst}$. This simple algorithm prevents updates while the fragment is migrating. It is efficient and easy to implement. However, the data might appear to be unavailable during the reorganization process. Due to this limitation, we ignore this algorithm from further consideration.

The second, allows concurrent updates against two copies of the migrating fragment: (a) one on $d_{src}$, termed primary, and (b) the other on $d_{dst}$, termed secondary. The secondary copy is constructed from the primary copy of the fragment. All read requests are directed to the primary copy. All updates are

---

[3] Some studies require each fragment of a file to be assigned to a different disk drive [29].

performed against both the primary and secondary copy. The migration process is a background task that is performed based on availability of bandwidth from $d_{src}$. It assumes some buffer space for staging data from primary copy to facilitate construction of its secondary copy. This buffer space might be provided as a component of the embedded device. Depending on its size, the system might read and write units larger than a block. Moreover, it might perform writes against $d_{dst}$ in the background depending on the amount of free buffer space. Once the free space falls below a certain threshold, the system might perform writes as foreground tasks that compete with active user requests [4].

## 5    Predict: Fragments to Migrate

Predict, the second step of our framework, may utilize a taxonomy of techniques for choosing what fragments to migrate. In this section, we detail two classes of greedy algorithms, each with a different objective:

1. **EVEN** strives to distribute the load uniformly across the disks by migrating fragments to minimize the difference between (a) the disk that has more than its fair share of system load, and (b) the disk that has less than its fair share.
2. **PYRAMID** maximizes the utilization of fastest disks by (a) organizing disks in a vertical hierarchy with the fastest disk appearing at the top of the pyramid, and (b) migrating fragments that impose the greatest load to the top of this hierarchy.

When a configuration consists of groups of disks with approximately the same bandwidth, ORE constructs clusters with each cluster containing the same bandwidth. This does not impact the design of EVEN. However, it modifies PYRAMID to become a hybrid approach. Same as before, PYRAMID organizes the clusters in a hierarchy with the cluster containing the fastest disk type appearing at the top of the hierarchy. Fragments that impose the highest load migrate to the top of the pyramid. Within a cluster, fragments are migrated using EVEN because the disks that constitute a cluster are of the same type.

To illustrate, assume a configuration with 100 disks of type A, each offering a bandwidth of 10 megabytes per seconds, and 2 disks of type B, each offering 100 megabytes per second. The first cluster, termed $C_1$, offers an aggregate bandwidth of 1000 megabytes per second. The second cluster, termed $C_2$, offers an aggregate bandwidth of 200 megabytes per second. This does not impact EVEN because it continues to treat each disk individually, migrating fragments to approximate an even distribution of workload. However, PYRAMID organizes these two clusters in a hierarchy with $C_2$ as at the top layer because it contains the fastest disks. It migrates fragments that impose the highest load to $C_2$. Within each cluster, it employs EVEN to approximate an even distribution of workload across the disks of that cluster.

In the following, we detail each approach and its variations.

## 5.1   EVEN: Constrained by Bandwidth

At the end of each time slice, EVEN computes the fair-share of system load for each disk drive. Next, it identifies the disk with (a) maximum positive load imbalance, termed $d_{src}$, and (b) minimum negative load imbalance, termed $d_{dst}$. (The concept of load imbalance is formalized in the next paragraph.) Amongst the fragments of $d_{src}$, it chooses the one with a load closest to the minimum negative load of $d_{dst}$. It migrates this fragment from $d_{src}$ to $d_{dst}$. This process repeats until either there are no source and destination disks or a new time slice arrives.

The maximum positive load imbalance pertains to those disks with an imposed load greater than their fair share. For each such disk $d_i$, its $\delta^+(d_i) = $ load$(d_i)$-Fairshare$(d_i)$. Positive imbalance of $d_i$ is defined as $\frac{\delta^+(d_i)}{Fairshare(d_i)}$. EVEN identifies the disk with highest such value as the source disk, $d_{src}$, and migrates its fragments to those disks with a negative load imbalance.

We define the minimum negative load imbalance for those disks with an imposed load less than their fair share. For each such disk $d_i$, its $\delta^-(d_i)$ equals load$(d_i)$-Fairshare$(d_i)$. Negative imbalance of $d_i$ is $\frac{\delta^-(d_i)}{Fairshare(d_i)}$. The disk with the smallest negative imbalance[4] is the destination disk, $d_{dst}$, and EVEN migrates fragments to this disk. EVEN identifies those fragments of $d_{src}$ with an imposed load approximately the same as $\delta^-(d_{dst})$ and migrates them to $d_{dst}$.

**EVEN$_{C/B}$: Constrained by Bandwidth with Cost/Benefit Consideration.** EVEN$_{C/B}$ extends EVEN, see Section 5.1, by quantifying the benefit and cost of each candidate migration from $d_{src}$ to $d_{dst}$. Section 5.3 describes how the system quantifies the cost and benefit of each candidate migration because it is general purpose and used by the PYRAMID variation of Section 5.2. EVEN$_{C/B}$ sorts candidate migration based on their net benefit, i.e., benefit - cost, migrating those that provide the greatest savings first. After each migration, the cost of each candidate migration is re-computed (because the migration might have changed this value) and the list is resorted. Section 6 shows this algorithm provides significant response time enhancements when compared with EVEN.

## 5.2   PYRAMID

PYRAMID migrates fragments with the highest load to the fastest disk drives. It constructs layers of storage devices and assigns the fastest to the top of the hierarchy. Fragments migrate up and down the pyramid based on their imposed load. We describe 3 variations of this algorithm. The performance results of Section 6 demonstrate the superiority of the last design, PYRAMID$_{BW,C/B}$.

**PYRAMID$_{SP}$: Constrained by Space.** PYRAMID$_{SP}$ migrates highest load fragments to the fastest disks until their storage capacity is exhausted. If the

---

[4] Given two disks, $d_1$ and $d_2$ with negative imbalance of -0.5 and -2.0, respectively, $d_2$ has the minimum negative load imbalance.

database size is smaller than the total storage capacity of devices then disks that constitute the lowest layer of this hierarchy might be completely un-utilized.

Its details are as follows. At the end of each time slice, this algorithm sorts fragments based on their imposed load. It maintains a sorted list of disks based on their available bandwidth. Next, it computes which fragments should reside on which disk by exhausting the storage capacity of disks at the highest layer. This is the target placement. PYRAMID$_{SP}$ compares this with the current placement and computes a collection of migrations to transform the current placement to the target placement. It migrates those that impact fragments with the highest load first. It terminates when (a) the new placement is realized or (b) a new time slice arrives.

By exhausting the storage capacity of fast disks, a migration with PYRAMID$_{SP}$ might translate into multiple migrations. For example, assume the storage capacity of disks 1 and 2 are exhausted. In order to switch the place of two equi-sized fragments, say 1.1 and 3.2, the system might perform 3 migration: migrate fragment 1.1 from disk 1 to disk 3, migrate fragment 3.2 from disk 2 to disk 1, and migrate fragment 1.1 to disk 2. Of course, this can be prevented as long as main memory is sufficiently large to hold either fragment 1.1 or 3.2 and partially written fragments can be restored in the presence of failures.

When a configuration consists of groups of disks with each disk group providing similar bandwidth, this algorithm constructs clusters of disks. Migration of fragments across the clusters is the same as before. Within a cluster, PYRAMID$_{SP}$ employs EVEN to migrate fragments from one disk to another, see Section 5.1.

**PYRAMID$_{BW}$: Constrained by Bandwidth.** PYRAMID$_{BW}$ migrates fragments with the highest load to the fastest disk drives with the objective to utilize the bandwidth of each layer in the hierarchy. Thus, even if the database is small enough to fit on the fastest disk, this algorithm utilizes the storage capacity of each layer. The amount of data assigned to each layer is proportional to its bandwidth.

Its detail is as follows. At the end of each time slice, PYRAMID$_{BW}$ sorts fragments and disks based on their imposed load and bandwidth, respectively. Next, using the bandwidth of each disk, it estimates the fraction of load that should be assigned to each disk to exhaust its bandwidth. This identifies which fragments should reside on which disk drive. If the current assignment realizes this new placement then the algorithm terminates. Otherwise, it migrates fragments to realize the new placement. It terminates when (a) the new assignment is realized or (b) a new time slice arrives.

**PYRAMID$_{BW,C/B}$: Constrained by Bandwidth with Cost/Benefit Consideration.** This algorithm extends PYRAMID$_{BW}$ by computing the cost and benefit of each candidate migration. It sorts these candidates based on their net benefit, performing those that provide greatest savings first. Note that once it migrates the first candidate in the list, the benefit of the other migrations might change. Thus, it re-computes the benefit of each candidate after performing one migration.

## 5.3   Evaluating Benefit and Cost of a Migration

This section describes an approach to quantify the benefit and cost of migrating a fragment $f_{i,j}$ from $d_{src}$ to $d_{dst}$. Its unit of measurement is time, i.e., milliseconds. The cost of migrating a fragment is the total time spent by $d_{src}$ to read the fragment and $d_{dst}$ to write the fragment.

The benefit of migrating $f_{i,j}$ is measured in the context of previous time slices. ORE hypothesizes a virtual state where $f_{i,j}$ resides on $d_{dst}$ and measures the improvement in average response time. In essence, it estimates an answer to the following question: "What would be the average response time if $f_{i,j}$ resided on $d_{dst}$?" By comparing this with the observed response time, we quantify the benefit of a migration. Of course, this number might be a negative value which means that there is no benefit to performing this migration. Note this methodology assumes the past access patterns resemble future access patterns.

We start by describing a methodology to estimate a response to the hypothetical "what-if" question. Next, we formalize how to compute the benefit. Subsequently, we present how much space is required to implement our methodology.

Our methodology to estimates a response to the "what-if" question assumes ORE is previewed to all block requests issued to the SAN switch and the status of each storage drive. ORE maintains one additional piece of information, namely the duration of overlap between two fragments, termed OVERLAP($f_{i,j}$, $f_{k,l}$). This information is maintained for each time slice. It estimates how long two requests referencing fragments $f_{i,j}$ and $f_{k,l}$ overlap with each other in time. It is used to detect correlations between requests referencing fragments $f_{i,j}$ and $f_{k,l}$. If there is a high correlation then these fragments should be assigned to different disks to minimize the impact of queuing delays. Below, we present a formal definition of OVERLAP.

In order to define OVERLAP and describe our methodology, and without loss of generality, assume that we are answering the "what-if" question in the context of one time slice. To simplify the discussion further, assume a homogeneous collection of disk drives. (This assumption is removed at the end of this section.) The average system response time, $RT_{avg}$, is a function of average response time observed by requests referencing each fragment. Assuming $F$ files, each partitioned into at most $G$ fragments, it is defined as:

$$RT_{avg} = \frac{\sum_{i=1}^{F} \sum_{j=1}^{G} RT_{avg}(f_{i,j})}{F \times G} \tag{3}$$

The average response time of a fragment, $RT_{avg}(f_{i,j})$, is the sum of its average service time, $S_{avg}(f_{i,j})$, and wait time, $W_{avg}(f_{i,j})$:

$$RT_{avg}(f_{i,j}) = S_{avg}(f_{i,j}) + W_{avg}(f_{i,j}) \tag{4}$$

$S_{avg}(f_{i,j})$ is a function of the disk it resides on and average requested block size. For each fragment, ORE maintains the average requested block size in the FragProfiler table. Thus, given a disk drive $d_{dst}$ and a fragment $f_{i,j}$, ORE can estimate $S_{avg}(f_{i,j})$ if $f_{i,j}$ resided on $d_{dst}$ (using the physical characteristics of $d_{dst}$).

To compute $W_{avg}$, note that each request has an arrival time, $T_{arvl}$. For each fragment $f_{i,j}$ residing on disk $d_i$, we maintain when the requests referencing $f_{i,j}$ will depart the system, $T_{depart}$. $T_{depart}$ is estimated by analyzing the wait time of the request in the queue of $d_i$. Upon the arrival of a request referencing fragment $f_{k,l}$, we examine all those fragments with a non-negative $T_{depart}$. For each, we set OVERLAP$(f_{k,l}, f_{i,j}, T_{arvl})$ to be the difference between $T_{arvl}(f_{k,l})$ and $T_{depart}(f_{i,j})$: OVERLAP$(f_{k,l}, f_{i,j}, T_{arvl})$= Max(0, $T_{depart}(f_{i,j}) - T_{arvl}(f_{k,l})$). For a time slice, OVERLAP$(f_{k,l}, f_{i,j})$ is the sum of the individual OVERLAP$(f_{k,l}, f_{i,j}, T_{arvl})$ where $T_{arvl}$ is during the time slice. In our implementation, we maintained OVERLAP$(f_{k,l}, f_{i,j})$ as an integer that is initialized to zero at the beginning of each time slice. Upon the arrival of a request referencing $f_{k,l}$, we increment OVERLAP$(f_{k,l}, f_{i,j})$ with OVERLAP$(f_{k,l}, f_{i,j}, T_{arvl})$. This minimizes the amount of required memory.

OVERLAP$(f_{k,l}, f_{i,j})$ defines how long requests referencing $f_{k,l}$ wait in a queue because of requests that reference $f_{i,j}$. Assuming that $f_{i,j}$ and $f_{k,l}$ are the only fragments assigned to disk $d_i$ and the system processes #Req$(f_{k,l})$ requests that reference $f_{k,l}$, the average wait time for these requests is:

$$W_{avg}(f_{k,l}) = \frac{OVERLAP(f_{k,l}, f_{i,j}) + OVERLAP(f_{k,l}, f_{k,l})}{\#Req(f_{k,l})} \qquad (5)$$

It is important to observe the following two details. First, self OVERLAP is also defined for a fragment $f_{k,l}$, i.e., OVERLAP$(f_{k,l}, f_{k,l})$. This enables ORE to estimate how long requests that reference the same fragment wait for one another. Second, this paradigm is flexible enough to enable ORE to maintain OVERLAP$(f_{k,l}, f_{i,j})$ even when $f_{k,l}$ and $f_{i,j}$ reside on different disks. ORE uses this to estimate a response time for a hypothetical configuration where $f_{i,j}$ migrates to the disk containing $f_{k,l}$. Third, ORE can estimate the response time of a disk drive for an arbitrary assignment of fragments to disks using Equation 3.

Based on Equation 4, there are two ways to enhance response time observed by requests that reference a fragment, $f_{k,l}$. First, migrate $f_{k,l}$ to a faster disk for an improved service time, $S_{avg}$. Second, migrate a fragment $f_{i,j}$ away from those disks whose resident fragments have a high OVERLAP$(f_{k,l}, f_{i,j})$.

Figure 1 shows the pseudo-code to estimate the benefit of migrating $f_{i,j}$ from $d_{src}$ to $d_{dst}$. ORE may compute this for $N$ previous time slices where $N$ is an arbitrary number. The only requirement is that the embedded device must provide sufficient space to store all data pertaining to these intervals.

Given $G$ fragments, in the worst case scenario, the system maintains $\frac{G^2 + G}{2}$ integer values. For example with a 1000 fragments (G=1000) and a 32 bit integer representation, in the worst case scenario, the system would store 4 megabytes of data per time slice. In our experiments, the amount of required storage was significantly less than this. With the 80-20 rule, we expect this to hold true for almost all applications. In Section 7, we describe how ORE can employ a circular buffer to limit the size of trace data that it gathers from the system.

1. the load imposed by fragment $f_{i,j}$ on $d_{src}$ is termed $load(f_{i,j}, d_{src})$.
2. the load imposed by fragment $f_{i,j}$ on $d_{dst}$ after migration is $load(d_{dst}) + load(f_{i,j}, d_{src})$.
3. Number of accesses processed by disk $d_{src}$ is $Access_{src}$
4. Number of accesses processed by disk $d_{dst}$ is $Access_{dst}$
5. Look-up the average response time of $d_{src}$ prior to migration, termed $RT_{src,before}$
6. Look-up the average response time of $d_{dst}$ prior to migration, termed $RT_{dst,before}$
7. Estimate the average response time of $d_{src}$ after migration, termed $RT_{src,after}$
8. Estimate the average response time of $d_{dst}$ after migration, termed $RT_{dst,after}$
9. Total response time savings of $d_{src}$ after migration is:
   $Savings_{src}=(Access_{src,after} \times RT_{src,after}) - (Access_{src,before} \times RT_{src,before})$.
10. Total response time savings of $d_{dst}$ after migration is:
    $Savings_{dst}=(Access_{dst,after} \times RT_{dst,after}) - (Access_{dst,before} \times RT_{dst,before})$.
11. Benefit of migrating $f_{i,j}$ is $Benefit(f_{i,j})=Savings_{src} + Savings_{dst}$.

**Fig. 1.** Pseudo-code to compute the benefit of a candidate migration

In our experiments, see Section 6, the maximum percentage error observed by our methodology was 23% when estimating the average response time of a request.

# 6   Performance Evaluation

We used a trace driven simulation study to quantify the performance of the proposed on-line re-organization algorithm. We start with a brief overview of the trace driven simulation model. Next, we present the obtained results and our observations.

The traces were gathered from a production Oracle database management system on a HP workstation configured with 4 gigabyte of memory, and 5

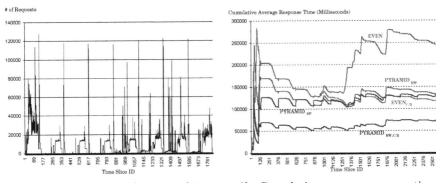

2a. No. of requests as a function of time    2b. Cumulative average response time

**Fig. 2.** Pattern of request arrival and system performance

terabytes of storage devices (283 raw devices). The database consisted of 70 tables and is 27 gigabyte in size. The traces were gathered from 4 pm, April 12 to 1 pm April 23, 2001. It corresponds to 23 million operations on the data blocks. The file references are skewed with approximately 83% of accesses referencing 10% of the blocks. Moreover, accesses to the tables are bursty as a function of time. This is demonstrated in Figure 2a, where we plot the number of requests to the system as a function of six minute intervals, termed time slices.

We used the Java programming language to implement our simulation model. It consists of 3 class definitions:

1. Disk: This class definition simulates a multi-zone disk drive with a complete analytical model for computing seeks, rotational latency, and transfer time. When a disk object is instantiated, it reads its system parameters from a database management system. Hence, we can configure the model with different disk models and different number of disks for each model. A disk implements a simplified version of the EVEREST file system.

2. Client: The client generates requests for the different blocks by reading the entries in the trace files.

3. SAN Switch: This class definition implements a simplified SAN switch that routes messages between the client and the disk drives. The file manager is a component of this module. This module services each request generated by a client.

   (a) File Manager: The file manager controls and maintains the placement of data across disk drives. It maintains the assignment of different files and their fragments across the disk drives. Given a request for a block of a file, this module locates the fragment referenced by the request and resolves which disk contains the referenced data. It consults with the file system of the disk drive to identify the appropriate cylinder and track that contains the referenced block.

The file manager implements the 3-step re-organization algorithm of ORE, see Section 4, and its alternative policies detailed in Section 5.

We conducted experiments with both a large configuration consisting of 283 raw devices that corresponds to the physical system that produced the traces and smaller configurations. The smaller configurations are faster to simulate. The performance results presented in this paper are based on one such configuration consisting of 9 disk drives. It consisted of 3 different disk models, forming 3 clusters of homogeneous disks: $C_1$, $C_2$, and $C_3$. Each cluster consisted of 3 disk drives. These disks correspond to those introduced in the late 2000, late 1998 and early 1997. Each disk in $C_1$ has a storage capacity of 180 gigabytes with a transfer rate of 40 megabytes per second (MB/sec). These were modeled after the high density, Ultra160 SCSI/Fibre-Channel disks introduced by Seagate in late 2000. Each disk in $C_2$ has a storage capacity of 60 gigabytes with a transfer rate of 20 MB/sec. Each disk in $C_3$ has a storage capacity of 20 gigabytes with a transfer rate of 4 MB/sec. These two models are similar to those described in [38].

We also analyzed different block sizes. The experimental results presented here are based on 128 kilobyte blocks. In Section 7, we summarize our observations based on smaller block sizes.

All experiments start with the same data placement, namely, a random distribution of fragments across all 9 disks.

**Performance Results:** Figure 2b shows the performance of alternative predict techniques using the trace. The x-axis of this figure denotes time, i.e., six minute time intervals termed time slices. The y-axis is the cumulative average response time. It is computed as follows. For each time slice, we compute the total number of requests and the sum of all response times till the end of that time slice. The cumulative average response time is the ratio of these two numbers, i.e., $\frac{total\ response\ time}{total\ requests}$. If during a time slice, no requests are issued then the cumulative average response time remains constant. This explains the flat portions of each curve in Figure 2b.

The y-axis of Figure 2b ranges from 12 milliseconds to 5 minutes. The maximum response time is very high given that (a) the average service time of the slowest disk is 68 milliseconds, and (b) the average utilization of the available bandwidth (for all 9 disks) is less than 10%. The high response time is because of the bursty nature of request arrivals, see Figure 2a. There are time slices that observe more than 100,000 requests in a matter of seconds. These requests reference a few tables and access the same disk to form long queues. The wait-time in these queues explains the high response times.

Figure 2b shows $PYRAMID_{BW,C/B}$ is superior to all the other techniques because it provides the best possible cumulative average response time. The second best technique is $EVEN_{C/B}$. Both use OVERLAP to identify those fragments that are referenced together and migrate them to different disks. This minimizes the length of queues observed at each disk drive. In general, using the concept of cost/benefit to migrate fragments reduces the maximum queue lengths by more than a factor of 2.

With our configuration, the database is small enough to fit on one of the three 180 gigabyte disks. $PYRAMID_{SP}$ migrates all file fragments to the 3 fastest disks by the $200^{th}$ time slice, rendering the six slower disks idle. Next, it uses EVEN to migrate the fragments amongst these 3 disk drives. Similar to EVEN and $PYRAMID_{BW}$, it observes queues longer than those seen by $EVEN_{C/B}$ and $PYRAMID_{BW,C/B}$, although it benefits from the speed of the fast disks to service these requests quickly (12 millisecond service time versus 18 and 68 milliseconds with the other two disk models).

The fact that the performance of $PYRAMID_{SP}$ is not as good as $EVEN_{C/B}$ and $PYRAMID_{BW,C/B}$ highlights the following interesting observation: migrating data to fast disks does not result in superior performance. A re-organization strategy that assigns a proportional amount of system workload to each device intelligently is a superior alternative.

# 7    Conclusion and Future Research Directions

This paper introduced ORE as a 3-step reorganization framework for embedded SAN file systems. We described several algorithms that decide what fragments to migrate to which disk. We employed a trace driven simulation study to quantify their performance trade-offs. Two algorithms, namely, EVEN$_{C/B}$ and PYRAMID$_{BW,C/B}$ provide the best cumulative average response time. There are several reasons for this. First, they migrate fragments with a high load to the faster devices. Second, they use the concept of OVERLAP to migrate two fragments that are referenced simultaneously to different devices in order to minimize the queuing delays. While we do not claim that these observations apply to all SAN applications, we expect them to hold true for those applications that issue requests in a bursty manner, exhibit a skewed data access pattern (80-20 rule [19]) with future access patterns resembling past access patterns.

The block size ($\beta$) impacts the behavior of ORE greatly. A small block size, e.g., 2 kilobyte, reduces bandwidth of fast disks dramatically because seek and rotational delays dominate the transfer time, see Equation 2. With the nine disk configuration of Section 6, a 2 kilobyte block size would force ORE to treat all disks as identical.

An intelligent technique such as PYRAMID$_{BW,C/B}$ that utilizes bandwidth of all devices is superior to one that simply migrates the data to the fastest devices (PYRAMID$_{SP}$). In our experiments, PYRAMID$_{BW,C/B}$ controls placement of data with the objective to minimize the likelihood of simultaneous requests referencing the same device, reducing formation of bottlenecks and hot spots.

The results presented in this paper are very promising and we plan to extend ORE in several ways. First, ORE should consider the availability requirement of a file $f_i$ when placing it across devices. For example, $f_i$ may specify that its mean-time-to-data-loss, $MTTDL(f_i)$, should exceed 200,000 hours, $MTTDL_{min}(f_i)$ = 200,000 hours. Assuming physical disk drives fail independent of one another, each disk has a certain failure rate [38,30,16], termed $\lambda_{failure}$. Its mean-time-to-failure (MTTF) is simply: $\frac{1}{\lambda_{failure}}$. When a file (say $f_j$) is partitioned into $n$ fragments and assigned to $n$ disks (say $d_1$ to $d_n$) then the data becomes unavailable in the presence of a single failure[5]. Hence, it is defined as follows [38,30,16]: $MTTDL(f_i) = \frac{1}{\sum_{i=1}^{n} \lambda_{failure}(d_i)}$. For example, if the MTTF of disk A and B is 1 million and 2 million hours, respectively, then the MTTDL of a file with fragments scattered across these two disks is 666,666 hours. This is important because ORE may not be able to spread the fragments of a file across all devices. Moreover, ORE might be forced to place those files with a high availability requirement on the newer disks with a high MTTF characteristics.

Second, we intend to investigate the design of an online capacity planner that consumes the maximum response time requirements of an application, detects

---

[5] There has been a significant amount of research on construction of parity data blocks and redundant data, see [38] that focuses on this for heterogeneous disks. This topic is beyond the focus of this study. In this paper, we control the placement without constructing redundant data.

when the system is not meeting this requirement, and suggests changes to the configuration to meet the specified response time. This capacity planner would be a component of the embedded device. It can detect when the response time requirement is being violated because it observes all request arrivals and departures. It can suggest hardware changes because the first step of ORE, monitor, gathers important details on how the resources are used.

## Acknowledgments

We wish to thank Anouar Jamoussi and Sandra Knight of BMC Software for collecting and providing traces used in this study. We also thank William Wang, Sivakumar Sethuraman, and Dinakar Yanamandala of USC for assisting with the implementation of our simulation model. This research was made possible by an unrestricted cash gift from BMC Software Inc., a fellowship award from the Annenberg Center for Communication, and NSF research grant IIS-0307908.

## References

1. K. Amiri, G. Gibson, and R. Golding. Highly Concurrent Shared Storage. In *Proceedings of the International Conference on Distributed Computing Systems*, April 2000.
2. K. Amiri, D. Petrou, G. Ganger, and G. Gibson. Dynamice Function Placement for Data-Intensive Cluster Ccomputing. In *Proceedings of the USENIX Annual Technical Conference*, June 2000.
3. T. Anderson, Y. Breitbart, H. Korth, and A. Wool. Replication, Consistency, and Practicality: Are These Mutually Exclusive? *Proceedings of ACM SIGMOD*, 27, 1998.
4. W. Aref, I. Kamel, T. Niranjan, and S. Ghandeharizadeh. Disk Scheduling for Displaying and Recording Video in Non-Linear News Editing Systems. In *Proceedings of Multimedia Computing and Networking Conference*, 1997.
5. R. H. Arpaci-Dusseau, E. Anderson, N. Treuhaft, D. E. Culler, J. M. Hellerstein, D. Patterson, and K. Yelick. Cluster I/O with River: Making the Fast Case Common. In *Proceedings of the Sixth Workshop on Input/Output in Parallel and Distributed Systems*, pages 10–22, Atlanta, GA, 1999. ACM Press.
6. S. Berson, S. Ghandeharizadeh, R. Muntz, and X. Ju. Staggered Striping in Multimedia Information Systems. In *Proceedings of ACM SIGMOD*, pages 79–90, 1994.
7. P. M. Chen and D. A. Patterson. Maximizing Performance in a Striped Disk Array. In *Proc. 17th Annual Int'l Symp. on Computer Architecture, ACM SIGARCH Computer Architecture News*, page 322, 1990.
8. G. Copeland, W. Alexander, E. Boughter, and T. Keller. Data placement in Bubba. In *Proceedings of ACM SIGMOD*, pages 99–108, 1988.
9. Asit Dan and Dinkar Sitaram. An Online Video Placement Policy Based on Bandwidth to Space Ratio (BSR). In *Proceedings of ACM SIGMOD*, pages 376–385, 1995.
10. D. DeWitt and J. Gray. Parallel Database Systems: The Future of High Performance Database Systems. *Communications of the ACM*, 35(6):85–98, 1992.

11. A. L. Drapeau, K. W. Shirrif, J. H. Hartman, E. L. Miller, S. Seshan, R. H. Katz, K. Lutz, D. A. Patterson, E. K. Lee, P. H. Chen, and G. A. Gibson. RAID-II: A high-bandwidth network file server. In *Proceedings of the 21st Annual International Symposium on Computer Architecture*, pages 234–244, 1994.

12. S. Ghandeharizadeh, D. Ierardi, and D. Kim. Placement of Data in Multi Zone Disk Drives. In *Proceedings of the Second International Baltic Workshop on Databases and Information Systems*, 1996.

13. S. Ghandeharizadeh, D. Ierardi, and R. Zimmermann. An Algorithm for Disk Space Management to Minimize Seeks. *The Computer Journal*, 57:75–81, 1996.

14. S. Ghandeharizadeh, D. Ierardi, and R. Zimmermann. Management of Space in Hierarchical Storage Systems. In M. Arbib and J. Grethe, editors, *A Guide to Neuroinformatics*. Academic Press, 2001.

15. S. Ghandeharizadeh, S. Kim, W. Shi, and R. Zimmermann. On minimizing startup latency in scalable continuous media servers. In *Multimedia Computing and Networking*, Feb 1997.

16. G. Gibson. Redundant Disk Arrays: Reliable, Parallel Secondary Storage, 1991.

17. G. A. Gibson and D. A. Patterson. Designing Disk Arrays for High Data Reliability. *Journal of Parallel and Distributed Computing*, 17(1–2):4–27, /1993.

18. L. Golubchik and R. R. Muntz. Fault Tolerance Issues in Data Declustering for Parallel Database Systems. *Data Engineering Bulletin*, 17(3):14–28, 1994.

19. J. Gray and G. Graefe. The 5 Minute Rule, Ten Years Later. In *SIGMOD Record*, volume 26, 1997.

20. J. Gray, P. Helland, P. O'Neil, and D. Shasha. The Dangers of Replication and a Solution. In *Proceedings of ACM SIGMOD*, pages 173–182, 1996.

21. J. Gray, B. Horst, and M. Walker. Parity Striping of Disk Arrays: Low Cost Reliable Storage with Acceptable Throughput. In *Proceedings of the VLDB Conference*, pages 152–162, September 1990.

22. J. Gray and A. Reuter. *Transaction Processing : Concepts and Techniques*. Morgan Kaufmann, 1992.

23. H. Hsiao and D. DeWitt. Chained Declustering: A New Availability Strategy for Multiprocessor Database Machines. In *Proceedings of 6th International Data Engineering Conference*, pages 456–465, 1990.

24. M. K. Lakhamraju, R. Rastogi, S. Seshadri, and S. Sudarshan. On-Line Reorganization in Object Databases. In *Proceedings of ACM SIGMOD*, pages 58–69, 2000.

25. E. K. Lee and C. A. Thekkath. Petal: Distributed Virtual Disks. In *Proceedings of the Seventh International Conference on Architectural Support for Programming Languages and Operating Systems*, pages 84–92, Cambridge, MA, 1996.

26. M. L. Lee, M. Kitsuregawa, B. C. Ooi, K. Tan, and A. Mondal. Towards Self-tuning Data Placement in Parallel Database Systems. In *Proceedings of ACM SIGMOD*, pages 225–236, 2000.

27. D. Petrou, K. Amiri, G. Ganger, and G. Gibson. Easing the Management of Data-Parallel Systems via Adaptation. In *Proceedings of the 9th ACM SIGOPS European Workshop*, September 2000.

28. P. Scheuermann, G. Weikum, and P. Zabback. "Disk Cooling" in Parallel Disk Systems. *Data Engineering Bulletin*, 17(3):29–40, 1994.

29. P. Scheuermann, G. Weikum, and P. Zabbak. Data Partitioning and Load Balancing in Parallel Disk Systems. *VLDB Journal*, 7(1), 1998.

30. D. P. Siewiorek and R. S. Swarz. *The Theory and Practice of Reliable System Design*. Digital Press, 1982.

31. A. Veitch, E. Riedel, S. Towers, and J. Wilkes. Towards Global Storage Management and Data Placement. Technical Report HPL-SSP-2001-1, Hewlett Packard Laboratories, March 2001.

32. R. Vingralek, Y. Breitbart, and G. Weikum. Snowball: Scalable Storage on Networks of Workstations with Balanced Load. *Distributed and Parallel Databases*, 6(2):117–156, 1998.

33. G. Weikum, C. Hasse, A. Moenkeberg, and P. Zabback. The COMFORT Automatic Tuning Project, Invited Project Review. *Information Systems*, 19(5):381–432, 1994.

34. M. Wiesmann, F. Pedone, A. Schiper, B. Kemme, and G. Alonso. Understanding Replication in Databases and Distributed Systems. In *Proceedings of 20th International Conference on Distributed Computing Systems (ICDCS'2000)*, pages 264–274, Taipei, Taiwan, R.O.C., 2000. IEEE Computer Society Technical Commitee on Distributed Processing.

35. J. Wilkes, R. Golding, C. Staelin, and T. Sullivan. The HP AutoRAID Hierarchical Storage System. In *Proceedings of the Fifteenth ACM Symposium on Operating Systems Principles*, pages 96–108, Copper Mountain, CO, 1995. ACM Press.

36. K. Wu, P. Yu, J. Chung, and J. Teng. A Performance Study of Workfile Disk Management for Concurrent Mergesorts in a Multiprocessor Database System. In *Proceedings of the VLDB Conference*, pages 100–110, September 1995.

37. X. Yu, B. Gum, Y. Chen, R. Wang, K. Li, A. Krishnamurthy, and T. Anderson. Trading Capacity for Performance in a Disk Array. In *Symposium on Operating Systems Design and Implementation*, October 2000.

38. R. Zimmermann and S. Ghandeharizadeh. HERA: Heterogeneous Extension of RAID. In *In Proceedings of the International Conference on Parallel and Distributed Processing Techniques and Applications (PDPTA 2000)*, June 2000.

# Towards Multimedia Fragmentation

Samir Saad, Joe Tekli, Richard Chbeir, and Kokou Yetongnon

LE2I Laboratory UMR-CNRS, University of Bourgogne
21078 Dijon Cedex, France
{samir.saad, joe.tekli}@khali.u-bourgogne.fr
{richard.chbeir, kokou.yetongnon}@u-bourgogne.fr

**Abstract.** Database fragmentation is a process for reducing irrelevant data accesses by grouping data frequently accessed together in dedicated segments. In this paper, we address multimedia database fragmentation by extending existing fragmentation algorithms to take into account key characteristics of multimedia objects. We particularly discuss multimedia primary horizontal fragmentation and provide a partitioning strategy based on low-level multimedia features. Our approach particularly emphasizes the importance of multimedia predicates implications in optimizing multimedia fragments. To validate our approach, we have implemented a prototype computing multimedia predicates implications. Experimental results are satisfactory.

**Keywords:** Multimedia fragmentation, Range and KNN operators, predicates implication, objects classification.

## 1 Introduction

Since the last two decades, multimedia data are of key importance in many application areas such as medicine, surveillance, cartography, meteorology, security, visual data communications, etc. Hence, the need for systems that can catalog, store, and efficiently retrieve relevant distributed multimedia data is becoming very high. Initially, research in multimedia management has been handled separately by database management and computer vision communities. As a result, different types of features have been used, in the literature, for multimedia data management. Low-level features such as color, texture, shape, layout, etc. are used by the computer vision research community, while meta-data and semantic based features are widely used by the database management community to describe data context and semantics. Emerging applications in distributed environments create an increasing demand on the performance of multimedia systems, requiring new data partitioning techniques to achieve high resource utilization and increased concurrency and parallelism. Several continuing studies are aimed at building distributed multimedia databases management systems MMDBMS [20]. Nevertheless, most existing systems lack a formal framework to adequately provide full-fledge multimedia operations.

Traditionally, partitioning techniques are used in distributed system design to reduce accesses to irrelevant data. Three main fragmentation techniques have been defined for relational databases: horizontal fragmentation HF, vertical fragmentation

Y. Manolopoulos, J. Pokorný, and T. Sellis (Eds.): ADBIS 2006, LNCS 4152, pp. 415–429, 2006.

(VF), and hybrid or mixed fragmentation (MF). These techniques have been recently extended for object oriented databases. However, multimedia data fragmentation issues haven't been addressed in current systems.

Multimedia fragmentation is a relatively complicated issue owing to the complexity of the multimedia data itself; different multimedia data types (video, audio, image and/or text), frequently used with various formats, as well as the intricacy of the description of physical and/or semantic multimedia data. In this paper, we address primary horizontal fragmentation in distributed multimedia databases and analyze the impact of multimedia operators and predicates. We particularly address multimedia predicates implication required in current fragmentation algorithms such as Make_Partition and Com_Min [2, 11, 12]. We also present our prototype with corresponding experimental results conducted to validate our approach.

The remainder of this paper is organized as follows. Section 2 briefly reviews background in DB fragmentation. Section 3 presents a motivation example. Section 4 details our multimedia fragmentation process. Section 5 presents our prototype and experimental tests. Finally, section 6 concludes and draws future directions.

## 2  Background

Fragmentation techniques for distributed DB systems aim to achieve high resource utilization and performance [5]. This is addressed by removing irrelevant data accessed by applications and by reducing data exchange among sites [1]. In this section, we briefly present traditional database fragmentation approaches, depicting the evolution from relational to object oriented DBMS, and focus on horizontal fragmentation algorithms. In essence, there are three fundamental fragmentation strategies: Horizontal Fragmentation (HF), Vertical Fragmentation (VF) and Mixed Fragmentation (MF).

HF underlines the partitioning of an entity/class in segments of tuples/objects verifying certain criteria. The generated horizontal fragments have the same structure as the original entity/class. Horizontal fragmentation is generally categorized in two types: Primary HF and Derived HF. PHF is the partitioning of an entity based on its attributes' values [12]. DHF denotes the partitioning of an entity (called member) based on links with other entities (called owners) [12]. In other words, it is the partitioning of an entity/class in terms of the PHF of another entity/class [1] taking into consideration their inner-links.

VF breaks down the logical structure of an entity/class by distributing its attributes/methods over vertical fragments, which would contain the same tuples/ objects with different attributes [1]. The unique tuple/object identifier (id) is kept in all vertical fragments [7] so that the DBMS can link related segments.

MF is a hybrid partitioning technique where horizontal and vertical fragmentations are simultaneously applied on an entity/class [11].

To the best of our knowledge, two main algorithms for the PHF of relational DBMS are provided in the literature: *Com_Min* developed by Oszu and Valduriez [12] and *Make_Partition* Graphical Algorithm developed by Navathe *et al.* [10] (used essentially for vertical fragmentation). The *Com_Min* algorithm generates, from a set of simple predicates applied to a certain entity, a complete and minimal set of predicates used to determine the minterm fragments corresponding to that entity. A minterm is a conjunction of simple predicates [2] associated to a fragment. *Make_Partition* generates minterm fragments by grouping predicates having high affinity towards one another. The number of minterm fragments generated by *Make_Partition* is relatively smaller than the number of *Com_Min* minterm fragments [15] (the number of minterm fragments generated by *Com-Min* being exponential to the number of simple predicates considered).

Similarly, there are two main algorithms for the PHF of object oriented DBMS: one developed by Ezeife and Barker [6] using Com_Min [12], and the other developed by Bellatreche *et al.* [2] on the basis of Make_Partition [10]. The use of Com_Min or Make_Partition is the major difference between them.

## 3  Motivation

In order to use current partitioning approaches, widely employed in traditional databases, for fragmenting multimedia data, several issues should be studied and extended. On one hand, to achieve fragmentation, current algorithms require as an input parameter [6] the database conceptual schema (CS). This requirement is not always fulfilled in some multimedia databases due to the unstructured (or semi-structured) and complex nature of multimedia data. On the other hand, multimedia queries contain new operators handling low-level and semantic features. These new operators should be considered when studying predicates and particularly predicate implications. For example, let us consider the following predicates used to search for photos similar to given photos in an Employee multimedia database as shown below.

| Predicate | P1 | P2 | P3 | P4 |
|---|---|---|---|---|
| Attribute | *Emp_photo* | *Emp_photo* | *Emp_photo* | *Emp_photo* |
| Operator[1] | *Range_Sim$_{\varepsilon 1}$* | *Range_Sim$_{\varepsilon 2}$* | *Range_Sim$_{\varepsilon 3}$* | *KNN* |
| Value | | | | |
| Parameter | $\varepsilon_2 > \varepsilon_1$ | $\varepsilon_2 > \varepsilon_1$ | $\varepsilon_3 > \varepsilon_1$ | K=3 |

In current approaches, the following predicates are considered different and analyzed separately:

- $P_1$ and $P_2$: two range queries with different parameters (radius)
- $P_1$ and $P_3$: two range queries with different parameters and values
- $P_3$ and $P_4$: two different operators

However, in multimedia applications, $P_1$ would also retrieve objects belonging to results of queries based on $P_2$ and $P_3$. Likewise, $P_4$ may return a subset of $P_3$'s results. Thus, we can say that $P_2$ and $P_3$ infer $P_1$ (denoted by $P_1 \rightarrow P_2, P_3$) and consider only the results returned by $P_2 / P_3$, thus eliminating $P_1$.

It is important to notice that ignoring such implications between predicates can lead, in multimedia applications, to higher computation costs when creating

---

[1] More details about multimedia operators will be given later.

fragments, bigger fragments which is very restrictive for multimedia storage, migration, and retrieval, as well as data duplication on several sites. In [2, 11], the authors have only highlighted the implication issue importance, but have not well detailed nor identified the various kinds of implications. These issues will be tackled in following paragraphs.

# 4  Multimedia Primary Horizontal Fragmentation

In this section, we start by introducing some concepts and definitions necessary to tackle multimedia primary horizontal fragmentation. We develop subsequently additional steps to be integrated in current approaches, allowing adequate multimedia data fragmentation processing.

## 4.1  Definitions

### 4.1.1  Multimedia Object
A multimedia object is described by a set of attributes, related to a set of meta-data. It can be formally depicted as a set of attribute ($a_i$) and value ($v_i$) doublets:

O $\{(a_1, v_1); (a_2, v_2), \ldots , (a_n, v_n)\}$. Multimedia attributes and values can be *simple* (like color = "red"), *complex* (color histogram, texture, shape, etc.) or the raw data (BLOB files) of multimedia objects.

### 4.1.2  Multimedia Type
A multimedia type allocates a set of attributes used to describe multimedia objects corresponding to that type: $T(a_1, a_2, a_3, \ldots , a_n)$. We consider that two objects, described by the same attributes, are of the same type.

### 4.1.3  Multimedia Query
A multimedia query is written as follows [2, 9]:
$q = \{(Target\ clause),\ (Range\ clause),\ (Qualification\ clause)\}$,   where:

- **Target clause**: contains multimedia attributes returned by the query
- **Range clause**: gathers the entities (tables/lasses) accessed by the query, to which belong *target clause* and *qualification clause* attributes
- **Qualification clause**: is the query restriction condition, a Boolean combination of predicates, linked by logical connectives $\land, \lor, \neg$

### 4.1.4  Multimedia Operators and Predicates
As mentioned before, multimedia information introduces new types of data and new operators and predicates. In the following, we explain multimedia operators and predicates related to low-level features. Note that semantic similarity operators are out of this paper's scope and will be detailed in future studies.

*4.1.4.1  Multimedia Operators.* In multimedia databases, objects are widely described using vector spaces with numeric attributes, such as shape or color descriptors. Thus, in order to retrieve multimedia data, dedicated similarity queries are used, involving *range queries* and/or *k-nearest neighborhood* operators. Formal definitions are given thereafter.

*4.1.4.1.1   Multimedia Range Query Operator.* A range query operator $\bar{\theta}$ returns the set of objects $V_j$ of an object value $V_i$ located within a certain range $\varepsilon$ from $V_i$ using a distance function $D$ (cfr. *Figure 1*). It can be formally written as:

$$\text{Range Query}(V_i, \bar{\theta}, \varepsilon) = N_{\bar{\theta}}^{\varepsilon}(V_i) = \{V_j / D(V_i, V_j) \le \varepsilon / \varepsilon \in \square \tag{1}$$

The function $D$ can be the classic Euclidean distance, a weighted Euclidean distance, a quadratic form distance, etc.

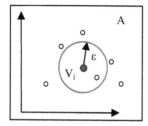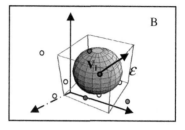

**Fig. 1.** Visualizations of a range query operator $\bar{\theta}$

A range query operator $\bar{\theta}$ has the following interesting properties, useful for optimizing the computation process:

- $N_{\bar{\theta}}^{\varepsilon_i}(V_i) \subseteq N_{\bar{\theta}}^{\varepsilon_j}(V_l)$ *if* $\varepsilon_i \le \varepsilon_j$
- *if* $N_{\bar{\theta}}^{\varepsilon_i}(V_i) \subseteq N_{\bar{\theta}}^{\varepsilon_j}(V_j)$ *and* $N_{\bar{\theta}}^{\varepsilon_j}(V_j) \subseteq N_{\bar{\theta}}^{\varepsilon_i}(V_l) \rightarrow N_{\bar{\theta}}^{\varepsilon_i}(V_i) \subseteq N_{\bar{\theta}}^{\varepsilon_i}(V_l) \ \forall \varepsilon_i, \varepsilon_j, \varepsilon_1$

*4.1.4.1.2   Multimedia KNN Operator.* A K-Nearest Neighborhood (KNN) operator $\bar{\theta}$ returns the set of K neighbors of an object value $V_i$ located into either a ranged or unlimited domain space, using a distance $D$ [3, 20]. It could be formally written as follows:

$$KNN(V_i, \bar{\theta}, k)_\varepsilon = N_{\bar{\theta}}^k(V_i)_\varepsilon = \left\{ V_{j=1..k} / D(V_i, V_j) \le D(V_i, V) \right\}$$
$$\forall \ V \notin N_{\bar{\theta}}^k(V_i), \text{ where } k \in \square \text{ and } Max(D(V_i, V)) \le \varepsilon / \varepsilon \in \square^* \cup \{\bot\} \tag{2}$$

If $\varepsilon = \bot$, the domain space is unlimited

As for range query operators, a KNN operator can be observed as a visual object in function of values dimensions. *Fig. 2* shows a ranged 2D KNN operator with k=3.

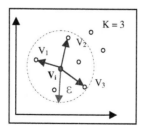

**Fig. 2.** Visualizations of a ranged 2D KNN operator $\vec{\theta}$

A KNN operator $\vec{\theta}$ has the following properties:

- $N_{\vec{\theta}}^{k_i}(V_i) \subseteq N_{\vec{\theta}}^{k_j}(V_i)$ *if* $k_i \leq k_j$
- *if* $N_{\vec{\theta}}^{k_i}(V_i) \subseteq N_{\vec{\theta}}^{k_j}(V_j)$ *and* $N_{\vec{\theta}}^{k_j}(V_j) \subseteq N_{\vec{\theta}}^{k_l}(V_l)$ $\rightarrow N_{\vec{\theta}}^{k_i}(V_i) \subseteq N_{\vec{\theta}}^{k_l}(V_l)$ $\forall k_i, k_j, k_l$

*4.1.4.2 Multimedia Predicates.* A multimedia predicate $\hat{P}$ is defined as follows:
$$\hat{P}_i = (A_i \; \theta_m \; V_i)$$
Where:
- $A_i$ is a multimedia attribute or object
- $V_i$ is a value in the domain of $A_i$ or a multimedia object

$\theta_m = \theta_t \cup \{\bar{\theta}, \vec{\theta}\}$ *where* $\theta_t$ *is* a traditional operator such as a comparison

operator $(=, <, \leq, >, \geq, \neq)$, or a set operator (contained-in, set-equality, ...), etc.

## 4.2 Steps for Multimedia Data Primary Horizontal Fragmentation

Before applying current fragmentation approaches, several steps should be executed in order to support and provide relevant multimedia data fragmentation. We suggest introducing the following pre-processing phase:

**Multimedia_fragmentation_pre-processing ()**

```
    Begin
                Multimedia_Types_Classification()          // detailed in section 4.2.1
                For each multimedia Type
                        Predicates_Grouping()              // detailed in section 4.2.2
                        Multimedia_Predicates_implication()  // detailed in section 4.2.3
                EndFor
    End
```

### 4.2.1  Classification of Multimedia Objects

By applying existing horizontal fragmentation algorithms to a multimedia database, we attain non consistent horizontal fragmentation criteria (minterms). Suppose that *Camera Position*, *Audio Frequency* and *Dominant Color* are three multimedia attributes describing Video, Audio and Image objects respectively. The following Boolean expression: *CameraPosition = "North West"*$\land$ *AudioFrequency = "6 KHz"* $\land$ *DominantColor = ((10; 10; 10), RGB)* is a non consistent minterm, specifying criteria on "heterogeneous" attributes describing multimedia objects of different types, therefore producing an empty horizontal fragment.

In order to attain coherent minterms, we need to gather related objects together. As mentioned before, we assume that multimedia objects having the same attributes are considered of the same type. The algorithm provided below is used for classifying objects, according to their corresponding types.

**Multimedia_Types_Classification ()**

```
        Input : MM        // multimedia objects
        Output : T_M      //set of multimedia types corresponding to objects in MM

        Begin
                For each Mo_i ∈ MM
                        If Mo_i.A ≠ all T_i.A              // Adding a new type corresponding to the object Mo_i
```

```
                New T_{n+1} / T_{n+1}.A = Mo_i.A      // if the type isn't considered yet in MM
                T_{n+1} = T_{n+1} U Mo
          Else
                T_i = T_i U Mo_i / Mo_i.A = T_i.A     // Adding the object Mo_i to its corresponding type
          Endif                                        // if the type is already identified
      Endfor
End
```

## 4.2.2 Predicate Grouping

It is also important to gather predicates into groups on the basis of operators. Using the algorithm below, two predicate groups are identified: multimedia and traditional. This separation will allow defining appropriate methods for multimedia implication:

$$P_i \xrightarrow{\theta_m} P_j \Leftrightarrow \begin{bmatrix} \overset{\Box}{P_i} \xrightarrow{\theta} \overset{\Box}{P_j} \\ P_i \xrightarrow{\theta_t} P_j \end{bmatrix} \qquad \xrightarrow{\theta} \quad \text{denotes a multimedia similarity implication}$$

$$\xrightarrow{\theta_t} \quad \text{denotes a traditional implication}$$

Recall that traditional implication is out of this paper's scope.

```
Predicates_grouping ()

      Input:  Q           //set of all user queries
              T_i         //a multimedia type
      Output:  P_j^i      //a query predicate defined on type T

               Ṗ_i        //set of multimedia predicates applied on T

               P_i        //set of traditional predicates applied on T

      Begin
              For each query Q_i ∈ Q

                    For each  P_j^i ∈ Q_i

                          If ( P_j^i ∈ P̂) then

                                    Ṗ_i  =  Ṗ_i  ∪ P_j^i
                          Else
                                    P_i  =  P_i  ∪ P_j^i
                          Endif
                    EndFor
              EndFor
      End
```

## 4.2.3 Multimedia Predicates Implication

Finding inference or implication between predicates is crucial to cutback the number of predicates involved in the fragmentation process [4, 11] (a large number of unnecessary fragments would notionally achieve low system performance). When a predicate $P_i$ implies a predicate $P_j$ (denoted by $P_i \rightarrow P_j$), $P_i$ can be removed from the minterm fragment to which it belongs and replaced by $P_j$. Predicate implication is taken into consideration in traditional algorithms, mainly in Com_Min [12] and Make_Partition algorithms [10]. In the following, we detail the rules that can be used to determine implication between low-level feature-based predicates, by using both: range query and KNN methods.

*4.2.3.1   Range Query Predicates Implication.* Two range query predicates $\overline{P_i}$ and $\overline{P_j}$ are in implication if:

$$\overline{P_j} \to \overline{P_i} \Leftrightarrow \left\{ 0 \leq D(V_i, V_j) \leq \varepsilon_i - \varepsilon_j \right\}$$

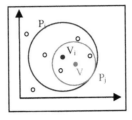

**Fig. 3.** 2D Range Query Predicates Implication

However, if $\varepsilon_i = \varepsilon_j$ and $D(V_i, V_j) \neq 0$ or if $\varepsilon_i - \varepsilon_j < D(V_i, V_j) \leq \varepsilon_i + \varepsilon_j$, then there is an intersection between $\overline{P_i}$ and $\overline{P_j}$. Therefore, $\overline{P_i}$ and $\overline{P_j}$ cannot be associated via implication.

*4.2.3.2   KNN Predicates Implication.* The KNN implications for ranged or unlimited domain space are identical and can only be computed as follows:

$$\overrightarrow{P_j} \to \overrightarrow{P_i} \Leftrightarrow \left\{ V_i = V_j \text{ and } k_i \geq k_j \right\}$$

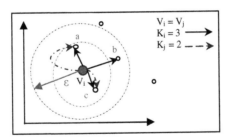

**Fig. 4.** KNN Predicates implication with identical values

Note that two KNN predicates $\overrightarrow{P_i}$ and $\overrightarrow{P_j}$ identified within two limited ranges $\varepsilon_i$ and $\varepsilon_j$ are not in implication (like for range queries) if:

$$\left\{ 0 < D(V_i, V_j) \leq \varepsilon_i - \varepsilon_j \text{ where } \varepsilon_i \text{ and } \varepsilon_j \in [0,1] \right\}$$

*4.2.3.3   Multimedia Predicates Implication.* Using the same reasoning, we consider that two multimedia predicates $\overline{P_i}$ and $\overline{P_j}$ are in implication if:

$$\overline{P}_j \to \overline{P}_i \Leftrightarrow \begin{cases} 0 \le D(V_i, V_j) \le \varepsilon_i - \varepsilon_j \text{ and } \left( \overline{P}_i \vee \overline{P}_j \in \{\overline{P}\} \text{ and } (\vec{\varepsilon} < \overline{\varepsilon}) \right) \\ OR \\ V_i = V_j \text{ and } k_i \ge k_j \end{cases}$$

The first condition allows computing the implication between either two range query predicates or a range query predicate and a ranged KNN predicate. $\vec{\varepsilon}$ is used to designate the range of KNN predicate, and $\overline{\varepsilon}$ to designate the radius of the range predicate. The second condition highlights KNN predicates implication.

The following algorithm generates sets of multimedia predicate implications, $IS_i$, corresponding to each multimedia type $T_i$. Note that every set element consists of a doublet of predicates $(P_i, P_j)$, meaning that $P_i$ implies $P_j$.

**Multimedia_Predicates_Implication ()**

**Input:**      $\overline{P}_i$          //set of M multimedia predicates applied on a multimedia type T

**Output:**    $IS_i$          //set of multimedia predicates implications applied on a type $T_i$

**Variable:**   $P_j^i$          //a query predicate defined on type T

**Begin**

    For each $P_j^i \in \overline{P}_i$

        If j≤M-1 then

            For each $P_{j+1}^i \in \overline{P}_i$

                If $(A_j = A_{j+1})$ then          //same attribute

                    If( $P_j^i$.operator $= \overline{\theta}$ and( $P_{j+1}^i$.operator $= \overline{\theta}$ or $P_{j+1}^i$.operator $= \vec{\theta}$ )) then

                        If ($\varepsilon_j > \varepsilon_{j+1}$ ) then          // $R_j R_{j+1}$ , $R_j K_{j+1}$

                            If $0 \le D(V_j, V_{j+1}) \le \varepsilon_j - \varepsilon_{j+1}$ then          // $P_{j+1}^i \to P_j^i$

                              $IS_i = IS_i \cup (P_{j+1}^i, P_j^i)$

                          Endif

                        Elseif ($\varepsilon_{j+1} > \varepsilon_j$ and $P_{j+1}^i$.operator $= \overline{\theta}$ ) then          // $R_j R_{j+1}$

                            If $0 \le D(V_{j+1}, V_j) \le \varepsilon_{j+1} - \varepsilon_j$ then          // $P_j^i \to P_{j+1}^i$

                              $IS_i = IS_i \cup (P_j^i, P_{j+1}^i)$

                          Endif

                      Endif

                  Elseif ( $P_j^i$.operator $= \vec{\theta}$ and $P_{j+1}^i$.operator $= \vec{\theta}$ ) then          // $K_j K_{j+1}$

                    If $D(V_i, V_j) = 0$ or $V_i = V_j$ then

                      If ($k_j \ge k_{j+1}$) then

                        $IS_i = IS_i \cup (P_{j+1}^i, P_j^i)$

                      Elseif ($k_{j+1} \ge k_j$) then

                        $IS_i = IS_i \cup (P_j^i, P_{j+1}^i)$

                      Endif

                  Endif

                Elseif( $P_j^i$.operator $= \vec{\theta}$ and $P_{j+1}^i$.operator $= \overline{\theta}$ ) then          // $K_j R_{j+1}$

                  If ($\varepsilon_{j+1} > \varepsilon_j$) then

                      If $0 \le D(V_{j+1}, V_j) \le \varepsilon_{j+1} - \varepsilon_j$ then          // $P_j^i \to P_{j+1}^i$

                        $IS_i = IS_i \cup (P_j^i, P_{j+1}^i)$

                    Endif

```
                        Endif
                    Endif
                Endfor
            Endif
        Endfor
        IS_i = Optimize(IS_i )
```

**End**

**Optimize ( IS_i)**

  **Input:** ISi                                  // set of multimedia predicates implications applied on a type T

  **Begin**
        For each  $( P_j^i, P_k^i ) \in$  IS_i

                For each  $( P_k^i, P_l^i ) \in$  IS

                    If  $( P_j^i \rightarrow P_k^i$ and $P_k^i \rightarrow P_l^i )$  then

                            $IS_i = IS_i \cup ( P_j^i, P_l^i )$

                    Endif
                EndFor
        EndFor
  **End**

### 4.2.4  Algorithm Complexity

The complexity calculations are carried out below on the basis of the worst case analysis. Suppose $n_f$ represents the largest number of possible fragments, $n_o$ represents the largest number of multimedia objects in a type or a fragment, $n_q$ the largest number of user queries, $n_t$ the largest number of types, $n_p$ the largest number of multimedia predicates, $n_i$ the largest cardinality of the sets $IS_i$, $n_v$ the largest feature vector dimension involved. Our fragmentation pre-processing algorithm is of time complexity of $O(n_t \times (n_o + n_q \times n_p + n_v \times n_p^2 + n_i^2) )$, which simplifies to $O(n_t \times (n_v \times n_p^2))$. Note that the polynomial (quadratic) nature of our features implication computation algorithm $(O(n_v \times n_p^2))$ dominates the complexity formulae and is experimentally demonstrated in our simulation prototype.

### 4.2.5  Computation Example

In the following, multimedia predicates (range query and KNN) will be illustrated in the same manner for the sake of simplicity:

$\overline{P} = A$ Similar($\varepsilon$) V    and    $\vec{P} = A$ Similar(k, $\varepsilon$) V    where:

  –   *A* is a multimedia attribute. In the present example, *A* stands for *Dominant Color* : *DC*
  –   *Similar* represents $\overline{\theta}$, the range similarity operator, when the number between brackets $\varepsilon$ denotes a real value such as $0.0 \leq \varepsilon \leq 1.0$ ; $\varepsilon$ designating the similarity range
  –   *Similar* stands for $\vec{\theta}$, the KNN operator, when the number between brackets k denotes an integer value ; k representing the number of neighboring objects to be returned by the KNN predicate within a range $\varepsilon$

*Figure 5* shows three images a, b and c characterized by their feature vector values $V_a$, $V_b$ and $V_c$ respectively ; V designating, for each image, its *Dominant Color* feature in RGB color space (vector dimension = 3).

We also consider the following two range query predicates:

  –   **P_1:** DC Similar($\varepsilon_1$) $V_1$ and **P_2:** DC Similar($\varepsilon_2$) $V_2$ (*DC: Dominant Color* ) where $V_1 = (22; 22; 22)$, $V_2 = (90; 10; 10)$, $\varepsilon_1 = 0.6$, and $\varepsilon_2 = 0.2$

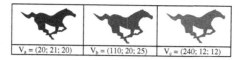

| $V_a = (20; 21; 20)$ | $V_b = (110; 20; 25)$ | $V_c = (240; 12; 12)$ |
|---|---|---|

**Fig. 5.** Sample images

Please note that in our similarity computations, we used the following weighted Euclidean distance function:

$$Dist(X,Y) = \frac{\sqrt{\sum_{i=1}^{N}(x_i - y_i)^2}}{\sum_{i=1}^{N}(x_i + y_i)} \in [0,1] \qquad \begin{array}{l} N = \text{Max (dim(X), dim(Y)), dim(X)} \\ \text{and dim(Y) being the dimensions} \\ \text{of vectors X and Y respectively.} \end{array}$$

Following our multimedia implication computation rules, predicate $p_2$ implies predicate $p_1$ $(0 \le Dist(V_1, V_2) \le \varepsilon_1 - \varepsilon_2)$ where:

–   $Dist(V_1, V_2) = ( (22-90)^2 + (22-10)^2 + (22-10)^2 )^{1/2}$ / $(22 +90 + 22 + 10 + 22 + 10) = 0.397$
–   and $\varepsilon_1 - \varepsilon_2 = 0.6 - 0.2 = 0.4$

A query utilizing predicate $P_1$ would return still regions a and b

–   $Dist(V_1, V_a) = 0.024$ ($< \varepsilon_1$, returned object)
–   $Dist(V_1, V_b) = 0.399$ ($< \varepsilon_1$, returned object)
–   $Dist(V_1, V_c) = 0.662$ ($> \varepsilon_1$)

Whereas a query invoking predicate $P_2$ would return still region b

–   $Dist(V_2, V_a) = 0.417$ ($> \varepsilon_2$)
–   $Dist(V_2, V_b) = 0.102$ ($< \varepsilon_2$, returned object)
–   $Dist(V_2, V_c) = 0.401$ ($> \varepsilon_2$)

One can clearly realize that the set of multimedia objects returned by $P_1$ ({a, b}) includes those returned by of $P_2$ ({b}). If taken into account, such implications would reduce fragment creation computation cost, fragment size and multimedia data duplication on multiple sites.

# 5   Prototype

To validate our approach, we have implemented a C# prototype called "Multimedia Implication Identifier" encompassing:

*   A relational database, storing multimedia objects via Oracle 9i DBMS, described following the multimedia meta-model M² (MPEG-7 compatible) developed by Chalhoub *et al.* in [4].
*   A set of interfaces allowing users to formulate simple and complex multimedia queries, providing the ability to select multimedia information.
*   Containers for storing user queries, enabling, via specific processes, the computation of query access frequencies which are basically used in the predicate affinity calculations.
*   Specific containers undertaking the storage of predicates, utilized by dedicated procedures to calculate predicate implications.

The prototype accepts, as input, multimedia queries. Automatic processes subsequently calculate query access frequencies, identify corresponding predicates, and compute for each multimedia type (represented by a table) its Predicate Usage

Matrix (PUM)[1] and its Predicate Affinity Matrix (PAM)[2] used to measure the affinity between predicates, the PAM taking into account our predicate implication steps.

Note that we chose to present multimedia implications in PAM matrixes, proposed by [15, 4], for the sake of clearness (PAMs being suitable structures for displaying predicate implications). Nevertheless, our algorithm is generic in the sense that it could be equally used with other primary horizontal fragmentation approaches, Com_Min [16] in particular.

## 5.1 Simulation Example

Among the various tests that were conducted, we present a simple simulation example comparing predicate affinities (PAM) obtained with and without the inclusion of our multimedia physical implication rules. In the following example, multimedia type "Still Region", designating motionless images, is selected for PUM and PAM calculations. Let $Q = \{q_{i = 0 \text{ to } 5}\}$ be a set of user queries defined on "Still Region" Type. Recall that we represent queries following paragraph 4.1.3.

$q_0$: { (MO); (StillRegion); (ObNature = "vehicule" $\wedge$
    DC Similar(0.3) ((12; 10; 13), (14; 15; 16), (20; 20; 20))) }
$q_1$: { (MO); (StillRegion); (ObNature = "vehicule" $\wedge$ ObColor = "red" $\wedge$
    DC Similar(0.2) ((12; 10; 13), (14; 15; 16), (20; 20; 20))) }
$q_2$: { (MO); (StillRegion); (ObNature = "truck" $\wedge$  ObColor = "red" $\wedge$
    DC Similar(0.1) ((9; 8; 7), (7; 8; 7), (10; 11; 10))) }
$q_3$: { (MO); (StillRegion); (ObNature = "vehicule" $\wedge$
    DC Similar(3) ((12; 10; 13), (14; 15; 16), (20; 20; 20))) }
$q_4$: { (MO); (StillRegion); (ObNature = "vehicule" $\wedge$  ObColor = "red" $\wedge$
    DC Similar(1) ((12; 10; 13), (14; 15; 16), (20; 20; 20))) }
$q_5$: { (MO); (StillRegion); (ObNature = "truck" $\wedge$    ObColor = "red" $\wedge$
    DC Similar(1) ((9; 8; 7), (7; 8; 7), (10; 11; 10))) }

Let $P = \{P_{i = 0 \text{ to } 8}\}$ be the set of predicates used by Q.

$P_0$: ObNature = "vehicule"
$P_1$: DC Similar(0.3) ((12; 10; 13), (14; 15; 16), (20; 20; 20))
$P_2$: ObColor = "red"
$P_3$: DC Similar(0.2) ((12; 10; 13), (14; 15; 16), (20; 20; 20))
$P_4$: ObNature = "truck"
$P_5$: DC Similar(0.1) ((9; 8; 7), (7; 8; 7), (10; 11; 10))
$P_6$: DC Similar(3) ((12; 10; 13), (14; 15; 16), (20; 20; 20))
$P_7$: DC Similar(1) ((12; 10; 13), (14; 15; 16), (20; 20; 20))
$P_8$: DC Similar(1) ((9; 8; 7), (7; 8; 7), (10; 11; 10))

P contains traditional predicates ($P_0$, $P_2$) as well as multimedia predicates ($P_1$, $P_3$, $P_4$, $P_5$, $P_6$, $P_7$, $P_8$). Note $P_1$, $P_3$ and $P_5$ are range query predicates (the number between brackets being a real value – similarity range ε), while $P_6$, $P_7$ and $P_8$ are KNN predicates (the number between brackets being an integer value – number of objects k to be returned by the predicate). Also note that *DC* represents a composite *Dominant*

---

[1] It contains the predicates used by each query as well as query access frequencies and is subsequently used as input to the PHF process adopted by [11, 2].

[2] Following [15, 4], the PAM is a square and symmetric matrix where each value aff($P_i$, $P_j$) can be numerical or non numerical. Numerical affinity represents the sum of the frequencies of queries which access simultaneously $P_i$ and $P_j$. Non numerical affinity underlines the implication relation between predicates $P_i$ and $P_j$.

*Color* feature vector stating the three consecutive dominant colors in an image, in RGB color space. For example, $DC_1$ of predicate $p_1$ underlines dominant colors C(12; 10; 13), C'(14; 15; 16) and C''(20; 20; 20).

By reading the updated PAM, one can clearly point out the multimedia implication rules defined in the paper:

- Predicate $P_3$ ($\varepsilon_3 = 0.2$, $V_3 = ((12; 10; 13), (14; 15; 16), (20; 20; 20)))$ implies $P_1$ ($\varepsilon_1 = 0.3$, $V_1 = ((12; 10; 13), (14; 15; 16), (20; 20; 20)))$ having:
    - $V_1 = V_3$ and $\varepsilon_1 > \varepsilon_3$
- Predicate $P_5$ ($\varepsilon_5 = 0.1$ "max", $V_5 = ((9; 8; 7), (7; 8; 7), (10; 11; 10)))$ implies    $P_1$ ($\varepsilon_1 = 0.3$, $V_1 = ((12; 10; 13), (14; 15; 16), (20; 20; 20)))$ having:
    - $\varepsilon_1 > \varepsilon_5$, $dist(V_1, V_5) \leq \varepsilon_1 - \varepsilon_5$
- No implication can be identified between predicates $P_3$ and $P_5$ having:
    - $dist(V_3, V_5) > \varepsilon_3 - \varepsilon_5$ (similarity circle intersection/exclusion)
- Predicate $P_7$ ($k_7 = 1$, $V_7 = ((12; 10; 13), (14; 15; 16), (20; 20; 20)))$ implies predicate $P_6$ ($k_6 = 3$, $V_6 = ((12; 10; 13), (14; 15; 16), (20; 20; 20)))$ having:
    - $V_6 = V_7$ and $k_6 > k_7$
- No implication can be identified between $P_6$ (or $P_7$) and $P_8$, having:
    - $V_8 \neq V_6$ (correspondingly $V_7$)

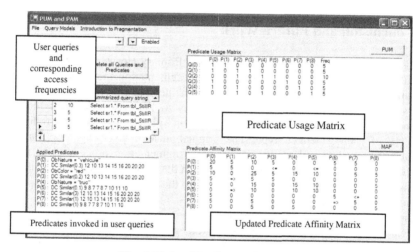

**Fig. 6.** Updated Predicate Affinity Matrix

Disregarding our multimedia implication rules would yield, in the present example, a PAM with only numerical affinities.

The PUM and uPAM make up the inputs to the NHP primary horizontal partitioning algorithm [11, 2], not being implemented yet in our prototype.

## 5.2  Timing Analysis

We have shown that the complexity of our physical similarity implication simplifies to $O(n_v \times n_p^2)$. We verified the formula experimentally, the timing results being presented in *Fig. 7*.

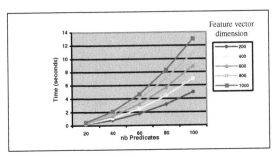

**Fig. 7.** Timing results

The experiment was carried out on a Pentium 4 PC (2.8 Ghz CPU, 798 Mhz bus, 512 MB RAM). One can see that the time to compute similarity implications grows in a polynomial (quadratic) fashion with the number of predicates involved. Our experiments also show that feature vector dimension affects time complexity, owing to predicate distance computations (weighted Euclidian distance).

## 6   Conclusion and Future Work

In this paper, we proposed an approach for the Primary Horizontal Fragmentation of multimedia databases, by extending existing fragmentation methods. Following the definition of a multimedia type, we identified the need to classify multimedia objects corresponding to the same type, in order to achieve consistent horizontal fragmentation criteria. The "Type Fragmentation" phase could be then followed by the PHF of each generated type. The original idea of emerging new multimedia operators allowed the adaptation of existing fragmentation procedures to partition multimedia data. We concentrated our efforts on the primary horizontal fragmentation of unstructured multimedia data, emphasizing the impact of multimedia predicate implications in optimizing multimedia fragments.

Future directions include the introduction of semantic-based multimedia predicates. Our future goals also incorporate generating a multimedia conceptual schema, including the derived horizontal fragmentation process, and optimizing, if possible, the used fragmentation methods (semantic implication is yet to be developed). Likewise, multimedia vertical fragmentation and XML fragmentation will be talked in upcoming studies.

## References

1. Baiao F, Mattoso M., A Mixed Fragmentation Algorithm for Distributed Object Oriented Databases. *9th Inter. Conf. on Computing Information*, Canada, 1998
2. Belatreche L, Karlapalem K, Simonet A., Horizontal class partitioning in object-oriented databases. *8th Inter. Conf. on Database and Expert Systems Applications* (DEXA' 97), Toulouse, September 1997
3. Braunmuller B, Ester M, Kreigel H. P., Sander J., Efficiently Supporting Multiple Similarity Queries for Mining in Metric Databases. *Proc. of the 16th Inter. Conf. on Data Engineering*, p.256, 2000

4. Chalhoub G, Saad S, Chbeir R, Yetongon K., A Multimedia Meta-Database Model for Distributed Multimedia DBMS. *WSEAS*, 2004
5. Chinchwadkar G.S., Goh A., An Overview of Vertical Partitioning in Object Oriented Databases. *The Computer Journal,* Vol. 42, No. 1, 1999
6. Ezeife C.I., Barker K., A Comprehensive Approach to Horizontal Class Fragmentation in a Distributed Object Based System. *Inter. Journal of Distributed and Parallel Databases*, 1, 1995. Kluwer Academic Publishers
7. Ezeife C.I., Barker K., Distributed Object Based Design: Vertical Fragmentation of classes. *Journal of Distributed and Parallel DB Systems*, 6(4): 327-360, 1998
8. Kosch H., Distributed Multimedia Database Technologies Supported by MPEG-7 and MPEG-21, Auerbach Publications, 280 p., 2004
9. Navathe S.B, Ceri S, Wiederhold G, Dou J., Vertical Partitioning Algorithms for Database Design. *ACM Transactions on Database Systems*, 9, 680-710, 1984
10. Navathe B, RA M., Vertical Partitioning for Database Design: a Graphical Algorithm. *1989 ACM SIGMOND Conf.*, Portland, p. 440-450, 1989
11. Navathe S.B, Karlapalem K, Ra M., A Mixed Partitioning Methodology for Initial Distributed Database Design. *Journal of Computer and Software Engineering*, 3(4): 395-426, 1995
12. Ozsu M.T, Valduriez P., Principals of Distributed Database Systems. Prentice Hall, Prentice Hall, 1991
13. Gertz M, Bremer J.M., Distributed XML Repositories: To-Down Design and Transparent Query Processing. Department of CS, University of California, 2004
14. Sub C., An approach to the model-based fragmentation and relational storage of XML-documents. Grundlagen von Datenbanken 2001:98-102
15. Sub C. et al., Data Modeling and Relational Storage of xml-based Teachware. GI Jahrestatung (1) 2001:378-387
16. Grosky W. I., Managing Multimedia Information in Database Systems,  Communications of the ACM, 1997, Vol. 40, No. 12, pp. 72-80
17. Synchronized Multimedia Working Group, www.w3.org/tr/rec-smil, 02-02-2006
18. SVG Working Group: www.w3.org/tr/svg., 02-12-2006
19. MovingPictureExperts Group: http://www.chiariglione.org/mpeg/standards/mpeg-7/mpeg-7.htm, 02-27-2005
20. Bernhard Braunmuller et al., Efficiently Supporting Multiple Similarity Queries for Mining in Metric Databases, *IEEE Trans. on Knowledge and Data Engineering,* v.13 n.1, p.79-95, January 2001

# Content Is Capricious: A Case for Dynamic System Generation

Hans-Werner Sehring, Sebastian Bossung, and Joachim W. Schmidt

Software Systems Institute (STS)
Hamburg University of Science and Technology (TUHH)
{hw.sehring, sebastian.bossung, j.w.schmidt}@tuhh.de

**Abstract.** Database modeling is based on the assumption of a high regularity of its application areas, an assumption which applies to both the structure of data and the behavior of users. Content modeling, however, is less strict since it may treat one application entity substantially differently from another depending on the instance at hand, and content users may individually add descriptive or interpretive aspects depending on their knowledge and interests. Therefore, we argue that adequate content modeling has to be *open* to changes, and content management systems have to react to changes *dynamically*, thus making content management a case for dynamic system generation.

In our approach, openness and dynamics are provided through a *compiler framework* which is based on a conceptual model of the application domain. Using a *conceptual modeling language* users can openly express their views on the domain's entities. Our compiler framework dynamically generates the components of an according software system. Central to the compiler framework is the notion of generators, each generating a particular module for the intended application system. Based on the resulting *modular architecture* the generated systems allow personalized model definition and seamless model evolution.

In this paper we give details of the system modules and describe how the generators which create them are coordinated in the compiler framework.

## 1 Introduction

Most data-intensive applications serve, one way or another, as information systems (ISs) and call for some kind of persistence technology. High volumes of data and large user communities require additional functionality (query support, concurrency, recovery etc.) which nowadays comes nicely packaged as off-the-shelves database models and database technology.

Database modeling is rather strict in the sense that it is based on the assumption of a high regularity of its application areas. This assumption applies to both the structure of data and the behavior of users. Therefore, database models rest on a small set of agreed upon computational base types (numbers, strings, ...) and a few structuring mechanisms (mostly records and sets) used to design schemata shared by the entire application and its community. In an

Y. Manolopoulos, J. Pokorný, and T. Sellis (Eds.): ADBIS 2006, LNCS 4152, pp. 430–445, 2006.
© Springer-Verlag Berlin Heidelberg 2006

enterprise database, for example, the view on a company employee is defined before employee records are instantiated, and users of the database have to share the company's view.

Content modeling, however, is more capricious since it may treat each represented entity substantially differently depending on the instance at hand, and content users may individually add descriptive or interpretive aspects depending on their knowledge and interests. For example, when considering a particular piece of art, some users may be interested in the artist who created it, the material used and the prices achieved while others are more concerned about details on the period in which it was created, its meaning, etc.

Therefore, we argue that adequate content models have to be *open* to changes, and content management systems have to be *dynamic* to reflect such model changes. In other words, content management systems are seen as a case for dynamic system generation while database management system usually get away with the technically less ambitious case of generic system implementation.

ISs inherit the restrictions of fixed schemata and a uniform user community from the underlying database technology. The development of ISs usually accommodates to these restrictions: in an intensive phase of domain analysis the database schema is defined once and for all. Application logic and presentation are implemented with respect to the schema and the domain model. Because IS implementation relies heavily on certain schema information, later changes to this schema affect all parts of an IS, an aspect nearly prohibitive to any effort of dynamic system evolution or to any attempt of system personalization.

For content management systems such inflexibility cannot be tolerated. Content is viewed by users in different contexts with individual conceptual models in mind. Furthermore, users have to be able to define suitable models or adapt existing ones during the lifetime of a content management system. Therefore, model changes have to be integrated dynamically, without additional development steps which include manual intervention.

In our approach, openness and dynamics of content management systems is provided through a *compiler framework* which is based on a conceptual model of the application domain. In our *conceptual modeling language* users can openly express their views on the domain's entities, and based on such views our compiler framework dynamically generates the components of the implementing software system. Central to the compiler framework is the notion of generators, each generating a particular module for the application system and collectively implementing the intended application. Based on the resulting *modular architecture* the generated system allows personalized model definition and seamless model evolution.

In this paper we give details about the system modules as well as the generators which create them. We also describe how the generators are interconnected in the compiler framework.

The paper is organized as follows: in sec. 2 we give a brief account of conceptual modeling for content-intensive application systems and of contemporary approaches to model-based system generation. The additional support required for openness and dynamics is outlined in sec. 3. In sec. 4 we discuss our contributions to implementing open and dynamic content management systems. A detailed description of our model compiler framework is finally presented in sec. 5. The paper concludes with a summary and a short outlook on future work. Related work is discussed where appropriate.

# 2   Application System Modeling

Automatic system generation is based on abstract models—of either an application domain or of software. Such models and appropriate software generation facilities enable open dynamic content management systems.

## 2.1   Conceptual Modeling

Conceptual modeling [10,8] is the activity of providing a model of an application domain. Conceptual modeling languages provide a domain vocabulary and avoid technical details as much as possible.

Starting system development with conceptual modeling thus avoids untimely consideration of technical constraints.

A conceptual model defines a vocabulary as a foundation for users and software developers. This way software uses the domain experts' vocabulary, and users are able understand the functionality of the developed software.

## 2.2   Model-Driven Development

Research and practice in software engineering led to a thorough understanding of IS development. The insights gained are leading towards approaches which allow to derive software from specifications. To this end, models are used as (more or less) formal specifications of software systems.

Two of the approaches which are currently discussed take a somewhat exteme position: domain-specific languages (DSLs) [4] and mappings between software models expressed in general purpose languages, e.g., the Model-driven Architecture propsal [13].

DSLs are abstract languages for one application domain which are intended to be used by domain experts. DSLs are not necessarily (computationally) complete. Instead they cover an area of an application domain with a clearly defined scope. DSLs have a fixed semantics within the application domain. This semantics is based on by prefabricated software components which provide implementations. Such software components can range from libraries to software generators [17].

General purpose languages serve the modeling of complete software systems. Often, languages which allow varying degrees of concreteness are used, e.g. the Unified Modeling Language (UML). During the generation process of a software system a series of model mappings is applied, leading from abstract to more concrete models. During the process details are added at every model stage. Usually, the series of models starts with less formal models which can be created in co-operation with domain experts. Approaches based on general purpose languages generally arrive at completely formal descriptions of the software to be generated. Therefore, the final step of creating code comes down to a transformation from the chosen language to a programming language.

## 2.3   Open Modeling and Dynamic System Evolution

As discussed in the introductory section content management systems need

 - a conceptual model which is open to different user views (openness) and
 - implementations which keep up with the opinions of the users (dynamics).

Therefore, a modeling language is needed which on the one hand allows domain experts to describe their application domain, and on the other hand is concrete enough to serve the purpose of automatic software generation.

An approach which is purely based on a DSL does not offer openness since it is constrained to a fixed set of concepts which are offered by the respective language and mapped to existing software components. Existing approaches which map models expressed in a general purpose language to each other do not account for dynamics. The additional information given for the mapping at every model stage generally prevents fully automatic system creation [2,5].

In contrast to the approaches discussed in the previous section we concentrate on the specific class of content management which is combined with conceptual models for the description of entities. Modeling is open to any application domain, while the restriction to systems with a common core functionality allows their dynamic generation.

Note that we have to consider two modeling facilities for openness and dynamics: for the *source* application domain we need a modeling language which is general enough to allow openness, meaning that it is not constrained to pre-defined concepts for the description of entities. The *target* software model has to be specific enough to allow dynamics by enabling automatic generation of content management systems.

# 3   Support for Openness and Dynamics

The requirements of openness and dynamics call for special support in both systems creation as well as in operation. In fact in open and dynamic systems the line between creation and operation is blurred.

## 3.1   Shortcomings of Manual Software Engineering

Data-intensive applications normally are developed in processes which bear resemblance with the waterfall process: As part of the analysis of an application domain a conceptual schema is created. Based on this schema, the whole of the system is implemented. This means that the application is manually linked to the schema by the implementation process. Obviously, any changes to the schema have an impact on all parts of the application.

Therefore, when openness and dynamics are required, the common approach of manually implementing a static conceptual schema is clearly unfeasible. Our approach can remedy the situation by open modeling and dynamic systems generation as is discussed in sec. 4. Model changes are considered the rule not the exception, and content management systems are created with evolution in mind.

### 3.2  Modeling Requirements

The conceptual modeling language is needed to mediate between two worlds: the application domain of a user and the later system implementation.

Our approach concentrates on content management but combines it with a conceptual model of the described entities. Entities are therefore modeled dualistically by medial content as well as a conceptual description (see sec. 4.1). The approach is thus applicable to a wide variety of application domains.

However, in order to support dynamic systems, the model given by the user has to be compiled into a running system without any human intervention. Our approach achieves this by means of a compiler framework running a set of generators as described in more detail in sec. 5. On top of the conceptual schema, some of the generators might require a few additional parameters to bridge the gap between a conceptual model and its implementation in a content management system. These parameters provide the information discussed in sec. 2.2 but are completely available before the generation.

### 3.3  System Requirements

The general requirements outlined above can be mapped to requirements to content management systems. In particular:

1. The conceptual schema needs to be available to users and users must be able to modify it.
2. The system must be up to date with any such modifications *automatically*, therefore any manual development is not possible.
3. The conceptual schema must be truly conceptual. In traditional systems development it is often the case that implementation decisions have to be made during the analysis phase for purely technical reasons (e.g., the length of fields because of restrictions in the database). Such information must be separated from the conceptual schema.

We describe in the next sections how these requirements are met by our approach.

## 4  Ingredients of Open and Dynamic Systems

The requirements put forward in sec. 3 cannot be met with standard contemporary information systems. Generic systems lack openness since application domain concepts have to be mapped to generic ones, and hand-coded systems lack

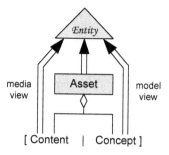

**Fig. 1.** Description capabilities of assets

dynamics since changes require an incremental engineering roundtrip. Our approach employs a conceptual modeling language, a modular system architecture, as well as automatic system generation to meet the requirements. The conceptual modeling language is covered in detail in previous work (see [14,15]) but will be outlined next. We then describe the modular architecture of generated content management systems and point out how these systems are created.

### 4.1   Conceptual Modeling Language

In our conceptual modeling language, entities are described by *asset classes*. These classes jointly describe a medial view (in the form of multimedia content, e.g., an image) and a conceptual view of the entity, see fig. 1. The conceptual view consists of characteristics (primitive attributes which are intrinsic to the entity), relationships to other asset classes, and constraints on the asset class. Classes are related in an inheritance hierarchy.

Asset classes are grouped into *asset models*, which usually deal with a particular application domain. Classes from one model can be imported into other models. The language supports openness by allowing the (partial) redefinition of imported classes to suite the task at hand. Anything that is not redefined stays the same as in the original.

Furthermore, the language provides means to create, modify, and delete instances as well as to query for them.

### 4.2   Modular System Architecture

The creation of a system in a dynamic manner can in some cases entail changes to its setup. The architecture of the system must therefore allow for flexible reconfiguration. A monolithic system is certainly not capable of such flexible change. Quite the contrary, we propose a modular system architecture that is built of many small modules. The kinds of modules for the most frequently occurring tasks are illustrated in fig. 2(a). All modules have a uniform interface and can be composed in layers. This makes it possible to always combine modules in the way most appropriate to the task at hand.

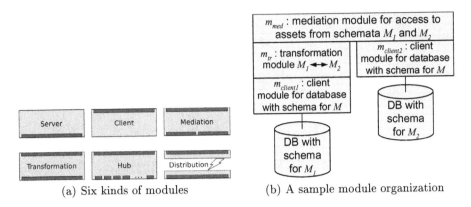

(a) Six kinds of modules          (b) A sample module organization

**Fig. 2.** Modules of generated content management systems

The module interface reflects the capabilities of the asset language to create, modify, delete and query for asset instances. Each module can thus express its functionality in terms of calls to the module(s) on the underlying layer.

A *component* is a combination of modules, usually arranged in layers. Components provide several services to their modules: resolution of identifiers, management of module lifecycles, and management of the proper organization of modules at system startup. Each module can use other modules and can also be used by several others. However, the setup of modules in a component always must be a directed acyclic graph.

Modules can be of several kinds, in particular:

- Components are accessed via *server modules* using standard protocols.
- The description data of asset instances is stored in third party systems, databases in most cases. Mapping asset models to schemata of such systems is done by *client modules.*
- A central building block of the architecture of generated content management systems is the mediator architecture [19]. In our approach it is implemented by modules of two kinds. The first are *mediation modules* which delegate requests to other modules based on the request.
- The other kind are *transformation modules.* By encapsulating mappings in such modules, rather than integrating this functionality into other modules, mappings can be added dynamically (compare [12]).
- *Hub modules* uniformly distribute calls to a larger number of underlying modules.
- By use of *distribution modules* components can reside at different physical locations and communicate by exchanging data.

These module kinds have been identified with respect to the requirements of content management systems. They provide basic services by the principle of Separation of Concerns. The functionality of a content management system is implemented by a *component configuration* which composes selected modules. For example, schema evolution leads to a combination of client, transformation, and mediation modules (indicated in figure 2(b), see [15] for details).

### 4.3   System Generation

The subdivision of a system into fine-grained modules as outlined above allows for flexible reconfiguration. This is necessary for a dynamic system, however not sufficient. Manual implementation of modules is unfeasible, as modules are usually highly schema dependent. System generation is therefore necessary to allow the system to be dynamic.

Several generative approaches (e.g., [18]) use loosely coupled generators. While this is fine for system generation under the supervision of a developer, generation in dynamic systems must happen without such intervention. We have therefore aimed at a tight, albeit flexible, coupling of generators. Given that our approach assembles systems of smaller modules, we can use generators which each create a particular type of module (e.g., a client module for persistence in relational databases). The generators are combined in a compiler framework which takes care of their proper setup and manages their interdependencies.

## 5   Model Compiler Framework

As argued in the previous section automatic software generation is necessary to allow dynamics of information systems with a fine-grained architecture.

There are different approaches to the problem of generating whole software systems which are composed of various parts that are produced by independent generators: (1) the generated software modules have to be adapted to be composable [7], (2) generic software modules are wrapped in a domain-specific way [11], (3) glue code to combine modules needs to be generated [3], or (4) the generators need to cooperate in order to create a consistent set of modules. As already indicated we favor the latter approach for content management systems.

Writing coordinated generators is a complex task, mainly because setting up an infrastructure for them [16] is difficult. Therefore, our model compiler for content management systems is designed as a framework with generators as extension points. In conjunction with a facility for code generation it constitutes a domain-independent meta-programming infrastructure [17].

### 5.1   A Framework Approach to Model Compilers

A typical compiler is divided into frontend and backend [1] to decouple source language recognition from target language generation. To this end, a compiler frontend creates an intermediate representation of the input definitions. Such an intermediate representation forms the input of a compiler's backend which generates code in the target language. This allows compiler setups for multiple targets as well as—at least in theory—to process different source languages.

The model compiler for our conceptual language is built in an object-oriented fashion. The classical division into frontend and backend has been translated into a framework architecture that allows to configure compilers for the generation of dynamic content management systems. This framework addresses the need to generate multiple targets in conjunction.

An instance of the compiler framework is defined by providing a parser, a dictionary proxy, several generators, and a configuration of the framework. This is detailed in the subsequent sections.

Alike a programming language compiler, which creates an intermediate code representation, the frontend in the compiler framework creates *intermediate model* representations. Starting from a class IntermediateModel the asset class definitions are available as an object graph.

Compilers use *symbol tables* to store information about the language constructs recognized. Our model compiler for content management systems builds on the concept of symbol tables, but extends it significantly: these tables are not only used in the frontend of a compiler, but they are the means by which generators communicate during the generation process.

Asset class definitions can be distributed: models are created by combining existing classes available to the modeler, and existing classes can be redefined (see section 4.1). Therefore, the model compiler needs access to asset classes which are not contained in the model at hand, but have been defined elsewhere. They are provided by *dictionaries* which store available class definitions.

Fig. 3 shows a UML sequence diagram of the frontend activities of a compiler run. This figure emphasizes the function of dictionaries. In the example an intermediate model im is created by the parser in the frontend. The definitions make reference to another model which is included as an intermediate model sm. In order to get access to it the parser requests it from the framework (sm=getModel). The framework contains a *dictionary proxy* to transparently access the known dictionaries. In the example there are two dictionaries. The first one does not know the requested model. The second one returns it as rm, and the dictionary proxy creates a local representation sm from rm.

Dictionary proxies are used to decouple a compiler configuration from the access to dictionaries. Dictionaries can be accessible by various means. For example, asset class definitions can be contained in local files or in resources accessible over a network. Dictionary proxies are a configurable part of the framework so that various alternatives can be realized.

Since a compiled model might be included into other models, it also has to be made available in a dictionary. In the example of fig. 3 the framework registers the model with the dictionary proxy (registerModel), which in turn inserts it into the first dictionary (createModel).

Dictionaries by themselves are content management systems which are generated from the asset meta model. This way, the compiler can use a proper component configuration. A variety of dictionary implementations can easily be created using the existing generators, e.g., dictionaries that store schemata in relational databases or XML databases. Furthermore, dictionaries can be equipped with a range of other functionality for, e.g., remote access.

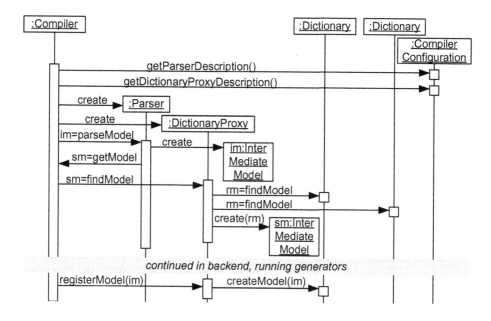

**Fig. 3.** Frontend of the model compiler with distributed dictionary

## 5.2   Parsers

In accordance with the classical architecture of compilers the intermediate model is used to distribute information between the compiler components. An intermediate model is created from an external representation. A parser makes the compiler independent of a particular linguistic form of an asset model, and there are parsers that retrieve asset model definitions from various sources.

A set of parsers is readily available for model compiler instances. The one most commonly used reads files containing asset language expression as defined in [15]. Other options are parsers for different syntactical forms, e.g. in XML, or parsers that adapt an internal model representation from modeling tools.

Additional parsers can be developed within the compiler framework. They have to fulfill an interface prescribed by the framework which requires them to produce an IntermediateModel instance.

## 5.3   Code Generators

The backend of a model compiler consists of generators. There is a correspondence between generators and the modules of content management systems. For each implementation of one of the module kinds introduced in sec. 4.2 there is at least one generator. Often there is more than one generator which contributes to the creation of a module. For example, client modules for database access are typically created by a pair of generators; one of them creates the database schema, the other one creates code to access the database as well as to store and retrieve asset instances.

In order to be integrated into the compiler framework, generators have to fulfill an interface. This interface mainly defines methods for a protocol by which generators communicate with the framework.

As part of this protocol parameters can be passed to generators as will be explained in the following sections. Generators take parameter values into account when generating a module.

The artifacts which are created by a generator to implement a module are reflected in the symbol table of the generator. The generators create their artifacts as a complex structure into which the symbol table provides named points of entry. Each generator fills its symbol table during its execution and passes the symbol table back to the compiler framework afterwards. The framework in turn gives available symbol tables to further generators making them the essential means of generator communication.

The symbol tables contain detailed structured information about the artifacts which were created by the respective generator. A typical behavior for a generator is for example to iterate over all asset classes from the intermediate model and all their attributes to generate a piece of code for each attribute. The symbol table will then contain a mappings from attributes to these pieces of code (e.g., access methods). The aim of symbol tables is to make access explicit for generators which rely on artifacts created by others (and most generators do). Without symbol tables, generators further down the chain would have to make assumptions about namings and would have to recover the corresponding pieces from the whole of the generated artifacts.

A complete system is normally built from artifacts in several languages. Different meta-programming facilities are available to the generators to create their output. This facilitates the creation of structured models of the artifacts and is therefore important to provide meaningful symbol tables. The structured models are converted into their concrete form as a side-effect of the generator execution. Such a concrete form are for example files containing source code of a particular programming language.

### 5.4  Framework Configurability

By providing generator implementations the backend of the compiler framework is enriched with additional functionality. Which generators are actually executed is determined by a *compiler configuration*, as are the frontend components (parser, dictionary proxy) used. Multiple configurations can be provided by system experts. Upon dynamic system generation a user chooses one of the available configurations for each compiler run.

For the frontend, the parser and the dictionary proxy (see fig. 3) can be chosen. They are provided as discussed in sections 5.1 and 5.2.

The backend configuration consists of two kinds of definitions: the generators to be used for creating a content management system and values of parameter to the generators.

For each configuration a set of generator implementations is given. This way generator instances out of the known generator implementations are chosen.

There may be more than one generator with the same implementation, for example, if two client modules for database access are needed in a content management system. In this case the two client modules are created by two instances of the corresponding generator. The generation results may differ because of different sets of parameter values.

Values for parameters which a generator might need are given as part of the configurations. Generators determine the parameters to use at runtime, and the framework will supply them with the values given in the configuration. This is part of the generator protocol introduced in the subsequent section.

## 5.5   Generator Control

Traditional compilers for programming languages include a backend for one generation target—executable binary code in most cases. In contrast a model compiler for content management systems has to consider several targets at a time, e.g., database schemata, database access code, application level code, and so on.

The multiple targets of a model compiler are addressed by the generators provided to the compiler framework as described in the previous section. The various artifacts a compiler creates are highly interrelated. Therefore, the execution of generators has to be scheduled in such a way that they create a working content management system.

Generators follow a specified protocol inside the compiler framework. Fig. 4 illustrates this protocol in the form of a UML sequence diagram. In this figure a compiler setup with three generators is shown. The APIGenerator is a standard generator which creates the uniform module interface (see sec. 4.2). An SQLSchemaGenerator produces a database schema for a relational database. Real setups use specialized generators which account for the peculiarities of concrete database management systems. The JDBCGenerator creates Java code for a client module which stores asset instances according to the given asset model in the database with the generated relational schema.

The grey box in fig.4 represents the compiler frontend as shown in fig. 3. It creates the intermediate model im which reflects the asset class definitions.

The extended symbol table concept described in sec. 5.1 is the primary means to coordinate generator executions. Depending on its configuration, the framework (here represented by the Compiler instance) creates the necessary generators. Each generator is asked for the symbol tables it needs as input, the symbol table it will produce as the result of a successful execution, and the configuration parameters it needs to be supplied with. Based on the information given by the generators the framework computes a schedule for generator execution that ensures the required data flow.

In the example of fig. 4 both the API and the SQL schema generator will not require any symbol tables as input. The JDBC generator generates a client module which implements the module API and accesses a database configured with the generated schema, thus it requires symbol tables which reflect the respective artifacts. Therefore, the JDBC generator needs both symbol tables created by the other generators (st1 and st2) and thus has to be executed last. Either the

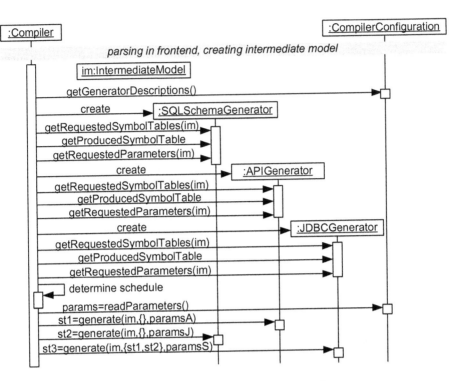

**Fig. 4.** Generator scheduling protocol

API or the SQL schema generator can be run first, or both can be run in parallel. Following the generator protocol the JDBC generator returns the symbol table st3 as announced by **getProducedSymbolTable**. This symbol table can be used by generators which want to employ the JDBC code.

Finally, the generators are run in the determined order (**generate** in fig. 4). They are provided with the required symbol tables and parameter values, and return a new symbol table.

Fig. 5 makes the data flow that takes place between the generators through symbol tables more explicit. The generators of a first schedule stage (API and SQL schema generators) are executed concurrently. Each of them creates some module artifacts and stores information about the generated artifacts in a particular symbol table. The symbol tables are available to the generator of the second schedule stage (the JDBC generator). The activity diagram in fig. 5 shows both control and data flow to point out the fact that the compiler framework computes a schedule for the generators instead of having them controlled by data flow alone. This way, the compiler framework can detect inconsistent configurations without actually running generators.

Generators are provided with the intermediate model when they request symbol tables (**getRequestedSymbolTables**) and parameters (**getRequestedParameters**). This way the choice of symbol tables and parameters can depend on the actual

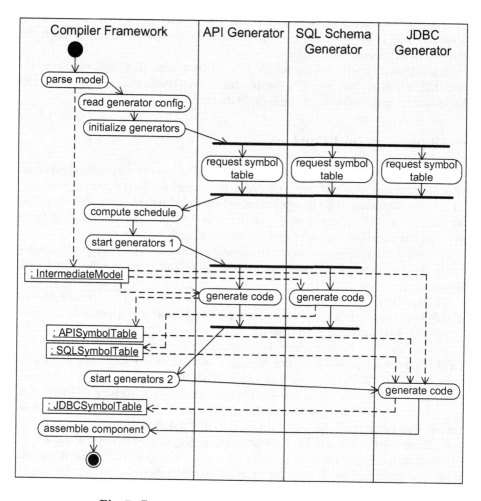

**Fig. 5.** Generator communication with symbol tables

asset class definitions. E.g., a schema generator needs type mappings for all asset class members. Therefore, it will gather the types used in asset class attributes and request the according SQL types which shall be used within a database. Because of the dynamic choice of symbol tables possible generator schedules can depend on the asset class definitions.

## 5.6   Component Assembly

When all generators have finished their tasks a system component is assembled from the generated modules and parameterizations of third party products. This includes two activities: actually building the modules and combining them in a component of a content management system.

Modules are built from the generated artifacts. Each generated artifact needs a special final treatment: source code needs to be compiled, database schemata have to be deployed, etc.

A component is created according to a given component configuration (see sec. 4.2) which determines the component's functionality on the basis of the basic functionality offered by the individual modules.

## 6    Summary and Outlook

Content management systems which describe domain entities by multimedia content have to take into account their users' views and working contexts. One way to do so is by means of a conceptual model provided by the users. In this paper we have presented a generative approach to the creation of content management systems that enables openness and dynamics of such systems.

As a solution to the problem of coordinating the various generators of software artifacts for a content management system a design for a compiler framework has been proposed.

Through application projects, we were able to verify that users are indeed enabled to provide their personalized perspective [9] and that a dynamic response to schema modifications is feasible [6].

In the future we hope to extend our approach in several respects. One of the focal points is a possible feedback of generator runs on the asset model. Giving such feedback will enable generators to interact with each other via the model to distribute any additional constraints that might be necessary to impose on the schema. An example of this is the length restriction of string fields. These restrictions can arise from the use of a relational database for persistence. However, these restrictions need to be respected by all parts of the application, e.g., in presentation logic. There is, therefore, a feedback loop from the client module generator providing additional information to the other generators. Currently such information which is important to all generators has to be defined in the asset model, violating its conceptual nature.

## References

1. Alfred V. Aho, Ravi Sethi, and Jeffrey D. Ullman. *Compilers: Principles, Techniques, and Tools.* Addison-Wesley, 1986.
2. Scott W. Ambler. *The Object Primer: Agile Model-Driven Development with UML 2.0.* Cambridge University Press, third edition, 2004.
3. Uwe Assmann. Meta-programming Composers In Second-Generation Component Systems. In J. Bishop and N. Horspool, editors, *Systems Implementation 2000 – Working Conference IFIP WG 2.4.* Chapman and Hall, 1998.
4. Don Batory, Bernie Lofaso, and Yannis Smaragdakis. JTS: Tools for Implementing Domain-Specific Languages. In *Proceedings Fifth International Conference on Software Reuse*, pages 143–153. IEEE, 1998.
5. Jorn Bettin. Model-Driven Software Development: An emerging paradigm for Industrialized Software Asset Development. Technical report, SoftMetaWare, 2004.

6. Sebastian Bossung, Hans-Werner Sehring, Patrick Hupe, and Joachim W. Schmidt. Open and Dynamic Schema Evolution in Content-intensive Web Applications. In José Cordeiro, Vitor Pedrosa, Bruno Encarnaçãom, and Joaquim Filipe, editors, *Proceedings of the 2nd International Conference on Web Information Systems and Technologies, WEBIST 2006*, pages 109–116. INSTICC Press, 2006.
7. Johan Brichau. *Integrative Composition of Program Generators*. PhD thesis, Vakgroep Informatica, Vrije Universiteit Brussel, 2005.
8. Michael L. Brodie, John Mylopoulos, and Joachim W. Schmidt, editors. *On Conceptual Modelling: Perspectives from Artificial Intelligence, Databases, and Programming Languages*. Topics in Information Systems. Springer-Verlag, 1984.
9. Matthias Bruhn. The Warburg Electronic Library in Hamburg: A Digital Index of Political Iconography. *Visual Resources*, XV:405–423, 2000.
10. Peter P. Chen. The Entity-Relationship Model – Toward a Unified View of Data. *ACM Transactions on Database Systems*, 1(1):9–36, 1976.
11. Gopal Gupta. A language-centric approach to software engineering: Domain specific languages meet software components. In *Electronic Proceedings of the CoLogNet Area Workshop Series on Component-based Software Development and Implementation Technology for Computational Logic Systems*, Technical University of Madrid (Spain), 19.-20. September 2002.
12. Mira Mezini, Linda Seiter, and Karl Lieberherr. Component integration with pluggable composite adapters. In *Software Architectures and Component Technology*. Kluwer, 2000.
13. Joaquin Miller and Jishnu Mukerji. MDA Guide Version 1.0.1. Technical Report omg/2003-06-01, OMG, June 2003.
14. Joachim W. Schmidt and Hans-Werner Sehring. Conceptual Content Modeling and Management: The Rationale of an Asset Language. In *Perspectives of System Informatics*, volume 2890 of *LNCS*, pages 469–493. Springer, 2003.
15. Hans-Werner Sehring and Joachim W. Schmidt. Beyond Databases: An Asset Language for Conceptual Content Management. In *Proceedings of the 8th East European Conference on Advances in Databases and Information Systems*, volume 3255 of *LNCS*, pages 99–112. Springer-Verlag, 2004.
16. Yannis Smaragdakis and Don Batory. Scoping Constructs for Program Generators. Technical Report CS-TR-96-37, Austin, Texas, USA, 1996.
17. Yannis Smaragdakis, Shan Shan Huang, and David Zook. Program generators and the tools to make them. In *PEPM '04: Proceedings of the 2004 ACM SIGPLAN Symposium on Partial Evaluation and Semantics-based Program Manipulation*, pages 92–100. ACM Press, 2004.
18. Pedro Valderas, Joan Fons, and Vicente Pelechano. Transforming Web Requirements into Navigational Models: An MDA Based Approach. In *Proc. ER05*, volume 3716 of *LNCS*, pages 320–336. Springer Verlag, 2005.
19. G. Wiederhold. Mediators in the Architecture of Future Information Systems. *IEEE Computer*, 25:38–49, 1992.

# Author Index

# Lecture Notes in Computer Science

For information about Vols. 1–4045

please contact your bookseller or Springer

Vol. 4094: O. H. Ibarra, H.-C. Yen (Eds.), Implementation and Application of Automata. XIII, 291 pages. 2006.

Vol. 4093: X. Li, O.R. Zaïane, Z. Li (Eds.), Advanced Data Mining and Applications. XXI, 1110 pages. 2006. (Sublibrary LNAI).

Vol. 4092: J. Lang, F. Lin, J. Wang (Eds.), Knowledge Science, Engineering and Management. XV, 664 pages. 2006. (Sublibrary LNAI).

Vol. 4091: G.-Z. Yang, T. Jiang, D. Shen, L. Gu, J. Yang (Eds.), Medical Imaging and Augmented Reality. XIII, 399 pages. 2006.

Vol. 4090: S. Spaccapietra, K. Aberer, P. Cudré-Mauroux (Eds.), Journal on Data Semantics VI. XI, 211 pages. 2006.

Vol. 4089: W. Löwe, M. Südholt (Eds.), Software Composition. X, 339 pages. 2006.

Vol. 4088: Z.-Z. Shi, R. Sadananda (Eds.), Agent Computing and Multi-Agent Systems. XVII, 827 pages. 2006. (Sublibrary LNAI).

Vol. 4085: J. Misra, T. Nipkow, E. Sekerinski (Eds.), FM 2006: Formal Methods. XV, 620 pages. 2006.

Vol. 4083: S. Fischer-Hübner, S. Furnell, C. Lambrinoudakis (Eds.), Trust and Privacy in Digital Business. XIII, 243 pages. 2006.

Vol. 4082: K. Bauknecht, B. Pröll, H. Werthner (Eds.), E-Commerce and Web Technologies. XIII, 243 pages. 2006.

Vol. 4081: A. M. Tjoa, J. Trujillo (Eds.), Data Warehousing and Knowledge Discovery. XVII, 578 pages. 2006.

Vol. 4080: S. Bressan, J. Küng, R. Wagner (Eds.), Database and Expert Systems Applications. XXI, 959 pages. 2006.

Vol. 4079: S. Etalle, M. Truszczyński (Eds.), Logic Programming. XIV, 474 pages. 2006.

Vol. 4077: M.-S. Kim, K. Shimada (Eds.), Geometric Modeling and Processing - GMP 2006. XVI, 696 pages. 2006.

Vol. 4076: F. Hess, S. Pauli, M. Pohst (Eds.), Algorithmic Number Theory. X, 599 pages. 2006.

Vol. 4075: U. Leser, F. Naumann, B. Eckman (Eds.), Data Integration in the Life Sciences. XI, 298 pages. 2006. (Sublibrary LNBI).

Vol. 4074: M. Burmester, A. Yasinsac (Eds.), Secure Mobile Ad-hoc Networks and Sensors. X, 193 pages. 2006.

Vol. 4073: A. Butz, B. Fisher, A. Krüger, P. Olivier (Eds.), Smart Graphics. XI, 263 pages. 2006.

Vol. 4072: M. Harders, G. Székely (Eds.), Biomedical Simulation. XI, 216 pages. 2006.

Vol. 4071: H. Sundaram, M. Naphade, J.R. Smith, Y. Rui (Eds.), Image and Video Retrieval. XII, 547 pages. 2006.

Vol. 4070: C. Priami, X. Hu, Y. Pan, T.Y. Lin (Eds.), Transactions on Computational Systems Biology V. IX, 129 pages. 2006. (Sublibrary LNBI).

Vol. 4069: F.J. Perales, R.B. Fisher (Eds.), Articulated Motion and Deformable Objects. XV, 526 pages. 2006.

Vol. 4068: H. Schärfe, P. Hitzler, P. Øhrstrøm (Eds.), Conceptual Structures: Inspiration and Application. XI, 455 pages. 2006. (Sublibrary LNAI).

Vol. 4067: D. Thomas (Ed.), ECOOP 2006 – Object-Oriented Programming. XIV, 527 pages. 2006.

Vol. 4066: A. Rensink, J. Warmer (Eds.), Model Driven Architecture – Foundations and Applications. XII, 392 pages. 2006.

Vol. 4065: P. Perner (Ed.), Advances in Data Mining. XI, 592 pages. 2006. (Sublibrary LNAI).

Vol. 4064: R. Büschkes, P. Laskov (Eds.), Detection of Intrusions and Malware & Vulnerability Assessment. X, 195 pages. 2006.

Vol. 4063: I. Gorton, G.T. Heineman, I. Crnkovic, H.W. Schmidt, J.A. Stafford, C.A. Szyperski, K. Wallnau (Eds.), Component-Based Software Engineering. XI, 394 pages. 2006.

Vol. 4062: G. Wang, J.F. Peters, A. Skowron, Y. Yao (Eds.), Rough Sets and Knowledge Technology. XX, 810 pages. 2006. (Sublibrary LNAI).

Vol. 4061: K. Miesenberger, J. Klaus, W. Zagler, A.I. Karshmer (Eds.), Computers Helping People with Special Needs. XXIX, 1356 pages. 2006.

Vol. 4060: K. Futatsugi, J.-P. Jouannaud, J. Meseguer (Eds.), Algebra, Meaning, and Computation. XXXVIII, 643 pages. 2006.

Vol. 4059: L. Arge, R. Freivalds (Eds.), Algorithm Theory – SWAT 2006. XII, 436 pages. 2006.

Vol. 4058: L.M. Batten, R. Safavi-Naini (Eds.), Information Security and Privacy. XII, 446 pages. 2006.

Vol. 4057: J.P.W. Pluim, B. Likar, F.A. Gerritsen (Eds.), Biomedical Image Registration. XII, 324 pages. 2006.

Vol. 4056: P. Flocchini, L. Gąsieniec (Eds.), Structural Information and Communication Complexity. X, 357 pages. 2006.

Vol. 4055: J. Lee, J. Shim, S.-g. Lee, C. Bussler, S. Shim (Eds.), Data Engineering Issues in E-Commerce and Services. IX, 290 pages. 2006.

Vol. 4054: A. Horváth, M. Telek (Eds.), Formal Methods and Stochastic Models for Performance Evaluation. VIII, 239 pages. 2006.

Vol. 4053: M. Ikeda, K.D. Ashley, T.-W. Chan (Eds.), Intelligent Tutoring Systems. XXVI, 821 pages. 2006.

Vol. 4052: M. Bugliesi, B. Preneel, V. Sassone, I. Wegener (Eds.), Automata, Languages and Programming, Part II. XXIV, 603 pages. 2006.

Vol. 4051: M. Bugliesi, B. Preneel, V. Sassone, I. Wegener (Eds.), Automata, Languages and Programming, Part I. XXIII, 729 pages. 2006.

Vol. 4049: S. Parsons, N. Maudet, P. Moraitis, I. Rahwan (Eds.), Argumentation in Multi-Agent Systems. XIV, 313 pages. 2006. (Sublibrary LNAI).

Vol. 4048: L. Goble, J.-J.C.. Meyer (Eds.), Deontic Logic and Artificial Normative Systems. X, 273 pages. 2006. (Sublibrary LNAI).

Vol. 4047: M. Robshaw (Ed.), Fast Software Encryption. XI, 434 pages. 2006.

Vol. 4046: S.M. Astley, M. Brady, C. Rose, R. Zwiggelaar (Eds.), Digital Mammography. XVI, 654 pages. 2006.